HTML 4 HOW-TO

THE DEFINITIVE HTML 4 PROBLEM-SOLVER

John Zakour, Jeff Foust, David Kerven

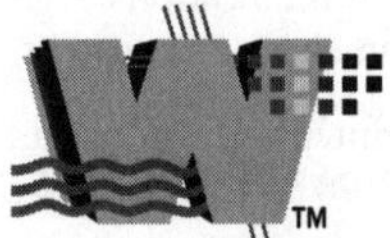

Waite Group Press™
A Division of
Sams Publishing
Corte Madera, CA

Publisher: Mitchell Waite
Associate Publisher: Charles Drucker
Acquisitions Manager: Susan Walton
Project Editor: Laura E. Brown
Content Editor: Scott Rhoades
Technical Editor: Ken Cox
Production Editor: Tonya R. Simpson
Copy Editor: Deidre Greene
Managing Editor: Brice P. Gosnell
Indexing Manager: Johnna L. VanHoose
Software Specialist: Dan Scherf
Production Manager: Cecile Kaufman
Production Team Supervisors: Brad Chinn, Andrew Stone
Cover Designer: Jean Bisesi
Book Designer: Jean Bisesi
Production: Shawn Ring, Michael Henry, Ayanna Lacey, Mary Ellen Stephenson
Indexer: Bruce Clingaman

Published by Waite Group Press ™.
200 Tamal Plaza, Corte Madera, CA 94925

Waite Group Press™ is a division of Sams Publishing.

Printed in the United States of America
97 98 99 10 9 8 7 6 5 4 3 2 1

Library of Congress Cataloging-in-Publication Data
Zakour, John
HTML 4 How-To / John Zakour, Jeff Foust, David Kerven.
p. cm.
Includes index.
ISBN 1-57169-125-1
1. HTML (Document markup language) I. Foust, Jeff. II. Kerven, David. III. Title.
QA76.76.H94Z35 1997 97-30091
005.7'2--dc21 CIP

International Standard Book Number: 1-57169-125-1

DEDICATION

To my parents, as after all, if it weren't for them, I wouldn't be here.
—John Zakour

To Mom.
—Jeff Foust

I would like to dedicate this book to my mother, Sheila Yoskowitz; my wife, Jenny Kerven; and my family.
—David Kerven

ABOUT THE AUTHORS

John Zakour is currently an HTML consultant and a freelance writer. Some of his writing—daily computer cartoons, the novel *The Doomsday Brunette*, and a new novel *Plutonium Blond*—can be found on Prodigy On-Line Service's World Wide Web pages. John majored in Computer Science at Potsdam State University. Upon completion of his studies at Potsdam, he worked as a database programmer for Cornell University. Upon his return to New York, he was a Web page designer for Cornell University's New York State Agriculture Experiment Station. As an HTML consultant, John also has a Web page. You can see it at `http://www.psnw.com/~jmz5/`.

Jeff Foust is a graduate student in planetary astronomy at M.I.T. A native of Council Bluffs, Iowa, he holds a B.S. in planetary science from Caltech. He has been exploring the Web and creating pages for it since the fall of 1993. His Shoemaker-Levy 9 impact page, with information and images of the impact of the comet on Jupiter, received national attention in *Astronomy*, *Macworld*, and *Wired* magazines. When not working on his thesis or using the Web, he has been active in a number of space-related ventures, including serving as editor of SpaceViews (`http://www.seds.org/spaceviews`), a monthly space journal. He is Webmaster for Web-Net (`http://www.web-net.org`), an organization bringing together people and businesses on the Web. Jeff is also a (frustrated) Boston Red Sox fan.

David Kerven was born in Jersey City, New Jersey, in 1967 and was raised in Livingston, New Jersey. He received his B.S. in electrical engineering from Johns Hopkins University and his Ph.D. in computer science from the University of Southwestern Louisiana. Dr. Kerven is currently living in Atlanta with his wife, Jenny. He is an assistant professor of computer science at Clark Atlanta University, where he teaches courses in software engineering and object-oriented programming principles. For the past six years, he has participated in hypermedia research and development, in the development of four hypermedia environments, and the development of CGI applications for World Wide Web-based adaptive tutorial/training systems. He currently serves as Webmaster of the Clark Atlanta University Computer Science Web server.

TABLE OF CONTENTS

CONTENTS

PART I
INTRODUCTION

CHAPTER 1

PART II
AUTHORING

CHAPTER 2

PART V
APPENDIXES

ACKNOWLEDGMENTS

To my wife, Olga, and my son Jay, who put up with me during those "one or two days" I was running behind schedule. To Ron, who was always there with computer advice. To Tom, who's always there with grammatical advice. To my ex-boss Linda, who would always let me take an hour or two off when I needed it.

—John Zakour

To Chris Lewicki and others at the University of Arizona chapter of Students for the Exploration and Development of Space (SEDS), who have created a first-class Web site (`http://www.seds.org/`) and provided me with space to experiment with Web designs for some time.

—Jeff Foust

I would first like to thank my wife, Jenny, for her loving forbearance and support throughout the entire writing process. In addition, I would like to thank the editors at Waite Group Press for their diligence and uncommon perseverance in wading through my unpolished drafts. Special thanks go to Troy Downing, who contributed How-To 13.8 on how to set up the MacHTTP server security. Finally, I would like to acknowledge the support of God, my family, and my department at Clark Atlanta University.

—David Kerven

PREFACE

Welcome to World Wide Web authoring. Surfing the Internet through the World Wide Web has escaped the confines of academia and is quickly becoming a common sport in boardrooms and family rooms. *HTML 4 How-To* will provide you with a road map to enter the dynamic environment of Internet publishing on the World Wide Web. Unlike existing HyperText Markup Language (HTML) documentation, *HTML 4 How-To* presents many real-world document development problems along with specific step-by-step solutions, explanations, and examples. With *HTML 4 How-To* as your guide, you can concentrate on developing your information rather than your implementation. To give you a jump start on the Information Superhighway, all sample documents, program code, and multimedia objects presented in the book are included on the CD-ROM.

The World Wide Web is expanding at an incredible pace. The basic building blocks of the World Wide Web are documents developed using HTML. The Internet traffic devoted to the retrieval of HTML documents is likewise increasing; in fact, high-traffic servers currently receive in excess of 1,000 accesses every hour. Both small- and large-scale HTML projects are being initiated daily by both individuals and large commercial entities. With this kind of volume usage, HTML has become the *de facto* development language for network-based hypermedia information.

From purchasing flowers in Maine to ordering a pizza in California, you will find more commercial ventures are beginning to enter this arena. Financial institutions, retailers, publishers, and other corporations are only beginning to explore the potential of the worldwide electronic community. *HTML 4 How-To* is not another manual, nor is it a technical specification; it is a guide that will give you direction for entering this rapidly growing environment and enhancing existing documents.

Each How-To in the book states a problem; describes the circumstances leading to the problem; develops a step-by-step solution; and delineates relevant tips, comments, warnings, and, occasionally, alternative solutions. Each How-To will walk you through the solution to a common development problem. *HTML 4 How-To* is not another style manual; instead, it is a user-oriented, goal-driven guide that will change the way you develop HTML documents. *HTML 4 How-To* provides everything you need to know to begin developing world-class HTML documents. So, jump into *HTML 4 How-To* and share your vision with the world.

Chapter 1, "Web Basics," introduces several key concepts about the World Wide Web. Most of this information should be familiar ground to prospective authors. The information serves as a review and a reminder while potentially filling gaps. The How-To's set the stage for the HTML 4 details to come.

Chapter 2, "HTML Basics," deals with the basic concepts of authoring documents in HTML 4. You will learn how to identify and construct simple HTML documents. The How-To's tell you how to begin to develop HTML documents. They also introduce you to several key HTML elements.

Chapter 3, "Adding HTML Physical Character Effects," continues by describing the various physical character effects possible with HTML 4. Each How-To walks you through the use of these character effects. Documented examples demonstrate the proper use of these elements while also addressing relevant stylistic issues.

Chapter 4, "Adding HTML Logical Character Effects," carries you beyond the physical effect to HTML 4's logical character effects. Although these effects do not require a visible change in your Web pages, many Web browsers do provide a visible indication of these elements. This chapter's How-To's demonstrate the effective usage of the logical character elements supported by HTML 4.

Chapter 5, "Tables," looks at the management, organization, and formatting of data using HTML 4 tables. Tables also support strict formatting of desired elements, such as images and text, by providing row/column alignment. The How-To's in this chapter instruct you in the use of HTML 4 table elements.

Chapter 6, "Lists," leads you through the myriad of list types supported by HTML 4. Lists serve an essential function in the organization of many HTML documents. The How-To's explain the different types of lists and styles available and provide step-by-step instructions on inserting each type of list into your pages.

Chapter 7, "Managing Document Spacing," takes a close look at the management of space in HTML 4 documents. How you space the information in your Web page substantially affects the impact of the page upon a viewer. HTML 4 provides several elements to control spacing. The How-To's in this chapter provide clear instructions on the use of these spacing elements.

Chapter 8, "Establishing Links," covers the creation of links in HTML 4 documents. Links are the glue that connect HTML documents around the world. Links potentially connect your Web page to both other Web pages and a variety of other Internet-based information. The How-To's in this chapter examine the creation of links to other Web pages and other network-based information.

Chapter 9, "Using Images in Your Documents," jumps into the topic of images. HTML 4 allows the incorporation of images directly into your Web pages in both the foreground and the background. This chapter also introduces the creation and use of imagemaps. Imagemaps enable you to click upon a particular location within the image and trigger a link associated with the location. The How-To's in this chapter step you through the process of image inclusion and imagemap construction.

Chapter 10, "Adding Externally Linked Multimedia Objects," delves further into the multimedia arena. This chapter examines how HTML 4 supports the inclusion of a variety of multimedia data types. The How-To's provide stylistic and technical information on the inclusion of these data types. The information in this chapter concentrates on the development and inclusion of multimedia objects accessed indirectly through links and external helper applications. However, much of the information is relevant in developing multimedia objects suitable for direct inclusion through the non-HTML 4 standard methods discussed in Chapter 18, "Direct Inclusion of Multimedia Objects."

Chapter 11, "HTML Interactive Forms," begins the examination of HTML forms. Authors use HTML forms to request data from viewers of pages. HTML provides a variety of input styles, such as text entry windows and lists of selections. The How-To's in this chapter explain the use of those HTML elements in form creation.

Chapter 12, "Server Basics," examines how to make HTML 4 documents available on the World Wide Web by establishing your own Web site. The How-To's in this chapter outline the various tasks required to accomplish this goal.

Chapter 13, "Handling Server Security," addresses the issue of providing security for your HTML documents. If you want to restrict access to a selection of your Web pages, you will likely find your answer in this chapter. Several of the procedures discussed might require the actions of your Web site administrator; however, many of the How-To's in this chapter provide instructions that you can use to restrict access to your Web pages.

Chapter 14, "The Common Gateway Interface (CGI)," offers information on gateway applications. Gateway applications process the data gathered by HTML forms, as described in Chapter 11. These applications generally produce dynamic documents based on the information available both on the server and through forms. The How-To's in this chapter examine the issues involved in creating gateway applications and provide instructions on and examples of how you can develop such applications.

Chapter 15, "Navigator and Internet Explorer HTML Extensions," presents a variety of features supported by Netscape's Navigator and Microsoft's Internet Explorer, two of the most popular Web browsers. These features enable you to extend beyond the bounds of the HTML 4 standard. However, these additional features are not without some cost in cross-browser compatibility. The How-To's in this chapter not only detail the use of these additional features but also discuss ways to minimize cross-browser incompatibility.

Chapter 16, "Cascading Style Sheets," explores the use of HTML cascading style sheets. Style sheets provide another means of specifying formatting constraints in Web pages. Furthermore, they allow for a differentiation of style among instances of a particular HTML element. Thus, Web pages might utilize multiple versions of the same HTML element with each particular use having a different style. Currently, only Microsoft's Internet Explorer and several experimental Web browsers support style sheets. However, in the near future, you might see them incorporated into the HTML standard. This chapter's How-To's cover the creation, use, and incorporation of HTML style sheets in your Web pages.

Chapter 17, "Web Programming with Java and JavaScript," introduces the use of Java and Javascript into your Web pages. Java applets are small programs that you may download via the Web. These applications run within browser environments that support Java, such as Navigator and Internet Explorer. Javascript allows the incorporation of scripted functions within your Web pages. Although HTML 4 supports the inclusion of Java applications, scripted functions are not yet a part of the standard. The How-To's in this chapter describe the current mechanisms for adding both Java and Javascript elements to your Web pages.

Chapter 18, "Direct Inclusion of Multimedia Objects," discusses the mechanisms currently used to support the direct inclusion of multimedia objects within a Web page. Both Netscape and Internet Explorer enable you to directly include multimedia objects within your Web pages. The How-To's in this chapter present methods of including various types of multimedia objects. These How-To's provide information on minimizing cross-browser incompatibilities, as well as the proper use of these features.

Chapter 19, "Frames," addresses this advanced means of controlling Web page layout. Frames enable you to control different portions of a "page" presented by a frames-capable browser using multiple HTML documents. This chapter's How-To's present the tricks and practices of using frames in Web page development.

Chapter 20, "Dynamic HTML," provides an introduction to layers, a powerful addition to HTML. Layers give page designers a host of new options such as the capability to position content at an exact position on a page, overlay content, hide or show content or portions of content, and create animation and movement without using Java. The How-To's in this chapter show you what's needed to take full advantage of this new HTML feature.

Chapter 21, "Dynamic Style Sheets and Fonts," provides a basic introduction to dynamic style sheets and their use in Web pages. Dynamic style sheets are a combination of cascading style sheets and JavaScript. The chapter's How-To's present a good overview of this new technology introduced in version 4 of Netscape Navigator.

Chapter 22, "Unsupported, Proposed HTML Features," presents many speculative HTML elements. The HTML language generates a wide variety of discussion leading to much speculation about the proper elements of the standard. The How To's in this chapter investigate modifications to the current standard.

Chapter 23, "Some of the Best Sites on the Web," takes you on a brief tour of Web pages where the authors have taken advantage of the unique aspects of HTML. There is a surfeit of pages on the Web that are cool; this chapter mentions the cream of the crop.

Just two years ago, few people had heard of the World Wide Web and still fewer knew of HTML. Now these terms have become almost commonplace, appearing in advertising and even nationally syndicated comic strips. Commensurate with this exposure, the Web has experienced, and is still experiencing, a rapid growth in size and usage.

Individuals and businesses who wish to keep pace with technology must learn the valuable skills necessary not only to use this medium but also to actively participate in the evolution of this medium through authoring. In a clearly defined, explicit how-to format, this book equips you to enter that arena confidently.

PART I

INTRODUCTION

CHAPTER 1

WEB BASICS

1

WEB BASICS

How do I...

1.1 Get on the Web from America Online?
1.2 Establish a connection to the Internet?
1.3 Find a Web browser?
1.4 Navigate via browser features?
1.5 Follow a link?
1.6 Open a location?
1.7 Find a Web authoring tool?
1.8 Find a home for my Web pages?
1.9 Get information about the evolution of HTML?
1.10 Design effective Web pages?

The World Wide Web, or simply the Web, has been called the "killer app" of the Internet. Certainly its capability to display text and graphics and provide access to other pages and information resources has made it the fastest-growing component of the Internet. You might already know how to explore the universe of information on the Web. But you might not know how to use the Web to display your own information to the world—information about you, your personal interests, or your business.

This chapter introduces you to the World Wide Web and guides you in getting onto the Web and ready to create your own Hypertext Markup Language (HTML) documents. This chapter is not intended to be a thorough introduction to the Web; other resources, both on the Web and in books, can provide more detailed explanations of the Web and how to use it. This chapter simply explains the basics of the Web, including how to find an access provider, how to find and use a browser, and how to find space for the Web pages you create. After you understand these basics, you can learn in future chapters how to create your own Web pages using HTML.

1.1 Get on the Web from America Online

Major online services—America Online, CompuServe, and Prodigy—now provide access to the World Wide Web. This How-To discusses how America Online's Internet service works and how you can use it to access the Web.

1.2 Establish a Connection to the Internet

Another way to access the Web is to get an account with an Internet service provider, or *ISP*. These accounts usually include access to the World Wide Web and other Internet resources, and often they provide space to store the Web pages you will be creating. This How-To explains how to find a local provider and get the kind of Internet access you need to explore the Web.

1.3 Find a Web Browser

As the Web has exploded, the number of browser programs—the programs you use to explore the Web—has increased. Now there are browsers for nearly every conceivable type of computer. These programs have also grown more sophisticated, to the point where they support advanced HTML features and extensions. This How-To explains how to find an appropriate Web browser for your computer.

1.4 Navigate via Browser Features

After you have Web access and a working browser, you must be able to move around on the Web. The easiest way to navigate on the Web is to use the features incorporated into your browser to move between pages. This How-To shows how to use these basic features to start moving around the Web.

1.5 Follow a Link

One very helpful feature the World Wide Web offers is the capability to move from page to page by selecting specific highlighted words, phrases, or images, which are called *links*. This How-To explains what links are and how you can use them to explore the Web.

1.6 Open a Location

Another way to move around in the Web is to go directly to a specific page using its address, or *URL* (universal resource locator). This How-To explains how to go directly to a specific location on the Web using basic features found in Web browsers.

1.7 Find a Web Authoring Tool

Seeing the variety of pages already on the Web might inspire you to create your own. One of the easiest ways to do this is to find an authoring tool, or HTML editor, that will enable you to create your own pages much as you would using a word processor, without worrying about the correct HTML tags to use. This How-To explains how authoring tools work and how to find them on the Internet.

1.8 Find a Home for My Web Pages

After you've created your pages, you need a place to store them so they can be accessed by other people on the Web. This usually involves finding an ISP that provides Web space for its customers. This How-To discusses how to look for a home for your Web pages.

1.9 Get Information About the Evolution of HTML

Your initial forays into the World Wide Web and page creation might pique your interest in the language of the Web, HTML, and its evolution. Resources on HTML and its development are available on the Web (in addition to what's in this book). This How-To shows you how to find information on the evolution and future of HTML.

1.10 Design Effective Web Pages

Even if you don't yet know anything about HTML, you can learn how to design effective pages. You can master many of the attributes of an effective page—its layout, design, and ease of use—before you learn HTML. This How-To offers helpful tips for designing effective Web pages.

1.1 How do I... Get on the Web from America Online?

COMPATIBILITY: NOT APPLICABLE

Problem

I plan to join America Online. How can I get on the World Wide Web using this service?

Technique

To use the World Wide Web from America Online, you need version 3+ of the America Online software, along with a modem.

Steps

The following steps show how to get onto the World Wide Web from America Online:

1. If you don't have version 3+ of the America Online (AOL) software on your hard disk, install it. The installation process is very easy and straightforward. Just follow the onscreen prompts. Be aware, however, that the AOL modem setting defaults to a Hayes modem configuration. If you have another brand of modem, make sure you change the AOL modem setting to match it.
2. After you install America Online 3+, start it up by double-clicking on the America Online icon. Sign on to America Online. This brings you to the Main menu.
3. Select Internet Connection from the Main menu. This brings you to the Internet Connection menu, which contains a series of Internet-related topics. Figure 1-1 shows this menu.
4. Select the World Wide Web icon.

   The America Online browser will load. Your screen will then resemble Figure 1-2.

How It Works

America Online makes getting on the World Wide Web surprisingly easy. Loading the 3+ software and browser gives you all the tools you need.

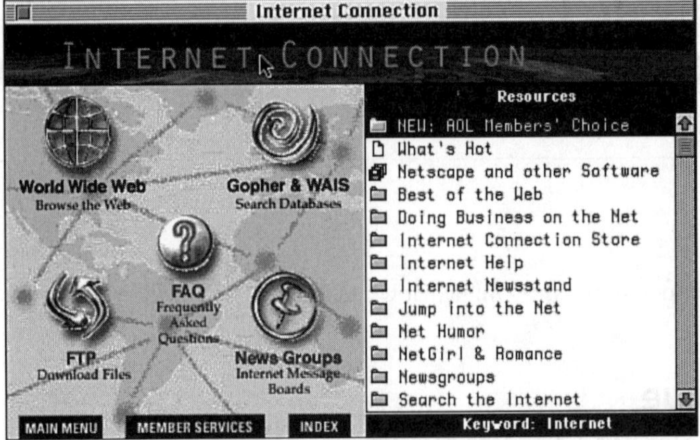

Figure 1-1 The Internet Connection menu on America Online

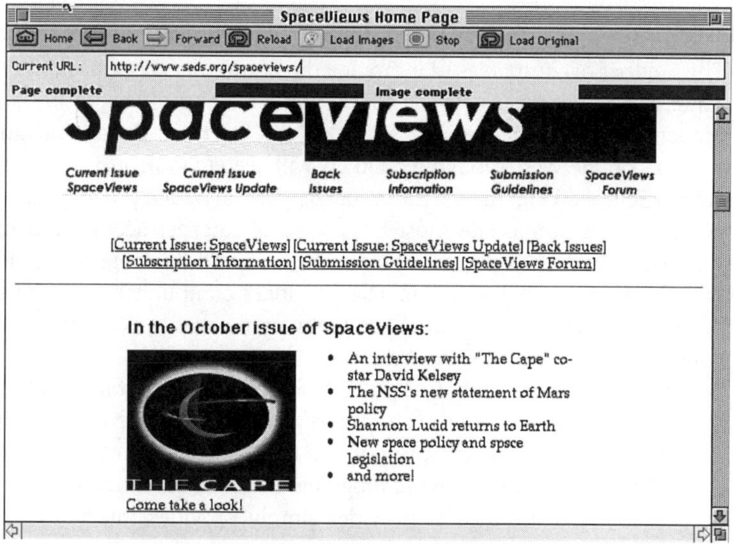

Figure 1-2 The America Online Web browser

Comments

If you have an older version of the America Online software, you will find the upgrade software in the Internet Connection section. The faster the modem you have, the better.

COMPLEXITY
BEGINNING

1.2 How do I... Establish a connection to the Internet?

COMPATIBILITY: ALL

Problem

Instead of using one of the online service providers, I'd like to get an account with a company that will provide me with direct Internet access. How can I get an Internet account, and what type of connection do I need to be able to access the Web?

Technique

The number of companies that provide direct Internet access is rapidly increasing. These companies are usually called Internet service providers, or ISPs; they offer an account on their systems and access to the Internet. To take advantage of the graphics on the Web, though, you likely will need to look into special connections, such as SLIP and PPP, that can turn your computer into a temporary site on the Internet.

A shell account is the most basic type of Internet access. You dial into the Internet provider's computer and use a command-line interface (such as UNIX or DOS) or a text-based menu. The provider's computer has all the software for e-mail, news, and other utilities. Your computer serves as a "dumb" terminal for the connection.

A Serial Line Internet Protocol (SLIP) or Point-to-Point Protocol (PPP) connection turns your computer into a temporary site on the Internet. You dial into the provider's computer as you would if you had a shell account, but instead of using that computer's software, you use programs on your own computer for e-mail, news, and other applications. The provider simply provides Internet access for your computer.

The Integrated Services Digital Network (ISDN) line is a new technology becoming available in many urban areas. These special phone lines provide connections that are much faster than those possible over ordinary phone lines. ISDN lines also feature two channels, so you can send a fax or talk on the phone while using your modem on the other channel. The speed can be expensive, though; installing an ISDN line in your home or office can cost several hundred dollars.

Steps

When establishing an Internet connection, first determine the level of access you require. This is covered in step 1. Steps 2 and 3 offer tips for finding providers in your area and determining which one best suits your needs.

1. First, determine the level of Internet access you need. Because a shell account limits you to the provider's text-based applications, you can use only a text-based browser such as Lynx. You can install software such as The Internet Adapter (TIA) in your shell account that enables it to mimic a SLIP/PPP connection, but this is not as efficient as using a real SLIP or PPP connection.

   If you plan to use a browser that displays graphics, such as Netscape, Mosaic, or Internet Explorer (see How-To 1.3), your best choice is a SLIP/PPP account so you can use the browser software on your own machine to explore the Web. You should get at least a 14.4K (14,400 baud) modem, and preferably a 28.8K modem, so that large files will transfer quickly to and from your computer.

If you plan to do some heavy-duty Web surfing and need more speed than a SLIP/PPP connection, consider an ISDN line. The setup cost can be steep; however, you can save money by being able to transfer large files very quickly, saving on access charges.

2. Next, you must identify the ISPs in your area. You can do this in several ways. Ask friends or colleagues who have Internet access about the providers they use or know about. If you have access to Usenet through another account (or know someone who does), locate the newsgroup `alt.internet.access.wanted` for current information on Internet providers. There are also resources on the Web if you or someone you know can access them. For example, the site `http://thelist.com/` provides a detailed list of hundreds of ISPs, broken down by area code in the U.S. and Canada and by country code outside North America. Many phone book yellow pages now also list ISPs.

3. After you're armed with a list of local ISPs, contact each of them and ask for information about the services they provide. Ask them about the following:

- ✔ The type of Internet services they provide (shell accounts, SLIP/PPP, ISDN).
- ✔ The monthly fee for their services.
- ✔ Whether they have an access number (or POP, Point of Presence) in your local calling area.
- ✔ Whether they add any per-hour charges for premium services or special types of connections.
- ✔ The highest modem speed they support. It should be at least 14.4Kbps, and preferably 28.8Kbps or even 56Kbps, which is now supported by many ISPs. Ask if there is a surcharge for the higher rates of speed.
- ✔ The amount of disk space they provide for each user and what the surcharge is if you need additional space.

Costs will vary from provider to provider and from area to area, depending on the local competition. As a rule of thumb, though, for a standard shell or SLIP/PPP connection, you will probably pay about as much per month as you would for cable TV. Of course, you are likely to find the Internet much more informative and educational than cable TV!

How It Works

ISPs usually buy access to fast 57.6K, T1, and T3 lines from larger network providers. ISPs then combine this network access with their own computers, along with banks of modems to handle incoming calls from customers like you, and sell you packages of Internet access based on this system.

Comments

If you live in a small city or rural area, there might not be any local ISPs in your area. In that case, you might want to investigate using one of the major online services or look into other services that provide long-distance Internet access (often through 800 numbers) for $5–$10 an hour.

The prices on faster 56Kbps modems are now starting to drop. You might want to consider this option if you would like more speed than a 28.8Kbps offers but do not want to invest in an ISDN line. Take note though that, as of this writing, a standard 56Kbps protocol still hasn't been agreed on, and not all ISPs support this speed.

COMPLEXITY
INTERMEDIATE

1.3 How do I... Find a Web browser?

COMPATIBILITY: ALL

Problem

I now have access to the Internet and the World Wide Web. Before I can start exploring, however, I need some kind of browser program to access the Web. How can I find one that best fits my needs?

Technique

Many Web browsers are now available, covering nearly all computer systems. Your system might already have a browser set up for your use; if not, there are plenty of options to choose from. Here are some of the more popular browsers:

- ✔ Netscape Navigator (see Figure 1-3) is far and away the most popular browser. More than 50 percent of all Web browsers now in use are Windows, Macintosh, and UNIX versions of Netscape. Netscape has taken the lead by providing its browser software at little or no cost and by developing HTML extensions that improve the graphics quality of Web pages.

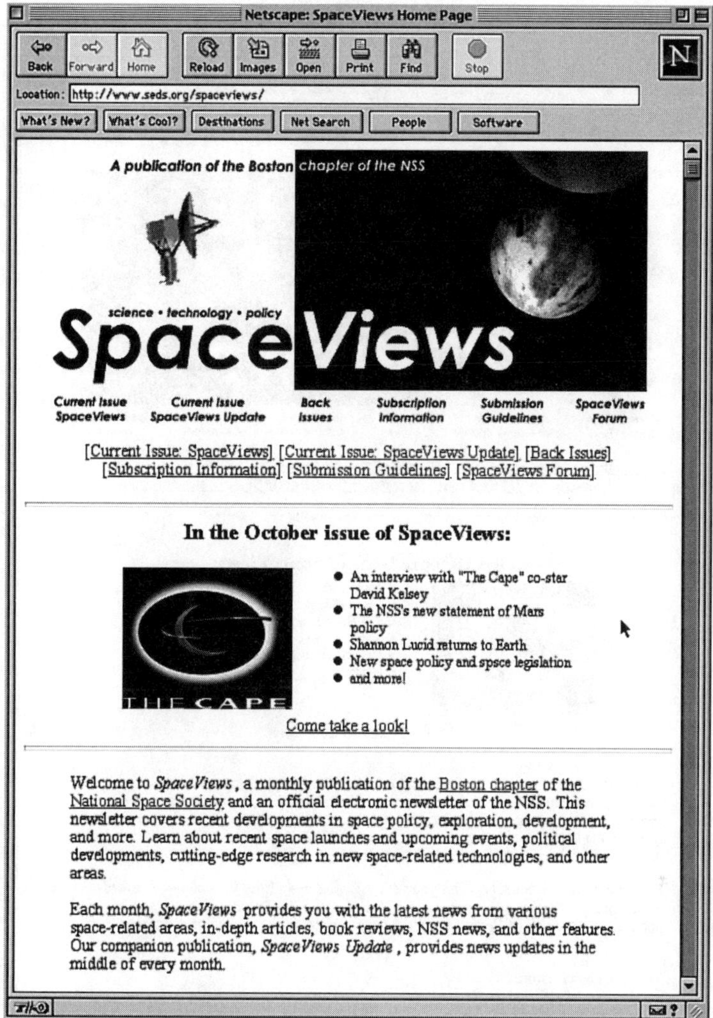

Figure 1-3 Netscape Navigator

- ✔ Microsoft provides Netscape with its strongest competition, Internet Explorer (see Figure 1-4). Versions of Internet Explorer for Windows and Macintosh machines are available free from the Microsoft Web site. The most recent versions of Internet Explorer have most of the same features as Netscape Navigator.

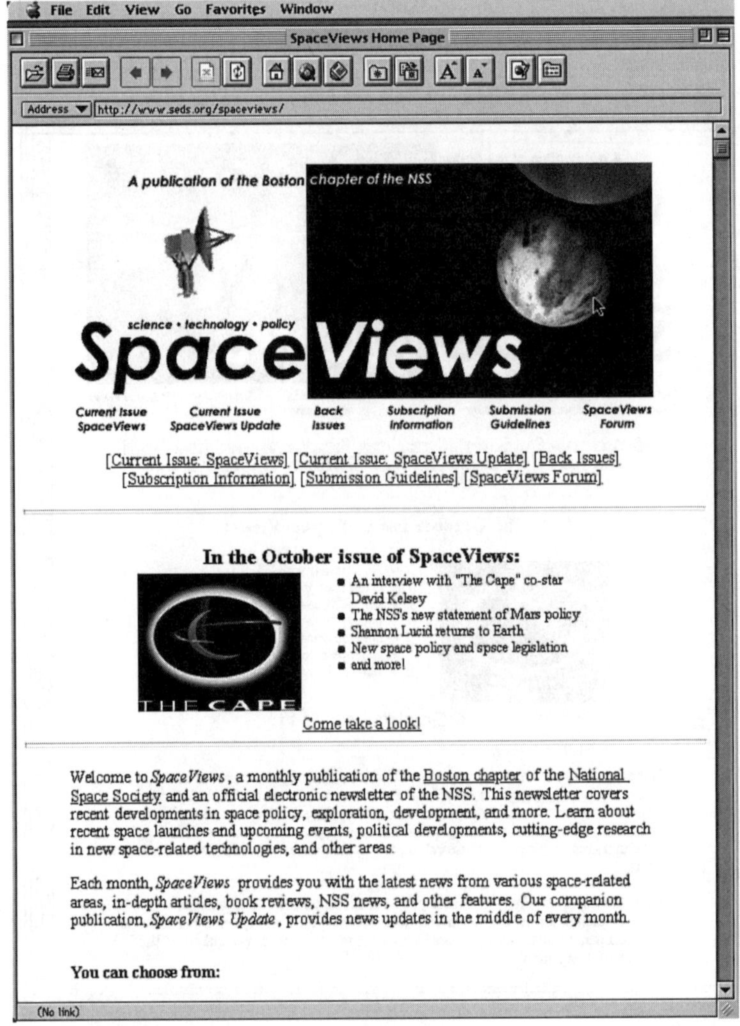

Figure 1-4 Microsoft Internet Explorer

- ✔ Mosaic, the browser that started the Web explosion, is still around (see Figure 1-5), although it is no longer as popular because of the development of Netscape. New versions of Mosaic are still being developed at the National Center for Supercomputer Applications (NCSA) at the University of Illinois, which offers Macintosh, UNIX, and Windows versions of the browser at no cost. Mosaic has also been licensed to several companies that are creating their own enhanced versions of the browser. Some people prefer Mosaic to its two more popular counterparts because they find it "less cluttered" with features.

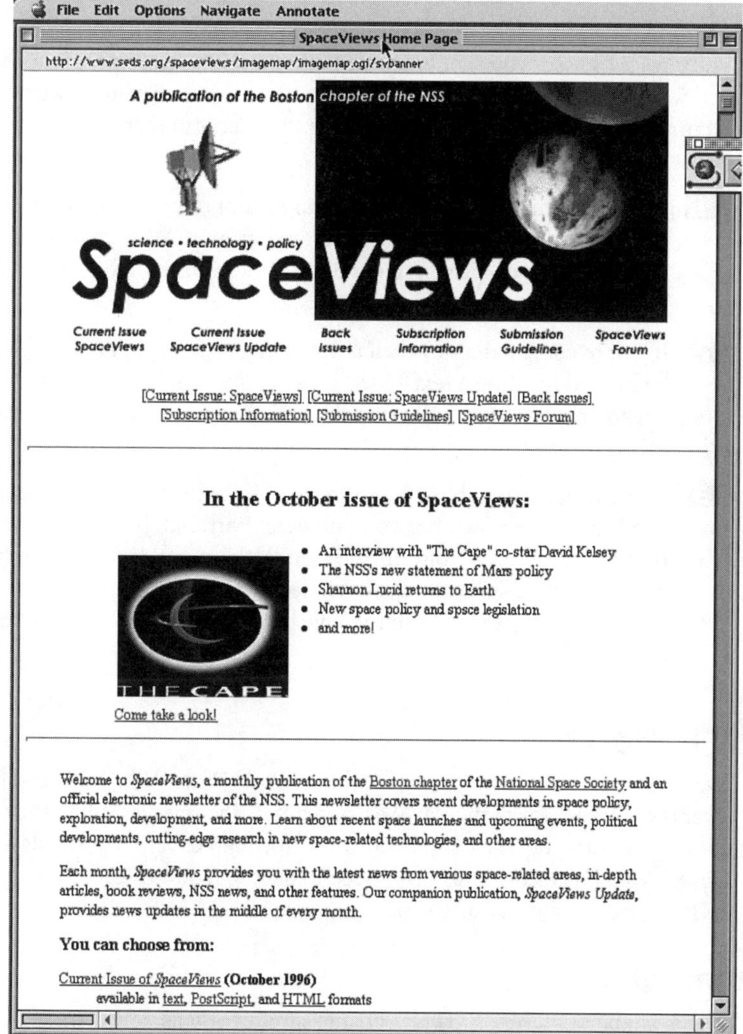

Figure 1-5 NCSA Mosaic

- ✔ For people limited to text-only access, either through a shell account or with DOS, the best option for Web access is still Lynx, a text-based browser. Although you cannot see the graphics used in Web pages with this browser, you can download these images for later viewing offline.

Steps

The type of browser you should use depends on the type of Internet access you have and what software, if any, is already configured on your system. Although Netscape is currently the most popular, several other browsers out there might better suit your needs, so it doesn't hurt to look around.

1. If you have an account through your school or employer, there's a very good chance that you already have one or more Web browsers available. Check with your local system administrator, or ask fellow users what browsers they use.
2. If you're using a dial-up shell account without any adapter software, you'll be limited to using a text-based browser such as Lynx. Your ISP might already have Lynx installed; check with the provider's support staff to see if this is the case.
3. If you're accessing the Internet from a SLIP/PPP or ISDN connection, you'll need to get your own browser software. Fortunately, there are many browsers to choose from. In addition to the popular ones listed here, you can find a detailed list of browsers for most computer systems in Appendix B, "WWW Resources." After you've installed the software, you're ready to explore the Web.

How It Works

Web browsers serve as the interface with the World Wide Web. They send out requests over the Internet for particular Web pages and documents. When they receive the files, they turn the HTML files into the formatted versions displayed on your screen. Web browsers are also equipped to handle requests for information by using FTP, Gopher, and other methods.

Comments

The availability of Web browsers changes frequently as new browsers are released and current ones are upgraded. Although Netscape is the current king of the browsers, a new browser could take its place at any time. This is an important point to keep in mind when you begin to design Web pages: Netscape uses several extensions to HTML that are not part of the standard HTML specification and are not supported by other browsers. If people stop using Netscape (or any other browser having its own extensions to HTML), the extensions in your page can no longer be used.

1.4 How do I... Navigate via browser features?

COMPATIBILITY: ALL

Problem

I have my browser program running and I'm starting to explore the Web. I want to be able to move around from page to page and return to my home page easily. How can I navigate on the Web using my browser's features?

Technique

Nearly all browsers offer a set of basic navigational features that enable you to go from page to page with a single mouse click or keypress. Browsers also enable you to go at any time to a home page that you can predefine.

Steps

Start up your browser. You will notice, either in the browser window or in one of the browser's menus, several commands such as Home, Forward, and Back. These commands enable you to move back and forth among the Web sites you've visited.

1. Most browsers feature a Home button or menu option. When this option is selected, the browser returns the user to its home page or the page that was automatically loaded when the browser started up. This is usually the home page of your ISP or the home page of the company that created the browser. Many browsers give you the option to change the default home page, usually by entering the appropriate address, or URL, of the page you want in the appropriate field of the Preferences dialog box (or by using another similar option).

2. To go from the current page to the previous page you viewed, use the Back button or menu option on most browsers. You can use the Back option to go all the way back to the home page of the browser.

3. Similarly, you can use the Forward option to go forward in the sequence of Web pages visited (called a *history*), all the way up to the most recent page you loaded. (You can use the Forward option only if you previously used the Back option to back up from the last page loaded.)

4. Although not strictly a navigational feature, the Reload or Refresh option offered on most browsers enables you to reload a Web page you previously viewed from the server. This is important if you've been using the Back and Forward commands but want to make sure that a page you loaded some time ago is the most recent version of the page. Reload is also useful if the page updates itself periodically or did not load properly the first time you accessed it.

How It Works

Web browsers store pages in memory. When a Forward or Back button is selected, the required page loads from memory. Because the page contents might have changed since you last loaded it, the Reload command enables you to bring up the page from the server and get any additions or corrections.

Comments

If you back up several pages in your Web browser and then select a different link to follow, any pages that are listed forward of the new page that you are viewing will be removed from your history of pages. That is, you can keep going backward and forward through your history of pages only until you choose a new page somewhere in the list. When you choose a new page, all the pages forward of that new page will be removed from memory.

1.5 How do I... Follow a link?

COMPATIBILITY: ALL

Problem

I've noticed that many words and phrases, and even some pictures, are highlighted on Web pages. I understand that these are called *links* and that they can take me to other places on the Web. How do I use a link to go from page to page?

Technique

Links use selected words or graphics (called *anchors*) to provide a gateway to another Web page, FTP site, Gopher menu, or other Internet resource. When you select the link, you are automatically taken to the new location.

Steps

1. If you're using a graphical browser such as Internet Explorer or Netscape, links appear as words that are highlighted or underlined. Graphics that serve as links have highlighted borders the same color as the highlighted text. To select a link, move the mouse cursor over the highlighted text or graphic and press the mouse button. The browser will automatically follow the link.

2. If you're using a text-based browser, links usually appear as either bold or underlined text or with numbers beside them. To select a link, either enter the number of the link or use the arrow keys to move the cursor to the link, and then press the appropriate key.

How It Works

The document stores the location of the link along with the text or graphic that serves as the anchor for the link. When a user selects a particular link, the browser loads the Web page or other file associated with that link.

Comments

Many browsers let the user display the destination of the link at the bottom of the screen (sometimes called the *message or status bar*) when the cursor passes over the link. This is a useful feature that lets you know exactly where the link goes and helps you decide whether to choose the link.

1.6 How do I... Open a location?

COMPATIBILITY: ALL

Problem

A friend told me about a great page on the Web. I don't know how I would find it using links, but my friend gave me something called a URL. How can I use this URL to open the page?

Technique

Another method of locating pages is to go directly to them using the page's universal resource locator (*URL*), which is nothing more than the address of the page. You type this URL into your browser to go directly to the page.

Steps

Before you can open a location, you must know the URL of the location. A typical Web URL looks something like this:

```
http://www.fake.com/homepage.html
```

The URL consists of the name of the protocol (HTTP for Web pages), the name of the computer on which the file is located, and the name of the file. Chapter 8, "Establishing Links," discusses URLs in greater detail.

After you have the URL for the page, choose the Open or Open Location command on most browsers, and then enter the URL in the appropriate dialog box. The browser goes directly to that page, loading the contents into the browser for you to view.

How It Works

When a user enters a URL into the Open Location command of a browser, the browser loads the page associated with that URL. This works just as if a link to that page had been selected, because links use URLs to define their destinations.

Comments

URLs can be used to describe more than just Web pages. They can be used for FTP sites, Gopher menus, Usenet newsgroups, electronic mail, and Telnet sites as well. All these types of URLs are discussed in greater detail in Chapter 8.

1.7 How do I... Find a Web authoring tool?

COMPATIBILITY: ALL

Problem

I'd like to get started creating Web pages, but for now I'd like to avoid learning about all the markup tags needed to create an HTML document. I understand there's a way around this by using an HTML editor, or authoring tool, that will enable me to create HTML documents in much the same way that I already use a word processor. How do I find one of these programs?

Technique

HTML editors, or authoring tools, are programs that enable people to create HTML documents for their Web pages without getting into the nuts and bolts of HTML. These programs use a format similar to a word processor or page layout program that allows people to enter text and graphics onto a page. In addition, many of the newer word processors, including WordPerfect and Microsoft Word, have HTML editing features. Many browsers such as Netscape Gold come with Web authoring tools built in. Although you still must know some basic HTML to use these programs, they do make it easier for beginners to create Web pages.

Steps

When selecting a Web authoring tool, you'll need to know how much memory and hard disk space you have available on your system so you can make sure the software will work.

1. Just as you did when looking for a Web browser, you might find that your Internet provider already has HTML authoring tools available for you to use. Ask your provider's support staff.

2. If your provider doesn't offer any authoring tools, you can search the Web, where you will find any number of authoring tools for Macintosh, UNIX, Windows, and other systems. A good place to start is `http://www.w3.org/hypertext/WWW/Tools/`. This page, provided by the World Wide Web Consortium, lists several editors, converters, and other tools to help you create HTML documents. It also offers links to more information and the locations from which you can download the software.

How It Works

A converter is a program that reads a file in one format (such as a standard word processor format) and converts it into an HTML document, with all the tags already added. An HTML editor is a program that works like a word processor and enables you to create HTML files by inserting HTML tags from menu items, instead of having to type them in.

Comments

Some editors claim to give you WYSIWYG (What You See Is What You Get). But remember, not all browsers display documents in the same way, and some browsers support HTML extensions that others do not. Thus, some browsers might be able to display documents the same way they appear to you while you're editing them, but others might not be able to do so. This is important to keep in mind when you are creating Web pages.

1.8 How do I... Find a home for my Web pages?

COMPATIBILITY: ALL

Problem

I've created some pages that I'd like to put on the Web for everyone to see. However, I need to put the pages somewhere accessible to anyone on the Web. How do I find a home for these pages?

Technique

Most ISPs give users space in which to put their Web pages, sometimes for an additional charge. If your provider doesn't offer Web space, there are some other options.

Steps

When you look for a place to store your Web pages, decide beforehand how much space you need for your pages and what other special options, such as CGI scripts, you'll need to have. You can then more intelligently choose a home for your pages.

1. The first place to check for Web storage space is with your ISP. ISPs often give a certain amount of Web space to their customers for little or no additional charge. Special services, such as scripts for forms in Web pages, might also be provided for an additional charge.

2. If you already have an account with your school or employer but don't have Web space, or if you are a subscriber to an online service that doesn't offer Web space to its customers, many ISPs will offer Web-only accounts at a special rate. Although you won't have a full account with the provider, you will have space for your Web pages and a method (often e-mail or FTP) to send new and updated versions of Web pages. The provider may also include other services, such as scripts, for an additional charge.

3. When looking for Web space with a provider, be sure to ask the following questions:

- ✔ How much space is available per user, and how much is charged for extra space?
- ✔ How easy is it to edit current pages and insert new pages (and whether this can be done online or via FTP or e-mail)?

- ✔ How much traffic is included, and what are the charges for extra traffic (*traffic* refers to the number of times your pages are accessed, usually measured in megabytes, where a 10-kilobyte page that is accessed 5,000 times would come to 50 megabytes of traffic)?
- ✔ What special services are available, such as script creation or graphic design, and how much does the provider charge for these services?

How It Works

ISPs usually provide some space for users to place Web pages. This space might be in a special directory, or it might be linked to the home directory of the user. Providers may also allow users to include special scripts, or programs, in specific directories on the server for interactive Web pages.

Comments

Although many providers offer special assistance in creating Web pages, this usually comes at a steep cost—often more than $25 an hour. A small investment of time learning HTML, like you're doing right now, can save you a lot of money in the long run when you create your own pages.

Another popular alternative for "housing" your Web pages is GeoCities: `http://www.geocities.com`. GeoCities is a company that offers free Web space to individuals. The Web pages are grouped by geographical areas, where each area represents a specific interest.

1.9 How do I... Get information about the evolution of HTML?

COMPATIBILITY: ALL

Problem

Now that I'm starting to use HTML, I'd like to learn more about how HTML has developed and what its future directions are. Where can I find this information on the Web?

Technique

Information on the current state and future plans of HTML is available on the Web, particularly from the World Wide Web Consortium (W3C).

Steps

1. To get information on the current level of standard HTML, check the URL `http://www.w3.org/`. This site provides links to documents describing the features of HTML that have been approved as an Internet standard and is currently supported by all browsers.

2. For a detailed description of universal resource locators, check the URL `http://www.w3.org/hypertext/WWW/Addressing/Addressing.html`. It explains all the various types of URLs and how you can use them in Web documents.

3. If you are interested in including some of the HTML extensions developed by Netscape, check the Netscape Extensions page at `http://home.netscape.com/assist/net_sites/index.html`. This page gives information about the extensions Netscape has provided for HTML, along with examples of advanced features such as tables, backgrounds, and dynamic documents.

How It Works

These links provide access to updated documents on the status of the current HTML draft, future HTML development, and how URLs work.

Comments

Some Netscape and Microsoft extensions to HTML are not currently part of either version of HTML, although some of the tags might be included in a later draft of HTML 4.*x*. Although a page that contains Netscape extensions can be read by other browsers, it will not be formatted in the same way it is in Netscape.

One of HTML's newest and most exciting features, Layers, is covered in Chapter 20, "Dynamic HTML." Currently Layers are supported only by Netscape 4.0 and Internet Explorer 4.0 or higher. (And each supports them in a slightly different manner.)

1.10 How do I... Design effective Web pages?

COMPATIBILITY: ALL

Problem

I want to make sure that the pages I create stand out (in a good way, of course), even though I'm just beginning to learn HTML. What are some of the basic techniques I must know to create effective Web pages?

Technique

Several fundamental aspects of designing a home page transcend HTML. These include layout, design, and ease of use. Here are some helpful tips you can use to create any kind of Web page, from the simplest page to advanced pages with forms, frames, and graphics.

Steps

Before you begin to design your Web pages, review the following pointers. They will help you sharpen the design of your pages and avoid embarrassing mistakes.

1. First, decide what you're going to say. It sounds obvious, but many Web pages (not to mention other types of publications) fail because they lack focus. The key points you want to present to the readers must be clear. If people become confused about what you're trying to say, they probably won't come back to other pages you create and will steer others clear of them as well. (Word-of-mouth is especially powerful on the Internet.)

2. After you've decided on the goals of your Web page, you must plan what to include on the page. Now is a good time to start subdividing your material by content. The material can either be put on separate pages or combined on one page, depending on your mode of presentation.

3. Unless your page is going to be very short, it helps to have an introductory page briefly describing the purpose of your Web site, what information is available, and how to get to it. This serves as both an introduction and a table of contents, allowing the reader to decide quickly whether the contents of the page are interesting enough to continue reading. Other pages, with more information about your topic, can be included as links on the introductory page. (See Chapter 7, "Managing Document Spacing," for more information on links.)

4. If possible, make each page you design relatively short. There should be no more than one or two screens of text and graphics per page. If the page is longer, readers will have to scroll repeatedly to read the whole page, which can disrupt the flow of the document. If you must create longer pages, include a table of contents and links to specific places within the document to make it easier for people to find information.

5. Don't overload a page with graphics. Graphics files can be very large, which means it takes much longer for a browser to load a page that includes them. The neat graphics you included on your page can take minutes for others to load. Although you might have a fast network connection, other people might have relatively slow access over a modem.

6. When creating your pages, keep in mind that they will be viewed by people using a wide variety of browsers, from text-only browsers to the latest versions of Mosaic, Internet Explorer, and Netscape. Thus, you probably want to conform to the HTML standards when composing your document so that it can be used by the largest possible number of readers. Also, do not make your page overly reliant on graphics. Some people use text-only browsers or turn off image loading (an option provided by many browsers to enable documents to load faster). This doesn't mean you shouldn't take advantage of graphics and HTML extensions, but in the process, be careful that you don't make the document unusable to many readers. If you do decide to make your pages "browser dependent," make sure you specify which browser you are catering to.

7. Before you announce your pages to the world, carefully check them over to make sure they are free of errors and bad HTML. Look at the pages with different browsers (or ask friends who use different browsers to look at the pages) and make sure everything looks right. Putting an error-laden, poorly designed set of pages on the Web can be very embarrassing.

How It Works

The proper design of Web pages is not that different from the proper design of printed materials. You want to make your point to your readers as succinctly as you can and with as few errors as possible.

Comments

Good style is largely in the eye of the beholder. What can appear stylish and hip to one person can appear ugly and boring or confusing to another. However, these pointers should help improve any Web pages you design because they transcend the content of the pages and focus on the basics of presentation.

PART II

AUTHORING

CHAPTER 2

HTML BASICS

2

HTML BASICS

How do I...

- **2.1 Recognize an HTML document?**
- **2.2 Convert word-processed documents to HTML?**
- **2.3 Convert other types of files to HTML?**
- **2.4 Create HTML documents with an authoring tool?**
- **2.5 Insert an HTML element?**
- **2.6 Build a simple HTML document?**
- **2.7 Include a comment?**
- **2.8 Add body text?**
- **2.9 Set the background color of my Web page?**
- **2.10 Set the color of the text in my Web page?**
- **2.11 Set the colors for the hypertext links in my Web page?**
- **2.12 Use an image as the background for my Web page?**
- **2.13 Insert special characters into a document?**
- **2.14 Create a home page?**
- **2.15 View my home page?**

The World Wide Web is an ever-growing online information space filled with a myriad of commercial, educational, and entertaining materials. These materials, in the form of hypermedia documents accessed through the Internet, can be located anywhere in the world. No matter where they originate, most Web documents are created using Hypertext Markup Language (HTML).

HTML *authoring* is the process of creating and defining such documents. HTML version 4.0 is the most recent version of this powerful authoring language; unless otherwise indicated, the term HTML refers to the language as a general entity, whereas HTML 4.0, HTML 3.2, HTML 3, and HTML 2 refer to specific versions of the language. This chapter begins to explore how you can use HTML to publish hypermedia documents on the World Wide Web.

You use HTML elements to define document structure and format. An HTML *element* is the inclusive region defined by either a single tag or a pair of tags. (Tags are described more completely in How-To 2.5.) A *tag* is a string in the language surrounded by a less-than (<) and a greater-than (>) sign. An opening tag is any tag in which the string does not begin with a slash (/); also, with these you might see a list of allowable attribute/value pairs within an opening tag. An ending or closing tag is a string that begins with a slash (/). Appendix A, "HTML Quick Reference," provides a quick reference to elements supported by HTML 4.0.

This chapter covers the recognition and creation of simple HTML documents. The detailed use of individual editors and converters is beyond the scope of this book, although several How-To's provide a brief introduction to them. You are also led through the processes for developing and viewing a simple home page.

The topics covered in this chapter introduce the essential basics of HTML authoring. Later chapters provide you with insights and examples. The information in this chapter will jump-start you into the publication of your own HTML documents.

2.1 Recognize an HTML Document

You can present information in a variety of forms: GIF images, WAV sound, or PostScript text. HTML documents format textual information with embedded markup tags that provide style and structure information. In this How-To, you will learn the structure of HTML documents and how to identify a document as an HTML document.

2.2 Convert Word-Processed Documents to HTML

You have been developing documents using word processors for a long time. Some of these documents are exactly the ones that you want to publish on the World Wide Web. Is there an easy way to transform these documents into HTML? In this How-To, you will learn how to convert word-processed documents to HTML pages automatically.

2.3 Convert Other Types of Files to HTML

You have been developing documents using a variety of text formatting languages. You have documents that you have developed in TeX and Scribe. You need to alter the markup tags to conform to HTML rather than the native formatting commands. Are there automatic tools to help with this task? In this How-To, you will learn how to convert text-formatted documents to HTML pages.

2.4 Create HTML Documents with an Authoring Tool

If you want to jump straight into authoring but don't want to become enmeshed in the details of HTML formatting, then this How-To might be your answer. It answers the question, "Is there a way to generate an HTML document without having to insert the formatting tags manually?" In this How-To, you will learn how to find and use HTML authorware.

2.5 Insert an HTML Element

Markup tags are the glue holding HTML documents together. These tags determine the various elements contained within your document. To a large extent, these elements define how the information in your document is treated and rendered. In this How-To, you will learn the process for placing this structural and formatting information into your HTML document.

2.6 Build a Simple HTML Document

HTML documents are the basis upon which the World Wide Web is built. Any attempt to author hypermedia objects for the World Wide Web will require the development of a suitable HTML document. This How-To provides step-by-step instructions for developing a simple HTML document. This simple example can serve not only as your first HTML document but also as your guide for developing well-structured HTML documents. In this How-To, you will learn how to build your first HTML page.

2.7 Include a Comment

Comments provide a mechanism for documenting the reasons you have developed a document the way that you have. You don't want this information presented to the viewer, but it should be available to those interested in the design and development process. In this How-To, you will learn how to format comments in HTML.

2.8 Add Body Text

The body is the meat of an HTML document. The body element represents the information content of a document. In this How-To, you will learn how to author the body of HTML pages.

2.9 Set the Background Color of My Web Page

Graphical browsers such as Navigator and Internet Explorer use a default background color when displaying Web pages. HTML enables you to pick a more appropriate color. In this How-To, you will learn how to specify a Web page's background color.

2.10 Set the Color of the Text in My Web Page

HTML enables you to override a browser's default color for displaying text. In this How-To, you will learn how to indicate your choice of text color.

2.11 Set the Colors for the Hypertext Links in My Web Page

Browsers usually display the links from your Web page to other pages in a different color from the surrounding text. HTML enables you to specify the particular color for browsers to use. You can use aspects of this capability to have links that your viewer has already visited seem to blend into the surrounding text or completely vanish from the page. In this How-To, you will learn how to select the colors a browser should use to display the links in your Web page.

2.12 Use an Image as the Background for My Web Page

Going beyond changing the background color of a Web page, you can select an image for browsers to use as wallpaper forming the background for your Web page. Just as in applying real wallpaper to a room, the browser paints the background of your Web page using as many copies of the specified image as necessary to provide complete coverage. In this How-To, you will learn how to modify your Web page to include a background image.

2.13 Insert Special Characters into a Document

A variety of symbols beyond the standard alphanumeric characters might be required in your HTML documents. In this How-To, you will learn how to include such characters so that they appear correctly in a viewing environment such as Mosaic or Netscape.

2.14 Create a Home Page

You have created a few simple pages; now you are ready to create a page of your own in which people can find information about you. This How-To walks you through the creation of a simple home page that can be expanded as your skill in HTML increases. In this How-To, you will learn how to create a basic home page.

2.15 View My Home Page

You have created an HTML document, but you have no idea what it will look like in Netscape or some other browser application. You must view the documents that you create to determine how they will appear when viewed, not only in your current browser but also in other browsers. In this How-To, you will learn how to view and test an HTML page.

2.1 How do I... Recognize an HTML document?

COMPATIBILITY: HTML

Problem

What is an HTML document? How do I create one? How can I tell that a document has been formatted using HTML? What are the telltale signs?

Technique

Formatted textual information can be stored in a variety of ways:

- ✔ Word-processed documents
- ✔ PostScript documents
- ✔ HTML documents
- ✔ DVI documents

HTML documents serve as the basis for information published on the World Wide Web. To determine whether a text file is an HTML document, you can check its document structure and look for the presence of HTML elements. These are the characteristics that identify an HTML document.

First, try to display the document using an HTML browser. If the text file is displayed properly within a browser's viewing window, then most likely the file is an HTML document.

Follow this by looking at the document with a text editor. Examine the file for HTML tags. A *tag* is a string in the language surrounded by a less-than (**<**) and a greater-than (**>**) sign. An *opening tag* is any tag in which the string does not begin with a slash (**/**). An *ending* or *closing tag* is a string that does begin with a slash (**/**). The region between an opening tag and a closing tag with the same string is referred to as an *element*.

Steps

This procedure determines whether a document is an HTML document. If at any particular step you determine that the file in question is or is not an HTML document, you are finished and need not continue with the remainder of the steps.

1. Use your favorite browser to try to view the document in question. You can do this with most browsers via either a menu option or a command-line argument. For example, with Netscape, you execute an Open Page or File from the File menu. With Lynx, you open the local file **/AMIHTM.HTM** by issuing the following command. Be sure that you have named the local file with the `.html` (or `.htm` for PC) filename extension. This indicates to most browsers that the local file is to be accessed as an HTML document.

```
lynx /amihtm.htm
```

If the document does not appear in the browser's display, then more than likely the file is not an HTML document. This is not a definitive test, however, because several possible conditions could potentially cause an HTML document not to appear.

2. Open the file in question using your favorite text editor. If the document fails to open due to an error indicating that the document is a binary document of unknown format, then you can conclude that the file is not an HTML document. All HTML documents are ASCII text documents. If you receive an error message indicating that the file contains lines that are too long, you should try to open the file using another editor with a greater line-length limit.

3. Examine the text file in the editor window. HTML 3.2 and later documents might begin with a document type tag identifying it as an HTML 3.2 or 4.0 document. Documents conforming to earlier versions of HTML can begin with just an **<HTML>** tag. Tags are used to delimit structural or formatting elements in HTML. An opening and a closing **<HTML>** tag should surround the entire document. You should also find opening and closing tags for **<HEAD>** and **<BODY>** elements. An HTML document should appear as shown in the following code:

```
<!DOCTYPE HTML PUBLIC "-//W3C//DTD HTML 3.2//EN">
<HTML>
<HEAD>
......
</HEAD>
<BODY>
......
</BODY>
</HTML>
```

4. If you find these statements in your document, you are looking at an HTML document. However, older HTML documents might not have these structural elements. Furthermore, the additional information in the document type tag will vary depending on the version of HTML and the language. This document type tag indicates HTML 3.2 with an English language flavor.

5. At this point, you are looking at either an old-style HTML document or some other ASCII text-based document—PostScript, for example. You should scan through the document looking for any of the HTML elements specified in Appendix A, "HTML Quick Reference." If no tags can be

found, the file is not an HTML document. If tags are present, then the file is likely an HTML document that was developed using a loose HTML specification. For example, the following code might represent an old-style HTML document:

```
<TITLE>Old Style Document</TITLE>
....
```

How It Works

As you begin authoring HTML documents, you might want to examine other authors' HTML documents and styles. Having a knowledge of the common architecture of HTML documents will allow you to analyze and adapt existing documents to suit your goals.

The first step in the identification process is to examine the document in question with an HTML browser such as Chameleon's WebSurfer. If the document fails to display, then that document likely is not in HTML. However, this is not certain. A few possible explanations for such a failure are

- ✔ A filename extension used for the file you are viewing that is inappropriate for an HTML document
- ✔ The remapping of the `.html` (or `.htm`) filename extension to indicate a type other than HTML
- ✔ An error in the HTML code of the document

Most browsers will not render a file as an HTML document, even though it is, unless the file is appropriately named. Without the suitable filename extension (usually `.html` or `.htm`), the browser might treat the document as simple plain text (or as whatever the configured default type is). If the document fails to display for this reason, make sure you add the appropriate extension to your file before trying to view it with your browser.

To correct the second situation, either remap the `.html` (or `.htm`) extension to indicate an HTML document or rename the file with the appropriate extension. If you plan to examine several local files, you might want to perform the latter operation through your browser's menus or through its configuration files.

Next, all HTML documents are text-based. In other words, you should be able to examine them with a standard text editor, such as EDIT on a PC or SimpleText on a Mac. If the document is a binary file, then, by default, it is not an HTML document.

In addition, all well-constructed HTML 3.2 and above documents conform to a common document structure. By examining the text of the file for architectural features, you should be able to make an initial judgment concerning a document. Figure 2-1 illustrates this common architecture.

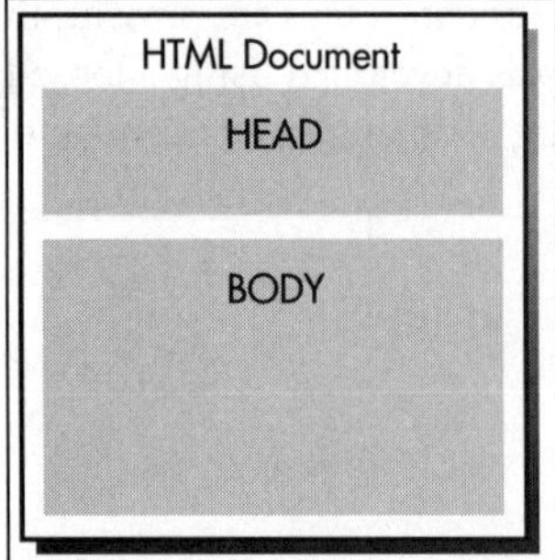

Figure 2-1 Structure of an HTML document

In some cases, this architectural information might not be sufficient to make an absolute determination, particularly for documents built on an earlier HTML standard. (See the "Comments" section.) In this case, you must examine the document for HTML elements. These elements can be of any type specified in Appendix A.

Comments

This procedure will work for any HTML document. Certain caveats should be kept in mind, however.

PC, UNIX, and Mac platforms use slightly different combinations of carriage returns and line feeds to designate the end of a line; therefore, if the text file you are trying to view was developed on a platform different from the one you are currently using, strange characters might appear at the end of text lines or the file might appear as a single long string of text. This latter situation might cause difficulties with text editors that have fixed line-length limits.

With respect to structural features, certain browsers such as Mosaic can scan and display less well-constructed HTML documents. These capabilities permit the display of HTML documents that conform to a looser standard.

Browser applications perform a two-step procedure for determining whether a file is an HTML document or some other data object. First, the browser examines the server response header sent with the data object. If a `Content-type: text/html` line is present, then the browser assumes that the document is HTML. If the browser cannot determine the object type from the server, either because the object did not come from a server (a local file) or because a server did not supply a complete response header, it examines the file's filename extension. By default, if the extension is `.html` (`.htm` for PC), the browser attempts to display the object as an HTML document. You can often configure the specific filename extensions used by a particular browser through menu options or configuration files.

Servers determine whether a file is an HTML document based solely on the filename extension. For HTML, the usual filename extension is `.html` (`.htm` for

PC-based servers). As is true with browsers, you can usually configure the filename extensions for a server. (See Chapter 12, "Server Basics," and Chapter 13, "Handling Server Security.")

2.2 How do I... Convert word-processed documents to HTML?

COMPATIBILITY: HTML

Problem

I don't want to begin authoring documents from scratch. I have already developed a whole bank of documents suitable for use on the World Wide Web using my word processor. Is there any way I can use these preexisting documents without having to re-create them using HTML?

Technique

Converters exist for many popular word processing packages. These converters accept word processor documents and generate appropriate HTML documents as output. This How-To provides step-by-step instructions for acquiring and applying an appropriate converter.

The process requires familiarity with the use of anonymous FTP or FTP URLs. Your first task is to identify an appropriate converter. Next, acquire the converter. Then, apply the converter to your existing documents. Finally, fine-tune your document in an HTML editing environment.

Steps

This procedure provides the necessary steps to acquire and use word processor document converters.

1. Determine the word processing application you used to develop your documents.

2. Find the converter you will need to use. Table 2-1 lists examples of some of these environments by software package and provides pointers to information concerning them. If you cannot find your particular word processor in Table 2-1, you might want to use a Web search application to find an applicable converter.

Table 2-1 Common word processor conversion applications

WORD PROCESSOR	CONVERTERS	AVAILABILITY
Word for Windows	rtftohtml	`http://www.sunpack.com/RTF/rtftohtml_overview.html`
WordPerfect	wptohtml	`http://www.keele.ac.uk/htmtools/wp/wptoht52/wptohtml.html`
FrameMaker	WebMaker	`ftp://ftp.alumni.caltech.edu/pub/mcbeath/web/miftran/`

3. Use an anonymous FTP or an FTP URL to acquire an appropriate converter package. Uncompress, unarchive, and install the converter application as appropriate for your platform.

   ✔ On a UNIX platform, use the **`uncompress`** and **`tar`** commands to uncompress and unarchive the converter.

   ✔ On a PC platform, the most common compression/archival program is ZIP. Use the unzip application to uncompress and unarchive the acquired converter.

   ✔ On a Mac platform, the common compression/archival program is StuffIt. Use the StuffIt program to uncompress and unarchive the converter.

4. Apply the converter to your word processed documents.

5. If you need to, use a text or HTML editor to fine-tune the converted documents.

How It Works

Many preexisting word processor documents might be suitable for use in the World Wide Web environment. Therefore, converter applications have been developed to take word processed documents and generate equivalent HTML documents from them. The first step in converting these documents is acquiring a suitable converter.

Several converters have been developed for this purpose. Table 2-1 provides references to several of them. Many commercial applications are also available.

After you install the converter, converting existing documents into HTML is just a matter of judiciously applying the converter application. This will lead to HTML documents that look the way they did within the word processing environment.

The final step of this procedure is to use an editing environment to fine-tune the converted document. This fine-tuning includes two parts: corrections and additions.

Corrections are sometimes necessary when the converter does not know how to deal with a particular type of formatting in the word processed file. You can make these corrections using any of the authoring environment methods discussed in How-To 2.4.

Additions are also likely because most word processors do not support hypertext linking. *Links* provide associative connections between HTML documents. These connections link a location in one document to a location within another document; HTML designates these locations using the anchor tags `<A...>...</A>`. Therefore, the addition of anchors to word processed documents is common. (See Chapter 8, "Establishing Links," for detailed information on the use of the anchor element.)

Furthermore, you may also add logical elements (in contrast to purely physical elements) at your discretion. Word processors usually support the conversion of physical elements, such as bold and italics (see How-To's 3.1 and 3.2); however, they do not support logical HTML elements, such as strong and emphasis (see How-To 4.2). Hence, desired logical elements need to be added after document conversion.

Finally, converters currently available do not support HTML level 4.0, and many do not support level 3.2 elements. Inclusion of such elements involves editing the converted document using the methods described in How-To 2.4.

Converters are by no means perfect; therefore, remembering to perform this final step in the procedure is important. Simply taking the results of a conversion and asking your Web site administrator to install the documents might lead to disappointing results. Check your documents thoroughly in Web browsers such as NCSA Mosaic, Microsoft's Internet Explorer, Netscape Navigator, and in HTML editing environments (as described in How-To 2.4).

Comments

The converters mentioned in this How-To do not make up a complete list. They do represent a sampling of converters for many popular word processors. To convert documents developed in a word processor not mentioned in Table 2-1, you might want to use any of the available Web search pages, such as AltaVista (`http://www.altavista.com`), Hotbot, (`http://www.hotbot.com`), Lycos (`http://lycos.cs.cmu.edu`), or Infoseek (`http://www.infoseek.com`).

Finally, not all converters are equal. The names of some commercially available products and contact information are provided in Table 2-2.

Table 2-2 The names of some commercially available converters

PRODUCT	FORMATS	CONTACT
Cyberleaf	FrameMaker, Interleaf, Word, WordPerfect	Interleaf, Inc.
FasTag	FrameMaker, Interleaf, Word, WordPerfect	Avalanche Development
TagWrite	FrameMaker, Interleaf, Word, Ventura Publisher, WordPerfect	Zandar Corp.

2.3 How do I...
Convert other types of files to HTML?

COMPATIBILITY: HTML

Problem

I have developed my documents using a document formatting language. I want to use these documents on my Web site. How can I use these documents with minimal additional effort? I've already inserted my formatting information through my development language. All I need is a way to transform that information into HTML.

Technique

Many documents have been developed through formatting languages such as PostScript, TeX, and troff. This How-To provides step-by-step instructions for acquiring and applying converters to such documents. These packages will accept documents developed in common formatting languages and generate appropriate HTML documents as output.

The process requires familiarity with the use of anonymous FTPs or FTP URLs. First, identify an appropriate converter. Next, acquire the converter. Then, apply the converter to your existing documents. Finally, fine-tune your document in an HTML editing environment.

Steps

The following steps are necessary to acquire and use document converters:

1. Determine the formatting language you used to develop your documents.

2. Table 2-3 shows examples of some of the available converters, listed by document formatting language, and provides pointers to information concerning them. Find the converter that you will need to use. Due to the dynamic nature of the Web, you might want to use a Web search page such as Lycos (`http://lycos.cs.cmu.edu`) to find an applicable converter if you need one for a document processing language not listed in Table 2-3.

Table 2-3 Common formatting language conversion applications

FORMATTING LANGUAGE	CONVERTERS	AVAILABILITY
TeX/LaTeX/Texinfo	latex2html	http://cbl.leeds.ac.uk/nikos/
		tex2html/doc/latex2html/
		latext2html.html
	texi2html	ftp://src.doc.ic.ac.uk/
		computing/informationsystems/
		www/tools/translator
PostScript	ps2html	ftp/pub/ps2html/ps2html-v2.html
Scribe	Scribe2html	ftp://gatekeeper.dec.com/pub/
		DEC/NSL/www/

3. Use anonymous FTP or an FTP URL to acquire an appropriate converter package. Uncompress, unarchive, and install the converter application as appropriate for your platform.

✔ On a UNIX platform, use the `uncompress` and `tar` commands to uncompress and unarchive the desired converter.

✔ On a PC platform, the most common compression/archival program is ZIP. Use the unzip application to uncompress and unarchive the acquired converter.

✔ On a Mac platform, the common compression/archival program is StuffIt. Use the StuffIt program to uncompress and unarchive the converter.

4. Apply the converter to your formatted documents.

5. Use the process described in How-To 2.4 to fine-tune the converted documents.

How It Works

Many preexisting documents might be suitable for use in the World Wide Web environment. Therefore, applications have been developed to convert such formatted documents to equivalent HTML documents. The first step in this process is acquiring a suitable converter. Table 2-3 names and references several of them.

Most document formatting languages support a similar suite of formatting commands. The primary difference is in the syntax of the language. After you install the converter, it will map documents in the source formatting language to HTML documents.

The final step of this procedure is to fine-tune the converted document using the editing facilities described in How-To 2.4. This fine-tuning includes both additions and corrections.

Most converters will not insert hypermedia links into your document. Because most document formatting languages such as PostScript and troff do not support hypertext links, links do not appear in documents of this type; consequently, direct translation of such documents will not include links. Any desired hypertext links need to be added by the author after conversion. Chapter 8, "Establishing Links," provides comprehensive information on link creation.

Despite their similarities, document formatting languages do not all provide the same structuring and formatting elements. You might want to add HTML elements to enhance the converted documents. For example, HTML supports logical elements as well as purely physical ones. The markup for a bolded statement (How-To 3.1) might carry over with no problem; however, if you want to specify emphasis elements (How-To 4.2) that will connote semantic as well as physical characteristics, you will have to add these by hand.

Corrections will sometimes be necessary when the converter does not know how to deal with a particular type of formatting element in the source document. The converter might generate either no element or an erroneous element in the HTML document. In either case, the document needs correction to maintain the desired formatting.

Comments

The list of converters mentioned in this How-To is not necessarily comprehensive. It contains a sampling of converters for many popular document formatting languages. To convert documents developed with a formatting language not mentioned in Table 2-3, you might want to use any of the available Web search engines.

As with word processor conversion programs, different converters support different inputs and outputs. Furthermore, converters have varying degrees of success in maintaining formatting integrity. Before you install a converter on your server, you should view a document converted by it using several browsing packages to guarantee that your document looks the way you want it to look. For consistency, you might want to compare this view to the appearance of the document in its original form.

Finally, basic elements can be automatically added to standard ASCII text files. One such program is asc2html. This application (reference **ftp://src.doc.ic.ac.uk/computing/information-systems/www/tools/ translators**) takes a plain text file and generates an HTML document with a simple body containing the file's data within a **<PRE>** element. (See How-To 7.6 for information on the **<PRE>** element.) A title is inserted based on the filename, and URLs in the data are converted into hypertext links.

2.4 How do I... Create HTML documents with an authoring tool?

COMPATIBILITY: HTML 2+

Problem

I want to start creating HTML documents, but I do not feel the need to learn every little HTML element. Some tools must exist that enable me to create a document without having to insert each and every tag manually. I see the relationship between text formatting languages such as PostScript and word processors. Why not a similar editor for HTML?

Technique

The editors used to create HTML documents tend to fall into three categories:

- ✔ Text editors: Manual insertion of HTML tags
- ✔ Text editors with macros/pull-down menu tag selection: Creation of HTML elements through application of macros/menu items on selected areas of text
- ✔ WYSIWYG (What You See Is What You Get) style: Tags inserted as with macro/menu-based approach; however, formatting displays as it will ultimately be rendered (see the "Comments" section concerning HTML WYSIWYG limitation).

This How-To examines these three classes of applications and gives a general means of acquiring them so you can use them to develop your documents.

Steps

The following procedures are broken down by these three categories. Each category provides the steps necessary to acquire an editor of this type for your platform, followed by a generic walk-through of the creation of a simple document.

The acquisition phase of each process is broken down by development platform. Furthermore, the use of anonymous FTP or FTP URLs is required to retrieve most of the HTML editors described.

Text Editors

1. Determine the development platform you want to use.
2. Find a text editor that you want to use. Table 2-4 lists examples of typical text editors by platform.

Table 2-4 Text editors by platform

EDITOR/ENVIRONMENT	PLATFORM(S)	AVAILABILITY
BBEdit-Lite	Mac	ftp://ftp.std.com/pub/bbedit/
		freeare/bbedit-lite-30.hqx
TeachText	Mac	Standard
EDIT	PC	Standard
Notepad	PC (Windows)	Standard
emacs	PC, UNIX	GNU archive sites
vi	PC, UNIX	PC archive sites, standard

3. Manually enter tags. Follow the procedure developed for creation of simple HTML documents defined in How-To 2.6.

Macro Packages and Editors with Pull-Down Menu Tag Selection

1. Determine the development platform you want to use.

2. Find an editor that you want to use. Table 2-5 lists examples of some of these editors by platform and provides pointers to information concerning them.

Table 2-5 Macro packages and editors

EDITOR/ENVIRONMENT	PLATFORM(S)	AVAILABILITY
Alpha	Mac	http://www.cs.umd.edu/~keleher/
		alpha.html
BBEdit Ext. 1	Mac	http://www.barebones.com/
BBEdit Ext. 2	Mac	http://www.uji.es/bbedit-html-
		extensions.html
HTML Assistant Pro	PC	Freeware version on the CD
HTMLed	PC (Windows)	ftp://ftp.std.com/src/pc/
		www/htmled12.zip
emacs HTML helper	PC, UNIX	http://www.santafe.edu/~nelson/
		tools/

Review the materials suggested in Table 2-5 before making your final decision.

3. Retrieve the desired editor from the location(s) suggested in Table 2-5.

4. Uncompress, unarchive, and install the software as and where necessary.

- ✔ On a UNIX platform, use the `uncompress` and `tar` commands to uncompress and unarchive the desired editor.
- ✔ On a PC platform, the most common compression/archival program is ZIP. Use the unzip application to uncompress and unarchive the desired editor.
- ✔ On a Mac platform, the common compression/archival program is StuffIt. Use the StuffIt program to uncompress and unarchive the desired editor.

You are now ready to begin.

5. Open the editor to start creating the document.
6. Type the text that is to appear in your document. Include all information content at this time.
7. Use the pull-down menus or the macros to insert appropriate HTML tags to create the desired document elements.
8. Save the document in a file with the filename extension indicating that the file content is an HTML document. This extension is usually `.html` (or `.htm`).

WYSIWYG Style

1. Determine the development platform you want to use.
2. Find the HTML editor that you want to use. Table 2-6 lists examples of some of these environments by platform and pointers to information concerning them.

Table 2-6 HTML editors

EDITOR/ENVIRONMENT	PLATFORM(S)	AVAILABILITY
HTML Editor	Mac	`http://dragon.acadian.ca:1667/`
		`~giles/HTML_Editor/`
		`Documentation.html`
GT_HTML.DOT	PC (Word for Windows)	`http://www.gatech.edu/`
		`word_html/release.htm`
Internet Assistant	PC (Word for Windows)	`http://www.microsoft.com/`
	(also on the CD)	`msword/internet/ia`
Netscape Navigator Gold	PC, Mac, UNIX	`http://home.netscape.com`
tkWWW	UNIX	`http://tk-www.mit.edu:8001/`
		`tk-www/help/`

3. Review the materials suggested in Table 2-6 before making your final decision. Note, due to the dynamic nature of the Web, many of these URLs will change so you may need to find them with your favorite search engine.
4. Retrieve the desired HTML editor from the location(s) suggested in Table 2-6.
5. Uncompress, unarchive, and install the software as and where necessary.
   - ✔ On a UNIX platform, use the **uncompress** and **tar** commands to uncompress and unarchive the converter. These applications are provided with the operating system.
   - ✔ On a PC platform, the most common compression/archival program is ZIP. Use the unzip application to uncompress and unarchive the acquired converter. Several ZIP applications are available through PC FTP sites, BBSs, and users' groups.
   - ✔ On a Mac platform, the common compression/archival program is StuffIt. Use the StuffIt program to uncompress and unarchive the converter. The StuffIt program is available through a variety of Mac FTP sites, BBSs, and users' groups.

   You are now ready to begin.
6. Open the HTML editor to start creating the document.
7. Use the menus and macros to format your document. Commands have an immediate effect on the way the information looks. Insert the desired information. Select formatting and linking tags from the available pull-down menus, hot keys, and macros.
8. Save the file with an appropriate filename extension indicating that the file is an HTML document.

How It Works

These procedures explain the three types of editing environments used to develop HTML documents. Deciding which type to use is a question of weighing priorities.

Due to its availability and familiarity, a text editor might be the easiest and quickest to use to develop documents; however, most text editors do not provide suitable support for HTML authors. This type of authoring requires the author to have a good working knowledge of HTML tags and syntax. The other two types of editing environments require some HTML knowledge for fine-tuning, but the bulk of development and tag insertion can be handled by the environment; on the other hand, these tools are more difficult or more expensive to obtain. Figure 2-2 displays an example of a text editor editing environment.

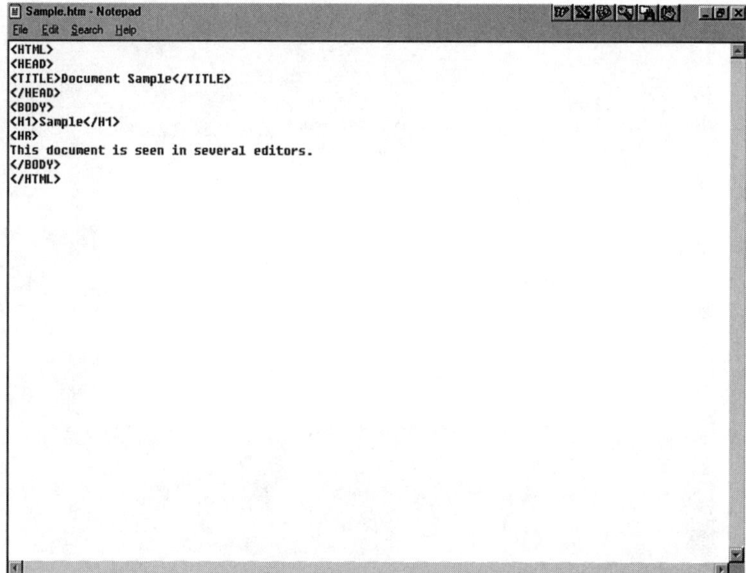
Sample.htm - Notepad
File Edit Search Help
<HTML>
<HEAD>
<TITLE>Document Sample</TITLE>
</HEAD>
<BODY>
<H1>Sample</H1>
<HR>
This document is seen in several editors.
</BODY>
</HTML>

Figure 2-2 HTML document creation with a text editor

With a pull-down menu/macro-type environment, you mark blocks of text and provide formatting information. How you format each block of text varies by editor. On the surface, this type of environment might seem ideal because it requires minimal knowledge of HTML syntax while making it easy to insert appropriate formatting tags and rendering information. However, knowledge gained in this type of environment might not be transferable. If you learn the macros and menu systems of a particular editor, that information might not apply in another authoring environment. Figure 2-3 shows an example of an environment of this type.

Finally, a WYSIWYG editor is useful because the document looks the same in development as it does when you are finished. However, unless the users accessing your documents are restricted to a particular browser application, the visible aspects of a document under development will not stand out as well. Figure 2-4 shows such an environment. The file **SAMPLE.HTM** on the CD contains the complete HTML source for the documents appearing in Figures 2-2, 2-3, and 2-4.

For additional information about a particular editor or editing environment, refer to the documentation for the package in question. Table 2-7 lists the various applications and the location of available documentation. Note, due to the dynamic nature of the Web, many of these URLs may change, so use your favorite search engine to find them.

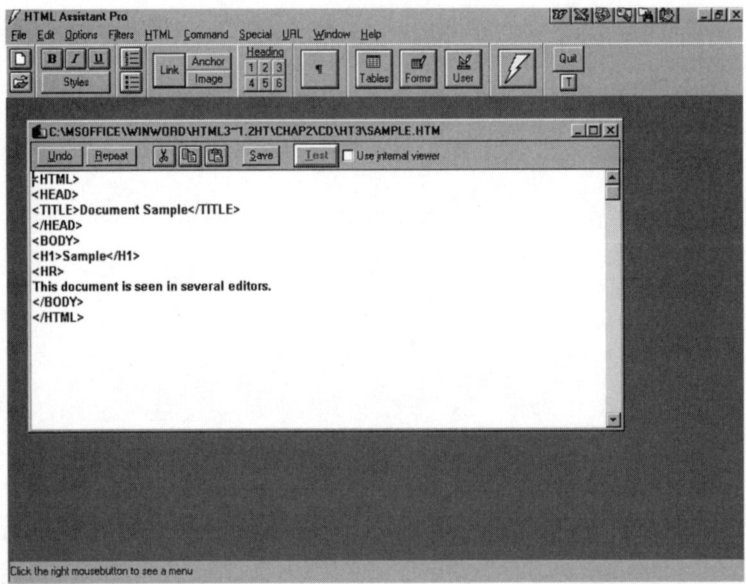

Figure 2-3 HTML document creation with a macro/menu editor

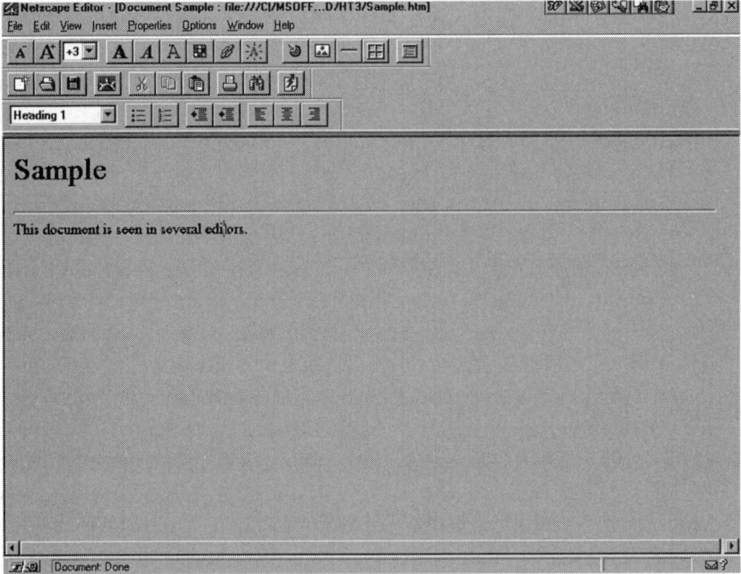

Figure 2-4 HTML document creation with a WYSIWYG editor

Table 2-7 Editor documentation

EDITING PACKAGE	PLATFORM(S)	DOCUMENTATION
Alpha	Mac	http://ww.cs.umd.edu/~keleher/alpha.html
BBEdit-Lite	Mac	ftp://ftp.std.com/pub/bbedit/freeware/bbedit-lite-30.hqx
BBEdit Ext. 1	Mac	http://www.york.ac.uk/~ld11/BBEditTools.html
BBEdit Ext. 2	Mac	http://www.uji.es/bbedit-html-extensions.html
HTML Editor	Mac	http://dragon.acadian.ca:1667/~giles/HTML_Editor/Documentation.html
GT_HTML.DOT	PC (Word for Windows)	http://www.gatech.edu/word_html/release.htm
HTMLed	PC (Windows)	http://info.cern.ch/hypertext/WWW/Tools/HTMLed.html
Internet Assistant	PC (Word for Windows)	http://www.microsoft.com/pages/deskapps/word/ia/support.htm
emacs	UNIX, PC	Within emacs, GNU archive sites
emacs HTML helper	UNIX, PC	http://www.santafe.edu/~nelson/tools/
vi	UNIX, PC	UNIX manual pages and external references
tkHTML	UNIX	http://www.infosystems.com/tkHTML/tkHTML.html
tkWWW	UNIX	http://tk-www.mit.edu:8001/tk-www/help/

Comments

The term *WYSIWYG* (What You See Is What You Get) is definitely a misnomer when applied to any particular HTML editor. What you see as an author might be significantly different from what a user gets when he or she accesses your document, so any claim that an HTML editor is WYSIWYG should be viewed with caution. WYSIWYG features should not be discounted, but you should actively test your documents in a variety of browsers to guarantee that your document design carries through to most, if not all, viewing environments.

Furthermore, even if you use a "higher-level" editor to abstract the lower-level HTML syntax, a general knowledge of HTML is useful for fine-tuning documents.

Many editor-generated documents could be improved through the judicious use of manual alterations made in a text editor.

Finally, many HTML 4.0 and 3.2 features have not been incorporated in many of the editors currently available. To include these features, you must use a text editor. So although you can create a document in any of the environments, in many editors placement of level 4.0 and 3.2 elements is possible only if you manually insert them.

2.5 How do I... Insert an HTML element?

COMPATIBILITY: HTML

Problem

I want to build documents that will be used and usable. How do I structure my documents? How do I specify logical grouping within the information? How can I get browsers to render my documents with the appropriate formatting?

Technique

HTML uses elements to define document formatting and structuring. Document elements are created via tags. Elements are defined by an opening tag and, if necessary, a closing tag.

An opening tag is composed of an element name followed by an appropriate series of attribute/value pairs between a less-than sign (**<**) and a greater-than sign (**>**). Closing tags are similar to opening tags in that they mark one end of an element; however, they differ in terms of syntax. A closing tag consists of an element name preceded by a slash (**/**). In addition, closing tags do not contain attribute/value lists.

Tagged elements follow four basic patterns:

✔ Empty element

```
<TAG>
```

✔ Empty element with attributes

```
<TAG ATTRIBUTE1="VALUE" ATTRIBUTE2="VALUE">
```

✔ Element with content

```
<TAG>
Enclosed Text
</TAG>
```

✔ Element with content and attributes

```
<TAG ATTRIBUTE1="VALUE" ATTRIBUTE2="VALUE">
Enclosed Text
</TAG>
```

Use an editing environment to add tags. The types of editing environments and the ways to acquire them for your development platform are described in How-To 2.4. The steps that follow indicate procedures for inserting tagged elements into your HTML documents through your editing environment. The insertion procedure is the same for all HTML elements.

Steps

How you insert tagged elements into HTML documents depends on the editing environment used to create the document. In a strictly text-based development environment, you insert all tags manually. With other editing environments, you add the tags through macros and/or menu selections provided by the software.

Either way, the resultant HTML document will have the appropriate elements included, demarcated by the appropriate tags.

1. Open the HTML document that you want to edit in your favorite editing environment. (See How-To 2.4, on editing environments.)

2. Locate the position in which you want to add the desired element. If the element that you want to add does not require any enclosed information (such as a horizontal rule, as described in How-To 7.1), go to step 3. Insert the text that will be enclosed between the opening and closing tags. An example of such a textual message is included in this code:

```
This text should appear in bold.
```

3. If you can't insert the desired tags by using a macro or menu options, skip to step 5. To insert an empty element, proceed to step 4. Select the body text you want to include in the element.

4. If the macros work by inserting opening and closing tags, follow the instructions in steps 5 and 6; when you are instructed to insert a tag manually, you should use the appropriate macro. Otherwise, use the appropriate macro or menu option to format the selected text as desired. For the sample text, the sentence would be highlighted and the macro or menu option for bold would be selected. You are now ready to proceed to step 7.

5. Move your insertion point to where you want the element to begin. Insert an opening tag at this location. The following code illustrates the insertion of an opening bold tag. (How-To 3.1 provides detailed information on the use of the bold tag.)

```
<B>This text should appear in bold.
```

To insert an empty element, insert the opening tag and proceed to step 7.

6. Move your insertion point to the end of the enclosed text and insert a closing tag at this location. The following code illustrates the insertion of a closing bold tag:

```
<B>This text should appear in bold.</B>
```

7. Save your document and continue adding elements by returning to step 2.

How It Works

The final product of this process is an HTML document with appropriate elements added. HTML documents are based on ASCII text; therefore, you should be able to view them as simple text, independent of how they appear in your editing environment. Each element should appear as an opening and a closing tag surrounding appropriate content information.

The following examples show a variety of possible opening tags:

```
<B>
```

This tag simply indicates the beginning of a bold element. The content information appearing between the opening and closing tags appears as bold text when displayed by a browsing package such as Mosaic. (See How-To 3.1 for information on bold elements.)

```
<HR>
```

This tag indicates the placement of a horizontal rule (line). Elements such as this one that do not require a closing tag are often referred to as *empty elements* because no content information is necessary. (See How-To 7.1 for information on the horizontal rule element.)

```
<META NAME="GENERATOR" CONTENT="Internet Assistant for Word ">
```

This HTML code represents another type of empty element: the *meta-information element*. This element provides supportive information about the document rather than a specific indication of how the document is presented. This element does not have content information between opening and closing tags; however, information content is represented as attribute/value pairs contained within the opening tag itself. (See How-To 2.6 for information on the **<META>** element.)

Elements that are not empty are concluded with a closing tag. For example, to close the bolding element **<B>**, the closing tag would appear as **</B>**.

In a text-based editing environment, all HTML tags must be inserted manually. When you want to include a particular element, you enclose the desired text with appropriate opening and closing tags.

In a macro/menu-based editing environment, tags, and consequently elements, are added to HTML documents through available macros and menu options. If elements are not supported by a particular editing environment, you can add them manually, as described for purely text-based editors.

WYSIWYG editors handle tag insertion in a manner similar to that used in a macro/menu-based environment; however, the tags for the elements might not be visible. Most character-level elements will be rendered as appropriate for the element. Bold elements appear in bold, as shown in Figure 2-5, rather than between `<B>...</B>` tags.

The addition of various elements can also be performed automatically by your editing environment. For example, a sample document developed using Microsoft's Internet Assistant will have the `<HTML>`, `<HEAD>`, `<BODY>`, and several `<META>` elements included automatically. The code for the HTML document seen in Figure 2-5 was developed in this editing environment and appears as follows. (The file `BOLD.HTM` on the CD also contains this HTML document.)

```
<HTML>
<HEAD>
<META NAME="GENERATOR" CONTENT="Internet Assistant for Word ">
<META NAME="BUILD" CONTENT="Feb 10 1995">
<META NAME="AUTHOR" CONTENT="">
<META NAME="CREATIM" CONTENT="1995:5:12:22:22:">
<META NAME="VERSION" CONTENT="1">
</HEAD>
<BODY>
<B>This text should appear as bold.</B>
</BODY>
</HTML>
```

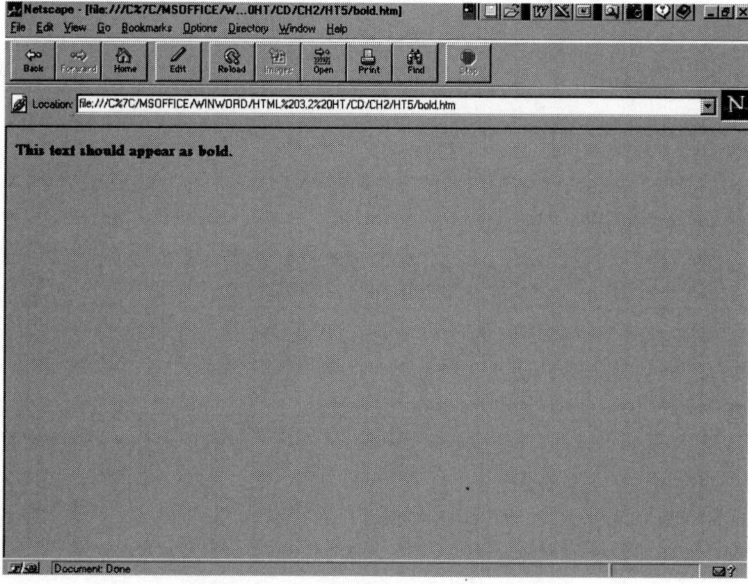

Figure 2-5 Document with bold tags inserted

NOTE

Later versions of Internet Assistant may insert the proper document type tag (for example, `<!DOCTYPE HTML PUBLIC "-//W3C//DTD HTML 3.2//EN">`).

Comments

Most WYSIWYG and macro/menu editing environments currently support HTML level 2 elements and many support level 3.2. Level 4.0 elements and extensions usually require the use of a text editor and manual insertion. This situation will change as additional HTML editors are developed.

A reference to HTML 3.2 and 4.0 standard elements appears in Appendix A, "HTML Quick Reference." The elements discussed in this How-To are delineated in Table 2-8. The Location field indicates the scope in which the element can appear.

Table 2-8 Summary of elements used

ELEMENT	LOCATION	PURPOSE
<HTML>...</HTML>	file	Defines the scope of an HTML document (see How-To 2.1).
<HEAD>...</HEAD>	HTML	Defines the head of an HTML document (see How-To 2.1).
<META...>	HEAD	Supplies meta-information (see How-To 2.6).
<TITLE>...</TITLE>	HEAD	Defines the title of an HTML document (see How-To 2.6).
<BODY>...</BODY>	HTML	Defines the body of an HTML document (see How-To 2.8).
<B>...</B>	BODY	Defines a bolded element (see How-To 3.1).
<HR>	BODY	Places a horizontal rule when displayed (see How-To 7.1).

2.6 How do I... Build a simple HTML document?

COMPATIBILITY: HTML 2+, INTERNET EXPLORER, NETSCAPE

Problem

I know how to browse the World Wide Web to find information, now I want to take the next step and add information of my own. Where do I start?

Technique

The following procedure creates a simple HTML document. This document illustrates the components you'll need to include to create your own meaningful, well-structured HTML documents.

The steps lead you through the definition of the overall HTML document and the construction of the head and body components. Several HTML elements and their use are introduced in the document development process.

Steps

The following guides you through the creation of a single HTML document titled My First Page. This document contains the single statement Hello World!.

You can follow these steps and alter the aforementioned strings to begin generating documents of your own.

1. Change directories to the location in which you want to develop your HTML documents. Create a new file in your favorite text editor. Be sure to choose a filename with an extension that indicates an HTML document to your browser.

```
edit first.htm
```

2. Begin with a document type tag and an `<HTML>` opening tag. Enter the following lines in your document:

```
<!DOCTYPE HTML PUBLIC "-//W3C//DTD HTML 3.2//EN">
<HTML>
```

3. Indicate that you are beginning the `<HEAD>` element of the document by issuing a `<HEAD>` opening tag. If a `<HEAD>` element is included, it must appear within an `<HTML>` element. The following line should appear next in your document:

```
<HEAD>
```

A complete list of elements that you might include within your `<HEAD>` element is provided in the "How It Works" section.

4. The `<TITLE>` element is used to indicate the title of an HTML document. `<TITLE>` tags are placed within the head component of a document. The title of the document is placed between the opening and closing `<TITLE>` tags. Add this `<TITLE>` element to your document:

```
<TITLE>My First Page</TITLE>
```

Use of this element is required in all HTML 3.2 and higher documents. This element usually will not have any visible effect within a browser's viewing window; however, the enclosed title might appear in the window title and/or the history list for the browser.

5. To end the head area, issue a <HEAD> closing tag.

```
</HEAD>
```

Thus, the <HEAD> element is nested within the <HTML> element.

6. At this point, you must develop the body of the document. A <BODY> opening tag indicates that this point has been reached. Enter the following line:

```
<BODY>
```

7. In this case, the body of the document is simply a text statement. More complex elements that can appear within the body component will be covered in other How-To's. For now, add the following statement to your file:

```
Hello World!
```

8. A </BODY> closing tag marks the end of the <BODY> element. Similar to the <HEAD> element, the <BODY> element is also completely nested within the <HTML> element. To end the <BODY> element, issue the closing tag in your document:

```
</BODY>
```

9. Finally, terminate the <HTML> element with an </HTML> closing tag. Add this to your document to complete your first HTML document.

```
</HTML>
```

10. Save the file. Remember to use the `.html` or `.htm` filename extension to indicate an HTML document.

How It Works

An HTML document consists of nested elements. An *element* is a document component enclosed between opening and closing tags. (Closing tags are not required for all elements.) The first tag indicates the type, version, and language of the particular document using a document type tag (for example, `<!DOCTYPE HTML PUBLIC "-//W3C//DTD HTML 3.2//EN">`). The outermost element is an <HTML> element, beginning with an <HTML> opening tag and ending with an </HTML> closing tag. The remainder of the document is nested within this element.

The two primary subcomponents nested within the <HTML> element are a <HEAD> and a <BODY> element. Both of these elements appear within an <HTML> element, but neither appears nested within the other.

The <HEAD> element of a document contains meta-information about the information contained in the <BODY> element. This meta-information usually does not have a direct visible effect within a browser's viewing window, but the browser does have access to this meta-information. The following elements can appear within the scope of a **<HEAD>** element:

- ✔ **<BASE>**: How-To 8.3 describes the use of this element in detail.
- ✔ **<ISINDEX>**: How-To 14.5 details the use of this element.
- ✔ **<LINK>**: How-To 8.4 fully describes the use of this element.
- ✔ **<META...>**: This element is used to specify additional meta-information not supported by another **<HEAD>** element or to specify additional information that should be sent by a server as part of a response header when the document is generated. (See Appendix G, "HTML Hypertext Transfer Protocol (HTTP).") Netscape's Client Pull (see How-To 15.9) is one example using this element (see Table 2-9).

Table 2-9 META element attributes and values

ATTRIBUTE	VALUE
CONTENT	Data associated with the name or HTTP-EQUIV
HTTP-EQUIV	HTTP response header field to generate with the value specified in the content
NAME	Name of the meta-information in content

- ✔ **<NEXTID...>** (an HTML 3 element not maintained in later versions of HTML): This element contains a single attribute/value pair within the tag. The **N** attribute takes a value of the form ***z123***, where ***z*** indicates an alphabetic character and ***123*** represents a three-digit number. Several HTML editing environments use this element to generate unique identifiers. You should not use this element when you are manually creating HTML documents.
- ✔ **<RANGE...>** (an HTML 3 element not maintained in later versions of HTML): This element enables you to define and name regions within the body of the document. This element uses several attribute/value pairs. These pairs are specified in Table 2-10.

Table 2-10 RANGE element attributes and values

ATTRIBUTE	VALUE
CLASS	Class of the region being defined
FROM	Name of the location within the body marking the beginning of the region
ID	Name that you want associated with the defined region
UNTIL	Name of the location within the body marking the end of the region

- ✔ **<STYLE...>...</STYLE>**: This element enables you to specify additional style and format information associated with particular elements in the document as well as the document as a whole. The desired style information is enclosed between the tags. The actual specification of style elements is still under development. Chapter 16, "Cascading Style Sheets," provides additional information on the use of the cascading style sheet type as supported in Microsoft's Internet Explorer and later versions of Netscape. The **<TYPE>** attribute of this element specifies the format of the style information provided. For example, the following style element specifies in text/css notation that the left margin for the **<BODY>** element is 1 inch:

```
<STYLE TYPE="text/css">
 BODY { margin-left: 1in }
</STYLE>
```

✔ **<TITLE>...</TITLE>**: You should use this element to specify the title of the document defined in the **<BODY>** element.

How-To 2.8 describes the creation of the **<BODY>** element in greater detail.

Creating an HTML document is therefore a process of nesting appropriate elements. The architecture of the sample HTML document (also on the CD in the **FIRST.HTM** file) is seen in Figure 2-6. Extending this, it can be seen that complex documents require deep levels of nesting. This is the code:

```
<!DOCTYPE HTML PUBLIC "-//W3C//DTD HTML 3.2//EN">
<HTML>
<HEAD>
<TITLE>My First Page</TITLE>
</HEAD>
<BODY>
Hello World!
</BODY>
</HTML>
```

The resultant rendering of this document appears in Figure 2-7. For the Mosaic browser, the **<TITLE>** element generates a document title that appears in the Title area of the user interface. The body appears as normal text in the display area.

Comments

A reference to the tags specified in the HTML 3 standard appears in Appendix A, "HTML Quick Reference." Table 2-11 shows the elements discussed in this How-To.

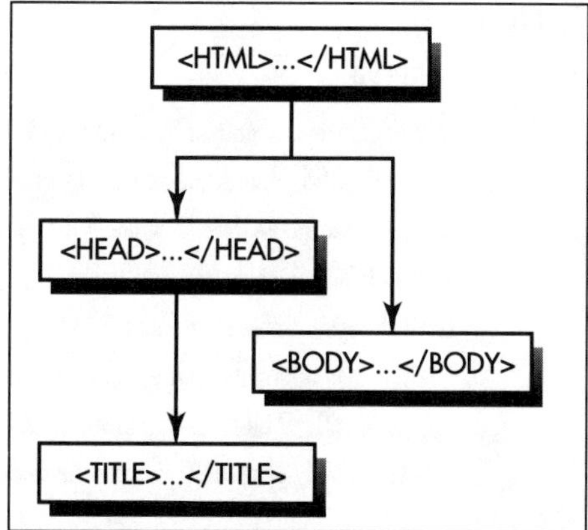

Figure 2-6 Architecture of a simple HTML document

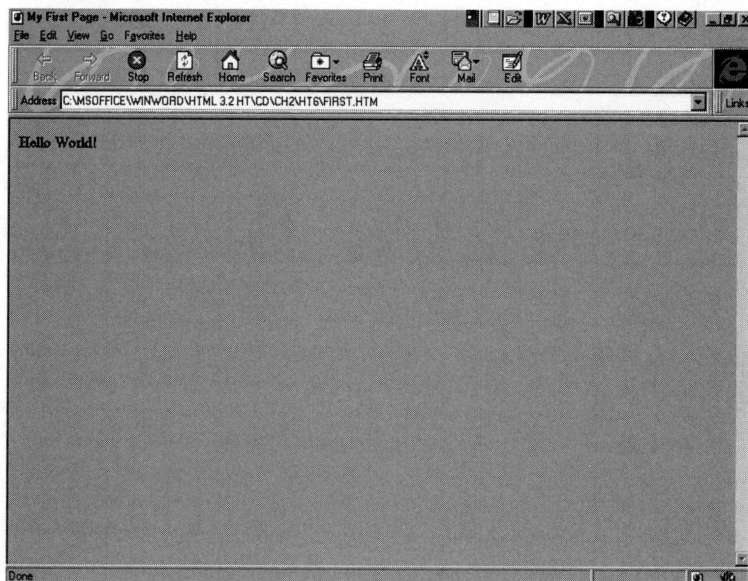

Figure 2-7 Rendering of a sample HTML document

Table 2-11 Elements used in this How-To

ELEMENT	LOCATION	PURPOSE
`<HTML>...</HTML>`	file	Defines the scope of an HTML document (see How-To 2.1).
`<HEAD>...</HEAD>`	HTML	Defines the head of an HTML document (see How-To 2.1).
`<META...>`	HEAD	Includes other meta-information about the document.
`<NEXTID...>`	HEAD	Used by HTML editors to generate unique IDs.
`<RANGE...>`	HEAD	Names a region within the document body.
`<STYLE...>...</STYLE>`	HEAD	Specifies style information for use in the document.
`<TITLE>...</TITLE>`	HEAD	Defines the title of an HTML document.
`<BODY>...</BODY>`	HTML	Defines the body of an HTML document (see How-To 2.8).

When authoring HTML documents, remember that how the final document appears will depend on the browser application. Each application will process HTML elements in its own way. For example, the Lynx browser renders the sample document slightly differently than Mosaic, as shown in Figure 2-8.

Notice that, even for this very simple document, significant differences exist in the rendering. You must keep this fact in mind while authoring, because your documents could potentially be viewed by any browser application. Therefore, authoring to maximize appearance quality in a particular browser might result in poor appearance in other applications. With this in mind, you might want to select a set

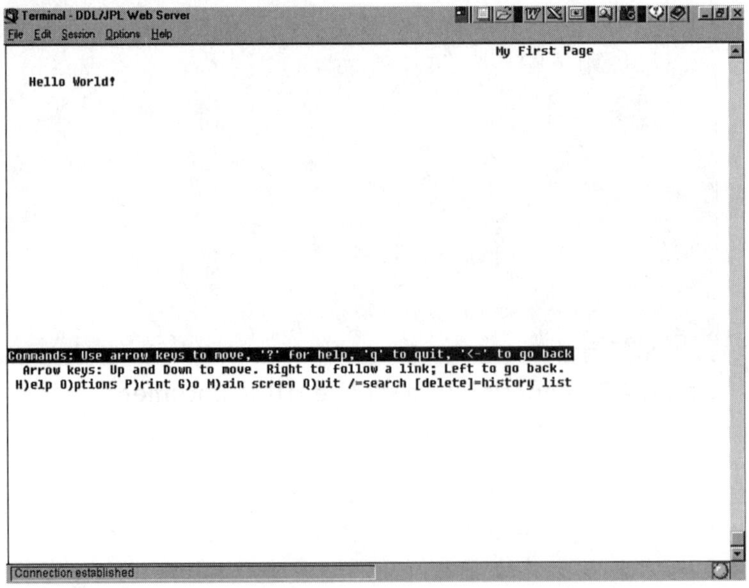

Figure 2-8 Rendering of sample HTML document in Lynx

of common browser applications, such as Internet Explorer, Mosaic, and Netscape, and try to maximize appearance quality in the common browsers while providing at least a minimal usability with other browsers.

2.7 How do I... Include a comment?

COMPATIBILITY: HTML

Problem

I want information about my documents to be available to me or to future authors. I want this information to be included in my HTML document, but I don't want it displayed to every casual viewer of the document.

Technique

HTML enables authors to include comments that reside in the document but do not appear when the document is rendered. The process involves the use of a construct similar to an opening tag. A comment can be viewed as a very specific type of logical element that is not visible to the common user.

The following procedure takes you through the process of creating comments within your HTML documents. Comments have two primary uses. First, they serve as a means for documenting design decisions you make while creating a document. Comments of this type become quite useful for maintenance and modification. Second, certain applications will use comments to include additional application-specific information within an HTML document.

Steps

Comment element insertion is similar in many respects to the insertion of other logical elements. The following process guides you through the insertion of comment elements using a typical editing environment that does not support comment inclusion via a macro or a menu mechanism. If yours does, you should refer to the documentation for your particular editing environment.

1. Open the HTML document you want to edit in your favorite editing environment. (See How-To 2.4 on editing environments.)

2. Locate the position in which you want to add your comment element.

3. Move your insertion point to this location.

4. Begin the comment tag by typing **<**.

5. The code for a comment continues with an exclamation point immediately following the < sign. The code for your comment should now appear as follows:

```
<!
```

6. The exclamation point is followed by two dashes. Insert these two dashes into your HTML document. No spaces should be placed between any of these characters.

```
<!--
```

7. Type the rest of your comment. Do not include a > sign within the body of your comment because this would be interpreted as the termination of your comment.

```
<!-- THIS IS A SAMPLE COMMENT
```

8. End your comment with a greater-than sign preceded by two dashes. Spaces can appear between these two dashes and the closing >.

```
<!-- THIS IS A SAMPLE COMMENT -->
```

9. The comment has now been added to your document. You are now ready to save your HTML document or continue developing the document. If you want to add further comments to this document, return to step 2 and proceed as before.

NOTE

You cannot nest comments. Also, comments can span multiple lines, although it is not recommended in practice due to lack of support in many browsers. Here is an example of a multiline comment:

```
<!--
 This is a multi-line comment. By definition it is
valid
 HTML 3.2; however, in practice, many viewers will
misinterpret
 it.
-->
```

How It Works

The addition of comments to documents that you are developing is generally considered good practice. For simple, self-explanatory documents, comments might not be necessary, but for more complex documents, comments are not only desirable but necessary.

HTML provides for comments by specifying an appropriate construct for their inclusion. Comments appear similar to standard HTML tags. In this way, applications scanning HTML documents can easily identify comments and treat them appropriately.

Comments are similar in structure to HTML opening tags. (For additional information on opening tags, see How-To 2.5.) The comment is enclosed in **<** and **>** signs. The first character after the less-than sign is an exclamation point (**!**). Two dashes immediately follow the exclamation point. This string indicates the beginning of a comment.

A comment is terminated by two dashes followed by the greater-than sign. Spaces can appear between the dashes and the terminating **>**. You can place the text of your comment within these stated bounds. Here are some sample comments and explanations:

```
<!-- This is a sample of a valid comment. -- >
```

This is a standard comment style. You should note that the space after the final pair of dashes does not alter the comment status.

```
<!--
 This is a multiline comment. By definition it is valid
 HTML 3; however, in practice, many viewers will misinterpret
 it.
-->
```

The preceding sample HTML segment represents a multiline comment. Many viewers do not handle this type of comment appropriately. A good practice would be to use the following HTML segment:

```
<!-- This is a multiline comment. By definition it is valid -->
<!-- HTML 3.2; however, in practice, many viewers will misinterpret -->
<!-- it. -->
```

This version will work with any viewer that supports comments, whereas the first one might fail with some browsing programs.

```
<!-- Commented HTML tags are often <B>misinterpreted</B> -->
```

Finally, you should not try to use comment syntax to surround existing HTML elements. The preceding sample code will be misinterpreted by most browser applications and yield undesirable effects. A better approach to making the desired text a comment appears in the following HTML segment:

```
<!-- Commented tags are often --><!-- B --><!-- misinterpreted --> ⇐
<!-- /B-->
```

This comment will be handled appropriately. To comment existing HTML tags, you must carefully examine the code being commented in each case.

Figure 2-9 shows how the comments that appear in the following HTML code might be rendered; the **COMMENT.HTM** file on the CD also contains this document. Note that this browsing and editing environment handles the multiline comment. However, it interprets that commented tag for a bold element as the termination of the comment.

```
<!DOCTYPE HTML PUBLIC "-//W3C//DTD HTML 3.2//EN">
<HTML>
<HEAD>
<TITLE>Comments, Comments, and More Comments</TITLE>
</HEAD>
<BODY>
<!-- This is a sample of a valid comment. -- >
<!--
 This is a multiline comment. By definition it is valid
 HTML 3; however, in practice, many viewers will misinterpret
 it.
-->
<!-- Commented HTML tags are often <B>misinterpreted</B> -->
</BODY>
</HTML>
```

Comments

Comments are not treated equally by various application programs. Some browsers ignore comments completely. Others treat them as potential directives or even as document content, depending on how the comment was entered. Some browsers might have a particularly difficult time with multiline comments.

Several applications use specially tailored comments for application-specific tasks. NCSA server-side includes (discussed in How-To 13.4) are an example of one such use. Another example is the internal tracking of documents by Microsoft's Internet Assistant. This application automatically inserts specially tailored comments to track documents created within its environment.

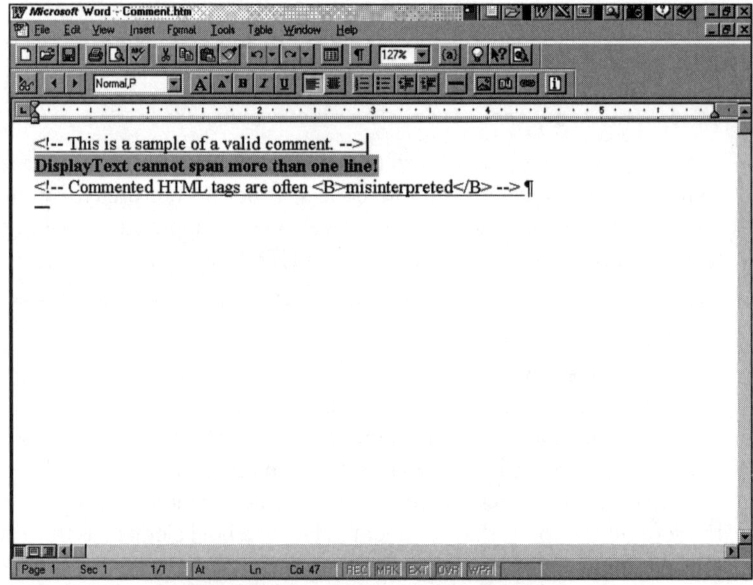

Figure 2-9 Appearance of the comments document in a browser without multiline comment support

A reference to HTML 4.0 standard elements appears in Appendix A, "HTML Quick Reference." The elements discussed in this How-To are delineated in Table 2-12. The Location field indicates the scope in which the element can appear.

Table 2-12 Elements used in this How-To

ELEMENT	LOCATION	PURPOSE
`<HTML>...</HTML>`	file	Defines the scope of an HTML document (see How-To 2.1).
`<!--...-->`	HTML	Represents an HTML comment element (see How-To 2.7).
`<HEAD>...</HEAD>`	HTML	Defines the head of an HTML document (see How-To 2.1).
`<TITLE>...</TITLE>`	HEAD	Defines the title of an HTML document (see How-To 2.6).
`<BODY>...</BODY>`	HTML	Defines the body of an HTML document (see How-To 2.8).
`<B>...</B>`	BODY	Represents a bolded element (see How-To 3.1).

2.8 How do I... Add body text?

COMPATIBILITY: HTML 2+, INTERNET EXPLORER, NETSCAPE

Problem

I want to add content to my HTML document. Where do I put this information? What limitations are there on the information I can add?

Technique

The **<BODY>** element represents the information content of an HTML document. This element defines the portion of your document that includes information that will be rendered in a browser's display area.

Such content can be composed of any valid nested elements, plus any pure text you want to include. The following procedure provides a step-by-step description for creating the meat of your HTML document.

Steps

Here are the basic tasks involved in beginning development of HTML document information content. This procedure assumes that you are using a simple text-based editor to author your HTML document. If that is not the case, you can tailor the procedure by ignoring steps that are handled implicitly by your environment. For example, if your environment automatically creates the **<BODY>** element, you can skip the step involving insertion of the **<BODY>** tag. You will need to reference the documentation for your particular editing environment to make such judgments.

1. Open the HTML document you want to edit in your favorite editing environment. (See How-To 2.4, on editing environments.)

2. Locate the position in which you want to begin adding content. This location will vary depending on your editing environment. In a text editor, this location is inside the scope of the <HTML> element and after the <HEAD> element.

3. Move your insertion point to this location.

4. If your document already contains a <BODY> element, proceed to step 5. Begin the content portion by inserting a <BODY> opening tag. You will begin your comment with the following code:

```
<BODY>
```

This opening tag can have several attribute/value pairs associated with it. These pairs are described in the "How It Works" section.

5. You now are ready to write the body of your HTML document. Enter any desired text and legal elements in the locations desired within the <BODY> element. Make any necessary corrections or additions. In Figure 2-10, the highlighted information represents the content added at this step in a text editor (Notepad). If you are creating this <BODY> element for the first time in this document, proceed to step 6; otherwise, continue with step 7.

6. End the body components of your HTML document with a <BODY> closing tag. This will end your <BODY> element.

```
</BODY>
```

NOTE

Keep in mind while editing that carriage returns in an HTML document do not necessarily imply carriage returns in the rendered document. Spaces and carriage returns in the text of the <BODY> element are largely ignored when displayed by browsers. Therefore, if you want to use spaces or carriage returns, you must use appropriate HTML elements to force them. (See Chapter 7, "Managing Document Spacing.")

7. You have now successfully added the <BODY> element of your HTML document. Save your document.

How It Works

The HTML <BODY> element represents the information content of your document. When you add or modify content, you alter this element.

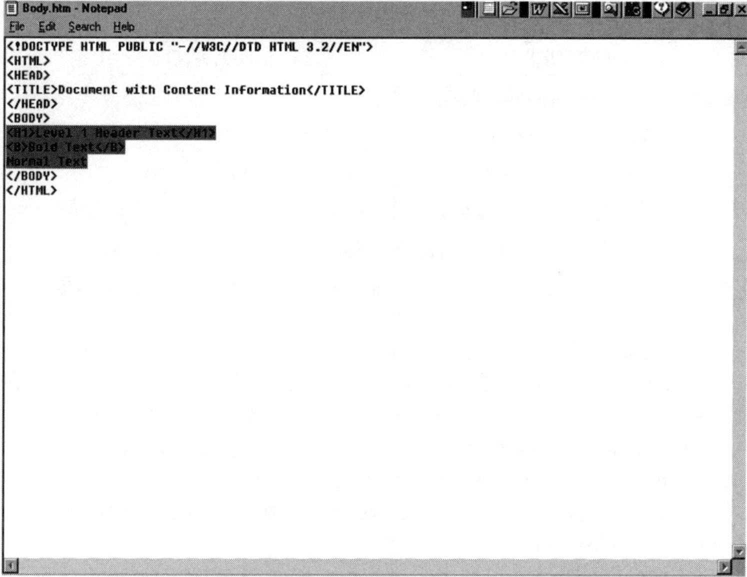

Figure 2-10 Content information

A **<BODY>** opening tag can contain a list of attribute/value pairs associated with the **<BODY>** element. The following list describes the valid attributes and their potential values:

- ✔ **ID="string"**: The **ID** attribute associates an identifier with the **<BODY>** element. Styles and hypertext links can use this value for addressing purposes. The value must be unique within the scope of the HTML document. HTML 3.2 and later do not include this attribute, but use of HTML style sheets (as described in Chapter 16, "Cascading Style Sheets") might require its presence.
- ✔ **LANG="aa.bb"** (HTML 3, not maintained in HTML 3.2): The **LANG** attribute defines the language standard used within the context of the **<BODY>** element. The value is composed of two period-separated components: the two-letter abbreviation for the language and the two-letter abbreviation for the country variation. For example, **LANG="en.uk"** indicates that the **<BODY>** element content should use the conventions associated with the English language as used in the United Kingdom.
- ✔ **CLASS="string"**: This attribute associates a class name with the **<BODY>** element. Searches and styles can use this class information.

HTML 3.2 and later provide several additional attributes for specifying a Web page's background, text color, and link colors. Separate How-To's address these attributes, as outlined in Table 2-13.

Table 2-13 Elements used in this How-To

ATTRIBUTE	FEATURE	HOW-TO
BGCOLOR	Page's background color	2.9
TEXT	Page's text color	2.10
LINK	Color of link text	2.11
ALINK	Color of text for activated link	2.11
VLINK	Color of text for previously visited links	2.11
BACKGROUND	Image to wallpaper a page's background	2.12

A **<BODY>** element can contain any textual information you want, as well as any element allowed within the scope of a **<BODY>** element. When you add text and elements to HTML documents, you are assumed to be in fill mode. The effect of this is that all text and many elements you enter will appear contiguously in the rendered document. Some nested elements cause a carriage return in the rendered document, whereas others do not. Issues of spacing in document presentation are covered more deeply in Chapter 7.

Each HTML document can have at most one **<BODY>** element. If all the information can be contained within a document's **<HEAD>** element, then the **<BODY>** component is not required. For example, Figure 2-11 shows a document that contains several nested elements as well as a single line of straight text. (See How-To's 4.1 and 3.1 for information on the heading, **<H1>**, and bold, **<B>**, elements, respectively.)

Here is the full HTML code for this document, which appears on the CD in the **BODY.HTM** file:

```
<!DOCTYPE HTML PUBLIC "-//W3C//DTD HTML 3.2//EN">
<HTML>
<HEAD>
<TITLE>Document with Content Information</TITLE>
</HEAD>
<BODY>
<H1>Level 1 Header Text</H1>
<B>Bold Text</B>
Normal Text
</BODY>
</HTML>
```

Compare this with Figure 2-11. Note that the carriage returns in the HTML code and the rendered document do not match. This is due to the way the browser interprets the level 1 heading element and the bold element. According to the viewer in Figure 2-11, a heading 1 element implies a carriage return in the rendered output, whereas a bold element does not.

Comments

This section introduces the basics of creating information content. Methods of including links, images, tables, lists, frames, layers, and other elements are clearly described in other portions of this book. Table 2-14 provides a quick reference to these locations.

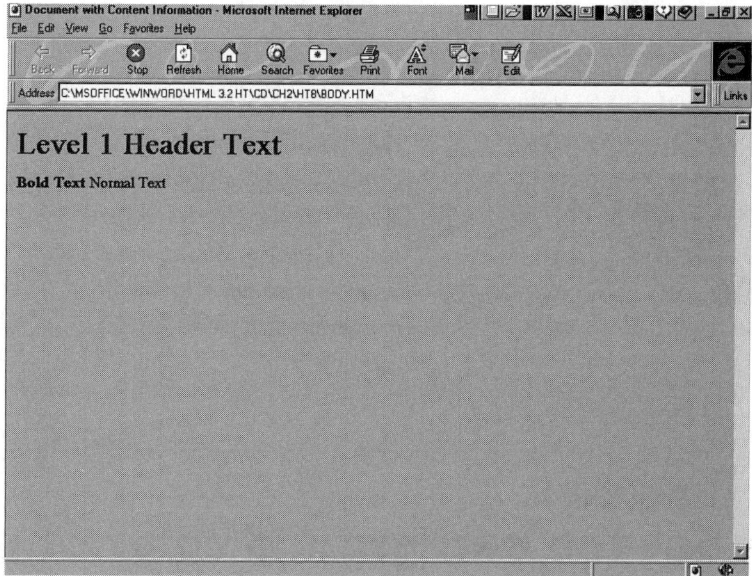

Figure 2-11 Document with content information

Table 2-14 Further references

INFORMATION TYPE	REFERENCE
Aligned text	Chapter 7, "Managing Document Spacing"
Physical character effects	Chapter 3, "Adding HTML Physical Character Effects"
Logical character effects	Chapter 4, "Adding HTML Logical Character Effects"
Comments	How-To 2.7
Images	Chapter 9, "Using Images in Your Documents"
Links	Chapter 8, "Establishing Links"
Lists	Chapter 6, "Lists"
Math symbols and effects	How-To's 20.11 and 20.12
Multimedia objects	Chapter 10, "Adding Externally Linked Multimedia Objects"
Special characters	How-To 2.13
Tables	Chapter 5, "Tables"
Frames	Chapter 19, "Frames"
Layers	Chapter 20, "Dynamic HTML"

A reference to the tags specified in the HTML 4.0 standard appears in Appendix A, "HTML Quick Reference." The elements discussed in this How-To are listed in Table 2-15. The Location field indicates the scope in which the element can appear.

Table 2-15 Elements discussed in this How-To

ELEMENT	LOCATION	PURPOSE
<HTML>...</HTML>	file	Defines the scope of an HTML document (see How-To 2.1).
<!--...-->	HTML	Represents an HTML comment element (see How-To 2.7).
<HEAD>...</HEAD>	HTML	Defines the head of an HTML document (see How-To 2.1).
<TITLE>...</TITLE>	HEAD	Defines the title of an HTML document (see How-To 2.6).
<BODY>...</BODY>	HTML	Defines the body of an HTML document (see How-To 2.1).
<B>...</B>	BODY	Represents a bolded element (see How-To 3.1).
<H1>...</H1>		Represents the <BODY> level 1 heading element (see How-To 4.1).

2.9 How do I... Set the background color of my Web page?

COMPATIBILITY: HTML 2+, INTERNET EXPLORER, NETSCAPE

Problem

I am tired of looking at the solid light-gray background of my home page. I want to add some life by changing its background color.

Technique

You can use two methods to alter the background color of your Web page. The first method involves the use of HTML style sheets; How-To 16.4 details this method. The more common method requires the addition of an attribute to the opening tag of a page's body element. HTML 3.2 and beyond provide the **BGCOLOR** attribute contained within the **<BODY>** opening tag for this purpose.

The value that you assign to this attribute instructs browsers to use a particular color as the background for your page. The following procedure walks you through the process of altering the background color of your Web page.

Steps

These steps guide you through the process of setting the background color of a Web page using the **BGCOLOR** attribute of the body element.

1. Open your Web page in a text editor. (A variety of HTML editors provide additional support for specifying background colors; see the "Comments" section for an example of this.)

2. Locate the opening tag of the body element for your page. This tag should appear as follows:

```
<BODY>
```

Your body element can include other attributes; if this is the case, simply add the new ones according to the next steps.

3. Move your insertion point after the `Y` in the tag. Enter the attribute name `BGCOLOR` and the equal sign. The tag displays how your body tag should look at this point:

```
<BODY BGCOLOR=>
```

4. After the equal sign, indicate the color that you want to use for the background of your Web page. You should place quotation marks around your color selection. Table 2-16 provides a list of commonly supported colors.

Table 2-16 HTML 3.2 and beyond's 16 defined colors (from the Original Windows palette)

COLOR	HEXADECIMAL TRIPLET	COLOR	HEXADECIMAL TRIPLET
Black	#000000	Green	#008000
Silver	#C0C0C0	Lime	#00FF00
Gray	#808080	Olive	#808000
White	#FFFFFF	Yellow	#FFFF00
Maroon	#800000	Navy	#000080
Red	#FF0000	Blue	#0000FF
Purple	#800080	Teal	#008080
Fuchsia	#FF00FF	Aqua	#00FFFF

The "How It Works" section explains the use of the hexadecimal triplets in this table. For example, if you wanted a yellow background color for your page, you would use the following opening tag:

```
<BODY BGCOLOR="yellow">
```

NOTE

HTML 3.2 and later versions enable you to select colors other than the predefined ones indicated in Table 2-16. The "How It Works" section explains this process. In addition, Appendix H, "HTML Color Table," provides a listing of other common colors and the appropriate values to use with the `BGCOLOR` attribute.

5. Save your Web page.

6. Test your Web page by loading it into a browser.

How It Works

HTML 3.2 and above enable authors to select a background color for Web pages. The specification of a background color attribute (BGCOLOR) in the body element opening tag is the most common method of accomplishing this task.

When a background color-capable browser interprets this attribute, it locates the color closest to the one requested among those colors it has available. It uses this closest match to paint the background color of the page. Commonly, browsers specify a set of predefined colors for use in Web pages, including those listed in Table 2-16.

HTML 3.2 and above also support another method of specifying a color based upon the red, green, and blue (RGB) components of the desired color. Using this method, a six-digit hexadecimal number represents the relative intensity of each component of the color. A two-digit hexadecimal number, ranging from 00 to FF (0–255 in decimal), represents the intensity level for each component color. A low value, say 00 or 01, indicates a dark RGB component, whereas a high value, say FE or FF, indicates a very bright RGB component.

Under this encoding, the value 000000 would indicate the color black and the value FFFFFF would indicate the color white. Any value in between, where the three components are the same, will produce a shade of gray.

After you have determined the appropriate RGB value for the color you want, you include that RGB value preceded by a pound sign (#) as the value for the BGCOLOR attribute. For example, the following tag could be used to create a slightly off-white background:

```
<BODY BGCOLOR="#FDFDFD">
```

NOTE

Microsoft's Internet Explorer and later versions of Netscape do not require the leading pound sign (#), but for cross-browser support, you should include it.

Microsoft's Internet Explorer supports a three-digit approach, where each digit has a value between 0 and F (0–15 in decimal), indicating the intensity of the particular RGB component. For example, the following tag could be used to specify a medium gray background:

```
<BODY BGCOLOR="#888">
```

NOTE

Netscape's Navigator browser does not support the three-digit hexadecimal format, only the six-digit one. So for cross-browser support, you should use either named colors or six-digit hexadecimal representations.

Appendix H provides a convenient list associating traditional color names with their respective RGB values. The CD contains sample pages using these body elements with a yellow background (from step 4), a slightly off-white background, and a medium gray background. These examples appear in the files **YELLOW.HTM**, **GRAY.HTM**, and **WHITE.HTM**, respectively. An example of a page without a specified background color appears in the file **NORMAL.HTM**.

Comments

The final step in the procedure can be crucial. First, using a particular background color might lead to difficulties in reading your page. For example, black text can be difficult to see on top of a dark background color, or an image included on the page might not appear properly against the new background. The latter situation is particularly relevant when dealing with transparent and translucent images. (See How-To's 9.5 and 9.17.)

Second, the appearance of colors varies depending on both the hardware and the software used by the viewer of your page. When adding a background color, you must remember that browsers use the closest match to select the color, and your color selection is therefore at the mercy of this matching routine.

Finally, because HTML 3.2 and beyond enable you to alter the color of various components of your Web page, you must view your page to ensure that your entire color scheme creates a page that is not only visually appealing but also legible.

Many HTML editors provide additional support for selecting background colors. For example, HTML Assistant Pro Freeware Edition for Windows (available on the CD) enables you to choose the color by selecting from a customizable palette. Figure 2-12 shows an example of this selection process. You access this feature by selecting the Special | Background Assistant menu option.

2.10 How do I... Set the color of the text in my Web page?

COMPATIBILITY: HTML 3+, INTERNET EXPLORER, NETSCAPE

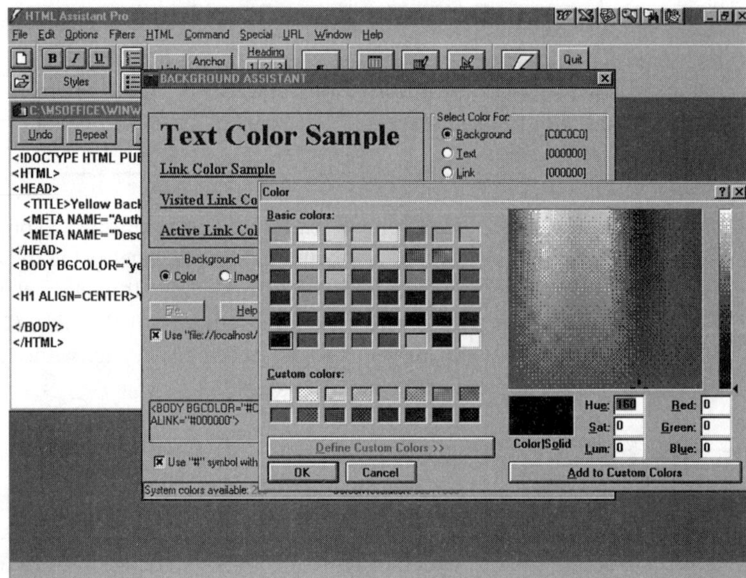

Figure 2-12 Altering a Web page's background color with HTML Assistant

Problem

Black text on a gray background looks dull on a Web page. I want to jazz up my page by changing the color of the text.

Technique

You can use several methods to alter the color of text on your Web page. The first method enables you to change the color of text in different areas of your documents; How-To 3.5 discusses this method. The next method involves the use of HTML style sheets; How-To 16.3 details this method. The last method is the easiest. This method requires the addition of an attribute to the opening tag of a page's body element. HTML 3.2 and 4.0 provide the `TEXT` attribute contained within the `<BODY>` opening tag for this purpose.

The value that you assign to this attribute instructs browsers to use a particular color to display the text in your page. The following procedure walks you through the process to alter the text color of your Web page.

Steps

These steps guide you through the process of setting the text color of a Web page using the `TEXT` attribute of the body element.

1. Open your Web page in a text editor. (See the "Comments" section for an example using an HTML editor.)

2. Locate the opening tag of the body element for your page. This tag should appear as follows:

```
<BODY>
```

Your body element can include other attributes; if this is the case, simply add the new ones described in the next steps.

3. Move your insertion point after the **Y** in the tag. Enter the attribute name **TEXT** and the equal sign. The following tag displays how your body tag should look at this point:

```
<BODY TEXT=>
```

4. After the equal sign, indicate the color that you want to use for the text of your Web page. You should place quotation marks around your color selection. Table 2-16 provides a list of HTML 3.2- and 4.0-supported, named colors; particular browsers might support additional named colors. For example, if you want purple text in your page, use the following opening tag:

```
<BODY TEXT="purple">
```

You can find a sample document using this body element on the CD located in the file **PURPLE.HTM**.

NOTE

HTML 3.2 and 4.0 enable you to select colors other than the predefined ones. The "How It Works" section explains this process; in addition, Appendix H, "HTML Color Table," provides a listing of other common colors and the appropriate values to use with the TEXT attribute.

5. Save your Web page.

6. Test your Web page by loading it into a browser.

How It Works

HTML 3.2 and 4.0 enable authors to select a background color for Web pages. The specification of a text color attribute (**TEXT**) in the body element opening tag is one way to accomplish this task.

When a browser interprets this attribute, it locates the color closest to the one requested among those colors it has available. It uses this closest match to display the text of the page. Usually, HTML 3.2 supports a set of predefined colors for use in Web pages, as indicated in Table 2-16.

HTML 3.2 and 4.0 also support another method of specifying a color based on the red, green, and blue (RGB) components of the desired color. Using this method, a six-digit hexadecimal number represents the relative intensity of each component of the color. A two-digit hexadecimal number, ranging from **00** to **FF** (**0–255** in decimal), represents the intensity level for each component color. A low value, say **00** or **01**, indicates a very dark RGB component, whereas a high value, say **FE** or **FF**, indicates a very bright RGB component.

Under this encoding, the value **000000** would indicate the color black and the value **FFFFFF** would indicate the color white. Any value in between, where the three components are the same, will lead to a shade of gray.

After you have determined the appropriate RGB value for the color you want, include the RGB value preceded by a pound sign (#) as the value for the **BGCOLOR** attribute. For example, the file **RED.HTM** on the CD contains the following tag to specify bright red text on a standard background:

```
<BODY TEXT="#FF0000">
```

NOTE

Microsoft's Internet Explorer and later versions of Netscape do not require the leading pound sign (#); however, for cross-browser support, you should include it.

Microsoft's Internet Explorer supports a three-digit approach, where each digit ranges from **0–F** (**0–15** in decimal) indicating the intensity of the particular RGB component. For example, the following tag would specify white text on the standard background:

```
<BODY TEXT="#FFF">
```

Figure 2-13 shows a page using this body element to set a white text color. The source for this page appears on the CD in the **WHITE.HTM** file.

NOTE

Netscape's Navigator browser does not support the three-digit hexadecimal format, only the six digit. So, for cross-browser support, you should use either named colors or six-digit hexadecimal representations.

Appendix H provides a convenient table associating traditional color names with their respective RGB values. In addition to the particular color examples, the CD provides the file **NORMAL.HTM** as an example of a page with standard text color.

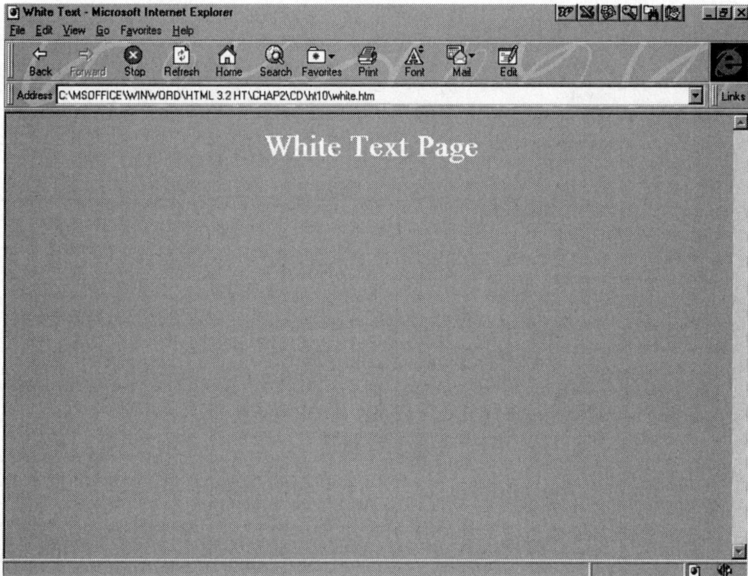

Figure 2-13 Using white text on a standard color background

Comments

The final step in the procedure can be crucial. First, the appearance of colors varies depending on both the hardware and the software of the viewer of your page. When selecting a text color, you must remember that browsers use a closest match to select the color and that your color selection is at the whim of this matching routine. Second, when altering both the text color and a document background using a specific color (see How-To 2.9) or a tiled image (see How-To 2.12), you must check that the text in your chosen color is still legible viewed against the background chosen.

The method discussed in this How-To describes the process for modifying your Web page using a text editor. Several WYSIWYG HTML editors are available that provide a more automated process for altering the color of your text. For example, with the Netscape Navigator Gold editor, you modify the color of your text by selecting a color from a customizable palette. Figure 2-14 shows an example of this selection process. You access this palette through the Properties|Document menu option.

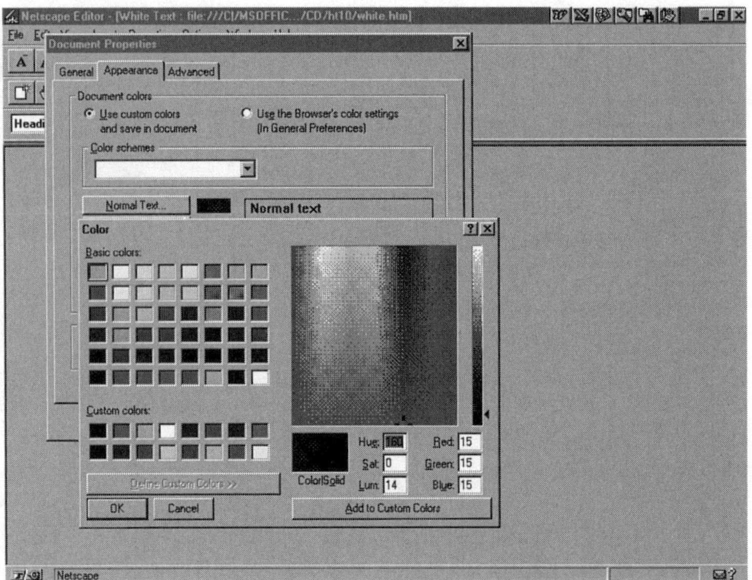

Figure 2-14 Selecting the text color for a Web page with Netscape Navigator Gold

COMPLEXITY
BEGINNING

2.11 How do I... Set the colors for the hypertext links in my Web page?

COMPATIBILITY: HTML 3+, INTERNET EXPLORER, NETSCAPE

Problem

I've changed my text color and background color, and my links no longer stand out to the viewer. How do I change the color of these links?

I want my links to fade into the remainder of the text after a reader has visited the link or, better yet, I want my links to disappear after a user has visited them.

Technique

HTML 3.2 and 4.0 enable you to select the color of your links, activated links, and previously visited links. The most common method of accomplishing this involves the addition of attributes to the opening tag of a page's body element. HTML 3.2 and 4.0 provide the **LINK**, **ALINK**, and **VLINK** attributes contained within the **<BODY>** opening tag for changing link color, activated link color, and visited link color, respectively.

The values that you assign to these attributes instruct browsers to use a particular color to display the links in your page. This procedure walks you through the process to alter the link colors of your Web page.

Steps

These steps guide you through the process of setting the link colors of a Web page using the link color attributes of the body element.

1. Open your Web page in a text editor. (See the "Comments" section for an example using an HTML editor.)

2. Locate the opening tag of the body element for your page. This tag should appear as follows:

```
<BODY>
```

Your body element can include other attributes; if this is the case, simply add the new ones as described in the following steps.

3. Move your insertion point to after the `Y` in the tag. Enter the attribute name for the link types that you want to change and an equal sign after each. The following tag displays how your body tag should look at this point if you want to modify the color of all links (normal, visited, and activated):

```
<BODY LINK= ALINK= VLINK=>
```

NOTE

Microsoft's Internet Explorer does not support the activated link attribute (`ALINK`). It ignores this attribute, so feel free to set it for cross-browser support purposes.

If you want to change the color of normal links and visited links only, your tag should appear as

```
<BODY LINK= VLINK=>
```

4. After the equal sign, indicate the color that you want to use for the links on your Web page. You should place quotation marks around your color selection. Table 2-16 provides a list of HTML 3.2- and 4.0-supported, named colors. For example, if you want purple links in your page, yellow activated links, and black visited links, use the following opening tag:

```
<BODY LINK="purple" ALINK="yellow" VLINK="black">
```

A sample document using this `<BODY>` opening tag appears on the CD in the file `PYB.HTM`. If you want to change the color of normal links to blue and visited links to green, your tag should appear as

```
<BODY LINK="blue" VLINK="green">
```

You can access a sample document using this tag by following the link contained in the file **PYB.HTM**. This link triggers the access of the **BG.HTM** file, also on the CD.

NOTE

HTML 3.2 and 4.0 enable you to select colors other than the predefined ones. The "How It Works" section explains this process; in addition, Appendix H, "HTML Color Table," provides a listing of other common colors and the appropriate values to use with the link color attributes.

5. Save your Web page.

6. Test your Web page by loading it into a browser.

How It Works

HTML 3.2 and 4.0 enable authors to select a background color for Web pages. The specification of link color attributes (**LINK**, **ALINK**, **VLINK**) in the body element opening tag is the common means of accomplishing this task.

When a browser interprets these attributes, it locates the colors closest to the ones requested among those colors it has available. It uses these closest matches to display the links of the page. HTML 3.2 and 4.0 directly support the use of the named colors in Table 2-16 in How-To 2.9.

HTML 3.2 and 4.0 also support another method of specifying a color based on the red, green, and blue (RGB) components of the color you want. Using this method, a six-digit hexadecimal number represents the relative intensity of each component of the color. A two-digit hexadecimal number, ranging from **00** to **FF** (**0–255** in decimal), represents the intensity level for each component color. A low value, say **00** or **01**, indicates a very dark RGB component, whereas a high value, say **FE** or **FF**, indicates a very bright RGB component.

Under this encoding, the value **000000** would indicate the color black and the value **FFFFFF** would indicate the color white. Any value in between, where the three components are the same, will lead to a shade of gray.

After you have determined the appropriate RGB value for the color you want, you include the RGB value preceded by a pound sign (**#**) as the value for the **BGCOLOR** attribute. For example, the document **RED.HTM**, found on the CD, uses the following tag to create a bright red link:

```
<BODY LINK="#FF0000">
```

NOTE

Microsoft's Internet Explorer does not require the leading pound sign (#), but for cross-browser support, you should include it.

Microsoft's Internet Explorer supports a three-digit approach, where each digit ranges from **0–F** (**0–15** in decimal), indicating the intensity of the particular RGB component. For example, the file **YELLOW.HTM**, included on the CD, contains the following tag to specify the use of yellow links:

```
<BODY LINK="#FF0">
```

NOTE

Netscape's Navigator browser does not support the three-digit hexadecimal format, only the six digit. So, for cross-browser support, you should use either named colors or six-digit hexadecimal representations.

Appendix H provides a convenient list associating traditional color names with their respective RGB values.

These features provide two useful tricks for HTML page designers with respect to previously visited links. First, by designating the visited link color attribute (**VLINK**) the same value as the text color attribute for a Web page, links will seem to fade into the surrounding text after a reader visits the target of that link. This trick is more effective where links are not indicated in another manner, such as through underlining. In some cases, as a Web page author, you can affect these additional indicators; for example, How-To 16.5 explains how you can remove the underlining of visited links using HTML style sheets. Figure 2-15 displays the use of this trick: Previously visited links simply blend into the surrounding text.

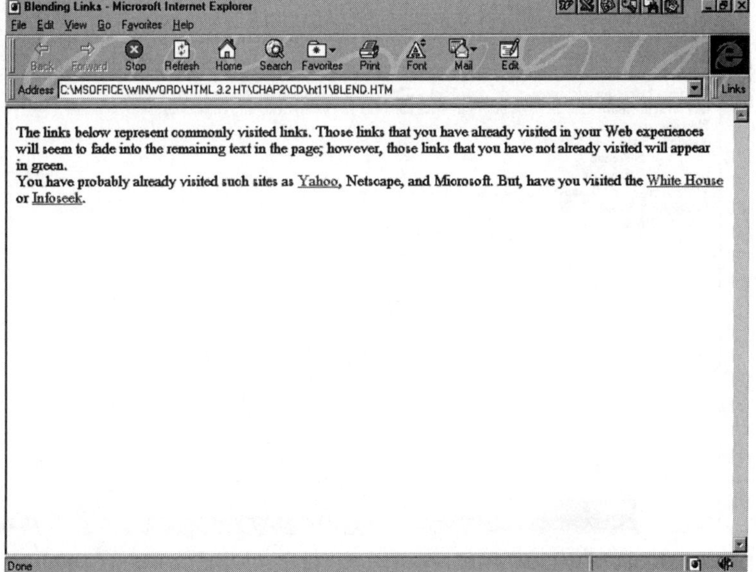

Figure 2-15 Blending previously visited links into the surrounding text

This particular example uses style sheet tricks to remove the underlining from previously visited links. File **BLEND.HTM** on the CD contains the complete HTML source for this document. The body element opening tag for this document appears as

```
<BODY BGCOLOR="white" TEXT="black" LINK="green" VLINK="black">
```

This tag instructs the browser to display standard text in black, link anchor text in green, and previously visited links in black. Therefore, after a viewer has followed a link, the browser displays this link in the same color as the rest of the text on all subsequent visits to this page.

The second neat trick involving visited links enables you to make links seem to vanish after they have been visited. As with the blending of links, this trick works best when browsers do not supply additional link indicators, such as underlining and changing cursors. You make links seem to disappear after they are visited by selecting the same color for both visited links and the background of the page. For example, the file **VANISH.HTM** on the CD, shown in Figure 2-16, uses the following body element opening tag:

```
<BODY BGCOLOR="white" TEXT="black" LINK="green" VLINK="white">
```

Unvisited links in the document appear green, whereas previously visited links disappear into the document background color. Therefore, by specifying the same color for both the **BGCOLOR** and **VLINK** attributes, you can make previously visited links disappear.

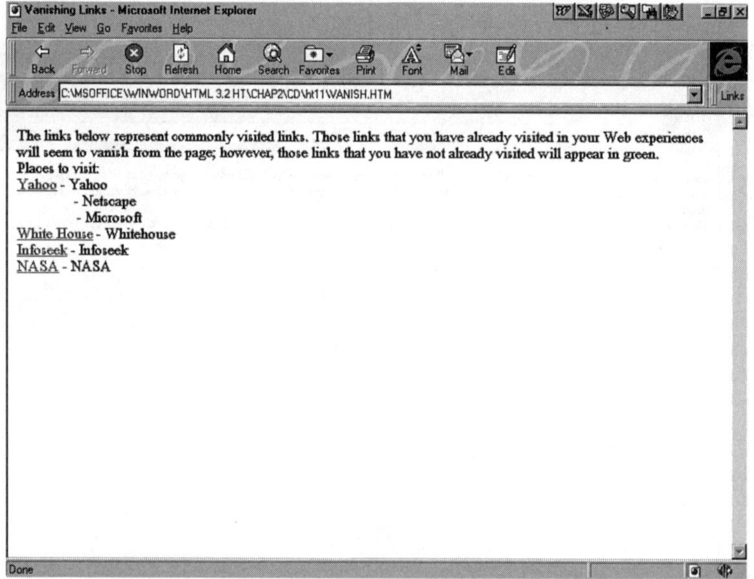

Figure 2-16 Vanishing previously visited links

Comments

The final step in this procedure can be crucial. First, the appearance of colors varies depending on both the hardware and the software being used by the viewer of your page. When selecting link colors, you must remember that browsers use a closest match to select the color and that your color selection is at the whim of this matching routine. Second, when altering both link colors and a document background using a specific color (see How-To 2.9) or a tiled image (see How-To 2.12), you must check that the links in your chosen color are still legible when viewed against your chosen background. Remember to check all three link states for appropriateness of the colors chosen.

The method discussed in this How-To describes the process for modifying your Web page using a text editor. Several HTML editors are available that provide a more automated process for altering the color of your links. For example, with HTML Assistant (available on the CD), you modify the color of your links by selecting a color from a customizable palette. Figure 2-17 shows an example of this selection process. You access this palette through the Special|Background Assistant menu option.

This method alters the color of links throughout your document. An alternative method enables you to change link colors in different areas of your documents; How-To 16.3 discusses how you can accomplish this using HTML style sheets. In addition, How-To 16.5 shows you how to remove link underlining.

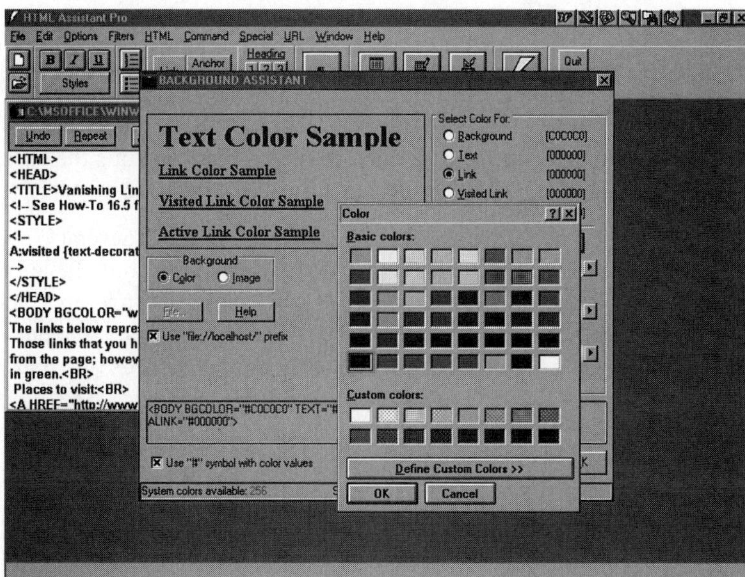

Figure 2-17 Selecting the link colors for a Web page with HTML Assistant

COMPLEXITY
BEGINNING

2.12 How do I... Use an image as the background for my Web page?

COMPATIBILITY: HTML 3+, INTERNET EXPLORER, NETSCAPE

Problem

I want something more interesting than a simple solid color background. I want to personalize my Web page by applying some wallpaper.

Technique

HTML 3.2 and 4.0 support the specification of an image that browsers should use as the background for a Web page. The browser uses as many copies of the specified image as are required to cover the width and height of the page.

First, you will need to find or create an image to use as a background. You then set the **BACKGROUND** attribute of your document's body element opening tag to specify this image file. You identify this image with an appropriate URL reference. You can also indicate whether you want the background to scroll with your page's text or to remain fixed with respect to the motion of the text. Internet Explorer is currently the only browser that supports fixed backgrounds, referred to as *watermarks*.

Steps

The following steps guide you through the process of setting the background of a Web page using the **BACKGROUND** attribute of the body element.

1. Locate a background image or create one yourself. Several Web sites provide images suitable for use as Web page backgrounds. Table 2-17 displays the names and URLs of several of these sites. Also, refer to Yahoo!'s list of background-related sites at `http://www.yahoo.com/Computers_and_Internet/Internet/World_Wide_Web/Page_Design_and_Layout/Backgrounds/`.

Table 2-17 Background image Web sites

SITE	URL
The Background Archive	`http://www.public.iastate.edu/~haley/bgnds.html`
Ender's Realm	`http://www.ender-design.com/rg/backidx.html`
Homepage Designs	`http://www.geocities.com/WallStreet/1679/backgrounds.html`
KPT Background Archive	`http://the-tech.mit.edu/KPT/bgs.html`

SITE	URL
My Background Farm	`http://www.missouri.edu/~c691759/Backgrounds.html`
Paul's Backgrounds	`http://funnelweb.utcc.utk.edu/~wallace/textures/textures.html`
Wallpaper Zone	`http://www.nitespots.com/wallpaper_zone/`
WebDesigns	`http://www.execpc.com/~jeffo/webdes/bckgrnd2.html`

For more information on the creation and modification of background images, see Chapter 9, "Using Images in Your Documents."

2. Open your Web page in a text editor. (See the "Comments" section for an example using an HTML editor.)

3. Locate the opening tag of the body element for your page. This tag should appear as follows:

```
<BODY>
```

Your body element can include other attributes; if this is the case, simply add the new ones as described next.

4. Move your insertion point to after the `Y` in the tag. Enter the attribute name `BACKGROUND` and the equal sign. The following tag displays how your body tag should look at this point:

```
<BODY BACKGROUND=>
```

5. After the equal sign, indicate the URL of the image that you want to use for the background of your Web page. You should place quotation marks around this URL. For example, if you want to use the image having the URL `http://www.mysite.edu/bg/marble.gif` as the background for your page, you would use the following opening tag:

```
<BODY BACKGROUND="http://www.mysite.edu/bg/marble.gif">
```

6. Decide whether you want the background to remain fixed with respect to the motion of your page's text when viewed with Internet Explorer. If you do want to turn on this feature, add the following attribute and value to your body element:

```
<BODY BACKGROUND="http://www.mysite.edu/bg/marble.gif" BGPROPERTIES=FIXED>
```

Browsers that do not support this attribute will generally ignore it.

7. Save your Web page.

8. Test your Web page by loading it into a browser.

How It Works

HTML 3.2 and 4.0 enable authors to select a background image for Web pages. Specifying a background image attribute (**BACKGROUND**) in the body element opening tag is one means of accomplishing this task.

When a browser interprets this attribute, it retrieves the indicated image file. It uses this image file to paint the background of the page. You will find that many images suitable for use as Web page backgrounds are freely available over the Web. Explore the sites provided in Table 2-17 and the sites listed in the Yahoo! Backgrounds category. Make sure to carefully read the instructions on each site where you download an image file: The site might require you to credit the creator of the image properly when you use it.

For example, Figure 2-18 shows the use of a background downloaded from the Ender's Realm background archive referenced in Table 2-17. The body element for this page also contains a mixture of attributes described in How-To's 2.9, 2.10, and 2.11.

Here is the opening tag of the body element for this page:

```
<BODY TEXT="#FFFF00" BACKGROUND="tex6.jpg" ⇐
LINK="red" VLINK="#FF0" ALINK="silver">
```

This particular open tag specifies that browsers should wallpaper the background of this page with the image **TEX6.JPG**. In addition, the browser should display text in yellow, links in red, active links in silver, and previously visited links in yellow. The HTML source for this page appears in the file **MARBLE.HTM** on the CD; the file **TEX6.JPG** stores the background image.

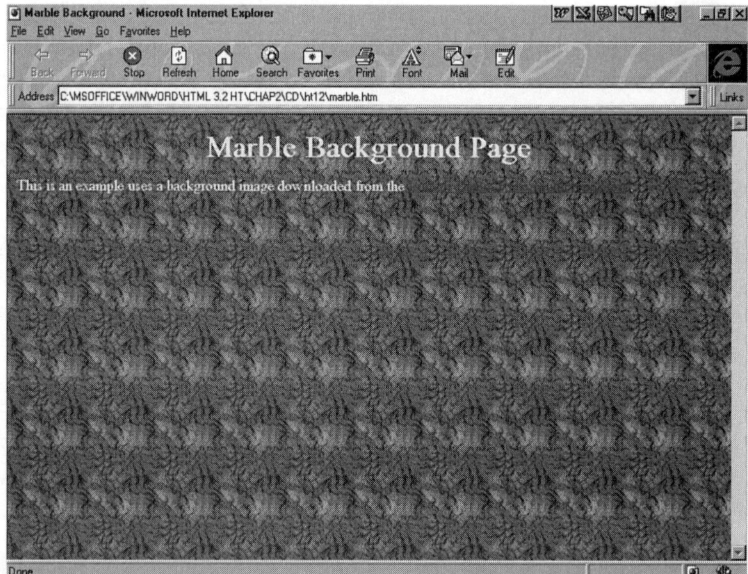

Figure 2-18 Applying a marble wallpaper to a Web page

An additional feature, currently supported by Microsoft Internet Explorer, enables you to keep the background fixed with respect to the motion of text when you scroll. The use of the **BGPROPERTIES** attribute with a value of **FIXED** turns on this feature. Most other browsers will simply ignore this attribute and treat the background in the standard fashion.

One neat trick: This feature enables you to choreograph your page content and background. Using this trick, you first create or retrieve an image larger than the visible portion of your page content, which does not necessarily imply a large image in terms of file size. You will want an image this large because browsers will tile the image if the image is smaller than the visible area in the browser. You can use this method to include a standard letterhead or border that will appear in all your Web pages. Unlike a letterhead that scrolls off the screen as the viewer reads your page, the text of the page flows over the letterhead while the letterhead remains constant.

For example, Figure 2-19 displays the top of a page with a sign indicating that more information is farther down. Figure 2-20 displays the same page at a point farther down. You should notice that the more indicator has not moved from its position, despite the scrolling of the page's content. This page's body element opening tag appears as follows:

```
<BODY TEXT="red" BGCOLOR="#FFFFFF" LINK="fuchsia" VLINK="#FFFF00"⇐
ALINK="#FF0000" BACKGROUND="more.gif" BGPROPERTIES=FIXED>
```

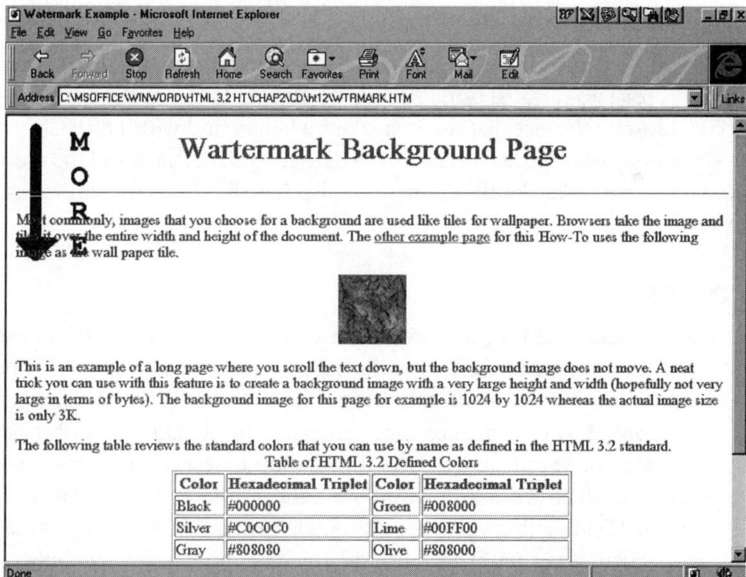

Figure 2-19 Using a watermark background—top of the page

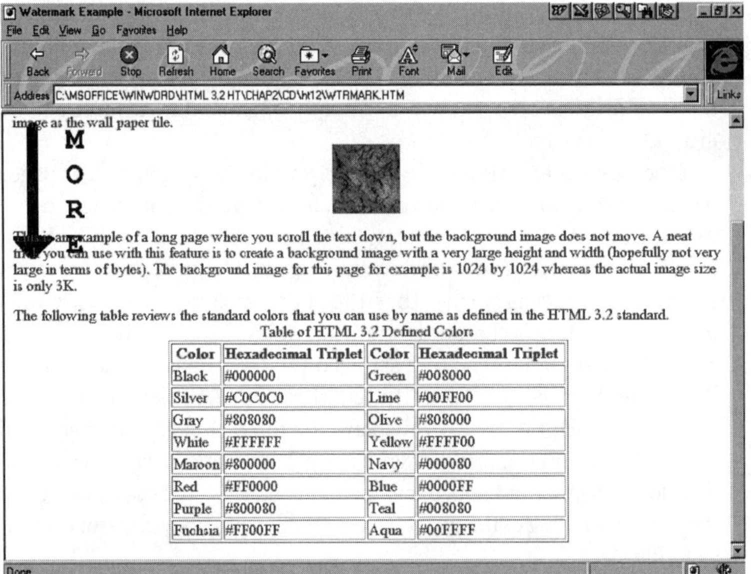

image as the wall paper tile.

This is an example of a long page where you scroll the text down, but the background image does not move. A neat trick you can use with this feature is to create a background image with a very large height and width (hopefully not very large in terms of bytes). The background image for this page for example is 1024 by 1024 whereas the actual image size is only 3K.

The following table reviews the standard colors that you can use by name as defined in the HTML 3.2 standard.

Table of HTML 3.2 Defined Colors

Color	Hexadecimal Triplet	Color	Hexadecimal Triplet
Black	#000000	Green	#008000
Silver	#C0C0C0	Lime	#00FF00
Gray	#808080	Olive	#808000
White	#FFFFFF	Yellow	#FFFF00
Maroon	#800000	Navy	#000080
Red	#FF0000	Blue	#0000FF
Purple	#800080	Teal	#008080
Fuchsia	#FF00FF	Aqua	#00FFFF

Figure 2-20 Using a watermark background—middle of the page

The CD contains the complete HTML code for this document in the file **WTRMARK.HTM**; you will also find the background image **MORE.GIF**. The image used in this page was created using Paint Shop Pro (included on the CD). You should note that, despite the fact that the image has a height and width of 1024 pixels, the file size is only 3KB. The body element opening tag specifies the use of the image **MORE.GIF** as a watermark background image. It also sets the colors for various aspects of this Web page.

Comments

The final step in this procedure can be crucial. Using background images requires you to examine the readability of the page's content closely. You might need to modify the color of your text and links (see How-To's 2.10 and 2.11) so that they can be read against your chosen background image. In addition, if your background image is transparent or translucent, you might want to test several background colors to determine which work best with your background image (see How-To 2.9).

Some HTML editors provide automatic generation of an appropriate body element opening tag with background image support. For example, Figure 2-21 shows the use of HTML Assistant's background assistant to select a background image. You access this dialog through the Special|Background Assistant menu option.

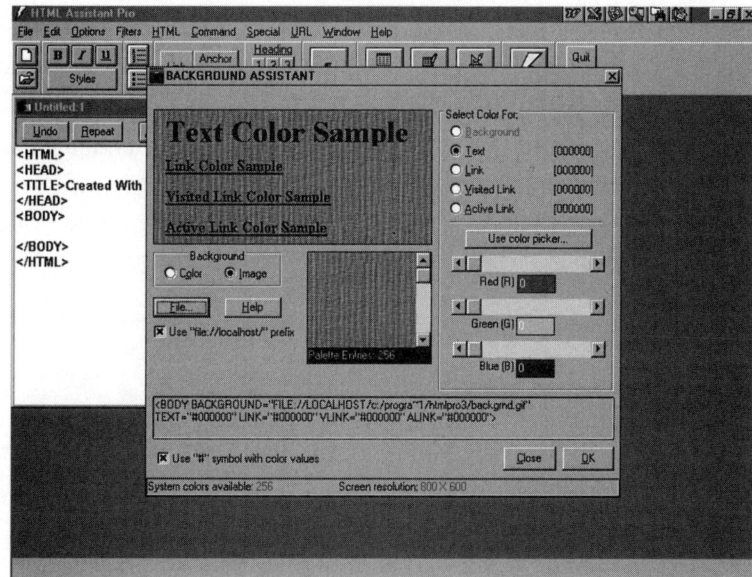

Figure 2-21 Selecting a background image using HTML Assistant

How-To 16.4 discusses a more advanced method for specifying background images, either for the entire document or for particular HTML elements. This alternative relies on the use of HTML style sheets.

COMPLEXITY
INTERMEDIATE

2.13 How do I... Insert special characters into a document?

COMPATIBILITY: HTML, INTERNET EXPLORER, NETSCAPE

Problem

I would like to use characters in my documents that are interpreted as HTML code. Not only that, I would like to include some words from a variety of languages. HTML supports the ISO Latin 1 character set, but my editing environment does not. How do I include these characters?

Technique

Any ISO Latin 1 character can be specified in an HTML document. HTML provides two reference types for including characters.

- ✔ Character references: Any character can be included through the use of its ISO Latin 1 character code.
- ✔ Entity references: Some frequently used characters have been assigned mnemonics. These characters can be included by specifying the appropriate mnemonic.

Steps

The following steps will enable you to insert special characters into your HTML documents. For character codes and entity references of specific special characters, see Table 2-18.

1. Open the HTML document you want to edit using your favorite text editor. (See How-To 2.4, on HTML editing environments.)
2. Locate the position in which you want to insert a special character in the text. This location varies depending on your editor. In a text editor, this location is usually within the document's body element.
3. Move your insertion point to this location.
4. Enter an ampersand (&) at this point in the code:

```
&
```

5. Follow the ampersand with either a character reference or an entity reference. (See Table 2-18.) If you use a character reference, the ampersand is followed by a pound symbol (#), followed by the decimal code for the desired character. If you use an entity reference, the ampersand is followed by the mnemonic for the character that you want to insert.

```
&#38
&amp
```

6. Finally, end the reference with a semicolon. The following sample code indicates the inclusion of two ampersands in the rendered HTML document:

```
&amp;
```

7. Save your document or continue editing.

How It Works

By using either a character or an entity reference, you can enter any ISO Latin 1 character into an HTML document. Many platforms do not support the full ISO Latin character set; therefore, HTML provides these two methods for including unsupported characters. Table 2-18 provides a list of ISO Latin characters beyond U.S. ASCII, as well as characters that hold particular significance in HTML.

Table 2-18 ISO Latin 1 character set—special characters and beyond ASCII

CHARACTER	CODE	ENTITY REFERENCE	COMMENT
"	34	"	HTML code
&	38	&	HTML code
<	60		HTML code
>	62	>	HTML code
_	161		
(	162		
£	163		
¤	164		
¥	165		
:¦	166		
§	167		
"	168		
©	169	©	Netscape & IE support
a	170		
«	171		
¬	172		
=	173		
®	174	®	Netscape support
–	175		
°	176		
±	177		
2	178		
3	179		
´	180		
µ	181		
¶	182		
·	183		
'	184		
¹	185		

continued on next page

continued from previous page

CHARACTER	CODE	ENTITY REFERENCE	COMMENT
º	186		
»	187		
¼	188		
½	189		
¾	190		
¿	191		
À	192	`À`	
Á	193	`Á`	
Â	194	`Â`	
Ã	195	`Ã`	
Ä	196	`Ä`	
Å	197	`Å`	
Æ	198	`Æ`	
Ç	199	`Ç`	
È	200	`È`	
É	201	`É`	
Ê	202	`Ê`	
Ë	203	`Ë`	
Ì	204	`Ì`	
Í	205	`Í`	
Î	206	`Î`	
Ï	207	`Ï`	
q	208		
Ñ	209	`Ñ`	
Ò	210	`Ò`	
Ó	211	`Ó`	
Ô	212	`Ô`	
Õ	213	`Õ`	
Ö	214	`Ö`	
x	215		
Ø	216	`Ø`	
Ù	217	`Ù`	
Ú	218	`Ú`	
Û	219	`Û`	
Ü	220	`Ü`	
s	221	`Ý`	
t	222	`Þ`	

CHARACTER	CODE	ENTITY REFERENCE	COMMENT
ß	223	ß	
à	224	à	
á	225	á	
â	226	â	
ã	227	ã	
ä	228	ä	
å	229	å	
æ	230	æ	
ç	231	ç	
è	232	è	
é	233	é	
ê	234	ê	
ë	235	ë	
ì	236	ì	
í	237	í	
î	238	î	
ï	239	ï	
_	240	ð	
ñ	241	ñ	
ò	242	ò	
ó	243	ó	
ô	244	ô	
õ	245	õ	
ö	246	ö	
÷	247		
ø	248	ø	
ù	249	ù	
ú	250	ú	
û	251	û	
ü	252	ü	
v	253	ý	
w	254	þ	
ÿ	255	ÿ	

Figure 2-22 shows the special ASCII characters—quotes, ampersand, greater-than, and less-than—that hold a particular significance in HTML. The quotes symbol is used to delimit attribute values. The ampersand is used to indicate a character or entity reference, and the greater-than and less-than signs are used to delimit HTML tags. A special entity is required for a nonbreaking space to differentiate it from a normal space. Both types of space are character code **32**, but a nonbreaking space implies that the text around the space should not be broken between lines.

HTML 3.2 and 4.0 also provide entity references for several non–ISO Latin 1 characters, such as the nonbreaking space. Table 2-19 outlines these entities.

Table 2-19 Entity references for non–ISO Latin 1 characters

CHARACTER	ENTITY REFERENCE	COMMENTS
Baseline dots	&ldots;	Three dots on the baseline
Center dots	&cdots;	Three dots on same level as a minus sign
Diagonal dots	&ddots;	Diagonal dots (top left to bottom right)
Dot fill	&dotfill;	Center dots filling column in an array
Em dash	&emdash;	Dash the length of an em space
Em space		Space size of point size of current spot
En dash	&endash;	Dash the length of an en space
En space		Space size of half the point size
Large space	&quad;	Huge space
Medium space	&sp;	Medium space
Nonbreaking space		ASCII 32, but with nonbreaking caveat
Thin space		Thin space
Vertical dots	&vdots;	Three vertical dots
Alpha	α	alpha
Beta	β	beta
Gamma	γ	gamma
Delta	δ	delta
Epsilon	ε	epsilon
Var Epsilon	&vepsilon;	var epsilon
Zeta	ζ	zeta
Eta	η	eta
Theta	θ	theta
Iota	ι	iota
Kappa	κ	kappa
Lambda	λ	lambda
Mu	μ	mu
Nu	ν	nu
Xi	ξ	xi
Omicron	ο	omicron
Pi	π	pi
Var Pi	ϖ	var pi

CHARACTER	ENTITY REFERENCE	COMMENTS
Rho	ρ	rho
Var Rho	ϱ	var rho
Sigma	σ	sigma
Var Sigma	&vsigma;	var sigma
Tau	τ	tau
Upsilon	υ	upsilon
Phi	φ	phi
Var Phi	ϕ	var phi
Chi	χ	chi
Psi	ψ	psi
Omega	ω	omega

Therefore, special characters and non-ASCII characters can be included in HTML documents through the use of either character or entity references. When a browser detects an ampersand (&) in your HTML code, it interprets the semicolon-terminated value that follows as a reference. If the first character beyond the ampersand is a pound symbol (#), the value is taken as a character reference so when the document is rendered, the character indicated by the code is drawn. Otherwise, the value is taken to be an entity reference. The browser maps this reference to the appropriate character.

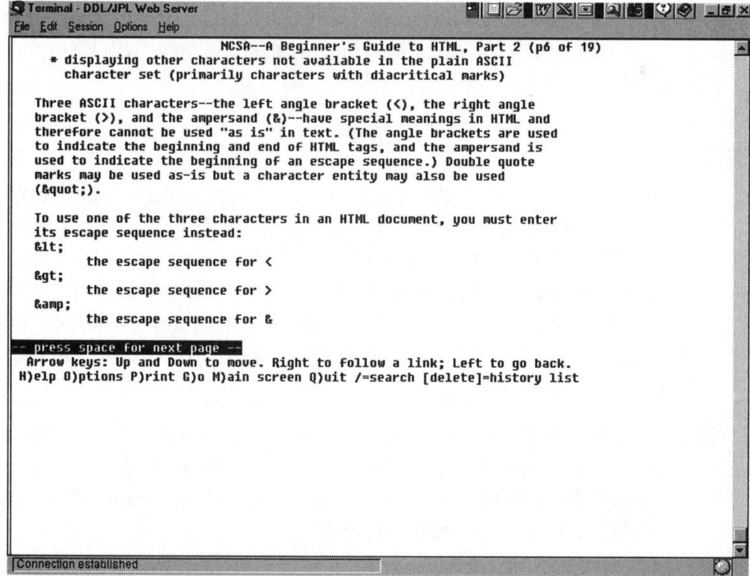
Terminal - DDL/JPL Web Server
File Edit Session Options Help

NCSA--A Beginner's Guide to HTML, Part 2 (p6 of 19)

* displaying other characters not available in the plain ASCII character set (primarily characters with diacritical marks)

Three ASCII characters--the left angle bracket (<), the right angle bracket (>), and the ampersand (&)--have special meanings in HTML and therefore cannot be used "as is" in text. (The angle brackets are used to indicate the beginning and end of HTML tags, and the ampersand is used to indicate the beginning of an escape sequence.) Double quote marks may be used as-is but a character entity may also be used (").

To use one of the three characters in an HTML document, you must enter its escape sequence instead:

<
the escape sequence for <

>
the escape sequence for >

&
the escape sequence for &

-- press space for next page --
Arrow keys: Up and Down to move. Right to follow a link; Left to go back.
H)elp O)ptions P)rint G)o M)ain screen Q)uit /=search [delete]=history list

Connection established

Figure 2-22 Special ASCII characters

Comments

Some browsers might understand entity references differently than others. Furthermore, some browsers might limit which references are supported. For example, certain text-based browsers might not support non-ASCII characters of any kind.

2.14 How do I... Create a home page?

COMPATIBILITY: HTML

Problem

I know some of the HTML basics, and I want to create a home page to provide information about myself to the World Wide Web community. I don't need anything very fancy just yet, but I would like to create and install a functional home page.

Technique

The home page creation process is very similar to the creation process defined in How-To 2.6. Use the same document structure as you would develop for any other HTML document, with a few additional elements included to mark the various sections.

Create the document with several sections. Create a contact information area, a biography area, and a modification date area. These areas will be separated by horizontal rules.

Steps

The following steps lead you through the creation of a single HTML document titled "Home Page of John Q. Public." This document will serve as your business card in the World Wide Web community.

This process assumes that you are using a normal text editor to create your document. If you use a different editor, some of the steps outlined might not be necessary; be sure to check the documentation for your particular editor to determine which steps apply.

1. Change directories to the location where you want to develop your HTML document. Open a file in your editor. (See How-To 2.4 on editing environments.) Be sure to choose a filename with an extension indicating an HTML document to your browser.

```
edit homepage.htm
```

2. Begin with a document type tag and an **<HTML>** opening tag. Enter the following lines in your document:

```
<!DOCTYPE HTML PUBLIC "-//W3C//DTD HTML 3.2//EN">
<HTML>
```

3. Indicate that you are beginning the header area of the document by issuing a **<HEAD>** opening tag. The following line should appear next in your document. The **<HEAD>** element must appear within the scope of an **<HTML>** tag.

```
<HEAD>
```

4. The **<TITLE>** element indicates the title of an HTML document. Place **<TITLE>** tags in the header component of a document. Place the document title between the opening and closing **<TITLE>** tags. Add this title element to your document. Substitute your own name for John's.

```
<TITLE>Home Page of John Q. Public</TITLE>
```

This element is required. Many browsers use this information to generate and display the title of the document. If you omit this element, browsers that require strict HTML adherence might not display your document.

5. To end the head area, issue a **<HEAD>** closing tag.

```
</HEAD>
```

6. At this point, you must develop the body of the document. A **<BODY>** opening tag is used to indicate that this point has been reached. Enter the following line of code:

```
<BODY>
```

7. The body of your document consists of three components. The first part includes your contact information. You might want to provide more or less information than the sample code, as determined by your needs.

```
<!-- Mark the beginning of this portion with a horizontal rule. -->
<HR>
<!-- Center your name as a level 1 header. -->
<H1 ALIGN="center">John Q. Public</H1>
<!-- Provide any desirable contact information. -->
999 Peachtree St.<BR>
Atlanta, GA 30314<BR>
USA<BR>
E-Mail: my_id@mysite.edu
```

8. The second portion of your document content includes your biographical statement.

```
<!-- Mark the beginning of this portion with a horizontal rule. -->
<HR>
<!-- Choose the heading text that you feel appropriate. -->
<H1>About Me</H1>
<!-- The formatting & information should be developed to suit your ⇐
needs. -->
This is the first paragraph in this section about myself.
I have been at MY BUSINESS for the past X years.
<P>
I am currently working on several projects.
These projects include...
```

As you learn more about HTML, you probably will enhance this portion with other HTML elements such as links, externally viewable objects, and inline images.

9. End your document by specifying the date and identifying the individual who last modified this document.

```
<!-- Mark the beginning of this portion with a horizontal rule. -->
<HR>
<!-- Substitute the appropriate information in your document. The date -->
<!--should appear in a long format with the month name written out -->
<!--since the order conventions for date abbreviations vary. -->
Last modified on CURRENT_DATE by YOUR_NAME (YOUR_E-MAIL)
```

10. Use a `<BODY>` closing tag to mark the end of the body element. Similar to the head element, the body element is also completely nested within the HTML element. To end the body element, issue the closing tag in your document.

```
</BODY>
```

11. Finally, end the `HTML` element with an `<HTML>` closing tag. Add this to your document to complete your first HTML document:

```
</HTML>
```

12. Save the file. Remember to use a filename extension that indicates an HTML document.

13. Try to view your home page using as many different browsing applications as you can.

14. If there are problems with the way items display, modify the document as appropriate.

15. When you feel that your home page is ready for the rest of the world, ask your site administrator to install your document on your Web site. Follow his or her instructions to install the document in your home directory.

How It Works

Use this procedure to develop an initial home page that will serve as your introduction to the World Wide Web community. This first attempt at a home page provides information about you and your interests to network browsers around the world.

The procedure described takes you through the development of a basic HTML document composed of an HTML element and the two nested head and body elements. The body element described contains three discrete components:

✔ Contact information: This section provides information on how people viewing the page can get in touch with you.

✔ Biographical information: This section gives you the opportunity to tell people about yourself. You can include information on what you have done, what you are doing, and what you are interested in doing.

✔ Creation/modification information: This final component should be included as a general practice in most HTML documents. Considering the fluidity of electronic information, the area gives your viewer an idea of how current your information content is.

Figure 2-23 displays how the home page developed in this procedure would appear in a browser.

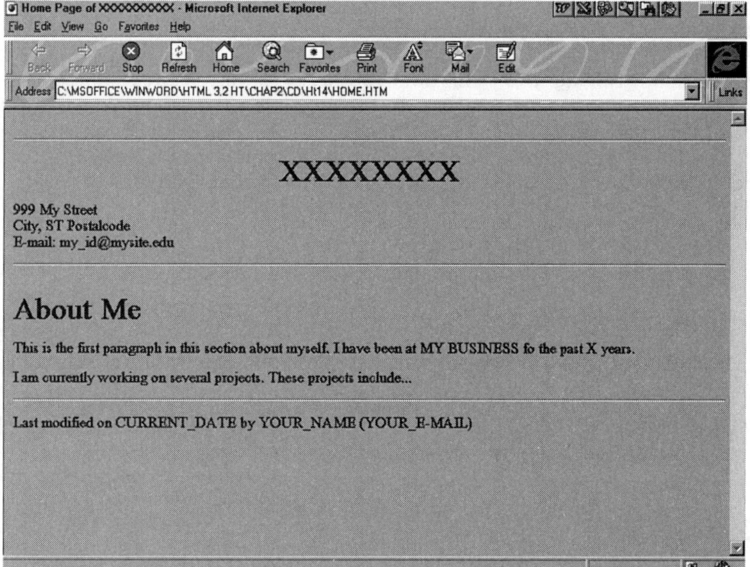

Figure 2-23 Home page example

Here is the complete HTML definition of this document:

```
<!DOCTYPE HTML PUBLIC "-//W3C//DTD HTML 3.2//EN">
<HTML>
<HEAD>
<TITLE>Home Page of John Q. Public</TITLE>
</HEAD>
<BODY>

<!-- Mark the beginning of this portion with a horizontal rule. -->
<HR>
<!-- Center your name as a level 1 header. -->
<H1 ALIGN="center">John Q. Public</H1>
<!-- Provide any desirable contact information. -->
999 Peachtree St.<BR>
Atlanta, GA 30314<BR>
USA<BR>
E-Mail: my_id@mysite.edu

<!-- Mark the beginning of this portion with a horizontal rule. -->
<HR>
<!-- Choose the heading text that you feel appropriate. -->
<H1>About Me</H1>
<!-- The formatting and information should be developed to suit your needs.
-->
<TAB INDENT=5>This is the first paragraph in this section about myself.
I have been at MY BUSINESS for the past X years.
<P>
<TAB INDENT=5>I am currently working on several projects.
These projects include...

<!-- Mark the beginning of this portion with a horizontal rule. -->
<HR>
<!-- Substitute the appropriate information in your document. The date -->
<!--should appear in a long format with the month name written out -->
<!--since the order conventions for date abbreviations vary. -->
Last modified on CURRENT_DATE by YOUR_NAME (YOUR_E-MAIL)

</BODY>
</HTML>
```

As you become more experienced with HTML, you can enhance this basic home page with a large assortment of elements. You will be able to include lists (see Chapter 6, “Lists”), multimedia objects (see Chapter 10, “Adding Externally Linked Multimedia Objects”), links to other pages (see Chapter 8, “Establishing Links”), and a variety of other advanced features.

Comments

When adding elements of your own, remember that the document you are creating can be viewed by thousands, if not millions, of people. During your document development, you should consider the variety of browsing environments in use, each with differing presentation capabilities.

A reference to the HTML 3.2 and 4.0 standard elements appears in Appendix A, "HTML Quick Reference." The elements discussed in this How-To are listed in Table 2-20.

Table 2-20 Elements used in this How-To

ELEMENT	LOCATION	PURPOSE
<HTML>...</HTML>	file	Defines the scope of an HTML document (see How-To 2.1).
<!--...-->	HTML	Represents an HTML comment element (see How-To 2.7).
<HEAD>...</HEAD>	HTML	Defines the head of an HTML document (see How-To 2.1).
<TITLE>...</TITLE>	HEAD	Defines the title of an HTML document (see How-To 2.6).
<BODY>...</BODY>	HTML	Defines the body of an HTML document (see How-To 2.1).
<B>...</B>	BODY	Represents a bolded element (see How-To 3.1).
 	BODY	Represents a line break (see How-To 7.4).
<H1>...</H1>	BODY	Represents a Level 1 heading element (see How-To 4.1).
<HR>	BODY	Places a horizontal rule when displayed (see How-To 7.1).
<P...>	BODY	Represents a paragraph break (see How-To 7.4).

2.15 How do I... View my home page?

COMPATIBILITY: BROWSER SPECIFIC

Problem

I have created my home page using an editor. I don't know how the document will appear in a browser until I actually view it. I'd like to take a look at the page in a few different browsers so that I get a feel for what other people will see when they view my page.

Technique

Use a browser to view your home page or any other page that you create. Browsers typically provide mechanisms for examining local HTML documents. There are three common interfaces used to perform this task.

- ✔ Command line: The path to the file that you want to open is passed to the browser application as a command-line argument.
- ✔ Open file: The browser application offers a menu option that accesses a local file.

✔ Open URL: The browser application has a menu option that enables you to open a URL. The protocol for a local file is simply **`file`**.

Procedures for opening local documents through these three interface types are provided in the "Steps" section.

Steps

The following methods open locally created documents for viewing within browser applications. Step-by-step instructions are provided for the three common interface types for specifying local files.

Consult the documentation for your particular browser application to determine which interfaces are appropriate. In all cases, your browser is assumed to be able to interpret the document that you are opening as HTML rather than as plain text.

Command Line

1. Be sure that you name the local file with the **`.html`** (or **`.htm`** for PC) filename extension. This indicates to most browsers that the local file is to be accessed as an HTML document whether it truly is or not.

2. Invoke your browser application with the file you want to open as a command-line argument. For example, to attempt to open the file **`MYHOME.HTM`** in the current directory using the Lynx browser, you would issue the following command:

```
lynx myhome.htm
```

Open File

1. Name the local file with the **`.html`** (or **`.htm`** for PC) filename extension. This indicates to most browsers that the local file is to be accessed as an HTML document whether the document truly is HTML or not.

2. Load your browser application.

3. Select the menu option or hot key for opening a local file.

4. The interface for entering the file information varies among browsers. Consult the browser documentation to determine how to complete this operation successfully. In Netscape Navigator and Microsoft Internet Explorer, a file selection dialog is presented; you can browse the local directory hierarchy until you find the file you want.

Open URL

1. Be sure that you named the local file with the **`.html`** (or **`.htm`** for PC) filename extension. This indicates to most browsers that the local file is to be accessed as an HTML document, whether the document truly is or not.

2. Load your browser application from the command line or an appropriate icon.

3. Select the menu option or hot key for opening a URL.

4. The interface for entering the file information will vary depending on your particular browser. You should consult the browser documentation to determine how to successfully complete this operation. In Lynx, you press G, and the system prompts you to enter the URL you want to open. If you want to open the local file `MYHOME.HTM` in the `path_info` directory, you enter this URL:

```
file://localhost/path_info/myhome.htm
```

How It Works

When opening a local file, your browser application determines how to treat the contents of a file based on the extension on the filename. The browser maps filename extensions to particular content types and will render the file as it deems appropriate. Your HTML files should have the `.html` extension (`.htm` on PC platforms).

The three methods examined for opening a local file accomplish the same task. The goal of the interface is to provide the browser with a path to the file that you want to open. The command-line interface method takes this information directly when the application is started.

Many browsers support an open local file function. Because most HTML documents require viewing before installation on a Web site, the ability to view a local file is extremely useful in the authoring process. Many individuals track private information through personal webs stored locally that are not accessible to the world. Figure 2-24 exhibits this interface method. The desired file can be selected from a file selection dialog window.

Local files can also be accessed via a standard Open URL facility. Specifying a `file` protocol type tells the browser that the desired files can be found in the local file system. The Go feature of the Lynx browser is displayed in Figure 2-25.

After the browser receives sufficient information to find the requested file, it tries to open it according to the information provided. The browser determines the display type of this file by mapping the filename extension to a suitable content type. The browser reads the content and then displays it according to the type determined. HTML 3.2 and 4.0 files display as HTML documents.

Comments

Different browser applications support different subsets of these interfaces for opening local documents. The documentation for your particular browser contains the information on how this task is performed.

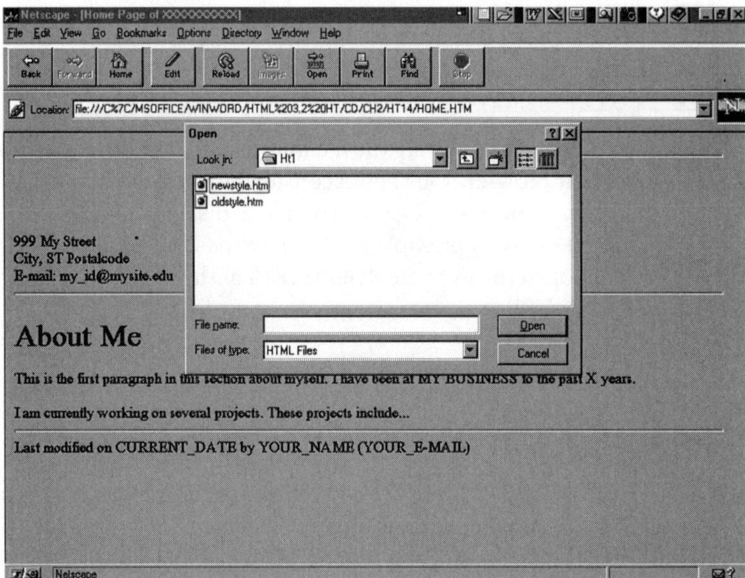

Figure 2-24 Netscape's Open Local facility

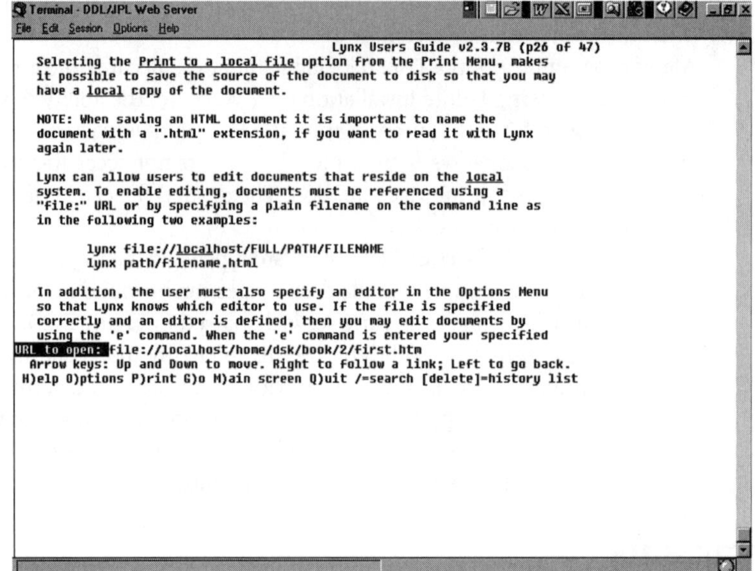

Figure 2-25 Lynx Go interface

If your HTML documents are being opened as plain text documents, the most likely reason is that your browser is not properly configured to treat these files as HTML documents. The browser determines whether a file contains an HTML document based on the filename extension of the file being accessed. The most commonly used extension to indicate an HTML file is `.html` (or `.htm` on the PC platform). If your files have this extension and still are not opening properly, check the configuration of your browser application. You might need to configure this extension to indicate an HTML document. For more information on this process, consult the documentation for your browser application.

CHAPTER 3

ADDING HTML PHYSICAL CHARACTER EFFECTS

3

ADDING HTML PHYSICAL CHARACTER EFFECTS

How do I...

When creating an HTML page, you will occasionally want to emphasize or otherwise set apart a word or phrase from the rest of the text. Just as word processors provide several styles—such as bold and italic—that can be used to alter the appearance of text, HTML offers a similar set of character effects. One type, physical effects, is designed to alter the appearance of the text displayed. The styles include bold, italic, and underline, as well as alterations in the size and color of the text. This chapter provides an overview of the physical character effects available in HTML 4.0.

3.1 Use Bold Font

When you create a document on a word processor, there are often specific words and phrases you want to emphasize to bring them to the attention of the reader. This is frequently done by making the characters bold. HTML lets you do the same thing. This simple How-To explains how to add bold text to your page.

3.2 Use Italic Font

Certain names and other text elements—names of books and movies, for example—require formatting in italics for proper style. You might also want to emphasize certain words in the text this way. This simple How-To explains how to place words and phrases in your page in italics.

3.3 Use a Fixed-Width Font

Samples of computer input and output, as well as other text items that require precise alignment, are often displayed in a fixed-width (or typewriter-style) font. This simple How-To explains how to add fixed-width text to your page.

3.4 Change Font Size

HTML 4.0 enables you to change the font size of the text in a document, making it larger or smaller to fit the needs of the document. This How-To explains how to use sets of tags to change the font size of text.

3.5 Change Font Color

HTML 4.0 has the capability to change the color of the text displayed in a document. This How-To explains how to change the font color in a document, either by using an exact color description or by specifying a basic color name.

3.6 Underline Text

Another way to emphasize text is to underline it. This is often done when italics and bold aren't available or do not fit the style of the document. This simple How-To explains how to underline words and phrases in your page.

3.7 Specify Strikethrough Formatting

Strikethrough formatting is often used to show examples of incorrect text, such as the incorrect input for a computer program. This How-To explains how to include strikethrough formatting in your pages.

3.8 Include Superscripts and Subscripts

Superscripts and subscripts are used to move text elements above or below the rest of the line. These are often used in footnotes and in mathematical and scientific formulas. This How-To explains how to add superscripts and subscripts to your page using the features of HTML 4.0.

3.1 How do I... Use bold font?

COMPATIBILITY: HTML 2+

Problem

I have some text I would like to emphasize by making it bold. How do I make text bold in HTML?

Technique

Making text bold in HTML is very easy. Simply by using the <B> tag, you can make any amount of text, from one letter to entire paragraphs, appear bold.

Steps

To make text bold, place the <B> tag at the beginning of the text and the </B> tag at the end:

```
This is normal text and <B>this is bold text.</B>
I only want to make the first letter of this <B>w</B>ord bold.
```

An example of bold and other physical styles as they are displayed in Netscape Navigator is shown in Figure 3-1. The same example as displayed in Microsoft Internet Explorer is shown in Figure 3-2. The code is also available on the CD-ROM as file 3-1.HTML.

How It Works

When a browser encounters a <B> tag, it displays the text contained between the <B> and the </B> tags as bold text. The browser does no other processing on the text.

Comments

Some browsers do not enable you to mix <B> with other tags, such as italics (<I>, see How-To 3.2). The <STRONG> tag (see How-To 4.2) often formats text in the same manner as <B>. Which one to use is up to you. See How-To 4.9 for a discussion about using styles effectively.

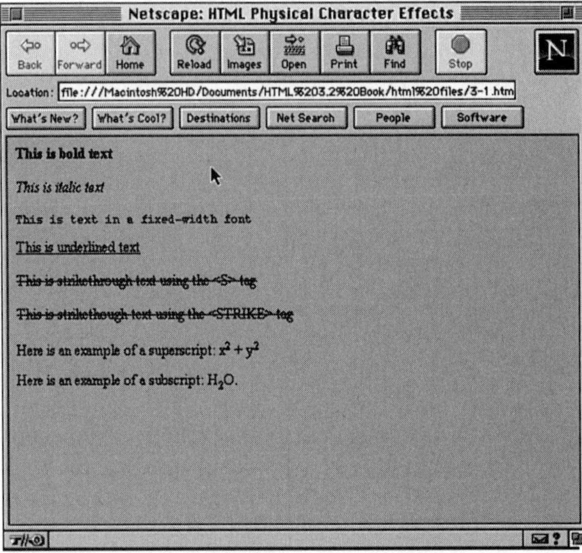

Figure 3-1 Examples of various physical character effects (Netscape Navigator)

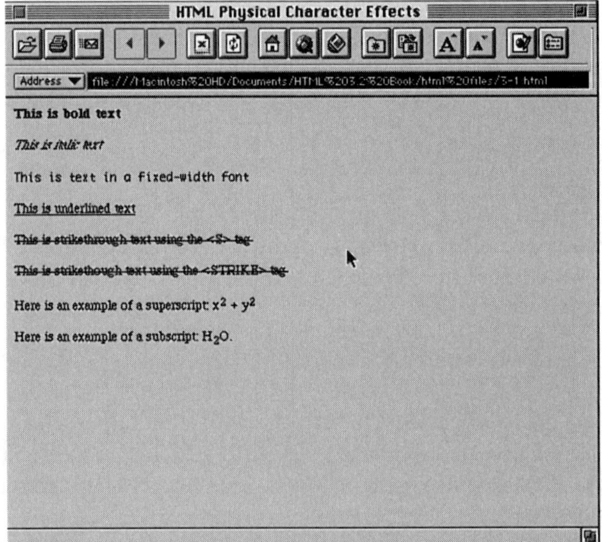

Figure 3-2 Examples of various physical character effects (Microsoft Internet Explorer)

3.2 How do I... Use italic font?

COMPATIBILITY: HTML 2+

Problem

I have some text, including the titles of some books, that I need to show in italics. How do I display text in italics in HTML?

Technique

Italicizing text in HTML is very easy. The **<I>** and **</I>** tags will italicize any amount of text contained between them.

Steps

To italicize text, place the **<I>** tag at the beginning of the text and the **</I>** tag at the end:

```
This is normal text and <I>this is italicized text.</I>

I only want to put the first letter of this <I>w</I>ord in italics.
```

Examples of italics and other physical styles are shown in Figures 3-1 and 3-2. This code is also available on the CD as file **3-1.HTML**.

How It Works

When a browser encounters an **<I>** tag, it displays the text contained between the **<I>** and the **</I>** tags in italics. The browser does no other processing on the text.

Comments

Some browsers do not enable you to mix **<I>** with other text style tags, such as **<B>**. The **<EM>** tag (see How-To 4.2) often formats text in the same manner as **<I>**. Which one you use is up to you.

COMPLEXITY
BEGINNING

3.3 How do I... Use a fixed-width font?

COMPATIBILITY: HTML 2+

Problem

I have some text that I would like to place in a fixed-width font to maintain the exact alignment of the words. How do I put words in a fixed-width font in HTML?

Technique

Putting text into a fixed-width font is very easy. Any text placed between the **<TT>** and **</TT>** tags (for teletype or typewritten text) will be rendered in a fixed-width font.

Steps

To place text in a fixed-width font, put **<TT>** at the beginning of the text and **</TT>** at the end of the text:

```
This is normal text and <TT>this is text in fixed-width font.</TT>
I only want to put the first letter of this <TT>w</TT>ord in fixed-width
font.
```

Examples of fixed-width font and other physical styles are shown in Figures 3-1 and 3-2. The code is also available on the CD in file **3-1.html**.

How It Works

When a browser encounters a **<TT>** tag, it renders the text between the **<TT>** and the **</TT>** tags in a fixed-width font. The actual fixed-width font used (such as Courier or Monaco) depends on the browser, and it can often be modified by the user. No other formatting of the text is done by the **<TT>** tag.

Comments

Some browsers don't enable you to combine **<TT>** with other text style tags, such as **<B>** and **<I>**, to format the same text. Because many browsers enable users to choose which fixed-width font to use when displaying text marked by **<TT>**, the displayed text might not appear to some users as it appears in your original.

3.4 How do I... Change font size?

COMPATIBILITY: HTML 3.2+

Problem

I need to include different-sized fonts in my documents. Most of the users accessing my documents will have browsers capable of rendering these fonts. How can I make the font size larger or smaller?

Technique

Font changes are accomplished by using elements that specify that the enclosed text should be rendered using a different font size.

Here are two methods of accomplishing this task. The first describes the use of the `<BIG>` and `<SMALL>` tags that are part of HTML 3.2 and above. The second describes the use of the `<FONT>` and `<BASEFONT>` tags, also part of HTML 3.2 and above, providing greater flexibility in font size changes.

Steps

1. Open the HTML document that contains the text size you want to change.

2. To make the font size smaller by an arbitrary amount, place the `<SMALL>` tag at the beginning of the text and the `</SMALL>` tag at the end:

```
This is normal text and <SMALL>small text.</SMALL>

I only want to decrease the font size of the first letter of this⇐
<SMALL>w</SMALL>ord.
```

3. Similarly, to increase the font size by an arbitrary amount, place the `<BIG>` tag at the beginning of the text and the `</BIG>` tag at the end of the text:

```
This is normal text and <BIG>big text.</BIG>

I only want to increase the font size of the first letter of this⇐
<BIG>w</BIG>ord.
```

4. You can use the `SIZE` attribute of the `<FONT>` tag to provide finer control over the size of the font used in the document. `SIZE` can be specified by any integer between `1` and `7`, with `3` as the usual default. For example, to place text in a very large font, use

```
<FONT SIZE=7>This text is very large</FONT>
```

5. You can change the font size of the entire document with the **BASEFONT** element at the beginning of the document. Use the **SIZE** attribute to change the default font size. For example, to create a document whose default font size is **2**, you would enter

```
<BASEFONT SIZE=2>
```

6. You can also use the **SIZE** attribute to change the font size relative to the default font size by using a + or – sign to indicate the change from the default size. For example, to place text in a font two sizes larger than the default size, use

```
<FONT SIZE="+2">This text is two sizes larger than the default</FONT>
```

Examples of changes to font size and color are shown in Figures 3-3 and 3-4. This code is also available on the CD as file **3-2.HTML**.

How It Works

When a browser encounters a **<BIG>** or **<SMALL>** element, it will render the text contained between the **<BIG>** and **</BIG>** (or **<SMALL>** and **</SMALL>**) tags by changing the font size by a predetermined amount. When a browser identifies the **<FONT>** tag, it reads the attributes and makes the required changes in the size or color of the font. When the browser reads the **<BASEFONT>** element, it adjusts all the text on the page to the font size specified by the **SIZE** attribute.

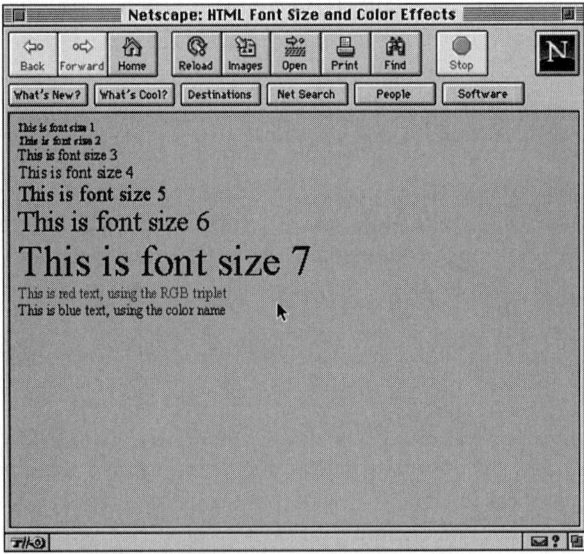

Figure 3-3 Examples of font size and color changes (Netscape Navigator)

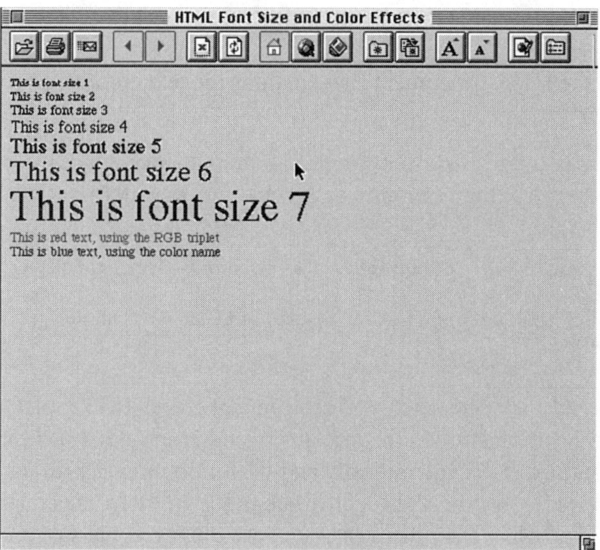

Figure 3-4 Examples of font size and color changes (Microsoft Internet Explorer)

Comments

Older browsers do not support any of the font tags, so they will not change the font size as specified by the tags. If you're looking to emphasize or otherwise call attention to certain passages of text, you'll want to consider using character effects such as bold and italics to make your point.

3.5 How do I... Change font color?

COMPATIBILITY: HTML 3.2+

Problem

I would like to change the color of the text on my page. Most of the users accessing my documents will have browsers capable of changing the color of text. How can I make the font different colors?

Technique

HTML 3.2 and above provide a way to change the color of text in a document. You can change the font color of selected portions of the text by using the **COLOR** attribute of the **<FONT>** tag.

Steps

1. Open the HTML document that contains the text color you want to change.
2. To specify the text whose color you wish to change, place the **<FONT COLOR>** tag at the beginning of the text and **</FONT>** at the end of the text.

```
This is normal text and <FONT COLOR>this is colored text.</FONT>

I only want to change the color of the first letter of this⇐
<FONT COLOR>w</FONT>ord.
```

3. To specify a specific color, you can use that color's RGB triplet, the hexadecimal combination of the red, green, and blue values of the color. This system uses **FF** for full intensity and **00** for no intensity. To use the RGB triplet values, set the **COLOR** attribute in the **<FONT>** tag equal to these values and place the pound (**#**) sign between the equal sign and the RGB triplet:

```
This is normal text and <FONT COLOR="#FF0000">this is red text.</FONT>

I only want to make the first letter of this⇐
<FONT COLOR="#FFFFFF">w</FONT>ord white.
```

4. An alternative to using the RGB triplets is to use one of a set of predefined color names that are part of HTML 4.0. A list of these colors can be found in Appendix H, "HTML Color Table."
5. To use these names, set the **COLOR** attribute in the **<FONT>** tag to equal them:

```
This is normal text and <FONT COLOR="red">this is red text.</FONT>

I only want to make the first letter of this⇐
<FONT COLOR="white">w</FONT>ord white.
```

6. The **COLOR** attribute can also be used with the **<BASEFONT>** tag in HTML 4.0 at the beginning of a document to define the default color for all text in the document:

```
<BASEFONT COLOR="#FF0000">
```

Examples of changes to font size and color are shown in Figures 3-3 and 3-4. This code is also available on the CD as file **3-2.HTML**.

How It Works

When a browser encounters a **<FONT>** tag that has defined a value for the **COLOR** attribute, it colors the text between the **<FONT>** and **</FONT>** tags using the color defined by the attribute.

Comments

The **COLOR** attribute to **<FONT>** is supported by more recent browsers, such as versions 2 and later of Netscape and Internet Explorer. Using the names of colors instead of RGB triplets was added to Netscape in version 3. Also note that, although the RGB triplets enable you to define millions of colors, many monitors are set up to display hundreds or thousands of colors. If the color requested isn't supported by the computer, the browser will pick the next closest color it can display.

3.6 How do I... Underline text?

COMPATIBILITY: HTML 2+

Problem

I have some text in my document that I would like to underline. How can I underline text in HTML?

Technique

Underlining text is a simple process in HTML. The **<U>** and **</U>** tags will underline any amount of text contained between them.

Steps

To underline text, place the **<U>** tag at the beginning of the text and the **</U>** tag at the end of the text:

```
This is normal text and <U>this is underlined text.</U>

I only want to underline the first letter of this <U>w</U>ord.
```

Examples of underlines and other physical styles are shown in Figures 3-1 and 3-2. This code is also available on the CD as file **3-1.HTML**.

How It Works

When a browser encounters a <U> tag, it underlines the text contained between the <U> and the </U> tags. The browser does no other formatting on the text.

Comments

Some browsers do not enable you to mix <U> tags with other tags, such as bold and italic, when trying to format the same word or phrase. Some browsers, such as versions of Netscape before 3, do not support underlined text.

COMPLEXITY
BEGINNING

3.7 How do I... Specify strikethrough formatting?

COMPATIBILITY: HTML 3.2+

Problem

As an example of what text should not be entered into a program, I would like to show the text in a strikethrough style, that is, with a horizontal line running through it. How can I use strikethrough style in HTML?

Technique

HTML 4.0 supports the use of the <S> tag, which converts any text placed between it and the corresponding </S> tag into strikethrough style.

Steps

1. To place text in strikethrough style, put the <S> tag at the beginning of the text and the </S> tag at the end of the text:

```
This is normal text and <S>this is strikethrough style text.</S>

I only want to strikethrough the first letter of this <S>w</S>ord.
```

2. An alternative method supported by some browsers is the <STRIKE> tag, which works in the same way as the <S> tag:

```
This is normal text and <STRIKE>this is strikethrough style text.⇐
</STRIKE>

I only want to strikethrough the first letter of this <STRIKE>w</STRIKE>ord.
```

Examples of strikethrough style are shown in Figures 3-1 and 3-2. The code is also available on the CD as file **3-1.HTML**.

How It Works

When a browser encounters an <S> or a <STRIKE> tag, it places the text between the <S> and </S> (or <STRIKE> and </STRIKE>) tags in strikethrough style by replacing the text with an identical font that has a horizontal line running through it.

Comments

Some browsers do not have access to a strikethrough font. If so, the browser might choose to use an alternative method for displaying the text. Because some older browsers support only either <S> or <STRIKE>, you should use both <S> and <STRIKE> around the text you want to place in strikethrough style:

```
Most browsers should display <STRIKE><S>this text</S></STRIKE> in⇐
strikethrough style.
```

3.8 How do I... Include superscripts and subscripts?

COMPATIBILITY: HTML 3.2+

Problem

I have a paper I want to convert to HTML that includes mathematical equations, chemical formulas, and numbered footnotes. These all require numbers to be placed in superscripts or subscripts. How do I create superscripted and subscripted text in HTML?

Technique

HTML 4.0 provides support for superscripts (text shifted above the normal level of the line) and subscripts (text shifted below the normal level of the line). The _{and} tags place any text between them below the level of the line, and in a smaller font when possible. The ^{and} tags place any text between them above the level of the line, also in a smaller font when possible.

Steps

1. Go to your document and identify the sections of the document to be displayed as subscript or superscript text.

2. To create a subscript, place the **_{** tag at the beginning of the text to be subscripted and the **}** tag at the end of the text to be subscripted:

```
The chemical formula of water is H<SUB>2</SUB>O.
```

3. To create a superscript, place the **^{** tag at the beginning of the text to be superscripted and the **}** tag at the end of the text to be superscripted:

```
A simple formula for a parabola is y = x<SUP>2</SUP>.
```

Examples of subscripts and superscripts are shown in Figures 3-1 and 3-2. The code is also available on the CD as file **3-1.HTML**.

How It Works

When a browser encounters a **<SUB>** tag, it shifts all the text between the **_{** and **}** tags below the level of the rest of the line and, depending on the browser, renders the text in a smaller size. When a browser encounters a **<SUP>** tag, it shifts all the text between the **^{** and **}** tags above the level of the rest of the line and, again depending on the browser, renders the text in a smaller size.

Comments

Because **<SUB>** and **<SUP>** were introduced with HTML 3.2, people using some pre-HTML 3.2 browsers, such as pre-2.0 versions of Netscape Navigator and Microsoft Internet Explorer, will not be able to see the subscripts or superscripts. To accommodate these users, an alternative for creating subscripts and superscripts in chemical formulas and mathematical equations is to create a graphic of the formula or equation in another program and to include the graphic in the page as an inline graphic. (See How-To 9.2.)

CHAPTER 4

ADDING HTML LOGICAL CHARACTER EFFECTS

4

ADDING HTML LOGICAL CHARACTER EFFECTS

How do I...

When you are creating an HTML page, you might want to emphasize or otherwise set apart a word or phrase from the rest of the text. HTML offers a set of tags called *logical character effects* that can be used not only to specify a particular formatting effect on the document text but to identify the meaning of the text as well. This chapter examines the logical character styles that are available in HTML 4.0, including headings, and shows you how to use character effects to improve the quality of a document.

4.1 Use Heading Styles

You often want to give your page a bold, distinct title to help readers identify it. Also, adding subheadings to a document to identify different areas of interest to readers is useful. This simple How-To explains how to add headings of various styles to your page.

4.2 Place Emphasis and Strong Emphasis

You might want to emphasize words or phrases in your pages, or you might want to strongly emphasize them, where it doesn't matter whether the text is bold, italicized, or underlined. This How-To explains how to emphasize and strongly emphasize key words and phrases in your pages, allowing different browsers to render those passages in their different ways.

4.3 Specify a Citation

If you are placing an essay or journal paper on the Web, you will want to include citations of other papers and documents. Instead of developing your own style to include citations, it is useful to mark a section of text as a citation and let the reader's browser do the specifying. This How-To explains how to mark text as a citation for this purpose.

4.4 Emphasize a Defined Term

Your page might include several terms that are defined in the text. This simple How-To explains how to use the `<DFN>` feature in HTML 4.0 to emphasize these words and phrases in your page.

4.5 Include Small Segments of Code and Variables

Often Web pages include references to computer code, specifically, the names of variables used in programs. These text elements are often best rendered in a format different from the rest of the text. This How-To explains how to use HTML tags to format text that includes computer code and variables.

4.6 Provide a Sample of Literal Characters

There are cases in which you want to include literal, otherwise unformatted, characters in your page. This How-To explains how to include samples of literal characters in your page.

4.7 Indicate Text as Keyboard Input

In the course of writing your page, you might want to insert brief sections of keyboard input, computer commands, or arguments. This How-To explains how you can format these text elements in HTML.

4.8 Specify an Address

There are many cases in which you want to specify the owner of a document and how to reach that person. This simple How-To shows how to specify the address of a person in an HTML document.

4.9 Spruce Up My Home Page with Character Effects

The character effects described in this chapter and Chapter 3, "Adding HTML Physical Character Effects," can be used to make a more impressive, interesting, and effective document. They can also be used to make a document ugly and difficult to read. This How-To suggests how you might best use these character effects to improve the look of your pages.

4.1 How do I... Use heading styles?

COMPATIBILITY: HTML 2+

Problem

I would like to include a title on my page. I would also like to include subheadings for various parts of my page, but I don't want these subheadings to be as large as the title. How do I include titles and headings of various sizes in my page?

Technique

HTML enables users to identify headings and subheadings in a document through the **<H*n*>** tag, where *n* is a number from 1 to 6. The largest heading is **<H1>** and the smallest is **<H6>**. You can also use attributes with these tags to align the headings with various parts of the page, or even to include images within the heading.

Steps

1. Go to your document and identify the words and phrases that will serve as titles and headings in the document.

2. To identify a section of text as a heading, place **<H*n*>** at the beginning of the text and **</H*n*>** at the end of the text, where *n* is replaced by an integer between 1 and 6:

```
<H1>This is an example of a level 1 heading</H1>
<H6>This is an example of a level 6 heading</H6>
```

3. To align a heading to the left, center, or right of the window using HTML 4.0, add the **ALIGN** attribute at the beginning of the heading. The default alignment is to the left.

```
<H1 ALIGN=LEFT>This is a level 1 heading aligned to the ⇐
left of the window</H1>
<H1 ALIGN=CENTER>This is a level 1 heading aligned to the ⇐
center of the window</H1>
<H1 ALIGN=RIGHT>This is a level 1 heading aligned to the ⇐
right of the window</H1>
```

An example of how headings appear in Netscape Navigator is shown in Figure 4-1. An example of how headings appear in Microsoft Internet Explorer is shown in Figure 4-2. The code for both examples is available on the CD-ROM as file `4-1.HTML`.

How It Works

When a browser encounters a heading tag, it automatically formats the text contained in the title according to its programming. This often includes changing the size of the text, making the text bold, and including carriage returns and line spacing. The exact way headings are formatted differs from browser to browser.

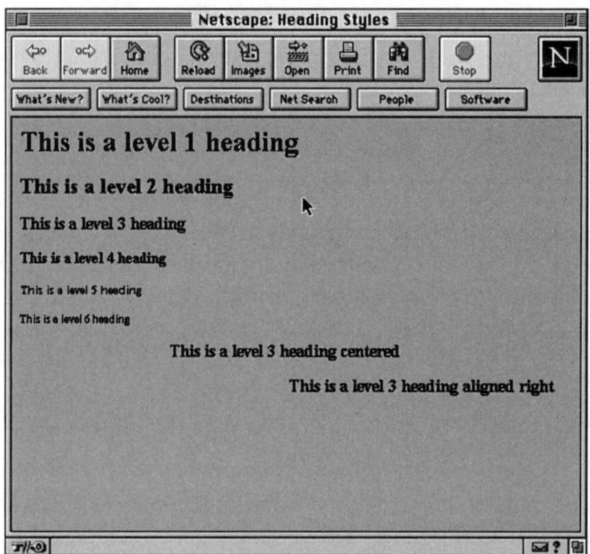

Figure 4-1 Various styles of headings (Netscape Navigator)

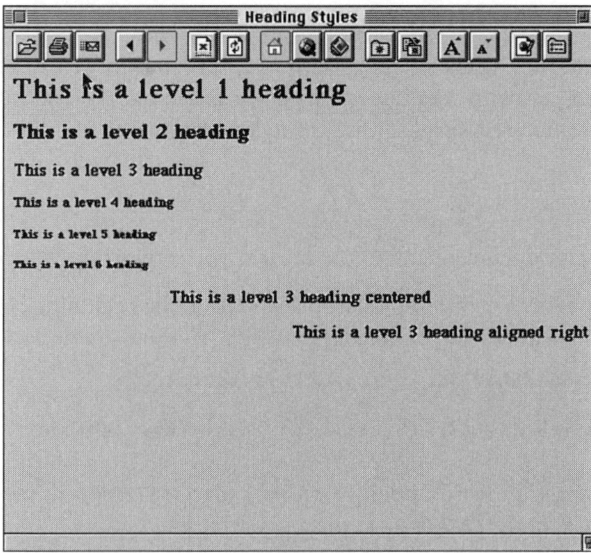

Figure 4-2 Various styles of headings (Microsoft Internet Explorer)

Comments

Because headings are rendered differently from browser to browser, be careful when referring to them by their appearance within a document. Also note that, as a rule, headings below level 3 are the same size as normal text, if not smaller, so their use as titles might not be very effective.

COMPLEXITY
BEGINNING

4.2 How do I... Place emphasis and strong emphasis?

COMPATIBILITY: HTML 2+

Problem

I would like to emphasize certain words and phrases on my page. However, I don't need a specific style applied to them, such as bold or italic. How can I emphasize generically or strongly emphasize text in HTML?

Technique

HTML supports the content-style tags **<EM>** and **<STRONG>** for generic emphasis and strong emphasis, respectively. These tags highlight specific areas of text without requiring the browser to use a specific physical style for them.

Steps

1. Open your document and locate the text you want to emphasize.
2. To emphasize a word or phrase, place **<EM>** at the beginning of the text and **</EM>** at the end of the text:

```
This is normal text and <EM>this is emphasized text.</EM>

I only want to emphasize the first letter of this <EM>w</EM>ord.
```

3. To emphasize a word or phrase strongly, place **<STRONG>** at the beginning of the text and **</STRONG>** at the end of the text:

```
This is normal text and <STRONG>this is strongly ⇐
emphasized text.</STRONG>

I only want to strongly emphasize the first letter of this ⇐
<STRONG>w</STRONG>ord.
```

An example of **<EM>**, **<STRONG>**, and other logical character effects, as displayed in Netscape Navigator, is shown in Figure 4-3. The same example, as displayed in Microsoft Internet Explorer, is shown in Figure 4-4. The code is also available on the CD as file **4-2.HTML**.

How It Works

When a browser encounters an **<EM>** tag, it emphasizes the text contained between the **<EM>** and **</EM>** tags using the browser's specific instructions for emphasized text. When a browser encounters a **<STRONG>** tag, it emphasizes the text contained between the **<STRONG>** and **</STRONG>** tags, once again using its specific instructions for strongly emphasized text.

Comments

Most browsers interpret **<EM>** the same as **<I>** (that is, they use italics) and **<STRONG>** the same as **<B>** (that is, they use bold). However, some browsers interpret these tags in different ways or enable the user to define the interpretation of **<EM>** and **<STRONG>**. How and where to use **<EM>**, **<STRONG>**, **<B>**, and **<I>** is discussed in How-To 4.9.

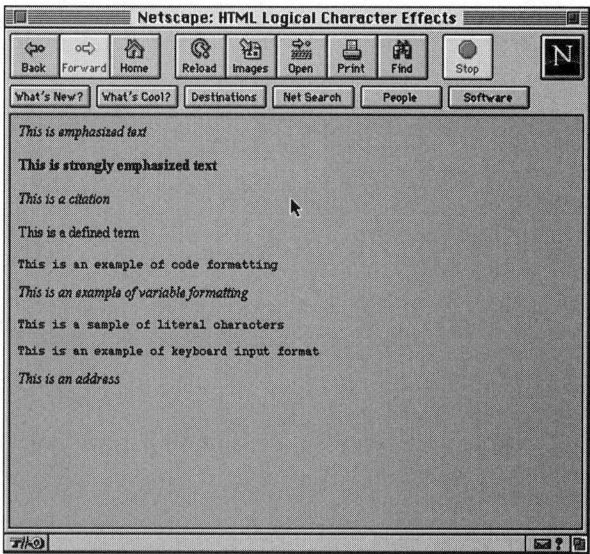

Figure 4-3 Examples of various logical character effects (Netscape Navigator)

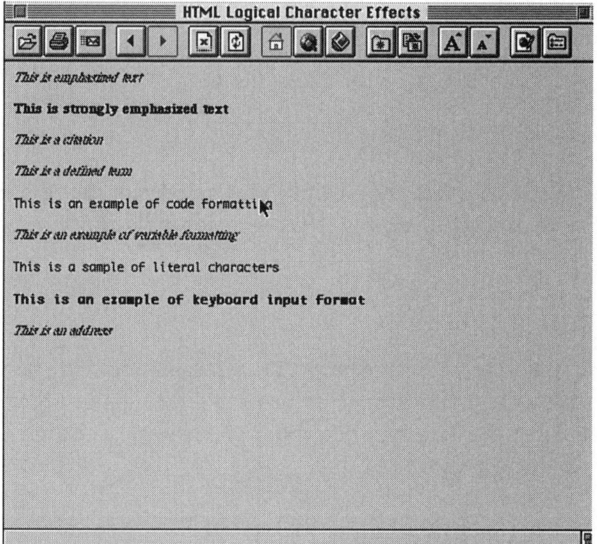

Figure 4-4 Examples of various logical character effects (Microsoft Internet Explorer)

4.3 How do I...
Specify a citation?

COMPATIBILITY: HTML 2+

Problem

I am putting an essay on the Web and I would like a simple way to format on the page the references to other papers. How can I format citations in HTML?

Technique

HTML makes formatting citations easy. The **<CITE>** tag will format a citation using a style built into each browser.

Steps

To format a citation, place the **<CITE>** tag at the beginning of the citation and **</CITE>** at the end of the citation:

```
Jane Doe's work showed how this could be accomplished <CITE>(Doe, ⇐
1998).</CITE>
```

Examples of citations and other content styles are shown in Figures 4-3 and 4-4. The code is also available on the CD as file **4-2.HTML**.

Technique

When a browser encounters the **<CITE>** tag, it formats the text between the **<CITE>** and **</CITE>** tags according to the style for indicating citations built into the browser.

Comments

Most browsers render the text marked by **<CITE>** in italics. However, because **<CITE>** is a content style, not a physical style, some browsers might be set to render such text differently. Keep this in mind when you are referencing a citation (or some part of a citation) using style tags.

4.4 How do I... Emphasize a defined term?

COMPATIBILITY: HTML 2+

Problem

I have several words and phrases that are defined in my pages. I would like to call attention to those words, but I don't specifically want to use bold, italic, or another style. How can I emphasize these words in HTML?

Technique

HTML supports the **<DFN>** tag, which is designed specifically for words and phrases that are defined in the text. The physical method of emphasizing the words is left up to the browser.

Steps

To mark a word or phrase that has been defined, place the **<DFN>** tag at the beginning of the text and **</DFN>** at the end of the text.

```
A batter has a <DFN>full count</DFN> when he has three balls and two ⇐
strikes.
```

Examples of definitions and other content styles are shown in Figures 4-3 and 4-4. The code is also available on the CD as file **4-2.HTML**.

How It Works

When a browser encounters a **<DFN>** tag, it changes the style of the text contained between the **<DFN>** and **</DFN>** tags. The style used is dependent on the browser, but it is usually either bold or italic.

Comments

Because the style is chosen by the browser and not by you, the defined terms might appear in a different style than you might anticipate. Therefore, be careful when you are referring to defined words based on their style.

4.5 How do I... Include small segments of code and variables?

COMPATIBILITY: HTML 2+

Problem

I have some samples of code from a program and some variables that I want to include in my page. I would like to format these to set them off from the rest of the text, but I don't want to go through a lot of work choosing a physical style. Is there an easy way to format code examples and variables in HTML?

Technique

HTML offers the **<CODE>** tag, which can be used to display sections of code from a program, usually in a fixed-width font, and **<VAR>**, which can be used to show variables from programs or other applications, often in italics.

Steps

1. Go to your document and locate the text you want to display as a variable or in code format.

2. To place a section of text in code format, place the **<CODE>** tag at the beginning of the text and the **</CODE>** tag at the end of the text:

```
The <CODE>goto 20</CODE> statement in the program should ⇐
be replaced to improve the programming style.
```

3. To display a word as a variable, place the **<VAR>** tag at the beginning of the text and the **</VAR>** tag at the end of the text:

```
The <VAR>count</VAR> variable keeps track of the number of ⇐
iterations of the loop.
```

Examples of the code and variable styles, as well as other content styles, are shown in Figures 4-3 and 4-4. The code is also available on the CD as file **4-2.HTML**.

How It Works

When a browser encounters a **<CODE>** tag, it places the text contained between the **<CODE>** and **</CODE>** tags in a style used by the browser for rendering code. This is usually a fixed-width font. When a browser encounters a **<VAR>** tag, it places the text contained between the **<VAR>** and **</VAR>** tags in the style used by the browser for variables. This is often italic.

Comments

Because <CODE> and <VAR> are not physical styles, how they are presented depends on the browser. Therefore, as with other content styles, be careful when you are referring to specific items based on their style.

4.6 How do I... Provide a sample of literal characters?

COMPATIBILITY: HTML 2+

Problem

I have some characters that I would like to show as a sample of literal, unformatted characters. How can I do this in HTML?

Technique

HTML offers the <SAMP> tag, which will display any text contained within the <SAMP> and </SAMP> tags as a sample of literal characters. This tag works in much the same way as <CODE> and <TT>, discussed earlier in this chapter.

Steps

To display text as a sample of literal characters, place the <SAMP> tag at the beginning of the text and </SAMP> at the end of the text:

```
This is an example of <SAMP>a sample of literal characters</SAMP>

In this case I only want to place <SAMP>o</SAMP>ne character in the sample.
```

Examples of sample text and other content styles are shown in Figures 4-3 and 4-4. The code is also available on the CD as file 4-2.HTML.

How It Works

When a browser encounters the <SAMP> tag, it formats the text contained between the <SAMP> and </SAMP> tags according to the rules built into the browser. Usually this means rendering the text in a fixed-width font, identical to the fonts used for <CODE> and <TT>, explained earlier, and <KBD>, explained in How-To 3.14.

Comments

Although text tagged with **<SAMP>** usually looks the same when rendered as text tagged with several other styles, it is best to use **<SAMP>** when referring to a specific sample, if for no other reason than to enable an indexing program to identify the tagged item properly.

4.7 How do I... Indicate text as keyboard input?

COMPATIBILITY: HTML 2+

Problem

On my page I would like to include some samples of input to a computer program. I would like to format these samples differently than the standard text is formatted. How can I do this in HTML?

Technique

The HTML keyboard style tag **<KBD>** enables you to mark text to be typed by the user. You can also use it to display computer commands and arguments, especially those to be entered by the user. The text tagged by **<KBD>** is usually shown in a fixed-width font.

Steps

To specify text that is to be keyboarded by the user, place the **<KBD>** tag at the beginning of the text and the **</KBD>** tag at the end of the text:

```
At the prompt enter the command <KBD>lpr output.txt</KBD>

Using the <KBD>-l</KBD> flag causes a long form of the directory to be ⇐
listed.
```

Examples of keyboard style and other content styles are shown in Figures 4-3 and 4-4. The code is also available on the CD as file **4-2.HTML**.

How It Works

When a browser encounters a **<KBD>** tag, it places everything between the **<KBD>** and **</KBD>** tags in keyboard style. Such text is usually rendered in a fixed-width font, but font style can vary among browsers.

Comments

Because <KBD> is a content style, its appearance can vary among browsers. The <KBD> style is also very similar to other styles, such as <CODE> and <SAMP>, so it can be used interchangeably with those styles. This will be discussed in more detail in How-To 4.9.

4.8 How do I... Specify an address?

COMPATIBILITY: HTML 2+

Problem

I want to include information about the author of a Web page. How can I specify an address of the author on a Web page?

Technique

The <ADDRESS> character effect is used to specify information about the creator or maintainer of a Web page. This information can include the name, e-mail address, phone number, mailing address, or other relevant information.

Steps

To specify text that is considered part of the address, place the <ADDRESS> tag at the beginning of the text and the </ADDRESS> tag at the end of the text:

```
This page was written by <ADDRESS>Jane Done</ADDRESS>.

<ADDRESS>Jane Doe / jane.doe@mycompany.com</ADDRESS>
```

Examples of the address effect and other logical character effects are shown in Figures 4-3 and 4-4. The code is also available on the CD as file **4-2.HTML**.

How It Works

When a browser encounters an <ADDRESS> tag, it places everything between the <ADDRESS> and </ADDRESS> tags in address style. Such text is usually rendered in italics, but font style can vary among browsers.

Comments

The <ADDRESS> tag is usually used at the bottom of the document to identify the author of the page. Because the <ADDRESS> tag doesn't allow any control over the formatting of its appearance, authors often find it preferable to use other styles to "sign" their pages in their own manner.

COMPLEXITY
INTERMEDIATE

4.9 How do I... Spruce up my home page with character effects?

COMPATIBILITY: HTML 2+

Problem

Now that I've learned about all these different styles, how can I use them most effectively to make my page more readable?

Technique

This problem is similar to the one encountered using fonts and type styles in word processors and page layout programs. With all the different styles available, there is a strong temptation to try them all. (After all, that's why they exist, right?) However, this can lead to pages that are aesthetically unpleasant and even difficult to read. This How-To contains some tips to help you use these styles effectively to spruce up your home page.

Steps

The following points will help you make the best use of physical or content styles in your Web pages:

1. Styles most effectively emphasize a point when used sparingly. If you make every other word bold or place large sections of text in italics, it becomes much harder to bring an important point to the attention of the reader.

2. In addition to diluting emphasis, frequent changing of styles from normal to bold to italics and so on makes it harder to read a document because your eyes must stop and adjust to the new type style before you can continue to read. Keep style changes to a minimum to avoid this problem.

3. There has been considerable discussion among WWW users and document creators about the appropriate use of `<B>` versus `<STRONG>` and `<I>` versus `<EM>`. On most browsers (but not necessarily all!), the tags do the same thing and are interchangeable. There is no single right way to use these tags. As a general rule, though, consider the following: Whenever you want to emphasize a word or phrase, use `<EM>` or `<STRONG>`. When the particular word or phrase requires a specific formatting, such as the title of a book or a specific name, use `<I>` or `<B>` instead. When in doubt, say out loud the sentence that contains the word or phrase in question. If you want to format the document to bring out the emphasis on the word or phrase as you would say it, use `<EM>` or `<STRONG>`.

4. HTML features another set of tags that are indistinguishable from one another when rendered on most browsers: **<TT>**, **<CODE>**, **<SAMP>**, and **<KBD>** all place text in a fixed-width format. Unlike the case described in step 3, things here are a bit more clear-cut. When you want to insert some code from a program, use the **<CODE>** tag. When you want to display the user input into a program, use the **<KBD>** tag. Use the **<SAMP>** tag when you want to display a sample of literal characters. Any other cases in which you need to display text in a fixed-width font can be handled by the **<TT>** tag. This division not only enables individual browsers to choose the best method for displaying information, it enables indexing programs that scan Web pages to identify any examples of code, input, and so on through the tags used. If nothing but **<TT>** were used for all fixed-width type purposes, the output would probably look the same on most browsers, but the indexing programs would have a much harder time finding code and input examples on Web pages.

5. When using tags to change the font size and color, keep in mind that some older browsers do not support these tags and won't change the text. Use these tags when other physical or logical effects won't emphasize the text in an acceptable way.

6. Due to differences in monitor resolution, text will not always appear the same size on different computers. As a rule of thumb, for a given font size specified with a **<FONT>** or **<BASEFONT>** tag (see How-To 3.4), the text will look bigger on Windows machines than on Macintosh computers. Keep this in mind before you change the font size to a very large or very small value.

Comments

With the judicious use of styles, you can easily spruce up your new home page and make it more interesting to read. Physical styles can improve the appearance of a page if care is taken with their use and it is understood that not all browsers will render physical styles in precisely the same way. The proper use of content styles will enable users to find the information of interest to them and will enable indexing programs to better catalog the contents of your pages.

CHAPTER 5

TABLES

5

TABLES

How do I...

Some powerful new techniques that started in HTML 3.2 improve your ability to display the information on your page. Among them are the new mathematical symbols that let you display simple and complex mathematical and scientific equations.

Table formatting commands added in HTML 3.2 and continued in 4.0 let you create tables and give you control over the size and alignment of the table contents. The How-To's in this chapter show you how to include math and tables effectively in your Web pages.

5.1 Include a Table

The `<TABLE>` element gives you the power to control the format and alignment of your information. You can place information into tables and be sure it will be properly aligned with the other information in the table, a great advantage when you're trying to display related information on a topic. This How-To gives the basics on including a table in your page.

5.2 Place a Caption in a Table

Captions are titles of tables, usually centered above the top of the table. This simple How-To explains how to add a caption to your table.

5.3 Insert a Table Heading

Table headings are the top row of the table and usually define what is in each column of the table. This How-To explains how to set up a table heading so you can easily identify the data in your table.

5.4 Define Data for a Cell or Table Element

After you've set up a table, you must be able to put data into it. In a table, data is stored in table elements, or *cells*. This How-To explains how to create cells and how to put your information into them.

5.5 Insert a Blank Data Cell

There are times when you might need to insert a blank cell into a table. This How-To explains two methods for doing this.

5.6 Create a New Row of Data

After you've begun to create table elements, you will want to put different items in different rows of the table. This How-To explains how to end one row of data and start a new row.

5.7 Define the Width of a Table Relative to the Browser Window

Sometimes you might want to base the size of your table on the size of the user's browser window. This How-To shows how to make the width of a table relative to the browser window.

5.8 Specify the Distance Between Cells

Occasionally you might need extra control over the placement of cells in your table. This How-To explains how to specify a distance between cells.

5.9 Set the Distance From the Cell Edge to the Cell Data

There are times when you might want to control the distance from a cell's edge to the cell's data. This How-To explains how to accomplish this.

5.10 Put a Table in My Home Page

When you've mastered the basics of creating tables, you'll no doubt be eager to include them in your pages. This How-To covers some tips and tricks for the effective use of tables, including some things you might not have thought of as tables.

5.11 Preset the Number of Columns in a Table for Faster Rendering

To speed table rendering, Netscape 4.0 enables you to specify the number of columns a table will have. This How-To shows you how to make the best use of this new table attribute.

COMPLEXITY
BEGINNING

5.1 How do I... Include a table?

COMPATIBILITY: HTML 3+

Problem

I have a collection of data that I would like to display as a table in my page. How do I define a table in HTML?

Technique

HTML 3.2 and 4.0 support tables, which enable you to control the row and column placement of information on your page. This How-To explains how to define a table in HTML by using the `<TABLE>` and `</TABLE>` tags. How to format the data to include in the table is covered later in the chapter.

Steps

1. Open your document. Identify where in the document you want to include a table. You might want to enter the table data into your document now, to serve as a guide when you add HTML `<TABLE>` tags later.

2. To specify data presented as a table, place the `<TABLE>` tag at the beginning of the data and `</TABLE>` at the end of the data:

```
<TABLE>
    <!-- Here's where the table information goes... -->
</TABLE>
```

3. HTML does not include, as a default, borders around the cells of the table. If you want to display the borders using the lines programmed into the browser, add the **BORDER** attribute to the **<TABLE>** tag:

```
<TABLE BORDER>
    <!-- Here's where the table information goes... -->
</TABLE>
```

4. As with other HTML elements such as headings, you can use the **ALIGN** attribute to control the horizontal location of the table on the page. The **ALIGN** attribute can take on the values shown in Table 5-1.

Table 5-1 Alignment options for tables

OPTION	DESCRIPTION
bleedleft	Flush with the left edge of the browser window
left	Flush with the left margin of the text
center	Centered between the left and right text margins
right	Flush with the right margin of the text
bleedright	Flush with the right edge of the browser window
justify	Fits the space between the left and right margins

For example, to center a table with a border, enter

```
<TABLE BORDER ALIGN=CENTER>
    <!-- Here's the data for the table... -->
</TABLE>
```

Or to place a borderless table flush against the left edge of the window, enter

```
<TABLE ALIGN=BLEEDLEFT>
    <!-- Here's the data for the table... -->
</TABLE>
```

5. When formatting a table, the browser automatically chooses a size for each column based on the text contained in each column. However, if you want to set a fixed size for each column, you can do so with the **COLSPEC** attribute in the **<TABLE>** tag. The **COLSPEC** attribute is followed by a series of letters and numbers; for example, **"L50 R30 C10"**. Here the letter stands for alignment of the text in the column: **L** for left, **C** for center, and **R** for right. The number is the width of the column. The units are set by the **UNITS** attribute, with the choices shown in Table 5-2.

Table 5-2 Options for the `UNITS` attribute

OPTION	DESCRIPTION
`en`	En units (1 en = ½ point = 1/144 inch): This is the default.
`relative`	Relative units: The browser sums the units to determine the relative width of each column.
`pixels`	Pixels on the browser display.

For example, to define three columns, each left-aligned and ½-inch wide, enter

```
<TABLE COLSPEC="L72 L72 L72">
    <!-- Table data goes here... -->
</TABLE>
```

To create a four-column table with the first three columns left-aligned and the fourth column right-aligned and half as wide as the others, enter

```
<TABLE UNITS=RELATIVE COLSPEC="L2 L2 L2 R1">
    <!-- Table data goes here... -->
</TABLE>
```

To create a table that has three columns, one left-aligned, one centered, and one right-aligned, each with a width of 100 pixels, enter

```
<TABLE UNITS=PIXELS COLSPEC="L100 C100 R100">
    <!-- Table data goes here... -->
</TABLE>
```

6. Similarly, you can control the width of the entire table by using the `WIDTH` attribute in the `<TABLE>` tag. Using the units defined by the `UNITS` attribute, the `WIDTH` attribute fixes the width of the table. If the `UNITS` attribute is set to `RELATIVE`, `WIDTH` interprets the number as the fraction of the distance between the left and right margins. For example, to set the width of a table to 4 inches (4×144=576 en), enter

```
<TABLE WIDTH=576>
    <!-- Table data goes here... -->
</TABLE>
```

To create a table that is centered on the screen and covers three-fourths of the distance between the left and right margins, enter

```
<TABLE ALIGN=CENTER UNITS=RELATIVE WIDTH=0.75>
    <!-- Table data goes here... -->
</TABLE>
```

How It Works

When a browser encounters a **<TABLE>** tag, it sets up the formatting to handle the data contained between the **<TABLE>** and **</TABLE>** tags. By reading the attributes contained between them, it knows where to override its default settings for creating tables, including the size and placement of the table.

Comments

The **BORDER** attribute tells the browser to use the lines defined within the browser; it is not possible to tell a browser to use a certain style of line or to use lines only on specific cells. If you use the pixel unit for **COLSPEC** and **WIDTH**, note that not all pixels are the same size, so something that formats one way on your browser might look different on another browser. It's probably better to stick to en and relative units to help ensure that formatting works the way you want it to.

5.2 How do I...
Place a caption in a table?

COMPATIBILITY: HTML 3+

Problem

I would like to add a title to the table in my page. I can do this with a heading, but is there a way to include a title as part of the table itself?

Technique

You can add a title, or a caption, to the top or bottom of your table by using the **<CAPTION>** tag. Any text contained between the **<CAPTION>** and **</CAPTION>** tags is aligned with the table and, depending on the browser, can also be specially formatted in bold or italic.

Steps

1. Open your document. Decide on an appropriate caption for your table. It can be a title or a brief description of the table.

2. Enter the text for your caption in the table between the **<TABLE>** and **</TABLE>** tags.

3. To add a caption to a table, place a **<CAPTION>** tag at the beginning of the caption text and a **</CAPTION>** tag at the end of the text. If you want the caption to appear above the table, place the caption above the data in the table:

```
<TABLE>
    <CAPTION>This is the table caption</CAPTION>
    <!-- Here's the table data... -->
</TABLE>
```

To place a caption below the table, put the caption text and tags below the table data but before the </TABLE> tag:

```
<TABLE>
    <!-- Here's the table data... -->
    <CAPTION>This is the table caption</CAPTION>
</TABLE>
```

4. You can format the text within the <CAPTION> tags just as you would any other text, using the markup tags described in Chapter 3, "Adding HTML Physical Character Effects." For example, to emphasize the caption of a table, enter

```
<TABLE>
    <CAPTION><EM>This is an emphasized caption!</EM></CAPTION>
    <!-- Here's the table data... -->
</TABLE>
```

You can also insert line breaks (as explained in Chapter 4, "Adding HTML Logical Character Effects") to control the layout of the caption:

```
<TABLE>
    <CAPTION>This is the top line of the caption<BR>
    and this is the bottom line of the caption</CAPTION>
    <!-- Here's the table data... -->
</TABLE>
```

How It Works

When a browser encounters the <CAPTION> tag inside a table, it places the text contained between the <CAPTION> and </CAPTION> tags either above or below the table, depending on where it encounters the caption. The caption is usually aligned with the table. Some browsers can also format the caption with bold or italics.

Comments

Because some browsers might format the caption, be careful when using text formatting tags such as <B> and <I> in the caption. These tags might be ignored by the browser, might override the default setting, or might be combined with the browser's format for the caption. For example, if a browser is programmed to render captions in bold text, placing <I> and </I> around your caption text might mean the caption appears in italics, remains in bold, or appears as bold italics.

5.3 How do I... Insert a table heading?

COMPATIBILITY: HTML 3+

Problem

In my table, I would like to have the top row consist of headings describing the contents of each column. I would like to set these headings off from the rest of the text. How can I accomplish this easily in HTML?

Technique

You can specify special heading cells in the table by using the **<TH>** tag. The text listed after the **<TH>** tag is considered part of the heading cell. You can use this tag anywhere in the table; the headings do not necessarily have to be at the top of a column. HTML also includes several sophisticated attributes that enable you to format your table headings precisely.

Steps

1. Open your document. Choose names for the heading cells. Heading cells can go across the columns or down the rows of your table, although for this example we will consider heading cells across the columns of a table.

2. Enter the word or phrase for each column heading in the table between the **<TABLE>** and **</TABLE>** tags.

3. For each column in your table, place a **<TH>** tag followed by the text for that column. For example, for a three-column table, enter

```
<TABLE>
    <CAPTION>Here's my table</CAPTION>
    <TH>Column 1<TH>Column 2<TH>Column 3
    <!-- Here's the data for the rest of the table... -->
</TABLE>
```

4. Although most browsers format the contents of heading cells differently from the rest of the text, you can still use normal text markup tags to alter the style of the heading. For example, to place the heading for the second column of this example in italics, enter

```
<TABLE>
    <CAPTION>Here's my table</CAPTION>
    <TH>Column 1<TH><I>Column 2</I><TH>Column 3
    <!-- Here's the data for the rest of the table... -->
</TABLE>
```

5. You can make a heading extend across more than one row or more than one column by using the **ROWSPAN** and **COLSPAN** attributes, respectively, in the **<TH>** tag. For these attributes, you state how many rows down or columns across you would like the heading cell to extend. For example, to make the heading for the second column extend over to the third column as well, enter

```
<TABLE>
    <CAPTION>Here's my table</CAPTION>
    <TH>Column 1<TH COLSPAN=2>Column 2
    <!-- Here's the data for the rest of the table... -->
</TABLE>
```

Similarly, to make the heading for column 1 extend down two rows, enter

```
<TABLE>
    <CAPTION>Here's my table</CAPTION>
    <TH ROWSPAN=2>Column 1<TH>Column 2<TH>Column 3
    <!-- Here's the data for the rest of the table... -->
</TABLE>
```

The uses of the **ROWSPAN** and **COLSPAN** attributes are discussed in greater detail in How-To 5.7.

6. You can use the **ALIGN** attribute inside the **<TH>** tag to define the alignment of the text within the header cell. The standard options of **LEFT**, **CENTER**, **RIGHT**, and **JUSTIFY** are available. To center the heading for the second column in this example, enter

```
<TABLE>
    <CAPTION>Here's my table</CAPTION>
    <TH ROWSPAN=2>Column 1<TH ALIGN=CENTER>Column 2<TH>Column 3
    <!-- Here's the data for the rest of the table... -->
</TABLE>
```

In addition to the standard alignment options, a fifth option, **decimal**, is also available. This is used to align the decimal points on each line of the cell if, for example, your cell has several lines of numbers (such as dollar amounts). If a line doesn't have a decimal point, the line is centered. You can use the **DP** attribute in the **<TH>** tag to define a decimal point if you want to use a character other than the default decimal point (**.**) symbol. An example of this would be using a colon like a decimal point to align a table of times, such as **1:15**, **2:45**, **3:30**, and so on.

7. In addition to the horizontal alignment just described, you can align text vertically within a cell by using the **VALIGN** attribute. There are four options for **VALIGN**, as shown in Table 5-3.

Table 5-3 Vertical alignment options for table cells

OPTION	DESCRIPTION
TOP	Aligns text at the top of the cell.
MIDDLE	Aligns text in the middle of the cell.
BOTTOM	Aligns text at the bottom of the cell.
BASELINE	Aligns all the text in a row with this alignment attribute set on a common baseline.

For example, to have the heading for the third column line up along the top of the cell, enter

```
<TABLE>
    <CAPTION>Here's my table</CAPTION>
    <TH>Column 1<TH>Column 2<TH VALIGN=TOP>Column 3
    <!-- Here's the data for the rest of the table... -->
</TABLE>
```

To have the first and third columns aligned on the same baseline while the second column is aligned in the middle of its cell, enter

```
<TABLE>
    <CAPTION>Here's my table</CAPTION>
    <TH VALIGN=BASELINE>Column 1<TH VALIGN=MIDDLE>Column 2 ⇐
    <TH VALIGN=BASELINE>Column 3
    <!-- Here's the data for the rest of the table... -->
</TABLE>
```

How It Works

The `<TH>` tag tells the browser that the text after that tag and before the next `<TH>` tag (or `<TD>` or `<TR>` tag, discussed next) is part of a cell that has been designated as a heading cell. Most browsers will format the text in a bold or emphasized style, although some will treat a heading cell the same as a data cell (see How-To 5.5).

Comments

When using the **ROWSPAN** and **COLSPAN** attributes to specify the size of rows, be careful you don't end up with overlapping cells. This could cause a table to be rendered in a way you didn't plan or to not display at all, depending on the browser.

HTML 3.2 added two more attributes that you can include in table heads and table cells:

- ✔ **WIDTH** enables the user to specify the width of a cell in pixels.
- ✔ **HEIGHT** enables the user to specify the height of cell in pixels.

COMPLEXITY
INTERMEDIATE

5.4 How do I... Define data for a cell or table element?

COMPATIBILITY: HTML 3+

Problem

Now that I've defined a table, added a caption, and set up headings for each column, I want to add my data to the table. How do I place data into table cells in HTML?

Technique

The process of adding data cells, or table elements, to your table is very similar to the technique used to add table headings described in How-To 5.3. The **<TD>** tag indicates that the text after it and before the next table-related tag is to be placed into a cell. As with **<TH>**, several sophisticated attributes can be used to control the placement and appearance of table cells.

Steps

1. Open your document. If you haven't done so already, enter the data you want to display in the table.

2. To place text in a data cell, put the **<TD>** tag in front of the text. The cell includes all the text that follows the data tag until it reaches another table-specific tag, such as **<TD>**, **<TH>**, and **<TR>**. Here is an example for the first row of a three-column table:

```
<TABLE>
    <CAPTION>The table caption</CAPTION>
    <TH>Column 1<TH>Column 2<TH>Column 3
    <TR><TD>Data 1<TD>Data 2<TD>Data 3
</TABLE>
```

(Don't worry about the **<TR>** tag right now because it is explained in detail in How-To 5.6. Basically, it creates a new row in the table.)

3. As with heading cells in a table, you can use formatting tags such as **<B>**, **<I>**, and **<EM>** to format the contents of a cell. Because data cells usually do not receive special formatting, unlike heading cells, this is a useful way to draw attention to a specific cell. For example, to highlight the data in the second column of this table, enter

```
<TABLE>
    <CAPTION>The table caption</CAPTION>
    <TH>Column 1<TH>Column 2<TH>Column 3
    <TR><TD>Data 1<TD><B>Data 2<B><TD>Data 3
</TABLE>
```

4. As described in How-To 5.3, you can use the **ROWSPAN** and **COLSPAN** attributes to identify data cells that have extended rows and columns. For example, to make the first data cell in the table extend over an extra column to the right, enter

```
<TABLE>
    <CAPTION>The table caption</CAPTION>
    <TH>Column 1<TH>Column 2<TH>Column 3
    <TR><TD COLSPAN=2>Data 1<TD>Data 3
</TABLE>
```

5. You can use the **ALIGN** attribute in **<TD>** to align the contents of the cell horizontally. As with **<TH>**, you can set **ALIGN** to **left**, **center**, **right**, **justify**, and **decimal**, the last one being used to align the contents of the cell by using the decimal point (or another character specified using the **DP** attribute, as discussed in How-To 5.3). For example, to center the contents of the third data cell in the table, enter

```
<TABLE>
    <CAPTION>The table caption</CAPTION>
    <TH>Column 1<TH>Column 2<TH>Column 3
    <TR><TD>Data 1<TD>Data 2<TD ALIGN=CENTER>Data 3
</TABLE>
```

6. You can also use the **VALIGN** attribute to align the contents of a cell vertically. As with heading cells, the options for **VALIGN** are **TOP**, **MIDDLE**, **BOTTOM**, and **BASELINE**. To set the contents of the first data cell along the top of the cell, enter

```
<TABLE>
    <CAPTION>The table caption</CAPTION>
    <TH>Column 1<TH>Column 2<TH>Column 3
    <TR><TD VALIGN=TOP>Data 1<TD>Data 2<TD>Data 3
</TABLE>
```

How It Works

When a browser encounters a **<TD>** tag in a table, it creates a new data cell in the table, placing all the text from the **<TD>** tag to the next table-related tag (**<TH>**, **<TR>**, **<CAPTION>**, **</TABLE>**) in the cell. Any formatting for the contents of the cell depends on the attributes set for the cell, as well as on any formatting tags contained within the cell.

Comments

As with the <TH> tag, you should take care when using **ROWSPAN** and **COLSPAN** with <TD> in your table. If you create overlapping cells by misusing the tags, your table will not be rendered correctly and it might not display at all, depending on the browser's settings.

COMPLEXITY
INTERMEDIATE

5.5 How do I... Insert a blank data cell?

COMPATIBILITY: HTML 3+

Problem

There are times when I would like to insert a blank cell into a table. How do I do that?

Technique

You add a blank cell by defining a cell that either has nothing in it or simply has a <BR> in it.

Steps

1. Open your document.
2. If you haven't done so already, create the table in which you want to include the blank cell.
3. Enter your blank cell by typing either of the following two lines:

```
<TD></TD>

<TD><BR></TD>
```

   Either method will give you a blank cell, but if you do not include the <BR> tag, the cell will not have any borders.

4. Check your table to make sure it looks like you want it to.

How It Works

When the browser finds a cell with nothing in it, that is exactly what it renders.

Comments

Figure 5-1 shows the difference between using the <BR> tag and not using it.

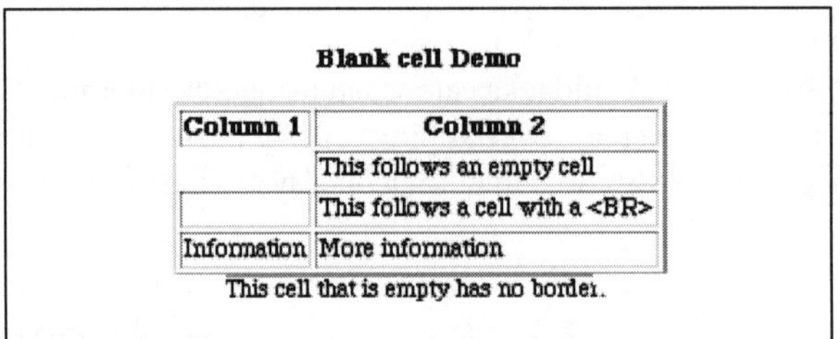

Figure 5-1 Using and not using the <BR> tag

COMPLEXITY
INTERMEDIATE

5.6 How do I...
Create a new row of data?

COMPATIBILITY: HTML 3+

Problem

Now that I can add data cells to my table, I would like to split the cells into rows. How can I divide the cells of my table into rows in HTML?

Technique

The `<TR>` tag creates a new row of cells in a table. You can use attributes with this tag to define the horizontal and vertical alignment of the contents of the row as well.

Steps

1. Open your document. If you have not already done so, enter the rest of the data for your table, using the `<TH>` and `<TD>` tags described in How-To's 5.4 and 5.5.

2. To help you decide the number and length of your rows (and to make it easier to correct errors in code later), enter carriage returns at the end of each row of data.

```
<TABLE>
     <CAPTION>The table caption</CAPTION>
     <TH>Column 1<TH>Column 2<TH>Column 3
     <TD>Data 1<TD>Data 2<TD>Data 3
     <TD>Data 4<TD>Data 5<TD>Data 6
</TABLE>
```

3. To specify the end of one row and the beginning of another, add the `<TR>` tag at the beginning of the new row:

```
<TABLE>
    <CAPTION>The table caption</CAPTION>
    <TR><TH>Column 1<TH>Column 2<TH>Column 3
    <TR><TD>Data 1<TD>Data 2<TD>Data 3
    <TR><TD>Data 4<TD>Data 5<TD>Data 6
</TABLE>
```

The `<TR>` tag at the beginning of the first row of the table is optional, but it helps ensure parallelism in the HTML code describing the table and does not upset the formatting of the table.

4. To set the horizontal alignment of all the cells of the row to the same value, use the `ALIGN` attribute in the `<TR>` tag. `ALIGN` in this context can take on the same values it can with the `<TD>` and `<TH>` tags: `LEFT`, `CENTER`, `RIGHT`, `JUSTIFY`, and `decimal`. To center the cells in the second row of data in the example, you can do the following:

```
<TABLE>
    <CAPTION>The table caption</CAPTION>
    <TR><TH>Column 1<TH>Column 2<TH>Column 3
    <TR><TD>Data 1<TD>Data 2<TD>Data 3
    <TR ALIGN=CENTER><TD>Data 4<TD>Data 5<TD>Data 6
</TABLE>
```

You can override the formatting for any cell in that row by setting the `ALIGN` attribute within the particular cell. For example, if you wanted the cell in the second column of the second data row aligned to the right side of the cell, and not centered like the rest of the text, you could do the following:

```
<TABLE>
    <CAPTION>The table caption</CAPTION>
    <TR><TH>Column 1<TH>Column 2<TH>Column 3
    <TR><TD>Data 1<TD>Data 2<TD>Data 3
    <TR ALIGN=CENTER><TD>Data 4<TD ALIGN=RIGHT>Data 5<TD>Data 6
</TABLE>
```

The alignment specified in the `COLSPEC` attribute in the table overrides any formatting you set with the `<TR>` tag, although you can override the `COLSPEC` alignment in individual cells.

5. You can set the vertical alignment of all cells in the row by using the `VALIGN` attribute in the `<TR>` tag. In heading and data cells, `VALIGN` takes on the values `TOP`, `MIDDLE`, `BOTTOM`, and `BASELINE`. For example, to set the vertical alignment of the second data row in the example to the middle of the cell, enter

```
<TABLE>
    <CAPTION>The table caption</CAPTION>
    <TR><TH>Column 1<TH>Column 2<TH>Column 3
    <TR><TD>Data 1<TD>Data 2<TD>Data 3
    <TR VALIGN=MIDDLE><TD>Data 4<TD>Data 5<TD>Data 6
</TABLE>
```

To override the vertical alignment for a row in a given cell, set the alignment within that particular cell. To set the middle cell of the second data row to a bottom alignment, you can use the following code:

```
<TABLE>
    <CAPTION>The table caption</CAPTION>
    <TR><TH>Column 1<TH>Column 2<TH>Column 3
    <TR><TD>Data 1<TD>Data 2<TD>Data 3
    <TR VALIGN=MIDDLE><TD>Data 4<TD VALIGN=BOTTOM>Data 5<TD>Data 6
</TABLE>
```

How It Works

When a browser encounters the <TR> tag, it creates a new row in the table and places the cells located between the <TR> and the next <TR> or the end of the table in that row. If alignment attributes are specified, they are applied to all the cells in that row unless individual cells (or the COLSPEC attribute in <TABLE>) contain information that overrides the alignment specified in <TR>.

Comments

If you set the column alignments using the COLSPEC attribute in the <TABLE> tag, then any horizontal alignment placed in the <TR> tags will be ignored. The order of precedence for defining cell alignments is

- ✔ <TH> and <TD>
- ✔ COLSPEC in <TABLE>
- ✔ <TR>

COMPLEXITY
INTERMEDIATE

5.7 How do I... Define the width of a table relative to the browser window?

COMPATIBILITY: HTML 3+

Problem

I would like to have my table occupy a certain percentage of the browser's window. How do I accomplish this?

Technique

You add a **WIDTH** attribute to the **<TABLE>** tag to specify the width of the table. You may set the width to either a percentage of the window or a number of actual pixels.

Steps

1. Open your document.
2. If you haven't done so already, create the table you would like to use.
3. Enter the **WIDTH** attribute into the **<TABLE>** tag. Set the width to the desired size. For example:

```
<TABLE WIDTH="50%">
...OTHER TEXT AND TAGS
</TABLE>
```

This tag will produce a table that occupies 50 percent of the browser.

4. View your document to make sure it looks like you think it should.

How It Works

The browser encounters the **WIDTH** attribute and renders the table according to the size given.

Comments

You can enter the width as a percentage, in which case it should be enclosed in quotes and include a **%**, or you can simply enter a number, in which case the browser will set the table width in actual pixels. Figure 5-2 shows a couple of different tables using the **WIDTH** attribute.

You can find more examples at **http://www.psnw.com/~jmz5/waite/tables.html**.

Table Width 50%

Salesperson	Sales
Bart	10000
Bob	5000
Boss	5

Table Width 75%

Salesperson	Sales
Bart	10000
Bob	5000
Boss	5

Figure 5-2 The use of the `WIDTH` attribute

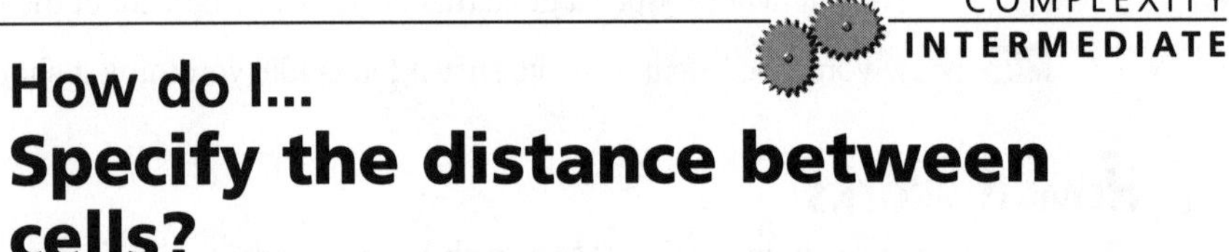

COMPLEXITY
INTERMEDIATE

5.8 How do I... Specify the distance between cells?

COMPATIBILITY: HTML 3+

Problem

I would like to have finer control over the distance between the cells of my table. How do I do this?

Technique

By adding the **CELLSPACING** attribute to the **<TABLE>** tag, you can control the space the browser shows between cells.

Steps

1. Open your document.
2. If you haven't done so already, create your table.
3. Modify the **<TABLE>** tag by adding the **CELLSPACING** attribute and a numeric value. The greater the value, the greater the distance between cells. For example:

```
<TABLE CELLSPACING=5>
...OTHER TEXT AND TAGS
</TABLE>
```

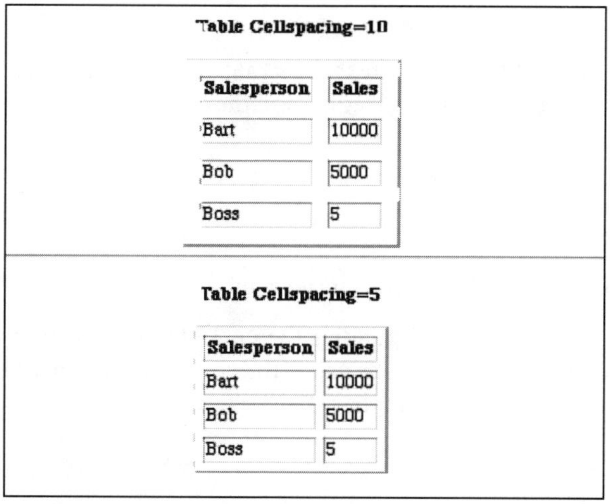

Table Cellspacing=10

Salesperson	Sales
Bart	10000
Bob	5000
Boss	5

Table Cellspacing=5

Salesperson	Sales
Bart	10000
Bob	5000
Boss	5

Figure 5-3 Tables using cell spacing

4. View your document to make sure it looks like you think it should.

How It Works

The browser creates the table with space between each cell, depending on the value of `CELLSPACING`.

Comments

`CELLSPACING`'s default value is `2`.

Figure 5-3 shows some examples of tables using cell spacing. You can see other examples at `http://www.psnw.com/~jmz5/waite/tables.html`.

COMPLEXITY
INTERMEDIATE

5.9 How do I...
Set the distance from the cell edge to the cell data?

COMPATIBILITY: HTML 3+

Problem

I would like to have finer control over the distance between the cell edges and the information inside them. How do I do this?

Technique

By adding the **CELLPADDING** attribute to the **<TABLE>** tag, you can control the space the browser shows between the cell edges and the cell's content.

Steps

1. Open your document.
2. If you haven't already done so, create your table.
3. Modify the **<TABLE>** tag by adding the **CELLPADDING** attribute and a numeric value. The greater the value, the greater the distance between the cells and the data. For example:

```
<TABLE  CELLPADDING=5>
...OTHER TEXT AND TAGS
</TABLE>
```

4. View your document to make sure it looks like you think it should.

How It Works

The browser creates the table with the space between each cell edge and the information in that cell, depending on the value of **CELLPADDING**.

Comments

CELLPADDING's default value is **1**.

Figure 5-4 shows some examples of tables using cell padding. You can see other examples at **http://www.psnw.com/~jmz5/waite/tables.html**.

COMPLEXITY
INTERMEDIATE

5.10 How do I... Put a table in my home page?

COMPATIBILITY: HTML 3+

Problem

Now that I know all the elements of a table in HTML, I would like to start adding tables to my pages. How can I use these tables to display my information effectively? What sort of tips and tricks can I use to make my tables look better?

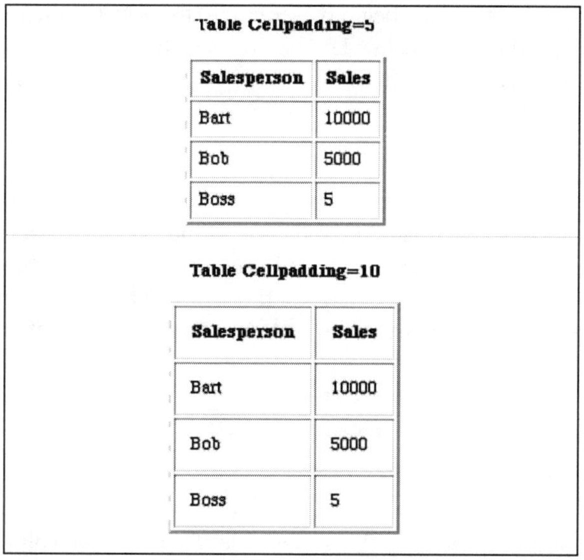

Table Cellpadding=5

Salesperson	Sales
Bart	10000
Bob	5000
Boss	5

Table Cellpadding=10

Salesperson	Sales
Bart	10000
Bob	5000
Boss	5

Figure 5-4 Tables using cell padding

Technique

Tables are a good way to control the layout and format of information on a Web page. A good way to learn how to create effective tables is to go through a few examples step by step to see how they are constructed.

Steps

These examples will give you an idea of how to create tables and use them to display different types of information.

1. First, look at a simple table that might be used by someone listing several products for sale and their prices. It might look like Table 5-4.

Table 5-4 Widget price list (September 1997)

ITEM	COST
Mini widget	$19.95
Widget	$29.95
Super widget	$39.95
Widget Royale (with cheese)	$79.95

To produce this table, begin by setting up the <TABLE> tags at the beginning and end of the list. Let the browser choose the size of the cells, and put a border around the table:

```
<TABLE BORDER>

</TABLE>
```

Now add a title as a caption at the top of the list. Again, let the browser choose the style for the caption; don't include any style tags here. For the sake of clarity, indent the contents of the <CAPTION> tag, as well as anything else contained between the <TABLE> tags, to help set it off from the rest of the code for the page.

```
<TABLE BORDER>
    <CAPTION>Widget Price List (September 1997)</CAPTION>

</TABLE>
```

Now add the heading cells for the table. There are two columns in this table, so create two heading cells using the <TH> tag. You can start off the row with the <TR> tag, although it is not explicitly required.

```
<TABLE BORDER>
    <CAPTION>Widget Price List (September 1997)</CAPTION>
    <TR><TH>Item<TH>Cost

</TABLE>
```

Now add the rows of items and their prices. Begin each row with the <TR> tag and put the <TD> tag in front of each item. Use italics (<I>) here to emphasize the phrase "with cheese."

```
<TABLE BORDER>
    <CAPTION>Widget Price List (September 1997)</CAPTION>
    <TR><TH>Item<TH>Cost
    <TR><TD>Mini Widget<TD>$19.95
    <TR><TD>Widget<TD>$29.95
    <TR><TD>Super Widget<TD>$39.95
    <TR><TD>Widget Royale <I>(with cheese)</I><TD>$79.95
</TABLE>
```

You've now made a full-fledged, complete table, although you could still tweak it a little bit to improve its appearance if you want. For example, if you include another item in the table with a price of more than $100.00, the formatting of the price column (which defaults to flush left) would be unattractive unless you set the alignment for the price cells to be flush right, as follows:

```
<TABLE BORDER>
    <CAPTION>Widget Price List (September 1997)</CAPTION>
    <TR><TH>Item<TH>Cost
    <TR><TD>Mini Widget<TD ALIGN=RIGHT>$19.95
    <TR><TD>Widget<TD ALIGN=RIGHT>$29.95
    <TR><TD>Super Widget<TD ALIGN=RIGHT>$39.95
    <TR><TD>Widget Royale <I>(with cheese)</I><TD ALIGN=RIGHT>$79.95
    <TR><TD>Mega Deluxe Widget<TD ALIGN=RIGHT>$109.95
</TABLE>
```

You could also use the **COLSPEC** attribute in the heading if you wanted to specify the size of the columns. Try this, using relative units and making the left column three times as wide as the right column, as follows:

```
<TABLE BORDER UNITS=RELATIVE COLSPEC="L3 R1">
    <CAPTION>Widget Price List (September 1997)</CAPTION>
    <TR><TH>Item<TH>Cost
    <TR><TD>Mini Widget<TD>$19.95
    <TR><TD>Widget<TD>$29.95
    <TR><TD>Super Widget<TD>$39.95
    <TR><TD>Widget Royale <I>(with cheese)</I><TD>$79.95
    <TR><TD>Mega Deluxe Widget<TD>$109.95
</TABLE>
```

The output of this table is shown in Figure 5-5. The code is available on the CD as file **5-5.HTML**.

2. Now try another type of table, which will show an effective way of using **COLSPAN** and **ROWSPAN**. Suppose you want to include the score from a baseball game in a Web page as a table. An example of a score is shown in Table 5-5.

Table 5-5 Today's game

TEAM	SCORE		
	R	H	E
Red Sox	8	11	0
Yankees	0	3	1

As you did in the first example, start with the **<TABLE>** tags and include the title of the table as the caption. For this example, do not include a border; all you want to do here is format the text the right way.

```
<TABLE>
    <CAPTION>Today's Game</CAPTION>

</TITLE>
```

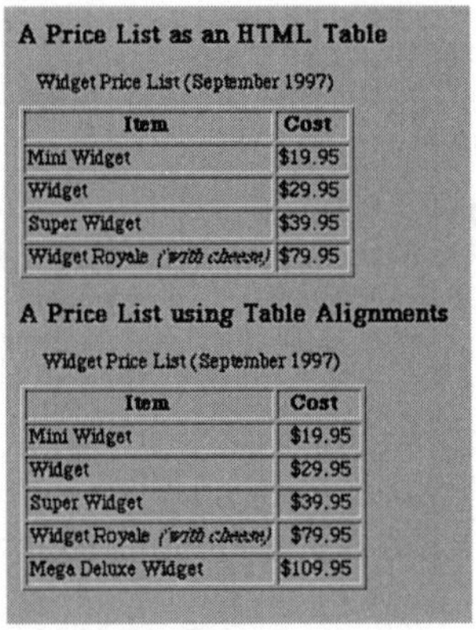

A Price List as an HTML Table

Widget Price List (September 1997)

Item	Cost
Mini Widget	$19.95
Widget	$29.95
Super Widget	$39.95
Widget Royale *(with cheese)*	$79.95

A Price List using Table Alignments

Widget Price List (September 1997)

Item	Cost
Mini Widget	$19.95
Widget	$29.95
Super Widget	$39.95
Widget Royale *(with cheese)*	$79.95
Mega Deluxe Widget	$109.95

Figure 5-5 A price list table in HTML

Before you proceed any further, sketch out how the rows and columns will be set up. It's clear that this table will have four columns: one for the name of the team and three for the various score categories (R, H, and E, which stand for Runs, Hits, and Errors). In this table, unlike the one in the previous example, there won't be an item for every cell. One way to deal with this would be to skip cells by including cell tags in the table but not putting any text in them. To do that, you immediately follow one table-related tag with another. Apply this to the first row of the table, where only two of the four columns contain any text, as follows:

```
<TABLE>
     <CAPTION>Today's Game</CAPTION>
     <TR><TH>Team<TH><TH>Score<TH>

</TABLE>
```

The second row is similar, but missing only one cell:

```
<TABLE>
     <CAPTION>Today's Game</CAPTION>
     <TR><TH>Team<TH><TH>Score<TH>
     <TR><TH><TH>R<TH>H<TH>E

</TABLE>
```

Finish the rest of the table using data cells for the team names and scores:

```
<TABLE>
     <CAPTION>Today's Game</CAPTION>
     <TR><TH>Team<TH><TH>Score<TH>
     <TR><TH><TH>R<TH>H<TH>E
     <TR><TD>Red Sox<TD>8<TD>11<TD>0
     <TR><TD>Yankees<TD>0<TD>3<TD>1
</TABLE>
```

The output of this table is shown in Figure 5-6. The code is available on the CD as file **5-6.HTML**.

This layout succeeds in skipping cells, but the result is less than aesthetically pleasing. The third column, which contains the number of hits, also includes the word **Score**. Because this word is much larger than the numbers or the letter H, the column is automatically sized wide enough to fit **Score**, which ends up disrupting the flow of the layout for the scores shown here. A solution to this problem is to use **COLSPAN**: You can define the top row to have only two columns, but have the second column of the row be three columns wide:

```
<TABLE>
    <CAPTION>Today's Game</CAPTION>
    <TR><TH>Team<TH COLSPAN=3>Score
    <TR><TH><TH>R<TH>H<TH>E
    <TR><TD>Red Sox<TD>8<TD>11<TD>0
    <TR><TD>Yankees<TD>0<TD>3<TD>1
</TABLE>
```

Note that when you add the **COLSPAN** attribute, you must delete the extra **<TH>** tags; if you don't, the table will include the extra columns and its flow will be disrupted. While you're at it, use the **ROWSPAN** attribute on the first cell in the first row (**Team**) to make it two rows deep:

```
<TABLE>
    <CAPTION>Today's Game</CAPTION>
    <TR><TH ROWSPAN=2>Team<TH COLSPAN=3>Score
    <TR><TH>R<TH>H<TH>E
    <TR><TD>Red Sox<TD>8<TD>11<TD>0
    <TR><TD>Yankees<TD>0<TD>3<TD>1
</TABLE>
```

Note that when you add the **ROWSPAN** attribute, you must delete the extra **<TH>** tag in the second row, which is no longer needed and would otherwise disrupt the layout of the table. Although this doesn't affect the layout as much as the **COLSPAN** attribute did, it makes it easier to change the alignment of the text in the cell. For example, if you want the word **Team** in that cell placed on the bottom of the cell instead of the top, you could write

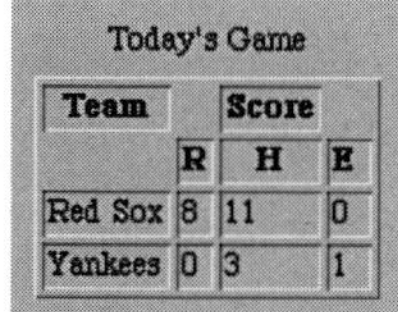

Team	Score		
	R	H	E
Red Sox	8	11	0
Yankees	0	3	1

Figure 5-6 A box score table made by skipping cells

```
<TABLE>
    <CAPTION>Today's Game</CAPTION>
    <TR><TH ROWSPAN=2 VALIGN=BOTTOM>Team<TH COLSPAN=3>Score
    <TR><TH>R<TH>H<TH>E
    <TR><TD>Red Sox<TD>8<TD>11<TD>0
    <TR><TD>Yankees<TD>0<TD>3<TD>1
</TABLE>
```

This is easier, and it is also better form, than making empty cells and moving text among the cells when you want to change the layout. The output of this table is shown in Figure 5-7 and is available on the CD as file `5-7.HTML`.

3. The examples shown here and elsewhere in the chapter assume you have short, one-line entries for the tables. However, there is no reason the tables need to have only short entries for each cell. You can use tables to format larger pieces of text and control their layout better than if you used line breaks, paragraphs, or other HTML features discussed in Chapter 4, "Adding HTML Logical Character Effects." For example, you want to format a troubleshooting guide for a product that will consist of a series of stated problems and a set of solutions for them. Here's how you can format this using a table.

First, create the `<TABLE>` tags and include the title of the table:

```
<TABLE BORDER>
    <CAPTION>Widget Troubleshooting Guide</CAPTION>

</TABLE>
```

The best way to format this would be to use two columns: one column with problems and the other with the corresponding solutions. Place heading cells into the table based on this.

```
<TABLE BORDER>
    <CAPTION>Widget Troubleshooting Guide</CAPTION>
    <TR><TH>Problem<TH>Solution

</TABLE>
```

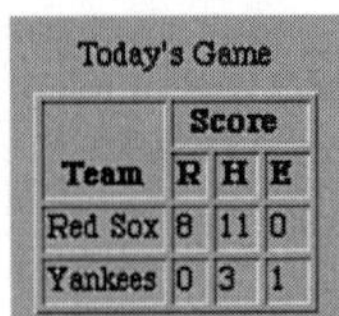

Today's Game

Team	Score		
	R	H	E
Red Sox	8	11	0
Yankees	0	3	1

Figure 5-7 A box score table made with `ROWSPAN` and `COLSPAN`

Now add the problems and the solutions. Add the text just as you would for any other table. Because HTML considers all text placed between the **<TD>** tag and the next table-specific tag as part of a single cell, you can easily put multiple lines of text into a single cell. For example:

```
<TABLE BORDER>
     <CAPTION>Widget Troubleshooting Guide</CAPTION>
     <TR><TH>Problem<TH>Solution
     <TR>
          <TD>Widget won't turn on
          <TD>Make sure the widget is plugged in. Also make sure
the power switch is in the on position. If the widget still will not
turn on, take your widget to the nearest repair shop for servicing.
<TR>
          <TD>Widget behaving erratically
          <TD>Press the reset button on the underside of the widget. If the
widget still behaves erratically, turn the power off and then back on.
If this does not work, take your widget to the nearest repair shop
for servicing.
</TABLE>
```

You can continue to do this, making table cells many lines long, if necessary. The only limit is the amount of your data (although style can play a part too).

The output of this code is shown in Figure 5-8. The code is available on the CD as file **5-8.HTML**.

How It Works

Browsers format tables based on their own predefined settings, plus any specific commands contained in the table. These commands give you considerable power to control the layout of the table.

Widget Troubleshooting Guide

Problem	Solution
Widget won't turn on	Make sure the widget is plugged in. Also make sure the power switch is in the on position. If the widget still will not turn on, take your widget to the nearest repair shop for servicing.
Widget behaving erratically	Press the reset button on the underside of the widget. If the widget stil behaves erratically, turn the power off and then back on. If this does not work, take your widget to the nearest repair shop for servicing.

Figure 5-8 A troubleshooting list as a table in HTML

Comments

As you have seen, tables are a powerful way to format text in your pages. Tables are versatile: Not only can they be shaped to display your information, but they are not just limited to plain text. Tables can be used to display graphics (Chapter 9, "Using Images in Your Documents") or forms (Chapter 11, "HTML Interactive Forms"), or to format lists of links to other documents (Chapter 7, "Managing Document Spacing"). Tables can include essentially any HTML element, including line breaks and paragraphs and even lists (Chapter 6, "Lists"). Tables take a little time to understand completely, but your effort will be rewarded by a better ability to control the layout and present your information. Adding colors to tables is discussed in Chapter 15, "Navigator and Internet Explorer HTML Extensions."

For an example of how changing different table attributes affects the table, check out the accompanying Web page at **http://www.psnw.com/~jmz5/waite/tables.html**.

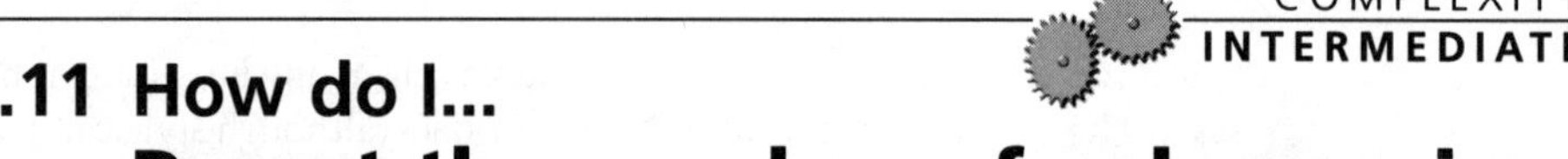

5.11 How do I... Preset the number of columns in a table for faster rendering?

COMPATIBILITY: NETSCAPE 4.0

Problem

I would like to speed up the rendering of my tables. What can I do to accomplish this?

Technique

By adding the **COLS** attribute to the **<TABLE>** tag, you are presetting the number of columns your table will have; this will enable Netscape 4.0 to render the table more efficiently.

Steps

1. Open your document.

2. If you haven't already done so, create your table.

3. Modify the `<TABLE>` tag by adding the **COLS** attribute and a numeric value. The numeric value should simply be the number of columns your table will have.

```
<TABLE  COLS=3 BORDER=1>
<!-- Table with 3 columns goes here ...-->
</TABLE>
```

4. View your document to make sure it looks like you think it should.

How It Works

The browser creates the table based on the number of columns you specified—it's as simple as that. Because the browser doesn't have to "do the math," so to speak, to figure out how many columns your table will have, the table is rendered more efficiently.

Comments

This attribute works only with Netscape 4.0 and there is very little documentation for it. With smaller tables, the differences between using the **COLS** attribute and not are barely noticeable.

CHAPTER 6

LISTS

6

LISTS

How do I...

- 6.1 Create a numbered list?
- 6.2 Specify the style and sequence of my numbering?
- 6.3 Create a bulleted list?
- 6.4 Modify the appearance of my bullets?
- 6.5 Create an unmarked list?
- 6.6 Create a menu list?
- 6.7 Create a directory list?
- 6.8 Create a glossary list?
- 6.9 Nest lists together?
- 6.10 Use lists to jazz up my home page?

A lot of information is best displayed in lists: ingredients for a recipe, your top 10 favorite albums, the outline for a presentation, the definitions for a set of terms. You can use tags such as `<P>` and `<BR>` (see Chapter 7, "Managing Document Spacing") to manage the placement of items in a document and create lists, but these tags are cumbersome and provide you with little flexibility to create the types of lists that best fit your information. Fortunately, HTML has other tags that let you create lists that include numbers, bullets, indentations, and other features. Moreover, HTML 4.0 includes attributes that give you even greater ability to create the best lists for your data. This chapter covers the various types of lists that can be generated in HTML and shows you how they can be used to create a more effective home page.

6.1 Create a Numbered List

Some information is ideally suited to be displayed in a numbered list: rankings, top 10 lists, step-by-step procedures. This simple How-To shows how you can create a numbered, or ordered, list that appears in a document, with the ranking automatically included.

6.2 Specify the Style and Sequence of My Numbering

There are many situations in which the standard style of numerical lists isn't the best way to present information. A different style of numbering is needed sometimes, as in outlines, and in other cases a numbered list should begin with a number other than 1. This How-To explores the ways you can alter the style and sequence of numbering used in an ordered list.

6.3 Create a Bulleted List

Some information is better suited to a point-by-point list: outlines, menus. Each item on such a list is usually marked with a point, or bullet, to set it apart from other elements of the list. This simple How-To shows you how to create a bulleted list.

6.4 Modify the Appearance of My Bullets

Sometimes the standard style of bullets isn't the way you want to present your data. HTML 4.0 provides alternatives to the standard bulleted list that give the writer some control over the bullets used. This How-To shows how to use those attributes to modify the appearance of bullets in these lists.

6.5 Create an Unmarked List

In some cases, neither a numbered list nor a bulleted list is appropriate for the information you want to include in a document. Sometimes the best type of list is one without any sort of number or mark in front of each item. This How-To explains how to create an unmarked list.

6.6 Create a Menu List

Lists, when combined with links to other documents or other locations in the same document, are often the best way to present the reader of a document with a menu of choices. This How-To explains how to use the menu feature to create menus in HTML versions predating HTML 3.2.

6.7 Create a Directory List

Some information takes the form of a list of entries from a directory: a list of files, a list of people, and so forth. This How-To explains how to use the directory feature in HTML versions predating HTML 3.2 to create a directory of that information.

6.8 Create a Glossary List

Creating a glossary—a list of words and their definitions—requires special formatting to achieve the best results. This How-To explains how to use features in HTML to create a glossary.

6.9 Nest Lists Together

Some elements of a list might in fact be lists themselves, such as entries in an outline. This How-To shows how to nest lists within lists, as well as how to mix different types of lists together.

6.10 Use Lists to Jazz Up My Home Page

With the knowledge of how to use lists, you can now create a better-structured home page that gives readers easier access to the information they need. This How-To provides some tips on style and explains how to add lists to a page effectively.

6.1 How do I... Create a numbered list?

COMPATIBILITY: HTML 2+

Problem

I have a set of data I would like to display as a list. I want each item in the list to be preceded by a number. However, because the order of the list items might change from time to time, I would like to have the numbers generated automatically so I don't have to spend time manually editing the number for each item. How can I create a numbered list in HTML?

Technique

HTML enables you to create a numbered, or ordered, list that will automatically generate numbers in front of each item in the list. The number placed in front of an item depends on the location of the item in the list: The first item gets the numeral 1, the second 2, and so on. You can do this by using the `<OL>` and `<LI>` tags, described in the "Steps" section.

Steps

1. Open your document. Identify the locations in your document where you want to include a list.

2. Place the items to be included in the list in your document. For clarity, separate each item with a carriage return, for example:

```
<H2>My Five Favorite Baseball Teams</H2>
Red Sox
Cubs
Royals
Dodgers
Indians
```

3. At the beginning of the list, place the `<OL>` (for ordered list) tag. At the end of the list, place the `</OL>` tag:

```
<H2>My Five Favorite Baseball Teams</H2>
<OL>
Red Sox
Cubs
Royals
Dodgers
Indians
</OL>
```

4. In front of each item in the list, place the `<LI>` (list item) tag:

```
<H2>My Five Favorite Baseball Teams</H2>
<OL>
<LI>Red Sox
<LI>Cubs
<LI>Royals
<LI>Dodgers
<LI>Indians
</OL>
```

5. Some browsers permit you to conserve space in a document by making a list more compact. A compacted list usually has less space between list entries and might use a smaller, more compressed font. To specify a compacted list, replace the `<OL>` at the beginning of the list with `<OL COMPACT>`:

```
<H2>My Five Favorite Baseball Teams (compact form)</H2>
<OL COMPACT>
<LI>Red Sox
<LI>Cubs
<LI>Royals
<LI>Dodgers
<LI>Indians
</OL>
```

Examples of numbered lists are shown in Figures 6-1 and 6-2. The code is also available on the CD-ROM as file **6-1.HTML**.

How It Works

When an HTML browser such as Mosaic or Netscape loads a numbered list such as the one just shown, it converts each `<LI>` it finds between the `<OL>` and the `</OL>` into a number; the first `<LI>` becomes the number 1, the second becomes 2, and so on. The browser also puts a carriage return just before the number to format the text better.

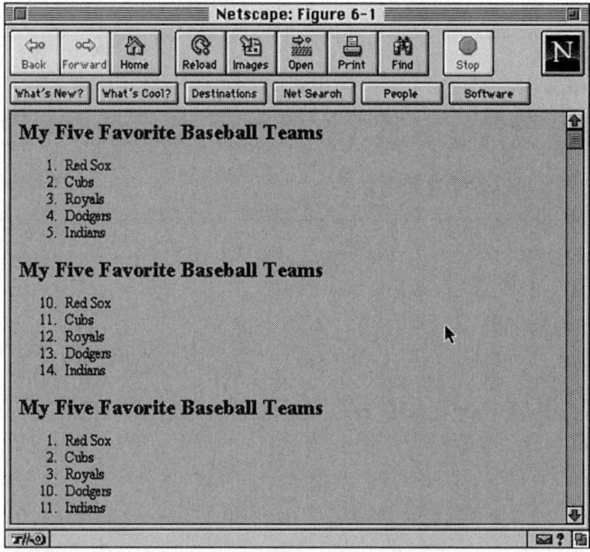

Figure 6-1 Examples of numbered lists

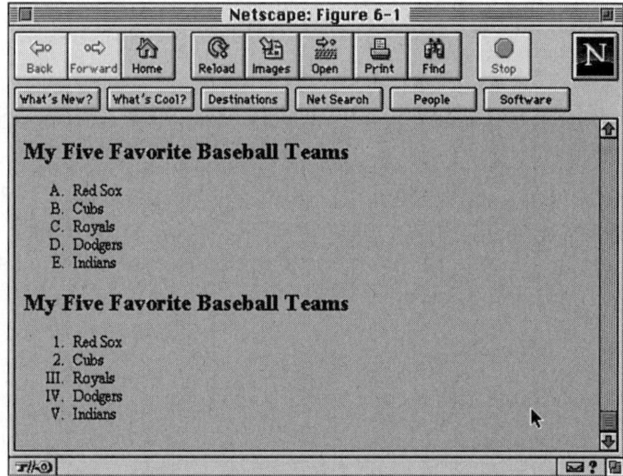

Figure 6-2 More examples of numbered lists

Comments

The `COMPACT` attribute is not well supported, so it might not give the results you expect when viewing it in popular browsers. With the list markup just described, all lists will begin with the number 1 and increment upward. The next section describes how to start at different numbers and how to use different numbering systems for ordered lists.

COMPLEXITY
BEGINNING

6.2 How do I... Specify the style and sequence of my numbering?

COMPATIBILITY: HTML 3.2+

Problem

I have a list that I don't want numbered in the conventional way. I'd like to be able to adjust the style of numbers used to create a table, and I would also like to start my lists at a number other than 1. How can I adjust the style and sequence of numbers in my numbered lists?

Technique

HTML 3.2 introduced several attributes that can be used with numbered lists. One enables you to alter the style of numbers used in the lists, whereas another sets the starting number of the lists.

Steps

1. Open your document. Create your ordered list in the manner described in How-To 6.1.

2. To start an ordered list at a number other than 1, place the **START** attribute on the **<OL>** tag at the beginning of the list. Set the attribute equal to the value of the first number in your list. For example, to create a list that begins with number 10, enter

```
<H2>My Five Favorite Baseball Teams</H2>
<OL START=10>
<LI>Red Sox
<LI>Cubs
<LI>Royals
<LI>Dodgers
<LI>Indians
</OL>
```

3. You can also use the **VALUE** attribute within the **<LI>** tag to change the numbering sequence within a list. For example, to start numbering a list at 1 but change to a higher value later in the list, enter

```
<H2>My Five Favorite Baseball Teams</H2>
<OL>
<LI>Red Sox
<LI>Cubs
```

```
<LI>Royals
<LI VALUE=10>Dodgers
<LI>Indians
</OL>
```

4. You can select the type of numbering system to be used with the **TYPE** attribute. Table 6-1 lists the possible values of the **TYPE** attribute.

Table 6-1 Values for the TYPE attribute

ATTRIBUTE VALUE	DEFINITION
A	Use uppercase letters (A, B, C, and so on).
a	Use lowercase letters (a, b, c, and so on).
I	Use uppercase Roman numerals (I, II, III, and so on).
i	Use lowercase Roman numerals (i, ii, iii, and so on).
1	Use standard numbers, the default (1, 2, 3, and so on).

For example, to use uppercase letters in a list, enter

```
<H2>My Five Favorite Baseball Teams</H2>
<OL TYPE=A>
<LI>Red Sox
<LI>Cubs
<LI>Royals
<LI>Dodgers
<LI>Indians
</OL>
```

5. You can also use the **TYPE** attribute within the **<LI>** tag to change the numbering scheme within a list. For example, to change from standard numerals to uppercase Roman numerals, enter

```
<H2>My Five Favorite Baseball Teams</H2>
<OL>
<LI>Red Sox
<LI>Cubs
<LI TYPE=I>Royals
<LI>Dodgers
<LI>Indians
</OL>
```

Examples of numbered lists are shown in Figures 6-1 and 6-2. The code is also available on the CD as file **6-1.HTML**.

How It Works

When an HTML browser encounters an ordered list with the **START** attribute set equal to some value, it starts the numbered list with that value. Similarly, when it encounters the **TYPE** attribute equal to some value, it matches the value with a predefined list of numbering types and uses the appropriate type to number the list. When the browser encounters a **TYPE** or **VALUE** tag in a list element, it changes the list numbering scheme according to the value set in the tag.

Comments

Because **TYPE**, **START**, and **VALUE** were all additions to HTML 3.2, they might not be supported by older browsers. There is currently no way in HTML to alter the rate of numbering, that is, to create lists that use only even or odd numbers or go down instead of up. Should you need to create such a list, you will be best off entering the numbers manually in an unmarked list (see How-To 6.5).

COMPLEXITY
BEGINNING

6.3 How do I... Create a bulleted list?

COMPATIBILITY: HTML 2+

Problem

I have a set of data that I would like to display as a list. I want to call attention to each item on the list by placing a bullet in front of it, and I would like to have the bullet created automatically so I don't have to design a special graphic. How can I create a bulleted list in HTML?

Technique

HTML enables you to create a bulleted, or unordered, list with the bullets automatically created and placed in front of each list item. The technique is very similar to the numbered list technique; the only difference is in the tags that are used at the beginning and the end of the list.

Steps

1. Open your document. Identify the locations in your document where you want to include a list.

2. Place the items to be included in the list in your document. For clarity, separate each item with a carriage return, for example:

```
<H2>My Five Favorite Baseball Teams</H2>
Red Sox
Cubs
Royals
Dodgers
Indians
```

3. At the beginning of the list, place the `<UL>` (for unordered list) tag. At the end of the list, place the `</UL>` tag:

```
<H2>My Five Favorite Baseball Teams</H2>
<UL>
Red Sox
Cubs
Royals
Dodgers
Indians
</UL>
```

4. In front of each item in the list, place the `<LI>` tag:

```
<H2>My Five Favorite Baseball Teams</H2>
<UL>
<LI>Red Sox
<LI>Cubs
<LI>Royals
<LI>Dodgers
<LI>Indians
</UL>
```

5. Some browsers permit you to conserve space in your document by making your list more compact. A compacted list usually has less space between list entries and can use a smaller, more compressed font. To create a compacted list, replace the `<UL>` tag at the beginning of the list with `<UL COMPACT>`:

```
<H2>My Five Favorite Baseball Teams (compact form)</H2>
<UL COMPACT>
<LI>Red Sox
<LI>Cubs
<LI>Royals
<LI>Dodgers
<LI>Indians
</UL>
```

Examples of bulleted lists are shown in Figure 6-3. The code is also available on the CD as file **6-2.HTML**.

How It Works

Just as it does for a numbered list, a browser converts each `<LI>` it finds between the `<UL>` and `</UL>` tags, in this case into a bullet. It also inserts a carriage return immediately before the bullet to format the text.

Comments

The actual shape and size of the bullet are determined by the browser; different browsers use different shapes for bullets. HTML 4.0 allows for some choice in selecting the type of bullets used (see How-To 6.4). When bullets are used in nested lists

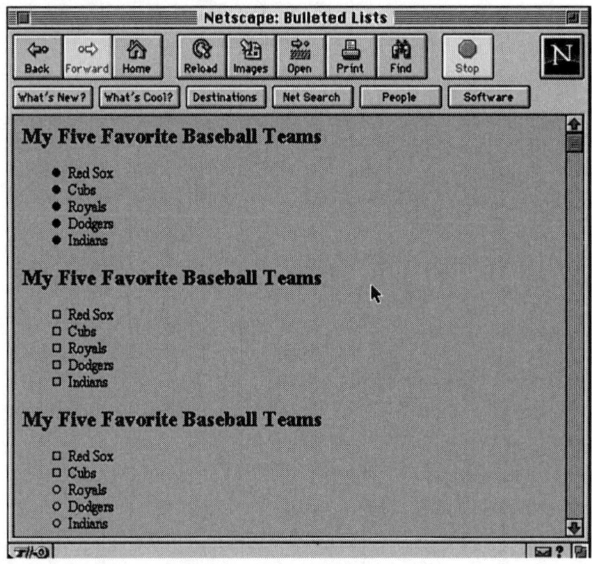

Figure 6-3 Examples of bulleted lists

(see How-To 6.9), different bullet shapes may be used at different levels of nesting; again, this depends on the browser. If you want to use a bullet with a specific shape or a special graphic, you should consider creating an inline image of the desired bullet (see How-To 9.2) and placing this in front of each item, using an unmarked list, as described in How-To 6.5.

COMPLEXITY
BEGINNING

6.4 How do I... Modify the appearance of my bullets?

COMPATIBILITY: HTML 3.2+

Problem

I would like to be able to replace the standard bullets used in my bulleted lists with another style. How can I alter the appearance of the bullets in HTML lists?

Technique

Attributes in HTML 4.0 enable you to alter the type of bullet used in an unordered list. You can easily select from several different styles of bullets with this feature.

Steps

1. Open your document. Create a bulleted list in the manner described in How-To 6.3.

2. To change the type of bullet used throughout the list, place the **TYPE** attribute in the **<UL>** tag at the beginning of the list. **TYPE** can have one of three values: **DISC**, **SQUARE**, or **CIRCLE**. For example, to create a bulleted list that uses squares as bullets, enter

```
<H2>My Five Favorite Baseball Teams</H2>
<UL TYPE=SQUARE>
<LI>Red Sox
<LI>Cubs
<LI>Royals
<LI>Dodgers
<LI>Indians
</UL>
```

3. You can change the type of bullet in the middle of the list by placing the **TYPE** attribute in the **<LI>** tag at the appropriate location in the list. To start with the disc style of bullets and then switch over to circles, use

```
<H2>My Five Favorite Baseball Teams</H2>
<UL TYPE=DISC>
<LI>Red Sox
<LI>Cubs
<LI TYPE=CIRCLE >Royals
<LI >Dodgers
<LI>Indians
</UL>
```

Examples of bulleted lists are shown in Figure 6-3. The code is also available on the CD as file **6-2.HTML**.

How It Works

When an HTML browser encounters an unordered list with the **TYPE** attribute set equal to some value, it matches the value with a predefined list of bullet types and uses the appropriate bullet to mark the list. When the browser encounters a **TYPE** tag in a list element, it changes the list bulleting scheme according to the value set in the tag.

Comments

Because **TYPE** was an addition to HTML 3.2, these features might not be supported by older browsers. Currently only circle, disc, and square bullets are available.

6.5 How do I... Create an unmarked list?

COMPATIBILITY: HTML 2+

Problem

I have a set of data that I would like to display as a list. I want to display this simply as a list of items separated by carriage returns, without numbers or bullets. How can I do this in HTML?

Technique

There are several ways to do this in HTML. Perhaps the simplest way is to insert line breaks, **
**, after each list element. Other techniques enable you to create unmarked lists and even set them off from the rest of the text. These methods are described next.

Steps

1. Open your document. Identify the locations in your document where you want to include a list.

2. To separate list items using line breaks, place **
** tags after each list element:

```
<H2>My Five Favorite Baseball Teams, using &lt;BR&gt;</H2>
Red Sox<BR>
Cubs<BR>
Royals<BR>
Dodgers<BR>
Indians<BR>
```

(The **<** and **>** are special key sequences that will print the **<** and **>** characters, respectively. They are used here because **<** and **>** are reserved for HTML commands.)

3. In HTML 2.0, you can create an identical list using the **<DL>** and **<DT>** tags:

✔ Place a **<DL>** (for descriptive list) at the beginning of the list and a **</DL>** at the end of the list:

```
<H2>My Five Favorite Baseball Teams</H2>
<DL>
Red Sox
Cubs
Royals
```

```
Dodgers
Indians
</DL>
```

✔ Place the <DT> tag in front of each item of the list:

```
<H2>My Five Favorite Baseball Teams, using &lt;DT&gt;</H2>
<DL>
<DT>Red Sox
<DT>Cubs
<DT>Royals
<DT>Dodgers
<DT>Indians
</DL>
```

4. To create a list that is indented from normal text, use the <DL> and </DL> tags at the beginning and end of the list, but use <DD> instead of <DT> before each list item:

```
<H2>My Five Favorite Baseball Teams, using &lt;DT&gt;</H2>
<DL>
<DD>Red Sox
<DD>Cubs
<DD>Royals
<DD>Dodgers
<DD>Indians
</DL>
```

The output generated by these different kinds of unmarked lists is shown in Figure 6-4. The code is also available on the CD as file **6-3.HTML**.

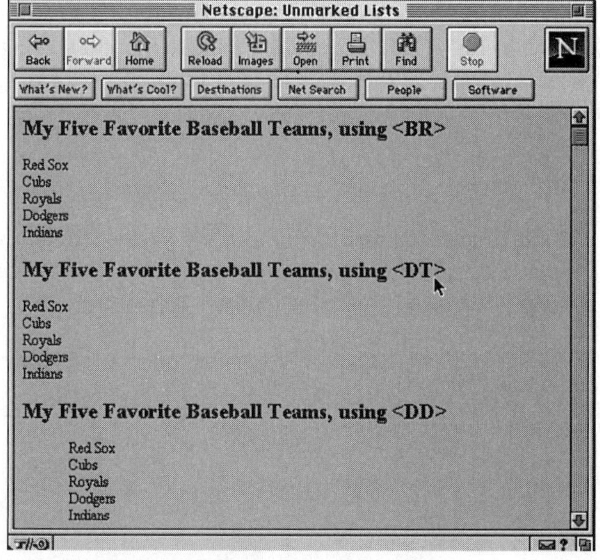

Figure 6-4 Examples of unmarked lists

How It Works

For the first kind of unmarked list, your browser simply replaces all the <BR> tags it finds with carriage returns. For the second kind of unmarked list, the browser replaces all the <DT> tags between the <DL> and </DL> tags with carriage returns. The browser does the same with the <DD> tags in the third kind of list, only it also includes a tab before the list item. The length of the indentation is set by the browser and can't be controlled within the document.

Comments

Although the <DT> and <DD> tags should be used together in glossary lists (see How-To 6.8), most major browsers will render lists using only <DT> or <DD> without problems.

COMPLEXITY
BEGINNING

6.6 How do I... Create a menu list?

COMPATIBILITY: HTML 2

Problem

I have a set of data that I want to display as a list. I want to show the items specifically as a menu of options for users to choose from. How do I do this in HTML?

Technique

HTML versions 2.0 and earlier support a tag called <MENU>, which enables list items to be displayed as a menu. HTML 3.2 and 4.0 include the <MENU> tag but do not support it to the same degree as they do <UL> and <OL>. For specific applications, though, it can be useful.

Steps

1. Open your document. Identify the locations in your document where you want to include a list. If you haven't done so already, enter the list items in the document, separated by carriage returns.

2. Place the <MENU> tag at the beginning of the list and the </MENU> tag at the end of the list:

```
<H2>My Five Favorite Baseball Teams</H2>
<MENU>
Red Sox
Cubs
Royals
Dodgers
Indians
</MENU>
```

3. In front of each item of the list, place an <LI> tag:

```
<H2>My Five Favorite Baseball Teams</H2>
<MENU>
<LI>Red Sox
<LI>Cubs
<LI>Royals
<LI>Dodgers
<LI>Indians
</MENU>
```

Figure 6-5 shows the output of this list. The code is also available on the CD in file **6-4.HTML**.

How It Works

As with other lists, a browser replaces all the **<LI>** tags between **<MENU>** and **</MENU>** with its predefined symbol or spacing. Often this is a bullet, so a list using the **<MENU>** tag frequently looks just the same as the bulleted list described in How-To 6.2.

Comments

<MENU> is not supported in HTML 3.2 or 4.0 to the same degree that other lists, such as **<OL>** and **<UL>**, are. Thus, any documents that include a **<MENU>** list might not format as expected when displayed on an HTML 3.2 or above compliant browser. However, if you are designing pages for a closed environment using older browsers, the **<MENU>** tag will continue to work and might be the best way to format your information.

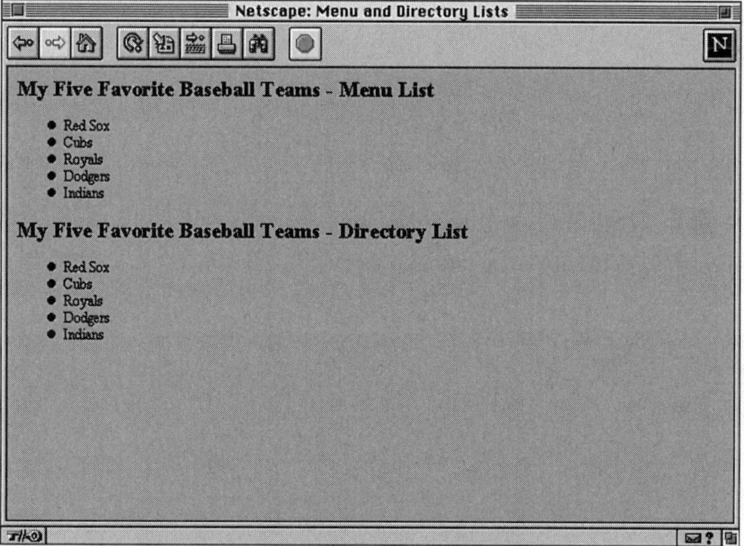

Figure 6-5 Examples of menu and directory lists

6.7 How do I... Create a directory list?

COMPATIBILITY: HTML 2

Problem

I have a set of data that I want to display as a directory of related items. How can I create a directory list in HTML?

Technique

HTML versions 2.0 and earlier support a tag called **<DIR>** that lists the items as if they were filenames in a computer directory. HTML 3.2 and 4.0 include the **<DIR>** tag but do not support it to the same degree as they do **<UL>** and **<OL>**. For specific applications, though, it can be useful.

Steps

1. Open your document. Identify the locations in your document where you want to include a list. If you haven't done so already, enter the list items in the document, separated by carriage returns.

2. Place the **<DIR>** tag at the beginning of the list and the **</DIR>** tag at the end of the list:

```
<H2>My Five Favorite Baseball Teams</H2>
<DIR>
Red Sox
Cubs
Royals
Dodgers
Indians
</DIR>
```

3. In front of each item, place an **<LI>** tag:

```
<H2>My Five Favorite Baseball Teams</H2>
<DIR>
<LI>Red Sox
<LI>Cubs
<LI>Royals
<LI>Dodgers
<LI>Indians
</DIR>
```

Figure 6-5 shows the output of this list. The code is also available on the CD in file **6-4.HTML**.

How It Works

As with other lists, a browser turns each **<LI>** tag into a predefined symbol or spacing. Most browsers interpret **<DIR>** lists by turning **<LI>** tags into carriage returns, making the lists another form of unmarked list (see How-To 6.5). Some browsers, such as Netscape, add a bullet in front of each item, turning directory lists into bulleted lists.

Comments

Because HTML 3.2 and 4.0 do not support the **<DIR>** tag to the same degree that they support other lists, such as **<OL>** and **<UL>**, any use of these tags in a document read by an HTML 3.2 or above compliant browser means the document might not format properly. Older browsers can still read and interpret these lists, though, so if you are designing pages for a closed environment using older browsers, this can be a useful way to display information.

COMPLEXITY
BEGINNING

6.8 How do I... Create a glossary list?

COMPATIBILITY: HTML 2+

Problem

I have a set of data that I would like to display as a list of terms and their definitions. I would like to emphasize the terms and set them apart from their definitions. How can I create such a glossary in HTML?

Technique

How-To 6.5 discusses the use of the **<DL>**, **<DT>**, and **<DD>** tags as a way to format an unmarked list. For an unmarked list, **<DT>** and **<DD>** are used separately, but they can be combined to create a glossary that emphasizes words and their definitions.

Steps

1. Open your document. Decide what information you would like to present as a glossary list.

2. Compile a list of terms and their definitions, separating them by carriage returns and tabs for clarity:

```
<H2>Some terms and definitions</H2>
Term 1
This is the definition for term 1
Term 2
This is the definition for term 2
```

3. Place the <DL> tag at the beginning of the list and the </DL> tag at the end of the list:

```
<H2>Some terms and definitions</H2>
<DL>
Term 1
This is the definition for term 1
Term 2
This is the definition for term 2
</DL>
```

4. Place the <DT> tag in front of each word to be defined:

```
<H2>Some terms and definitions</H2>
<DL>
<DT>Term 1
This is the definition for term 1
<DT>Term 2
This is the definition for term 2
</DL>
```

5. Place the <DD> tag in front of each definition:

```
<H2>Some terms and definitions</H2>
<DL>
<DT>Term 1
<DD>This is the definition for term 1
<DT>Term 2
<DD>This is the definition for term 2
</DL>
```

6. Some browsers allow you to conserve space in your document by making your list more compact. A compacted list usually has less space between list entries and may use a smaller, more compressed font. To create a compacted list, replace the <DL> tag with the <DL COMPACT> tag:

```
<H2>Some terms and definitions (compact form)</H2>
<DL COMPACT>
<DT>Term 1
<DD>This is the definition for term 1
<DT>Term 2
<DD>This is the definition for term 2
</DL>
```

Figure 6-6 shows the output of these lists. The code is also available on the CD as file **6-5.HTML**.

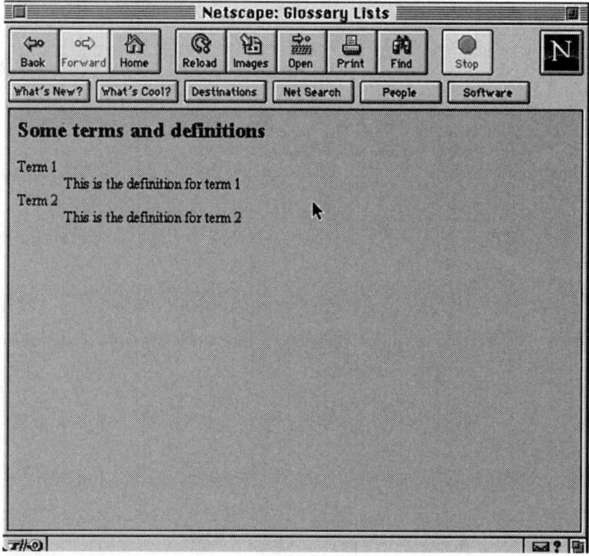

Figure 6-6 Example of a glossary list

How It Works

The browser software converts each **<DT>** found between the **<DL>** and **</DL>** tags into a carriage return. The browser converts the **<DD>** tags into a carriage return and an indentation.

Comments

HTML 3.2 and 4.0 require that, whenever you use the **<DL>** and **</DL>** tags, you also use both the **<DD>** and **<DT>** tags in the list. Although this makes it more difficult to create unmarked lists (see How-To 6.5), it has no effect here, because glossary lists need both types of tags to provide the best formatting. Note that the **COMPACT** attribute is not widely supported among the major browsers, so it might not produce the results expected.

6.9 How do I... Nest lists together?

COMPATIBILITY: HTML 2+

Problem

I have a set of data that I would like to display as an outline so that each main heading has subheadings and so forth. Can I use nested lists to create a formatted outline in HTML?

Technique

HTML makes it easy to nest lists. Lists can be inserted within lists and then be interpreted by a browser as sublists and set off from the main list. Examples of different kinds of nested lists are provided in the "Steps" section.

Steps

Open your document. Identify the lists in your document you would like to nest, decide what type of list you would like to create, and follow the steps for the given type of list.

Numbered List

1. For a numbered list, enter the items for each list level, using carriage returns to set them apart and tabs to show the level of nesting of each item in the outline:

```
<H2>An Example of Nested Lists</H2>
Point 1
Subpoint 1
      Subsubpoint 1
      Subsubpoint 2
      Subsubpoint 3
Subpoint 2
Subpoint 3
Point 2
Subpoint 1
Subpoint 2
Point 3
```

2. For the top-level list, place an <OL> at the beginning of the list, an </OL> at the end of the list, and an <LI> in front of only the top-level points:

```
<H2>An Example of Nested Lists</H2>
<OL>
<LI>Point 1
 Subpoint 1
        Subsubpoint 1
        Subsubpoint 2
        Subsubpoint 3
 Subpoint 2
 Subpoint 3
<LI>Point 2
 Subpoint 1
 Subpoint 2
<LI>Point 3
</OL>
```

3. For each sublist, place an <OL> at the beginning of the sublist, an </OL> at the end of the sublist, and an <LI> in front of each list item for that particular sublist. Continue this process for all the sublists.

```
<H2>An Example of Nested Numbered Lists</H2>
<OL>
<LI>Point 1
<OL>
 <LI>Subpoint 1
      <OL>
       <LI>Subsubpoint 1
       <LI>Subsubpoint 2
       <LI>Subsubpoint 3
      </OL>
 <LI>Subpoint 2
 <LI>Subpoint 3
</OL>
<LI>Point 2
<OL>
 <LI>Subpoint 1
 <LI>Subpoint 2
</OL>
<LI>Point 3
</OL>
```

The output of this list is shown in Figure 6-7. The code is available on the CD in file **6-6.HTML**.

Bulleted List

The technique to create bulleted lists is exactly the same as that for a numbered list, except that the <OL> and </OL> tags are replaced with <UL> and </UL>:

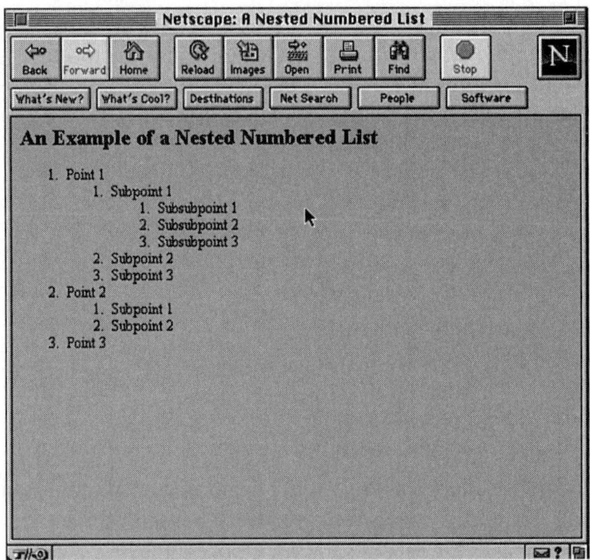

Figure 6-7 A nested numbered list

```
<H2>An Example of Nested Bulleted Lists</H2>
<UL>
<LI>Point 1
          <UL>
          <LI>Subpoint 1
                <UL>
                <LI>Subsubpoint 1
                <LI>Subsubpoint 2
                <LI>Subsubpoint 3
                </UL>
          <LI>Subpoint 2
          <LI>Subpoint 3
          </UL>
<LI>Point 2
          <UL>
          <LI>Subpoint 1
          <LI>Subpoint 2
          </UL>
<LI>Point 3
</UL>
```

Figure 6-8 shows the output of a nested bulleted list. The code is available on the CD in file **6-7.HTML**.

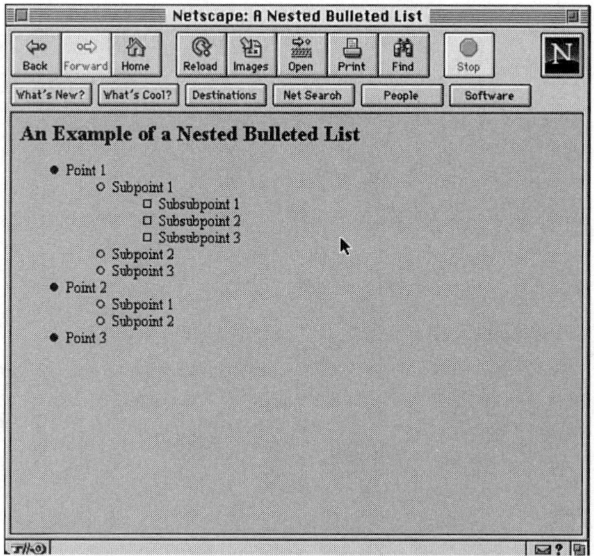

Figure 6-8 A nested bulleted list

Menu List

For menu lists, follow the steps as shown for a nested bulleted list, and use **<MENU>** and **</MENU>**:

```
<H2>An Example of Nested Menu Lists</H2>
<MENU>
<LI>Point 1
           <MENU>
           <LI>Subpoint 1
                  <MENU>
                  <LI>Subsubpoint 1
                  <LI>Subsubpoint 2
                  <LI>Subsubpoint 3
                  </MENU>
           <LI>Subpoint 2
           <LI>Subpoint 3
           </MENU>
<LI>Point 2
           <MENU>
           <LI>Subpoint 1
           <LI>Subpoint 2
           </MENU>
<LI>Point 3
</MENU>
```

Figure 6-9 shows the output of this list, which usually appears just the same as a nested bulleted list. The code is available on the CD in file **6-8.HTML**. Note that **<MENU>** is not a well-supported part of HTML 3.2 or 4.0.

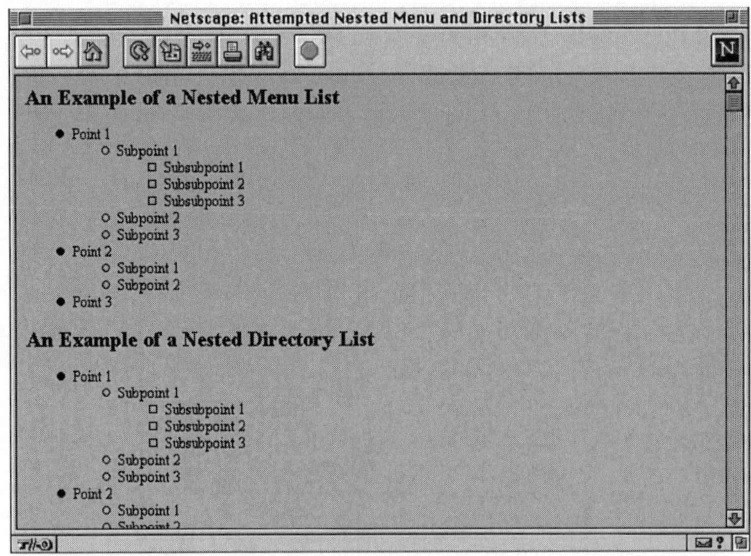

Figure 6-9 Attempts at nested menu and directory lists

Directory List

Most browsers, such as Netscape, display nested directory lists like menu lists, which look like nested bulleted lists.

To create a directory list, follow the steps as shown for nested menu lists, and use **<DIR>** and **</DIR>**:

```
<H2>An Example of Nested Directory Lists</H2>
<DIR>
<LI>Point 1
           <DIR>
           <LI>Subpoint 1
                   <DIR>
                   <LI>Subsubpoint 1
                   <LI>Subsubpoint 2
                   <LI>Subsubpoint 3
                   </DIR>
           <LI>Subpoint 2
           <LI>Subpoint 3
           </DIR>
<LI>Point 2
           <DIR>
           <LI>Subpoint 1
           <LI>Subpoint 2
           </DIR>
<LI>Point 3
</DIR>
```

The output of this list is shown in Figure 6-9. The code is available on the CD in file **6-8.HTML**. Note that **<DIR>** is not a well-supported part of HTML 3.2 or 4.0.

Unmarked List

You cannot create nested unmarked lists using the **
** tag, because there is no way for the browser to know what list level each item belongs to. However, by using the **<DL>** and **</DL>** list tags and either the **<DT>** or **<DD>** tag for each list item, you can create a nested unmarked list.

For a simple nested unmarked list, use **<DL>** and **</DL>** at the beginning and end of each list and sublist and **<DT>** in front of each list item:

```
<H2>A Nested Unmarked List Using &lt; DT &gt;</H2>
<DL>
<DT>Point 1
           <DL>
           <DT>Subpoint 1
                  <DL>
                  <DT>Subsubpoint 1
                  <DT>Subsubpoint 2
                  <DT>Subsubpoint 3
                  </DL>
           <DT>Subpoint 2
           <DT>Subpoint 3
           </DL>
<DT>Point 2
           <DL>
           <DT>Subpoint 1
           <DT>Subpoint 2
           </DL>
<DT>Point 3
</DL>
```

Figure 6-10 shows the output of this nested unmarked list. The code is available on the CD in file **6-9.HTML**.

For a nested unmarked list that is indented from the rest of the text, use **<DD>** in place of **<DT>** in the preceding example:

```
<H2>A Nested Unmarked List Using &lt; DD &gt;</H2>
<DL>
<DD>Point 1
        <DL>
        <DD>Subpoint 1
               <DL>
               <DD>Subsubpoint 1
               <DD>Subsubpoint 2
               <DD>Subsubpoint 3
               </DL>
        <DD>Subpoint 2
        <DD>Subpoint 3
        </DL>
<DD>Point 2
        <DL>
        <DD>Subpoint 1
        <DD>Subpoint 2
        </DL>
<DD>Point 3
</DL>
```

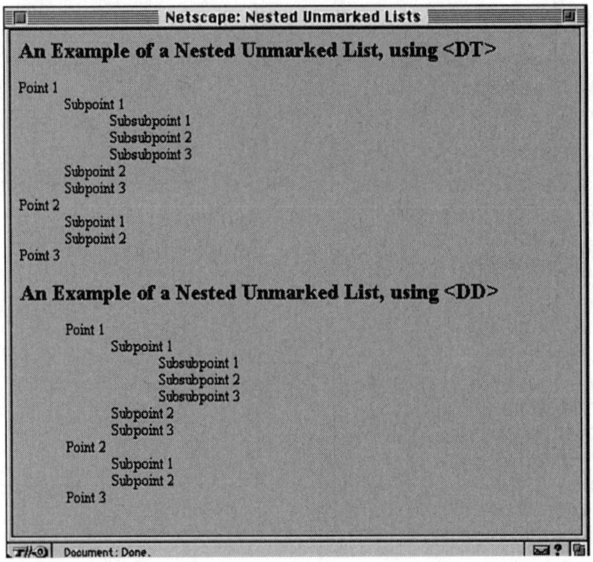

Figure 6-10 Examples of nested unmarked lists

Figure 6-10 shows the output of this unmarked nested list. The code is available on the CD in file **6-9.HTML**. You can also mix the **<DT>** and **<DD>** tags to create nested glossary lists.

Combining Lists

You can combine and nest different kinds of lists. The following example shows how to nest a bulleted list within a numbered list, which in turn is nested within an unmarked list:

```
<H2>A Nested List Using Unmarked, Numbered, and Bulleted Elements</H2>
<DL>
<DT>Point 1
           <OL>
           <LI>Subpoint 1
                   <UL>
                   <LI>Subsubpoint 1
                   <LI>Subsubpoint 2
                   <LI>Subsubpoint 3
                   </UL>
           <LI>Subpoint 2
           <LI>Subpoint 3
           </OL>
<DT>Point 2
           <OL>
           <LI>Subpoint 1
           <LI>Subpoint 2
           </OL>
<DT>Point 3
</DL>
```

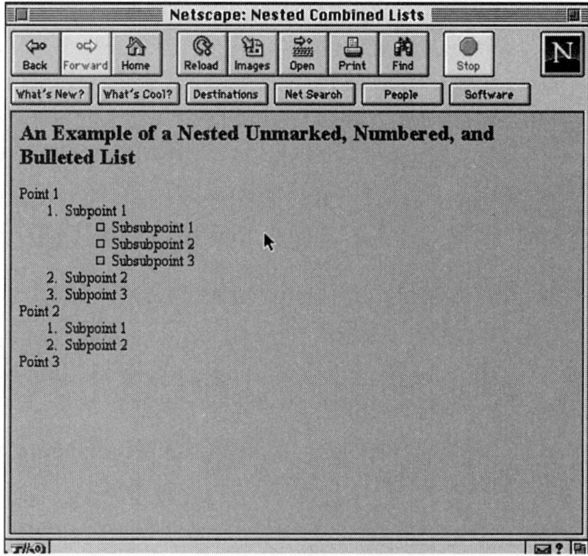

Figure 6-11 A nested combined list

Figure 6-11 shows the output of this combined nested list. The code is available on the CD in file **6-10.HTML**.

Be careful when mixing nested unmarked lists inside other types of lists. In some browsers, if you use the **<DT>** tag to mark list items in the unmarked list, the items might appear on the next higher list level. If you were to replace the bulleted sublist in this example with an unmarked list using **<DT>** in front of each list item, you might get an aesthetically unpleasant result. By using **<DD>** in place of **<DT>**, you get a better result.

How It Works

When a browser encounters a tag that marks the beginning of a new list before it encounters a tag that marks the end of the current list, it considers the contents of the new list to be a sublist nested inside the current list. The browser then formats the sublist accordingly. The format of the sublist can vary from browser to browser.

Comments

Different browsers use different styles to format nested lists. Some browsers mix letters and numbers in different levels of nested numbered lists, and some browsers use bullets of different shapes and sizes for different levels of nested bulleted lists. Therefore, when designing your pages, be careful when referring to specific list items by number or bullet, because the reader might not see the same number or bullet that you do. Also note that when mixing lists, some browsers will use the bullet or number style appropriate to that level, even if this is the first list of that type being used. Be cautious about making references to specific numbers or bullets.

6.10 How do I... Use lists to jazz up my home page?

COMPATIBILITY: HTML 2+

Problem

I would like to add lists to my home page so that I can better present my information. How can I effectively use lists to jazz up my home page?

Technique

Like any aspect of HTML, lists can be used and abused. The right way to use lists varies depending on what information you want to put into a list.

Steps

1. Avoid very long lists. Long lists are boring and difficult to read, and it's hard for the user to find a particular piece of information in them. Instead, break up any long lists into smaller lists, subdivided by topic. This is where nested lists can be useful.
2. Maintain parallelism in your lists. Don't change verb tenses or make other style changes in the middle of a list.
3. Along those lines, keep each list item about the same length. Lists can be made of short, one-word elements or long, paragraph-length statements, but the two shouldn't be combined.

How It Works

These tips help make your lists more effective by allowing a user to find the information of interest to him or her quickly. By grouping list items into related groups and by using parallel structure, you make it easier for a user to sort through the information provided.

Comments

Proper use of lists and good list style help set good Web pages apart from the rest. With a little practice, you'll soon be able to create all sorts of useful lists for your pages.

CHAPTER 7

MANAGING DOCUMENT SPACING

7

MANAGING DOCUMENT SPACING

How do I...

- **7.1 Add a horizontal line to an HTML document?**
- **7.2 Align text on a line using tables?**
- **7.3 Center text?**
- **7.4 Manage vertical spacing: paragraphs versus line breaks?**
- **7.5 Stop a browser from breaking a line at a critical point?**
- **7.6 Include preformatted text in my Web page?**
- **7.7 Insert a block quotation?**
- **7.8 Create divisions in my Web page?**
- **7.9 Exploit tables to arrange images, embedded objects, and text?**
- **7.10 Use transparent images to manage layout control?**
- **7.11 Create columnar text spanning a table?**
- **7.12 Space my home page?**

How you lay out or space your page is important in making a Web page that is tight and readable. Spacing is often initially overlooked when planning a Web page, which can be a mistake. A page that is properly spaced is easier to read and, therefore, visited more often by readers. A poorly spaced page might cause readers to miss information that is either too far off a page or too clumped together with other information to be noticed. This chapter will help you create an easy-to-read home page.

7.1 Add a Horizontal Line to an HTML Document

Horizontal lines separate distinct sections of documents. This How-To shows you how to add horizontal lines to your documents.

7.2 Align Text on a Line Using Tables

Tables can align text to go along the top or the bottom of a table row, a useful feature in formatting text. This How-To explains how to set the table formatting in HTML 4.0.

7.3 Center Text

An important aspect of document spacing and layout is the ability to center text on a page. This How-To shows the various ways to center text in HTML 4.0.

7.4 Manage Vertical Spacing: Paragraphs Versus Line Breaks

Two of the simplest tags in HTML are the paragraph, `<P>`, and line break, `<BR>`, tags. This How-To shows you the difference between the two tags and when you might want to use each one.

7.5 Stop a Browser From Breaking a Line at a Critical Point

Because of the differences in user preferences in browsers and among browsers themselves, text might be broken at different places in a Web page for different viewers, which can create unintended formatting problems. This How-To shows how to tell a browser not to break a line at an important place in a document.

7.6 Include Preformatted Text in My Web Page

All text delimited by `<PRE>` tags is displayed by a browser in a fixed-width font, including any white space within that text. This simple How-To shows you how to make the best use of the `<PRE>` tag.

7.7 Insert a Block Quotation

A block quotation is a long quotation from a book, speech, or other source that is set off from the rest of the document with different spacing and margins. This simple How-To shows how to format a section of text in a document as a block quotation.

7.8 Create Divisions in My Web Page

Divisions enable the Web page designer to group together blocks of text and other objects in a Web page and give that section, or division, special formatting. This How-To explains how to include these divisions in your Web page.

7.9 Exploit Tables to Arrange Images, Embedded Objects, and Text

One of the most powerful tools to control the layout of a Web page is tables. Different objects, such as text, images, and other multimedia features, can be arranged on the page in the manner chosen by the designer. This How-To shows how to use tables to create these advanced layout effects.

7.10 Use Transparent Images to Manage Layout Control

A special trick for controlling layout in a Web page is the use of transparent images that, while remaining invisible, force the page layout to shift. This How-To shows how to use transparent images to create a desired layout for a page.

7.11 Create Columnar Text Spanning a Table

Another feature of tables is the ability to place text in separate columns to give a Web page the feel of a magazine or newspaper. This How-To explains how to use tables to place text in multiple columns.

7.12 Space My Home Page

At first, spacing of a page might seem trivial. However, proper spacing can lead to a page that is easier to read and is therefore read more often. Improper spacing can make a reader skip over important information intentionally or unintentionally. This How-To helps you space your page in a user-friendly manner.

7.1 How do I... Add a horizontal line to an HTML document?

COMPATIBILITY: HTML 2+

Problem

I want to separate the credits for my page from the other information on my page. I see other pages that use horizontal lines to do this. How can I add a horizontal rule or line to my document?

Technique

Add horizontal lines to documents by using the **<HR>** (horizontal rule) tag. HTML 4.0 includes several attributes for **<HR>** that enable the user to change the width, thickness, and appearance of horizontal lines.

Steps

1. Open the HTML document in which you want to include horizontal lines.
2. Decide where you want to add a horizontal rule. In the example shown next, a horizontal rule separates the page's body from its footer. This is a common use for horizontal rules.
3. Enter an **<HR>** tag wherever you want to place a horizontal rule. For example:

```
<Html>
<HEAD><TITLE>My Example</TITLE></HEAD>
<Body>
<H2>How to add a horizontal rule to a document</H2>
Horizontal lines or rules are added to documents through the
use of the
HR tag. They are very easy to use and can make a document
look quite
professional. Horizontal Rules are so easy to add that some
people may
get carried away with their use. This is something you
should be careful
with. Still, <b>experiment</b>!  Have fun!
<P>
<P>
<HR>
This page was created by John Smith on 1/1/98. It was last
modified
on 6/1/98
</Body>
</Html>
```

4. You can change the thickness of the line in HTML 4.0 with the **SIZE** attribute. Set the **SIZE** attribute to an integer equal to the desired thickness of the line in pixels. The default thickness is typically 2. For example, to include a line with thickness 5 in this document, you would replace the **<HR>** with

```
<HR SIZE=5>
```

5. You can alter the width of the line by adding the **WIDTH** attribute to **<HR>**. **WIDTH** can be set to either the number of pixels wide the line should be or the percentage of the browser window's width the line should span. For example, to create a line 100 pixels wide, you would enter

```
<HR WIDTH=100>
```

Instead you wanted a line that goes across 60 percent of the screen, you would enter

```
<HR WIDTH="60%">
```

Note that you put quote marks around **60%** to be sure you don't confuse the browser by putting in a symbol that is neither a number nor a letter.

6. Most popular browsers show a horizontal line generated by **<HR>** as a type of shaded 3D line. However, if you would prefer to have your line appear as a simple black line, you can add the **NOSHADE** attribute to the **<HR>** tag. To create a line of size 5 that is 100 pixels across and appears only as a black line, you would enter

```
<HR SIZE=5 WIDTH=100 NOSHADE>
```

7. You can control the alignment of the horizontal rule on the page using the **ALIGN** attribute for **<HR>**. **ALIGN** can be set to **LEFT**, **RIGHT**, or **CENTER** for alignment to the left, right, or center of the screen, respectively. For example, to create a horizontal rule that is 80 percent of the screen width and aligned to the right side of the screen, you would enter

```
<HR WIDTH="80%" ALIGN=RIGHT>
```

8. Microsoft Internet Explorer version 3.0 and later enables you to control the color of the horizontal rule with the **COLOR** attribute to **<HR>**. Set the **COLOR** attribute to the name of RGB value of the desired color for the rule. To create a red horizontal rule, you would enter

```
<HR COLOR="#FF0000">
```

An example of the various types of horizontal lines is shown in Figure 7-1. The code for this figure is available on the CD-ROM as file **7-1.HTML**.

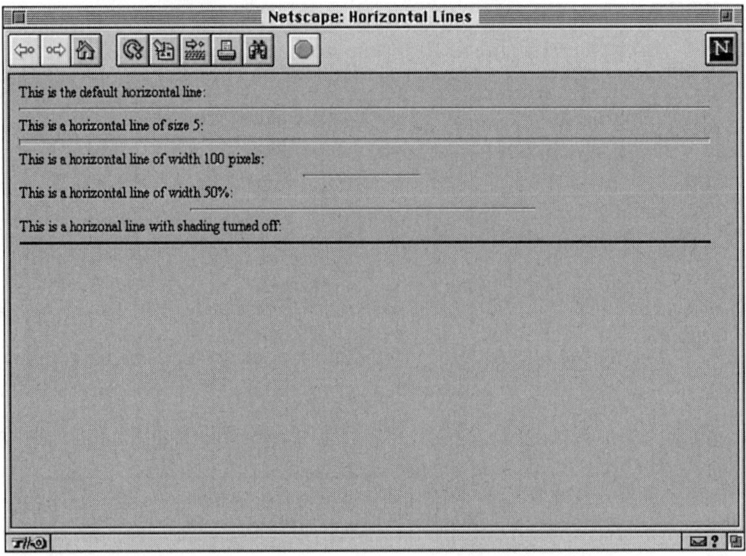

Figure 7-1 Examples of horizontal rules in HTML

How It Works

When a browser encounters an **<HR>** element, it generates a line on the page using the size, thickness, and color specified by the attributes in the tag.

Comments

The real trick here is not adding the line but deciding where the line should go and, for that matter, how many lines you should have on a page. The latter is largely a matter of taste. Some people believe you should use no more than two horizontal lines per page. Others believe the more the merrier. There are some standard places where horizontal lines are often used in documents:

- ✔ Around forms, to separate the form from the rest of the document
- ✔ At the end of a document, to separate information about the document (date created, author, and so on) from actual information contained in the document

It is possible to get carried away with horizontal lines, making your document harder to read and bigger than it should be. Be yourself, but use caution.

The **COLOR** attribute for **<HR>** is only supported by Microsoft Internet Explorer version 3.0 and later; other browsers will ignore the attribute. The **COLOR** attribute is not included in the most recent draft of HTML 4.0.

COMPLEXITY
INTERMEDIATE

7.2 How do I... Align text on a line using tables?

COMPATIBILITY: HTML 3.2+

Problem

I have some text in a table that I would like to align with the top or bottom of the table. How can I do this in HTML?

Technique

HTML 4.0 includes the **VALIGN** attributes to HTML, which enables you to specify how you want text aligned in a table. This is particularly useful with tables that have multiple cells of varying heights per row.

Steps

1. Open the HTML document with the table cells you want to align with the top or bottom of the row.

2. To align the text to the top of the row, place the **VALIGN=TOP** attribute in each table cell in that row. For example, in a three-cell row:

```
<TABLE>
<TR>
<TD VALIGN=TOP>
This is the text for the first cell of the table.
</TD>
<TD VALIGN=TOP >
This is the text for the second cell of the table. This cell
has more text that the first cell so that it takes more space
in the table.
</TD>
<TD VALIGN=TOP >
This is the text for the third cell of the table., which isn't as long
as the second cell.
</TD>
</TR>
</TABLE>
```

3. To align text to the bottom of the row, replace the **VALIGN=TOP** in the preceding example with **VALIGN=BOTTOM**:

```
<TABLE>
<TR>
<TD VALIGN=BOTTOM>
This is the text for the first cell of the table.
</TD>
<TD VALIGN=BOTTOM >
This is the text for the second cell of the table. This cell
has more text that the first cell so that it takes more space
in the table.
</TD>
<TD VALIGN=BOTTOM >
This is the text for the third cell of the table., which isn't as long
as the second cell.
</TD>
</TR>
</TABLE>
```

4. To center the contents of cells in a table, use the **VALIGN=MIDDLE** attribute. For example, in a three-cell row:

```
<TABLE>
<TR>
<TD VALIGN=MIDDLE>
This is the text for the first cell of the table.
</TD>
<TD VALIGN=MIDDLE >
This is the text for the second cell of the table. This cell
has more text that the first cell so that it takes more space
in the table.
</TD>
<TD VALIGN=MIDDLE >
This is the text for the third cell of the table., which isn't as long
as the second cell.
</TD>
</TR>
</TABLE>
```

An example of text alignment in tables is shown in Figure 7-2. The code for this figure is available as file **7-2.HTML**.

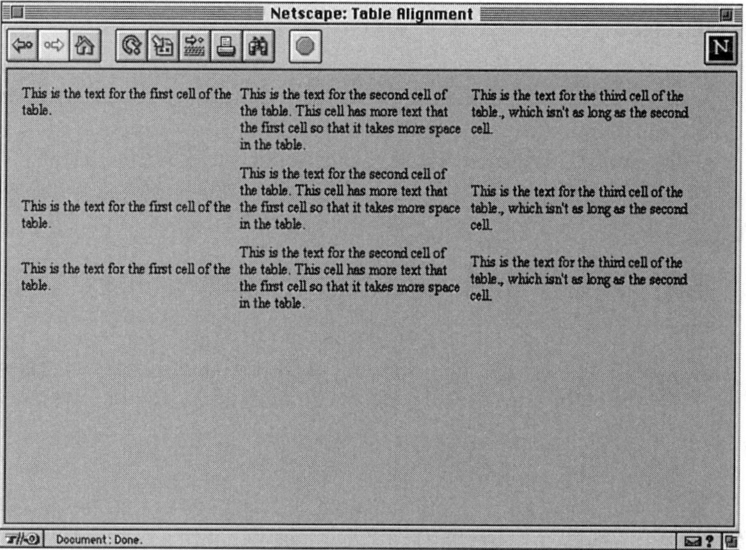

Figure 7-2 Vertical text alignment in tables

How It Works

When a browser encounters the **<VALIGN>** tag in a table cell, it will align the contents of the table cell with the top or bottom of the cell. The size of the cell is determined by the contents of all the cells in the row.

Comments

In addition to the **TOP**, **MIDDLE**, and **BOTTOM** values, **VALIGN** can also be set to **BASELINE**. This aligns the contents of the table cell with a specific baseline. Note that **BASELINE** is not officially part of HTML 4.0, but is supported by some browsers.

COMPLEXITY
BEGINNING

7.3 How do I... Center text?

COMPATIBILITY: HTML 3.2+

Problem

I want to draw attention to a section of text by centering it in the browser window. How can I do this in HTML?

Technique

There are several methods to center text using HTML 4.0. The **<CENTER>** and **<DIV ALIGN=CENTER>** tags enable you to center whole blocks of text and other Web page elements. Other text tags, such as **<H>** and **<P>**, now support the **ALIGN** attribute, which can be used to center the text contained within those tags.

Steps

1. Open the HTML document that contains the text you want to center.
2. One method of centering text is the **<CENTER>** tag. To use this, place the **<CENTER>** tag at the beginning of the text and the **</CENTER>** tag at the end of the text. An example of centered text using **<CENTER>** is

```
<CENTER>This line is centered.</CENTER>
```

3. You can achieve identical results with the **<DIV ALIGN=CENTER>** tag. Place the **<DIV ALIGN=CENTER>** tag at the beginning of the text to be centered and the **</DIV>** tag at the end of the text. Here is an example of centered text using **<DIV ALIGN=CENTER>**:

```
<DIV ALIGN=CENTER>This line is centered.</DIV>
```

   Further uses of the **<DIV>** element are explained in How-To 7.8.

4. The **ALIGN** attribute can be used to center headings (see How-To 4.1). To do this, insert the **ALIGN=CENTER** attribute at the beginning of the header tag:

```
<H3 ALIGN=CENTER>This heading is centered</H3>
```

5. The **ALIGN** attribute can also be used to center individual paragraphs (see How-To 7.4). To do this, insert the **ALIGN=CENTER** attribute at the beginning of the paragraph tag:

```
<P ALIGN=CENTER>This paragraph is centered</P>
```

An example of the various types of centered text is shown in Figure 7-3. The code for this figure is available as file **7-3.HTML**.

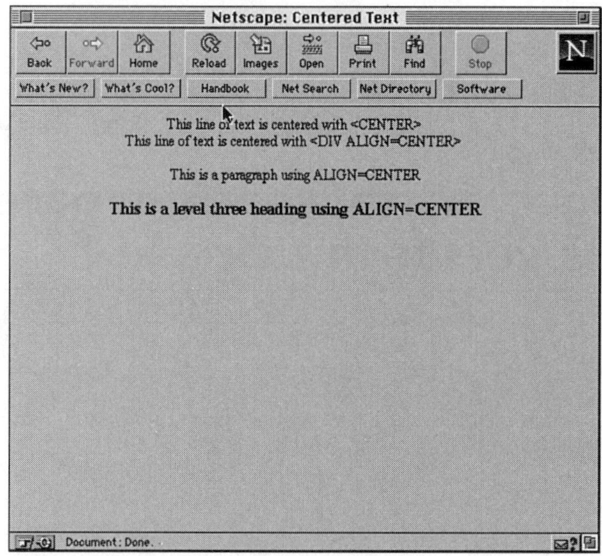

Figure 7-3 Centered text in HTML

How It Works

The **<CENTER>** and **<DIV ALIGN=CENTER>** tags work in the same way: They tell the browser to center all the text, as well as any other page elements, located between the opening and closing centering tags. Likewise, the **ALIGN=CENTER** attribute instructs the browser to center the contents of the heading or paragraph.

Comments

Why does HTML 4.0 have both **<CENTER>** and **<DIV ALIGN=CENTER>** tags, when they both do the same thing? The **<CENTER>** element was introduced by Netscape in an earlier version of its browser, even though the tag was not included in any draft version of HTML 3.0. Because **<CENTER>** gained widespread acceptance by Web page designers looking for ways to center parts of documents, **<CENTER>** was first included in HTML 3.2 and retained in HTML 4.0 as a synonym for **<DIV ALIGN=CENTER>**.

7.4 How do I...
Manage vertical spacing: paragraphs versus line breaks?

COMPATIBILITY: HTML 2+

Problem

How can I tell when I should use a new paragraph tag, <P>, and when I should use a line break tag,
?

Technique

Normally, a browser displays text across the available area of your text window. Text starts on a new line only when a complete word cannot be displayed on the current line. You have two methods of controlling where text breaks: the paragraph, <P>, and the line break, <BR>, tags. Which one you use is sometimes determined by personal taste and sometimes by the situation. Use a <P> tag to start a new paragraph, to which you can assign new attributes if you want. Most browsers also place an extra space after a <P>. A <BR> causes the browser to maintain the current paragraph attributes but to start placing text on a new line. The <BR> element is useful for such things as separating items in a list and breaking up lines of a song or a poem.

Steps

1. Create an HTML document with the text editor of your choice.

2. In the document, decide where you want to use new paragraphs and where you want to use simple line breaks. Usually it is pretty clear where to use each. A <P> tag is used wherever you would start a new paragraph if you were using a word processor. Use a line break, <BR>, if you want to keep information grouped together within the same paragraph but on separate lines. For example, you would not want a name and address to be in separate paragraphs, but you would want them to be on separate lines.

   The format of the new paragraph tag can be as simple as the following because this tag does not need to be closed:

```
<P>text
```

3. Although the simple tag is fine in most cases, the paragraph tag was expanded in HTML 3.2 to include alignment of the paragraph. This format is

```
<P ALIGN=RIGHT | LEFT | CENTER> text </P>
```

The text and images between the **<P>...</P>** tags are aligned to either the right, left, or center of the window depending on the option you select. Which format you choose is determined by personal taste and by the browser you are using.

4. The format of the break tag is also simple:

```
<BR>
```

However, this tag has been expanded on for use when you are working with images and text that are aligned. See Chapter 9, "Using Images in Your Documents," for more details.

The following code was used to create the sample document in Figure 7-4, which illustrates some of the differences between **
** and **<P>**:

```
<HEAD>
<TITLE>Demo of Paragraph <P> vs. Line
        Breaks<BR></TITLE>
</HEAD>
<BODY>
This is the first line. A simple paragraph tag.&lt;P&gt;<P>
Second line. Line break &lt;BR&gt;<BR>
This is the third line.
<P align=center>
Remember a browser normally does not break a sentence until it no longer has
room to display the current word in the window. A new paragraph tag causes
a new paragraph to begin, to which new attributes can be assigned. A line
break tag causes a line break, giving you a little more control of
things.</P>
<P ALIGN=left>
Here is a paragraph aligned to the left. The text flows until it comes to
the end of the window, or a new paragraph tag or line break. This line is
followed by a line break.&lt;BR&gt;<BR>
Notice the difference between that line and this one ended by a new
paragraph &lt;P&gt;.<P>
This is the next line.
Unordered list with paragraphs between items:
```

continued on next page

continued from previous page

```
<UL>
<LI>One&lt;P&gt;<p>
<LI>Two&lt;P&gt;<p>
</UL>
<P>
Unordered list with line breaks:
<UL>
<LI>One&lt;BR&gt;<br>
<LI>Two&lt;BR&gt;<br>
</UL>
</BODY>
</HTML>
```

An example of the uses of `<BR>` and `<P>` is shown in Figure 7-4. The code for this figure is available as file `7-4.HTML`.

How It Works

A browser displays text across the current line of the window until one of the following things happens:

- ✔ There isn't enough room on the current line to display the current word.
- ✔ A `<BR>` tag is encountered, in which case the browser starts a new line in the same paragraph.
- ✔ A `<P>` tag is encountered, in which case the browser not only begins a new paragraph but also enables the document creator to assign new paragraph attributes to the text that follows.

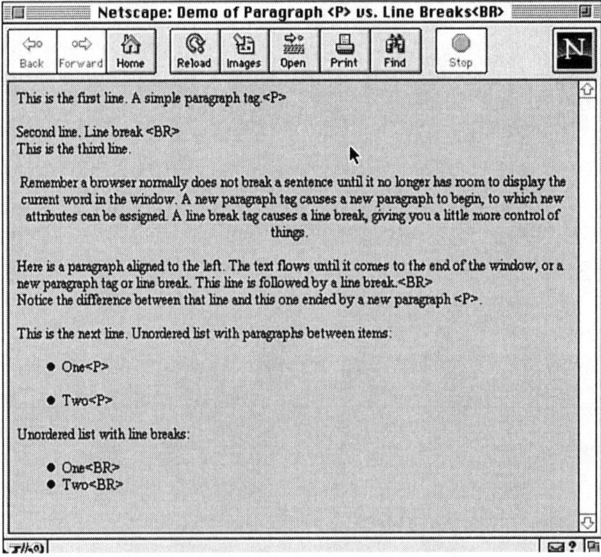

Figure 7-4 Various uses of `<BR>` and `<P>`

Comments

With the structure of the <P> tag, some people think it is a nice touch to close paragraphs with </P>. Although this might be good practice, it is not necessary because the browser assumes that a </P> tag exists when a new <P> or other similar tag is encountered in the document. Explicitly including a </P> tag is useful, though, when you are making changes to the alignment of paragraphs from one to the next.

Also, remember that the exact way a paragraph is displayed is governed by a combination of factors, such as the browser used, the style sheet setup, and various other tags.

COMPLEXITY
BEGINNING

7.5 How do I... Stop a browser from breaking a line at a critical point?

COMPATIBILITY: NETSCAPE NAVIGATOR, INTERNET EXPLORER

Problem

I have a section of text that must remain together and not have a line break in the middle of it. Is there a way I can keep a line from breaking in HTML?

Technique

You can use the <NOBR> tag to specify that a line should break at a particular point, which ensures that a section of text that follows will remain together on a single line.

Steps

1. Open the HTML document with the text you want to keep from breaking.
2. Just before the text in question (that is, at the point where you do not want the line to break), place the <NOBR> tag. For example, to make sure the phrase that begins to look like it is getting very long is not broken, you can enter

```
While this line  <NOBR> looks like it is getting very long, we can use
HTML to make sure a section of text stays all on one line.
```

3. At the end of the text segment that should remain unbroken, place the `</NOBR>` tag:

```
While this line  <NOBR> looks like it is getting very long, we can use
HTML to make sure a section of text stays </NOBR> all on one line.
```

An example of a nonbreaking line is shown in Figure 7-5. The code for this figure is available as file **7-5.HTML**.

How It Works

When a browser encounters the `<NOBR>` tag, it will place the text between it and the `</NOBR>` on a new line if there is not enough space on the current line for the designated text. The text will remain on the current line if there is enough room for it.

Comments

The `<NOBR>` tag is not widely supported by older browsers, so they might not ensure that lines will remain unbroken, as in this example.

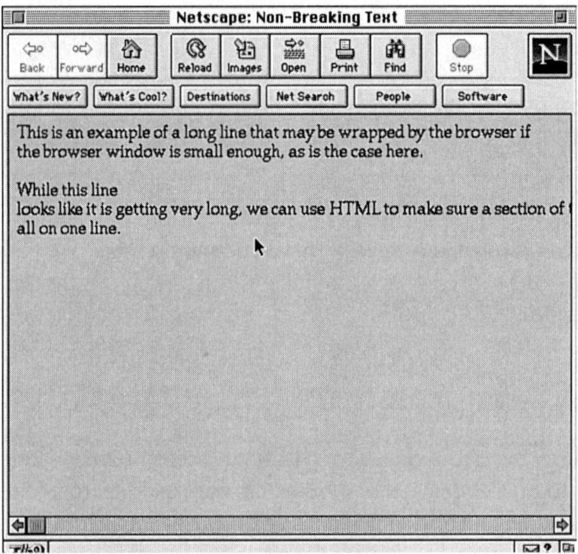

Figure 7-5 Nonbreaking lines

COMPLEXITY
BEGINNING

7.6 How do I... Include preformatted text in my Web page?

COMPATIBILITY: HTML 2+

Problem

I see a lot of pages in which the author includes rows of text evenly displayed in a monospace font, in which all the letters are the same width. How do I do this?

Technique

You can use the **<PRE>...</PRE>** tags to display preformatted blocks of text with a fixed-space font. When they appear inside **<PRE>** tags, white space, line breaks, and tabs are also displayed. Placing text between the **<PRE>** tags enables you to set up a sort of "poor man's" table, and it is also useful for simulating program listings.

Steps

1. Open the HTML document that contains the text that should retain its original formatting.

2. Place a **<PRE>** tag at the beginning of the preformatted text and a **</PRE>** tag at the end of the preformatted text, for example:

```
<PRE>
             <B>Gross sales</B>
Salesman                        Sales Ranking
Tim                              $10,000                  2
Tom                              $ 5,000                  3
Tammy                            $20,000                  1
<P><P><P>
These figures reflect the last quarter of 95. The first column of numbers
was created with spaces, the second with tabs. There are also carriage
returns in this paragraph within the sentences that would continue past the
screen.
</PRE>
```

In the chart, the first set of numbers is separated by spaces and the second set by tabs, because tabs are not ignored in text that appears between the preformatted text tags.

Notice after each salesperson's sale figures how the carriage returns work. Also notice how the bold `<B>` tags still work inside the <PRE> tags, but the new paragraph tags, `<P>`, are ignored.

An example of preformatted text is shown in Figure 7-6. The code for this figure is available as file `7-6.HTML`.

How It Works

The browser displays all text between the `<PRE>...</PRE>` tags in a fixed-width font without ignoring carriage returns and tabs. The next example shows the difference between how the same information is displayed when it appears between `<PRE>...</PRE>` tags and when it does not appear between `<PRE>...</PRE>` tags. The results can be seen in Figure 7-6.

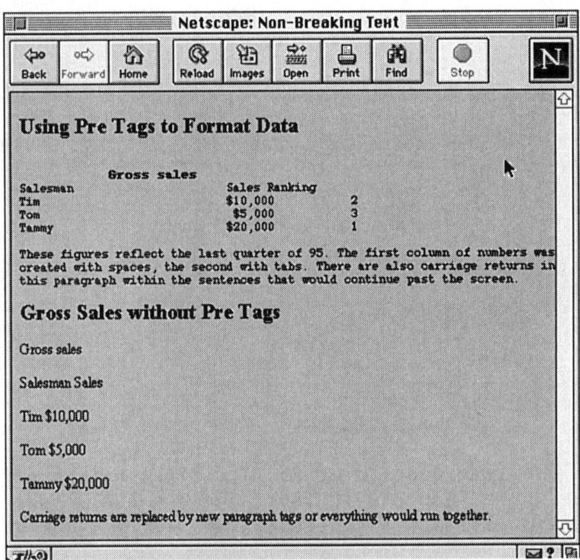

Figure 7-6 Preformatted text

```
<HTML>
<HEAD>
<TITLE>Preformatted text example</TITLE>
</HEAD>
<BODY>
<H2>Gross Sales By Sales People</H2>
<HR>
<PRE>
              Gross sales                <BR>
Salesman                        Sales<BR>
Tim                            $10,000<BR>
Tom                             $5,000<BR>
Tammy                          $20,000<BR>
Each line has a carriage return after it. Also notice what happens ⇐
to this line.
</PRE>
<HR>
<H2>Gross Sales without Pre Tags</H2>
<HR>
              Gross sales                <P>
Salesman                        Sales<P>
Tim                            $10,000<P>
Tom                             $5,000<P>
Tammy                          $20,000<P>
</HR>
Carriage returns are replaced by new paragraph tags or everything would ⇐
run together.
</BODY>
</HTML>
```

Comments

Although the `<PRE>...</PRE>` tags can be useful for quick-and-dirty tables, the advent of `<table>` tags in HTML 3.2 made creating tables with `<PRE>` somewhat less desirable. Probably the biggest use for `<PRE>` now is displaying program listings in documents. `<PRE>` can also be useful in forms if you want to have fields line up underneath one another.

7.7 How do I... Insert a block quotation?

COMPATIBILITY: HTML 2+

Problem

I have a long quotation that I want to include in my Web page. I would like to set it off from the rest of the text of the document. How can I include a block quotation in my Web page?

Technique

HTML supports the **<BLOCKQUOTE>** tag, which enables the user to specify that a specific block of text be formatted like a block quotation in a book, usually with indented margins on both the left and right sides.

Steps

1. Open the HTML document that contains the text that will be formatted as a block quotation.

2. Place a **<BLOCKQUOTE>** tag at the beginning of the pertinent text and a **</BLOCKQUOTE>** tag at the end of the text, for example:

```
Here is the documentation on the tag from the W3C:
<BLOCKQUOTE>
insert text here
</BLOCKQUOTE>
```

3. HTML 4.0 includes an attribute for **<BLOCKQUOTE>** that enables users to include the URL for the document from which the quotation comes. To take advantage of this new feature, include the **CITE** attribute to the **<BLOCKQUOTE>** tag and set it equal to the desired URL, for example:

```
Here is the documentation on the tag from the W3C:
<BLOCKQUOTE CITE="http://www.w3.org/">
insert text here
</BLOCKQUOTE>
```

An example of a block quotation is shown in Figure 7-7. The code for this figure is available as file **7-7.HTML**.

How It Works

When a browser encounters the **<BLOCKQUOTE>** tag, it formats the text contained between the **<BLOCKQUOTE>** and the **</BLOCKQUOTE>** tags using its rules for block quotations. Usually this means indenting the text at both the left and right margins to give an appearance similar to block quotations in books.

Comments

Many Web page authors use **<BLOCKQUOTE>** to give the text on their pages more white space between the margins and the edge of the browser window. Because this trick can also be done with tables, it is not of as great use as it once was. Also, many older browsers might not simply indent the text, but will use a different formatting technique. The **CITE** attribute to **<BLOCKQUOTE>** is a new addition to HTML 4.0 and is not widely supported, even by newer browsers.

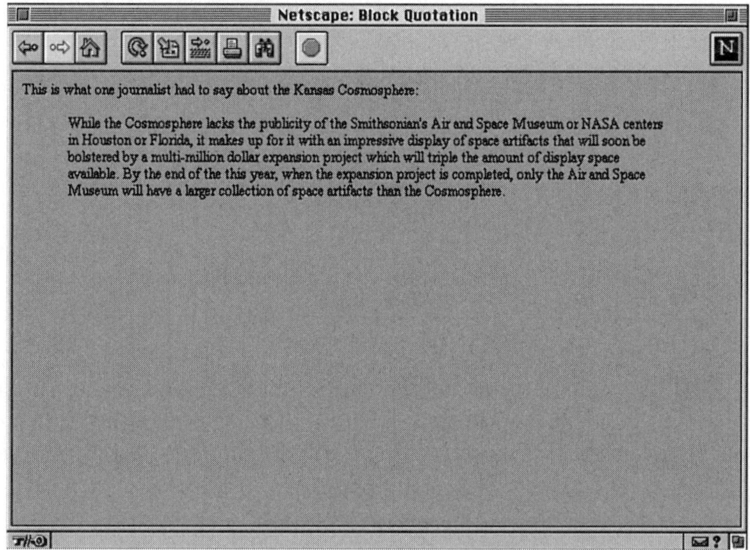

Netscape: Block Quotation
N
This is what one journalist had to say about the Kansas Cosmosphere:
While the Cosmosphere lacks the publicity of the Smithsonian's Air and Space Museum or NASA centers in Houston or Florida, it makes up for it with an impressive display of space artifacts that will soon be bolstered by a multi-million dollar expansion project which will triple the amount of display space available. By the end of the this year, when the expansion project is completed, only the Air and Space Museum will have a larger collection of space artifacts than the Cosmosphere.

Figure 7-7 Example of a block quotation

7.8 How do I... Create divisions in my Web page?

COMPATIBILITY: HTML 3.2+

Problem

I would like to divide my Web page into several different sections, each with its own formatting rules. How can I do this in HTML 4.0?

Technique

HTML 4.0 includes the `<DIV>` element for creating divisions in Web pages. These divisions can be used to set the alignment for an entire section of a Web page.

Steps

1. Open the HTML document to which you want to add sections.
2. Place the `<DIV>` tag at the beginning of the section you want to create in your document. Place the `</DIV>` tag at the end of the section:

```
<DIV>
This is the first section of my Web page.
</DIV>
<DIV>
This is the second section of my Web page
</DIV>
```

3. You can use the **ALIGN** attribute to set the alignment of the text within the section. **ALIGN** can be set to **LEFT**, **CENTER**, or **RIGHT**. For example, to left-align the first section of the page and right-align the second section, enter

```
<DIV ALIGN=LEFT>
This is the first section of my Web page.
</DIV>
<DIV ALIGN=RIGHT>
This is the second section of my Web page.
</DIV>
```

Examples of the various alignments of divisions are shown in Figure 7-8. The code for this figure is available as file **7-8.HTML**.

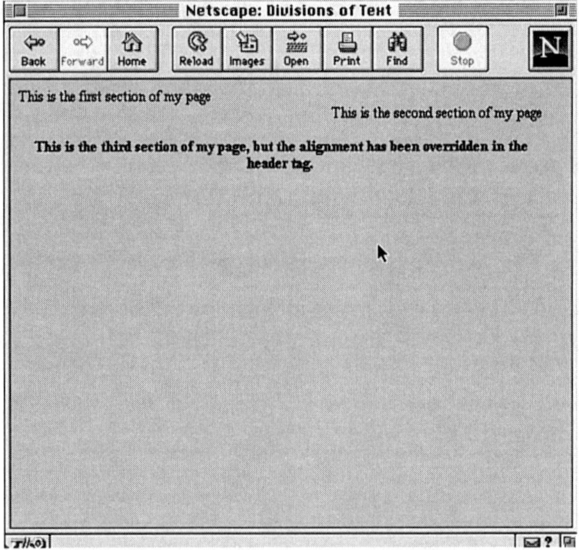

Figure 7-8 Examples of divisions in HTML

How It Works

When a browser encounters the **<DIV>** tag, it will take all the text located between the **<DIV>** and **</DIV>** tags and format it according to the instructions contained in the attributes of the **<DIV>** tag, such as alignment.

Comments

The **<DIV>** tags provide the default alignment for the text contained within them. That alignment can be overridden by specifying the alignment of a header or paragraph within the division. You can still center a heading in a division even if the division is set to align right. See Figure 7-8 and the file **7-8.HTML** for an example.

COMPLEXITY
BEGINNING

7.9 How do I...
Exploit tables to arrange images, embedded objects, and text?

COMPATIBILITY: HTML 3.2+

Problem

I would like to have more control over the location of the images, text, and other objects that make up my Web page. How can I do this using tables?

Technique

Tables provide a powerful way to control the layout of a Web page. You can insert sections of text, images, and other objects in table cells and control exactly where the items will appear on the browser window.

Steps

1. Open the HTML document that contains the text, images, and other objects that you will format. Because there is a wide variety of possible ways to use tables to control format, we will show just one example here: placing text around an image.

2. Decide how you want to lay out the display. In this case we want to have text around an image, so we need table cells containing text above, below, and to the left and right of an image. This will require three rows of table cells, so set up the table like this:

```
<TABLE>
<TR>
<!-- table row 1 -->
```

continued on next page

continued from previous page

```
</TR>
<TR>
<!-- table row 2 -->
</TR>
<TR>
<!-- table row 3 -->
</TR>
</TABLE>
```

3. With the rows laid out, you can now decide how many table cells you need. We described putting text on four sides of an image, so we will need four table cells, plus a cell for the image. We'll place a single cell each in the top and bottom rows, then span the table and place three cells in the middle row of the table:

```
<TABLE>
<TR>
<TD COLSPAN=3>
<!-- table row 1, top cell -->
</TD>
</TR>
<TR>
<TD>
<!-- table cell for left text -->
</TD>
<TD>
<!-- table cell for image -->
</TD>
<TD>
<!-- table cell for right text -->
</TD>
</TR>
<TR>
<TD COLSPAN=3>
<!-- table row 3, bottom cell -->
</TD>
</TR>
</TABLE>
```

4. With the table cells laid out, you can now go in and place the images and text in the appropriate cells:

```
<TABLE>
<TR>
<TD COLSPAN=3>
This is the text for the top row of the table. This text will span across
the entire width of the cell because of the COLSPAN attribute in thetable
cell tag.
</TD>
</TR>
<TR>
<TD>
This is text for the left side of the image. This text is⇐ below the top
row text and above the bottom row text.
```

```
</TD>
<TD>
<IMG SRC="myimage.gif" ALT="My Image" WIDTH=100 HEIGHT=100>
</TD>
<TD>
This is text for the right side of the image. This text is below the top
row text and above the bottom row text.
</TD>
</TR>
<TR>
<TD COLSPAN=3>
This is the text for the bottom row of the table. This text will span
across the entire width of the cell because of the COLSPAN attribute in the
table cell tag.
</TD>
</TR>
</TABLE>
```

5. After you have the basic layout set up, you can tweak the layout by setting the `VALIGN` and `WIDTH` attributes of the table cells.

An example of the table-based layout described here is shown in Figure 7-9. The code for this figure is available as file `7-9.HTML`.

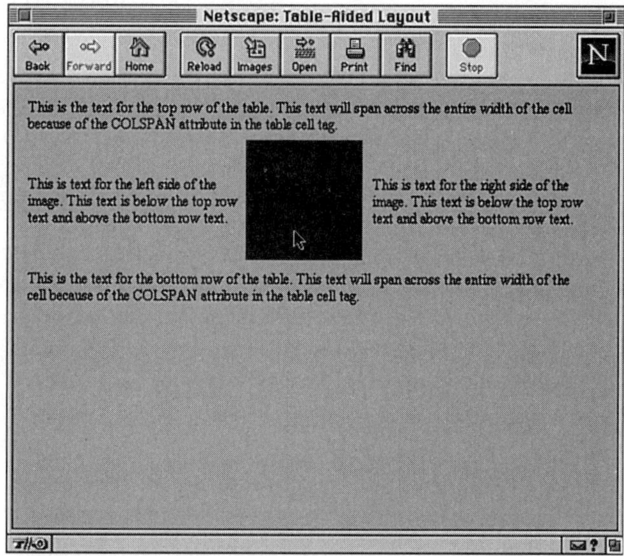

Figure 7-9 An example of a table-based layout

How It Works

When a browser encounters a table, it sets up the table according to the values set in the attributes (if any), the numbers of rows and columns, and the contents of the table cells themselves. Table cells do not have to contain merely words: Images and other objects are valid in cells.

Comments

In this example, we did not include a table border. For layouts like these, the table borders are not useful and can even be distracting to the layout of the page. Note that the detailed formatting used here will go to waste on older browsers that don't support tables.

COMPLEXITY
INTERMEDIATE

7.10 How do I... Use transparent images to manage layout control?

COMPATIBILITY: HTML 3.2+

Problem

I've heard that it's possible to use transparent images to control the layout of a Web page. How do I do this?

Technique

It's possible to use a transparent image (an image that takes up space on the browser screen but cannot be seen by the user) to shift the location of text and other page elements in the browser window. Although the use of images in Web pages in general is discussed in Chapter 9, "Using Images in Your Documents," this How-To shows how to include transparent images for layout control.

Steps

1. Open the HTML document whose layout you want to alter.

2. Before you make any changes to the document, you first need a transparent image that you will use in the layout. One example, a 1 pixel by 1 pixel transparent GIF file, is included on the CD as file **CLEARPIX.GIF**. Place this image in the same folder or directory as the HTML file you plan to edit.

3. Immediately in front of the text you want to move, insert the HTML tag `<IMG SRC="clearpix.gif" ALT="">`. This is the HTML code for inserting an image in the document. For example:

```
This is a normal line of text in this document.<BR>
<IMG SRC="clearpix.gif" ALT="">This is an indented line of text.<BR>
```

The syntax of the `<IMG>` tag is discussed in complete detail in Chapter 9.

4. In this example, if you want to indent the second line by a number of pixels, you could use the `HEIGHT` and `WIDTH` attributes to `<IMG>` to expand the size of the image to the desired width. For example, to move the second line in 100 pixels, set the `WIDTH` attribute to 100 while setting `HEIGHT` to 1:

```
This is a normal line of text in this document.<BR>
<IMG SRC="clearpix.gif" ALT="" WIDTH=100 HEIGHT=1>This
is an indented line of text.<BR>
```

5. Another method of doing the same thing would be to use the `HSPACE` (horizontal space) and `VSPACE` (vertical space) attributes. They do not resize the image but create a blank border of the specified size around the image. Thus, if the attribute were set to *n*, the image would become $2n+1$ pixels tall or wide. You could indent the line in the preceding example 101 pixels by replacing the `WIDTH` and `HEIGHT` tags with `HSPACE=50` and `VSPACE=1`:

```
This is a normal line of text in this document.<BR>
<IMG SRC="clearpix.gif" ALT="" HSPACE=50 VSPACE=1>This is an indented ⇐
line of text.<BR>
```

6. Similarly, you could use transparent images to alter the vertical layout of a page by adjusting `HEIGHT` and `VSPACE` instead of `WIDTH` and `HSPACE`. In the following example, a second line of text is placed far below the first line:

```
This is a normal line of text in this document.<BR>
<IMG SRC="clearpix.gif" ALT="" WIDTH=1 HEIGHT=100><BR>
This is a line of text far below the first.<BR>
This is a normal line of text in this document.<BR>
<IMG SRC="clearpix.gif" ALT="" HSPACE=1 VSPACE=50> <BR>
This is a line of text far below the first.<BR>
```

Examples of the use of transparent images are shown in Figure 7-10. The code for this figure is available as file `7-10.HTML`.

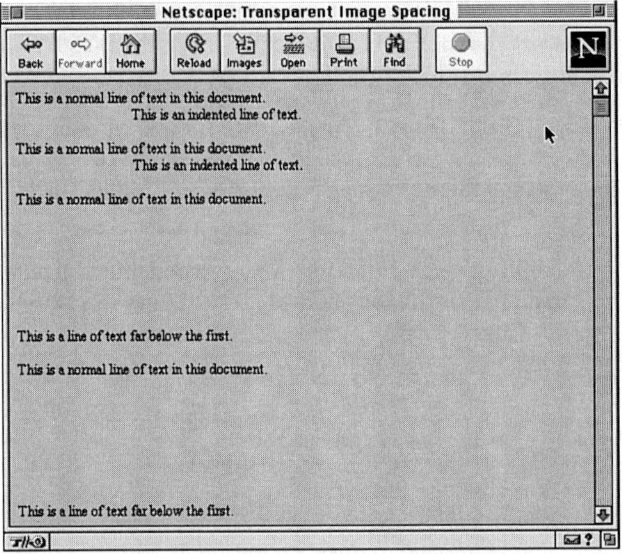

Figure 7-10 Examples of transparent images controlling layout in HTML

How It Works

When a browser encounters the **<IMG>** tag, it loads the named image. It scales the image according to the **HEIGHT** and **WIDTH** attributes found in the tag and adds a clear border around the document using the **<VSPACE>** and **<HSPACE>** tags. This graphic then alters the location of the remaining text in the document, even though this transparent image cannot be seen.

Comments

For this "trick" to work, the browser must be loading images. If the browser has the autoloading of images turned off, the space on the page can still be reserved (because of the **HEIGHT** and **WIDTH** tags), but an icon that represents an image will appear. This technique will not work for text-only browsers, such as Lynx.

7.11 How do I... Create columnar text spanning a table?

COMPATIBILITY: HTML 3.2+

Problem

I would like to format the text on my Web page like a newspaper or magazine, splitting it into several columns that appear side by side on the screen. Is there a way to do this in HTML?

Technique

You can use a table (see Chapter 5, "Tables") to split the layout of a page into several columns and place text in each column to create a multicolumn layout.

Steps

1. Open the HTML document with the text you want to place in multiple columns.

2. Create the table by entering a `<TABLE>` tag at the beginning of the text and `</TABLE>` at the end of the text:

```
<TABLE>
<!-- this is where your text goes -->
</TABLE>
```

3. Because we are concerned with splitting the text into several columns and don't have any concern about rows, we'll create only a single row. Place a `<TR>` tag just after the `<TABLE>` tag and a `</TR>` tag just before the `</TABLE>` tag:

```
<TABLE>
<TR>
<!-- this is where your text goes -->
</TR>
</TABLE>
```

4. Now we need to add the **<TD>...</TD>** tags that define the columns. You will need a table cell for each column. For the case of a two-column layout, you would need two sets of **<TD>...</TD>** tags, with the split between columns about halfway through the text. You would use something like the following:

```
<TABLE>
<TR>
<TD>
<!-- this is where the first half of your text goes -->
</TD>
<TD>
<!-- this is where the second half of your text goes -->
</TD>
</TR>
</TABLE>
```

You would use similar setups for other multiple column layouts: For a three-column layout, for example, you would use three sets of **<TD>...</TD>** tags.

5. To make sure all the text is aligned at the top of the table, insert the **VALIGN=TOP** attribute in each **<TD>** statement:

```
<TABLE>
<TR>
<TD VALIGN=TOP>
<!-- this is where the first half of your text goes -->
</TD>
<TD VALIGN=TOP>
<!-- this is where the second half of your text goes -->
</TD>
</TR>
</TABLE>
```

6. You can also use the **WIDTH** attribute of **<TD>** to control the width of the cell. In this example, if you wanted the first cell to be 250 pixels wide and the second to be 350 pixels wide, you would enter

```
<TABLE>
<TR>
<TD VALIGN=TOP WIDTH=250>
<!-- this is where the first half of your text goes -->
</TD>
<TD VALIGN=TOP WIDTH=350>
<!-- this is where the second half of your text goes -->
</TD>
</TR>
</TABLE>
```

An example of a two-column format is shown in Figure 7-11. The code for this figure is available as file **7-11.HTML**.

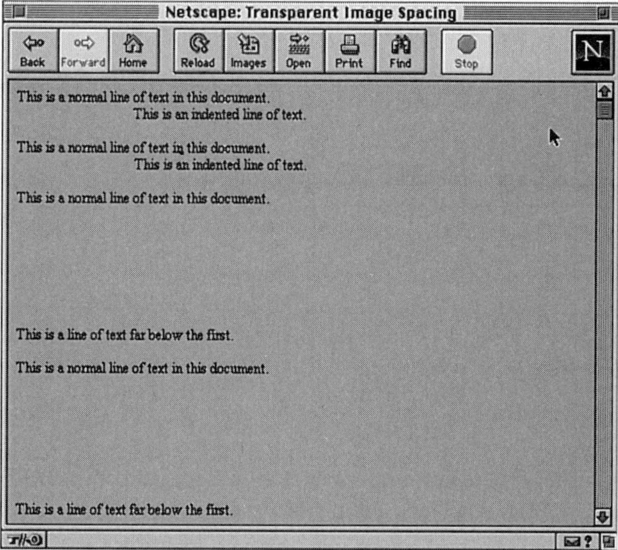

Figure 7-11 A two-column layout using tables

How It Works

This is another application of tables, which are discussed in greater detail in Chapter 5, "Tables." The content of each table cell is a block of text, which can span many paragraphs. The table cells are placed in a single row, and the **`VALIGN=TOP`** attribute makes sure the text is aligned at the top, a precaution in case the cells are of different lengths.

Comments

One precaution when creating tables is to keep the number of columns used to a minimum. If the person viewing a page with many columns has a small screen, either each browser will be very narrow, making it hard to read, or the table will extend past the right end of the browser window, requiring the user to scroll horizontally as well as vertically.

7.12 How do I... Space my home page?

COMPATIBILITY: NOT APPLICABLE

Problem

How can I make a home page so that it is easily readable, yet compact enough that readers don't have to scroll a lot?

Technique

The technique used here is a mixture of good judgment, common sense, and personal taste. Spacing is often a matter of personal taste. Bad spacing is easy to identify: If you can't read your page, nobody else can either. Good spacing is a bit harder to identify. You wrote your page, so you can tell where everything is, but that doesn't mean that another reader will be able to. Have a few people read your page and give you feedback on it. Here are also a few pointers to follow that will help make your page flow smoothly and be easy to read:

- ✔ Be consistent with your spacing.
- ✔ Be consistent with how you use horizontal lines.
- ✔ Feel free to ignore these points. After all, it is your page. Just remember, though, that if things run together or are spaced too far apart, readers might miss something you want them to read.

Steps

The following steps give general instructions on how to space your page. Feel free to follow or ignore any suggestions given.

1. Decide which type of spacing and horizontal line rules you want to use, if any.

2. Incorporate these rules into your pages. The following document is a very simple home page about poetry. It uses an **<HR>** tag to separate the two poems and another **<HR>** to separate the footer from the main text body of the page. It also uses **
** tags to cause each verse of the poem to appear on a separate line.

```
<HTML>
<HEAD>
<TITLE>My Page of Poems</TITLE>
<BODY>
</HEAD>
```

```
<H2>My Poetry Page</H2>
Here are a couple of my favorite poems:<P>
This one from my childhood:
<P ALIGN=CENTER>
Mary had a little lamb<BR>
Its fleece was white as snow<BR>
Everywhere that Mary went the lamb was sure to go!<BR>
</P>
<HR>
This one from my adulthood:
<P ALIGN=CENTER>
Roses are Red<BR>
Violets are Blue<BR>
I love you<BR>
<HR>
<CITE>
This page is maintained by: J. Smith.
</CITE>
</BODY>
</HTML>
```

3. Experiment to see what you think works best.

How It Works

You blend elements, tags such as **<P>**, **
, and **<HR>, and different levels of headers to create a page that is pleasing to the eye, informative, and yet not too long. It is helpful to have a set of rules that govern the use of certain tags. For example:

- ✔ Use **<HR>** after a level heading.
- ✔ Use **<HR>** before any footer or trailer information.
- ✔ Use **<HR>** to separate distinct items.
- ✔ Use two **<P>** elements to separate new sections.
- ✔ Use **
** between lines of addresses.
- ✔ Always start a page with a title displayed as a level 1 header.

Comments

For the most part, pages can be broken down into three sections:

- ✔ Heading information, which might include a snappy logo or information about who and where you are
- ✔ Body content that includes information or links to information you find important
- ✔ Footer information such as where to reach you, when the document was last updated, links to sites directly related to your page, and an e-mail address

CHAPTER 8

ESTABLISHING LINKS

8

ESTABLISHING LINKS

How do I...

8.1 Interpret a URL?
8.2 Understand a relative URL?
8.3 Add a base for relative URLs within the body of a document?
8.4 Specify a relationship between this document and other resources?
8.5 Create a link to a local page?
8.6 Create a link to other pages?
8.7 Send data to an HTTP server via a URL?
8.8 Create a link to a specific part of a page?
8.9 Create a link to an FTP site?
8.10 Create a link to a Gopher site?
8.11 Create a link to a Telnet site?
8.12 Create a link to a WAIS site?
8.13 Create a link to a Usenet newsgroup?
8.14 Create a link to electronic mail?
8.15 Create links to pages in other users' home directories?

8.16 Add links to lists and tables?

8.17 Add links to my home page?

With only a small amount of markup, you can format text files for effective presentation on the World Wide Web. This alone makes HTML and WWW a good way to publish documents over the Internet. But it captures only a small fraction of the potential of the World Wide Web. Imagine being able to give the reader of your document the ability, with a single keypress or mouse click, to move to another part of your document, another document on your computer, or Internet resources around the world. HTML provides the ability to add links to other documents and resources. You'll learn about links in this chapter, starting with some background about how links work and progressing through a series of methods to connect other documents to your own.

8.1 Interpret a URL

Universal Resource Locators, or *URLs*, are what World Wide Web browsers use to locate files on the Internet. This How-To explains the various parts of a URL and shows how to construct URLs to point to various kinds of documents.

8.2 Understand a Relative URL

If you have a number of pages located on your computer placed in various directories, relative URLs let you identify their location without typing the entire pathname of the file. This How-To explains how relative URLs work and how you can create relative URLs for your own needs.

8.3 Add a Base for Relative URLs Within the Body of a Document

If a page contains relative URLs and is transferred from one location to another, the relative URLs will no longer work in the new location. This How-To explains how to get around this problem by specifying a base for these URLs within the body of your page.

8.4 Specify a Relationship Between This Document and Other Resources

A page you're developing might be one of a set of related pages, and you might want to show how a particular page fits in with the other pages. This How-To explains how to specify relationships between a page and other pages and resources.

8.5 Create a Link to a Local Page

The simplest type of link is linking a page you've created with other pages and files on your computer. This simple How-To shows how to link together the pages you've created on your computer.

8.6 Create a Link to Other Pages

The World Wide Web connects thousands of pages around the world. This How-To shows how to connect your page to any number of pages around the world.

8.7 Send Data to an HTTP Server via a URL

When using forms or keyword searches, there are instances when you want to pass some information on to an application on a specific computer. This How-To explains how to attach keyword information to a URL to be passed on to an application.

8.8 Create a Link to a Specific Part of a Page

When creating a page, especially a very long page, you might want to provide links to other parts of the page to make it easy for readers to move around the document. This How-To explains how to create links to a specific part of a page.

8.9 Create a Link to an FTP Site

File Transfer Protocol (FTP) is a popular method of transferring files across the Internet. FTP servers are located around the world, with information on a wide range of topics including, no doubt, information useful for your pages. This How-To explains how to link an FTP site to your page.

8.10 Create a Link to a Gopher Site

Gopher provides an easy-to-use, menu-based interface to information resources on the Internet. This How-To explains how to link a Gopher site, and specific items at the site, to your page.

8.11 Create a Link to a Telnet Site

Some sites on the Internet provide information by Telnet, requiring a user to log on to the computer to access information. This How-To explains how to link a Telnet site to your page.

8.12 Create a Link to a WAIS Site

The Wide Area Information Servers (WAIS) technology is a method of providing searchable databases on the Internet, making them useful for finding specific items of information. This How-To explains how to link a WAIS site to your page.

8.13 Create a Link to a Usenet Newsgroup

Thousands of Usenet newsgroups cover every conceivable topic under the sun, as well as many inconceivable topics. This How-To explains how to link a Usenet newsgroup to your page.

8.14 Create a Link to Electronic Mail

It's often useful for people to contact you or other people concerning the contents of your page. One way to do this is to make it possible for readers to automatically e-mail people. This How-To explains how to link electronic mail to your page.

8.15 Create Links to Pages in Other Users' Home Directories

You might want to include links to pages located in the directories of other users on a multi-user machine. Instead of specifying the full pathname for the page, you can use a shortcut to create a link to that page. This How-To explains how to create a simple link to a page in another user's directories.

8.16 Add Links to Lists and Tables

Lists and tables provide ways to organize information efficiently. They can be combined with links to create easy-to-use menus of options. This How-To explains how to add links to the lists and tables in your page.

8.17 Add Links to My Home Page

Links can be simple and fun to add to your pages, but if done incorrectly, they can make your page difficult to understand or use. This How-To explains how to add links to your page that will increase the information content of your page and make it more fun to read.

8.1 How do I... Interpret a URL?

COMPATIBILITY: HTML 2+

Problem

I want to include links in my page, and I understand that I'll need to use URLs. However, I'm unfamiliar with the structure and composition of URLs—what goes into them and where. How do I interpret a URL?

Technique

HTML uses Universal Resource Locators, or URLs, to provide a simple, consistent way of accessing information using a wide variety of protocols. A URL consists of three main items: a protocol code, the address of the computer with the desired file (or an e-mail address or newsgroup name), and the location and filename of the file containing the information.

Steps

The following steps illustrate how to interpret a URL:

1. The first part of a URL is the protocol. The protocol indicates what method should be used to obtain the requested information. There are seven main

protocols, listed in Table 8-1, which are discussed in greater detail later in the chapter.

Table 8-1 URL protocols

PROTOCOL	DESCRIPTION
ftp	File Transfer Protocol (FTP)
gopher	Gopher
http	Hypertext Transfer Protocol (HTTP)
mailto	Electronic mail
news	Usenet news
telnet	Telnet
wais	Wide Area Information Servers (WAIS)

2. For five of the seven protocols (FTP, Gopher, HTTP, Telnet, and WAIS), the protocol is followed by a colon and two forward slashes (//). Immediately following the slashes is the address of the computer that is host to the relevant information. Some examples are

```
http://www.stateu.edu
ftp://ftp.widgets.com
gopher://info.stateu.edu
```

For the **mailto** protocol, the protocol is followed by a single colon and an e-mail address.

```
mailto:john@stateu.edu
mailto:help@widgets.com
```

For the **news** protocol, the protocol is followed by a single colon and the name of a Usenet newsgroup, although some browsers let you specify a remote computer from which to obtain newsgroup articles, in a manner such as HTTP, FTP, and Gopher.

```
news:alt.widgets
news:comp.infosystems.www.users
news://news.stateu.edu/sci.astro
```

3. For protocols other than **mailto** and **news**, the address of the computer is followed by the path to the desired file or directory. Some examples are

```
http://www.stateu.edu/pub/teams/yankees.html
ftp://ftp.widgets.com/etc/images/widget1.gif
gopher://info.stateu.edu/00/pubinfo/good%20restaurants
```

How It Works

When a browser encounters a URL, it first checks the protocol to determine what method the program must use to get the information. The browser then gets the address of the computer (or newsgroup name or e-mail address), accesses the site, and uses the path information in the URL to find the file and bring a copy back to the browser's computer.

Comments

Some browsers don't support some URL protocols such as `news` and `mailto`; such browsers require additional software or connections to work properly. A browser must be configured to use a communications program to use any Telnet URLs, and it must have access to a WAIS server or be able to use a WAIS server elsewhere as a proxy to use any WAIS URLs.

To understand the structure of URLs better, you might want to look at the URLs contained in a variety of Web pages. Those URLs will provide additional examples of how URLs are constructed.

COMPLEXITY
INTERMEDIATE

8.2 How do I... Understand a relative URL?

COMPATIBILITY: HTML 2+

Problem

When I've looked at some World Wide Web pages, I've seen URLs that don't have a protocol of any kind. Instead, they are just a filename or some kind of path. How do these kinds of URLs work?

Technique

When a URL does not begin with a protocol, that means it is referencing a file local to that computer (or possibly a file based on another computer; see How-To 8.3). Pathnames can be used to find files in directories other than the base directory.

Steps

To understand the following examples better, refer to Figure 8-1. This figure is a graphical representation of the directory structure used in the examples.

1. To access a file located in the same directory the current page is in, use only the name of the file as the URL. For example, if you are in `page1.html` and you want to go to `page2.html`, simply enter

```
page2.html
```

If you are in **page6.html** and you want to access **info.txt**, enter

```
info.txt
```

2. For files located in subdirectories of the current page's directory, include the subdirectory name(s), separated from the filename by a forward slash (/). For example, to get from **page1.html** to **page3.html**, enter

```
info/page3.html
```

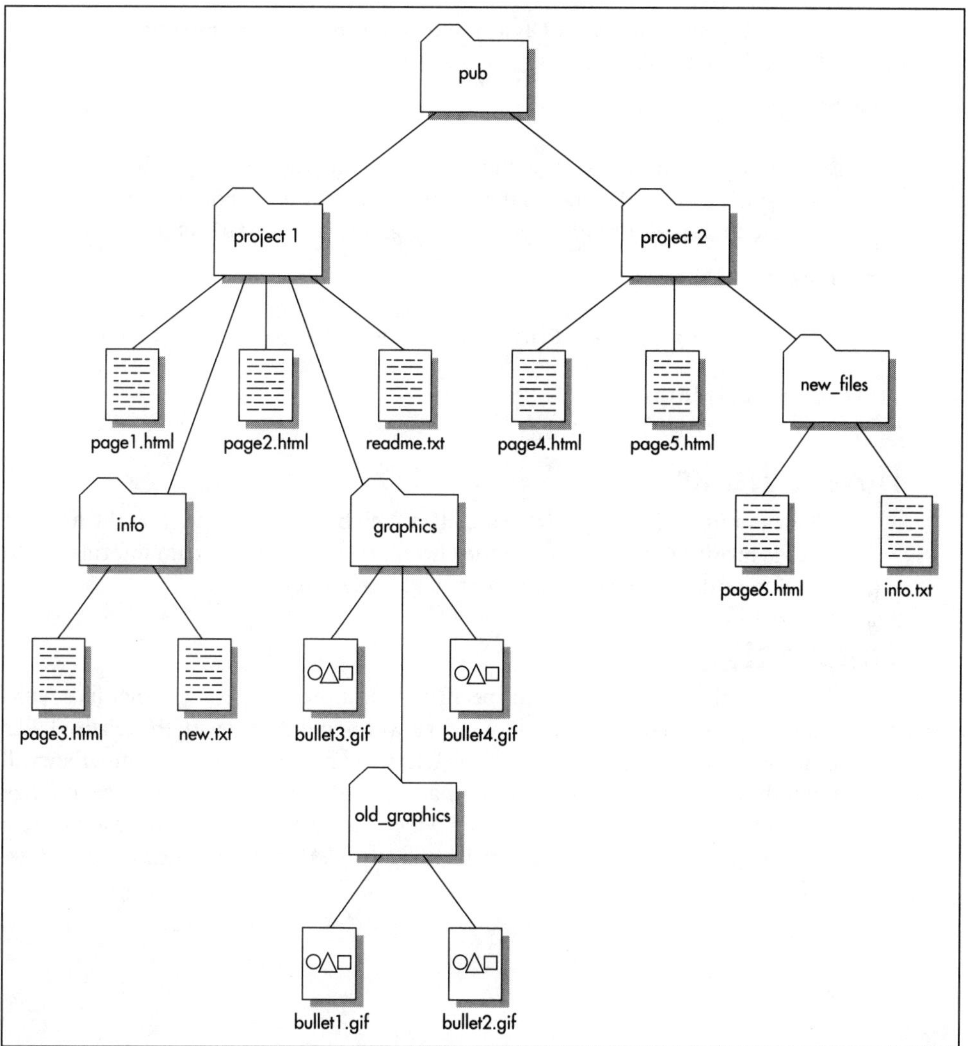

Figure 8-1 A sample directory structure

To get from **page2.html** to the file **bullet2.gif**, enter

```
graphics/old_graphics/bullet2.gif
```

3. For files located in parent directories (directories above the directory of the current page), use a double period (**..**) separated from the filename by a forward slash for each level up. For example, if you want to get back to **page4.html** from **page6.html**, enter

```
../page4.html
```

If you are in **bullet2.gif** and you want to access **readme.txt**, you will need to enter

```
../../readme.txt
```

4. You can combine steps 2 and 3 to access files located in directory branches separate from the branch the current directory is in. For example, if you are in **page4.html** and you want to go to **page2.html**, enter

```
../project1/page2.html
```

If you are in **page6.html** and you want to open **new.txt**, enter

```
../../files/project1/info/new.txt
```

How It Works

When a protocol is omitted from a URL, a Web browser assumes that the location given is relative to the location of the current page. It uses the path information to move up or down directories to locate and retrieve the file.

Comments

Relative URLs are a great way to specify the location of pages and other files without having to write out a full pathname. However, if the page with the relative URLs is moved to another directory, then the URLs will no longer work because they will point the way to files and directories that are not in the same relative location they originally were (unless, of course, all the files and directories are moved along with the page). You can solve this problem by using the **<BASE>** element described in How-To 8.3.

8.3 How do I... Add a base for relative URLs within the body of a document?

COMPATIBILITY: HTML 2+

Problem

I need to move a page with several relative URLs in it. However, I can't move the files along with the page and I don't want to spend the time editing the page to insert the new, longer pathnames for these files. How can I define a base for URLs in my document?

Technique

HTML has an element called **<BASE>** that can be included in the heading of a document to specify the base for all the relative URLs in the document. This enables you to move your page around without breaking the relative URLs, or permits you to use shortcuts in your URLs if you must reference several files from the same location.

Steps

1. Open your document and go to the heading section (between the **<HEAD>** and **</HEAD>** tags; see Chapter 2, "HTML Basics," for background information about headings in HTML documents).

2. Inside your page heading, insert the **<BASE>** tag. Inside the **<BASE>** tag, include the attribute **HREF** and set it equal to the full path for the desired directory, assuming that directory is located on the same computer as the page. For example, if you want to set the base for relative URLs to the directory **/pub/projects/data/**, enter

```
<HEAD>
<TITLE>My Page</TITLE>
<BASE HREF="/pub/projects/data/">
</HEAD>
```

3. If the desired base for your URLs is located on another computer, include the full URL, including the protocol and name of the computer. If, for example, the base is on a Web server at **www.stateu.edu** in the directory **pub/images**, you would enter

```
<HEAD>
<TITLE>My Page</TITLE>
<BASE HREF="http://www.stateu.edu/pub/images/">
</HEAD>
```

4. Or if the base is located on the FTP server **ftp.stateu.edu** in the directory **/pub/images**, the code would be

```
<HEAD>
<TITLE>My Page</TITLE>
<BASE HREF="ftp://ftp.stateu.edu/pub/images/">
</HEAD>
```

How It Works

The **<BASE>** element tells the browser to append the URL contained in it to any relative URLs located in the document. The contents of the **<BASE>** element are ignored for any URLs in the document that are fully formed, that is, that have protocols specified.

Comments

You can set the **<BASE>** element only once in a document, in the header. The **<BASE>** element does not work outside of the header. Therefore, if you have two sets of relative URLs for which you want to specify separate bases, you can use the **<BASE>** element for only one set. You must edit the other set to include the full pathnames and protocols.

COMPLEXITY
INTERMEDIATE

8.4 How do I... Specify a relationship between this document and other resources?

COMPATIBILITY: HTML 2+

Problem

I'm creating several Web pages that are all related to one another. I would like to be able to specify the relationship of each page to other pages for possible use by Web browsers. How can I specify a relationship between pages in HTML?

Technique

Use the **<LINK>** element in the header of an HTML document to identify relationships between documents and other resources. These relationships include preceding and following documents, tables of contents, indexes, and other document parts. The **<LINK>** element can also identify the author of a document.

Steps

1. Open your document and go to the heading section (between the **<HEAD>** and **</HEAD>** tags).

2. Place the **<LINK>** element in the header of a page.

```
<HEAD>
<TITLE>My Page</TITLE>
<LINK>
</HEAD>
```

3. The **<LINK>** element supports two kinds of attributes, **REL** and **REV**. **REL** indicates a relationship between the current document and a document listed in the element using the **HREF** attribute (as in How-To 8.3). The **REL** attribute can take on several different values. The most common ones, which have been reserved in HTML, are listed in Table 8-2.

Table 8-2 Values for the REL attribute in <LINK>

VALUE	DESCRIPTION
Bookmark	A specific section of a document
Copyright	A document with copyright information
Glossary	A glossary document
Help	A help document
Home	The home page or top of a hierarchy
Index	An index document
Next	The next document in a series
Previous	The previous document in a series
TOC	A table of contents document
Up	The parent document to the current one

A common use for these attributes is to identify the previous and next pages in a sequence of documents. For example, if your current page is the document **page4.html** and you want to identify the previous document (**page3.html**) and the next document (**page5.html**), you could use

```
<HEAD>
<TITLE>Page 4</TITLE>
<LINK REL=Previous HREF="page3.html">
<LINK REL=Next HREF="page5.html">
</HEAD>
```

Note that each reference is contained in a separate `<LINK>` element in the header.

4. The `REV` attribute is the opposite of `REL`. Instead of specifying another document's relationship to the current page, it specifies the current page's relationships to other pages. Applying this to the example results in the following:

```
<HEAD>
<TITLE>Page 4</TITLE>
<LINK REV=Next HREF="page3.html">
<LINK REV=Previous HREF="page5.html">
</HEAD>
```

You are now saying that this document (`page4.html`) is `page3.html`'s next document and `page5.html`'s previous document, instead of saying that `page4.html`'s previous document was `page3.html` and `page4.html`'s next document was `page5.html`. Confusing? This kind of confusion can be avoided by using one of the two attributes to specify relationships. `REL` is the attribute of choice for most people.

5. `REV` has found another use as a way to identify the author of the page. This can be done by placing the e-mail address of the author in a `mailto` URL (see How-To's 8.1 and 8.14 for more information about `mailto` URLs) and setting it equal to `REV`.

```
<HEAD>
<TITLE>Page 4</TITLE>
<LINK REV="mailto:jfoust@mit.edu">
</HEAD>
```

How It Works

The browser reads and stores the information contained in the `<LINK>` elements regarding the location of related files. Some browsers enables users to select those documents using a toolbar or other techniques.

Comments

`<LINK>` elements are a good way to indicate relationships among documents, but many Web browsers ignore the information contained in them. If you want to be sure that all readers have the ability to go to the files you've referenced in the `<LINK>` elements, you should include the links in the body of your page. Techniques for including these links are discussed starting in the next How-To.

8.5 How do I... Create a link to a local page?

COMPATIBILITY: HTML 2+

Problem

I would like to link one page I've created with another page, which is also located on my computer. How can I create a link in one of my pages that references a local page in HTML?

Technique

HTML uses the **<A>** and **</A>** tags to identify areas of the text that serve as anchors for links to other files. The **HREF** attribute in the **<A>** tag lists the location of the page or other resource.

Steps

1. Open your document. Decide what documents you would like to link to the current document.

2. Identify the word or phrase in your page that you want to use as an anchor for the link. Place the **<A>** tag at the beginning of the anchor and the **</A>** tag at the end of the anchor.

```
I enjoy watching <A>baseball</A>, but I'm not a good player.

I've visited <A>New York</A> a few times.
```

3. Inside the **<A>** tag, place the **HREF** attribute and set it equal to the filename of the other page, provided the destination page is located in the same directory as the page you're working on. The filename should be enclosed in double quotation marks.

```
I enjoy watching <A HREF="baseball.html">baseball</A>, but I'm not ⇐
a good player.

I've visited <A HREF="newyork.html">New York</A> a few times.
```

4. If the destination page is located in a subdirectory of the directory that contains your current page, you can indicate the path by including the subdirectory name(s) in the **HREF** attribute, separating the subdirectory names from each other and the filename with a forward slash (**/**), as shown in How-To 8.2:

```
I enjoy watching <A HREF="sports/baseball.html">baseball</A>, but I'm ⇐
not a good player.

I've visited <A HREF="usa/cities/east-coast/newyork.html">New York</A> ⇐
a few times.
```

5. If the destination page is located in a directory above the directory of your current page, you can go up the directory structure by using (`..`), two periods without any spacing between them, as shown in How-To 8.2.

```
I enjoy watching <A HREF="../baseball.html">baseball</A>, but I'm not ⇐
a good player.

I've visited <A HREF="../../newyork.html">New York</A> a few times.
```

6. Links can retrieve more than just other pages. You can include sounds, graphics, text files, and even compressed binary files in a link. For example, to include a link to a text file, enter

```
I have some <A HREF="info.txt">older information</A> about this subject.
```

Or to include a link to an image, enter

```
I took a <A HREF="gcanyon.gif">picture</A> of the Grand Canyon from ⇐
the South Rim.
```

Figure 8-2 shows some examples of links. The code is included on the CD-ROM as file `8-2.HTML`.

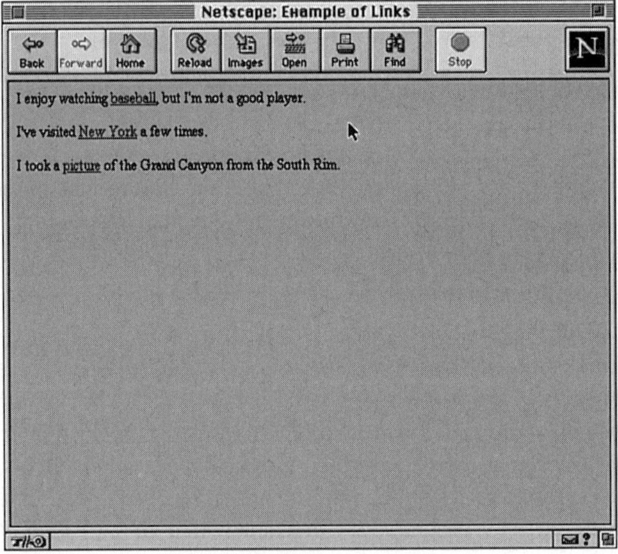

Figure 8-2 Examples of links

How It Works

The <A> and </A> tags tell the browser to identify the text contained between them as a link, which is usually done by highlighting or underlining the text. The **HREF** attribute provides the location of the file the browser should load if the link is selected. If the location of the file includes directory information, the browser assumes the location is given relative to the location of the current page. The **<BASE>** element (How-To 8.3) can be used to set that location to another path or even to another computer.

Comments

When a browser encounters a link to a file other than another WWW page, the browser decides how to deal with the file. Most browsers display a text file in the same manner as an HTML file (although with no formatting) and launch a helper application for other files: a graphics program for an image, an audio program for a sound file, and so on. This depends on the availability of a compatible external application. If no application exists on the reader's computer to handle a file, the file cannot be viewed or heard, although it can be saved for later use. Thus, when including links to images, sounds, and animation, try to use common formats for these files whenever possible.

8.6 How do I... Create a link to other pages?

COMPATIBILITY: HTML 2+

Problem

I would like to include a link to a page that has a lot of information relevant to my page. However, the page is located on another computer, so I can't use a link to a local page. How can I create a link to a page on another computer?

Technique

Using the Hypertext Transfer Protocol (HTTP), you can connect to one computer and transfer a copy of a document on that computer to a browser running on another computer by placing the URL of the document in the anchor of a link and using the **HREF** attribute.

Steps

1. Open your document. Locate the words or phrases to be used for the links.

2. Identify the text you want to use as a link by placing the `<A>` tag at the beginning of the anchor text and the `</A>` tag at the end of the anchor text.

```
I enjoy watching <A>baseball</A>, but I'm not a good player.

I've visited <A>New York</A> a few times.
```

3. Place the `HREF` attribute in the `<A>` tag and set it equal to the URL of the page. (See How-To 8.1 for more information about URLs.) Enclose the URL in double quotation marks.

```
I enjoy watching <A HREF="http://www.stateu.edu/sports/baseball.html">⇐
baseball</A>, but I'm not a good player.

I've visited <A HREF="http://www.stateu.edu/cities/newyork.html">⇐
New York </A> a few times.
```

4. This technique can transfer other types of files, such as text files and images. For example, to transfer a text file, simply use that file's pathname in the URL:

```
I have some <A HREF="http://www.stateu.edu/info/info.txt">older ⇐
information</A> about this subject.
```

Or to transfer an image, use the image file's pathname.

```
I took a <A HREF="http://www.stateu.edu/images/scenic/gcanyon.gif">⇐
picture</A> of the Grand Canyon from the South Rim.
```

5. You can use an `http` URL without a filename at the end for some special cases. Doing this displays the default page in the directory (usually named `index.html` or `default.html`, depending on how the HTTP server on that computer is configured), if it exists. Otherwise, it displays the contents of the directory, with the filenames linked to the files. For example, to load the default file on a subdirectory of `www.stateu.edu`, enter

```
I've created a new <A HREF="http://www.stateu.edu/pub/users/john/">home ⇐
page</A> in my user's directory.
```

How It Works

The `http` in the URL tells a browser to use the Hypertext Transfer Protocol to locate and transfer the file listed in the URL. The browser displays the page just like a local file. For text files, images, and other files, the browser uses the URL to locate the file and then transfers a copy using HTTP. The browser then displays the contents of the file or transfers the file to the appropriate external application.

Comments

Web servers often use different filenames for the default file. For example, CERN HTTPD uses `default.html`, whereas NCSA HTTPD uses `index.html`. On computer systems that support only three-letter file extensions, the filenames would be `default.htm` or `index.htm`, respectively. Some browsers might be configured to use a specific name instead of either of these two; check the server documentation or ask the webmaster of the site for specific information.

COMPLEXITY
INTERMEDIATE

8.7 How do I... Send data to an HTTP server via a URL?

COMPATIBILITY: HTML 2+

Problem

I'm developing a form to include in a page using a search keyword, and I want to be able to send the results to a server to be processed by a program there. Is there a way to include that response or other information in a URL to send to a server?

Technique

It is possible to include keywords or other basic pieces of information in a URL. A question mark is placed at the end of the URL for an application, followed by the data. Browsers usually do this automatically when they submit data.

Steps

1. Open your document. Locate the words or phrases for the links to the HTTP server.

2. If you want to include a keyword or other data in a link, first create an anchor in the text appropriate to the data you want to send. For example, to create a pair of links that will send the answers yes or no to a question, enter

```
<H3>Do you want to subscribe to our magazine?</H3>?
<UL>
<LI><A>Yes!</A>
<LI><A>No thanks</A>
</UL>
```

3. Use the `HREF` attribute to add a link to a program on an HTTP server that will receive the data. (For now, don't worry about the specifics of the program. Forms and CGI applications are covered in Chapter 11, "HTML Interactive Forms," and Chapter 14, "The Common Gateway Interface (CGI)," respectively.) If, for example, the program is called "response" and is located on the HTTP server at **www.stateu.edu**, your code would look like this:

```
<H3>Do you want to subscribe to our magazine?</H3>?
<UL>
<LI><A HREF="http://www.stateu.edu/applications/response">Yes!</A>
<LI><A HREF="http://www.stateu.edu/applications/response">No thanks</A>
</UL>
```

4. Now add to the end of the URL a question mark and the keyword you want sent to the application. For this example, let the responses be yes and no.

```
<H3>Do you want to subscribe to our magazine?</H3>?
<UL>
<LI><A HREF="http://www.stateu.edu/applications/response?yes">Yes!</A>
<LI><A HREF="http://www.stateu.edu/applications/response?no">No ⇐
thanks</A>
</UL>
```

How It Works

The browser interprets anything in a URL after a question mark to be data that is sent to a URL. The application referenced in the URL then receives the keyword as input and processes it accordingly.

Comments

The example shown here can actually be done better with forms. See Chapter 11 to find out how to create forms for your pages, and see Chapter 14 to see how to write applications to process the data. When keyword searching is enabled (using the **<ISINDEX>** tag in the header, as shown in Chapter 14), the question mark and keyword are added automatically and don't need to be included manually in the URL.

COMPLEXITY
INTERMEDIATE

8.8 How do I... Create a link to a specific part of a page?

COMPATIBILITY: HTML 2+

Problem

I have a long document that I am converting into a WWW page using HTML. I want to use a table of contents to refer to the various sections of the document so the reader can quickly refer to those sections. I would also like to be able to refer to different sections of the document from other pages. How can I create a link to a specific part of a page in HTML?

Technique

The **NAME** attribute used in the anchor tag identifies a section of a page. Users can then access this section via a link from within the document or from other documents.

Steps

1. Open your document. Identify the words or phrases that will serve as links. Also decide what sections of the document you want links to lead to.

2. To identify a section of a document, place the **<A>** and **</A>** tags at the beginning of the section. Include the **NAME** attribute in the **<A>** tag and set it to the name you want to give the section. Enclose the name in double quotation marks. Unlike the **<LINK>** tags, there is no need to include any text between the **<A>** and **</A>** tags.

```
<A NAME="section1"></A>
<H1>Section 1</H1>
<!-- text of section 1 -->
```

3. To include a link to the named section elsewhere in your page, create a link as described in How-To 8.5 and set **HREF** equal to the name of the section as defined by the **NAME** attribute. Enclose the name in double quotation marks and precede it with a pound symbol (**#**) to differentiate it from the name of another document.

```
You will find the relevant background information in ⇐
<A HREF="#section1">section 1</A>.
```

4. To include a link to the named section from another local document, create a local link as described in How-To 8.5 and include the name of the section, preceded by the pound symbol (#), in the location of the link defined by the HREF attribute.

```
You will find the relevant background information in ⇐
<A HREF="report.html#section1">section 1</A>.
```

5. For documents located on other computers, the process is similar. Attach the name of the section, preceded by the pound symbol (#), to the end of the URL for the document.

```
You will find the relevant background information in ⇐
<A HREF="http://www.stateu.edu/documents/report.html#section1">⇐
section 1</A>.
```

How It Works

When a browser loads a URL with a # symbol, it looks for the section of the document with an anchor tag matching the name after the # symbol. The browser then displays the loaded page, with the beginning of the named section at the top of the screen.

Comments

When used to create links, the <A> tag must include text. When <A> tags are used merely to identify a section of a document, text is not necessary. This is because the tag is being used only to mark a section of a document for later use in a link, not to function as a link to another document. There is no need to include text between the tags, because this text is not highlighted and cannot be used to jump to another document or section of a document.

8.9 How do I... Create a link to an FTP site?

COMPATIBILITY: HTML 2+

Problem

I've found a file that I would like to include as a link in my page. However, the file is not accessible on the World Wide Web, only by anonymous FTP. How can I add a link to a file on an FTP site?

Technique

You can construct a URL for the file located on the FTP site and include that in a standard HTML link. The link will function like a link to a page or other document accessible via HTTP.

Steps

1. Open the document and find the words or phrases you want to use as links.

2. To construct the URL, you must know the name of the site where the file is located and the path for the file (that is, the directory in which the file is located). For example, to access a file named **contents.txt** located on the server **ftp.stateu.edu** in the directory **pub/info**, you would use this URL:

```
ftp://ftp.stateu.edu/pub/info/contents.txt
```

To access the image file **gcanyon.gif** from **ftp.stateu.edu** in the directory **pub/photos/arizona**, you would use this URL:

```
ftp://ftp.stateu.edu/pub/photos/arizona/gcanyon.gif
```

3. You can now include either of these URLs in a link by setting the **HREF** attribute of the link equal to the URL.

```
The <A HREF="ftp://ftp.stateu.edu/pub/info/contents.txt">contents</A>
of the directory can be easily viewed.

I took an incredible ⇐
<A HREF="ftp://ftp.stateu.edu/pub/photos/arizona/gcanyon.gif">⇐
photo</A> of the Grand Canyon during my last trip there!
```

4. You can use FTP URLs to access entire directories and display their contents in the browser window. To do this, include the pathname to the directory in the URL, but do not add a filename to the end of the URL.

```
My <A HREF="ftp://ftp.stateu.edu/pub/photos/">photos directory</A> ⇐
contains a lot of pictures I took while on vacation in Arizona.
```

Figure 8-3 shows an example of an FTP directory accessed in HTML.

5. By default, the FTP URL uses anonymous FTP. However, you can create an FTP URL that uses nonanonymous FTP. To do so, include the username and password, separated by a colon, in front of the address of the FTP site. Include the **@** symbol between the password and the computer address. To access the FTP server at **ftp.stateu.edu** as user weather using the password **stormy**, you would use the following code:

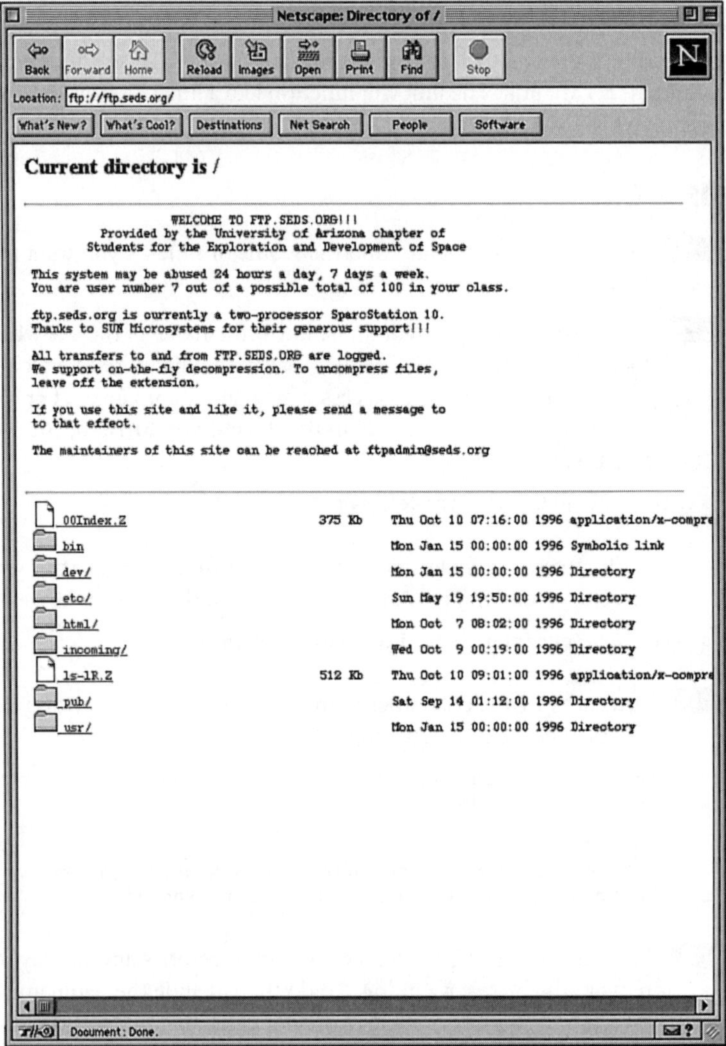

Figure 8-3 An FTP site as viewed in a Web browser

```
There is an archive of ⇐
<A HREF="ftp://weather:stormy@ftp.stateu.edu/pub/weather/">weather⇐
data </A> that includes satellite photos and updated forecasts.
```

How It Works

When a link with an FTP URL is selected, the browser opens an FTP connection with the specified computer. It goes to the appropriate directory and copies the file. The file then appears in the browser window or in an external application, depending on the type of file retrieved.

Comments

Unlike manually FTPing files, there is no need to specify whether to transfer a file as a binary, or ASCII, file. The browser checks the suffix of the file. If it matches a suffix associated with binary files, the file is transferred as a binary file. Otherwise, it is transferred as a text file. Also, unless a username and password are specified, most browsers automatically log in to the FTP site as anonymous and transfer a string, usually your e-mail address, as the password. If you do include a nonanonymous FTP URL in your page, remember that the password is available for anyone to view, so don't put the password to your account there. This should be used only for special, limited-use accounts for which passwords can be distributed freely.

8.10 How do I... Create a link to a Gopher site?

COMPATIBILITY: HTML 2+

Problem

I would like to reference a file stored on a Gopher server for my page. How can I add a link to a Gopher server? Can I go directly to the file or do I have to go through the directory structure of the Gopher server?

Technique

Several years ago, Gopher servers were a popular method of making information easily available to Internet users. Even with the rapid growth of the World Wide Web, many Gopher servers are still in use and contain information you might want to reference on your page. This can be done with a Gopher URL, either to the top-level directory or directly to the file.

Steps

1. Open the document and find the words or phrases you want to use as links.

2. Define the anchor text in your page using the **<A>** tag.

```
There is a <A>Gopher site</A> with more information on baseball.
```

3. To construct a URL for the top-level directory of a Gopher server, take the address of the Gopher site and attach **gopher://** to the front of it, such as **gopher://gopher.stateu.edu**. You can then set the **HREF** attribute in the link tag equal to this URL.

```
There is a <A HREF="gopher://gopher.stateu.edu">Gopher site</A> with
more information on baseball.
```

4. To construct a URL for a specific file or directory on a Gopher server, you must know the full path to it. To get this information, you will need to check the Gopher server and find the URL for it (usually available by selecting the Display technical information about this item option in most Gopher programs). As a rule, files have a `/00/` in their URL after the name of the server, directories have a `/11/` after the name of the server, and spaces in file or directory names are represented in the URL by the code `%20`. For example, to reference a file on a Gopher server, enter

```
There is a <A HREF="gopher://gopher.stateu.edu/00/teams/yankees.txt">⇐
file</A> with more information on the New York Yankees.
```

To reference a directory on a Gopher server, enter

```
There is a <A HREF="gopher://gopher.stateu.edu/11/teams">directory</A>
with information on all the major league baseball teams.
```

To reference a file with a space in its name, enter

```
There is a <A REF="gopher://gopher.stateu.edu/00/teams/the%20yankees">⇐
file</A> with information on the New York Yankees.
```

How It Works

When a Gopher link is selected, the browser contacts the site given in the URL using the `gopher` protocol and returns the information requested, either a file or a directory. The browser displays the file based on its rules for file types; text files usually display in the window, but image and sound files retrieved by `gopher` are sent to the appropriate external application. If a directory is retrieved, it appears in the window, with each directory item serving as a link to another Gopher item.

Comments

Before including a link to a specific directory or file on a Gopher server, be sure to check the exact URL for the file. Different servers use different methods of defining paths to files and directories, and the name of the file or directory given in the Gopher menu might be entirely different from the real name and location of the resource.

COMPLEXITY
INTERMEDIATE

8.11 How do I... Create a link to a Telnet site?

COMPATIBILITY: HTML 2+

Problem

I would like to create a link to an Internet resource accessible only by Telnet. I don't know how to include all the information, with the username and port number as well, in the URL. How do I create a link to a Telnet site in HTML?

Technique

A Telnet URL is similar to those used for FTP and Gopher sites. You can specify the port number, the username, and the password for logging in to the site.

Steps

1. Open the document and find the words or phrases you want to use as links.

2. As with other links, first specify the anchor text for the link in your document. Place the **<A>** tag at the beginning of the anchor and the **</A>** tag at the end of the anchor.

```
The State University <A>weather server</A> provides updated forecasts
and weather conditions.
```

3. To create a standard Telnet login using the standard port and not specifying the username or password, place **telnet://** in front of the address of the site, such as **telnet://suvax.stateu.edu**. You can now set the **HREF** attribute in the anchor tag equal to this URL.

```
The State University <A HREF="telnet://suvax.stateu.edu">weather server⇐
</A> provides updated forecasts and weather conditions.
```

4. Many special services offered by Telnet operate from a nonstandard port. To specify the port to which to Telnet, place a colon after the address of the site and add the port number after the colon.

```
The State University <A HREF="telnet://suvax.stateu.edu:3000">weather ⇐
server</A> provides updated forecasts and weather conditions.
```

5. To specify the username to be used when logging in to the Telnet site, place the username in front of the site address and separate the two with the @ symbol.

```
The State University <A HREF="telnet://weather@suvax.stateu.edu">weather⇐
server</A> provides updated forecasts and weather conditions.
```

6. To provide a password as well as a username, place a colon after the username and insert the password between the colon and @ symbol.

```
The State University <A HREF="telnet://weather:stormy@suvax.stateu.edu">⇐
weather server</A> provides updated forecasts ⇐
and weather conditions.
```

How It Works

When a Telnet link is selected, the browser starts up a Telnet session using the Telnet program set by the browser. The port number, username, and password, if provided, are used to establish the connection.

Comments

To be able to use a Telnet link, a browser must be able to access a Telnet program on the browser's computer; otherwise, the link cannot be used. The Telnet program that the browser uses is defined by the browser and can usually be changed by the reader. Because URLs are freely available and not encrypted, placing the password for an account in a URL creates a serious security hazard to that computer, unless the account is especially designed to be used solely for special applications. When in doubt, do not place the password to a computer account in a URL.

COMPLEXITY
INTERMEDIATE

8.12 How do I... Create a link to a WAIS site?

COMPATIBILITY: HTML 2+

Problem

I would like to access a WAIS database of information relevant to a topic on my page. How can I include a link to a WAIS server on my page?

Technique

WAIS provides the ability to conduct keyword searches on a variety of databases. You can include a link to a WAIS URL in your document that enables users to search a specific database on a topic or topics.

Steps

1. Open the document and find the words or phrases you want to use as links.

2. Identify the anchor for the link. Place the `<A>` tag at the beginning of the link and `</A>` at the end of the link.

```
You can also search a <A>database</A> of reports and other information
on this topic.
```

3. Create the URL for the WAIS database by adding the protocol tag `wais://` in front of the name of the server. Include information on the location of the database after the name of the server. If the WAIS server is running on a port other than the standard port (210), include the port number after the address of the computer and separate the two items with a colon. Set the `HREF` attribute in the anchor tag equal to this URL.

```
You can also search a ⇐
<A HREF="wais://server.stateu.edu/report-database.src">database</A>⇐
 of reports and other information on this topic.

You can also search a ⇐
<A HREF="wais://server.stateu.edu:8001/report-database.src">⇐
database</A>of reports and other information on this topic.
```

4. To specify a keyword for a WAIS search, include the keyword at the end of the URL and separate it from the name of the database with the question mark symbol. To search for all documents that contain the keyword `baseball`, enter

```
You can also search a ⇐
<A HREF="wais://server.stateu.edu/report-database.src?baseball">⇐
database </A> of reports and other information on this topic.
```

How It Works

The `wais` protocol tag in a URL informs the browser to start a WAIS search on the given database using the keyword, if provided. The browser then returns the results of the search in the window, often listing the filenames of the documents that have the given keyword and providing links to the files.

Comments

Many browsers either do not support WAIS searches or require that special software be installed to run the searches. Fortunately, not many WAIS databases are available, and few people include links to WAIS databases in their pages. There has been some development of software that enables users to conduct WAIS searches using forms. (See Chapter 11, "HTML Interactive Forms," for more information on how forms work.) This method will probably supersede the `wais` protocol tag in HTML.

8.13 How do I... Create a link to a Usenet newsgroup?

COMPATIBILITY: HTML 2+

Problem

I want to reference a Usenet newsgroup that is relevant to the subject of my page. How do I create a link to a Usenet newsgroup in HTML? Does the reader need special newsreading software to access the newsgroup?

Technique

Usenet newsgroups, forums for discussion on a wide range of topics, can be accessed from a page. No special software is needed, and the titles of the articles usually appear as a list of links to the articles themselves within the Web browser after the user specifies the address of a news server.

Steps

1. Open the document and find the words or phrases you want to use as links.

2. As with other links, mark the anchor text for the link. Place the **<A>** tag at the beginning of the anchor text and the **</A>** tag at the end of the anchor text.

```
A number of <A>discussions</A> about the Big Bang are in progress.
```

3. You can create the URL for the newsgroup by appending the name of the newsgroup to the protocol tag **news:**. You can then set the **HREF** attribute equal to this URL.

```
A number of <A HREF="news:sci.astro">discussions</A> about the Big Bang
are in progress.
```

4. In some cases, you can refer to a specific server for newsgroup articles. The URL in this case is constructed much like the URL for Web or FTP sites, with the name of the server followed by the name of the newsgroup.

```
A number of <A HREF="news://news.state-u.edu/sci.astro">discussions</A>
about the Big Bang are in progress.
```

This is not a feature of HTML 4.0, but is supported by Microsoft Internet Explorer and Netscape Navigator.

How It Works

When a news URL is selected, the browser accesses the newsgroup from its newsfeed. The titles of the unread articles (articles you have not yet read) appear in the window, serving as links to the full text of the articles.

Comments

To use a news link successfully, the reader's browser must have access to a newsfeed, and unless the server is specified in the URL, the newsgroup in question must be carried by the browser's newsfeed. Keep this in mind when you are creating links to local, limited-distribution newsgroups. If you include links to Seattle-area newsgroups, for example, it's unlikely that a reader in Boston has a newsfeed that carries these newsgroups and hence won't be able to access them.

8.14 How do I... Create a link to electronic mail?

COMPATIBILITY: HTML 2+

Problem

I would like to include a link that will let readers send e-mail to me with their comments about my page. I want to keep this simple and not take the time and trouble of creating a form and software to parse the form. How can I include a link to electronic mail in HTML?

Technique

HTML includes a URL tag called **mailto**, which identifies the address to which e-mail should be sent. If the link is selected, the browser will start a mail program to send a message to the recipient listed in the URL.

Steps

1. Open the document and find the words or phrases you want to use as links.

2. Identify the anchor text to be used for the link by placing the **<A>** tag at the beginning of the anchor and the **</A>** tag at the end of the anchor.

```
Send me <A>e-mail</A> with your comments about my page.
```

3. Create the URL for the link by placing the protocol tag **mailto:** in front of the e-mail address to which mail should be sent. Set the **HREF** attribute in **<A>** equal to this URL.

```
Send me <A HREF="mailto:nobody@stateu.edu">e-mail</A> with your comments
about my page.
```

4. Netscape versions 2 and later enable you to specify the subject of the message in the **mailto** tag. This information will appear in the **Subject:** line of the mail message when the mail window appears. To include this, enter a question mark (**?**) after the e-mail address, then the word **subject**, an equal sign, and the desired subject line for the message. For example, to include a subject line called **My Comments** in the example, you would enter

```
Send me <A HREF="mailto:nobody@stateu.edu?subject=My Comments">e-mail⇐
</A> with your comments about my page.
```

How It Works

When a **mailto** link is selected, the browser starts up its electronic mail program (as defined by the browser), setting the **To:** line in the message to the address given in the URL.

Comments

The **mailto** URL works successfully only if the browser has access to an electronic mail program. The program used can usually be set by the user. Using forms (see Chapter 11, "HTML Interactive Forms") is often a better way to get feedback on a page because it doesn't require the use of an external program. The subject line addition to the **mailto** URL that works in Netscape will not work in most other browsers (one exception is Microsoft Internet Explorer 3.02 when used in conjunction with Microsoft Internet Mail), and it might even make the link useless for the user. Take care when using it in an open environment.

8.15 How do I... Create links to pages in other users' home directories?

COMPATIBILITY: HTML 2+

Problem

I'd like to access some pages located in another user's directory. However, I would like to be able to shorten the length of the URL and not type the full path to the page. Is there a way I can easily create links to pages in other users' home directories?

Technique

On UNIX file systems, it is possible to abbreviate the path to a user's home directory by using the username preceded by the tilde (~) symbol. This can be used on local and remote systems to shorten the length of the URL of a page.

Steps

1. Open the document and find the words or phrases you want to use as links.

2. Specify the anchored text in your document. Place the **<A>** tag at the beginning of the anchor and **</A>** at the end of the anchor.

```
There's more information on the topic on <A>John's page</A>.
```

3. If the page is located in another user's directory on the same computer as your page, you can reach that user's home directory by using the username preceded by a tilde. For example, to access a page in user John's home directory, enter

```
There's more information on the topic on <A HREF="~john/info.html>⇐
John's page</A>.
```

You can also access another user's subdirectories by including them in the URL. For example, if the page listed here were located in the subdirectory **pub**, you would enter

```
There's more information on the topic on <A HREF="~john/pub/info.html>⇐
John's page</A>.
```

4. This technique also works for pages in users' directories on other computers. If John's page is located on the computer **www.stateu.edu** in his home directory, you could create the following link to it:

```
There's more information on the topic on ⇐
<A HREF="http://www.stateu.edu/~john/info.html>John's page</A>.
```

If the page is located in a subdirectory, it could be accessed by including the directory path in the URL.

```
There's more information on the topic on ⇐
<A HREF="http://www.stateu.edu/~john/pub/info.html>John's page</A>.
```

How It Works

The ~ symbol in the URL tells the browser to go to the home directory or to the listed subdirectory of the specified user and retrieve the document.

Comments

The ~ notation works only for computer systems that support multiple users and use UNIX or a variation of UNIX. Also, for a document to be retrievable in this way, its author must have given permission by making the contents of the directory readable by all users.

8.16 How do I... Add links to lists and tables?

COMPATIBILITY: HTML 2+ (LISTS), HTML 3+ (TABLES)

Problem

I would like to create a menu for the reader by organizing a set of links to different pages. It seems that the best way to do this is with a list or a table. How can I add links to lists and tables in HTML?

Technique

You can add links to lists and tables just as you would to ordinary text on a page. Each list item or table entry can serve as a link to a different page, FTP site, and so on.

Steps

1. Open the document and decide what information you would like to display in lists or tables and what resources you would like to link to a different page, FTP site, and the like.

2. Create the list or table, including all the list items and table entries, just as you would with an ordinary list or table. For example, a list might look like this:

```
<UL>
    <LI>Boston Red Sox
    <LI>New York Yankees
    <LI>Toronto Blue Jays
</UL>
```

A similar table might be formatted as follows:

```
<TABLE BORDER=1>
<TR><TH>Team<TH>Wins<TH>Losses
    <TR><TD>Boston Red Sox<TD>90<TD>72
    <TR><TD>New York Yankees<TD>88<TD>74
    <TR><TD>Toronto Blue Jays<TD>77<TD>85
</TABLE>
```

3. Now add the links where appropriate in the list or table, just as you would in the text of a document.

```
<UL>
    <LI><A HREF="redsox.html">Boston Red Sox</A>
    <LI><A HREF="yankees.html">New York Yankees</A>
    <LI><A HREF="bluejays.html">Toronto Blue Jays</A>
</UL>
<TABLE BORDER=1>
<TR><TH>Team<TH>Wins<TH>Losses
    <TR><TD><A HREF="redsox.html">Boston Red Sox</A><TD>90<TD>72
    <TR><TD><A HREF="yankees.html">New York Yankees</A><TD>88<TD>74
    <TR><TD><A HREF="bluejays.html">Toronto Blue Jays</A><TD>77<TD>85
</TABLE>
```

Figure 8-4 shows the output of this list and table. The code is available on the CD-ROM as file `8-4.HTML`.

How It Works

Links in lists and tables are treated the same as links elsewhere in a document. You can add links of all types that function exactly the same as links in other parts of a document.

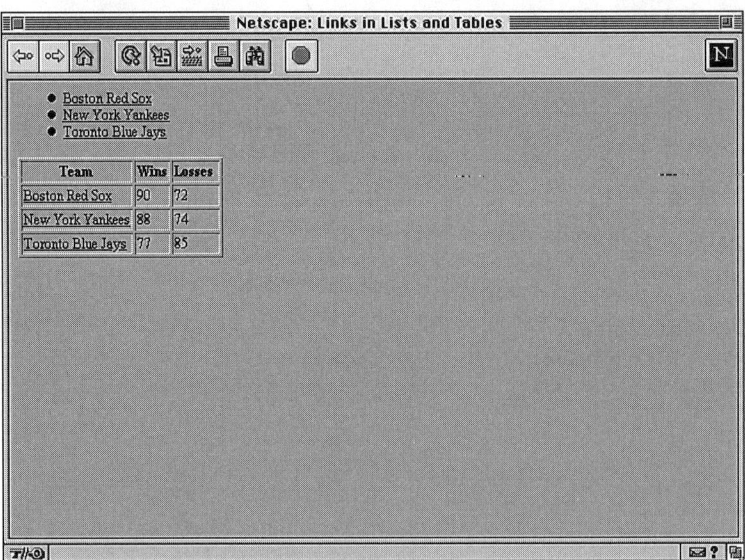

Figure 8-4 Examples of lists and tables with links

Comments

A good way to use links in lists and tables is to create a table of contents or a menu of choices for the reader. This works best if each link is given one line of the list or one entry in the table. Links can extend over multiple list or table entries, but they become less useful that way.

COMPLEXITY
INTERMEDIATE

8.17 How do I... Add links to my home page?

COMPATIBILITY: HTML 2, HTML 3+

Problem

I now know all about creating links in a page. However, I'm not sure how to put them into my document—that is, where they should go, how they should relate to the text of my document, and so on. How can I effectively add links to my home page?

Technique

There are many ways links can be used in a page. Consequently, there are many ways links can be misused as well. Some common problems with the use of links are described next, along with solutions to those problems.

Steps

These steps assume you know the basics of constructing links. These tips will help you use that knowledge to create effective ones.

1. First and foremost, a link must have some text or graphics (see How-To 9.12) that a reader can select. The following link might be to the best resource on the World Wide Web, but it will be useless for the reader of the document because, with no text between the anchor elements, there is no way to select the link:

```
<A HREF="http://www.stateu.edu/cool.html"></A>
```

Always make sure there is some relevant text between the anchor elements to permit readers to select the link.

An exception to this is when the **NAME** attribute is used in the anchor. Because the **NAME** attribute identifies only a specific location in a document and is not itself a link to another resource, the following usage is valid:

```
<A NAME="section1"></A>
```

In fact, this is often the best way to identify sections of a page without including additional text.

2. One of the most common problems with links, and one of the most annoying, is what is often called the *click here* syndrome. An example of code with this problem might look like this:

```
<A HREF="coolpic.gif">Click here</A> for a cool picture I took!
```

There are several problems with this statement. First, it disrupts the flow of a document. To understand this better, look at the following example:

```
The St. Louis Browns were one of baseball's most infamous teams.
<A HREF="badteams.html">Click here</A> for information on other bad
teams in baseball history. They appeared in only one World Series, in
1944, when most of baseball's stars were in the armed forces during
World War II. For more information on the World Series, click
<A HREF="series.html">here</A>. Their Series opponents were their
hometown rivals, the St. Louis Cardinals. All the games in that series
were played in one stadium, Sportsman's Park, the home stadium for both
teams. <A HREF="sportsman.gif">Click here</A> for a picture of
Sportsman's Park.
```

(This paragraph is shown in Figure 8-5. The code is available on the CD-ROM as file **8-5.HTML**.)

Imagine reading this without being able to access the links. All the `click here` statements disrupt the flow of the paragraph. Although it's thoughtful of the writer to explain what all the links are, the extra

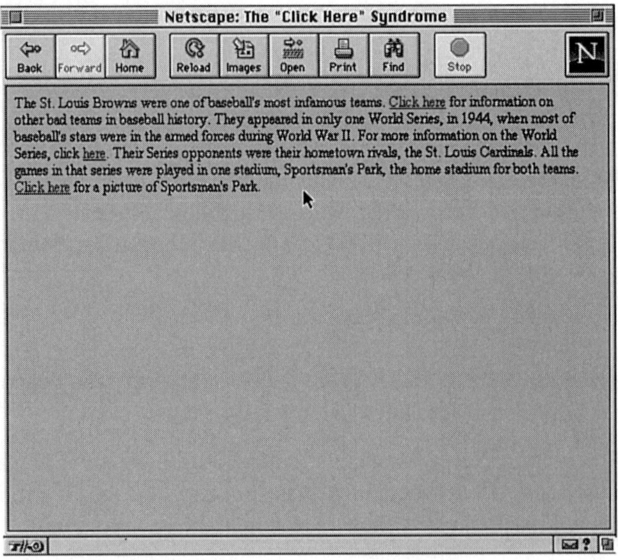

Figure 8-5 The `click here` syndrome

sentences make it harder to understand the main points of the paragraph. A solution to this problem is to use relevant words and phrases in the paragraph as anchors for the links. This will be discussed in more detail shortly.

Another problem with the **`click here`** statement is that it assumes that all readers of the page are using a graphical Web browser. Many people access the Web using a text-based browser such as Lynx. For these users, links are usually selected by a number, not by using a mouse, so the **`click here`** terminology is not useful for them, and it could even be confusing.

3. Another problem with links, at an extreme from the **`click here`** problem, are poorly labeled links. Ideally, the anchor phrase and the context of that phrase within the document should indicate where, in general, the link will lead. However, it's not uncommon for links to refer to resources that don't clearly follow from the anchor text. For example:

```
The St. Louis Browns were one of baseball's most infamous
<A HREF="badteams.html">teams</A>. They <A HREF="series.html">
appeared</A> in only one World Series, in 1944, when most of baseball's
stars were in the armed forces during World War II. Their Series
opponents were their hometown rivals, the St. Louis Cardinals. All the
games in that series were played in one <A HREF="sportsman.gif">stadium
</A>, Sportsman's Park, the home stadium for both teams.
```

(This paragraph is shown in Figure 8-6. The code is available on the CD-ROM as file **8-6.HTML**.)

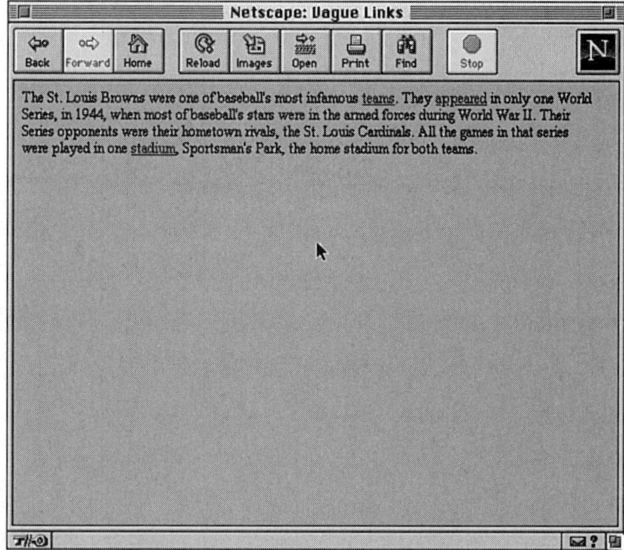

Figure 8-6 An example of vague links

The problem here is not a profusion of **click here** statements but of vague links. If a user reads this and sees the word **teams** in the top line linked, he or she might not know where that link leads: a list of bad teams, a list of all the teams in baseball, or general information about teams.

There is a middle ground between these two problems, a way to incorporate links into a document smoothly and still make it clear from the context of the document what the function of each link is. The sample paragraph, reworked, illustrates the solution.

```
The St. Louis Browns were one of baseball's most
<A HREF="badteams.html">infamous teams</A>. They appeared in only one
<A HREF="series.html">World Series</A>, in 1944, when most of baseball's
stars were in the armed forces during World War II. Their Series
opponents were their hometown rivals, the St. Louis Cardinals. All the
games in that series were played in one stadium, <A HREF="sportsman.gif">
Sportsman's Park</A>, the home stadium for both teams.
```

(This paragraph is shown in Figure 8-7. The code is available on the CD-ROM as file **8-7.HTML**.)

The **click here** statements have been eliminated and the function of the links is clearer. Seeing **infamous teams** linked, for example, suggests to the reader that the link probably leads to some specific information on bad teams. In some cases you might need to rewrite the text slightly to use this technique, but it is best if links can derive their meaning from the context of the document.

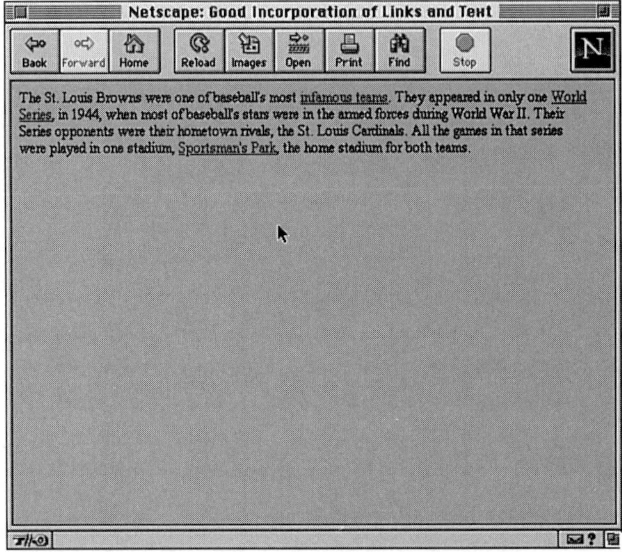

Figure 8-7 Good incorporation of links in text

4. Similarly, it is often useful to add explanatory information when using links in lists. Using short link names in a list of links might make it easy to create the list, but it might make it hard for a reader to decipher what each option specifically offers. For example, consider this list of links:

```
<H3>Menu of Options</H3>
<UL>
<LI><A HREF="intro.html">Introduction</A>
<LI><A HREF="techdata.html">Technical Data</A>
<LI><A HREF="prices.html">Price List</A>
<LI><A HREF="comments.html">Comments</A>
</UL>
```

Reading this, you can get some idea of what each link leads to, but it's hard to tell what information each option has, short of selecting it. Adding a bit of description can help a user better understand the contents of each list option. A good way to do this is with a glossary list (see Chapter 6, "Lists"). Applying a glossary list to this example would create the following:

```
<H3>Menu of Options</H3>
<DL>
<DT><A HREF="intro.html">Introduction</A>
<DD>A welcome message from the President and some background material ⇐
about widgets.
<DT><A HREF="techdata.html">Technical Data</A>
<DD>Technical specifications for all 13 types of widgets we sell
<DT><A HREF="prices.html">Price List</A>
```

```
<DD>A complete list of prices for all widgets and information ⇐
on special sales
<DT><A HREF="comments.html">Comments</A>
<DD>How to send us your comments and suggestions
</DL>
```

This list gives the reader a much clearer idea of the functionality of each link. These two lists are shown in Figure 8-8. This code is available on the CD-ROM as file **8-8.HTML**.

How It Works

The key to using links is to incorporate them into the text of your document as smoothly as possible, but without obscuring their meaning. The examples given show that, with some practice, this can be done.

Comments

Links make the World Wide Web just that: a web of information spanning the globe. By incorporating links to other documents in your pages (and, invariably, having your pages included as links in other people's documents), you can spin your own little section of the World Wide Web.

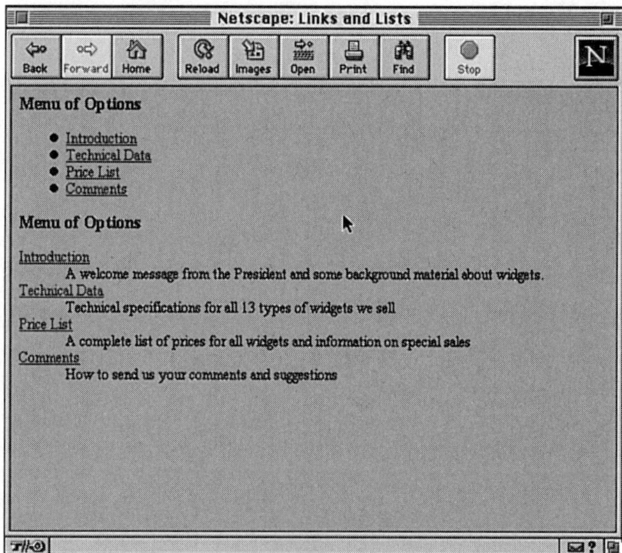

Figure 8-8 Bad and good ways to include links in lists

CHAPTER 9

USING IMAGES IN YOUR DOCUMENTS

9

USING IMAGES IN YOUR DOCUMENTS

How do I...

One key feature that distinguishes the World Wide Web from other parts of the Internet is images. Images, when used correctly, can liven up a Web page. This chapter shows numerous ways in which you can add images to make your HTML documents more interesting to read and to look at.

9.1 Build an Icon to Use in an HTML Document

Icons liven up an HTML document and help make a page more concise and compact by replacing a lot of words with one picture. This How-To shows how you can create icons for your documents.

9.2 Add an Inline Image

Now that you know how to create an icon, you must include it in your HTML documents. This How-To shows how easy it is to add images to your documents.

9.3 Align Images and Text Using the Advanced Tags

This How-To shows you several options you can use when aligning text and images in your documents.

9.4 Use the <ALT> Tag for Nongraphical Browsers

Sometimes a reader looking at your document is using a browser that can't view images or that has image loading turned off. This How-To shows how to use the **<ALT>** tag to put up a text description in place of an image.

9.5 Include an Image with a Transparent Background

Standard inline images display on a browser with white space around the edges. Although this is sometimes acceptable, it can look unprofessional at times. This How-To shows how to make an image's background transparent so it will blend in with the document.

9.6 Create an Interlaced Inline Image on My Page

Standard GIF images load from top to bottom. This is fine, but somewhat bland. Interlacing enables an entire image to load in a complete but low-resolution form, then build up to higher and higher resolution. This How-To shows how to make GIF images into interlaced images and suggests strategies for using them.

9.7 Create a Thumbnail Version of an Image

Thumbnail versions of images are not as large and as time-consuming to load as full-fledged versions of images. Therefore, there are times when it is beneficial to display a thumbnail copy of an image on a page. This How-To shows several ways to create thumbnail images.

9.8 Use an Image as a Link

Replacing or augmenting a text link with an image that links to another document can be a nice touch. This How-To shows how to use images as links.

9.9 Create a Background Pattern for My Page

HTML 3.0 and on up have the feature of being able to change your background color. This How-To demonstrates how to change the background on your pages to be virtually anything you find pleasing.

9.10 Create a Server-Side Clickable Imagemap

Clickable images or imagemaps are often used in place of text menus or as interactive maps. They are images that link a user to certain spots, depending on where the user clicks on that image. They add a nice graphical touch to your user interface. This How-To shows how to add imagemaps to documents.

9.11 Include Client-Side Imagemaps

Client-side clickable images are alternatives to server-side clickable images. They function the same way as server-side imagemaps, only they have the advantage of not needing a Common Gateway Interface (CGI) script to execute them because the browser handles the processing. This How-To shows how to add these types of imagemaps to documents.

9.12 Color Reduce an Image

You often will find that an image has more colors (or has allocated space for more colors) than needed. This makes your image larger than it needs to be and slows down the transmission of your pages. This How-To explores ways of reducing the number of colors in images.

9.13 Use `WIDTH` and `HEIGHT` Attributes with an Image

By using **`WIDTH`** and **`HEIGHT`** attributes with an image, you can speed up the image's transmission to a browser. This will make your pages load faster. This simple How-To shows how to use these attributes.

9.14 Scale an Image on My Page

By changing the original **`WIDTH`** and **`HEIGHT`** attributes with an image, you can effectively scale the image. This simple How-To shows how to use these attributes.

9.15 Use a Small or Low-Resolution Image While a Larger One Loads

Often it is nice to have a smaller image load before a larger image loads. This not only gives readers something to look at while the larger image loads, but it lets your page load any text that might be around the image, thus allowing readers a nice look at your page while they wait for the larger image to load. This simple How-To shows how to use this technique.

9.16 Speed Image Transmission

For the most part, the faster a Web page loads, the better. This How-To will explore techniques you can use to speed transmission of your Web pages.

9.17 Create an Animated GIF

Animated GIFs bring life to a Web page without using any CGI scripting or Java. This How-To shows how to create and use animated GIFs in Web pages.

9.1 How do I... Build an icon to use in an HTML document?

COMPATIBILITY: HTML

Problem

My documents work fine, but I would like to make them look snappier by adding icons. How can I create one or more icons that I can use later in my documents?

Technique

Icons are small graphical images saved in Graphical Interchange Format (GIF). Icons are usually small—either 64×64 or 32×32 pixels—but there is no set rule on this. They are created much as you would create any other image for your computer, using a graphics program. You create and save the image in GIF or you create the image in another format and then convert it to GIF. Finally, you transfer the GIF image to your server.

Steps

The following procedure shows you a general process of how to create icons or any graphic image. The actual process will vary depending on the software you use and the machine you are on, but the concepts remain the same.

1. Lay out your image on paper. Decide what you want to show and how you want it to look. Unless you are a talented artist, it is best to start simply. Something like the little balloon (a circle with a line) shown in Figure 9-1 is good for learning purposes.

2. Decide which graphics program you would like to use. Almost any graphics package available can be made to work. There are also several programs whose sole purpose is to facilitate the creation of images on the Web. The decision of which to use is usually a matter of availability and personal preference. Several features, though, do come in handy when creating images for the Web: the ability to easily control the pixel size of an image or the number of colors the image can have, for example, and the ability to save in GIF. You might want to take these factors into account before choosing your program. One popular program available for the Macintosh that meets all these standards is GraphicConverter. One popular program for the UNIX and PC worlds is GIFTOOL.

3. Open a new image. It is best to set the pixel size and the number of colors at the beginning. Pixel size is the number of horizontal and vertical squares that you use to create the image. The unwritten standard seems to be either 64×64 or 32×32, but like most other things on the Web, there are no set rules, only conventions or suggestions. If your image fits in a 1-inch by 1-inch square, you should be in pretty good shape. When choosing colors, keep the number as low as possible because the more colors you use, the bigger the image will be and the longer it will take to load. Use four or five colors to create an image that looks nice and is fairly colorful, but is not very large.

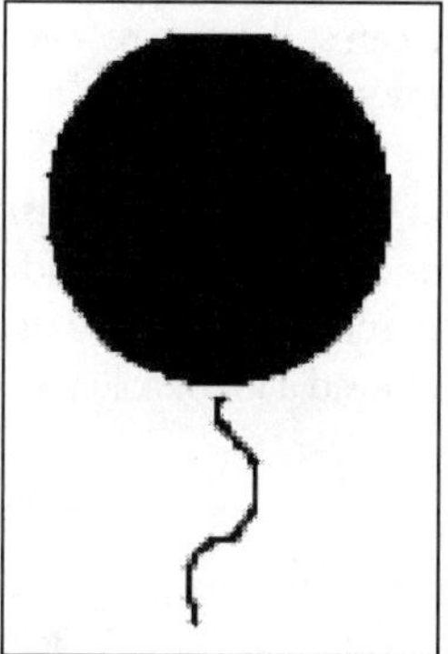

Figure 9-1 A simple image to use for an icon

4. Use whatever tools your application offers to draw your image. This is where no book in the world can help you. If you have artistic ability, go crazy! Even if you have no artistic ability, creating something like the balloon used in this example should be fairly simple.

5. When you are satisfied with your icon, save the image. If your program enables you to pick the format in which to save, choose GIF. If GIF is not available, then TIFF and PICT make good alternatives because they are easy to convert to GIF. It is best to save the image with a short, descriptive name. For our example, something like **BALLOON.GIF** works well.

6. If your graphics program does not have a GIF option to save in, find one of the many available GIF converter programs and convert the image to GIF. Some possible choices for converting images to GIF are GIFConverter for the Macintosh, GIFTOOL for UNIX and PC machines, and the PBMPLUS library, available for several UNIX environments. All these programs work in the same way: You open up **BALLOON.tiff** (for example), then save it in GIF format as **BALLOON.GIF**.

7. If your finished GIF icon is on a different machine than your server, transfer the icon to the appropriate machine. You will then be ready to go.

How It Works

There is no trick to this. Icons are just like any other graphic you create with your computer. The only difference between an icon you create for your Web pages and an icon you see on your computer's windows is that your icon is saved in GIF.

Comments

Even if you have absolutely no artistic ability, you can still create nice-looking images for icons by using graphical text. Figure 9-2 shows an example of using graphical text as an icon.

GIF stands for Graphical Interchange Format, which loosely translates to "This format is readable by a wide number of different machines." GIF and Joint Picture Experts Group (JPEG) are the two most popular and recognized image formats on the Web. GIF is usually used for images that do not need a lot of colors (such as icons).

WEB!

Figure 9-2 A graphical text icon can spice up a page and is easy to create

JPEG is usually used for photo-quality images. These differences are discussed in greater detail in How-To 9.16.

It should also be pointed out that there is no one right way to convert an image to GIF. Although all the tools mentioned in steps 2 and 6 can work a little differently, they all do work.

If you do not want to create any images of your own (or would like to supplement your own images with others), many extensive collections of public domain icons are available on the Web. To find these, use either Yahoo! or AltaVista and search for **`icons`**.

You can find Yahoo! at **`www.yahoo.com`**.

You can find AltaVista at **`www.altavista.digital.com`**.

Finally, if you would like to have a personalized banner created for your Web page, you can find a "banner generator form" at **`www.coder.com/creations/banner/`**. The banner generator is a snap to use and you can make many unique banners and graphical text icons. Simply follow these general steps:

1. Go to the banner generator form Web site (see the preceding paragraph).
2. In the text box provided, enter the text you would like to turn into a banner.
3. Select the fonts, colors, and other options you would like to set. The site's choices are rather extensive.
4. Submit the banner. It will be generated for you in a matter of minutes (at the most).
5. Follow the link to your new banner and then, if you like what you see, download it to your local machine. You then can use the banner wherever you see fit.

The banner generator site is free, easy to use, and enables you to generate many unique banners. It is one of the more useful sites on the Web.

9.2 How do I... Add an inline image?

COMPATIBILITY: HTML

Problem

I have an HTML document and I have an image that's saved as GIF. How do I include this image in my document?

Technique

Adding an image to an HTML document is surprisingly easy. You must create the image either with a graphics program or by scanning or downloading an existing image from another Web site. After you have the image, save it in GIF. Then use the **<IMG SRC>** tag to include the image in your document.

Steps

The following procedure shows you how to add images to your documents:

1. Create the GIF image you want to include in your document. For learning purposes, it is best to keep the image simple, such as **BALLOON.GIF** used in the previous How-To. If you are unsure how to create this image, refer to How-To 8.1.

2. Create the HTML document that will eventually hold the image. Again, for learning purposes, it is best to keep this document simple. For example:

```
<HTML>
<HEAD><TITLE>My First Image</TITLE></HEAD>
<BODY>
<H1>My First Image</H1>
This is a picture of a balloon:
</BODY>
</HTML>
```

3. Add the image to your document with the **<IMG SRC>** tag. This tag is an empty tag with the basic format

```
<IMG SRC="URL">
```

Other optional attributes that can be added to this tag are discussed later in this chapter.

After you add the tag, the document will resemble the following:

```
<HTML>
<HEAD><TITLE>My First Image</TITLE></HEAD>
<BODY>
<H1>My First Image</H1>
This is a picture of a balloon:
<IMG SRC ="BALLOON.GIF">
</BODY>
</HTML>
```

4. Save your HTML document as a text document, giving it a meaningful name such as **balloon.html**.

5. Make sure everything looks the way you think it should by viewing the document with either the Open Local or Open File command in your browser. If all went well, your document should resemble Figure 9-3.

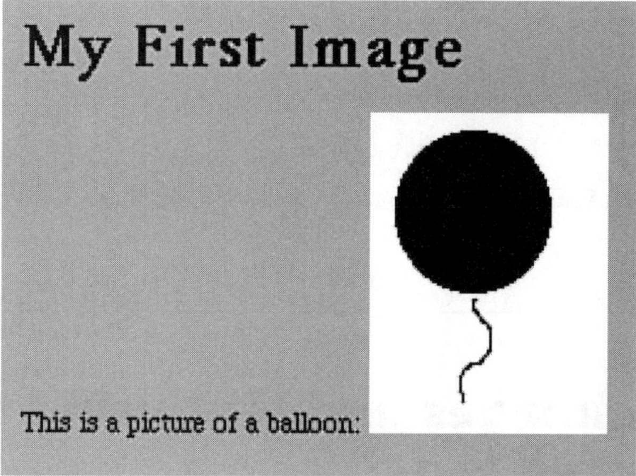

Figure 9-3 The balloon in a document

6. Transfer the completed HTML document and the GIF file to the server where they will reside, and inform your system administrator about the presence of the new document.

How It Works

Whenever a browser encounters the `<IMG SRC ="URL">` tag, it tries to display the image addressed by the URL. If the image is in GIF or JPEG format, the browser displays it on the screen without using a helper application. This creates the effect of the image being "inline" in your document.

Comments

For this example, the URL of the image was a very simple relative address because the image resides in the same directory as the document. This is not always the case. You can use any image at any URL, even if it doesn't reside on your server.

The image tag has grown and expanded probably more than any other tag in HTML. The following list shows other attributes and options you can include inside the tag. The less obvious of these will be dealt with in greater detail in later sections.

- ✔ `alt`: Alternative text to display for nongraphic browsers
- ✔ `align`: Aligns the graphic with the surrounding text, where values include `left`, `right`, and `center`
- ✔ `vwidth`: The amount of spacing above and below an image and surrounding text
- ✔ `hwidth`: The amount of spacing between an image and surrounding text

- ✔ **border**: Sets a border around a graphic, where the greater the number, the thicker the border
- ✔ **width**: Sets the width of the image
- ✔ **height**: Sets the height of the image
- ✔ **lowsrc**: Specifies a low-resolution version of the image to load first

9.3 How do I... Align images and text using the advanced tags?

COMPATIBILITY: HTML 3.2+

Problem

I have an HTML document with an inline image. I would like to wrap some text to the left of one image and to the right of another. How do I accomplish this?

Technique

HTML 2 allows for simple aligning of text and images by adding the **ALIGN** attribute to the **<IMG SRC>** tag. HTML 3 expanded this attribute by adding left and right options. When you use these options, text flows down the right or left side of an image aligned to them. The text flow continues until either the text passes the image, the text ends, or the browser encounters a **<BR CLEAR="left|right|all">** tag.

Steps

The following steps show you how to use the advanced text and picture alignment capabilities in your documents and what effect each of these alignment options has on images and text.

1. Create a GIF image you want to include in your document. The **BALLOON.GIF** image used earlier in this chapter can serve as an example.

2. Create the HTML document that will eventually hold the image. To help illustrate the point, this example contains two versions of the image:

```
<HTML>
<HEAD><TITLE>Practicing with Align</TITLE>
<BODY>
<H1>My First Image</H1>
Here is a picture:
<!-- picture goes here -->
```

```
Here is another picture:
<!-- another goes here -->
</BODY>
</HTML>
```

3. Replace the comments with `<IMG SRC>` tags.

```
<IMG SRC ="BALLOON.GIF">
```

4. Add the **ALIGN** option to the `<IMG SRC>` tag. The basic format of this tag with the **ALIGN** option is

```
<IMG ALIGN=TOP|MIDDLE|BOTTOM SRC"URL">
```

HTML 3 added **left** and **right** to these. The **left** option puts the image on the left side of the browser and then aligns any adjacent text to this image. The **right** option does the opposite. The two image tags look like this:

```
<IMG ALIGN=LEFT  SRC="BALLOON.GIF">
<IMG ALIGN=RIGHT  SRC="BALLOON.GIF">
```

5. Place any descriptive text around the first image.

6. Insert the `<BR CLEAR="left">` command at the spot in the descriptive text where you want the text to stop flowing around the image.

7. Place any descriptive text around the second image.

8. Insert the `<BR CLEAR="right">` command at the spot in the text where you want the text to stop flowing around the second image. When you are finished, the document should resemble the following:

```
<HTML>
<HEAD><TITLE>Practicing with Align</TITLE>
<BODY>
<H1>Netscape align</H1>
Here is a picture aligned left:<P>
<IMG ALIGN=LEFT SRC="BALLOON.GIF">
This is a balloon. Balloons float in the air. Balloons come in many
colors and sizes. Balloons can now even be given as GIFts for birthdays
and such. Balloons are cool.
<P>
Just put in a new paragraph so you could see the results.
<BR CLEAR=LEFT>
Here is the same picture aligned right:
<!-- No new paragraph marker so you can see the difference -- if any -->
<IMG ALIGN=RIGHT SRC="BALLOON.GIF">
This is a second balloon. It is identical to the first except for its
position on the screen. Text flow can look very good, especially when
using better images than smiley faces.
<BR CLEAR=RIGHT>
This text should no longer flow around the image.
</BODY>
</HTML>
```

9. Make sure everything looks the way you think it should by viewing the document locally with your browser. If all went well, your document should resemble Figure 9-4.

10. After you decide which `ALIGN` option you prefer, save your HTML document as a text document.

11. If necessary, transfer the completed HTML document and the GIF file to the server where they will reside and inform your system administrator or webmaster about the presence of the new document and file.

How It Works

Wherever a browser comes across an `<IMG SRC>` tag, the browser displays that image on the screen without a helper application if the image is in GIF or JPEG format. If there is no `ALIGN` option included in the tag, the image is not associated with any text. If there is an `ALIGN left` or `right` option, any text in the same paragraph as the `<IMG SRC>` tag will flow into that image until either the text surpasses the image, the text runs out, or the browser encounters a corresponding `<BR CLEAR = "left|right|all">` tag.

Comments

These extensions to this attribute add a great deal of power to the `<IMG SRC>` tag. When combined with the `<TABLE>` tags, these expressions can make an HTML document appear much like a multiple column document such as you might create with

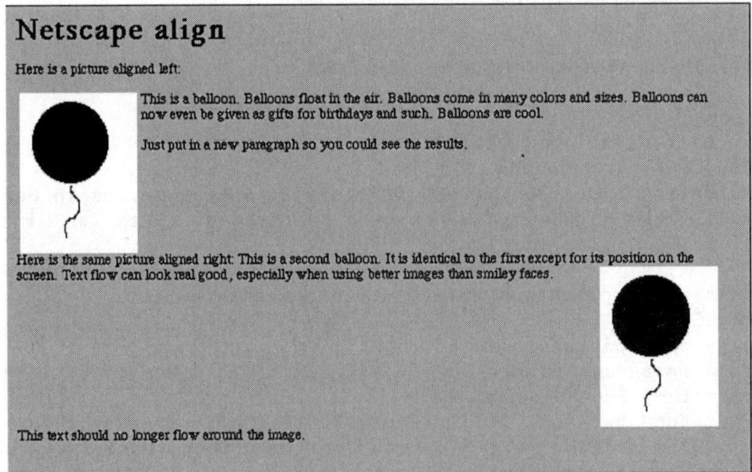

Figure 9-4 The images aligned with text in a document

a desktop publishing package. By combining these tags with frames (Chapter 19, "Frames") and dynamic HTML (Chapter 21, "Dynamic Style Sheets and Fonts") you can push your Web site beyond traditional desktop publishing.

9.4 How do I... Use the <ALT> tag for nongraphical browsers?

COMPATIBILITY: HTML

Problem

I have an HTML document with an image in it. How can I show people with nongraphical browsers that there is an image in my document?

Technique

You add images to documents with the **<IMG SRC>** tag. To inform nongraphical browsers (or a browser with image loading turned off) that there is an image in your document, include the **ALT** option in the tag, setting the **ALT** attribute to a text message that tells users what they are missing.

Steps

The following procedure shows you how to use the **ALT** attribute in your documents:

1. Create a GIF image you want to include in your document. For now, let's stick with the balloon, **BALLOON.GIF**.
2. Create the HTML document that will eventually hold the image. At first, keep this document simple, like the document used in the previous section.
3. Add the image to your document with the **<IMG SRC>** tag. The document should resemble the following:

```
<HTML>
<HEAD><TITLE>An Alt Example</TITLE></HEAD>
<BODY>
<H1>An Alt Example</H1>
This is a picture of a balloon:
<IMG SRC ="BALLOON.GIF">
</BODY>
</HTML>
```

4. Add the **ALT** option to the **<IMG SRC>** tag. The format of the **<IMG>** tag with the **ALT** option is

```
<IMG ALT="some text" SRC = "URL">
```

which in the sample document becomes

```
<IMG ALT="a picture of a balloon goes here" SRC ="BALLOON.GIF">
```

The result is something like Figure 9-5 when viewed through a nongraphical browser.

5. Save your HTML document as a text document.

6. Make sure everything looks the way you think it should by viewing the document with either the Open Local, Open File, or Open Page or File command in your browser.

7. If necessary, transfer the completed HTML document and the GIF file to the server on which they will reside and inform your system administrator about the presence of the new document.

How It Works

Whenever a browser comes across an **<IMG SRC>** tag, the browser tries to display the image if it is in GIF or JPEG format. If the browser is unable to display the image, it replaces it with any text found in the **ALT="text"** attribute.

Comments

It is considered good Net manners to use the **ALT** attribute whenever possible. This way, people using nongraphical browsers, such as Lynx, will still get the general idea of how a page is meant to be laid out. It is also a good idea to test how your **<IMG ALT SRC>** tags work by turning off automatic image loading in your browser and then checking out your documents.

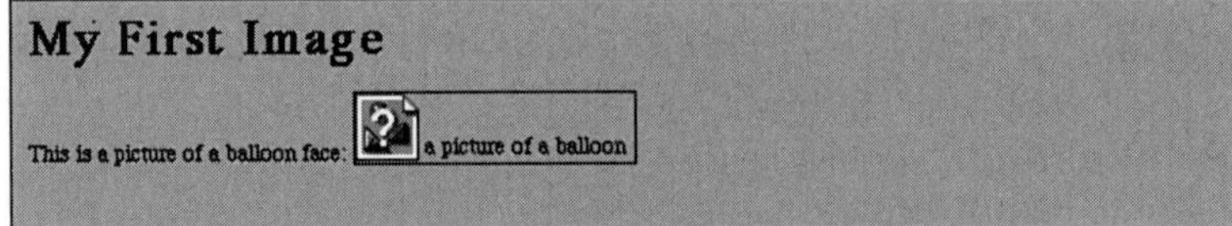

Figure 9-5 Use of the ALT attribute

9.5 How do I... Include an image with a transparent background?

COMPATIBILITY: HTML

Problem

Now I have an inline image in my HTML document, but there is a lot of white space around it. How do I remove this white space so my image will have a transparent background that blends in better with my page? In other words, how can I make the background of my image always match the background of the browser that is displaying it?

Technique

With the right tools, creating an image with a transparent background is only slightly more complicated than creating an image without one. You still follow the same process to create the image, but you must add an extra step or two. After you create the image, you must fill in the areas that you want to be transparent with a color that is not used anywhere else in the image. Then set that fill color to be the transparent GIF color and save the image in GIF89a format.

Steps

The following procedure gives you a general overview of what you must do to create a transparent image. How you create the image depends on the machine you are working on and the tools you are using, but the basic procedure remains the same.

1. Lay out your image on paper. Decide what you want to show and how you want it to look. For learning purposes, it is best to start with something simple like the balloon (**BALLOON.GIF**) used throughout this chapter.

2. Decide which graphics program to use. Your choices are almost endless because almost any available graphics program will work. There are also several utility programs around whose sole purpose is the creation of transparent images on the Web. The decision of which to use is usually a matter of availability and personal preference. Several features come in handy when creating images for the Web. Some of these are listed here:

   - ✔ The ability to control the pixel size of an image easily
   - ✔ The number of colors the image can have

- ✔ The ability to select a transparent color
- ✔ The ability to save in GIF89a format

You might want to take these into account before deciding on the package you want to use. Programs such as GraphicConverter for the Macintosh and GIFTOOL for UNIX and PCs are popular and inexpensive choices.

3. Open up a new image. It is best to set the pixel size and the number of colors at the outset. Pixel size is the number of horizontal and vertical squares that you use to create the image. When choosing colors, keep the number as low as possible. The more colors you use, the bigger the image will be and the longer it will take to load. Use four or five colors to create an image that looks nice and is fairly colorful, but is not very large.

4. Draw your image. The file **BALLOON.GIF** should be very simple to create. It is a circle with a line attached.

5. Fill in the area you want to make transparent with a color not used in the image. It does not matter what the color is as long as it is not used elsewhere in the image.

6. Set the transparent GIF color to the color you filled with. This is done slightly differently depending on the application you are using. For example, with GraphicConverter for the Macintosh, this setting can be found at the bottom of the Colors item found in the Picture menu.

7. Save your image in the GIF89a format. For this example, the new image is named **balloonT.GIF**. In practice, you do not need to use an altered name to differentiate between transparent and nontransparent images.

8. If your finished image is on a different machine than your server, transfer the icon to the appropriate machine.

How It Works

The color you use as the transparent color is automatically set to whatever a browser looking at that image happens to have as its background, the effect being that your image blends in perfectly with the background.

Comments

The only difference between a transparent GIF and a nontransparent GIF is the format in which the two are saved. The HTML tags are identical, for example,

```
<HTML>
<HEAD><TITLE>Transparent Demo</TITLE>
<BODY>
```

```
<H1>Transparent Demo</H1>
This is a balloon:
<IMG SRC="balloon.GIF">
This is a transparent balloon:
<IMG SRC="balloonT.GIF">
</BODY>
</HTML>
```

The tags are identical except for the URL, but the results are quite different, as shown in Figure 9-6.

It is easy to turn an existing image into a transparent GIF. Open the image, and then perform steps 5 and 6.

People often use transparent GIFs to add unique horizontal rules in a document. For example, if you want to have a red, white, and blue horizontal rule in one of your pages, instead of using the `<HR>` command (which doesn't allow for color), you can use the following procedure:

1. Use a graphics program to create a red, white, and blue line.
2. Save the line as a transparent GIF, naming it something like `CLINE.GIF`.
3. Insert the following `<IMG SRC>` tag into the document where you want to place the line:

```
<IMG SRC="CLINE.GIF">
```

This causes the browser to insert the red, white, and blue line wherever it finds this tag. It should be noted, though, that some people consider using images for horizontal lines to be a waste of server time because it takes longer to load a graphical image than it does to load a line drawn with the horizontal rule tag `<HR>`. Still, this is a personal call. If you want a colorful line on your page, go ahead and make one. It is, after all, your page.

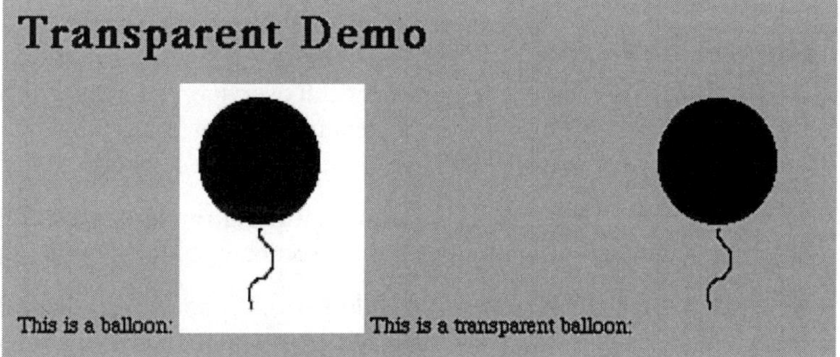

Figure 9-6 A comparison between transparent and nontransparent images

Finally, note that, due to the number of choices you have when converting an image to a transparent GIF, this chapter has only touched the surface. Following are other options you might want to consider:

- ✔ GIFTOOL: Available for UNIX and DOS machines
- ✔ The PBMPLUS library: Available for UNIX machines
- ✔ GraphicConverter or Transparency: Available for the Macintosh

9.6 How do I... Create an interlaced inline image on my page?

COMPATIBILITY: NETSCAPE, INTERNET EXPLORER

Problem

I have a document with an inline image that works fine, but my image loads from top to bottom. I occasionally see other people's images loading progressively: First a complete rough image appears, and then this image becomes finer and finer. How can I get my images to appear like this?

Technique

The technique used to make an image appear gradually is called *interlacing*. With the right tools, you can easily convert a normal image to an interlaced GIF image. GIFConverter on the Macintosh and GIFTOOL for UNIX and PC machines can convert a graphic from any number of formats to an interlaced GIF.

Steps

The following procedure gives you a general overview of what you must do to create an interlaced image. Some of the details for doing this depend on the machine and the tools you are using. Still, the basic procedure remains the same.

1. Find or create an image you want to turn into an interlaced GIF. The `BALLOON.GIF` file from the previous section would work well as an example.

2. Decide which program you would like to use to convert the image to an interlaced GIF. There are many available options across the three major platforms. Some of the major choices are GIFConverter for the Macintosh, GIFTOOL for UNIX machines and PCs, and the PBMPLUS tools for UNIX machines.

3. Open the image.
4. Save the image as an interlaced GIF. This procedure differs depending on the application you are using, but it is usually very easy to figure out. In GIFConverter, for example, you click the interlaced box that appears in the Save As dialog box.
5. View the image locally with your browser to make sure it looks the way you think it should.
6. If necessary, transport the image to your server.

How It Works

There really isn't much work for you to do here. The tool performs the conversion. When a browser loads the new interlaced image, the entire image appears gradually, going from a low-resolution outline to the finished image. You really don't need to know more than that.

Comments

The steps shown in this How-To vary depending on what graphics program you use and what system you are on; still, the technique is the same. Interlacing is so easy to accomplish that you might get carried away and have too many interlaced images on a page. The main advantage to interlacing comes when displaying larger images on the screen. An interlaced image will display a low-resolution "preview" of the image while the larger image loads. This enables a reader to view the rest of the page as the image finishes loading. Smaller images (such as the sample image) should probably not be interlaced, because they load pretty quickly. You should never interlace a background image because nobody wants to see your background load four times. Feel free to experiment, but try not to go overboard.

9.7 How do I... Create a thumbnail version of an image?

COMPATIBILITY: HTML

Problem

I have a large image that some people might be interested in seeing, while others might not. How can I make a thumbnail version of this image?

Technique

Thumbnail images are no different from any other images you see on the Web. They just happen to be smaller. You can make one by using any graphics program that has scaling capability to shrink the image to thumbnail size. You can then make the thumbnail image work like a button your viewer clicks to load the original image. This technique is shown in How-To 9.8.

Steps

The following procedure gives you a general overview of what you must do to create a thumbnail image. How you create the image depends on the machine and the tools you are using. Still, the basic procedure remains the same.

1. Find or create an image you want to turn into a thumbnail. For this example, use **BALLOON.GIF** from the previous section.

2. Decide which program you would like to use to scale (or resize) the image to thumbnail size. Almost any graphics program has the capability to scale images. Choose a graphics program that both scales images and saves them in GIF.

3. Open the image with the graphics program of your choice.

4. Find and select the scale option.

5. Set the new, smaller size of your image. How this works might differ slightly from application to application, but it always involves changing the percentage of the object's size. In this case, the object is being shrunk to 30 percent of its original size.

6. Save the smaller image as GIF or in some format that you can easily translate to GIF. Make sure you give the new image a distinct but related name such as **BALLON_S.GIF**. The name **BALLON_S.GIF** is less likely to be confused with the original than **BALLOONS.GIF**, but readers using Macintosh, Windows 95, or UNIX should feel free to use a longer, more distinctive name.

   The following document will resemble Figure 9-7 when viewed through a browser:

```
<HTML>
<HEAD><TITLE>Thumbnails</TITLE></HEAD>
<BODY>
<H1>Thumbnails</H1>
This is the original: <IMG SRC="BALLOON.GIF">
This is the resized thumbnail: <IMG SRC="BALLON_S.GIF">
</BODY>
</HTML>
```

7. If necessary, transfer the finished image to your server machine.

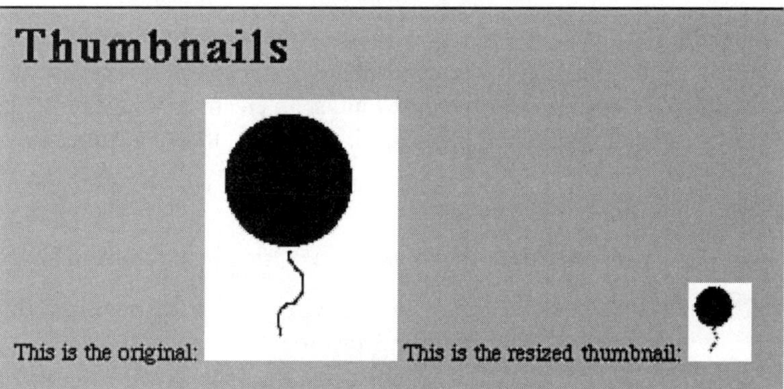

Figure 9-7 The thumbnail version of the balloon graphic

How It Works

There isn't anything tricky here. The thumbnail version of the image is nothing more than a scaled-down version of the original. The most difficult task in this How-To is choosing which software package to do the work in.

Comments

One of the best uses for thumbnails is as clickable images that lead to the full-sized image. How-To 9.8 shows how to make them work that way.

Many programs, such as Adobe Photoshop and GraphicConverter, automatically create thumbnails of images when you save them. You can copy these thumbnails and paste them into your own documents. Consult your system's documentation for instructions on how to do this.

Finally, if you want to display a smaller-scaled version of an image without actually creating a separate smaller image, you can use the `WIDTH` and `HEIGHT` attributes in the `<IMG>` tag to scale the element. How-To's 9.13 and 9.14 show you how to accomplish this.

9.8 How do I... Use an image as a link?

COMPATIBILITY: HTML

Problem

I have noticed that Web authors often use images for links, either in place of text or along with text. How can I do this?

Technique

Using an image as a link to another image or document is very easy. Image links are no different from regular hypertext links. To create an image link, place the **<IMG SRC>** tag with the URL of the image between **<A HREF = "URL">...</A>** tags.

Steps

The following procedure shows you step by step how to use an image as a link:

1. Find or create the image you want to use. For this example, the **BALLON_S.GIF** image from How-To 9.7 is a good choice.

2. Decide what you want the image to link to. In this case, the small balloon image links to an HTML document containing the full-sized balloon image and a description of balloons.

3. Create the base HTML document that will contain the link. The document, kept small, would look something like this:

```
<HTML>
<HEAD><TITLE>My First Image Link</TITLE>
<BODY>
<H1>My first image link</H1>
This is a small balloon:
<IMG SRC="BALLON_S.GIF"> click on it to go to a page with a larger
 balloon.<p>
</BODY>
</HTML>
```

4. Add the link. If the document to which you want to link is called **bal_info.html**, then the link would be

```
<A HREF="bal_info.html><IMG SRC="BALLON_S.GIF"></A>
```

This is fairly straightforward. If you understand hypertext links, you should have no trouble at all with this structure. The hypertext that is normally placed between the **<A HREF>...</A>** tags is in this case replaced by an **<IMG SRC>** tag. The document now looks like this:

```
<HTML>
<HEAD><TITLE>My First Image Link</TITLE>
<BODY>
<H1>My first image link</H1>
This is a small balloon:
<A HREF="bal_info.html><IMG SRC="ballon_s.GIF"></A>click on it to go
to a page with a larger balloon<p>
</BODY>
</HTML>
```

When viewed through a browser, the page looks much like Figure 9-8. As you can see, the small balloon image is highlighted, which means it is a link. Selecting that image sends the browser off to whatever URL is specified in the **<A HREF="URL">** tag.

5. Save your document as a text file. Give it any name that is simple, yet descriptive and unique. In this case, **ball_lnk.html** is acceptable.
6. View the document locally with your browser.
7. Make any fine-tuning changes needed, and then save the document.
8. If necessary, transfer the finished document and image to your server and inform your system administrator about the presence of the new document and image.

How It Works

When a browser comes across the **<A HREF="URL">...</A>** tags, it uses any text or valid URL of an image as the anchor for that tag, thus making text and images interchangeable for links. When a reader selects the hyperimage, he or she will be brought to the URL set with the **<A HREF="URL">** tag.

Comments

It is also possible to combine text and images between the **<A HREF="URL">...</A>** tags.

Note that people using Macintosh, Windows 95, and UNIX systems should feel free to use variable and document names that contain more than eight characters, plus a three-letter tag.

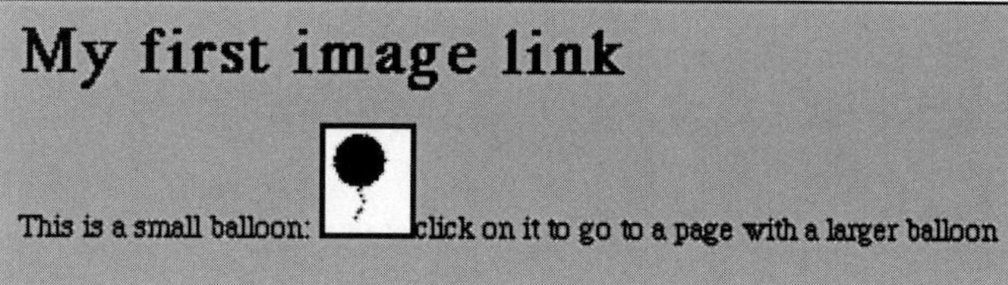

Figure 9-8 An image being used as a link

9.9 How do I... Create a background pattern for my page?

COMPATIBILITY: NETSCAPE, INTERNET EXPLORER

Problem

I see a lot of pages on the Web that appear in my browser with different backgrounds than the standard gray. How can I change the background on my page?

Technique

Change backgrounds by using the **BACKGROUND** attribute. The **BACKGROUND** attribute was added to HTML 3 as an extension to the **<BODY>** tag. You can use the **BACKGROUND** attribute to set the URL of a GIF that will be used as the document's background.

Steps

The following steps show how you can add a unique background to your documents:

1. Decide what kind of background you would like to use. Remember, you will place text on top of this background, so it is best to keep it light and simple.
2. Select the graphics program of your choice. You can use any graphics program, but it saves a conversion step if you use a program that can save images in GIF.
3. Open a new image.
4. Set the document size to something relatively small. A 1-inch by 1-inch square works well.
5. Select a small color palette. It is best to stick with 4 or 16 colors.
6. Create a new image. Here artistic skill helps, but it is possible to do a fairly nice job with very little ability. Remember, keep the colors light. Also, remember that this color box is repeatedly juxtaposed on the background, so strive for something that will flow smoothly. Experiment until you come up with something you like.
7. When you have something you like, save it as GIF, for example, **BACKGR.GIF**.

8. Add the **BACKGROUND** attribute to any **<BODY>** tag in any document where you want to have **BACKGR.GIF** be the background color. The format of this is

```
<BODY BACKGROUND="backgr.GIF"> Document here!</BODY>
```

How It Works

When Netscape or Internet Explorer encounters a **BACKGROUND** attribute, it sets the screen's background to the GIF file specified by that background.

Comments

Backgrounds look nice, but do have a cost: speed. Loading a background image increases the amount of time your page takes to load. The speed factor is the reason why it is best to keep the background simple.

To check out possible background colors, go to **http://www.infi.net/wwwimages/colorindex.html** or search Yahoo! or your favorite Web searching site for backgrounds.

COMPLEXITY
INTERMEDIATE

9.10 How do I... Create a server-side clickable imagemap?

COMPATIBILITY: HTML 2+

Problem

There are places on the Web that use clickable pictures for menu bars and navigational tools. How can I add such clickable images to my own documents?

Technique

Clickable images or imagemaps are not all that different from regular inline GIF images. The only real difference is that imagemaps have had hot spots assigned to them. *Hot spots* are areas of the image that link to certain URLs when you click on them. Hot spots are often assigned through a utility imagemap program whose sole function is to assist you in setting the coordinates for hot spots. You inform a browser that an image is a clickable imagemap by appending the **ISMAP** attribute to an **<IMG SRC>** tag. This tag appears between **<A HREF="URL">...</A>** tags that contain the URL of the text file that contains the imagemap coordinates. The browser then uses CGI to parse the results and figure out where to establish the link.

Steps

The following procedure gives you a general overview of what you must do to create an imagemap. How you create it depends on the machine you are using, the tools you have available, and the type of server your system is on. Still, the basic procedure remains the same.

1. Find or create a suitable image for your imagemap. This image can be as big and as complicated as you would like it to be. However, the less complicated it is, the easier it will be for the user to figure out what he or she can or can't click on, and the less time-consuming it will be to load. Imagemaps place a significant burden on the server and do have a delay time while the server processes your click, so frequent "misclicks" can be frustrating. For this example, the simple phrase **`W E B !`** is a good choice. It should be easy to create with any graphics program, plus it has four distinct parts—each character—that are easily differentiated from one another. Call this image **`WEB.GIF`**.

2. Now that you have the image, you must map out the location of the hot spots. You need some way of telling the server that the pixels of the image between these points lead to this URL. The area of the hot spot can be square, round, or a polygon. You must compute the boundaries of each hot spot. For each area you want to make a hot spot, you must find the coordinates and then define the URL to which these coordinates will link. Figure 9-9 depicts some sample coordinates for the **`web.GIF`** image.

Although you can do all this by hand, it is usually preferable to use a utility program to map out areas for you. There are many tools to choose from, depending on what platform you are using. On the Macintosh, WebMap is a good public domain choice. On Windows and X Window systems, MapEdit is a popular choice. All these utilities work in the same way: They present you with a series of familiar tools that let you capture the coordinates of the parts of the image you want to use as hot spots. Figure 9-10 shows WebMap in action.

3. After you have mapped out the boundaries of your imagemap, save these boundaries as a text file, naming it **`WEB.MAP`**. The **`WEB.MAP`** file for the preceding example making each letter selectable will look like this:

```
default DEFALT.HTM
rect w.htmL 27,1 99,66
rect e.htmL 121,2 168,62
rect b.htmL 188,2 233,68
rect X.HTML 257,0 279,73
```

4. Transfer the **`WEB.MAP`** text file to the server.

5. Create the HTML base document that will contain the imagemap.

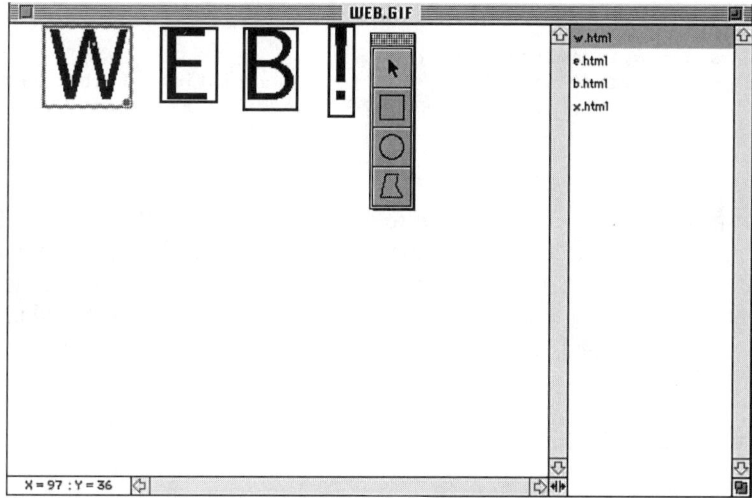

Figure 9-9 Coordinates for the `WEB.GIF` image

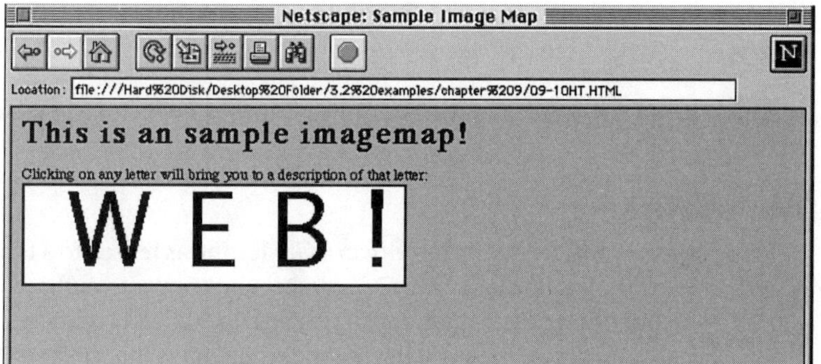

Figure 9-10 The finished image map

6. Now that you have the document, enter the **<IMG SRC>** tag inside an **<A HREF>** tag:

```
<A HREF="/cgi-bin/imagemap/WEB.MAP"><IMG SRC="WEB.GIF" ISMAP></A>
```

The **ISMAP** attribute at the end of the **<IMG SRC>** tag is the key here. That tells the browser that this GIF file is a clickable imagemap and that the text file named at the end of the **<A HREF>** tag should be the file fed to the imagemap CGI to interrupt clicks. The complete document would look like this:

```
<HTML>
<HEAD>
<TITLE>Sample Image Map</TITLE>
```

continued on next page

continued from previous page

```
<BODY>
<H1>This is a sample imagemap!</H1>
Clicking on any letter will bring you to a description of that letter:
<A HREF="/cgi-bin/imagemap/WEB.MAP"><IMG SRC="WEB.GIF" ismap></A>
</BODY>
</HTML>
```

7. Create any of the linked-to documents that you might need. This example would need five more documents: one for each letter, one for the exclamation point, and one default document that is returned when the user clicks on a spot that is not a hot spot. The document names should match the ones used in the map file. A sample document might look like this:

```
<HTML>
<HEAD>
<TITLE> W!!</TILE>
</HEAD>
<BODY>
<!-- This document is W.HTML -->
You selected the W -- the 23rd letter of the alphabet.<P>
</BODY>
</HTML>
```

8. If necessary, transfer the HTML document(s) to your server.

9. Ask your system administrator to activate your new imagemap document.

How It Works

An imagemap is really nothing more than a GIF file that is related to a text file through your server's CGI imagemap. The CGI can be a bit tricky if you have to write it—luckily, all the major servers come with this interface already written for you, so all you have to do is access it. When the browser encounters the **`<ISMAP>`** tag, it relates the GIF file in the tag to the text document pointed to by the URL in the `<A HREF="URL">` tag.

Comments

Because of the overhead involved, some systems don't enable their users to have imagemaps in their documents. It is a good idea to check with your system administrator before starting an imagemap.

Imagemaps vary slightly from server to server. NCSA deals with the coordinates of hot spots a little differently than CERN. If you use the proper tools, these differences will be largely handled for you. Still, it is always a good idea to consult with your server system's documentation or with your system's webmaster before starting an imagemap.

Finally, Netscape and Internet Explorer both support *client-side imagemaps*. Client-side imagemaps are like server-side imagemaps but the browser, not the server's CGI application, resolves the links. For more on client-side imagemaps, check out How-To 9.11.

9.11 How do I... Include client-side imagemaps?

COMPATIBILITY: NETSCAPE, INTERNET EXPLORER

Problem

I want to develop an imagemap, but I don't have the time or the know-how to write a CGI application that will read an imagemap and return the appropriate page. How can I include a simple imagemap on my page?

Technique

Netscape and Microsoft's Internet Explorer support client-side imagemaps in which the different regions of the image are specified within the document or in another HTML document. The syntax is similar to that for the **SHAPE** attribute. No CGI applications are required to read client-side imagemaps. Therefore, they work even while not connected to the Internet, which is handy for examining local Web pages.

Steps

1. Open your document, and then load an image with a viewer such as Photoshop that enables you to get the pixel locations from the image so you can specify image locations in the links.

2. Identify areas on the image that you want to serve as links. As of this writing, the only shape supported is a rectangle. Note the pixel locations of the upper-left and lower-right corners of the rectangle.

3. In the HTML document, insert the **<MAP>** and **</MAP>** tags. Use the **NAME** attribute for **<MAP>** to give a unique name for the imagemap. For example, to create an imagemap named **mymap**, you would enter

```
<MAP NAME="mymap">
</MAP>
```

4. Between the **<MAP>** and **</MAP>** tags, insert an **<AREA>** tag. There should be one **<AREA>** tag for each link on the map. If your imagemap has three areas, enter

```
<MAP NAME="mymap">
<AREA>
<AREA>
<AREA>
</MAP>
```

5. The **SHAPE** attribute of **<AREA>** identifies the shape of the area in the imagemap. Because rectangles are the only currently supported shape, **SHAPE** can have only one value, **"RECT"**.

```
<MAP NAME="mymap">
<AREA SHAPE="RECT">
<AREA SHAPE="RECT">
<AREA SHAPE="RECT">
</MAP>
```

6. The **COORD** attribute identifies the boundaries of the area on the imagemap. For **"RECT"**, **COORD** has four values, separated by commas: the x coordinate of the upper-left corner, the y coordinate of the upper-left corner, the x coordinate of the lower-right corner, and the y coordinate of the lower-right corner. The following is an example of three rectangles in different areas of the image:

```
<MAP NAME="mymap">
<AREA SHAPE="RECT" COORD="10,10,30,50">
<AREA SHAPE="RECT" COORD="50,50,70,70">
<AREA SHAPE="RECT" COORD="90,90,120,95">
</MAP>
```

7. For each area, the **HREF** attribute identifies the URL of the document that should be loaded if that area is selected by the user. The document can be a local file or a document on another server. Adding **HREF** attributes to the preceding example gives us

```
<MAP NAME="mymap">
<AREA SHAPE="RECT" COORD="10,10,30,50" HREF="info.html">
<AREA SHAPE="RECT" COORD="50,50,70,70" HREF="projects/info/data.html">
<AREA SHAPE="RECT" COORD="90,90,120,95" HREF="http://www.widgets.com/">
</MAP>
```

8. You can reference the imagemap information to an image on the page by adding the **USEMAP** attribute to the **<IMG>** element. **USEMAP** is set equal to the name of map information from the **NAME** attribute of **<MAP>**. For example, if the file **IMAGEMAP.GIF** serves as the imagemap, using the information from the last step, you would enter

```
<IMG SRC="IMAGEMAP.GIF" ALT="An imagemap" USEMAP="#mymap">
```

9. The map description does not have to be in the same document as the imagemap itself. If the map description is stored in the file **maps.html** in the same directory as the file with the imagemap, you can use

```
<IMG SRC="IMAGEMAP.GIF" ALT="An imagemap" USEMAP="maps.html#mymap">
```

How It Works

When a user clicks on an image that includes the **USEMAP** attribute, Netscape reads the corresponding imagemap description contained within the **<MAP>** element. If the user selects an area described by one of the **<AREA>** tags, the browser loads the document identified by the **HREF** attribute.

Comments

Not all browsers support client-side imagemaps, so people using some browsers cannot access those imagemaps. Because the **USEMAP** attribute takes precedence over ordinary links, there are two ways to work around this. One way is to enclose the image in a link that references a standard imagemap routine:

```
<A HREF="/cgi-bin/imagemap.cgi"><IMG SRC="IMAGEMAP.GIF" ALT="An imagemap"
 USEMAP="#mymap"></A>
```

This method requires that you have an imagemap CGI application configured and have set up the appropriate description files for that application. Another approach is to include a link to a document that gives an error message and informs the user that the imagemap can be accessed only by browsers that support client-side imagemaps:

```
<A HREF="error.html"><IMG SRC="IMAGEMAP.GIF" ALT="An imagemap"
 USEMAP="#mymap"></A>
```

You can find updated information about client-side imagemaps in Netscape at `http://www.netscape.com/assist/net_sites/html_extensions_3.html`.

COMPLEXITY
INTERMEDIATE

9.12 How do I... Color reduce an image?

COMPATIBILITY: HTML

Problem

My images are quite big and my page takes longer to load than I would like. I understand I might be able to use color reduction techniques to make my images smaller. How do I do this?

Technique

This is an interesting problem, and there really is more than one solution to it. None of the solutions involve HTML, however, but rather involve planning how many actual colors to use when creating your image, and then deciding on the type of format to use for your images. The latter choice will be based on, and is sometimes governed by, the first. The fewer the colors you use to create your image, the smaller that image will be.

Steps

The following steps show how you can choose a format for your image that will allow for the maximum reduction in the number of colors used while keeping your image looking good.

1. Create your image, either by hand or with a scanner.
2. Decide on the format in which you want to save the image. Your two main choices are GIF and JPEG. Each has its own strengths. It is a general rule of thumb that you use GIF for images that are small and do not need a lot of colors to look good. This is because graphics programs such as Photoshop enable you to index the colors of a GIF file, in effect permitting the image to store only the colors it needs, thus making the image smaller. JPEG is considered best for photographs, because the compression method it uses usually loses very little in quality with photographs, while it still creates an image that is smaller than the comparable image as a GIF.
3. Add the image to a HTML document with the `<SRC>` tag.

How It Works

You will need to experiment. Some images will look better in GIF, others in JPEG. You will also need to experiment with the number of colors. If the image is a GIF, you can use Photoshop or another graphics program to optimize the image by indexing the colors. If the image is a JPEG, you might find that medium compression yields an acceptable image.

Comments

The goal here should be to get the best image that takes up the least possible space. Sometimes the choice of what format to use is easy. If you want to display more than 256 colors, then you must use JPEG, because GIF allows only up to 256 colors. If you are dealing with an image that needs only a few colors, such as an icon, GIF will usually give you better quality and can be optimized so the image is actually smaller than its JPEG counterpart. The really tricky part is choosing a format for an image that uses up to 256 colors. Generally, the GIF version will look better but will be bigger, although this doesn't always hold true. Many times, which format you use and how you reduce the colors will depend on personal preferences.

Remember that you cannot optimize a file through the use of HTML tags; you must rely on a graphics program to do such things as indexing and compression.

For online examples of these concepts, feel free to check out `http://www.psnw.com/~jmz5/waite/graphics.html`.

9.13 How do I... Use WIDTH and HEIGHT attributes with an image?

COMPATIBILITY: NETSCAPE, INTERNET EXPLORER

Problem

My images take longer to load than I would like. I understand I can speed this process up if I use the **WIDTH** and **HEIGHT** attributes when I load the image. How do I do this?

Technique

You use the **WIDTH** and **HEIGHT** attribute in the **<IMG>** tag to control automatically the width and height of the image that will load.

Steps

The following simple procedure shows how to load images with the **WIDTH** and **HEIGHT** attributes:

1. Create or find the image you want to include in an HTML document.
2. Use a graphics program to determine the height and width of the image. This information is readily available with most software packages.
3. Add the **<IMG>** tag and include the proper **WIDTH** and **HEIGHT** attributes, for example:

```
<IMG  WIDTH=256 HEIGHT=269 SRC="SLOW.GIF">
```

4. View the document to make sure the image loads correctly.

How It Works

If the **WIDTH** and **HEIGHT** attributes are not included, the browser will calculate the size of all images it loads "on the fly." If you include these attributes in an **<IMG>** tag, the browser then uses the values given to define the size of the object. The browser can then load the image faster.

Comments

When you have a lot of images on a page, using these attributes can make a noticeable difference in speeding up the loading of a page.

You can see an online example at **http://www.psnw.com/~jmz5/waite/demoall.html**.

9.14 How do I...
Scale an image on my page?

COMPATIBILITY: NETSCAPE, INTERNET EXPLORER

Problem

I would like to present different sized versions of the same image on a page without having to save the image multiple times. How do I do this?

Technique

To scale an image, you use the **WIDTH** and **HEIGHT** attribute in the **<IMG>** tag. But instead of using the image's original size, you change the values to reflect the new size.

Steps

The following simple procedure shows how to load images with the **WIDTH** and **HEIGHT** attributes.

1. Create or find the image you want to scale in an HTML document.

2. Decide what size you would like to make the object; then do the math. For example, if you want to scale the object down 50 percent, cut the object's original **WIDTH** and **HEIGHT** attributes in half.

3. Add the **<IMG>** tag and include the scaled **WIDTH** and **HEIGHT** attributes. For example, here's how to scale the image used in How-To 9.13:

```
<IMG  WIDTH=128 HEIGHT=135 SRC="SLOW.GIF">
```

4. View the document to make sure the image loads correctly. Figure 9-11 shows one example of using scaling.

How It Works

If the **WIDTH** and **HEIGHT** attributes given with the **<IMG>** tag do not match the image's actual size, the browser scales the image to match the attributes before it renders the image.

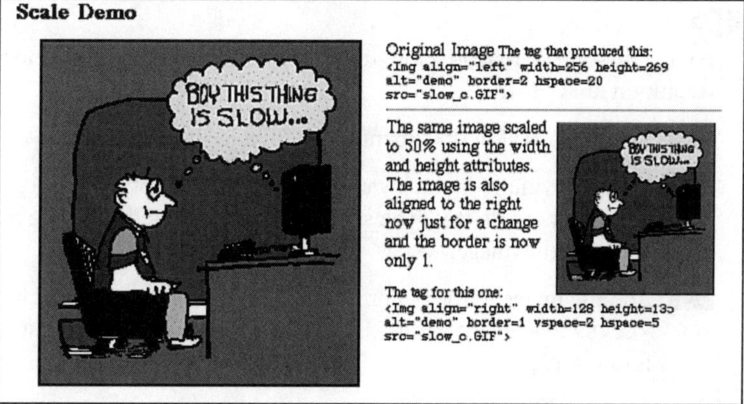

Figure 9-11 A scaling example

Comments

Netscape and Microsoft's Internet Explorer do a nice job of scaling images as long as you keep the ratios consistent.

You can see an online example at **http://www.psnw.com/~jmz5/waite/demoall.html**.

9.15 How do I... Use a small or low-resolution image while a larger one loads?

COMPATIBILITY: NETSCAPE

Problem

I have a big image that takes a while to load. I would like readers to be able to see a smaller version of this image while they wait for the large version to load. How do I do this?

Technique

You can load a smaller, lower-resolution image by placing a **<LOWSRC>** element inside an **<IMG>** tag. The browser will load any image **<LOWSRC>** points to before it loads the image the **<SRC>** element points to. This image will load in the same place the larger image will eventually occupy.

Steps

Follow these steps to load a low-resolution version of an image before the higher-resolution image loads.

1. Create the HTML document that will hold the image.
2. Create the image and a lower-resolution version of the image. There are many ways to do this. The simplest is probably reducing the number of colors in the image.
3. Add the image to the document by using the `<IMG>` tag and including a `<LOWSRC>` element and URL besides the normal `<SRC>` element and URL, for example:

```
<IMG LOWSRC="SLOW.GIF SRC="SLOWC.GIF">
```

4. View your document to make sure everything works correctly and that the `<LOWSRC>` images load before the one named in the `<SRC>` element.

How It Works

When the browser spots the `<LOWSRC>` element, it loads the image associated with that element. This enables other items on your page to load. After those are loaded, the regular image will load.

Comments

The image pointed to by `<LOWSRC>` does not have to be smaller than the normal image. The browser does not check this. `<LOWSRC>` can make a nice alternative to interlacing. `<LOWSRC>` can really make a difference if you have an especially large image to load.

You can find samples of this tag in use at **`http://www.psnw.com/~jmz5/waite/demoall.html`**.

COMPLEXITY
INTERMEDIATE

9.16 How do I... Speed image transmission?

COMPATIBILITY: HTML

Problem

My page has a lot of images and can take a long time to load. How can I speed image transmission?

Technique

There are many different methods you can use to make sure your page loads as fast as possible. These methods all were mentioned in the preceding sections, including color reduction, using **WIDTH** and **HEIGHT** attributes, and using interlacing or **<LOWSRC>**.

Steps

The following steps give some possible ways you can speed the transmission of your page:

1. Optimize your images so they use the fewest colors or the greatest compression and still look good. Often you can successfully use far fewer colors than you might believe.
2. Use **WIDTH** and **HEIGHT** attributes in **<IMG>** tags to speed up the loading process.
3. Avoid large background images that slow down the loading process. Background images should, for the most part, be small and subtle. Also, remember never to interlace a background image.
4. If you would like your readers to get an overview of your page while the larger images load, consider using interlacing or **<LOWSRC>**.
5. Experiment to find what works best for you.

How It Works

The process is actually based on a simple given: The smaller the images, the faster they will load. And if you supply **WIDTH** and **HEIGHT** attributes, you save the browser from having to compute these; therefore, the page will load faster. Interlacing and **<LOWSRC>** don't make your page load faster, but because they enable the user to view the layout of the page quicker than if these options were not used, the page seems to load faster.

Comments

What methods you use depends greatly on your personal preference and your target audience. If your target audience consists mostly of people using 28.8 or 14.4 modems (and remember, due to system loads and other factors, these modems will often not be effectively producing these speeds), you will want to be considerate with bandwidth and not put a lot of high-resolution images on your page. Also, remember that a lot of little images can also take time to load. One good way to anticipate how fast your page will load is to assume 1 second for every KB of text and graphics a page has. A general rule of thumb is that the total of all the images on your page should not exceed 40–50KB, though many of the most popular sites on the Web use far more bandwidth than this. This rule, like most other Web design rules, is very flexible and left up to the designer's personal taste.

9.17 How do I... Create an animated GIF?

COMPATIBILITY: NETSCAPE, INTERNET EXPLORER

Problem

I want to add some life to my Web page, but I don't have time to learn Java or CGI scripting. I've noticed that a lot of pages have cool animated icons. How can I add these types of icons to my pages?

Technique

One GIF file is actually able to hold many different images. By varying each of these images slightly, you can in effect perform animation by simply putting a GIF on the screen with an `<IMG>` tag. The process works much like an animation flip book changing from one image to another, thus giving the illusion of motion.

Steps

The following steps show you a general way to create animated GIFs:

1. Create the different versions of the image you want to animate. To keep it simple, each image should be the same size and use the same colors. Label each of these images in sequence, for example, **IMAGE.GIF**, **IMAGE02.GIF**, **IMAGE03.GIF**. Figure 9-12 shows one possible series. This example will produce an animated count up from 1 to 3.
2. Open a new file with whatever animated GIF tool you are using. The GIF Construction Set is a popular choice for the PC world. GifBuilder is a popular choice in the Mac world.
3. Load each image of the sequence, in order, into the new file.
4. For each image, set it to delay or stay on the screen for 1/100 of a second.
5. Decide how many times you want the image to loop and set that.
6. Set any other attribute you want to change from the default.
7. Save the new image as GIF. It is best to use a name that corresponds to the sequence names that make up the file.

8. Use the GIF image in an HTML document with a simple **<IMG>** tag. For example:

```
<IMG SRC="IMAGE,gif">
```

How It Works

When Netscape or Internet Explorer sees a GIF89a file that contains more than one image, it cycles through those images at a speed set by the user for the number of loops set by the user.

Comments

Too many animated GIFs on a page can be annoying and can cause cache problems.

This is a generalized way to create an animated GIF. The process will differ a bit depending on what tools you use. GIF Construction Set is a popular choice in the PC world and GifBuilder is a popular choice in the Mac world. You can find them by going to your Web search engine of choice and searching for their names.

GIF Construction Set 3.2 (the version available from the Web site as of this writing) makes creating animated GIFs extremely easy through the use of the Animation Wizard, which can be found in the File menu. This wizard prompts you along each step of the way needed to create an animated GIF, making the entire process quite painless.

There are also numerous collections of public domain animated GIFs online. To find them, use Yahoo! or your favorite Web search engine.

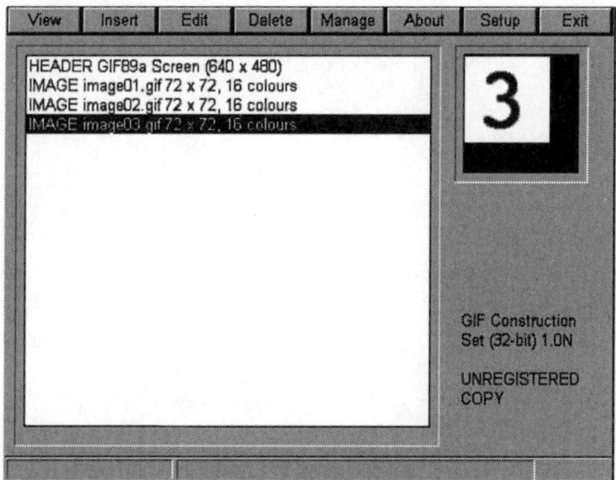

Figure 9-12 The sequence of images for an animation done with the GIF Construction Set

CHAPTER 10

ADDING EXTERNALLY LINKED MULTIMEDIA OBJECTS

10

ADDING EXTERNALLY LINKED MULTIMEDIA OBJECTS

How do I...

10.13 Make my VRML world more realistic?

10.14 Spin a VRML object?

10.15 Include animated textures on VRML objects?

Multimedia information is generally more intuitive and more informative than plain textual information. However, HTML 4.0 provides only limited means for including multimedia objects in your documents. This chapter explores the use of links to include this type of information in your document indirectly. Some of this information is also relevant to the development of multimedia for direct inclusion using nonstandard methods discussed in Chapter 18, "Direct Inclusion of Multimedia Objects."

Many types of information cannot be represented directly in HTML 4.0. For example, although most browsers support images within HTML documents using `<IMG>` elements (see Chapter 9, "Using Images in Your Documents"), only a limited number of types, usually Graphical Interchange Format (GIF) and Joint Pictures Experts Group (JPEG), are directly supported. Furthermore, HTML does not provide any direct support for the inclusion of other media types, such as audio or animation.

Processed data, such as PostScript or DVI files, cannot be included directly in HTML documents either. If a converter is available, you can translate this data to HTML (see How-To 2.7). However, converters generally create a single HTML document rather than a component suitable for inclusion in an HTML document.

Links provide a means for indirectly including both multimedia information and processed data. When a reader triggers a link to such information, the requested item is retrieved as any other file would be. However, when the browser receives an object that is not HTML or some other type that it directly interprets, it uses a helper application to render the object in an appropriate manner. If the user's hardware or software does not support the particular media type retrieved, then the object is not displayed.

This chapter explains the use of links that enable you to include a variety of information objects not directly supported by HTML. The procedures for including these objects, along with pointers to helper applications for displaying these objects, are provided. Table 10-1 summarizes the location of the relevant How-To's corresponding to various types of multimedia files and processed data files. How-To 10.1 provides a general approach to, as well as a complete example of, incorporating external objects into an HTML document.

Table 10-1 Multimedia objects covered in this chapter

INFORMATION TYPE	STORAGE FORMAT	HOW-TO'S	FILENAME EXTENSION
Application	DVI	10.9	`.dvi`
Application	PostScript	10.8	`.ps`
Audio	AIFF	10.6 and 10.7	`.aiff(.aif)`
Audio	AU	10.6	`.au`

INFORMATION TYPE	STORAGE FORMAT	HOW-TO'S	FILENAME EXTENSION
Audio	WAV	10.6 and 10.7	.wav
Image	GIF	Chapter 9 and 10.2	.gif
Image	JPEG	Chapter 9 and 10.2	.jpeg(.jpg)
Image	PNM	10.2	.pnm, .pbm, .pgm
Image	PICT	10.2	.PICT
Image	RGB	10.2	.rgb
Image	TIFF	10.2	.tiff(.tif)
Image	PNG	10.2	.png
Video	AVI	10.4 and 10.5	.avi
Video	MPEG	10.4 and 10.5	.mpeg(.mpg)
Video	QUICKTIME	10.4 and 10.5	.mov
x-world	VRML	10.10–10.15	.wrl

10.1 Add Links to Multimedia in My Home Page

You have a variety of multimedia objects and you want to include these objects in your home page. You want your place on the World Wide Web to be more dynamic and exciting. In this How-To, you will learn how to build a home page with linked multimedia.

10.2 Add an External Image

HTML supports inline images, and browsers implement this support for a limited number of image formats. You want to be able to include images in other formats in your HTML documents. In this How-To, you will learn how to incorporate external images in your HTML pages.

10.3 Convert Among Image Formats

You want to make your documents with large inline images more efficient. You have added images that can be viewed through an external viewer, but you want to include some of these as inline images. What must you do to show the images on your HTML page? In this How-To, you will learn how to convert among image formats.

10.4 Insert a Video

You want to include video clips in your HTML pages. How do you include them in your documents? What kind of support do readers need so they can view this information? In this How-To, you will learn how to add digital video to your pages.

10.5 Convert Among Video File Formats

What types of video file formats are there? How do you convert a file from one to another? Readers can view your video clips with a helper application, but you need the clip in another format so that you can edit it with your current hardware and software. In this How-To, you will learn how to convert among video formats.

10.6 Insert a Sound File

You want to include a voice description of the current document. The text and pictures do not totally convey the point you are trying to make with the current document. How do you include this sound file? And how do you tell your readers how to access this information? In this How-To, you will learn how to place sound files in your HTML pages.

10.7 Convert Among Audio File Formats

A variety of audio file formats has been developed on several different platforms. You must convert from one format to another easily so that you can efficiently edit and tailor the audio that you include in your documents. In this How-To, you will learn how to convert among sound file formats.

10.8 Include a PostScript Document

Much of your documentation is in the PostScript format. You want to build HTML documents that provide Web-based access to these PostScript files. How do you include PostScript documents in your HTML documents? In this How-To, you will learn how to access PostScript files from your HTML pages.

10.9 Include a Device-Independent (DVI) File

You have written documents using the TeX formatting language. You know you can convert these documents to HTML, but they are more useful to you as either TeX or DVI files. How do you provide access to your DVI files from HTML documents? In this How-To, you will learn how to provide access to DVI files from your HTML pages.

10.10 Find a VRML Browser

The Virtual Reality Modeling Language (VRML), like HTML, serves as a basis for network-based documents. As with HTML Web pages, you need a suitable browser to view these documents. In this How-To, you will learn how to locate a browser, or plug-in, suitable for use on your platform.

10.11 Create a VRML Document

The intricacies of VRML are beyond the scope of this book. However, an introduction to the recognition and creation of such documents will provide you with a glimpse into this growing area of Web documents. In this How-To, you will learn how to create a basic VRML document and how to recognize such a document if you retrieve one.

10.12 Locate Prebuilt VRML Objects

Authors throughout the Internet have developed a wide variety of VRML objects. A large number of such objects are freely (or not so freely) available for your use in your own worlds. In this How-To, you will learn about several repositories containing reusable VRML objects.

10.13 Make My VRML World More Realistic

VRML worlds often do not create a realistic environment. Several methods exist to improve the realism in your VRML worlds. In this How-To, you will learn how to use level of detail (LOD) and textures to improve the realism of your creation.

10.14 Spin a VRML Object

The current VRML standard does not provide support for any independent motion within worlds, but many new VRML browsers and plug-ins support independent object motion. In this How-To, you will learn how to include simple moving objects within your VRML world.

10.15 Include Animated Textures on VRML Objects

Textures applied to VRML objects enhance the realism of objects; however, textures can also convey additional, mobile information. By using an animated GIF image as a texture, you can project this animation onto the surface of any VRML object. In this How-To, you will learn how to apply an animated GIF image to a VRML object.

COMPLEXITY
INTERMEDIATE

10.1 How do I... Add links to multimedia in my home page?

COMPATIBILITY: HTML

Problem

I would like to introduce myself to the world. Can I include a voice welcome and introduction on my home page? Better yet, can I include a small video segment of myself stating who I am and what I do? How do I add multimedia elements to my home page?

Technique

You can incorporate multimedia objects into a home page. The use of tailored anchor elements to access helper applications for specified file types is the key to this process. Each multimedia file or processed data file added to an HTML 4.0 document, with the exception of inline images, active Java applets, or ActiveX controls, is added in this manner.

Steps

The following steps lead you through the creation or modification of a single HTML document titled "Home Page of Me." This document will serve as your business card in the World Wide Web community.

This process assumes that you are using a normal text editor for your document creation. If you use a different kind of editor, some of the steps outlined might not be necessary; be sure to check the documentation for your editor to determine which steps apply.

Step-by-step instructions are provided here to modify a home page, or any page, to include multimedia objects of all types.

1. Change directories to the location where you want to develop your HTML documents. Open the file containing your HTML home page in your favorite text editor.

```
edit homepage.htm
```

2. If you have not created a home page for yourself, review How-To 2.14 to help you create a home page.

3. Follow the procedure identified in Table 10-1 that is appropriate for the media type you want to include. For example, you might want to include a voice introduction to yourself or your Web pages in a home page constructed through the procedure in How-To 2.14

```
USA<BR>
E-Mail: my_id@mysite.edu
<A HREF="http://www.mysite.edu/~me/audio/intro.au">
<IMG SRC="/icons/sound.xbm" ALT="[Audio Icon]">
Welcome Message</A> (1.2 MB AU Audio)<BR>
```

or include an image of your project group that can be viewed with a helper application.

```
I am currently working on several projects with
<A HREF="http://www.mysite.edu/~me/group.jpg">group gold</A> (1.4 MB
JPEG).
These projects include...
```

4. Save the file. Remember to use the `.html` or `.htm` filename extension to indicate an HTML document.

5. Try to view your home page using as many different browsers as you have access to.

6. If there are problems with the way items display, modify the document as appropriate.

7. When you feel that your home page is ready for the rest of the world, ask your site administrator to install your document on your Web site, or follow his or her instructions to install the document in your home directory.

How It Works

Multimedia elements other than inline images are added to HTML documents by specifying links that refer to the required files. HTML does not support direct inclusion of such files. Therefore, to develop your multimedia home page, you must create or acquire appropriate multimedia or processed data files, install them on your Web server, and provide access to them via links from your home page.

If your software and hardware permit it, you might want to include a small video or audio segment introducing yourself. Or you might include a reference to a photo of your project team. Your imagination is the only limit to what you can accomplish.

After you have created or acquired suitable multimedia and processed data files, test them extensively to make sure they work exactly as you want, then install them on the server. Chapter 12, "Server Basics," discusses installation of documents on a server.

Use the procedures in this chapter to develop a multimedia home page that will serve as your introduction to the World Wide Web community. You should feel free to experiment with including other elements to create a home page suited to your interests and goals. However, for ease of understanding, the following example extends the home page developed in How-To 2.14:

```
<!DOCTYPE HTML PUBLIC "-//W3C//DTD HTML 3.2//EN">
<HTML>
<HEAD>
<TITLE>Home Page of John Q. Public</TITLE>
</HEAD>
<BODY>

<!-- Mark the beginning of this portion with a horizontal rule. -->
<HR>
<!-- Center your name as a level 1 header. -->
<H1 ALIGN="center">John Q. Public</H1>
<!-- Provide any desirable contact information. -->
999 Peachtree St.<BR>
Atlanta, GA 30314<BR>
USA<BR>
E-Mail: my_id@mysite.edu<BR>
<A HREF="http://www.mysite.edu/~me/audio/intro.au">
<IMG SRC="/icons/sound.xbm" ALT="[Audio Icon]">
Welcome Message</A> (1.2 MB AU Audio)

<!-- Mark the beginning of this portion with a horizontal rule. -->
<HR>
<!-- Choose the heading text that you feel appropriate. -->
<H1>About Me</H1>
<!-- The formatting and information should be developed to suit your needs.
-->
This is the first paragraph in this section about myself.
I have been at MY BUSINESS for the past X years.
<P>
I am currently working on several projects with
<A HREF="http://www.mysite.edu/~me/group.jpg">group gold</A> (1.4 MB JPEG).
```

continued on next page

continued from previous page

```
These projects include...

<!-- Mark the beginning of this portion with a horizontal rule. -->
<HR>
<!-- Substitute the appropriate information in your document. The date ⇐
should -->
<!-- appear in a long format with the month name written out since the ⇐
order -->
<!-- conventions for date abbreviations vary. -->
Last modified on CURRENT_DATE by YOUR_NAME (YOUR_E-MAIL)

</BODY>
</HTML>
```

You can now add links to your own multimedia and processed data files. Standard HTML 4.0 anchor elements can be used to specify these hypermedia links (see Chapter 8, "Establishing Links"). The preceding document contains two such example links. Figure 10-1 shows how this document would appear with one of these links activated.

The selection of the link triggers a request for the file specified in the anchor element. If the request is successful, this server generates a response that includes both the type of the requested file and its contents.

Servers maintain a database that maps filename extensions to information types to generate type information sent to browsers. Therefore, take care to ensure that

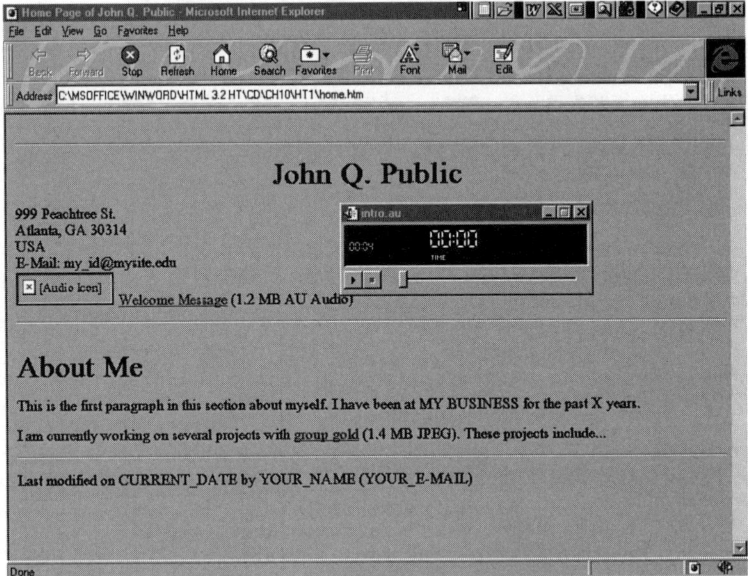

Figure 10-1 Rendering of a multimedia home page

the proper filename extensions are used. Chapter 12 and Appendix C, "MIME," provide further information on document installation and document types.

When a browser receives a file from the server, it determines how to present the data based on the type of information provided by the server. Most browsers will directly render only text and HTML documents in their display window. Helper applications display information of other types. This process is illustrated in Figure 10-2.

Comments

When adding elements of your own, remember that the document you are creating might be viewed by thousands, if not millions, of people. You should consider the variety of browsers with differing presentation capabilities during your multimedia document development.

Additional object types and suitable viewers can be added in the same way you would add the file types discussed in this chapter. For example, you can include virtual reality files by configuring the browser to launch an appropriate external viewer when it encounters a virtual reality file, creating links to appropriate objects, and installing a helper application capable of displaying the file. For more information on virtual reality files, see How-To's 10.10 through 10.15.

Several popular browsers support additional, nonstandard mechanisms for including multimedia objects within a Web page. See Chapter 17, "Web Programming with Java and JavaScript," and Chapter 18, "Direct Inclusion of Multimedia Objects," for additional information on these methods.

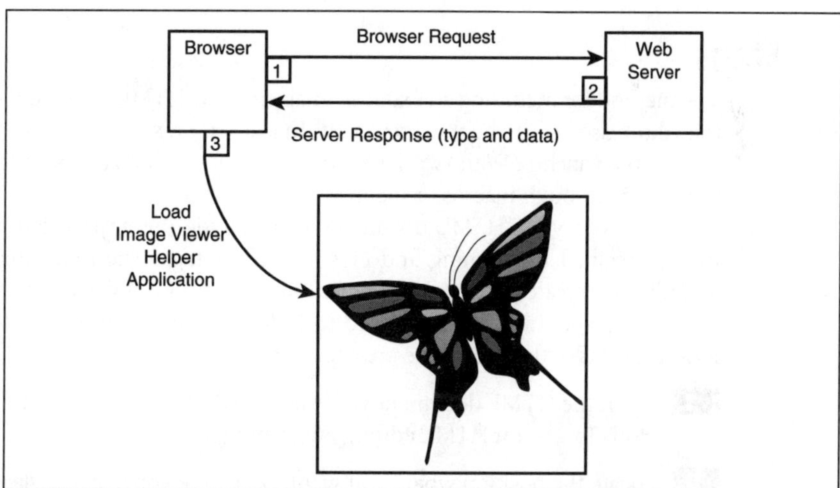

Figure 10-2 Retrieval and rendering process of external objects

10.2 How do I... Add an external image?

COMPATIBILITY: HTML

Problem

With inline images (Chapter 9, "Using Images in Your Documents"), I am limited to GIF images, X bitmap files, and JPEG images. I would like to include images in other formats. I know that I cannot include them directly because HTML does not support other image formats. However, I need to make these image objects available.

Technique

You can provide access to images not supported through the inline `<IMG>` HTML element by establishing a link to the desired image. When a reader selects a link, the browser retrieves the linked file from the server where it is stored and displays it. If the browser does not support direct display of the file, it uses a helper application. If no qualified helper application is available, the user usually has the choice of deleting the file or saving it for later use.

The following procedure shows how to include links to external images in your HTML documents.

Steps

The method for including an external image in your HTML document depends on the editor used to create the document. In a strictly text-based editor, you manually insert an anchor. With WYSIWYG or macro/menu-based editors, you might add the anchor through macros or menus.

Either way, your HTML document will include the appropriate anchor element, specified by opening and closing anchor tags. The following procedure assumes you create your anchor element in a text editor. If you are not using a text editor, you should consult your editor's documentation to determine whether modifications of the procedure are necessary.

1. Open the HTML document you want to edit in your HTML editor. (See How-To 2.4, on HTML editing environments.)

2. Locate the position where you want to include your image. Place the cursor at this location.

3. Insert the text that you want to enclose between the opening and closing anchor tags. If the image file is large, let the reader know. An example of such a message is

```
owl image (1.2 MB JPEG)
```

4. Place the insertion point where you want the anchor to begin. Insert an opening anchor tag at this location. Minimally, this should include the target of the link and the URL of the image you want to include. You include this URL as the value of an `HREF` attribute. The following code shows an opening anchor tag:

```
<A HREF="http://www.mysite.edu/images/owl.jpeg">owl image (1.2 MB JPEG)
```

5. Place the insertion point after the enclosed text. Insert a closing anchor tag. The following code shows a complete anchor element for the sample image:

```
<A HREF="http://www.mysite.edu/images/owl.jpeg">owl image</A>
(1.2 MB JPEG)
```

6. Save your document, or continue adding elements by returning to step 2.

How It Works

Most browsers support GIF and X bitmap images within a document using the HTML `<IMG>` element. When this element was added to HTML, GIF was one of the most widely used image formats. Recently, support for direct inclusion of JPEG images has become standard in several popular browsers.

Because many images are available in a variety of other file formats, you can use an external image viewer to access images in these formats in HTML documents, as shown in Figure 10-3.

Many different image formats exist, and you must have a suitable viewer if you want to view images of a particular type. Generic viewers can recognize and display images in a variety of formats. Consequently, it is easier to use image viewers of this type than to require a separate viewer for each image format.

You access an external image by activating an HTML anchor that links to such an image. This anchor provides no information to the reader about the size and format of the linked image. Therefore, a useful practice is to specify both the format and the size of the image in the text of the document. The format information enables the reader to decide whether he or she has an image viewer that can display the linked image. The size information enables the reader to decide whether he or she wants to wait the amount of time the image will take to download.

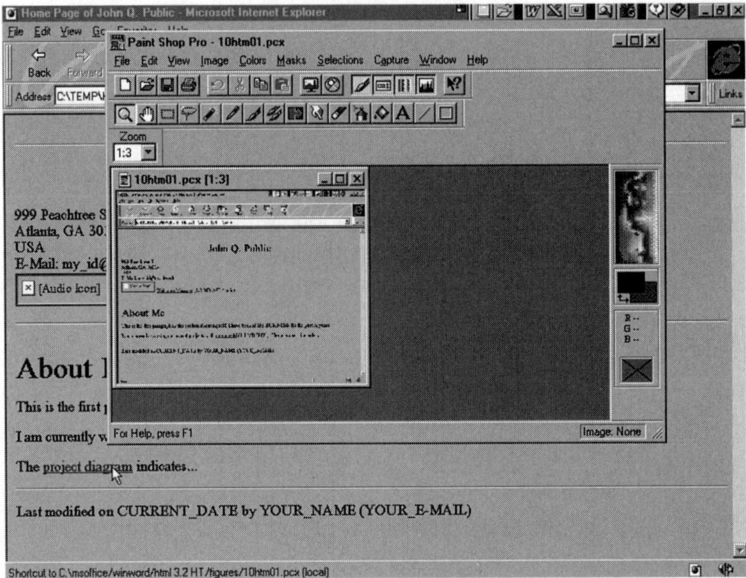

Figure 10-3 Browser and image viewer helper application

A common practice is to provide a smaller inline version of the image as part of the anchor for the linked image. This thumbnail image gives the user a preview of the larger external image. See How-To 9.7 for detailed information on the proper use of thumbnail images.

When a browser receives an image file from a server, it determines how to display the image based on the format of the image data. Most browsers directly display plain text and HTML documents. Other types of information, such as images, are shown by helper applications.

Comments

The anchor elements in this How-To use only the **HREF** attribute. Chapter 8, "Establishing Links," provides additional information to HTML 4.0 anchor elements, including information on other available attributes. Appendix A, "HTML Quick Reference," provides a quick reference on HTML 4.0 anchor elements. See How-To 10.1 for a complete example of incorporating external images into HTML documents.

For external images to be displayed properly, both the browser accessing the image and the server providing the image must be configured properly. Your Web site administrator is responsible for properly configuring your server. Instructions for configuring server support for external images are provided in How-To 12.6.

Configuring a browser to support external images requires either the modification of its configuration files or the alteration of a helper program list from the program's menu. You must examine your browser documentation to determine the procedure to configure support for external images.

Table 10-2 lists some suitable image viewers. You need the proper application for your computer system to view non-inline images. This is not a comprehensive list. If a suggested application does not meet your needs, use a Web search engine such as Infoseek (`http://www.infoseek.com`) to find a more suitable application.

Table 10-2 Common image viewing applications

PLATFORM	APPLICATION	LOCATION
Mac	JPEGView	`ftp://ftp.ncsa.uiuc.edu/Mosaic/Mac/Helpers/`
PC	LviewPro	`http://www.lview.com/`
PC	PaintShop Pro	`http://www.jasc.com` (also on the CD-ROM)
UNIX	xv	`ftp://ftp.cis.upenn.edu/pub/xv`

COMPLEXITY
INTERMEDIATE

10.3 How do I... Convert among image formats?

COMPATIBILITY: HTML

Problem

I have a set of image files in a variety of formats. I would like to put them into formats appropriate for display on Web pages. How can I convert these images into the right formats?

Technique

Many images are created and stored in a format that is not the best for your desired use. Fortunately, converters exist for several popular image formats.

First, identify an appropriate converter. Next, acquire the converter. Use it to convert your images. Finally, view your converted image using an image viewer to determine whether the image's integrity was maintained through the conversion process.

Steps

The following step-by-step procedure shows how to acquire and use an image converter. The listed converters accept images stored in particular file formats and generate appropriate image files as output.

1. Determine the original image file format as well as the format that you want to use for your converted image.

2. Find the converter you want. Table 10-3 lists some common converter applications. If you cannot find a suitable converter among them, you might want to use a Web search application to find an appropriate converter.

Table 10-3 Common image formatting conversion applications

PLATFORM	CONVERTERS	LOCATION
PC, Mac, UNIX	Adobe Photoshop	`http://www.adobe.com/prodindex/`
	Adobe Systems, Inc.	`photoshop/main.html`
PC	PaintShop Pro	JASC, Inc., `http://www.jasc.com/`, also on the CD-ROM
PC	Graphic Workshop	`http://www.mindworkshop.com/`
		`alchemy/gww.html`
Max	Graphic Converter	`http://members.aol.com/lemkesoft/`
UNIX	PBMPLUS	`ftp://wuarchive.wustl.edu/graphics/`
		`graphics/packages/NetPBM/`
UNIX (X-Window)	xv	`ftp://ftp.cis.upenn.edu/pub/xv/`

3. Use anonymous FTP or an FTP URL to acquire an appropriate converter. Uncompress, unarchive, and install the converter application as appropriate for your computer platform.

On a UNIX platform, use the **`uncompress`** and **`tar`** commands to uncompress and unarchive.

On a PC platform, the most common compression/archival program is ZIP. Use the unzip application to uncompress and unarchive.

On a Mac platform, the most common compression/archival program is StuffIt. Use the StuffIt program to uncompress and unarchive.

4. Convert your image file.

5. Examine the results of your image conversion in a suitable viewer. Edit the converted image if necessary.

6. Use the process described in How-To 10.2 to include external images in your HTML document. Use the procedures in Chapter 9, "Using Images in Your Documents," to use inline images.

How It Works

Image objects are created with a variety of applications and stored in many image formats. Many applications save in a single format. This format might not be suitable for use on your World Wide Web pages.

Most image formats provide essentially the same information. Therefore, converting the different formats is only a matter of translating the information from the source format to the target format. Depending on the conversion being performed, however, the converter might perform a more complex transformation in which information from the source image must be used to calculate or modify data to generate the target.

You might want images in different formats for several reasons. First, if you want to include an inline image, the image must be stored in GIF or JPEG format. Therefore, the first reason you might need an image converter is to generate a GIF or JPEG image from an image in some other format. After you have converted the image to GIF or JPEG, you can include the image inline using the **<IMG>** element, as described in Chapter 9, or as an external image by including a reference to the image using an anchor, as specified in How-To 10.2.

Furthermore, you might want to use a converter program to generate thumbnail images to provide a preview of images that can be seen with a viewer. To do this, use the editing capabilities of the converter to shrink the entire image or to clip a relevant portion. Save the new image or image portion as a GIF or JPEG image. Include the new thumbnail as an inline image in an anchor element. For example, if you have a 2MB JPEG image of an owl and you create a 15KB GIF thumbnail version of the same image, you could include the following code as a link to the original image:

```
<A HREF="http://www.mysite.edu/images/owl.jpeg">
<IMG SRC="http://www.mysite.edu/images/owl.gif" ALT="Owl Image"
ALIGN=bottom>
(2 MB JPEG)
</A>
```

Finally, you might want to remove inline images and provide access to them via an external viewer. GIF might not be the most compact format for the particular image. You can use a converter to store the image in a variety of formats and determine which will be the most efficient external image. The time it takes to download a particular page has an effect on the usability of that page by a reader. If your page takes an excessively long time to retrieve, the reader is less likely to wait for the download to complete and is very unlikely to visit the page again.

Comments

Several of the packages mentioned in Table 10-3 enable you to edit and modify the images you convert. You can use these features to fine-tune the image and to generate an altered version of the image. You might want to generate thumbnail images for use as links to other media types such as movie segments or audio.

When you convert an image file, make sure that you provide the correct filename extension on the newly generated image file. The filename extension is used by servers and browsers to determine the type of data being accessed. Table 10-4 lists the common filename extensions for a variety of image types. The third column displays the Multipurpose Internet Mail Extensions (MIME) types that browsers and servers use to send information on image types.

Table 10-4 Image file formats and common filename extensions

IMAGE FORMAT EXTENSION	FILENAME	MIME TYPE
GIF	.gif	image/gif
Image exchange format	.ief	image/ief
JPEG	.jpeg, .jpg, .jpe	image/jpeg
PICT	.pict, .pct	image/pict
TIFF	.tiff, .tif	image/tiff
Portable Image	.pnm	image/x-portable-anymap
Portable Bitmap	.pbm	image/x-portable-bitmap
Portable Graymap	.pgm	image/x-portable-graymap
Portable Pixmap	.ppm	image/x-portable-pixmap
Portable Network Graphics	.png	image/png
RGB	.rgb	image/x-rgb
X Window-Dump	.xwd	image/x-xwindowdump
X Bitmap	.xbm	image/x-xbitmap
X Pixelmap	.xpm	image/x-xpixmap

Appendix C, "MIME," provides more complete information about the use of MIME types in the World Wide Web environment.

10.4 How do I... Insert a video?

COMPATIBILITY: HTML

Problem

I want to include movie segments in my HTML 4.0 documents. However, HTML does not directly support the inclusion of video. Is there a way to provide access to my video object from my HTML 4.0 documents?

Technique

You cannot insert video segments directly into standard HTML 4.0 documents, but you can include links to video files. The movie object is retrieved and displayed by a helper application.

You can acquire a video object in one of three ways:

✔ Download an existing clip.

✔ Copy royalty-free clip video (much like clip art packages).

✔ Create video clips yourself.

The first two approaches are easiest; archives and CD-ROM clip libraries are widespread. The third option requires access to more specialized hardware and software. If you have access to such equipment, familiarize yourself thoroughly with the documentation provided with your hardware and software before you begin.

Steps

The following procedure lets you create links to video files. Depending on your editor, you can either insert the appropriate tags manually or use the macro or menu features of your editor. In either case, the HTML document will contain the appropriate anchor element. These directions assume you are using a text editor to add the element.

1. Open the HTML document you want to edit.
2. Locate the position where you want to place the link to the desired video object. Move the cursor to this location.
3. Insert the anchor text between the opening and closing anchor tags. An example is

```
The flight (10MB MPEG Video) of the owl is quite graceful.
```

4. Place the insertion point where you want the anchor to begin. Insert an opening anchor tag at this location. Minimally, this should include the URL where the image file is located, using the `HREF` attribute. The following example shows an opening anchor tag:

```
The <A HREF="http://www.mysite.edu/images/flight.mpeg">flight (10MB
MPEG Video) of the owl is quite graceful.
```

5. Move your insertion point to the end of the enclosed text. Insert a closing tag. The following example shows the full anchor element and surrounding text:

```
The <A HREF="http://www.mysite.edu/images/flight.mpeg">flight</A> (10MB
MPEG Video) of the owl is quite graceful.
```

6. Save your document, or return to step 2 to continue adding elements.

How It Works

HTML 4.0 does not directly support the inclusion of digital video. The digital video category includes both animation and movie clips. You can include video objects in an HTML document through links to the desired video file. The browser uses an external viewer to display the movie segment. Figure 10-4 shows a browser and the helper application used to display a video object.

When you create a link to a video clip, include the size and type specifications for the video clip referenced in or near the anchor text. The reader uses this information to determine whether he or she wants to download and view the referenced video clip.

You can also use a thumbnail image to indicate the content of the video. You could even convert the first frame of the video clip to a GIF image file and reduce it; then you could include it in your document as a link to the video clip. This might not be easy with some MPEG files due to compression. MPEG file compression works by storing the difference between two frames rather than storing the identical portions of the frames twice; therefore, extracting a single frame might require the processing of all preceding frames. For example, if you have a movie clip of an owl in flight, you could use a thumbnail of an owl to provide visual information describing the content of the movie. One example of how this could be done in HTML is

```
<A HREF="http://www.mysite.edu/images/owl.mpeg">
<IMG SRC="http://www.mysite.edu/images/owl.gif" ALT="Owl Image"
ALIGN=bottom>
(10 MB MPEG)
</A>
```

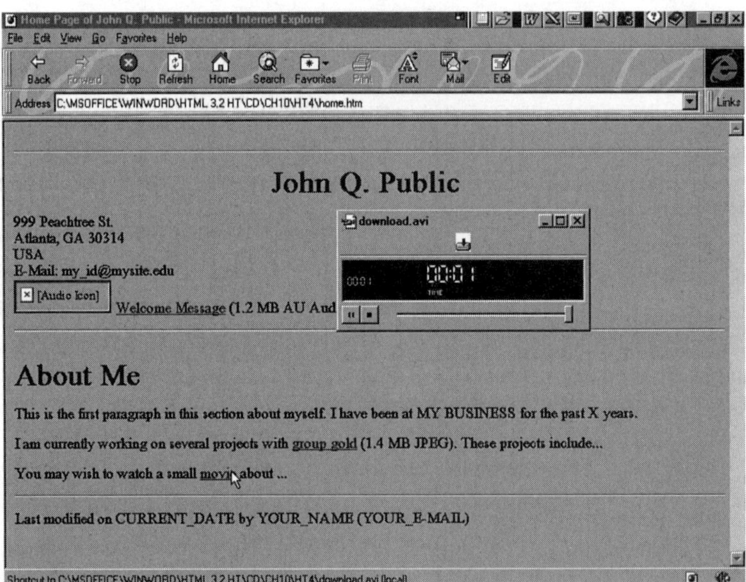

Figure 10-4 Browser and movie viewer helper application

When a user activates a link to a video file, the browser requests the specified file. The server responds with both type and data information from the requested movie file. When a browser receives this information, it displays the movie with the helper application appropriate for the movie type.

Therefore, you must install video files on your Web site or have your Web administrator install them. When these files are properly installed, you can create links to them using the standard HTML 4.0 anchor element. Install video objects in either MPEG or QuickTime format. These formats are the most widely supported by browsers in any computer platform.

Comments

Chapter 8, "Establishing Links," provides a detailed discussion of the use of the HTML 4.0 anchor element. Appendix A, "HTML Quick Reference," provides a handy reference to this element and a list of valid attributes. See How-To 10.1 for a general discussion of including external objects, as well as an example within a complete HTML document.

Both the browser accessing the video file and the server providing the files must be configured properly. Your Web site administrator is responsible for the proper server configuration. Instructions for configuring server support for video clips are provided in How-To 12.6.

In addition, browsers that are intended to access video files must have a video helper application installed and configured. How you configure your browser to support helper applications differs from browser to browser. You might need to edit a configuration file used by the browser, or you might need to enter the proper information by selecting a Preferences (or similar) option from one of your browser menus. Read your browser's documentation to determine the procedure for configuring your browser to use helper applications for movie files.

Table 10-5 lists some video players you can use. You need suitable hardware, a viewer, and a properly configured browser to view video files. This list is not comprehensive. If a suggested application does not meet your needs, use a Web search engine to try to find a more suitable helper application.

Table 10-5 Common video player applications

PLATFORM	APPLICATION (FORMATS)	LOCATION
Mac	Sparkle (MPEG)	`ftp://ftp.ncsa.uiuc.edu/Mosaic/Mac/`
		`Helpers/`
Mac	FastPlayer	`ftp://ftp.ncsa.uiuc.edu/Mosaic/`
		`Mac/Helpers/`
PC	Mpegplay (MPEG)	`http://www.winsite.com/info/pc/win3/`
		`desktop/mpegw32g.zip`

continued on next page

continued from previous page

PLATFORM	APPLICATION (FORMATS)	LOCATION
PC	Qtw (QuickTime)	ftp://wuarchive.wustl.edu/systems/
		ibmps/win3/misc/qtwin110.zip
UNIX	xanim (MPEG, QuickTime)	ftp://crl.dec.com/pub/X11/
		contrib/applications/
UNIX	mpeg_play (MPEG)	ftp://mm-ftp.cs.berkeley.edu/
		pub/mpeg/play

Several browsers support nonstandard means for directly including video files within a Web page. Chapter 18, "Direct Inclusion of Multimedia Objects," introduces you to the use of these inclusion mechanisms.

COMPLEXITY
ADVANCED

10.5 How do I... Convert among video file formats?

COMPATIBILITY: HTML

Problem

My video files are not as generically useful across computer platforms as I want them to be. I need to convert my movie files to a more useful format.

Technique

MPEG and QuickTime are the most common video formats on the World Wide Web. If you have Windows AVI format movies or Macintosh-specific QuickTime clips, you must convert them to either MPEG or "flattened" QuickTime. Macintosh-specific QuickTime movies exploit certain features of the Macintosh hardware and software; *flattening* a QuickTime movie removes these dependencies so that the movie supports cross-platform viewing.

Steps

This procedure outlines the process for acquiring converters and using them to convert video files. These converters accept video files in a particular format and save them in a different video file format.

The process requires a familiarity with the use of anonymous FTP or FTP URLs. Your first task is to identify an appropriate converter. Next, you must acquire the converter and apply it to your existing documents. Finally, you should examine the result of the conversion process.

1. Determine the format of your video files and the format to which you want to convert.

2. Find a suitable converter. Table 10-6 lists some software packages and points to their location on the Internet. If you cannot find a converter that meets your needs in the table, use a Web search engine to find a suitable converter.

Table 10-6 Common video format conversion applications

VIDEO FORMAT	CONVERTERS	LOCATION
MPEG to QuickTime	Sparkle (Mac)	ftp://ftp.ncsa.uiuc.edu/Mosaic/
		Mac/Helpers/
QuickTime to MPEG	Qt2Mpeg (Mac)	http://www.prism.uvsq.fr/public/
		wos/multimedia/files/qt2mpeg.sit.hqx
AVI, QuickTime	Mac Video for	http://www.prism.uvsq.fr/public/
	Windows (MAC)	wos/multimedia/files/vfw11.sit
QuickTime flattener	Flatten MooV(Mac)	http://hyperarchive.lcs.mit.edu/
		HyperArchive/Abstracts/gst/mov/
		HyperArchive.html
AVI to MPEG	XingCD (PC)	Xing Technology
QuickTime flattener	QFlat (PC)	ftp://venice.tcp.com/pub/anime-manga/
		software/viewers/qtfat.zip
QuickTime to MPEG	Qt2Mpeg (UNIX)	http://www.prism.uvsq.fr/public/wos/
		multimedia/files/qt2mpeg.zip

3. Acquire an appropriate converter package from an FTP site or software store. Install the converter application, as appropriate for your platform.

4. Convert your video files.

5. Use a viewer to examine the video files. The displayed video should be very close to the original. If there are notable flaws, edit or convert the original to create a suitable video file in the correct format.

6. Use the process described in How-To 10.4 to include videos in HTML 4.0 documents.

How It Works

The video clips that you find or create come in different formats, but for generic use on the World Wide Web, you want these objects in either QuickTime (flattened) or MPEG format. Currently, viewers for these formats are available across multiple platforms.

If your clips are in another format, you should acquire an appropriate converter and convert the clips to a suitable format. Then view these files using a suitable helper application to assure that information was not lost or significantly altered in the conversion process.

If you have access to a video editing application, you might want to adjust your videos. For MPEG video, you can use the MpegUtil program available for the UNIX platform (`http://www.comp.lancs.ac.uk/computing/users/phillip/mpegUtil.html`). The Adobe Premiere program serves as an editor for QuickTime movies on both the Macintosh and PC/Windows platforms (`http://www.adobe.com/prodindex/premiere/main.html`). Also, a shareware application called QuickEditor for QuickTime editing is available for the Macintosh (`http://www.umich.edu/~archive/mac/powermac/` or `http://hyperarchive.lcs.mit.edu/HyperArchive/Abstracts/gst/mov/HyperArchive.html /gst/mov/`).

When you are satisfied with the results of the conversion or editing, you are ready to install the documents on your Web site. You now should be able to make your video files accessible by referencing them in anchor elements, as described in How-To 10.4.

Comments

Even if your files are in a suitable format, you must decide whether you want to provide video and, if so, in which format(s). The biggest limitation for MPEG video is that, although the MPEG format does support an audio track, most players do not. Until recently, the QuickTime standard was viewed primarily as a Macintosh-specific format, which limited the availability of viewers for other platforms. Furthermore, the requirement that QuickTime movies be flattened for cross-platform use adds an additional step in the development process. Weigh these factors when deciding on the format that you ultimately use.

When you convert a video file, make sure you provide the correct filename extension for the newly generated video file. The filename extension is used by servers and browsers to determine the format of the file. Table 10-7 lists the common filename extensions for a variety of video file types. Browsers and servers communicate data type information using MIME types; the MIME types for several video file formats appear as well.

Table 10-7 Video file formats and common filename extensions

IMAGE FORMAT	FILENAME EXTENSION	MIME TYPE
Microsoft Video Format	`.avi`	`video/msvideo`
MPEG Format Video	`.mpeg, .mpg, .mpe`	`video/mpeg`
QuickTime Format Video	`.qt, .mov`	`video/quicktime`

Appendix C "MIME," provides more complete information on the use of MIME types on the World Wide Web.

10.6 How do I... Insert a sound file?

COMPATIBILITY: HTML

Problem

I would like to include sound clips in my home page. How can I provide links to sound files?

Technique

HTML does not enable you to include audio files in your pages. However, you can create a link to an application that will play a specified sound file.

The most commonly used audio file type on the World Wide Web is Sun's AU audio file format. The AU standard supports several types of encoding for sound samples. The most prevalent sample encoding is 8-bit m-law. The sound quality derived from this encoding is not as high as with other formats, but use of other formats such as AIFF, IFF, WAV, or MPEG audio yields audio segments that are not as portable. As multiplatform support grows for these other sound formats, the use of the formats that provide higher quality audio will also increase.

Steps

The following instructions let you create links to sound files in your HTML documents. This procedure assumes that you use a text editor to edit your page. If this is not the case, consult your editor's documentation to determine any necessary changes in the procedure.

1. Open the HTML document you want to edit in your favorite text editor.

2. Place the insert cursor at the position where you want to create a link to the desired sound file.

3. Insert the text that you want to enclose in the anchor element. When transferring large files, you should specify the file size to warn the reader. An example of such a message is

```
Hoot of an Owl (2 MB AU Audio)
```

4. Position the insertion point where you want the anchor element to begin. Insert an opening anchor tag at this point. Minimally, this tag should include the URL where the sound file is located. Use the **HREF** attribute to specify this value. The following example shows the insertion of an opening anchor tag:

```
<A HREF=http://www.mysite.edu/sounds/owl.au>Hoot of an Owl (2 MB AU
Audio)
```

5. Move the insertion point to the end of the enclosed text. Insert a closing anchor tag. The following example shows a complete anchor element linking to a sound file:

```
<A HREF=http://www.mysite.edu/sounds/owl.au>Hoot of an Owl</A> (2 MB AU
Audio)
```

6. You can also use a thumbnail image to indicate the nature of the audio file. For example, if you have an audio clip of an owl hooting, you could use a thumbnail image of an owl to provide a visual cue to what the audio file contains, as in the following example:

```
<A HREF="http://www.mysite.edu/sounds/owl.au">
<IMG SRC="http://www.mysite.edu/images/owl.gif" ALT="Owl Image" ⇐
ALIGN=bottom>
(2 MB AU Audio)
</A>
```

7. You can also use an icon to indicate the type of object rather than its contents. The following code might be used to include an icon for the same audio file:

```
<A HREF=http://www.mysite.edu/sounds/owl.au>
<IMG SRC="http://www.mysite.edu/icons/sound.gif" ALT="Sound Icon" ⇐
ALIGN=bottom>Hoot</A>  of an Owl (2 MB AU Audio)
```

8. Save your document, or continue adding elements by returning to step 2.

How It Works

When you create a link to a large file, such as an audio clip, you should include in the text near the anchor, or as part of it, the size and type of the file. The reader can use this information to decide whether the file is a suitable size and format to retrieve.

When the reader selects a link, the link triggers the retrieval of the object specified in the anchor element. If the request is successful, the server sends a response containing both the type of the requested file (audio/*) and the file itself (audio data).

To perform this task, the server maintains a database that maps filename extensions to information types. If you use audio files on your Web site, make sure you use the proper filename extensions. Chapter 12, "Server Basics," provides information on configuring your server to transmit sound files properly.

When a browser receives a file from the server, the browser determines how to display the object based on the type of the file. Most browsers process only pure text and HTML documents in their display window. Other types of information are presented to the reader by prespecified helper applications.

Comments

Chapter 7, "Managing Document Spacing," provides a detailed discussion of the various attributes that might be used with the anchor element.

For audio files to be served and rendered correctly, both the browser accessing the object and the server providing the audio object must be configured properly. Your Web site administrator will be responsible for the proper configuration of your server. Instructions for configuring server support for audio are provided in How-To 12.6.

Configuring a browser to support audio usually requires either modifying configuration files or changing a list of helper programs in the browser's menu. Consult your browser's documentation to determine how to configure helper applications for playing audio files. Several browsers support nonstandard means for directly including video files within a Web page. Chapter 18, "Direct Inclusion of Multimedia Objects," introduces you to the use of these inclusion mechanisms.

Table 10-8 lists some audio players suitable for use as helper applications. You will need suitable hardware such as a sound card and speakers or headphones, a program that plays sound files, and a browser that is configured to support audio.

Table 10-8 Common audio player helper applications

PLATFORM	APPLICATION	LOCATION
Mac	SoundMachine (AU,	`ftp://ftp.ncsa.uiuc.edu/Mosaic/`
	AIFF, AIF)	`Mac/Helpers/`
PC	WHAM (AU, WAV,	`ftp://wuarchive.wustl.edu/systems/`
	AIFF, IFF)	`ibmpc/win3/sounds/wham133.zip`
UNIX	showaudio (Metamail)	`ftp://thumper.bellcore.com/pub/nsb/`
	(AU, AIFF, AIF)	

This is not a comprehensive list. Should a suggested application not meet your needs, use a Web search engine such as Lycos (`http://www.lycos.com`) or AltaVista (`http://altavista.digital.com/`) to find a more suitable helper application.

COMPLEXITY
ADVANCED

10.7 How do I... Convert among audio file formats?

COMPATIBILITY: HTML

Problem

I want to save my homemade audio files in a format that most Web users can access. How do I do this?

Technique

You can acquire audio files in several ways:

- ✔ You can digitally record voice data through a microphone connected to many multimedia computer systems.
- ✔ You can use royalty-free audio clips from purchased packages.
- ✔ You can download audio files from bulletin boards or the Internet.
- ✔ With appropriate hardware and software, you can digitally record sound directly from a CD-ROM reader.

Audio files come in several formats. The most popular audio format used in the World Wide Web environment is Sun's AU. If you have audio in other formats, you might want to convert it to AU.

If AU sound quality is sufficient for your task, you should convert your sound file to the AU format. If you require higher quality, the two standards most commonly used other than the AU format files are the AIFF and WAV formats. Audio files stored in these formats are likely to have better sound quality than AU files.

The price of using WAV or AIFF formats rather than AU is reduced portability. If a browser supports audio, it most likely supports the AU format. In addition, the higher-quality audio usually requires more storage, resulting in a longer transmission time. This is a particular disadvantage for people with slow Internet connections.

After you decide on the format you want to use, acquire the appropriate converter and convert your audio files. You should then play these audio files using a suitable helper application to assure that information was not lost or significantly altered in the conversion process.

When you are satisfied with the results of the conversion, you are ready to install the documents on your Web site. You now should be able to access these audio information objects through appropriately constructed anchor elements, as described in How-To 10.4.

The process requires a familiarity with the use of anonymous FTP or FTP URLs. You must first identify an appropriate converter. Next, acquire the converter and apply it to your existing documents. Finally, you should examine the result of the conversion process.

Steps

The following shows you how to acquire converters and use them to convert audio files:

1. Determine the source and target file format of your audio information object.
2. Find the converter that you will need to use. Table 10-9 gives examples of some of these environments by software package and pointers to information concerning them. If you cannot find the file formats and platforms that you require in Table 10-9, you might want to use a Web search application to find an appropriate converter.

Table 10-9 Common audio format conversion applications

AUDIO FILE FORMAT	CONVERTERS	LOCATION
WAV, SND, AIFF	SoundApp (Mac)	`http://hyperarchive.lcs.mit.edu/`
		`HyperArchive/Abstracts/gst/snd/`
		`HyperArchive.html`
SND to AU	m-law (Mac)	`http://hyperarchive.lcs.mit.edu/`
		`HyperArchive/Abstracts/gst/snd/`
		`HyperArchive.html`
AU, WAV,	SOX (UNIX/PC)	`ftp://ftp.cs.ruu.nl/pub/MIDI/PROGRAMS/`
AIFF, SND		

3. Use anonymous FTP or an FTP URL to acquire an appropriate converter package. Uncompress, unarchive, and install the converter application as appropriate for your platform.
4. Apply the converter to your source audio files.
5. Use the process described in How-To 10.6 to include audio objects.

How It Works

The file formats available store sound like digital samples of the sound rather than the original analog signal—that is, like a CD rather than a record—and the size of the sample stored in part determines its quality.

Audio file conversions are often lossy; when converting from a higher-quality format to a lower one, loss of information occurs, particularly if the source uses 16-bit encoding and the target uses 8-bit or the source is stereo and the target is mono. In these cases, you can convert the file in only one direction. Trying to reverse the process will lead to audio segments in the original file format, but with significantly reduced sound quality.

Sound editors will enable you to modify sound files. Use such tools to tailor sounds or to mask out distortions. The WHAM application specified in Table 10-8 provides extensive sound editing capabilities for the PC platform. PlayerPro enables the same kind of audio editing on the Macintosh platform.

Comments

After generating a new audio file, make sure you save the file with the correct filename extension. The filename extension specifies the type of file being accessed. Table 10-10 lists the common filename extensions for a variety of audio information object types. Servers and browsers use MIME types to pass information concerning transmitted files.

Table 10-10 Audio file formats and common filename extensions

AUDIO FORMAT	FILENAME EXTENSION	MIME TYPE
AU 8-bit, m-law	.au, .snd	audio/basic
AIFF	.aiff, .aif	audio/x-aiff
Microsoft Audio	.wav	audio/x-wav
RealAudio	.ra, .ram	audio/x-pn-realaudio
RealAudio plug-in	.rpm	audio/x-pn-realaudio-plugin

Appendix C, "MIME," provides more complete information on the use of MIME types in the World Wide Web environment.

COMPLEXITY
INTERMEDIATE

10.8 How do I... Include a PostScript document?

COMPATIBILITY: HTML

Problem

I have a document archive consisting of a set of PostScript files. I need to keep these documents in this format so I can print them when required. Converting all of them to HTML 4.0 would mean that I would have to maintain the integrity of both sets of documents when changes are made. Can I provide access to my existing archive through HTML documents?

Technique

PostScript is one of the most commonly used printer languages. You can develop and maintain PostScript documents using many different applications. To avoid converting PostScript documents to HTML and maintaining two independent document sets containing the same information, you can use only the original PostScript files.

The disadvantage of this approach is that PostScript documents do not support hypermedia links. The advantages are that the documents are ready to print and only one set of documents needs to be updated. You will need to decide whether to store your documents as PostScript, HTML, or both.

You can create a link to a PostScript file in an HTML document rather than converting the PostScript file to an HTML document. (See How-To 2.3 for information about document conversion.) When a reader selects the link, the browser retrieves the PostScript file and displays it in a suitable viewer. You need not convert your PostScript documents to HTML to allow World Wide Web access, thus obviating the need to have two sets of the same documents.

When creating a link to a PostScript document, you should indicate in or near the text of the anchor element that the object referenced is a PostScript document. If a reader's browsing environment will not render PostScript documents, then he or she does not need to bother trying to trigger the link. Furthermore, you should specify the approximate length of the document referenced. This allows individuals with a slow network connection to make an informed decision about whether to trigger the link.

Steps

The following procedure shows how to link a PostScript file to your HTML documents. If you are creating HTML pages using an editor other than a text editor, consult your documentation to determine the correct procedure for adding an anchor element.

1. Open the HTML document you want to edit in your favorite text editor.
2. Move the cursor to the position where you want to add a link to a PostScript file.
3. Insert the text that you want enclosed between the opening and closing anchor tags.
4. Move your insertion point to where you want the anchor to begin and then insert an opening anchor tag. The **HREF** attribute of this tag should specify the URL of the PostScript file. The following example shows an opening tag for such an anchor element:

```
Printer ready version of this document is
<A HREF="http://www.mysite.edu/papers/owl.ps">available. (1.2 MB)
```

5. Insert a closing anchor tag after the enclosed text. The following example shows a complete anchor element of this type:

```
Printer ready version of this document is
<A HREF="http://www.mysite.edu/papers/owl.ps">available</A>. (1.2 MB)
```

6. You can use an icon in the anchor to indicate the type of the linked file. The following code might be used to include an icon for the same PostScript file:

```
Printer ready version of this document is
<A HREF="http://www.mysite.edu/papers/owl.ps">available
<IMG SRC="http://www.mysite.edu/icons/psdoc.gif" ALT="PostScript Icon"
ALIGN=bottom>
</A>. (1.2 MB)
```

7. Save your document or continue adding elements. Add additional links to PostScript files by returning to step 2.

How It Works

Select a link to request the file specified in the anchor element. If the request is successful, the server sends a response containing both the file's MIME type (application/PostScript) and the file itself.

To perform this task, the server maintains a database that maps filename extensions to MIME types. Therefore, if you use PostScript files on your Web site, make sure you use the proper filename extensions. Chapter 12, "Server Basics," provides more information on configuring servers to support PostScript documents.

When a browser receives a PostScript file from the server, it determines how to display the file based on the MIME type sent by the server. Most browsers directly display only pure text and HTML documents. Helper applications display other information types, such as PostScript documents. Figure 10-5 shows the results of triggering a link to a PostScript document.

Comments

Chapter 8, "Establishing Links," provides a detailed discussion of HTML hypertext links. This How-To uses only the `HREF` attribute of the anchor element, but you might want to include others as you see fit.

To provide access to PostScript documents on a server, you must properly configure the server to transmit PostScript files. Your Web site administrator is responsible for the proper configuration of your server; instructions for configuring a server to support PostScript documents are provided in How-To 12.6.

In addition, any browser that wants to access the PostScript documents must also be configured for direct rendering or, more likely for using a helper application, to display the file. Consult your browser's documentation to determine the procedure for configuring helper applications for PostScript files.

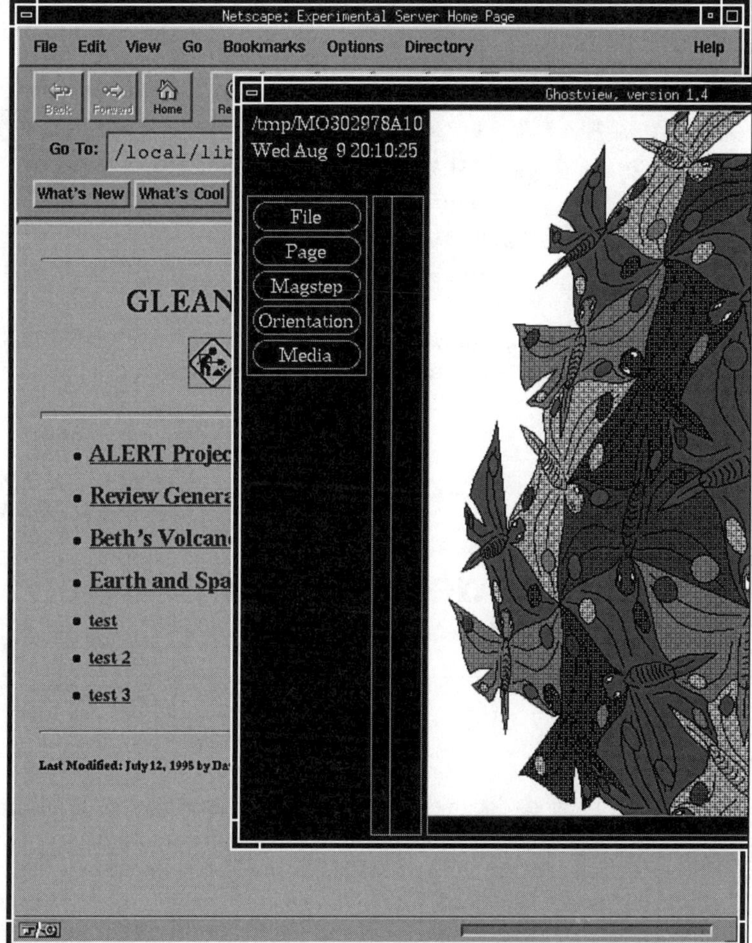

Figure 10-5 Browser and PostScript viewer helper application

Table 10-11 lists some PostScript viewers for several platforms. To view PostScript files, you will need suitable hardware, a helper application, and a browser configured to view PostScript documents.

Table 10-11 PostScript display applications

PLATFORM	APPLICATION	LOCATION
Mac	Mac Ghostscript	`http://hyperarchive.lcs.mit.edu/`
		`HyperArchive/Abstracts/gst/grf/`
		`HyperArchive.html`

continued on next page

continued from previous page

PLATFORM	APPLICATION	LOCATION
PC	gsview and gs*exe	ftp://gatekeeper.dec.com/pub/micro/
	(both required)	pc/winsite/win3/util/gsview
UNIX	ghostview	ftp://ftp.cs.wisc.edu/pub/ghost/
		gnu/ghostview*.gz
	ghostscript	ghostscript*.gz
	ghostscript fonts	ghostscript-fonts*.gz

Table 10-11 does not provide a comprehensive list. If a suggested application does not meet your needs, you can use a Web search engine to find a more suitable helper application.

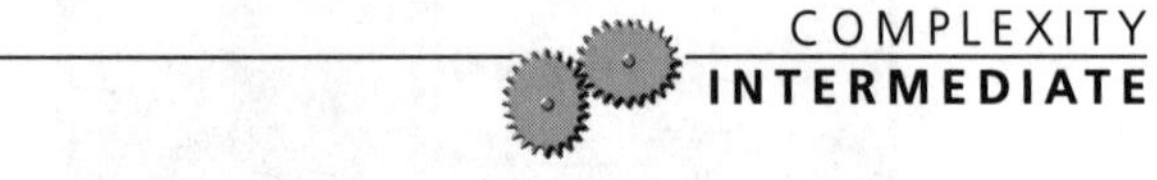

10.9 How do I... Include a device-independent (DVI) file?

COMPATIBILITY: HTML

Problem

Most of my previous documents were developed using the TeX formatting language. DVI files are generated by processing TeX documents. I have an archive of all my DVI files ready to print, and I would like to use HTML documents to provide online access to this archive. I don't want to have to maintain both the HTML and DVI documents. Is there a way I can use the DVI files without converting the entire archive to HTML?

Technique

TeX files can be converted to HTML documents (see How-To 2.3 for information about converting documents). However, two separate sets of documents would require twice as much maintenance. You can maintain a single set of TeX documents with their associated DVI files ready. These DVI files then can be accessed from HTML documents.

To accomplish this, create a link that, when selected, causes the browser to retrieve the DVI file and present it to the reader via a suitable viewer.

Steps

How you include an external object, such as a DVI file, in your HTML page depends on the editing environment used to create the document. These steps assume that you manually insert the anchor element with a text editor. For other editor types, consult your editor's documentation on how to add anchor elements.

The following step-by-step procedure shows how to create a link to a DVI file:

1. Open the HTML document you want to edit in your text editor.
2. Position the cursor where you want to add the DVI file.
3. Insert the text that you want enclosed in the anchor element.
4. Move the cursor to where you want the anchor element to begin and insert an opening anchor tag. Set the **HREF** attribute in this tag to the URL of the DVI file that you want to include. The following example shows such an opening tag:

```
Device Independent (DVI) version of this document is
<A HREF="http://www.mysite.edu/papers/owl.dvi">available. (2 MB)
```

5. Move the insertion point to the end of the anchor text. Insert a closing anchor tag. The following code shows a complete anchor element linking to a DVI file:

```
Device Independent (DVI) version of this document is
<A HREF="http://www.mysite.edu/papers/owl.dvi">available</A>. (2 MB)
```

6. You can use an icon in the anchor to indicate the type of the linked file. The following code might be used to include an icon for the same DVI file:

```
Printer ready version of this document is
<A HREF="http://www.mysite.edu/papers/owl.dvi">available
<IMG SRC="http://www.mysite.edu/icons/dvidoc.gif" ALT="DVI Icon" ⇐
ALIGN=bottom>
</A>. (2 MB)
```

7. Save your document, or continue adding elements by returning to step 2.

How It Works

Before WYSIWYG-style editors, formatted documents were developed using tags to mark the various formatted elements in the documents. Various document formatting languages were developed for this purpose: troff, runoff, and TeX. The TeX formatting language provides such features as incorporation of mathematical expressions, tabular formatting, and font changes.

The TeX application creates DVI files when it processes source files. You can use the DVI files to display or print the formatted document in any number of environments. In most cases, the DVI file needs to be translated to the display device's particular formatting language.

For those who want to provide access to their TeX documents on the World Wide Web, there are two options.

The first option is to convert the TeX documents to HTML. This approach leads to two sets of documents, each of which requires maintenance when one document is altered. In addition, HTML does not support all the capabilities of TeX.

The second approach is to maintain the original TeX documents and generate new DVI files as the TeX documents are updated. In this way, the documents are maintained only once and the DVI files are available to be shown on any display capable of processing a DVI file, as well as being accessible via links in HTML documents.

Selecting the link initiates a server request for the DVI file specified in the anchor element. If the request is successful, the server issues a response containing both the data type and the data itself.

To do so, the server maintains a database that maps filename extensions to information types. Therefore, if DVI files are installed on your Web site, be sure you use the proper filename extensions. Chapter 12, "Server Basics," provides information on configuring a server to support DVI files.

When a browser receives a DVI file from the server, it determines how to display the file based on the type of information provided by the server. Most browsers directly support only pure text and HTML documents in their display windows. Information on other types is displayed by prespecified helper applications. Figure 10-6 shows the result of activating a link to a DVI file.

Comments

HTML 4.0 anchor elements support a variety of attributes, although this How-To uses only the `HREF` attribute. For your purposes, you might need to use other attributes. Chapter 8, "Establishing Links," provides detailed information on HTML 4.0 anchor elements.

Although not as common as the other media types described in this chapter, DVI files require both server and browser configuration. Your Web site administrator is responsible for the proper configuration of your server. How-To 12.6 provides instructions for configuring server support for DVI files.

In addition to having your Web site administrator configure the server, you must configure browsers to support DVI files. Consult the documentation for your browser to determine the procedure for configuring helper applications such as a DVI viewer.

Table 10-12 lists some suitable DVI viewers for use as helper applications. You must have suitable hardware, a DVI viewer, and a browser that is configured properly.

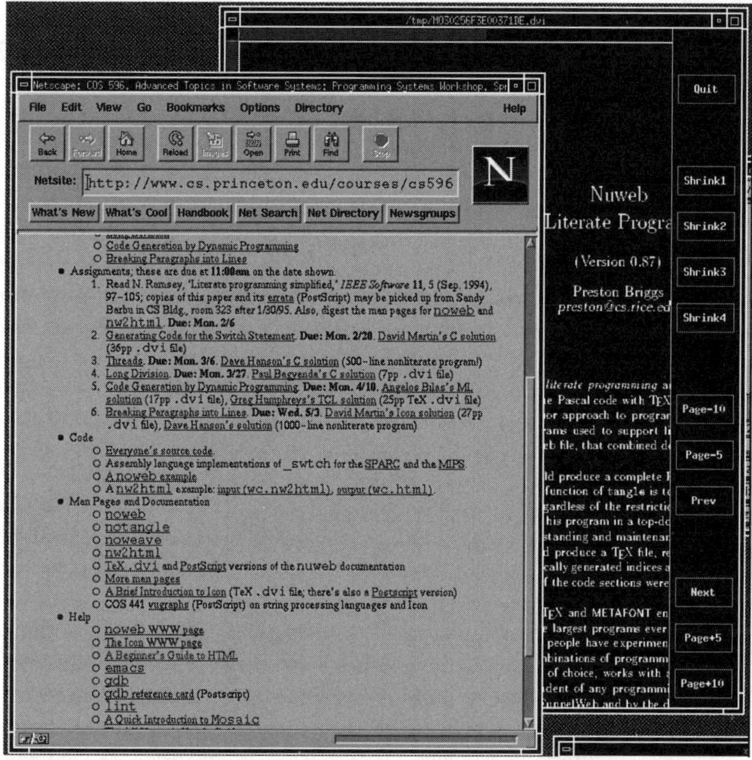

Figure 10-6 Browser and DVI viewer helper application

Table 10-12 DVI viewer applications

PLATFORM	APPLICATION	LOCATION
Mac	dvi-preview	http://www.tex.ac.uk/tex-archive/systems/mac/mactex/
PC	TrueTex (Commercial)	http://www.tex.ac.uk/tex-archive/systems/win32
UNIX	xdvi	http://www.tex.ac.uk/tex-archive/systems/unix

Table 10-12 does not provide a comprehensive list. If a suggested application does not meet your needs, use a Web search engine to find a more suitable helper application.

10.10 How do I... Find a VRML browser?

COMPATIBILITY: VRML

Problem

While surfing the Web, I have found sites providing 3D information. I need a viewer to explore and examine these 3D models and virtual worlds. How can I find a VRML browser?

Technique

The Virtual Reality Modeling Language (VRML, pronounced "vermel") provides a platform-independent means of specifying three-dimensional models and constructs. Servers can easily distribute such models across the World Wide Web. In fact, specific constructs in the language provide the ability to create links to other worlds or Web pages.

VRML documents are becoming increasingly abundant on the World Wide Web. Consequently, a need for VRML viewers has developed, driving the creation of numerous products running on a variety of hardware and software platforms.

Figure 10-7 shows a world rendered using a VRML viewer integrated into a browser. Figure 10-8 displays a world using a standalone VRML viewer.

Steps

The following procedure shows how to acquire a VRML browser and configure your Web browser to recognize VRML worlds:

1. Examine Table 10-13 to find a VRML viewer to meet your hardware and software requirements.

2. Download or purchase the VRML viewer you have selected.

3. Follow the applicable installation instruction for your VRML viewer.

4. If the VRML viewer's installation process does not automatically configure your Web browser, configure your browser to launch this viewer when it receives a document with the MIME type `x-world/x-vrml`. (For more information on MIME types, see Appendix C, "MIME.") This configuration process is browser specific.

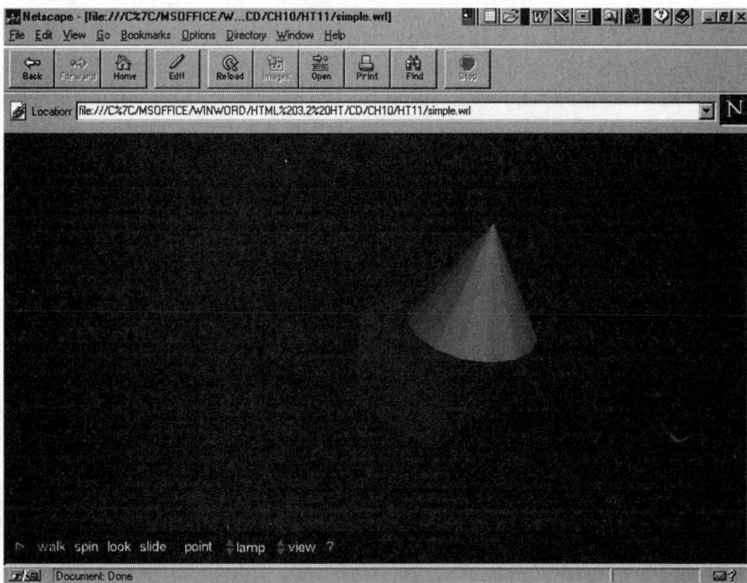

Figure 10-7 VRML world using plug-in

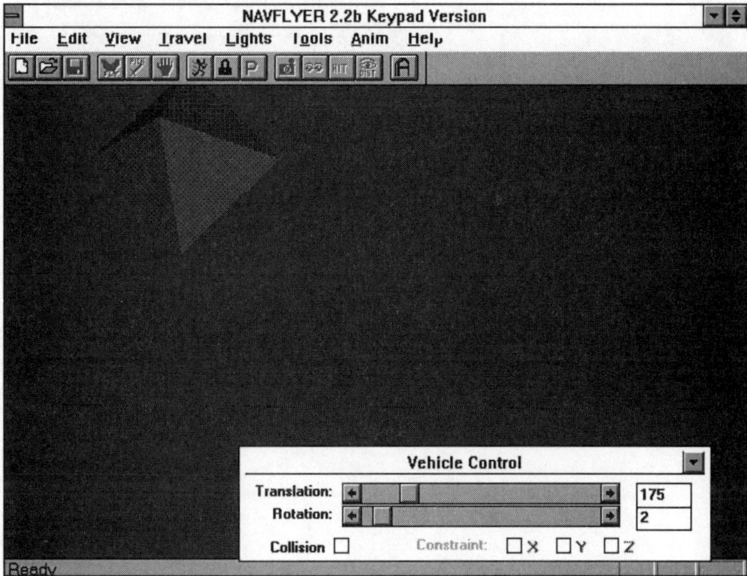

Figure 10-8 VRML world using standalone viewer

How It Works

Web servers transmit VRML worlds in the same way that they transmit any other objects, such as audio files. The server signals the browser that it is sending a VRML world. The browser recognizes this signal and runs an appropriate VRML viewer.

A large variety of VRML browsers have been developed recently. Table 10-13 lists several available VRML viewers by software and hardware type.

Table 10-13 VRML browsers

PLATFORM	VRML BROWSER	URL
cross-platform	VRweb	`http://www.iicm.tu-graz.ac.at/Cvrweb`
cross-platform	WebSpace	`http://webspace.sgi.com//`
Mac/PowerMac	Virtus Voyager	`http://www.virtus.com/files/mac/apps`
PC/Windows 3.1, NT, 95	Pioneer	`http://www.caligari.com/products/pioneer.html`
PC/Windows 3.1, NT, 95	NAVFlyer 2.2b	`ftp://yoda.fdt.net/pub/users/m/micgreen`
PC/Windows 3.1, NT, 95	VR Scout	`http://www.chaco.com/vrscout/`
PC/Windows 3.1, NT, 95	WorldView	`http://www.intervista.com/`
PC/Windows NT, 95	GLView	`http://www.glview.com/`
SGI/IRIX 5.2	i3D	`http://www.crs4.it/~3diadm/i3d-announce.html`
SGI/X Window	WebView	`http://www.sdsc.edu/projects/vrml/tools/webview/help/`
SGI, Sun/X Window	WebOOGL	`http://www.geom.umn.edu/software/weboogl/`

Comments

VRML worlds and associated image files can be large, so do not be too surprised at experiencing delays if you are accessing the Web over a 14.4K modem. For additional information on viewers and VRML software, see URL `http://rosebud.sdsc.edu/vrml`.

COMPLEXITY
INTERMEDIATE

10.11 How do I... Create a VRML document?

COMPATIBILITY: VRML

Problem

I want to create three-dimensional spaces for the World Wide Web community to visit. How does VRML provide this capability? How do I author VRML documents?

Technique

You author VRML documents using either a text editor or a three-dimensional modeling application. VRML enables you to specify three-dimensional objects in an ASCII text file. Using a text editor, you can create a VRML document by stringing together appropriate VRML constructs. Alternatively, you can graphically create three-dimensional spaces using suitable software that saves in VRML format.

Steps

You can create VRML documents in one of two ways. You can use a VRML editing environment to create three-dimensional spaces graphically or you can directly create a VRML document by inserting VRML constructs in a text file.

Three-Dimensional Editing Environment

Recently, many three-dimensional modeling packages have been developed for the creation of VRML documents. The following procedure outlines the steps for acquiring and installing a modeler suitable for your hardware and software platform:

1. Find a modeler suitable for your software and hardware platform. Table 10-14 summarizes several available modeler packages.

Table 10-14 VRML modelers

PLATFORM	MODELER	URL
Mac	STRATA	http://www.strata3d.com:80/html/
	StudioPro Blitz	strata_studiopro.html
Mac/PC	Virtus	http://www.virtus.com/products_wtp.html
	WalkThrough Pro	
PC	Pioneer	http://www.caligari.com/products/pioneer.html
PC	Spinner	http://www.3dweb.com/
PC	trueSpace 3	http://www.caligari.com/products/ts3/

continued on next page

continued from previous page

		`ts3_feat.html`
SGI	WebSpace Author	`http://webspace.sgi.com/WebSpaceAuthor/`
		`index.html`

2. Download or purchase the selected software.

3. Follow the instructions provided to install your modeler software.

4. Configure your Web browser to launch this application if your modeler will also serve as your default VRML viewer.

5. Open your modeler application and create your three-dimensional model.

6. Save your model to a file with the `.wrl` filename extension. If your modeler supports a variety of formats, select VRML.

Text Editor Creation

VRML documents contain standard ASCII text. This text represents the various constructs available through VRML. The following steps lead you through the VRML document creation process using a text editor:

1. Open a new document in your text editor.

2. Insert the following line. This line indicates that the file contains ASCII-based VRML constructs.

```
#VRML V1.0 ascii
```

3. Add desired VRML elements until you have created your desired scene. A variety of commonly used elements appears in the "How It Works" section.

4. Save the document. Use the `.wrl` filename extension when you save to indicate that the file is a VRML document.

In either case, add a link to your created world from a portion of a relevant Web page or use the nonstandard methods for direct inclusion discussed in Chapter 18, "Direct Inclusion of Multimedia Objects."

How It Works

Using a modeler is the easier of the two construction methods. A modeler enables you to create your three-dimensional information space visually. You can see on the screen how your model will look when it is rendered. For example, Figure 10-9 shows a scene composed of three visible objects: a cylinder, a torus, and a cube. This scene was built using the Fountain modeler (now called Pioneer; see reference in Table 10-14). The VRML file for this scene is available on the accompanying CD in the `COMPLEX.WRL` file.

The challenge you face when creating a VRML document with a 3D modeling package is learning how to draw in a three-dimensional space. If you are familiar with CAD packages or other 3D environments, the transition is fairly easy. The user interfaces of these VRML environments vary significantly. The primary source of information on these products is documentation provided online either with the package or via the Web and your own experience with the product. As you become more comfortable with the package, your productivity and accuracy will improve.

Ultimately, when you finish building your 3D scene, you save it to a VRML file. Many modelers support a variety of output formats. For access over the World Wide Web, you should save your scene in VRML. The standard filename extension used to indicate a VRML scene is `.wrl`. Use this extension when saving each of your scenes.

You can create or modify a VRML document using a text editor. The VRML format saves 3D information in standard ASCII text and stores 3D scenes in a hierarchy of nodes referred to as a *scene graph*. The scene graph specifies both the objects in the scene and the order in which those objects are evaluated. Nodes earlier in the scene graph can affect nodes later in the scene.

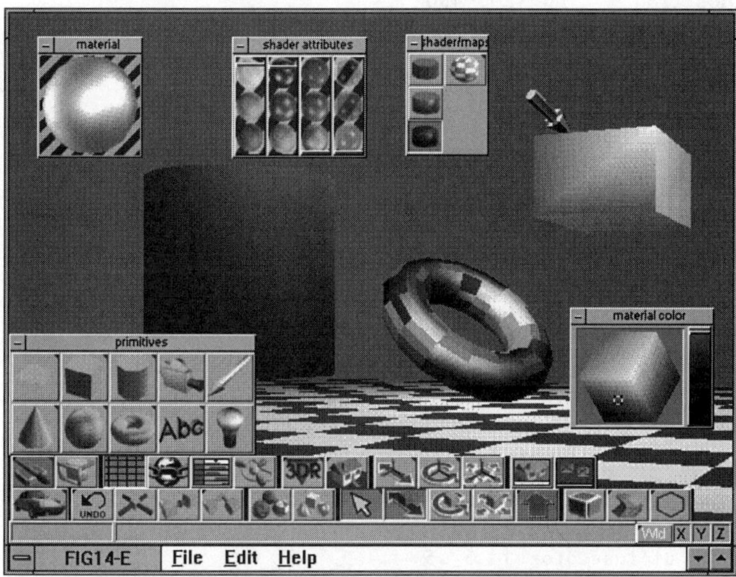

Figure 10-9 Scene created with a 3D modeler

Each VRML node has several general characteristics:

- ✔ Name: Each node can have a unique name associated with it.
- ✔ Type: Each node has a particular type, such as cube or translation.
- ✔ Parameters: Each node has a set of parameters specifying the specific characteristics of the individual node. For example, a sphere node would have a radius parameter.
- ✔ Child nodes: Nodes may contain other nodes, thereby creating the hierarchical structure of a scene graph.

The standard format for specifying a node in a VRML scene graph is ***ObjectName ObjectType { Parameters Children }***. For example, the following nodes specify a scene containing a pinkish cone, a purple cube, and a perspective camera. Figure 10-10 displays this scene in a VRML browser. A pound sign (**#**) indicates that the remainder of a line is a comment. This VRML source code also appears on the CD in the **SIMPLE.WRL** file.

```
#VRML V1.0 ascii

Separator { # 1st Grouping
    PerspectiveCamera { # Establish Perspective
        position    160 -200 430
    }

    Separator { # position, color, and place cube
        Transform { # set position
            translation 160 -200 -2
        }
        Material { # set color
            diffuseColor .3 .1 .3
        }
      Cube { # create a cube using established color at specified position
            width 100
            height 100
            depth 100
        }
    }

    Separator { # position, color, and place cone
        Transform { # set position
            translation 120 -80 50
        }
        Material { # set color
            diffuseColor 1 .5 .5
        }
      Cone { # create a cone using established color at specified position
            bottomRadius 50
            height 80
        }
    }
}
```

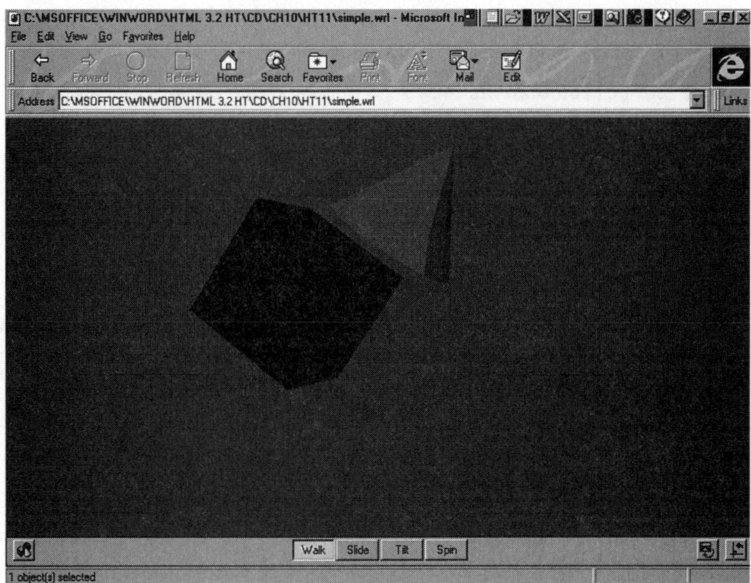

Figure 10-10 Small scene created by a text editor

A `Separator` node represents the root of the hierarchy. This node has a `PerspectiveCamera` child and two `Separator` children. The `camera` object indicates to the VRML browser the initial perspective of the scene. Each of the two `Separator` children contains three children: `Transform`, specifying the base location objects; `Material`, specifying the material used to draw objects (purple and pink, respectively); and a visible object (for example, `Cube` and `Cone`).

VRML nodes fall into four broad categories: shapes, properties, groups, and WWW. The following list details several of the more widely used node types. For a complete description of VRML version 1, see URL `http://rosebud.sdsc.edu/vrml` or check out *VRML Construction Kit* (Waite Group Press). Lengths and distances in VRML are measured in scaled meters.

Shapes

✔ `AsciiText`: This object type defines a string of characters. The commonly used parameters of this type are `string` and `justification`. The `justification` property has three possible values: `LEFT`, `CENTER`, or `RIGHT`. For example, to create a centered string object displaying `"I love VRML"`, you could use the following object:

```
AsciiText { string "I love VRML" justification CENTER }
```

✔ `Cone`: This creates a cone object in the scene graph. The `height` and `bottomRadius` properties set the cone's parameters. For example, the following node describes a cone that is 20 meters high and has a base with a radius of 10 meters:

```
Cone { height 20 bottomRCadius 10 }
```

- ✔ **Cube**: Use this node type to create a cubic object. The **height**, **width**, and **depth** properties of this node need not have the same value. For example, the specification of a 40×20×20 box in VRML would appear as

```
Cube { height 40 width 20 depth 20 }
```

- ✔ **Cylinder**: A node of this type creates a cylinder in the scene graph. This shape has a **height** and a **radius** property. The following line creates a cylinder with a base radius of 5 and a height of 25:

```
Cylinder { radius 5 height 25 }
```

- ✔ **Sphere**: You can create a sphere object with this node type. The only required property of this node type is a **radius**. For example, use the following line to create a sphere of radius 75:

```
Sphere { radius 75 }
```

Properties

- ✔ **FontStyle**: The **FontStyle** node type takes three parameters: **size**, **style**, and **family**. A **FontStyle** node affects all text in objects appearing after and below it in the scene graph hierarchy until another **FontStyle** node supersedes it. The possible values of the **style** property are **NONE**, **BOLD**, and **ITALICS**. The values of **family** are **SERIF**, **SANS**, and **TYPEWRITER**. The following node sets the font to serif, bold, 10 point:

```
FontStyle { size 10 style BOLD family SERIF }
```

- ✔ **Material**: This node describes the material used to render all shapes after and below it in the scene graph. The most commonly used property is **diffuseColor**, which, specified as an RGB triplet, sets the color used to draw shapes. Each value in the color triplet ranges from **0** to **1**, indicating the intensity of the color component. For example, to color shapes red, use the following **Material** node:

```
Material { diffuseColor 1 0 0 }
```

- ✔ **Transform**: This node establishes the relative location used to place shapes appearing below or after the **Transform** node in the scene graph. Two useful properties of this node type are **translation** and **scaleFactor**. The following node sets the translation to four meters in the positive x direction and scaling of two in the y direction only. (In scaling, x and z values are set to **1** to indicate no scaling.)

```
Transform { translation 4 0 0 scaleFactor 1 2 1 }
```

✔ `PerspectiveCamera`: A `PerspectiveCamera` node establishes a viewpoint for the scene. If only one such camera is specified, browsers often take this as the initial view of the scene. The most commonly set property of this node type is `position`, specifying the location of the camera. The following camera is positioned at x, y, z coordinates 25, 72, –200:

```
PerspectiveCamera { position 25 72 -200 }
```

Groups

✔ `Group`: This node contains an ordered list of other VRML nodes. The property nodes accumulate as they are traversed in the order. This accumulated information is passed back to the parent of the group node in the scene graph.

```
Group {
    ...          # object 1
    ...          # object 2
    }
```

✔ `Separator`: A `Separator` node is like a `Group` node. It contains an ordered list of child nodes. The difference between a separator and a group is that the accumulated property information in a separator is discarded at the end of the separator. The parent node continues with the accumulated transformations, in effect, prior to the separator.

```
Separator {
    ...          # object 1
    ...          # object 2
    }
```

WWW

✔ `WWWAnchor`: This node type works exactly like a `separator` object, except that it supports several additional properties: `name`, `description`, and `map`. The value of the `name` property indicates the URL to load when a child of this grouping node is selected. The value of the `description` property can be used by a VRML browser to display a description of the URL linked through the name property. The `map` property can have one of two values: `NONE` or `POINT`. A `POINT` value indicates that the coordinate selected in the scene should be appended to the URL specified by the `name` property. This capability gives rise to the possibility of a 3D imagemap.

```
WWWAnchor {
    name "http://rosebud.sdsc.edu/vrml"
    description "Link to VRML Repository"
    ...          # object 1
    ...          # object 2
    }
```

- ✔ `WWWInline`: This node enables a VRML document to incorporate another VRML document located at a specified URL. Use the **name** property to assign this URL value. For example, to include the world located at `http://www.mysite.edu/myworld.wrl`, you would use the following node in the scene graph:

```
WWWInline { name "http://www.mysite.edu/myworld.wrl" }
```

Using these nodes, you can successfully create and edit VRML worlds. This list serves as a brief introduction to the nodes and node properties available in VRML. For a complete specification of VRML, examine URL `http://www.sdsc. edu/vrml`.

Comments

VRML is still experimental. Consequently, many browsers and modelers speak slightly different dialects of VRML. Several also provide additional proprietary constructs.

When authoring, keep in mind that VRML documents can rapidly become very large. The larger the file, the longer a Web browser takes to download and present it. Consequently, users with a low bandwidth network connection, such as a 14.4K modem, will experience significant delays in viewing your VRML documents.

In addition, the complexity of your VRML document and the processing power of the viewer's machine affect the speed of rendering. A VRML document that renders and updates quickly on an SGI Reality Engine might take considerably longer to display and update on a 486 machine.

10.12 How do I... Locate prebuilt VRML objects?

COMPATIBILITY: VRML

Problem

I don't want to create my worlds from scratch. How do I find VRML objects that I can use in the worlds that I create?

Technique

A variety of 3D objects is available through several sites on the Internet. These sites offer free, and not-so-free, 3D objects that you can use to construct VRML worlds.

You can use prebuilt objects to jump-start your world-building process. Start by connecting to one of the following sites. Select and download a desired object. Then incorporate that object into your VRML world.

Steps

The following procedure walks you through the identification, retrieval, and use of prebuilt VRML objects available over the Internet.

1. Connect to a VRML object repository site. Table 10-15 lists several as potential starting points, or you can use one of the many Web search tools to pinpoint repositories on your own.

Table 10-15 Sampling of VRML object repository sites

SITE NAME	URL
New College vrmLab	`http://www.newcollege.edu/vrmLab`
Grafman's VRML Gallery	`http://www.graphcomp.com/vrml`
VRML Repository	`http://www.sdsc.edu/vrml/objects.html`
UK-VR SIG	`http://www.dcs.ed.ac.uk/~mxr/objects.html`

2. Select and download the object(s) you want.
3. Either reference the downloaded object as a **`WWWInline`** node or insert the contents of the downloaded object directly into your VRML world.
4. Save the VRML world.

How It Works

Just as image, audio, and video clip archives have developed over the years, VRML object repositories are beginning to appear. Table 10-15 lists several of these sites.

Reuse of existing objects will save you considerable time in the development process. The files that you download contain the developed objects. You can incorporate the object into your world in one of two ways:

- ✔ **`WWWInline`**: This node enables you to incorporate another VRML document located at a specified URL. Use the **`name`** property to assign this URL value. For example, to include the VRML object **`dnld_object.wrl`**, you would use the following node in the scene graph:

```
WWWInline { name "dnld_object.wrl" }
```

- ✔ Textual copying: Within your VRML page, directly insert the VRML code from the downloaded file that describes the object you want to use. You should use this method when the downloaded file contains multiple objects, of which you want to use only one.

See How-To 10.11 to flesh out the world you are creating. You might also want to consult the remainder of the How-To's in this chapter for more advanced VRML effects.

Comments

You should carefully read the rights and restrictions notice of the site from which you obtain 3D objects. Most sites allow free use of objects for noncommercial purposes, but some sites might apply further restrictions. If in doubt, contact the site administrator or the object author for further guidance.

As with any VRML space, you can include the world in a Web page using a link as described in How-To 10.1 or the nonstandard methods of multimedia object incorporation discussed in Chapter 18, "Direct Inclusion of Multimedia Objects."

COMPLEXITY
INTERMEDIATE

10.13 How do I... Make my VRML world more realistic?

COMPATIBILITY: VRML

Problem

My VRML worlds seems to lack realism. Are there any ways that I can make my world appear more realistic to people wandering through it?

Technique

This How-To describes two methods of improving the realism of VRML worlds:

- ✔ `Level of detail` nodes: `Level of detail` (`LOD`) nodes enable you to specify alternative representation of groups of objects in your world. When a viewer enters your world, the version of this group of objects that he or she sees is dependent on his or her relative distance to that group of objects.
- ✔ `Texture` nodes: `Material` nodes provide a basic means for specifying the appearance of different objects in your world. These materials do not provide the variety and randomness encountered in the real world. `Texture` nodes enable you to specify an image to use as wrapping paper over the surface of an object.

You can use the following procedures to add these features to your VRML worlds.

Steps

The following two procedures provide step-by-step instructions for adding more realism to your worlds by adding `level of detail` nodes and `texture` nodes.

Level of Detail

1. Open your VRML document in a text editor.
2. Move the insertion point to just before the group of objects for which you want to add alternative levels of detail representation.
3. Start an `LOD` node by typing the following:

```
LOD {
```

4. Determine the distance at which you want the alternative representations to switch. For example, you might want the most detailed representation seen when a viewer is within 25 meters of the group, the next most detailed when the user is between 25 and 75 meters, and the least detailed when the viewer is beyond 75 meters.
5. Translate this into a `range` attribute of the `LOD` node by determining the switch points. Insert the appropriate `range` attribute. For the example in step 4, the switch points are `25` and `75`, so you would enter the following `range` attribute:

```
range [25,75]
```

6. Place the current representation of your chosen group into a new `separator` group.

```
Separator {
     # Your Chosen Group of Objects
}
```

7. Create a representation for each distance range specified; you will need the number of switch points in the `range` attribute, plus one. Select the position of the current representation among these alternatives and create the remaining representations, each in its own `separator` group.
8. Arrange the alternative representations from the representation seen at the closest range to the representation seen at the farthest range.
9. End the `LOD` node with a closing curly brace.

```
}
```

10. Save your VRML document.
11. Test your VRML document.

Texture Mapping

1. Find or create a texture map image that you want to wrap around a VRML object. See How-To 10.12 for information on finding existing texture

images. See Chapter 9, "Using Images in Your Documents," for more information on images in general. The How-To's dealing with background images may be particularly useful.

2. Open your VRML document in a text editor.

3. Place each VRML object upon which you want to apply the texture within a `Separator` node of its own.

```
Separator {
    # Your Chosen Object(s)
}
```

4. Add a `Texture2` node to the node before which you want to apply the texture. The `filename` attribute of the texture node should contain the URL of the chosen texture. For example, to select the `wood.gif` image as the texture for the remaining objects within the `separator` group, you might use the following:

```
Separator {
    Texture2 {
        # Specify the URL of the texture
        filename "wood.gif"
    }
    # Your Chosen Object(s)
}
```

5. Save your document.

6. Test your document.

How It Works

Two areas in which VRML worlds fall short of reality are the lack of shifting perspectives as a viewer approaches an object and the lack of irregularities in VRML object surfaces. The two node types discussed in this How-To improve the realism in these areas.

`LOD` nodes enable you to alter the representation of a group of VRML objects selectively based on the distance of the viewer from that group of objects. As a viewer approaches the group of objects, the representation alters in the specified manner. This effect gives the impression that the details of the particular portion of the scene are clarifying as the viewer approaches. Obviously, a finite number of alternative representations is not a substitute for the smooth clarification of detail in the real world, but the use of `LOD` nodes provides an improvement.

`Texture` (`Texture2`) nodes provide a simulation of the irregularities found in real-world surfaces. Simply using `material` nodes to define the composition of object surfaces leads to objects with seemingly smooth, perfect exteriors. Using an appropriate image to wrap the object gives the object a more natural or realistic appearance. As with `LOD` nodes, `texture` nodes are not perfect, but they do improve realism.

Using textures does require a trade-off. Objects with texture maps take marginally longer to draw. Furthermore, each additional texture used within a world requires the browser to download a separate image file.

Comments

An added benefit of using **LOD** nodes is the speed of rendering distant objects. Because objects farther away from the viewer require less detail, the VRML representation will be simpler, requiring fewer, less detailed objects. The net effect of this is that the VRML browser or plug-in requires less time to render those distant objects while reserving computational resources for positioning and drawing detailed nearer objects.

As with any VRML space, you can include the world in a Web page using a link as described in How-To 10.1 or the nonstandard methods of multimedia object incorporation discussed in Chapter 18, "Direct Inclusion of Multimedia Objects."

COMPLEXITY
INTERMEDIATE

10.14 How do I... Spin a VRML object?

COMPATIBILITY: VRML 2

Problem

I want to add some motion to the worlds I am creating. A static world just doesn't reflect the world I want to put on display. How do I add at least some motion to my world?

Technique

VRML 2 provides the **SpinGroup** node. The **SpinGroup** node enables you to specify a group of VRML objects to be set in continuous motion.

Items that you want to spin in a particular manner will be grouped within a **SpinGroup** node. Use multiple **SpinGroup** nodes within a single world to set objects in motion subject to different constraints.

Steps

The following steps walk you through the process of adding a **SpinGroup** node to your VRML world:

1. Open your VRML world in a text editor.

2. Move your insertion point to the location just before the objects that you want to set in motion subject to the same rotational constraints.

3. Insert a `SpinGroup` node around this group of objects.

```
SpinGroup {
    # Objects to Set in Motion
}
```

4. Insert a `rotation` attribute at the beginning of your `SpinGroup` node.

```
SpinGroup {
    rotation 0 1 1 .2

    # Objects to Set in Motion
}
```

5. Save your document.

6. Test your document.

How It Works

The `SpinGroup` node places its contents in motion according to the parameters specified in the node's `rotation` attribute. This spin group acts much like a separator in terms of grouping objects in the VRML scene. The fact that the visible objects within the group are in motion makes the visual effect of this grouping significantly different.

The `rotation` attribute of the `SpinGroup` node controls the axes of rotation and the speed at which the objects within the group move. The `rotation` attribute requires four value parameters. The first three values represent the x, y, and z axes of the object, where a 1 value indicates that the object will rotate about that axis and a 0 value indicates no rotation about that axis. The fourth value is a decimal value representing the rotational speed of the spin. The greater the absolute value of this number, the faster the spin. The positivity or negativity of this value determines whether the group spins toward the positive or negative ends of the axes selected for rotation.

For example, Figure 10-11 shows the following `SpinGroup` node:

```
SpinGroup {
    rotation 0 1 1 .2

    Separator {
            Translation {
                    translation 160 -200 -2
        }
        Material {
            diffuseColor .3 .1 .3
        }
            Cube {
            width 100
            height 100
            depth 100
        }
        }
    }
```

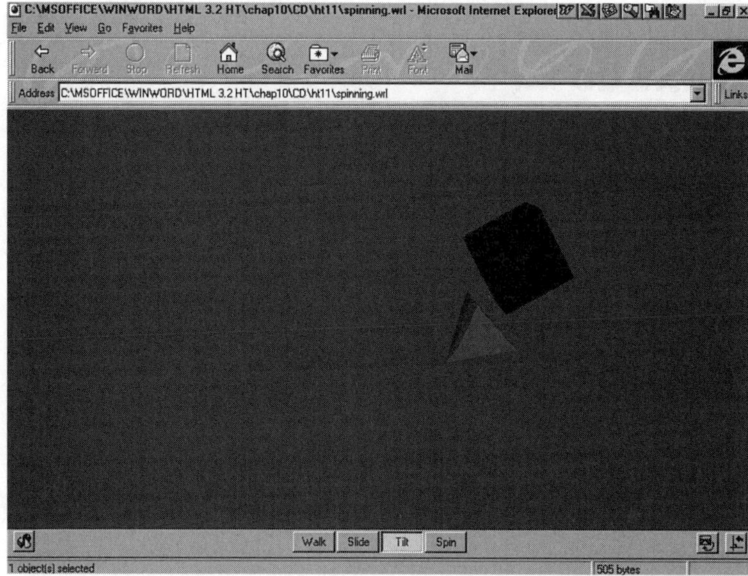

Figure 10-11 Spinning cube with stationary cone

The spin group adapts the cube created in the simple demonstration world created in How-To 10.11. Loading this VRML world into an appropriate viewer, you will notice that the cube is now in motion, spinning on its y and z axes.

The complete source for the VRML world shown in Figure 10-11 appears on the CD in the **SPINNING.WRL** file. The file **TWOSPIN.WRL** sets both the cone and the cube in motion in opposite directions.

Comments

Spin groups might not work with older VRML browsers or plug-ins. The **SpinGroup** node is part of the VRML 2 specification. If you do not have an enhanced VRML 1 browser or a VRML 2 browser, you might want to pick one up. Both Netscape Navigator and Microsoft Internet Explorer, through appropriate plug-ins or ActiveX controls, support this feature.

As with any VRML space, you can include the world in a Web page using a link as described in How-To 10.1 or the nonstandard methods of multimedia object incorporation discussed in Chapter 18, "Direct Inclusion of Multimedia Objects."

10.15 How do I... Include animated textures on VRML objects?

COMPATIBILITY: VRML

Problem

I would like the surface of a VRML object to shift and move as the viewer watches. How can I project an animation onto the surface of a VRML object?

Technique

This technique is very similar to the one described for standard texture images in How-To 10.13. The primary difference lies at the front end in the construction of the texture image.

VRML browsers that support animated textures expect the GIF files specified in a particular format. This How-To walks you through the process required to create a multiple-image GIF file suitable for use as an animated surface texture. You will need an appropriate image manipulation program that supports GIF to construct the proper image. See Chapter 9, "Using Images in Your Documents," and How-To's 10.2 and 10.3 for additional information on image editors.

You will first create an appropriate image. Then you will use the procedure in How-To 10.13, defining the use of texture nodes to insert the new texture into your VRML document.

Steps

The following procedure walks you through the creation of a multiple-image GIF file suitable for use as an animated texture. The last instruction has you insert this image as a texture in your VRML document using the procedure described for this purpose in How-To 10.13.

1. Plan out the animation that you want to project onto a VRML object surface. Define the size and number of frames. You should use single-size, square frames. For example, each of the frames in the animation developed in Figure 10-12 is 128×128 pixels.

2. Create each frame as a separate image of your chosen size.

3. Merge the frames into a single image with a width equal to the width of a frame and a height equal to the height of a frame times the number of frames. For example, the combined image in Figure 10-12 is 128 pixels in width and 512 pixels in height.

4. Set the background color of the combined image to the desired color of the VRML object onto which you will project the animation.

5. Save the combined image as a GIF89a format image.

6. Specify this image within a texture node by using the proper procedure defined in How-To 10.13.

How It Works

VRML browsers support the use of multiple image GIF files as textures. Therefore, you must construct or locate a suitable multiple image GIF file. Following this procedure, PaintShop Pro was used to create the four separate GIF files found on the CD: `HTM8.GIF`, `HTM9.GIF`, `HTM10.GIF`, and `HTM11.GIF`. These four GIF files were combined into the `htmani.gif` file seen in Figure 10-12.

You should note that the background of the combined image was altered from the original four. This was required to maintain the purple color of the cube in the world displayed in Figure 10-13. The VRML world displayed in Figure 10-13 uses the multiple image GIF file seen in Figure 10-12 as the texture for the spinning cube seen in Figure 10-11 in How-To 10.14. Without this background modification, the black background of the multiple image GIF file might override the material node within the VRML world.

The `ANISPIN.WRL` file on the CD contains the complete source code for the animation seen in Figure 10-13.

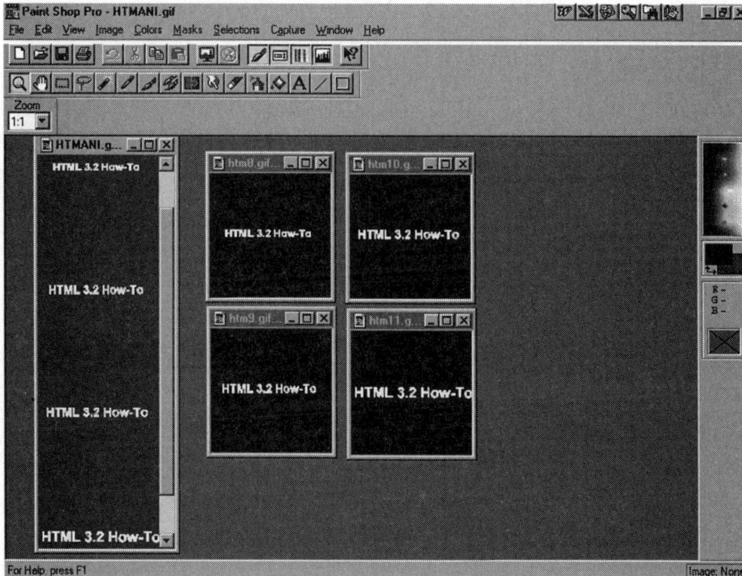

Figure 10-12 Animated texture construction

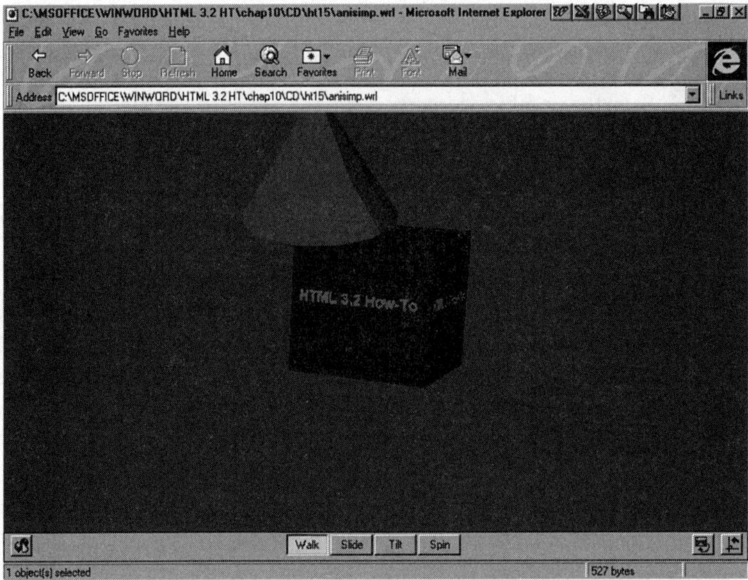

Figure 10-13 Spinning cube with animated texture

Comments

The latest VRML specification contemplates significantly greater flexibility in the type of moving imagery projectable onto visible object surfaces. For example, you might project an MPEG or QuickTime movie onto the surface of a VRML cone or any other visible VRML object.

As with any VRML space, you can include the world in a Web page using a link as described in How-To 10.1 or the nonstandard methods of multimedia object incorporation discussed in Chapter 18, "Direct Inclusion of Multimedia Objects."

CHAPTER 11

HTML INTERACTIVE FORMS

11

HTML INTERACTIVE FORMS

How do I...

You've come this far with HTML and are proceeding along just fine. You know how to create a nice-looking home page that has links to lots of other pages all over the WWW. The thing is, so far the information has been flowing in only one direction. You have been able to show people who read your pages whatever is on your mind, but your readers have had no way of giving you feedback. They can't let you know how they like your page or what they would like you to do differently. That is where forms come into play. You can include forms in your HTML document that allow your readers to send you input in a variety of different ways.

The form creation process is actually twofold. The first part is to include the HTML tags in your document that create the form. This first part is often referred to as the *front end*. The second part of the process involves creating a script in a language such as Perl, Java, server-side JavaScript, or C that processes the information contained in the form. This part of the process is called the *back end*. This chapter deals mainly with the first part, or front end, of the form creation process.

11.1 Create a Basic Form

Before you can let a user interact with your documents, you must create a basic form. This How-To shows you how to add the tags needed to create a startup form that lets a user enter lines of text.

11.2 Add a Text Box to a Form

There are instances when a user is going to want to enter more than one line of text at a time. This How-To shows you how to add scrollable text boxes of any size to your forms.

11.3 Add Check Boxes to a Form

Sometimes you want to let a user check off various options or choices. This How-To shows how to add check boxes to a form.

11.4 Add Radio Buttons to a Form

Sometimes you would like to let a user choose only one option among many from a list, such as pushing the buttons on a radio, where selecting one item deselects any other item that had been selected. This simple How-To shows how to add radio buttons to your forms.

11.5 Add Password Fields to a Form

There are times when you want a user to enter sensitive information into a field, but you want to disguise this input so a passerby or onlooker cannot read it. This How-To shows the process used to create password fields in which user-supplied information is replaced by asterisks.

11.6 Add Pull-Down Menus to a Form

Sometimes you might want to let a user select from several options or choices but show only the currently selected choice on the form. This simple How-To lets you add pull-down menus to your forms.

11.7 Add a File Selector Dialog Box to a Form

There are times when you would like a user to select a file from among a group of files. This How-To shows you how to add a file selector dialog box to a form.

11.8 Add a Single Line Text Field to a Form

Often you might want the user to input only a single line of code. This simple How-To shows you how to add single line prompts to your forms.

11.9 Use a Clickable Image as a Submit Button

At times you might want to spruce up your forms by using an image for the Submit button. This simple How-To shows you how to use an image for your Submit button.

11.10 Pass Information Between Forms

When creating dynamic documents, you might want to pass information from a current form to another form that you will build based partly on information from the current form. This How-To shows how to add hidden fields that can be used to store information to pass from one form to another.

11.11 Choose a Request Method to Send Data to the HTTP Server

Now that you have a complete form, you need a way for a reader to say, "I'm finished," and then deliver the information contained in the form to the HTTP server. This How-To will show you how to submit a form and how to pick the submission method that is right for you.

11.12 Process a Form

Now that you have a complete form all ready to go, you need a way to bridge the gap between the HTML document that contains the form and the HTTP server that will process the form. This How-To gives you a basic rundown on how to create a Common Gateway Interface (CGI) script that will send and process a form.

COMPLEXITY
INTERMEDIATE

11.1 How do I... Create a basic form?

COMPATIBILITY: HTML 2+

Problem

I would like to add forms to my documents so I can receive user feedback and create more dynamic documents. How do I do this?

Technique

Creating a form isn't all that difficult. You create forms as part of an HTML document by including the **<FORM>** tag, along with its associated tags that create

- ✔ Text fields
- ✔ Check boxes
- ✔ Radio buttons
- ✔ Pop-up menus

The form is later submitted to the HTTP server by using either the **GET** or the **POST** method. The form can then be processed by a script.

Steps

The following procedure shows you how to create a form and include it in a document:

1. Open a new file with any editor or word processor you choose. Make sure that whatever tool you use is capable of saving documents as text or ASCII, depending on the environment you are in.

2. Create a base HTML document. This document consists of the items needed to make an HTML document. This base document should include

   - ✔ **<HTML>...</HTML>** tags
   - ✔ **<HEAD>...</HEAD>** tags
   - ✔ **<TITLE>...</TITLE>** tags
   - ✔ **<BODY>...</BODY>** tags

   Your document should resemble the following:

```
<Html> <Head>
<Title>Input Form</Title>
</Head>
<Body>
</Body>
</Html>
```

3. Put two horizontal rule **<HR>** tags in the body of your document. Your form will go between these two tags. This step is entirely optional, but it helps the form stand out more. Your document should now look something like this:

```
<HTML> <HEAD>
<TITLE>Input Form</TITLE>
</HEAD>
<BODY>
```

```
<HR>
My form will go here!
<HR>
</BODY>
</Html>
```

4. Add the `<FORM>...</FORM>` tags to your document. The basic tag syntax is

```
<FORM METHOD="Get or Post" ACTION="URL" ENCTYPE="type">
Field definitions
</FORM>
```

The `<FORM>` tag tells a browser that there is a fill-in-the-blank form in this HTML document.

The **METHOD** attribute states the method to be used when you send the form to the server. The two acceptable methods are **GET** and **POST**. **GET** sends the information entered in the form to the server at the end of the URL. **POST** sends the information entered in the form to the server as a data body. **GET** is the default method, but **POST** is the method preferred by many HTML designers.

The **ACTION** attribute gives the address of the script that will process the form. This script can be written in almost any language; Perl and C are two popular choices.

The **ENCTYPE** attribute specifies how the data is to be encoded. This attribute applies only if you use the **POST** method, and even then, there is only one possible value, the default value **"application/w-www-form-urlencoded"**. The **ENCTYPE** attribute is included here only so that you recognize it if you see it.

The **METHOD**, **ACTION**, and **ENCTYPE** attributes are all optional; however, for the sake of clarity, it is best if you always include the **METHOD** and **ACTION** attributes.

Now your document and form will look like this:

```
<HTML> <HEAD>
<TITLE>Input Form</TITLE>
</HEAD>
<BODY>
<HR>
<FORM METHOD=POST ACTION="/cgi-bin/MY_SCRIPT">
My form will go here!
</FORM>
<HR>
</BODY>
</Html>
```

Figure 11-1 shows how this document will look when viewed with a browser. It doesn't look like much yet, but you have built a strong base on which to construct the rest of your form.

5. Add an `<INPUT>` tag so you can accept some input from a reader. The `<INPUT>` tag is a standalone tag. The syntax for this is

```
<INPUT TYPE="type" NAME="NAME" SIZE="number" VALUE="value">
```

Many kinds of `<INPUT>` types are available, but you are going to start with the most basic kind, a text entry field. To create a text entry field in a document, include the following between the `<FORM>...</FORM>` tags:

```
<INPUT TYPE="text" NAME="NAME" SIZE=30 VALUE="John Smith">
```

6. Put some text around the `<INPUT>` tag to give readers an idea of what you expect them to enter in the space provided. The document should now look like this:

```
<HTML> <HEAD>
<TITLE>Input Form</TITLE>
</HEAD>
<BODY>
<HR>
<FORM METHOD=POST ACTION="/cgi-bin/MY_SCRIPT">
Enter your name here :
<INPUT TYPE="text" NAME="NAME" SIZE=30 VALUE="John Smith">
</FORM>
<HR>
</BODY>
</Html>
```

Now you're getting somewhere. You have a form on the screen into which a reader can enter information.

7. Finish off this first form by giving the user a chance to either submit this information or reset the information and enter something else. This is done by using the `<INPUT>` tag and setting `TYPE` to either `"SUBMIT"` or `"RESET"`, for example:

```
<INPUT TYPE="SUBMIT" NAME="SUBMIT_BUTTON" VALUE="Submit">
<INPUT TYPE="RESET" NAME="RESET_BUTTON" VALUE="Oops">
```

My form will go here!

Figure 11-1 The form's starting point

Here, the **TYPE** attribute tells the browser what kind of button you are dealing with. **NAME** is a variable that you can access later when referring to this information. **VALUE** is what is written in the button. Adding these lines to your document, you will have

```
<HTML> <HEAD>
<TITLE>Input Form</TITLE>
</HEAD>
<BODY>
<HR>
<FORM METHOD=POST ACTION="/cgi-bin/MY_SCRIPT">
Enter your name here:
<INPUT TYPE="TEXT" NAME="NAME" SIZE=30 VALUE="John Smith">
<INPUT TYPE="SUBMIT" NAME="SUBMIT_BUTTON" VALUE="Submit">
<INPUT TYPE="RESET" NAME="RESET_BUTTON" VALUE="OOPS">
</FORM>
<HR>
</BODY>
</Html>
```

8. Save the document as a text or ASCII file. It is a good idea to give the document a reasonable name, such as **sampform**, along with an **.htm** or an **.html** extension. By saving the document in this manner, you can view it through either the Open Local or Open File commands in your browser. When viewed in this manner, the document should look very much like Figure 11-2.

How It Works

The **<FORM>...</FORM>** tags tell the browser to expect various **<INPUT>** tags between these two tags. These tags, along with other HTML tags and anything else that's valid in an HTML document, all make up a fill-in-the-blanks form (from now on referred to simply as a form). When the reader presses the Submit button, the contents of the form are sent to the HTTP server in a data stream in the form of

```
action?name=value&name=value
```

Comments

What has been created so far is a framework to gather information—the front end of the form. This enables you to interact with a reader, but you still need a script to

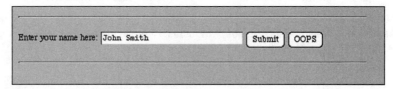

Figure 11-2 A simple but workable form

process this information. The script is dealt with briefly later in this chapter and in greater detail later in the book.

11.2 How do I... Add a text box to a form?

COMPATIBILITY: HTML 2+

Problem

After I have a form in my HTML document, I would like to let readers enter more than one line of text at a time. How do I do this?

Technique

When you are familiar with setting up a basic form, adding parts to this form is quite easy. To make a text box that creates a scrollable text field on the screen, insert the **<TEXTAREA>...</TEXTAREA>** tags somewhere between the **<FORM>...</FORM>** tags. You may have as many **<TEXTAREA>** tags as needed, and you may include other HTML tags between these tags.

Steps

The following steps show how to add **<TEXTAREA>** tags to your forms:

1. Decide on the number of text boxes you need and how you are going to lay them out on the form. The number of text boxes used on a form is normally quite easy and straightforward to determine: One or two is usually sufficient. Add a text box every place you think a reader needs a lot of room to write something. The layout is a matter of personal taste and preference. Don't be surprised if the actual layout you end up with is different from the one you first envisioned.

2. Open the HTML document that contains the form to which you want to add the text box. You may open the document in any text editor or word processor you feel comfortable using. In this case, you will expand on the document used in How-To 11.1.

3. Add the **<TEXTAREA>...</TEXTAREA>** tags between the **<FORM>...</FORM>** tags. The basic syntax is

```
<TEXTAREA NAME="NAME" ROWS="number of rows" COLS="number of columns">
 any default text </TEXTAREA>
```

The variable in the **NAME** attribute is what you will use to refer to this **<TEXTAREA>** when you later reference it in a script. The **ROWS** attribute is set to an integer for the number of rows the text box has. The **COLS** attribute is set to an integer for the number of columns the text box will have. The text between the **<TEXTAREA>...</TEXTAREA>** tags is the text that initially appears in the text box.

For this example, you will create a text box called **COMMENTS** that is 5 rows long and 60 columns wide. This should give the reader sufficient area to voice an opinion. If the reader needs more space, the box will scroll. Use this command sequence:

```
<TEXTAREA NAME="COMMENTS" ROWS=5 COLS=60>Your comments go here</TEXTAREA>
```

4. Put some text near the **<TEXTAREA>** tag to give the reader a better idea of what to enter.

The document should now resemble this:

```
<HTML> <HEAD>
<TITLE>Input Form</TITLE>
</HEAD>
<BODY>
<HR>
<FORM METHOD=POST ACTION="/cgi-bin/MY_SCRIPT">
Enter your name here: <INPUT TYPE="text" NAME="NAME" SIZE=30 VALUE="???">
<TEXTAREA NAME="COMMENTS" ROWS=5 COLS=60>Your comments go here</TEXTAREA>
<INPUT TYPE="submit" NAME="SUBMIT_BUTTON" VALUE="SEND ME">
<INPUT TYPE="reset" NAME="RESET_BUTTON" VALUE="OOPS">
</FORM>
<HR>
</BODY>
</Html>
```

5. Enter any other text or HTML tags to help clarify the document and make it easier to read. For this document, use a level 2 heading tag to let people know what to expect, plus a couple of paragraph tags to space things out a little more.

```
<HTML> <HEAD>
<TITLE>Input Form</TITLE>
</HEAD>
<BODY>
<H2>INPUT FORM -- Textarea</H2>
<HR>
<FORM METHOD=POST ACTION="/cgi-bin/MY_SCRIPT">
Enter your name here: <INPUT TYPE="text" NAME="NAME" SIZE=30 VALUE="???">
<P>
What do you think:<TEXTAREA NAME="comments" ROWS=5 COLS=60>Your comments
 go here</TEXTAREA>
<P>
<INPUT TYPE="SUBMIT" NAME="SUBMIT_BUTTON" VALUE="Submit">
<INPUT TYPE="RESET" NAME="RESET_BUTTON" VALUE="OOPS">
</FORM>
<HR>
</BODY>
</Html>
```

6. Save the document as text. Remember to give it a reasonable, clear name such as `sampform.html`.

7. Use Open File or Open Local on your browser to make sure your form looks the way you expect it to. If all went well, it will look like Figure 11-3.

How It Works

The **<FORM>...</FORM>** tags tell the browser to expect form **<INPUT>** tags between these two tags. The **<TEXTAREA>...</TEXTAREA>** tags create a space where a user may enter data within this form. When the user presses the Submit button, the information contained in the text area will be sent to the HTTP server. The information can later be accessed by referring to the name assigned to the text area with the **NAME** attribute.

Comments

The appearance of forms is certainly not carved in stone and is largely a matter of personal taste. Some people like to wrap their forms in **<PRE>...</PRE>** tags. This gives them more control over where they place items in the form. If you don't like how your text box looks, experiment with it. Try changing the values for **ROWS** and **COLS** in the **<TEXTAREA>** tag. You might also want to try moving the text box around the form some. The look of a form is very much a matter of individual taste.

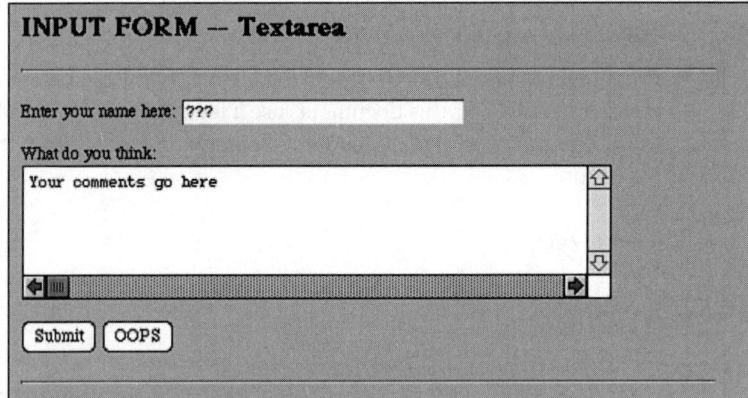

Figure 11-3 The form complete with a text field

11.3 How do I... Add check boxes to a form?

COMPATIBILITY: HTML 2+

Problem

Now that I have a form in my HTML document, I would like to be able to let users make choices while using it. How do I do this?

Technique

Check boxes enable a user to click on several choices from a list. They are added to forms in much the same manner as text boxes. To create a check box, insert an **<INPUT>** tag between the **<FORM>...</FORM>** tags. Inside the **<INPUT>** tag, set **TYPE** to **"checkbox"**. You can have as many check boxes as needed.

Steps

The following steps show how to add check boxes to forms:

1. Decide how many check boxes you are going to need and how you are going to lay them out on the form. The number of check boxes you need is usually pretty straightforward, because you should have a pretty good idea of how many lists of choices you want to give a reader. The layout is a matter of personal taste and preferences. Don't be surprised if the actual layout you end up with is different from the one you first envisioned. In this example, you will have two groups of check boxes: one so readers can select colors they like from a list and another so readers can pick foods they like. Just for fun, lay out one group horizontally and the other vertically.

2. Open the HTML document that contains the form to which you want to add the check boxes. You will be expanding on the document used in How-To 11.1.

3. Add the **<INPUT>** tag for the first check box between the **<FORM>...</FORM>** tags. In the **<INPUT>** tag, set the **TYPE** to **"checkbox"**. The basic syntax for this is

```
<INPUT TYPE="checkbox" NAME="NAME" VALUE="value" [CHECKED] > "Text"
```

The **TYPE** attribute declares that this field is a check box. The variable in the **NAME** attribute is how you will refer to this check box when you later reference it with a script. The **VALUE** attribute is what this check box is set to when it is checked. The **CHECKED** attribute is optional and tells the browser to show this check box as checked when it is first viewed. **"Text"** is for whatever text you want to associate with each particular check box.

The tags for the color check boxes look like this:

```
<INPUT TYPE="checkbox" NAME="COLOR_CHECK1" VALUE=0>Red
<INPUT TYPE="checkbox" NAME="COLOR_CHECK2" VALUE=0>Blue
<INPUT TYPE="checkbox" NAME="COLOR_CHECK3" VALUE=0>Yellow
<INPUT TYPE="checkbox" NAME="COLOR_CHECK4" VALUE=1 CHECKED>Green
```

The tags for food check boxes look like this:

```
<INPUT TYPE="checkbox" NAME="FOOD_CHECK1" VALUE=0>Lobster <P>
<INPUT TYPE="checkbox" NAME="FOOD_CHECK2" VALUE=0>Spam<P>
<INPUT TYPE="checkbox" NAME="FOOD_CHECK3" VALUE=1 CHECKED>Chocolate<P>
```

4. Put some header text near the check boxes so readers have a good idea of what you want them to do.

5. Enter any other text or HTML tags to help clarify the document and make it easier to read. The document should now resemble this:

```
<HTML> <HEAD>
<TITLE>Input Form -- Check Boxes</TITLE>
</Head>
<BODY>
<H2>INPUT FORM check boxes</H2>
<HR>
<FORM METHOD=POST ACTION="/cgi-bin/MY_SCRIPT">
Enter your name here: <INPUT TYPE="text" NAME="NAME"
SIZE=30 VALUE="???"><p>
What colors do you like:
<INPUT TYPE="checkbox" NAME="COLOR_CHECK1" VALUE="yes">Red
<INPUT TYPE="checkbox" NAME="COLOR_CHECK2" VALUE="yes">Blue
<INPUT TYPE="checkbox" NAME="COLOR_CHECK3" VALUE="yes">Yellow
<INPUT TYPE="checkbox" NAME="COLOR_CHECK4" VALUE="yes" CHECKED>Green
<P>
What foods do you like:
<P>
<INPUT TYPE="checkbox" NAME="FOOD_CHECK1" VALUE="yes">Lobster <P>
<INPUT TYPE="checkbox" NAME="FOOD_CHECK2" VALUE="yes">Spam<P>
<INPUT TYPE="checkbox" NAME="FOOD_CHECK3" VALUE="yes" CHECKED>
Chocolate<P>

<INPUT TYPE="submit" NAME="SUBMIT_BUTTON" VALUE="Submit">
<INPUT TYPE="reset" NAME="RESET_BUTTON" VALUE="OOPS">
</FORM>
<HR>
</BODY>
</HTML>
```

6. Save the document as text or ASCII.

7. Use the Open File or Open Local command on your browser to make sure your form looks the way you expect it to. If all goes well, it will look very much like Figure 11-4.

How It Works

The **<FORM>...</FORM>** tags tell the browser to expect form **<INPUT>** tags between these two tags. The **<INPUT>** tag, when **TYPE** is set to **"checkbox"**, creates a check box for the user to click on to select that particular item. The check box toggles between on and off as the user clicks it. If a particular check box is selected, then the variable name that refers to that check box will be set to that value. When the user presses the Submit button, the information contained in the form will be sent to the HTTP server. To see what check boxes were selected and not selected, you can use the names assigned with the **NAME** attribute and check their values.

Comments

Although check boxes can be physically grouped together on the page or form, it is usually not a good idea to group them together under one variable name. It is possible to have more than one check box checked at any given time, so it is a good idea to give each check box its own unique variable name. It is also best to keep the value assigned to the box when it is checked something simple. We usually choose **Yes**. The example shows one group of check boxes running across the page and the other group running down the page. This is done purely to illustrate the number of ways you can present check boxes. Experiment to find the presentation you prefer.

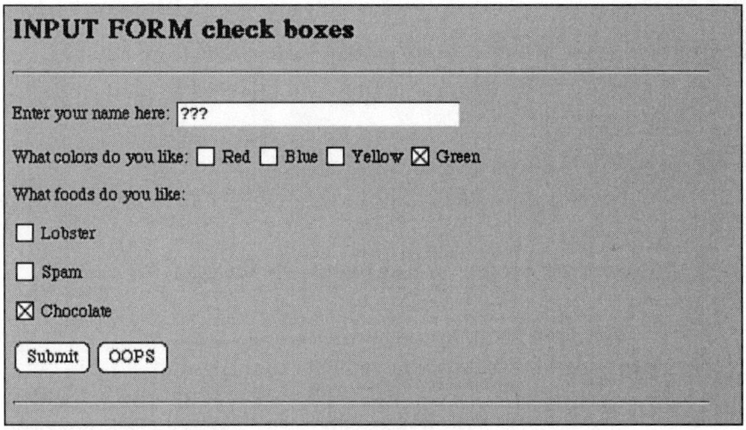

INPUT FORM check boxes

Enter your name here: ???

What colors do you like: ☐ Red ☐ Blue ☐ Yellow ☒ Green

What foods do you like:

☐ Lobster

☐ Spam

☒ Chocolate

Submit | OOPS

Figure 11-4 The form complete with check boxes

11.4 How do I...
Add radio buttons to a form?

COMPATIBILITY: HTML 2+

Problem

Now that I have a form in my HTML document, I would like to use radio buttons in it so I can let a user pick just one item out of a list. How do I do this?

Technique

Radio buttons are added to forms in much the same manner as check boxes are. To create a radio button that enables a user to click only one of several choices from a list, insert an **<INPUT>** tag between the **<FORM>...</FORM>** tags. Inside the **<INPUT>** tag, set **TYPE** to **"radio"**. You may have as many radio buttons as needed, and you may include other HTML tags between these tags.

Steps

The following steps show how to add radio buttons to forms:

1. Decide how many radio buttons you need and how you are going to lay them out on the form. The number is usually quite easy and straightforward to determine. The layout is a matter of personal taste and preferences. In this example, you will use one group of radio buttons for a reader to pick a favorite color and another for the reader to pick a favorite food.

2. Open the HTML document that contains the form to which you want to add the radio buttons. For this example, start with the document used in How-To 11.1.

3. Add the **<INPUT>** tag for the first radio button between the **<FORM>...** **</FORM>** tags. In the **<INPUT>** tag, set **TYPE** to **"radio"**. The basic syntax for this is

```
<INPUT TYPE="radio" NAME="NAME" VALUE=value [CHECKED] > "Text"
```

The **TYPE** attribute declares this field a radio button. The variable in the **NAME** attribute is how you will refer to this group of radio buttons when you later reference them in a script. The **VALUE** attribute is what this radio button is set to when it is checked. The **CHECKED** attribute is optional and tells the browser to show this radio button as checked when it is first displayed. **"Text"** is for whatever text you want to associate with each particular button.

The tags for the favorite color radio buttons look like this:

```
<INPUT TYPE="radio" NAME="COLOR_RADIO" VALUE=1>Red
<INPUT TYPE="radio" NAME="COLOR_RADIO" VALUE=2>Blue
<INPUT TYPE="radio" NAME="COLOR_RADIO" VALUE=3>Yellow
<INPUT TYPE="radio" NAME="COLOR_RADIO" VALUE=4 CHECKED>Green
```

The tags for the favorite food radio buttons look like this:

```
<INPUT TYPE="radio" NAME="FOOD_RADIO" VALUE=1>Lobster <P>
<INPUT TYPE="radio" NAME="FOOD_RADIO" VALUE=2>Spam<P>
<INPUT TYPE="radio" NAME="FOOD_RADIO" VALUE=3 CHECKED>Chocolate<P>
```

4. Put some heading text near the radio buttons so readers have a good idea of what you want them to do.

5. Enter any other text or HTML tags to help clarify the document and make it easier to read. The document should now resemble this:

```
<HTML> <HEAD>
<TITLE>Input Form</TITLE>
</HEAD>
<BODY>
<H2>INPUT FORM radio buttons</H2>
<HR>
<FORM METHOD=POST ACTION="/cgi-bin/MY_SCRIPT">
Enter your name here:
<INPUT TYPE="text" NAME="NAME" SIZE=30 VALUE="???"><p>
What is your favorite color:
<P>
<INPUT TYPE="radio" NAME="COLOR_RADIO" VALUE=1>Red
<INPUT TYPE="radio" NAME="COLOR_RADIO" VALUE=2>Blue
<INPUT TYPE="radio" NAME="COLOR_RADIO" VALUE=3>Yellow
<INPUT TYPE="radio" NAME="COLOR_RADIO" VALUE=4 CHECKED>Green
What is your favorite food:
<P>
<INPUT TYPE="radio" NAME="FOOD_RADIO" VALUE=1>Lobster
<INPUT TYPE="radio" NAME="FOOD_RADIO" VALUE=2>Spam
<INPUT TYPE="radio" NAME="FOOD_RADIO" VALUE=3 CHECKED>Chocolate

<INPUT TYPE="submit" NAME="SUBMIT_BUTTON" VALUE="Submit">
<INPUT TYPE="reset" NAME="RESET_BUTTON" VALUE="OOPS">
</FORM>
<HR>
</BODY>
</HTML>
```

6. Save the document as text or ASCII.

7. Use the Open File command or Open Local command on your browser to make sure your form looks like Figure 11-5.

INPUT FORM radio buttons

Enter your name here: ???

What is your favorite color:

Red Blue Yellow Green What is your favorite food:

Lobster Spam Chocolate Submit OOPS

Figure 11-5 The form complete with radio buttons

How It Works

The `<FORM>...</FORM>` tags tell the browser to expect form `<INPUT>` tags between these two tags. The `<INPUT>` tag, when the `TYPE` attribute is set to `"radio"`, creates a radio button for the user to click to select that choice. You can select only one radio button at a time from among any group of buttons associated with the same name. If a particular radio button is clicked, the variable name that refers to that group of radio buttons is set to that button's particular value. When the user presses the Submit button, the information contained in the form is sent to the HTTP server. To see what radio button was selected, check the variable's value with a script.

Comments

Although radio buttons greatly resemble check boxes, there is one big difference: Only one radio button from any group of radio buttons can be selected at a time. Therefore, only one name is assigned to the entire group of buttons.

COMPLEXITY
INTERMEDIATE

11.5 How do I...
Add password fields to a form?

COMPATIBILITY: HTML 2+

Problem

I would like users to enter their password so I can verify that they are who they say they are. How can I let them type their password so a nosy onlooker will not be able to read it?

Technique

Password fields in forms are displayed as text fields in which the entered text is shown as asterisks. To create a password field, insert an **<INPUT>** tag between the **<FORM> ...</FORM>** tags. Inside the **<INPUT>** tag, set the **TYPE** to **"password"**. You can have as many password fields as you want, but you usually need only one.

Steps

The following steps show how to add password fields to forms:

1. Decide how you would like to lay out your form. You will probably want to use only the name and password fields until you can verify that the user is actually who he or she claims to be.

2. Open the HTML document that contains the form to which you want to add the password field. Once again, use the basic document created in How-To 11.1.

3. Add the **<INPUT>** tag for the password field between the **<FORM>... </FORM>** tags. In the **<INPUT>** tag, set the **TYPE** to **"password"**. The basic syntax for this is

```
<INPUT TYPE="password" NAME="VARIABLE_NAME" SIZE="number"
 VALUE="initial value">
```

The **TYPE** attribute declares this field as a password text box. The variable in the **NAME** attribute is what you will refer to when you later want to check what's been entered here. **SIZE** is the length of the password text field. The **VALUE** attribute is what this field is initially set to—for example,

```
<INPUT TYPE="password" NAME="PASSWRD" VALUE=secret>
```

4. Put some descriptive text near the field so the reader has a good idea of what you expect him or her to enter.

5. Enter any other text or HTML tags to help clarify the document and make it easier to read. The document should now resemble the following:

```
<HTML> <HEAD>
<TITLE>Input Form</TITLE>
</HEAD>
<BODY>
<H2>INPUT FORM passwords</H2>
<HR>
<FORM METHOD=POST ACTION="/cgi-bin/MY_SCRIPT">
Enter your name here: <INPUT TYPE="text" NAME="NAME" SIZE=30
VALUE="???"><p>
What is your password:
```

continued on next page

continued from previous page

```
<INPUT TYPE="password" NAME="PASSWRD" VALUE=secret>
<P>
<INPUT TYPE="submit" NAME="SUBMIT_BUTTON" VALUE="Submit">
<INPUT TYPE="reset" NAME="RESET_BUTTON" VALUE="OOPS">
</FORM>
<HR>
</BODY>
</HTML>
```

6. Save the document as text or ASCII.

7. Use the Open File command or Open Local command on your browser to make sure your form looks like Figure 11-6.

How It Works

The `<FORM>...</FORM>` tags tell the browser to expect form `<INPUT>` tags between these two tags. The `<INPUT>` tag, when `TYPE` is set to `"password"`, is a text field with text displayed as asterisks. When the user presses the Submit button, the information contained in the form is sent to the HTTP server. To see what was entered in the field, use the name assigned with the `NAME` attribute.

Comments

Password fields are, for all intents and purposes, text fields. Instead of displaying what the user typed, however, the text displays as asterisks. You will still need a script to analyze this password. For information about creating a script, see How-To 11.12.

INPUT FORM passwords

Enter your name here: ???

What is your password: ••••••

[Submit] [OOPS]

Figure 11-6 The form complete with a password field

11.6 How do I... Add pull-down menus to a form?

COMPATIBILITY: HTML 2+

Problem

I would like to allow a reader to select one item from a list of items while the screen is showing only the currently selected item on the form. How can I do this?

Technique

Use the `<SELECT>...</SELECT>` tags to create a pull-down menu inside a form. To create a pull-down menu, insert the `<SELECT>` tags between the `<FORM>` tags. Label each option that can be selected separately with an `<OPTION>` tag. The form can include other HTML tags and elements.

Steps

The following steps show how to add pull-down menus to forms:

1. Decide which items you want to place in pull-down menus and how you want to place these items in your form. Sticking with the food motif, you will create one menu that lets a reader pick a food.

2. Open the HTML document that contains the form to which you want to add the pull-down menu. For now, expand on the document used in How-To 11.1.

3. Add the `<SELECT>...</SELECT>` tags between the `<FORM>...</FORM>` tags. Then add each `<OPTION>` tag between the `<SELECT>` tags:

```
<SELECT NAME="NAME">
<OPTION> An option
.....</SELECT>
```

The variable in the **NAME** attribute is what you will refer to when you later want to reference this menu. You have one `<OPTION>` tag for every item in the menu. You may not use any HTML markup tags between these options.

```
<SELECT NAME="MY_PULL_DOWN">
<OPTION>Lobster
<OPTION>Spam
<OPTION>Chocolate
</SELECT>
```

4. Put some descriptive text near the menu so the reader has a good idea of what you want him or her to do.

5. Enter any other text or HTML tags to help clarify the document and make it easier to read. The document should now resemble this:

```
<HTML> <HEAD>
<TITLE>Input Form </TITLE>
</HEAD>
<BODY>
<H2>INPUT FORM pulldown menus</H2>
<HR>
<FORM METHOD=POST ACTION="/cgi-bin/MY_SCRIPT">
Enter your name here: <INPUT TYPE="text" NAME="NAME" SIZE=30
VALUE="???"><p>
Pick a food:
<SELECT NAME="MY_PULL_DOWN">
<OPTION>Lobster
<OPTION>Spam
<OPTION>Chocolate
</SELECT>
<P>
<INPUT TYPE="submit" NAME="SUBMIT_BUTTON" VALUE="Submit">
<INPUT TYPE="reset" NAME="RESET_BUTTON" VALUE="OOPS">
</FORM>
<HR>
</BODY>
</HTML>
```

6. Save the document in text or ASCII format.

7. Use the Open File command or Open Local command on your browser to make sure your form looks something like Figure 11-7.

How It Works

The **<FORM>...</FORM>** tags tell the browser to expect associate form tags between these two tags. The **<SELECT>...</SELECT>** tags tell the browser to display the text

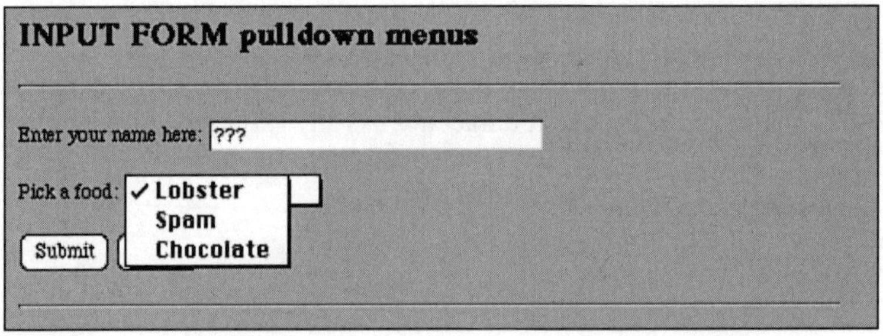

Figure 11-7 The form complete with a pull-down menu

next to each `<OPTION>` tag as a choice in a pull-down menu. When the user presses the Submit button, the information contained in the form is sent to the HTTP server. To see what was entered in the field, use the name that was assigned with the **NAME** attribute. In a pull-down menu, the variable used with the **NAME** attribute is actually assigned the value in the selected **<OPTION>** tag.

Comments

Pull-down menus are a kind of cross between check boxes and radio buttons because they are usually associated with one value. However, it is possible to have more than one option selected at a time. Many people like pull-down menus because pull-down menus do not use as much space on the screen as check boxes or radio buttons.

COMPLEXITY
INTERMEDIATE

11.7 How do I... Add a file selector dialog box to a form?

COMPATIBILITY: NETSCAPE 3.0

Problem

Now that I have a form in my HTML document, I would like to be able to give users a way to choose a document to be attached to the file's contents that will be sent to the server. How do I do this?

Technique

File selector dialog boxes are added with the **<INPUT>** tag. To create a file selector dialog box that enables a user to select a file from a list of files in a directory, insert an **<INPUT>** tag between the **<FORM>...</FORM>** tags. Inside the **<INPUT>** tag, set `TYPE` to **"file"**.

Steps

The following steps show how to add file selector dialog boxes to forms:

1. Decide the layout of your form on paper. In this simple example, you will use one text field and one file selector field.

2. Open the HTML document that contains the form to which you want to add the file selector dialog boxes. For this example, start with the document used in How To 11.1.

3. Add the `<INPUT>` tag for the first dialog box button between the `<FORM>... </FORM>` tags. In the `<INPUT>` tag, set `TYPE` to `"file"`. The basic syntax for this is

```
Text<INPUT TYPE="file" NAME="NAME" SIZE="width of field" VALUE="value"
ACCEPT="MIME contents types"  >
```

The `TYPE` attribute declares that this field will hold a filename selected from a dialog box button. The variable in the `NAME` attribute is how you will refer to this file when you later reference it in a script. The `VALUE` attribute is the default value of this field. The `SIZE` attribute sets the width of the field that will hold the filename. The `ACCEPT` attribute enables the user to limit the types of files that can be attached.

The tags for use in this example look like this:

```
<INPUT TYPE="file" NAME="FILEAT" VALUE="Cool File">
```

4. Put some heading text near the field that will contain the name of the file selected so readers have a good idea of what you want them to do.

5. Enter any other text or HTML tags that might help clarify the document and make it easier to read. The document should now resemble the following:

```
<HTML> <HEAD>
<TITLE>Input Form</TITLE>
</HEAD>
<BODY>
<H2>INPUT FORM File Dialog Box</H2>
<HR>
<FORM METHOD=POST ACTION="/cgi-bin/MY_SCRIPT">
Choose the file you wish to attach: <INPUT TYPE="file"
 NAME="FILEAT" SIZE=30 VALUE="COOL FILE"><p>
<P>
<INPUT TYPE="submit" NAME="submit_button" VALUE="Submit">
<INPUT TYPE="reset" NAME="reset_button" VALUE="Oops">
</FORM>
<HR>
</BODY>
</HTML>
```

6. Save the document as text or ASCII.

7. Use the Open File command or the Open Local command on your browser to make sure your form looks like Figure 11-8.

How It Works

The `<FORM>...</FORM>` tags tell the browser to expect form `<INPUT>` tags between these two tags. The `<INPUT>` tag, when the `TYPE` attribute is set to `"file"`, creates a field to hold a value and a button for the user to click to call up a dialog box that

INPUT FORM -- Textarea

Enter your name here: ???

File: Browse...

Submit OOPS

Figure 11-8 The form complete with a file selector dialog box

will, in turn, let the user select a file for a directory. When the user presses the Submit button, the information contained in the form is sent to the HTTP server.

Comments

Note that the **ACCEPT** attribute is not supported by all browsers.

COMPLEXITY
INTERMEDIATE

11.8 How do I... Add a single line text field to a form?

COMPATIBILITY: HTML 2+

Problem

Now that I have a form in my HTML document, I would like to let the user enter just one line of text. How do I do this?

Technique

Single line text fields are added to forms with the **<INPUT>** tag. To create a single line text field that enables a user to enter a single line of text, insert an **<INPUT>** tag between the **<FORM>...</FORM>** tags. Inside the **<INPUT>** tag, set **TYPE** to **"text"**. You can have as many single line text fields as needed, and you can include other HTML tags between these tags.

Steps

The following steps show how to add single line text fields to forms:

1. Decide how many text fields you need and how you are going to lay them out on the form. The number is usually quite easy and straightforward to determine. The layout is a matter of personal taste and preference. In this example, you will use just one single line text field.

2. Open the HTML document that contains the form to which you want to add the single line text field. For this example, start with the document used in How-To 11.1.

3. Add the `<INPUT>` tag for the first text field between the `<FORM>...</FORM>` tags. In the `<INPUT>` tag, set the `TYPE` to `"text"`. The basic syntax for this is

```
<INPUT TYPE="text" NAME="NAME" VALUE=value SIZE="length of the field">
```

The `TYPE` attribute declares that this field is a simple text field. The variable in the `NAME` attribute is how you will refer to this single line text field when you later reference it in a script. The `VALUE` attribute is what this field is initially set to. The `SIZE` attribute is used to set the width of the field.

4. Put some heading text near the single line text field so readers have a good idea of what you want them to do.

5. Enter any other text or HTML tags that might help clarify the document and make it easier to read. The document should now resemble the following:

```
<HTML> <HEAD>
<TITLE>Input Form</TITLE>
</HEAD>
<BODY>
<H2>INPUT FORM SINGLE LINE TEXT FIELD</H2>
<HR>
<FORM METHOD=POST ACTION="/cgi-bin/MY_SCRIPT">
Enter your name here: <INPUT TYPE="text" NAME="NAME" SIZE=30
 VALUE="???"><p>
<P>
<INPUT TYPE="submit" NAME="submit_button" VALUE="Submit">
<INPUT TYPE="reset" NAME="reset_button" VALUE="Oops">
</FORM>
<HR>
</BODY>
</HTML>
```

6. Save the document as text or ASCII.

7. Use the Open File command or the Open Local command on your browser to make sure your form looks like Figure 11-9.

How It Works

The `<FORM>...</FORM>` tags tell the browser to expect form `<INPUT>` tags between these two tags. The `<INPUT>` tag, when the `TYPE` attribute is set to `"text"`, creates a field to hold a line of text. When the user presses the Submit button, the

INPUT FORM -- Single line text prompt

Enter your name here: ???

Submit OOPS

Figure 11-9 The form complete with a single text line

information contained in the form is sent to the HTTP server. To access that information, use the **NAME** variable's value with a script.

Comments

Text is the default value type of the **<INPUT>** tag.

COMPLEXITY
INTERMEDIATE

11.9 How do I...
Use a clickable image as a Submit button?

COMPATIBILITY: HTML 2+

Problem

Those text Submit buttons on forms are boring looking. I would like to liven up my form by using an image as my Submit button. How do I do this?

Technique

Using an image as your Submit button is surprisingly easy. To create a graphical Submit button, insert an **<INPUT>** tag between the **<FORM>...</FORM>** tags. Inside the **<INPUT>** tag, set **TYPE** to **"image"**.

Steps

The following steps show how to use images as Submit buttons in forms:

1. Decide what type of image you would like to use as your Submit button, and then create it with your favorite graphics program. Remember, for compatibility, it is best to use a GIF file.

2. Open the HTML document that contains the form to which you want to add the Submit button. For this example, start with the document used in How-To 11.1.

3. Add the `<INPUT>` tag for the graphical Submit button between the `<FORM>` `...</FORM>` tags. In the `<INPUT>` tag, set `TYPE` to `"image"`. The basic syntax for this is

```
<INPUT TYPE="image" SRC="url of the graphio" NAME="SUBMIT"
VALUE="Go for it" >
```

The `TYPE` attribute declares that the image pointed to by `SRC` is to be used as the Submit button. The `NAME` and `VALUE` attributes will be used by nongraphical browsers to render a Submit button.

4. Enter any other text or HTML tags to create the form that will hold the information to be submitted.

```
<HTML> <HEAD>
<TITLE>Input Form </TITLE>
</HEAD>
<BODY>
<H2>INPUT FORM CLICKABLE IMAGES FOR SUBMIT</H2>
<HR>
<FORM METHOD=POST ACTION="/cgi-bin/MY_SCRIPT">
Enter your name here: <INPUT TYPE="text" NAME="NAME" SIZE=30
VALUE="???"><p>
<INPUT TYPE="image" SRC="button.gif" NAME="SUBMIT_BUTTON"
 VALUE="Go for it!">
<INPUT TYPE="reset" NAME="RESET_BUTTON" VALUE="OOPS">
</FORM>
<HR>
</BODY>
</HTML>
```

5. Save the document as text or ASCII.

6. Use the Open File command or the Open Local command on your browser to make sure your form looks like Figure 11-10.

How It Works

The `<FORM>...</FORM>` tags tell the browser to expect form `<INPUT>` tags between these two tags. When the `TYPE` attribute is set to `"image"`, a button is created on the form that will contain the image pointed to by the `SRC` attribute. The image will function as the Submit button for the form. When the user selects this button, it acts as if the user had just pressed a standard Submit button as it sends the information to the URL named in the action attribute in the `<FORM>...</FORM>` tag.

Comments

This feature is a nice addition to HTML because it can help liven up forms. Remember to include the `NAME` and `VALUE` attributes for nongraphical browsers.

Figure 11-10 The form with an image used as a Submit button

COMPLEXITY
INTERMEDIATE

11.10 How do I... Pass information between forms?

COMPATIBILITY: HTML 2+

Problem

I want to build two forms and have something in the second form be contingent on something entered in the first form. Because a form is not accessible again after it is submitted, how can I do this?

Technique

It is possible to pass information between forms with hidden fields. These fields can be accessed by a CGI program or script even after the form has been submitted to determine what course of action to take in building a second form.

Steps

The following steps give a general description of how you can pass information from one form to another. For more complete information on this topic, see Chapter 13, "Handling Server Security."

1. Create an HTML document. For this example, use the one from How-To 11.1.
2. Enter the holder for the hidden field. A hidden field is created with the **<INPUT>** tag much like a text field.

```
<INPUT TYPE="hidden" NAME="HIDDEN_FIELD"  VALUE="info">
```

Here the **TYPE** attribute is set to **"hidden"** so a reader cannot see the field. The **NAME** attribute is set to whatever name you want to use to access this field with later. The **VALUE** attribute is any information you want to carry in this field.

```
<HTML> <HEAD>
<TITLE>Input Form</TITLE>
</HEAD>
<BODY>
<HR>
<FORM METHOD=POST ACTION="/cgi-bin/my_script">
Enter your name here: <INPUT TYPE="text" NAME="NAME" SIZE=30
 VALUE="John Smith">
<INPUT TYPE="hidden" NAME="HIDDEN_FIELD"  VALUE="info">
<INPUT TYPE="submit" NAME="SUBMIT_BUTTON" VALUE="Submit">
<INPUT TYPE="reset" NAME="RESET_BUTTON" VALUE="OOPS">
</FORM>
<HR>
</BODY>
</HTML>
```

This form looks identical to the form created in How-To 11.1 when displayed by a browser.

3. After the form is submitted to the server, use a script to refer to the field.

How It Works

When you place a hidden field inside the **<FORM>...</FORM>** tags, you create space to hold information. The reader will not see or use this space, but a script can use it. You can access this field as you would any other field.

Comments

This is a very general introduction to this topic, with just enough information to let you recognize it when you see it later. It is very easy to create the hidden field on the form. To use this field, though, you need a script written in Perl, C, or some other language. There is an example of this technique and more information on hidden fields in Chapter 14, "The Common Gateway Interface (CGI)."

11.11 How do I... Choose a request method to send data to the HTTP server?

COMPATIBILITY: HTML 2+

Problem

Now that my form is all ready to go, what method should I use to send the information to the HTTP server, and how do I tell the form to send this information?

Technique

First, decide whether you are going to use the **GET** or **POST** method. This is largely a matter of personal preference, but the consensus seems to be that you should use **POST**. Use the **<INPUT>** tag to create a Submit button. When the user selects this button, the information in the form is sent to the HTTP server.

Steps

The following steps give a general overview of the procedure used to decide which method you want to use when submitting information from a form to a server:

1. Decide what you want to include in your form and how you want your form to be laid out. For this example, use a simple form that asks a reader for his or her name and comments.

2. Decide which method you want to use to post your information. You have two choices: **GET** or **POST**. Sometimes this choice is dictated by the type of server your system is using, in which case it is a good idea to call your system administrator and see if he or she recommends either of the two methods. If not, then the choice is a matter of your preference. The **POST** method seems to be the most common choice.

   The **GET** method passes the contents of the form as a string in a query URL. The server places this string into the environment variable **query_string**.

   The **POST** method sends the contents as a data block through the standard input stream of the CGI script named in **ACTION**. The length of this string is stored in the environment variable **content_length**.

   No matter which method you choose, the data will still be encoded the same: **field1=content&field2=content&**.

3. Create your HTML document, complete with a form.

```
<HTML><HEAD><TITLE>A Simple Sample Form</TITLE></HEAD>
<BODY>
<HR>
<FORM METHOD=POST ACTION="$ME/post">
Name: <INPUT TYPE="text" NAME="INPUT_NAME" SIZE=30
VALUE="???">
<P>Comment:<TEXTAREA NAME="TEXT_COMMENTS" ROWS=5 COLS=50>
</TEXTAREA>
<P><INPUT TYPE="submit" NAME="SUBMIT_BUTTON" VALUE="SEND">
<HR>
</FORM>
</BODY>
</HTML>
```

4. Save your document in text or ASCII format.

5. Read How-To 11.12 to see how you can process this and other forms.

How It Works

Selecting the Submit button passes the information in the form to the server. For this example, if a user entered `John Smith` for `input_name` and `Nice WWW site!` for `text_comments`, these would be sent to the server as

```
input_name=John+Smith&text_comments=Nice+WWW+site!
```

It is then up to the CGI script processing the form to parse out the data.

Comments

There is much information online that addresses choosing between the `GET` and `POST` methods. To see what NCSA has to say, access the following URL: `http://hoohoo.ncsa.uiuc.edu/docs/setup/admin/NCSAScripts.html`.

11.12 How do I... Process a form?

COMPATIBILITY: HTML 2+

Problem

Now that I have created this great form, how can I let somebody actually use it over my Web server? Then, how can I process the information they send me?

Technique

Information stored in a form is sent to the HTTP server as part of a data stream, either as part of a URL or as a data block. It is possible to use environment variables to extract the user input from this data stream. Processing a form requires a CGI script to act as a go-between among the HTML, the HTTP server, and the information sent in the form. This script can be written in any high-level language your site supports. Favorite choices are Perl and C. This very simple sample script is broken into three parts:

- ✔ The first part looks at the arguments sent to the server in the URL and determines what actions to take.
- ✔ The second part displays the form for a user to interact with.
- ✔ The third part extracts and decodes the form's information, after which it processes that information.

Steps

The following procedure uses a form created from techniques used in previous sections of this chapter to show one method of capturing and then using information from forms:

1. Develop a form that you want to use. For this example, we will use a very simple three-item form:

```
<HTML><HEAD><TITLE>A Simple Sample Form</TITLE></HEAD>
<BODY>
<HR>
<FORM METHOD=POST ACTION="$ME/post">
Name: <INPUT TYPE="text" NAME="INPUT_NAME" SIZE=30
VALUE="???">
<P>Comment:<TEXTAREA NAME="TEXT_COMMENTS" ROWS=5 COLS=50>
</TEXTAREA>
<P><INPUT TYPE="submit" NAME="SUBMIT_BUTTON" VALUE="Submit">
<HR>
</FORM>
</BODY>
</HTML>
```

2. Create a CGI script in the editor or word processor of your choice. The CGI script in this example is broken up into three parts. The first part, or main program, sets up the routine and decides whether the server should send the reader a form to fill out or whether the reader has sent the server a form to process. The Perl code for this script immediately follows.

The first part of the script is actually broken up into two sections. The first section takes care of the overhead:

```
#!/usr/bin/perl
$ME = "HTTP://MY_SERVER/cgi-bin/SAMPFORM.CGI";
$PATHINFO = $ENV{PATH_INFO};

print <<EOF;
Content-type: text/HTML

EOF
```

The first line tells the Perl compiler that this is a Perl script. The next line sets up the address given in the **<FORM>** tag's **ACTION** attribute. You should replace the **MY_SERVER** with your server's URL. The third line grabs the path information from the environment variable **path_info**. This information is used in the next section of the script to determine whether the program should send the user a form to fill out or whether the user has sent information from the form. The next four lines initialize the server to expect an HTML document.

```
if ($PATHINFO eq "") {
  &send_form;
} elsif ($PATHINFO =~ m|^/post|){
  &post_form;
}
exit 0;
```

These lines use the path information to determine what course of action the script is to take. If the path information is blank (""), that means send the user a form to fill out. If the information contains a string that contains the word **POST**, that means the user has seen the form and pressed the Submit button on the form, and now it is time to process the information in the form.

3. The next part of the script is the **send_form** subroutine. This part outputs to the HTTP server the form you want the reader to see.

```
sub send_form
{
  print <<EOF ;
<HTML><HEAD><TITLE>A Simple Sample Form</TITLE></HEAD>
<BODY>
<HR>
<FORM METHOD=POST ACTION="$ME/post">
Name: <INPUT TYPE="text" NAME="INPUT_NAME" SIZE=30 VALUE="???">
<P>Comment:<TEXTAREA NAME="TEXT_COMMENTS" ROWS=5 COLS=50> </TEXTAREA>
<P><INPUT TYPE="submit" NAME="SUBMIT_BUTTON" VALUE="Submit">
<HR>
</FORM>
</BODY>
</HTML>
EOF
}
```

This is straightforward. The HTML document prints to the server, allowing a user to interact with the form.

4. The final part of the script is the **post_form** subroutine. This is put into action after the user has submitted the form. This subroutine reads the form's input from the standard input stream, splits the input into appropriate fields and values, and then removes any strange characters the server might have added when it encoded the input. You now are free to access the information contained in the form via the names assigned to each field.

```
sub post_form
{
# Get the input.
  read(STDIN, $BUFFER, $ENV{'CONTENT_LENGTH'});
  # Split the name-value pairs.
  @pairs = split(/&/, $buffer);
  foreach $PAIR (@pairs)
  {
    ($NAME, $VALUE) = split(/=/, $pair);
# Un-Webify plus signs and %-encoding
    $VALUE =~ tr/+/ /;
    $VALUE =~ s/%([a-fA-F0-9][a-fA-F0-9])/pack("C", hex($1))/eg;
    $FORM{$NAME} = $VALUE;
  }
```

Without diving too much into Perl (there are other Waite Group Press books on that subject), we will say here that this code reads the contents of the standard input into a variable called **$buffer**. The string in **$buffer** is a **content_length**—bytes long string of continuous data sent like this:

```
INPUT_NAME=john+smith&text_comments=nice+web+server
```

The next few lines of code use the **split** command to separate variables and their values. The lines after that remove those **+** signs from the value and translate any encoded characters.

```
  print <<EOF ;
<HTML>
<HEAD><TITLE>Here's what was input</TITLE></HEAD>
<BODY>
The name entered was: $FORM{'INPUT_NAME'}. <P>
Their comments are $FORM{'TEXT_COMMENTS'}.
</BODY></HTML>
EOF
```

The final part of this routine outputs another HTML document that uses the information sent in the form. To use the person's name in the form, refer to it as **$FORM{'INPUT_NAME'}**. This **$FORM{'INPUT_NAME'}** is replaced in the outputted HTML document by **John Smith**.

5. The script is now complete. Save it with whatever name you think best describes it. For this example, simply call it

```
sampform.cgi
```

6. If you created your script with a word processor or editor on a system other than the system on which your server resides, you will need to transfer the script to the appropriate spot on your server system. Check with your system administrator for information on how to do this for your particular system.

7. When the script is on the server, change the access rights to the script. Most HTML documents do not need a user to execute them, but CGI scripts do. The mode should be changed to

```
chmod 755 sampform.cgi
```

8. A script that will not run on your server will not work. Compile the script to make sure there are no errors. To compile the script, type either

```
sampform.cgi
```

or

```
perl sampform.cgi
```

If all went well, this should output something that looks like this:

```
Content-type: text/HTML

<HTML><HEAD><TITLE>A Simple Sample Form</TITLE></HEAD>
<BODY>
<HR>
Send me your comments:<BR>
<FORM METHOD=POST ACTION="MY_SERVER/cgi-bin/SAMPFORM.CGI/post">
Name: <INPUT TYPE="text" NAME="INPUT_NAME" SIZE=30 VALUE="???">
<P>Comment:<TEXTAREA NAME="TEXT_COMMENTS" ROWS=5 COLS=50> </TEXTAREA>
<P><INPUT TYPE="submit" NAME="SUBMIT_BUTTON" VALUE="Submit">
<HR>
</FORM>
</BODY>
</HTML>
```

9. Access the CGI script over the Web by using the Open Location command in your browser's menu. Then enter the URL specified by the **METHOD** action. For example, to use the CGI script used in the sample, type

```
HTTP://MY_SERVER/cgi-bin/sampform.cgi
```

replacing **MY_SERVER** with your server's URL. When first accessed, the form should look much like Figure 11-11.

10. When the form is submitted, the screen will look like Figure 11-12.

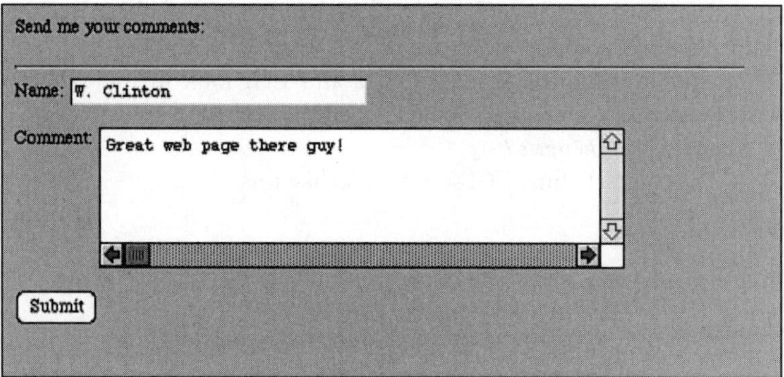

Figure 11-11 The form served by the sample script

How It Works

The first part of the script sets the table and checks the `path_info` environment variable to see whether the server has sent anything to the script. If nothing was sent, the script sends an HTML document for the browser to display. If the path information contains `POST`, the server has sent a form that must be processed. The fields are encoded, so they must first be separated and then stripped of all the characters the system adds. After this, the information in the fields can be accessed by referring to their variable names. An in-depth analysis of how CGI and forms interact goes beyond the scope of this chapter and is covered in Chapter 13, "Handling Server Security." Yet you do not need a total understanding of the form and CGI interaction to use forms successfully.

Comments

Not all system administrators allow users to have their own CGI scripts. It is a good idea to check with your system administrator before starting. Not only will he or she be able to tell you whether you can place scripts on your server, but the administrator can probably also point you in the right direction. The script given here is a bare-bones script. It doesn't have any error checking or safety precautions built into it. In addition, the form could have contained other types of form tags. Still, it should

Figure 11-12 The form's information after it has been processed

give you the basic idea of how CGI and forms interact with each other. Experiment by plugging in your own forms.

For more information on forms and CGI look in the Yahoo! directory at **http://www.yahoo.com/Computers_and_Internet/Internet/World_Wide_Web/Programming/Forms/**.

The complete final CGI script looks like this:

```
#!/usr/bin/perl
#
# This is a CGI script which lets users interact with a form.
# If the CGI PATH_INFO passed to us is empty, then we just
# return an HTML document with a form allowing the user to post
# feedback. If the CGI PATH_INFO is set to post, the user's feedback
# is shown to them
#
#
# URL for this script (without arguments) on this server. Note: if this
# server were using WN this URL would look slightly different with NCSA
#    "http://address/cgi-bin/name"
#
# Note: the examples use variable names in upper case as per
# the WPG standard only here variable names are in lower case
# as in the Perl standard
#
# Note: I am using my server's actual URL in this example

$me = "http://zeb.nysaes.cornell.edu/cgi-bin/SAMPFORM.cgi";

# Get the argument from the URL.

$pathinfo = $ENV{PATH_INFO};

# Start out by sending a content-type for the document we'll be returning.

print <<EOF;
Content-type: text/html

EOF

# See what we're supposed to be doing.

if ($pathinfo eq "") {
  &send_form;
} elsif ($pathinfo =~ m|^/post|){
  &post_form;
}
exit 0;

# &send_form; returns a menu of available options for this gateway
#script.

sub send_form
{
#
# The form for them to interact with -- you can plug your own in
# here...
```

```
#
  print <<EOF ;
<HTML><HEAD><TITLE>A Simple Sample Form</TITLE></HEAD>
<BODY>
Send me your comments:<BR>
<HR>
<FORM METHOD=POST ACTION="$me/post">
Name: <INPUT TYPE="text" NAME="input_name" SIZE=30 VALUE="???">
<P>Comment:<TEXTAREA NAME="text_comments" ROWS=5 COLS=50> </TEXTAREA>
<P><INPUT TYPE="submit" NAME="submit_button" VALUE="Submit">
<HR>
</FORM>
</BODY>
</HTML>
EOF

}
# post_form; show them what they entered

sub post_form
{
# Get the input.
  read(STDIN, $buffer, $ENV{'CONTENT_LENGTH'});
  # Split the name-value pairs.
  @pairs = split(/&/, $buffer);
  foreach $pair (@pairs)
  {
    ($name, $value) = split(/=/, $pair);
# Un-Webify plus signs and %-encoding
    $value =~ tr/+/ /;
    $value =~ s/%([a-fA-F0-9][a-fA-F0-9])/pack("C", hex($1))/eg;
    $form{$name} = $value;
  }
#
#The form we're outputting based on what the user gave us -- you
#can modify this to meet your requirements
#
  print <<EOF ;
<HTML>
<HEAD><TITLE>Here's what was input</TITLE></HEAD>
<BODY>
The name entered was: $form{'input_name'}. <P>
Their comments are $form{'text_comments'}.
</BODY></HTML>
EOF
}
```

Note that JavaScript can also be used to handle form processing and interaction. A few examples of using JavaScript to interact with forms can be found in How-To 17.7, How-To 17.10, and How-To 17.11. An in-depth review of JavaScript is beyond the scope of this book, but these sections should give those interested in exploring the use of JavaScript a good start.

PART III

SERVING

CHAPTER 12

SERVER BASICS

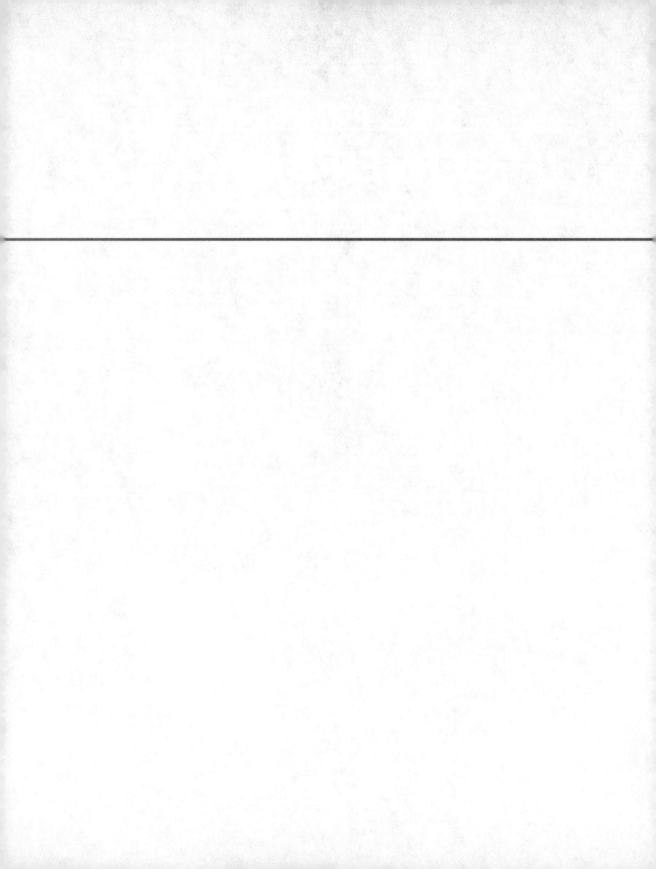

12

SERVER BASICS

How do I...

A Web server is an application that listens to the Internet, awaiting connections and requests from Web browsers and other user agents such as search engines. The server examines a request and, if it is appropriate, supplies the requested services. For most casual users, this abridged description is enough. However, if you are developing your own Web site, you will find the How-To's in this chapter of great benefit.

Browsers use the *Hypertext Transfer Protocol* (HTTP) to communicate with servers. This is a generic protocol language developed specifically for the transmission of hypertext documents across the Internet. Whenever you specify a URL with the HTTP prefix, you are requesting the use of this protocol to transmit the referenced document. Browsers send an appropriate HTTP request to the specified server.

Servers respond to user agent requests with a two-part response. The first component of the response, the *response header*, contains a variety of information about the server handling the request and the file or data being sent. For example, the type information is in the response header; this information is used by many browsers to determine whether a helper application or an appropriate plug-in is needed to process the object sent. The second part of the response is the *message body*. The content of this component is the actual data from the requested file, whether it is an HTML document, an AIFF audio segment, or data of some other type.

This chapter introduces information necessary for establishing and maintaining a Web site. This includes directions for server configuration, document installation, and the addition of file types. The examples concentrate on the NCSA HTTPD server package, which serves as the basis for both other UNIX-based servers, such as Netscape's Commerce Server, and servers for other platforms, such as WinHTTPD for Windows 3.1 and Website for Windows NT. Several How-To's also examine the installation and configuration of Netscape's FastTrack server.

Chapters 13, "Handling Server Security," and 14, "The Common Gateway Interface (CGI)," discuss server security and gateway application development, respectively.

12.1 Choose Server Software

After you decide that you are going to establish a server, you must select and find the appropriate server software. What is appropriate depends upon several factors such as hardware, operating system, and reliability. This How-To will help you make the right choice.

12.2 Install Server Software

Each server software package will have its own installation guide and requirements. The general installation tasks are similar; however, specific installation details are slightly different from server to server. This How-To examines in detail the installation process for the HTTPD server software developed by NCSA.

12.3 Install a Netscape FastTrack Server

Netscape's server software provides an easy-to-use, entry-level server for the Windows 95/NT and UNIX markets. This How-To examines in detail the installation process for the Netscape FastTrack server software.

12.4 Configure the Server

Each Web site has its own requirements and restrictions. Therefore, simply downloading and installing the software might not be enough to establish a working Web site. This How-To provides information about configuring an HTTP server for your site. The specifics of configuring an NCSA HTTPD server are discussed in detail.

12.5 Configure a Netscape FastTrack Server

Unlike NCSA-type servers that require direct editing of configuration files, the FastTrack server uses a separate administration server to support configuring of the primary Web server. The administration server provides an HTML form-based interface for configuring the primary server. This How-To examines the use of the FastTrack Web interface to configure a server.

12.6 Register Additional MIME Types

Documents of various types can be stored on HTTP servers. Servers specify document types using Multipurpose Internet Mail Extension (MIME) types. The server must know the type of each document so that it can perform its tasks appropriately. If you add a document of a new type to the server, you must register this new type. This How-To describes how to register new types.

12.7 Install Documents

The primary purpose of the server is to respond to requests for documents. To do so, the server must know where documents are stored. This How-To provides directions for installing documents on an NCSA HTTPD server or on derivative servers such as WinHTTPD.

12.8 Start or Stop the Server

The server must be active to receive requests from clients. You activate the server by starting it and deactivate it by stopping it. These functions are performed as required for maintenance of the server. This How-To describes how you stop and start a UNIX server.

12.9 Register My Server

When your server site runs properly, you will want to let others know it exists. The instructions in this How-To outline a procedure for introducing your site to the World Wide Web community.

12.1 How do I... Choose server software?

COMPATIBILITY: ANY SERVER

Problem

How do I choose server software for my Web site? What are the issues involved? Why is one platform or server more efficient or reliable than another? I need to know what my options are and how I can evaluate them.

Technique

The purpose of server software is to respond to client requests appropriately. This involves listening for client requests (perhaps simultaneous requests), evaluating them, and generating suitable responses.

To choose the software that best suits your needs, you must first evaluate the capabilities of your hardware and operating system. Use the evaluation in steps 1 through 3 to determine whether your platform is adequate for your needs or whether you should move to a different platform.

When you have determined your optimal hardware and operating system platform, consider the various server software packages. Select the package that best meets your needs according to the criteria that appear in step 4.

Finally, acquire your chosen server software, either from the manufacturer or by using FTP.

Steps

This How-To presents step-by-step instructions for evaluating and selecting an appropriate server software package to meet the needs of your Web site. To acquire a particular package, you must be familiar with the use of anonymous FTP or FTP URLs (unless the chosen package is a commercial product, in which case you will need to contact the appropriate vendor). Appendix F, "Summary of Selected Server Software," provides a summary of several available server packages.

1. Identify your hardware platform. This list specifies several hardware platforms suitable to a Web server site:

- ✔ Apple Macintosh computer and compatibles
- ✔ IBM PCs, PC compatibles
- ✔ Sun, SGI, Digital, and other UNIX workstations

2. Identify the operating system(s) running on your hardware platform. You might need to consult your system's manuals to determine this information. Server software has been developed for the following operating systems:

- ✔ MacOS
- ✔ UNIX
- ✔ MS Windows 3.1 environment
- ✔ MS Windows 95 environment
- ✔ MS Windows NT environment

3. Your hardware and operating system greatly affect your choice of server software because each HTTP server has been engineered for a single platform. If you have a choice of operating systems, the following list shows, in descending order, the optimal choices in operating systems for a server site. This order assumes similar processing and memory capabilities on the hardware. The "How It Works" section discusses the basis for this order.

- ✔ UNIX
- ✔ MS Windows 95 environment, Windows NT, MacOS
- ✔ Windows 3.1

4. Based on your platform, you are now ready to select a server. You must think about the features you want to support on your server. Some of these key issues are described next.

Hardware and software platform support: This criterion places the first restriction upon your choice of server packages. Appendix F provides a brief summary of server software packages by operating system. Each description in this appendix ends with a URL that provides additional information on the specified server.

Security: Different server packages provide different levels and types of security. Levels of security range from restricting access to the entire server to restricting access to individual documents. Access can be restricted by machine address, username and password, or both.

Gateway interface compliance: Many applications work in conjunction with HTTP server software. These applications serve as gateways between a Web server and resources available at the server site. A common interface specification for such applications is the Common Gateway Interface (CGI), which is explained in Chapter 14, "The Common Gateway Interface (CGI)." (For current release information, see **http://hoohoo.ncsa.uiuc.edu/cgi/overview.html**.) However, different servers support this interface to varying degrees, ranging from full compliance to no gateway application support at all.

Firewall support: Firewalls are another type of security feature. A firewall limits Internet traffic between machines inside and outside the firewall. Running behind a firewall limits your selection of server packages.

Search capabilities: What kind and depth of search capability do you want built into the server software? Additional search capabilities can be built with gateway applications; however, certain server packages directly support searching.

File inclusion support: File inclusion enables your server to incorporate files from your server site into the HTML documents it distributes. For example, this feature could be used to include a standard business letterhead on all the HTML documents at your site.

Request types supported: HTTP supports many request types. The most common type is the **get** request, supported by most servers. (Appendix G, "HTML Hypertext Transfer Protocol (HTTP)," provides detailed information on additional request types.) Requests for HTML documents are usually the result of **get** requests from browsers.

5. After you select a list of criteria, you are ready to choose among the various HTTP server software packages available for your platform. Consult Appendix F for a brief description of many commonly used servers.

6. Contact the server software manufacturer or use FTP to acquire your chosen server software. The example demonstrates how you might use anonymous FTP to acquire the NCSA HTTPD server from a UNIX machine. Open an FTP connection to the **ftp.ncsa.uiuc.edu** site. Then enter

```
glean dsk 151 >ftp ftp.ncsa.uiuc.edu
Connected to ftp.ncsa.uiuc.edu.
220 curley FTP server (Version wu-2.4(25) Thu Aug 25 13:14:21 CDT 1994) ⇐
ready.
```

7. When prompted, enter the name **anonymous**. For a password, enter your e-mail address.

```
Name (ftp.ncsa.uiuc.edu:dsk): anonymous
331 Guest login ok, send your complete e-mail address as password.
Password:
230 Guest login ok, access restrictions apply.
```

8. Change directories to the location of the current version of HTTPD by entering the following command:

```
ftp> cd Web/httpd/UNIX/ncsa_httpd/current
```

9. Change the transfer mode to binary using the **binary** command.

```
ftp> binary
200 Type set to I.
```

10. Issue the appropriate **get** command to retrieve the server package appropriate for your UNIX platform.

```
ftp> get httpd_1.5.2a_export_solaris2.4_sparc.tar.Z
200 PORT command successful.
150 Opening BINARY mode data connection for httpd_1.5.2a_export_⇐
solaris2.4_sparc.tar.Z (958569 bytes).
226 Transfer complete.
local: httpd_1.5.2a_export_solaris2.4_sparc.tar.Z remote: httpd_1.5.2a_⇐
export_solaris2.4_sparc.tar.Z
958569 bytes received in 104 seconds (9 Kbytes/s)
```

How It Works

If you are establishing a Web site to provide information to the World Wide Web community, consider several platform issues. First, your server site must run reliably 24 hours a day. You cannot know at what time or from what location accesses will be made; therefore, your hardware and operating system platform must run reliably on a constant basis (or as constantly as possible).

In addition, your server should be efficient. You want to be able to service many incoming requests as quickly as possible. Popular sites service as many as 1,000,000 requests an hour. These requests could be spaced over the entire hour or within a single minute. In a perfect world, closely spaced or even simultaneous requests would be serviced as quickly as those made at wider intervals. Your hardware and software will have a significant effect on this performance.

Finally, you should consider the maintenance of a server on your platform. A server should be easily maintained and updated. Keep in mind that, in some cases, ease of maintenance decreases as the number of supported features increases.

With these needs in mind, the available server platforms can be prioritized from most to least suitable as follows: UNIX; Windows NT, Windows 95, or MacOS; and Windows. The UNIX operating system features true multitasking, the capability to run many processes at the same time. This capability makes it possible for an HTTP server to answer many simultaneous requests. Furthermore, the UNIX operating system provides a clear separation between user processes, such as an HTTP server, and operating system tasks, such as a printer manager. This capability improves the reliability of your server significantly. Your server will remain intact under high system loads and will have a reduced likelihood of system crashes. Finally, the UNIX platform was the first to be used for HTTP server development; consequently, many new features and capabilities are added to UNIX servers before they reach servers for other platforms.

Windows NT, Windows 95, and MacOS are about equally desirable. They support servers that, in general, are easier to configure, particularly if you are unfamiliar with UNIX. They also support both multitasking and task separation, although not as strongly as these features are supported in UNIX. Unless you are managing an excessively popular site with a large number of gateway applications running, server performance on these platforms competes nearly on a par with UNIX servers. Although the performance of MacOS servers may lag a little behind that of Windows 95 and NT servers, MacOS servers are much more secure than Windows or UNIX servers and are almost impossible to break into.

Finally, DOS and Windows are the least favorable for establishing a stable Web site. Neither of these environments supports true multitasking, nor do they support task separation particularly well. Windows systems simulate a limited form of multitasking, but not to the same degree as UNIX. The lack of true multitasking leads to sluggish response time, which increases quickly with the number of requests. The lack of task separation leads to reduced reliability in general; user applications can cause system crashes that place your Web site out of commission until the system is rebooted. System crashes for a single user are annoying, but system crashes for your Web site mean that your site is dead to the world.

For some of the platforms just mentioned, server selection is limited; however, for several a significant selection is available with varying capabilities. Therefore, consider the features you want to support when choosing your platform and server.

Comments

Ultimately, the decisions regarding hardware, operating system, and server platform hinge on personal choice. Many Web administrators agree that HTML documents are best distributed over the Web through the combination of a UNIX-based machine and either the NCSA or CERN HTTP servers. Both of these servers are freely available from URLs `http://hoohoo.ncsa.uiuc.edu/docs/Overview.html` and `http://www.w3.org/hypertext/WWW/Daemon/Status.html`, respectively.

Finding a UNIX machine is not as difficult a task as it might sound. The Linux operating system is a UNIX clone that has been developed for PC-compatible computers. This operating system is freely available, and information can be found at URL `http://sunsite.unc.edu/mdw/linux.html`. Seriously consider this option for establishing a reliable, low-cost Web site. Even though Linux will run on a 386 platform, you can greatly increase the reliability and efficiency of your Web site if you have a 486 or Pentium-based system, preferably one with more than 16MB of RAM.

COMPLEXITY
INTERMEDIATE

12.2 How do I... Install server software?

COMPATIBILITY: UNIX-BASED SERVER

Problem

I have selected and acquired my server software. Now I must install it correctly on my system. NCSA HTTPD server software is one of the most commonly used UNIX-based server packages; it has been ported to a variety of other platforms and is the basis for several other popular servers. How do I install this package?

Technique

Server software is usually acquired in a compressed archive. This software must then be uncompressed and unarchived to an appropriate location on your hard disk. If a suitable executable copy of the server software has been acquired, the process is complete; otherwise, the server software package must be compiled before use.

This How-To explains how to install the NCSA HTTPD server. A similar process is required by most UNIX server packages; examine your documentation to learn how to install your server software.

Steps

The steps outline the procedure for installing the NCSA HTTPD server on a UNIX system; many of the instructions given for this server will also apply to other platforms. These instructions are also suitable for updating server software.

1. If you have a compressed archive version of this program, you must first uncompress the archive file; if the file is not compressed, proceed to step 2. Use the following command to uncompress the server archive:

```
uncompress httpd_1.4.1_sunos4.1.3.tar.Z
```

2. Unarchive your server software archive. Install the software in an appropriate location on your hard disk. (If you have already unarchived and installed your server software in a suitable location, proceed to step 3.)

This step varies by platform; however, in general, you should place your server software in a location that you can easily access and maintain. The following example shows the installation of the NCSA HTTPD software in the `/usr/local` directory:

```
glean# ls
adm     include
bin     lib
conf     man
etc     typescript
httpd_1.4.1_sunos4.1.3.tar
glean# tar xf httpd_1.4.1_sunos4.1.3.tar
glean# ls
adm     httpd_1.4.1_sunos4.1.3.tar
bin     include
conf     lib
etc     man
httpd_1.4.1     typescript
```

3. This step is optional, but it is recommended for platforms capable of creating aliases. Create an alias to the location where you installed your server software. This link can be referenced when starting your server rather than the installation directory created in step 2. Therefore, when you update the server, your references to your server application need not change. When an update is made, install the new version as specified in steps 1 and 2 and link the update to the old alias. This process is shown in the example, which demonstrates the creation of an alias for a server installation under UNIX, followed by an update to point to a new server installation.

```
glean# ls -l
total 10
lrwxrwxrwx   1 root            10 Jun 15 15:36 httpd -> httpd_1.3R
drwxr-sr-x   2 root           512 Jun 15 15:36 httpd_1.3R
drwxr-sr-x   8 524            512 May 21 23:37 httpd_1.4.1
glean# rm httpd
```

continued on next page

continued from previous page

```
rm: remove httpd? y
glean# ln -s httpd_1.4.1 httpd
glean# ls -l
total 10
lrwxrwxrwx  1 root         11 Jun 15 15:38 httpd -> httpd_1.4.1
drwxr-sr-x  2 root        512 Jun 15 15:38 httpd_1.3R
drwxr-sr-x  8 524         512 May 21 23:37 httpd_1.4.1
```

4. Finally, create the root directory of your data tree. The root directory is the base of your document hierarchy, the top-level directory where you place most of your Web documents. If you plan to run multiple servers providing access to multiple hierarchies, select several locations. Choose these locations based on the goals for the particular data tree. For most situations, you'll need to choose a hard disk with adequate space for your documents. If your data tree will be relatively static and development has already been completed, you should have a good idea how much disk space is required; however, if the document tree is dynamically changing and growing, you might need to link space from a large drive to your chosen location. The example demonstrates this task on a UNIX platform.

```
glean# df
Filesystem    kbytes    used    avail    capacity    Mounted on
/dev/sd3a     32791     4102    25410     14%      /
/dev/sd3d     281599     168051     99469     63%      /usr
/dev/sd3e     47185     6347    38479     14%      /var
/dev/sd3g     516811     484585     6386     99% ⇐
/export/tools/sparc.sunos.4
/dev/sd3h     807204     40134     726710     5%     /export/home/00
swap        281280     16    281264     0%     /tmp
schemer:/export/home/00/users/dsk
         1255494     546059     646661     46%     /tmp_mnt/home/dsk
schemer:/export/home/00/users/omonroe
         1255494     546059     646661     46%     /tmp_mnt/home/omonroe
glean# mkdir /export/home/00/htdocs
glean# ls -F /export/home/00
ht1/     htdocs/         lost+found/   shen@         users/
```

How It Works

Installing server software is usually a straightforward process. Configuring and administering the server is where the complexity increases. You can acquire server software through either anonymous FTP or via an FTP URL. How-To 12.1 provides an example of using anonymous FTP to acquire server software. Figure 12-1 shows how you could use Netscape and an FTP URL to acquire the same server package.

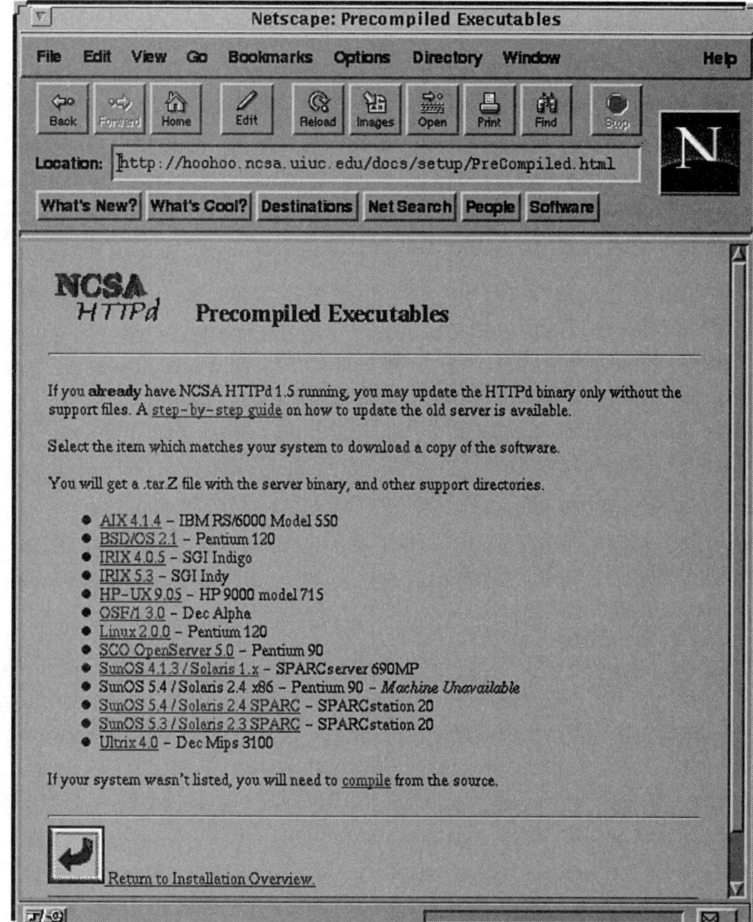

Figure 12-1 Acquiring NCSA HTTPD with an FTP URL

Software packages are often stored on archive sites in compressed and archived formats. In the UNIX world, compression and archival support often use two separate utilities. For PCs and Macintoshes, these functions are usually supported through the same application. For proper installation, the package must be uncompressed and unarchived.

Where you place the server software package is often determined by convenience; you will need to have access to the configuration files as well as the executable programs. The space required by the server software is fairly fixed; therefore, you won't need large amounts of extra disk space beyond the server software requirements.

You might want, however, to retain enough space to install the next version of the software when it becomes available. Earlier, step 3 showed you how to prepare for such an eventuality. Creating a link to the installation directory and specifying server-related files with respect to this link makes such upgrades easier to manage; all you'll need to do is replace the link to the old version with a link to the new version.

Finally, choose a location to serve as the root of your data tree. Most servers provide a way to address HTML documents and other Web objects outside this hierarchy. However, for security, most documents should reside in this location. The more documents outside this controlled area, the higher the security risk. If you plan to run multiple independent servers from your computer, choose several such locations. Figure 12-2 shows a diagram of a UNIX directory hierarchy and displays a potential choice for the root of a data tree.

This choice usually depends on the amount of free disk space in a particular partition. If you expect your Web site to grow, extra space is essential. If your document set is fixed, free disk space might not be as important.

Comments

Many servers—such as OS2HTTPD, WinHTTPD, Website, and Apache—are based on the NCSA HTTPD server; consequently, the installation procedures given above for the UNIX HTTPD server apply to them as well. The specific methods of decompression and extraction vary depending on platform, but decompression and extraction will generally be required. Still, be careful to read the specific installation instructions provided with your server software.

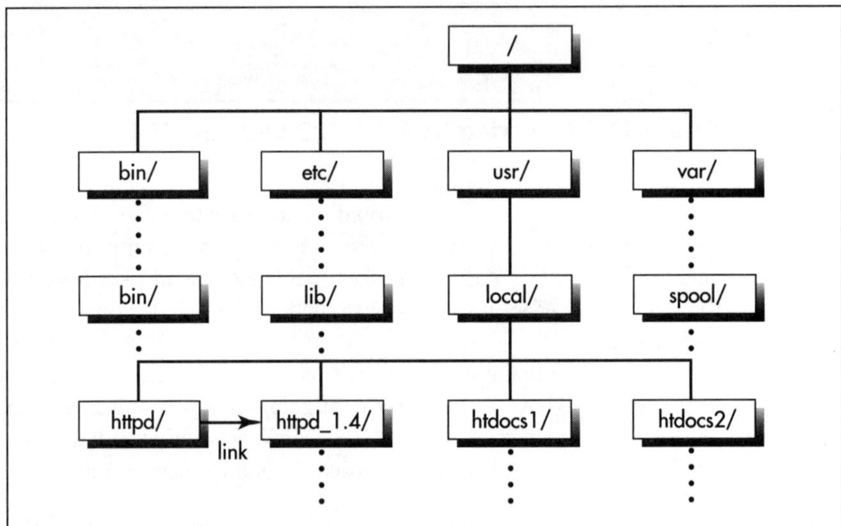

Figure 12-2 UNIX NCSA HTTPD directory hierarchy diagram

Keep in mind that server software development is an ongoing process; therefore, both software and documentation can change from one day to the next. You should pay attention to the developments and evolution of the server package you choose and make upgrades as new products become available and stable.

COMPLEXITY
INTERMEDIATE

12.3 How do I... Install a Netscape FastTrack server?

COMPATIBILITY: NETSCAPE FASTTRACK SERVER

Problem

I've purchased a Netscape FastTrack server for my hardware and operating systems platform. I now need to install the products so that I can begin providing my HTML documents to the world.

Technique

The Windows installation process involves the self extraction of the archive file provided by Netscape. Invoking this file begins the installation. When the file extraction process is complete, the familiar Windows software Setup Wizard allows completion of the installation. This application requests the information necessary to minimally install the FastTrack server. The Setup Wizard will then automatically complete the installation.

Steps

These steps outline the procedure for installing the Netscape FastTrack server on a Windows 95 system. The process for installation on a UNIX system more closely resembles the process described in How-To 12.2.

1. Netscape distributes the FastTrack server by FTP as a self-extracting archive. By double-clicking on the file in Windows Explorer, you trigger the decompression and installation of the server software. The archive file unpacks itself and launches the setup program.

2. When the Netscape FastTrack Server Installation dialog box appears, select Yes to continue. The Welcome screen should appear.

3. Click Next from the Welcome screen to continue. The Software License Agreement should appear.

4. Click Accept to accept the agreement. If you choose not to accept, the installation process ends.

5. The setup program requests that you select the location to which to install the server. Choose the default location, enter another directory, or select the Browse option to pick a directory.

6. Click Next to continue with the installation. The setup program copies the necessary files to the specified directory.

7. Click Next to continue with the installation. The Configure Netscape FastTrack Server screen should appear. The configuration information required in the next several steps provides FastTrack with the minimal configuration information necessary to complete installation. (How-To 12.5 describes how to modify and extend this minimal configuration information.)

8. The application requests the complete name of the server host. Enter the fully qualified domain name of your server machine and click Next.

9. Enter the administration password. Also, select either the default administration username, `admin`, or select one of your own. Click Next to continue.

10. Finally, at the prompt enter the location of your primary document directory. Select the default, enter a directory, or browse through the directories and make your selection. Click Next to continue.

11. At the Finish screen, click Finish to complete installation. The installation procedure completes itself by installing several items to the Windows 95 Start menu as well as a new icon in the Windows control panel.

How It Works

The basic installation process on the Windows platforms conforms to standard installation of most Windows-based software. If you are installing Netscape FastTrack on a UNIX system, the installation process will more closely resemble the process described in How-To 12.2.

Netscape provides its server software as a self-extracting, self-installing archive file. The installation process begins when this archive file is executed from Windows Explorer, the software installer in the control panel, or a command line. The file first extracts the necessary files into the system's temporary area. When this is complete, the file invokes the standard Setup Wizard. The only information necessary to complete the first portion of the process is the name of the directory in which the setup program should install the server software, as shown in Figure 12-3. You should select a location on your hard disk with at least 16MB of free space to store the necessary server files.

The setup program continues by placing the necessary server files in the specified directory. The setup program screen tracks the status of the installation process. Figure 12-4 displays a sample tracking of an installation of the FastTrack server.

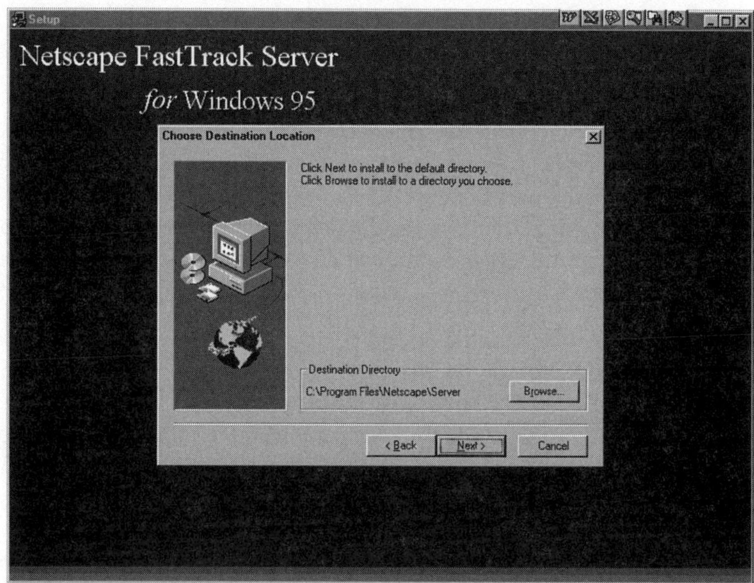

Figure 12-3 Setup procedure requesting the destination directory

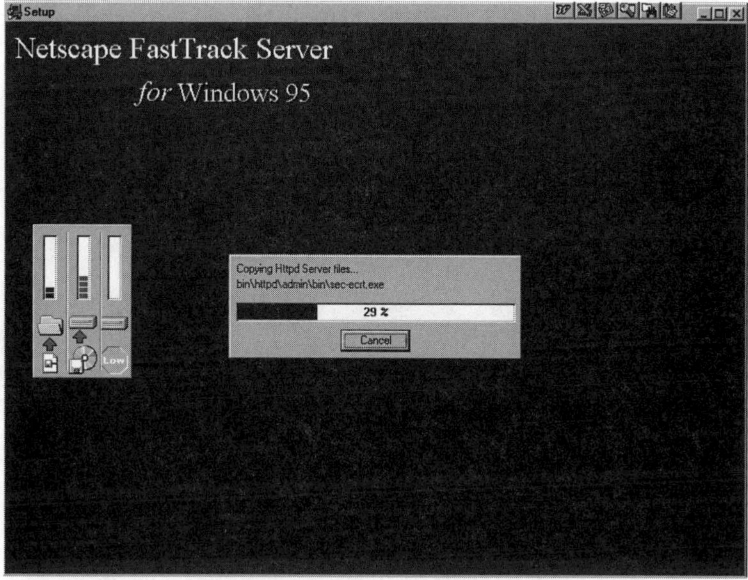

Figure 12-4 Setup installation tracking screen

The Setup Wizard proceeds by requesting minimal configuration information necessary for proper installation. Installation requires three pieces of essential configuration information:

- ✔ Server name: Installation requires the specification of the Internet name of the machine running the server. This must include both the hostname and the domain name. Figure 12-5 displays the screen used to enter this information. Either confirm the default name provided or enter the proper name for the server host. Clicking Next confirms the choice currently specified.
- ✔ Administrator username and password: The FastTrack server allows administration of the Web servers running on a host machine through the use of a special Web server running on the host machine. This administration Web server supports the creation and administration of information Web servers on the host machine. Access to the administration Web server is initially limited to individuals using the username and password specified at this stage. Figure 12-6 shows the dialog window that requires this information. Initial configuration of the server requires the use of this username and password. How-To 12.6 describes this configuration process using the administration server.
- ✔ Document directory location: The installation process requires the location of the document root directory. This directory is the location where the server locates documents that clients, usually Web browsers, request.

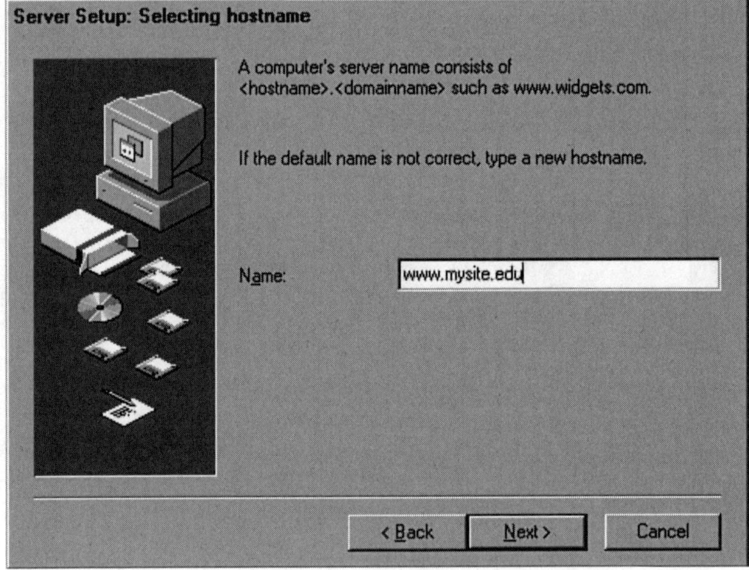

Figure 12-5 Specifying the server hostname

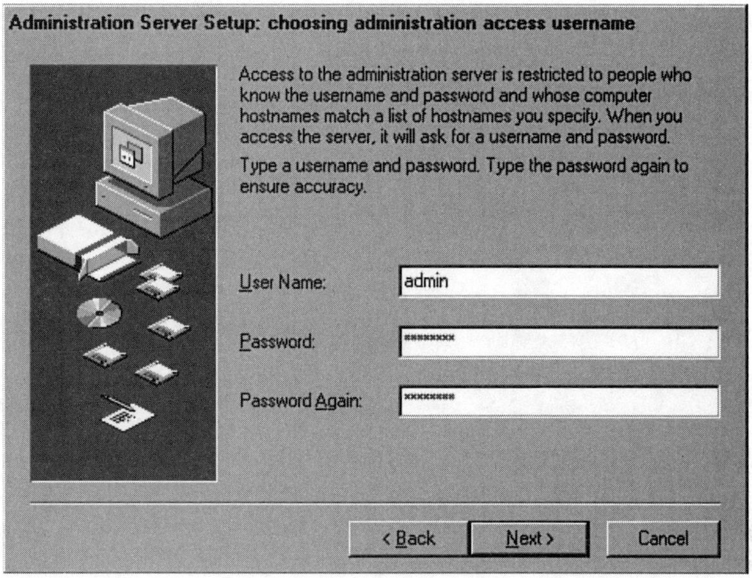

Figure 12-6 Specifying the administrator's username and password

> Choosing this directory requires an analysis of current disk use on your host machine and an estimate in bytes of the expected amount of information to be supplied by the server. Although it is possible to move the document directory and reconfigure the server, proper selection of a document root directory can reduce the need for this task. Figure 12-7 displays the dialog box that configures the document directory location.

After the setup program performs the minimal configuration, the installation completes itself with the creation of several menu and control panel items. The installation application creates menu items for running the administration server, accessing the FastTrack release notes, and uninstalling the FastTrack server. New Control Panel icons allow the control of all FastTrack servers running on the particular machine. For example, Figure 12-8 displays this server's control console.

When installation is complete, the next task is server configuration (see How-To 12.5).

Comments

The operating system platform often determines the degree of automation involved in the installation of the server software. In the Windows world, automatic installation of software tends to be the norm, whereas in the UNIX world, a more controlled manual process dominates. The procedures found in this How-To and How-To 12.2 provide examples from both ends of this spectrum.

In the end, either method suffices to get the job done.

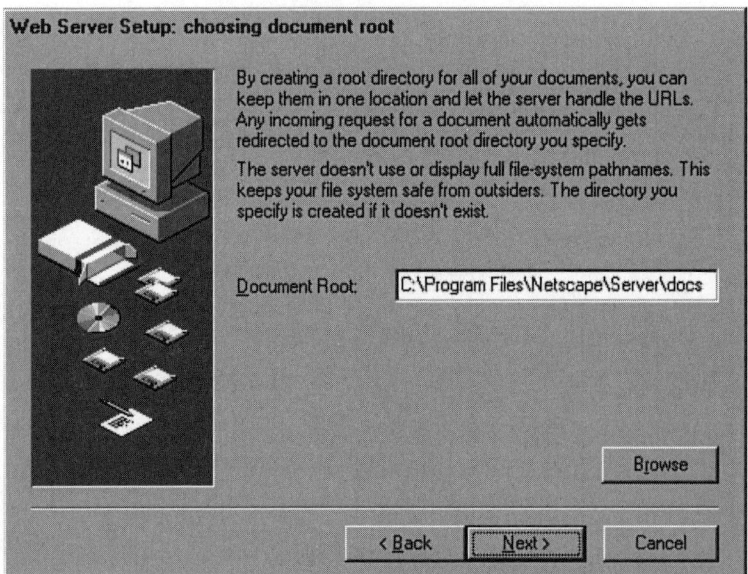

Figure 12-7 Specifying the document directory location

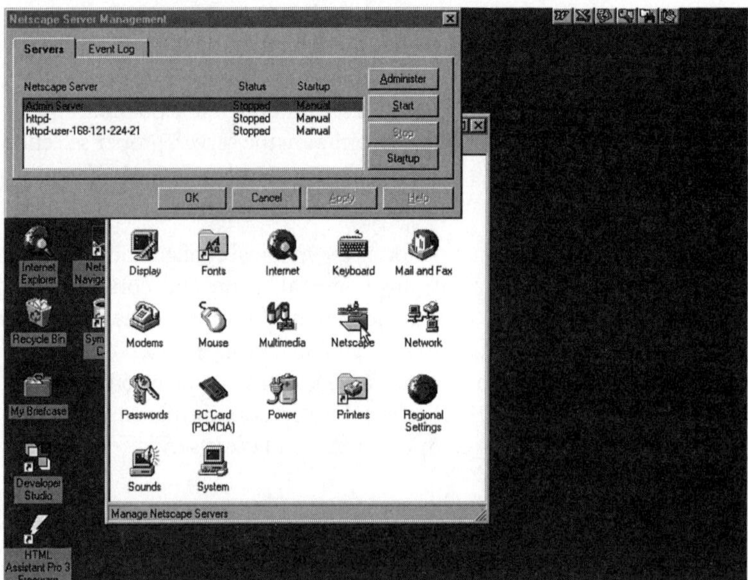

Figure 12-8 Access the Netscape Server Management control panel through the Windows Control Panel

12.4 How do I... Configure the server?

COMPATIBILITY: HTTPD-BASED SERVERS

Problem

I must tailor the server environment to my needs. What are the various attributes that I must set? Where are they located, and what values do they take? Can I configure multiple servers to run on the same machine?

Technique

HTTPD servers require three general types of configuration:

- ✔ Server configuration
- ✔ Resource configuration
- ✔ Security configuration

These three configurations tell the server how it should run, what resources it has at its disposal and where they are, and who has access to which resources. The manner in which these configurations are performed can vary among servers; however, most servers require at least the first two to be done before startup.

The following procedure provides instructions for performing the first two of the three types of configurations for the NCSA HTTPD server. Initial security configuration is also described for this package. (Configuring and maintaining server security is covered in detail in Chapter 13, "Handling Server Security.") To perform tasks specific to other software, read the documentation for your server software.

Steps

The following procedures provide instructions for configuring an NCSA HTTPD server. The individual steps walk you through tasks in the configuration process. For further information on configuring an NCSA HTTPD server, see NCSA's online documentation at URL **`http://hoohoo.ncsa.uiuc.edu/docs/setup/Configure.html`**. Configuration of the WinHTTPD server software is very similar, so hints for configuring this server are included in the steps as well. The configuration of these server packages entails including the correct commands in the correct configuration file. Configuration file commands are also referred to as *directives*.

Choosing a Directory

You must provide a directory for each independent server running on your host machine. This directory contains the configuration files, log files, and possibly unique icons and gateway applications associated with the particular server.

Change directories to the location where you want to configure the server. If this is your primary server, the configuration directory can be the same as your installation directory. To configure a second server properly, you must copy the necessary configuration files to another location. The example demonstrates the creation of a new directory for configuring a second NCSA HTTPD server.

```
glean# cd /usr/local
glean# ls
adm     conf     httpd     include          man
bin     etc     httpd_1.4.1     lib
glean# mkdir httpd2
glean# cp -r httpd/conf httpd2
glean# ls httpd2/conf
access.conf-dist          mime.types
httpd.conf-dist          srm.conf-dist
glean# mkdir httpd2/log
```

Server Configuration

After you have chosen or created a configuration directory, you must perform any necessary server configuration tasks. For NCSA HTTPD, this process involves editing the **httpd.conf** file. (For WinHTTPD, this is the **httpd.cnf** file.)

1. Open **httpd.conf** in your favorite text editor.

2. Configure (UNIX HTTPD only) the **ServerType** directive. This directive can take one of two values: **standalone** or **inetd**. **standalone** configures the server to run by itself, whereas **inetd** specifies that the server be controlled by the **inetd** process, an application that monitors various network functions. Standalone servers tend to run more efficiently than **inetd**-controlled servers due to reduced overhead. To establish a standalone server, make sure the following line appears in the configuration file:

```
ServerType standalone
```

Servers using **inetd** require a slightly different configuration approach than standalone servers do. Examine URL **http://hoohoo.ncsa.uiuc.edu/docs/ setup/Configure.html** for more information on configuring an **inetd** server.

3. Assign a port number for the server. The default port for HTTP servers is port 80. To use this port, you must start the server as the privileged user, **root**. Port numbers less than 1023 are reserved for the various network services provided by the UNIX operating system. Some common port

choices for servers are 1080, 8000, and 8080. To configure a server to listen at port 8080, issue the `Port` command:

```
Port 8080
```

4. UNIX enables you to start several server processes running at startup. Specify the initial number and the maximum number using the `StartServers` and `MaxServers` directives. The default values for these directives are, respectively, `5` and `20`. You can change these values depending on your hardware capabilities and the volume of traffic you expect. The following lines establish these default values:

```
StartServers 5
MaxServers 20
```

5. Assign (in a UNIX HTTPD configuration) the user- and group names for the individual who runs the HTTPD process. For security, you might not want the server to run with the privileges of the individual who is executing the HTTPD process; you probably do not want the server to run as the privileged user, `root`—even if `root` actually starts the server. To configure the server to run as if it were run by username `me` and group `mygroup`, issue the following directives in the configuration file:

```
User me
Group mygroup
```

You can specify the values for these directives by user- or group names or by user or group numbers. If you use numbers, precede the specific number with the pound sign (`#`).

6. Next, set the name (e-mail address) of the individual administering this server with the `ServerAdmin` directive. The following line sets `me@www.mysite.edu` as the administrator for this server:

```
ServerAdmin me@www.mysite.edu
```

7. Add a line to specify the base address of the directory in the file system you will use to store the various server files. For example, the following line in your configuration file would establish `/usr/local/http2` as the base location for your server files:

```
ServerRoot /usr/local/http2
```

8. Specify the location of the various log files used by the server. Specify where the error, transfer, agent, and referrer logs are located. If the specified path does not begin with a slash (`/`), the path is relative based on the path specified with the `ServerRoot` directive. Use the following lines to set these locations:

```
ErrorLog logs/error_log
TransferLog logs/access_log
AgentLog logs/agent_log
RefererLog logs/referer_log
```

9. Specify where the process ID for the primary server process will be stored. Use the **PidFile** directive to specify this information. As with the log files, this specification can be either relative to the server root directory or absolute.

```
PidFile logs/httpd.pid
```

10. Specify how the server refers to itself by using the **ServerName** directive. Many Web sites use servers with names beginning with **www**. However, simply placing this name in the configuration file will not make this file usable by the outside world. To accomplish this, you must contact your network administrator to set up the new name as an alias for your machine. The following line would establish **www.mysite.edu** as the name of a server:

```
ServerName www.mysite.edu
```

11. When you have finished the configuration, save this file and configure the server resources.

Resource Configuration

Next, you must configure the resources available to the server. This involves telling the server where it can locate a variety of resources. You can configure this aspect of the NCSA HTTPD server by editing the **srm.conf** file (WinHTTPD: **srm.cnf**).

1. Open **srm.conf** in your favorite text editor.

2. Set the location of your data tree with the **DocumentRoot** directive. For example, the following line sets the document root to be located in the **/export/home/00/htdocs** directory:

```
DocumentRoot /export/home/00/htdocs
```

3. Specify the subdirectory of individual user directories visible to this server. This subdirectory is commonly called **public_html**. (This particular directive is not supported by WinHTTPD.) If you want the subdirectory accessible by the server to be referred to as **www_docs**, you would issue the following directive:

```
UserDir www_docs
```

If someone wanted to access a document called **doc.htm** from the home directory of **user** through your server, he or she would use the URL **http://www.mysite.edu/~user/doc.htm**.

4. The `DirectoryIndex` directive specifies the name of the default file to open when none is given in a URL addressing the site. If an individual accesses your server without specifying a particular file (for example, `http://www.mysite.edu/`), the server responds with a predefined default file. The default name used by NCSA HTTPD is `index.html` (WinHTTPD: `index.htm`). If a directory does not have a prewritten index, a directory index may be generated dynamically. The following code specifies that the default directory index is in a file named `index.htm`:

```
DirectoryIndex index.htm
```

5. The access control information for each directory is stored in a single file. Configure the name of this file with the `AccessFileName` directive. The default specification appears as

```
AccessFileName .htaccess
```

See Chapter 13 for information on how to use directory-level access control files.

6. You can register additional document types provided by this server. Several methods for performing this task are described in detail in How-To 12.6.

7. If the server cannot determine the document type of a requested file, it provides a default type in the response to the request. Use the `DefaultType` directive to designate the default document type that the server uses. In most cases, the MIME type `text/plain` is an appropriate value for this attribute. (See Appendix C "MIME," for additional information on MIME types.) You could use the following line of code to designate this default type:

```
DefaultType text/plain
```

8. You may associate icons with particular document types. For example, a folder icon could be associated with a directory. HTTPD-based servers come with several specified default icons that you may optionally replace or extend with your own. When you issue the `AddIcon` directive, specify the filename extension with which you want to associate an icon, as well as the location of the icon on the hard disk. Specify this location using any path aliases that you established for this server with `Alias` directives. For example, to establish an alias for the `icons` directory in the `/usr/local/http2` directory and then associate an icon with movie files, issue the following set of directives:

```
Alias /icons/ /usr/local/etc/httpd/icons/
AddIcon /icons/movie.xbm .mpg .qt
```

NCSA HTTPD enables you to establish up to 20 separate directory aliases for your server.

9. HTTPD-based servers provide a special alias for the directory containing CGI applications. (See Chapter 14, "The Common Gateway Interface (CGI)," for a detailed description of CGI programs.) Specify this location with the `ScriptAlias` directive. For example, if you want to specify `/cgi-bin/` as the alias for this directory and the actual location of this directory is `/usr/local/httpd/cgi-bin`, use the following line of code in your configuration file:

```
ScriptAlias /cgi-bin/ /usr/local/httpd/cgi-bin/
```

10. Save this configuration file and proceed with the security configuration.

Security Configuration

Finally, you must configure security. The steps in this section provide a method for configuring an HTTPD-based server with limited security. This represents a bare-bones configuration that enables you to get your server up and running. For advanced security configuration and security configuration of other servers, see Chapter 13 along with the documentation for your server software.

You can configure the security of an NCSA HTTPD server by editing the `access.conf` file (WinHTTPD: `access.cnf`).

1. Open `access.conf` in your favorite text editor.

2. Specify the location of the standard server script directory. The entry contained in the distribution file assumes a default location. The default entry appears in the following code:

```
<Directory /usr/local/etc/httpd/cgi-bin>
Options Indexes FollowSymLinks
</Directory>
```

   To modify this entry, change the `/usr/local/etc/httpd/` portion of the directory path to wherever you placed the script directory. This is usually in the server root directory (`ServerRoot`) in a subdirectory called `cgi-bin`.

3. Modify the second directory element to point to the root of your data tree. The default entry appears as

```
<Directory /usr/local/etc/httpd/htdocs>
```

   Modify this entry to point to the directory defined as the root of your document hierarchy (`DocumentRoot`).

4. Save this configuration file.

You have completed the configuration of your server and are now ready to start the server and begin serving HTML documents to the World Wide Web community.

How It Works

Server configuration entails establishing values required for the server to run properly. The server must know who should own the server process, where various server files are located, who the server administrator is, and a variety of other information. This information forms the constraints under which the server runs.

Resource configuration involves specifying information about the data tree. This task includes providing a reference to the root of the document hierarchy. It involves establishing mappings for additional document types. Many times, server specific, as well as general, aliases can be established for directories and documents in the data tree. The preceding steps specify a minimum resource configuration. Additional modifications can be made to tune the server more extensively. For more detailed information on configuring the server resource map file for HTTPD-based servers, refer to the available online documentation.

If you have chosen a server that, by default, allows access to documents, you need not concern yourself too much with security configuration unless you want to place restrictions on some portion of your data tree. Information about security configuration for particular server packages is described in Chapter 13. If you have a server that denies access, such as WN (see Appendix F, "Summary of Selected Server Software"), you must configure security before you start your server. In this case, examine your server documentation to establish your security properly.

When the server initially runs, it reads the commands from the configuration files. These directives establish the constraints under which the server runs. Each server on your system requires a full set of configuration files tailored to specify the constraints and capabilities that you want.

When you alter a configuration file, the server must be stopped and restarted for the configuration changes to take effect. Because the configuration files are read only when the server is initially run, the changes are not seen until the server restart causes the configuration files to be read anew.

Comments

The configuration files and formats for servers derived from NCSA HTTPD, such as WinHTTPD, Apache, and OS2HTTPD, are quite similar to those of their parent. Consequently, you can usually use the procedures just defined to configure these servers.

Certain variations exist between platforms, however. You should examine the documentation for your package, keeping an eye out for these differences. Most server packages have considerable online documentation to help you with the configuration process.

The online documentation provides you with up-to-the-minute information on the current status of your server software. If you have waited even a few days to install the package you downloaded, a better version might have become available in the intervening time.

COMPLEXITY
ADVANCED

12.5 How do I... Configure a Netscape FastTrack server?

COMPATIBILITY: NETSCAPE FASTTRACK SERVER

Problem

Installing the FastTrack server provided only minimal configuration information. I need to add an alias for additional directories on my server. I would like to create specific configuration styles applicable to selected portions of my server. And I must create a server capable of listening to another Internet port.

Technique

Two methods exist to configure a FastTrack server. The first method involves the direct editing of the FastTrack configuration files, namely the **magnus.conf** file and the **obj.conf** file. Although the format and commands differ, this process closely resembles the configuration of an NCSA server described in How-To 12.4. The online documentation provided with FastTrack explains the specific commands for use in these files.

The second method uses the administration server that provides menu-based access to the configuration of all FastTrack servers running on a host machine. When the administration server is invoked, the administrator selects a server to configure. Upon selection, the administration server displays the administration menu for the chosen server. From this menu, the administrator can configure all aspects of the chosen server.

Steps

The steps outline the procedure for configuring the Netscape FastTrack server on a Windows 95 system. Beyond the initial extraction of the distribution files, the Windows 95 installation process is similar to those for both Windows and UNIX. These instructions also provide directions for running additional servers on the same host machine.

1. Invoke the administration Web server in one of the following three ways:

- ✔ Enter the URL for the administration Web server using Netscape Navigator.
- ✔ Select the Netscape icon from the Windows Control Panel.
- ✔ Choose the Start | Programs | Netscape | Administer Netscape Server item from the Windows Start menu.

2. If you do not want to create a new server on this host, proceed to step 5. Select the Install a New Netscape FastTrack Server button.

3. Enter the requested information:

Server name: This must include the complete Internet hostname and domain name.

Port number: This specifies the port to which the new server should listen.

Server identifier: This name identifies the new server within the scope of the administration Web server.

Document root: This directory will serve as the root of primary document repository for the new server.

4. Select the OK button to complete the creation of the new server. At the success screen, select Configure Your New Server to configure the new server.

5. View the current settings of your server by selecting the View Server Settings option in the System Settings window, which examines the current configuration of the server.

6. Select the items from the displayed settings that require alteration. The common items that you might want to change include

- ✔ Primary document directory: This directory will serve as the root of the primary document repository for the new server.
- ✔ Additional document directories: This allows the association of aliases for specific directories on the host machine.
- ✔ Port number: This specifies the port to which the new server should listen.
- ✔ Error log: This gives the location of the error log file for this server.
- ✔ Default MIME type: If the server cannot determine the type of a file, the server uses this type.
- ✔ Access log: This gives the location of the access log file for this server.
- ✔ Configuration style creation: Configuration styles provide a method for reusing and reapplying a configuration to a particular subset of documents on the Web server.

NOTE

Each menu in the administrator provides access to help that is tailored to the specific configuration information under review.

7. Whenever configuration information changes, select OK to submit the specified changes.

8. Select Save to confirm the changes. Changes do not take effect until they are applied. If you are finished changing the configuration, proceed to step 9; otherwise, return to step 6.

9. After you have entered all desired configuration changes, click the Apply button at the top-right corner of the administration Web server main directory. This will stop and restart the Web server, incorporating the changed configuration.

How It Works

The administration Web server provided with the Netscape FastTrack server is the primary means of configuring a server. You access the server locally either by invoking the Programs|Netscape|Administer Netscape Server options from the Windows Start menu or by selecting the Administer button on the Netscape Server Management control panel, available from the Windows control panel. Figure 12-9 displays these two methods of starting the administration Web server. These two methods both result in the launching of Netscape Navigator Gold, which provides the access to the server. From remote sites, launch Netscape Navigator Gold and directly access the administration Web server using its URL; this URL is **http://*server_name*:5709**, by default.

Navigator prompts you for a username and password to access the administration Web server. If the username and password are accepted, the main administration page appears in the browser, as shown in Figure 12-10. From this page, you can

- ✔ Create a new server on the current host machine.
- ✔ Remove a server from the current host machine.
- ✔ Configure the administration server.
- ✔ Turn a server on or off.
- ✔ Configure a server on the current host machine.

How-To 12.8 discusses the various methods of turning servers on and off. Chapter 13, "Handling Server Security," addresses configuration issues specific to server security. Selecting the server removal provides a fill-out form through which any server, including the administration server, can be removed from the host machine; removal of the administration server is not advisable unless you plan to remove all FastTrack servers from the host machine.

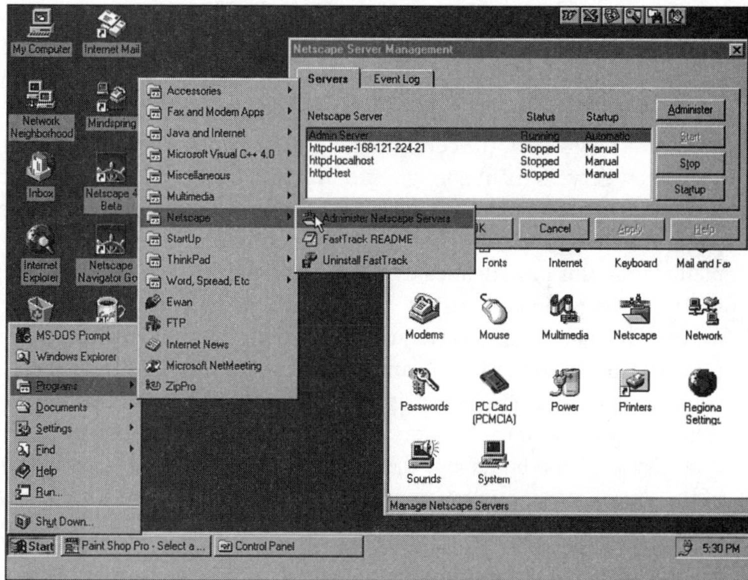

Figure 12-9 Access the FastTrack administration server

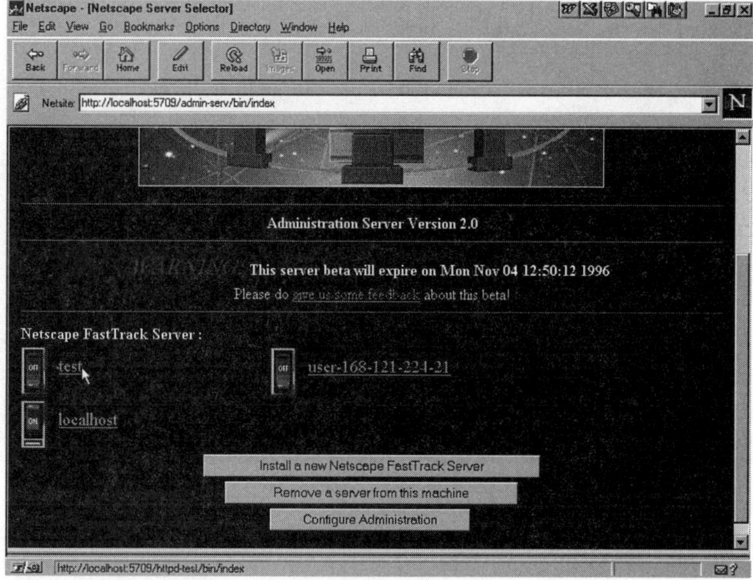

Figure 12-10 Access administration functions through the administration server main access page

A single host machine can run multiple instances of the FastTrack server. The Install a New Server option provides a form-based interface to this creation process, as displayed in Figure 12-11. This form provides the minimal configuration information necessary to establish the new server. Submission of this form triggers the installation of the new server; the confirmation screen seen in Figure 12-12 provides access to the new server's main configuration page.

Figure 12-13 displays a typical server administration page. The administration page provides access to all the commonly configured aspects of the server. The top menu bar in this page delineates configurable areas. Initially, the page appears with system settings menu items set. The available system settings appear in the far-left frame. The right frame contains the configurable information pertinent to the topic selected in the top menu and the subtopic selected from the left frame. A particularly useful subtopic under system settings is View Server Settings. Not only does this subtopic summarize the current server settings, it also provides links to windows that allow modification of these current settings. Figure 12-14 displays an example of the View Server Settings frame within the context of the administration page.

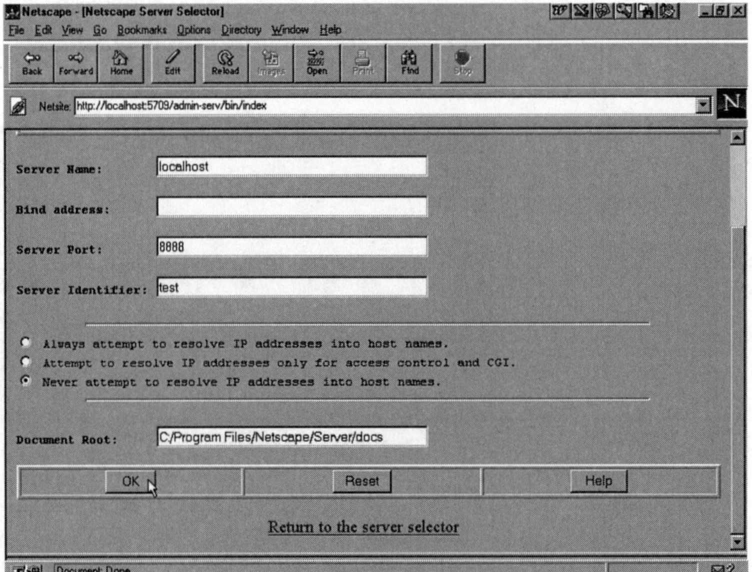

Figure 12-11 Provide minimal configuration information through the Install New Server page

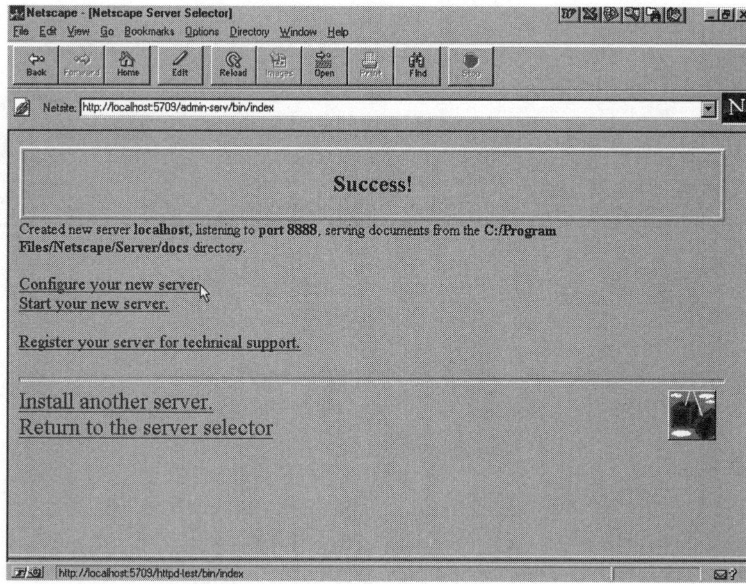

Figure 12-12 Complete configuration process accessible from the Successful Installation page

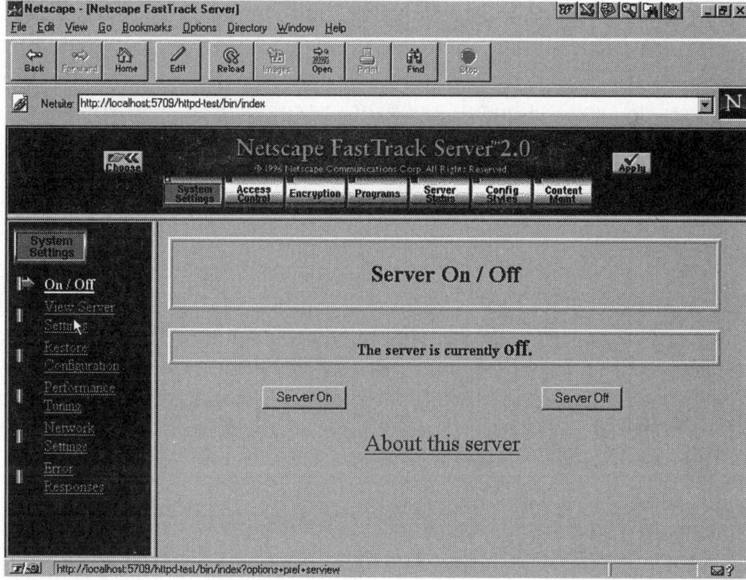

Figure 12-13 Configure a server through its administration page

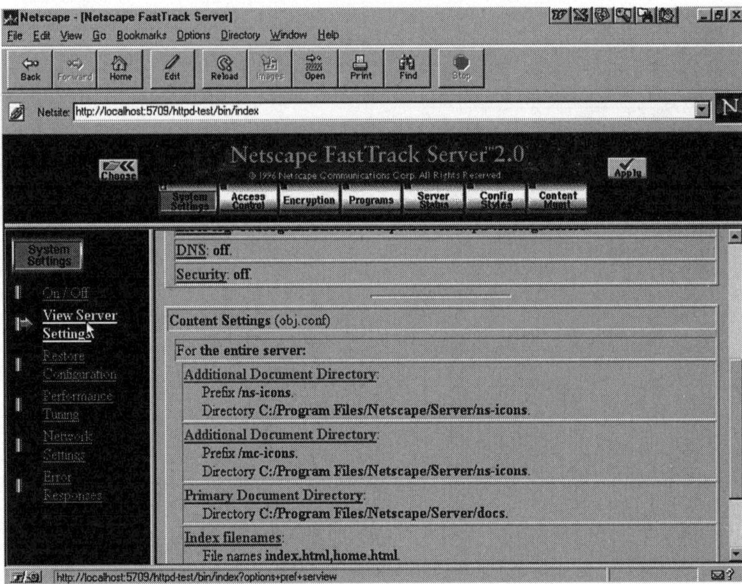

Figure 12-14 Viewing server settings provides a handy means to access commonly configured server attributes

The other top frame menu items allow configuration of other essential areas of the server. The Access Control and Encryption items are discussed in How-To's 13.9 and 13.10. The Programs item supports the configuration of various types of server-side application programs such as common gateway applications (discussed in Chapter 14, "The Common Gateway Interface (CGI)"), server-side Java applications, and other types of server-side applications. The Server Status item provides access and summarizes the various activity logs for the server. The Config Styles menu items allow the creation, deletion, and modification of configuration styles. A configuration style is a named set of configuration settings that can be attached to multiple portions of a particular server's document directories. Finally, the Content Mgmt menu items support miscellaneous configuration options dealing with the document base of the server. These items permit the modification of the default types of documents in directories (subject to the constraints), the specification of forwarding URLs, and the creation of aliases to secondary document directories, to name several of the most commonly configured subtopics.

Modifications can either be applied immediately upon specification of each configuration item or saved for application at once after all modifications are complete. After each modification, a confirmation form appears in the configuration frame (bottom right). This form allows several options: Go back to before requesting the change, undo the requested change, save the requested change, and save and apply the requested change. Figure 12-15 shows a typical confirmation form. After all configuration changes are complete, they must be applied using the Apply button in the top frame menu, if they have not already been applied individually.

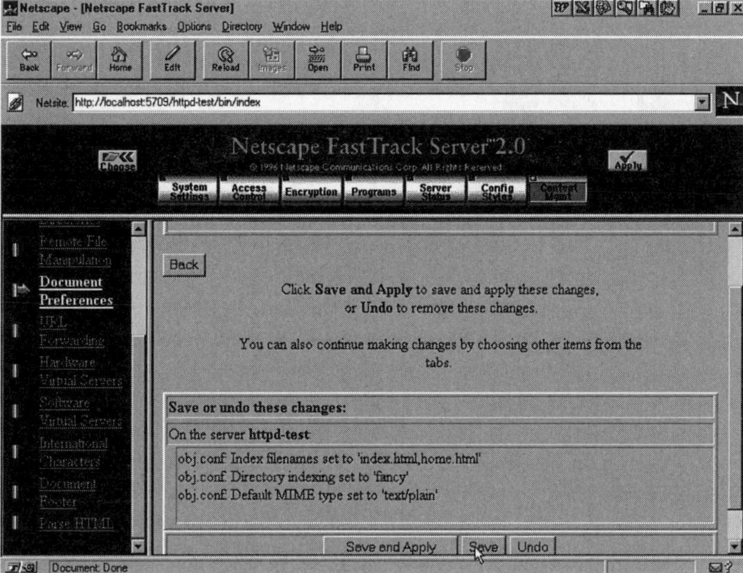

Figure 12-15 Confirmation forms allow for immediate or delayed application of configuration changes

Selecting the Apply button places the Apply window in the bottom-right frame. This frame provides buttons labeled Apply Changes and Load Configuration Files. The second option applies if the configuration files (`magnus.conf` or `obj.conf`) were modified manually and required reloading to establish the correct current configuration information. Selecting the Apply button results in the application of all previously saved configuration changes. Figure 12-16 presents the results of submitting a series of saved changes. The FastTrack server, like the servers in How-To 12.4, requires a shutdown and restart process for changes to take effect. One nice aspect of FastTrack is that this process occurs automatically upon the application of configuration changes through the administration server.

Comments

The administration server system described in this How-To provides an easy interface to the Netscape FastTrack configuration files. Using a text editor also allows configuration. The FastTrack server uses two primary configuration files, named by default `magnus.conf` and `obj.conf`. Configuration information for a particular server can be entered manually. See the online documentation accompanying FastTrack for the formats of these configuration files.

If the administration server suits your needs, you should use this server rather than editing manually. Besides providing a user interface, the forms supporting administration place some constraints on how the configuration information can be changed. Manual modification of the configuration files does not impose such

Figure 12-16 Results of the application of configuration changes to the server

constraints. The trade-off in using these methods is the ease of modification using the administration server versus the flexibility achieved through complete control over configuration edits.

COMPLEXITY
INTERMEDIATE

12.6 How do I... Register additional MIME types?

COMPATIBILITY: HTTPD-BASED SERVERS, NETSCAPE FASTTRACK

Problem

When I access some documents with a browser, the documents display as a strange mix of control characters because they are a type of file my server won't support. I would like to add documents of this type on my Web site and have them supported by my server. How do I configure the server to support this new document type?

Technique

MIME types are used by Web servers and clients to specify the document type of files. This type of information is provided to a client through a content type field sent in a server response. The server determines the file type by examining a document's filename extension. This filename extension maps into an internal table that associates filename extensions with document types.

You can modify this table of associations in three ways. This How-To takes you through each method.

Steps

You can use the following three methods to modify or extend the document types that your NCSA HTTPD server can serve properly:

✔ Types file modification

✔ Resource map file modification

✔ Access file modification

Types File Modification

The types file is commonly located in the configuration subdirectory. The file supplied with the NCSA HTTPD and Netscape FastTrack distributions is called **mime.types**. The name of this file can be configured in an NCSA server configuration file (**httpd.conf**) using the **TypesConfig** directive.

1. Open the types configuration file in your favorite text editor. This file will be named either **mime.types** or whatever you have specified in the server configuration file using the **TypesConfig** directive.

2. The types configuration file lists the file types recognized, one per line. The MIME type (see Appendix C, "MIME") is followed by the filename extension that will be associated with that type. Comments in this file appear following a pound sign (**#**) in the line.

3. If you want to add a new document type, add a new line to this configuration file. For example, if you want to provide support for Excel spreadsheets using an NCSA server, add the following line:

```
application/excel              xls
```

or using a Netscape FastTrack server, add the following line:

```
type=application/excel         exts=xls,xl
```

4. If you want to modify an existing entry, move to the type you want to modify and edit the line. For example, to modify the **text/html** line to accept both **.html** and **.htm** as acceptable extensions, for an NCSA server, change the following line:

```
text/html     html
```

to this:

```
text/html     html htm
```

or, using a Netscape FastTrack server, change the following line:

```
type=text/html          exts=html
```

to this:

```
type=text/html          exts=html,htm
```

5. After you have made the alterations you want, save this configuration file; then restart the server to see the changes you have made.

Resource Map File Modification

You can add or modify types using an NCSA server resource map file. Issue `AddType` directives to extend or supersede the default types provided through the types configuration file. In a FastTrack server, you can add or modify types using the object configuration file (`obj.conf`) for the server: Issue the `ObjectType` directive to accomplish this task.

1. For an NCSA Web server, open the server resource map file in your text editor. This file is named `srm.conf`, or whatever you specified in the server configuration file using the `ResourceConfig` directive. For an NS FastTrack server, open the object configuration file; the default name for this file is `obj.conf`.

2. This file contains a series of directives defining the various resources available to the server. Each line is either a comment or a directive. Comments in this file follow a pound sign (#).

3. To add a new document type or to supersede any default types, add a new line to this file. For example, to provide support for Excel spreadsheets, add the following line to this file:

```
AddType        application/excel        .xls
```

or, using a Netscape FastTrack server, add the following line:

```
ObjectType fn=type-by-exp exp=*.xls type=application/x-excel
```

4. To add server-wide support for CGI applications outside the specified script directory or server-side includes, issue the following `AddType` directives:

```
# Add support for CGI application through recognition of the cgi ⇐
extension.
AddType        application/x-httpd-cgi        .cgi
# Add support for server side includes through use of the shtml ⇐
extension.
AddType        text/x-server-parsed-html        .shtml
```

5. After you have made the desired changes, save the file. Restart the server to see the changes you have made.

Access File Modification

You can modify or extend the supported types by changing the access control files, either in the global access control file or at the individual directory level. The types defined in this manner are available only in the designated directories. Such types will supersede those defined in the types configuration file or the server resource map file.

1. Open the access control file in your text editor. The global access control file is named `access.conf` or whatever you specified in the server configuration file using the `AccessConfig` directive. The per-directory access control file is in the directory you want to affect and is called either `.htaccess` or whatever filename you specified using the `AccessFileName` directive in the server resource map file.

2. To add a new document type or supersede any default types, add a new line to the file. For example, if you want to provide support for Excel spreadsheets, add the following line:

```
AddType         application/x-excel         .xls
```

If you are modifying the global access configuration file, make sure you are adding the type within the appropriate `<Directory>` element(s).

3. If you want to add directory-level support for CGI applications outside the designated script directory or server-side includes, you can issue the following `AddType` directives:

```
# Add support for CGI application through recognition of the cgi ⇐
extension.
AddType         application/x-httpd-cgi         .cgi
# Add support for server side includes through use of the shtml ⇐
extension.
AddType         text/x-server-parsed-html         .shtml
```

4. Save the file and restart the server to see the changes.

How It Works

The file specified in the server configuration file using the `TypesConfig` directive indicates the default MIME types an NCSA server uses (see Appendix C). A Netscape FastTrack server locates this file using the `load-types` function of `Init` in the object configuration file. This file defines the base types that will be served. This set of types is usually left unaltered and can be used by several servers to define the supported base types. This approach affects all servers that look to this file for types definitions.

The types added through the resource configuration file affect only the individual server using that configuration file. These added types extend the allowable types over the entire server. For example, you could use this method to make a single server capable of serving Excel spreadsheets while other servers running on the same computer could not.

Finally, you can use the access configuration file modification approach for more fine-tuned control than for an entire server. Modifications through this method have an effect on only the directories specified. If the method is used in a directory-level access control file, then the extensions or modifications are available only when accessing a document in that directory.

The object configuration file in a Netscape FastTrack server supports the finer granularity configuration of types.

Comments

In general, determine which method you will use to add types based on how widely you want to support the new type. Most types can be added at the resource configuration level, unless you are particularly worried about security, in which case global or directory-level access control might be the more suitable option. This is particularly true for types such as CGI applications; as the Web site administrator, you might want to limit the location of such files to either the script directory or several controlled locations.

In addition, all three methods require you to stop and restart the server for the changes to take effect.

12.7 How do I... Install documents?

COMPATIBILITY: ANY SERVER

Problem

I have created Web pages and would like to make them accessible to the World Wide Web community. I already have access to a Web site (see How-To's 12.1 through 12.5). How do I install my HTML documents on this site?

Technique

The approach used to install documents on a server site will vary by hardware and software platform. In general, you install documents by placing copies of these documents in a predefined area of the file system allocated for this purpose. On operating systems that support file-level access control, the access protection of the documents must be set properly.

With many servers, documents can also be placed in preconfigured user directories. The following steps outline the installation of a document on an NCSA HTTPD server.

Steps

The steps define two procedures. The first describes the mechanism a Web site administrator could use to install documents in the main document area of the server. The second instructs users how to install documents in their home directories that are accessible by the server.

Document Root Installation

If you are a Web site administrator, you can use the following method to install documents in the data tree. The location of this document hierarchy is specified in the NCSA server resource file using the **DocumentRoot** directive. In the Netscape FastTrack **obj.conf** file, use the **NameTrans** directive.

1. Examine the documents. Identify the type of each document. If the document type is not supported by your server, either reconfigure the server to support the desired type (see How-To 12.4) or let the author of the document know that the document type is not supported.

2. View each document that is to be placed on your server in an appropriate viewing environment such as a browser or image viewer. Verify documents of all types before you install them on your server.

3. After you have checked the documents, move them to an appropriate location in the document hierarchy. If you were to install the file **hello.htm** in the **welcome** subdirectory of the **DocumentRoot**, **/export/home/00/htdocs**, you could use the following UNIX command:

```
mv hello.htm /export/home/00/htdocs/welcome
```

4. Check the permissions settings for the document. You must set these permissions so that the user running the server has read and execute permission on the document. For example, the following command sets the protection of the **hello.htm** document to allow all users to read and execute the document:

```
chmod +rx hello.htm
```

For more information on the UNIX **chmod** command, consult a UNIX reference manual.

5. The document is now accessible through your HTTPD-based server. If you are running a server such as WN that, by default, denies access to documents, configure the access control to the document to provide the desired access level. This enables your server to service requests for this document.

User Directory Installation

The following process outlines the steps required to install documents in your home directory. Documents installed in this manner are subject to constraints established by your Web site administrator.

1. Contact your Web site administrator to determine whether documents in your home directory can be supported through your server. If this option is not supported, you must have the site administrator install the documents that you develop. If documents can be served from your home directory, you must know which subdirectory to use. Your site administrator can provide this information.

2. If you do not already have the designated subdirectory in your home directory, you will need to create it. The default subdirectory specified by the NCSA HTTPD server is the **public_html** directory. Under UNIX, the following command, issued in your home directory, creates such a directory:

```
:mkdir public_html
```

The following statement would be placed on the Web site to explain to users of the system that there is a communications malfunction. In any case, the following lines would be added to the server's object configuration files:

```
NameTrans fn=document-root root="C:/Program Files/Netscape/Server/docs"
```

3. Examine the documents. Identify the type of each document. You might have to ask your site administrator which document types are supported by your server. If the document type is not supported, either ask your site administrator to reconfigure the server to support the desired type or attempt to support the document type yourself using a per-directory access control file (see How-To 12.4). The latter option might not be available, depending on the configuration of the global access file. If you cannot support the type on your own, either attempt the former or redevelop the document using a supported type.

4. You should view each document that is to be placed on your server in an appropriate viewing environment such as a browser or an image viewer. Check that you are not putting incorrect or improper documents on your server.

5. Move the documents to the appropriate subdirectory of your home directory. For example, to install the file **hello.htm** from your home directory, use the following UNIX command.

```
mv hello.htm public_html
```

6. Check the permissions settings for the documents you install. These permissions must be set so that the user running the server has at least read and execute permission on the documents. For example, the following command sets the protection of the `hello.htm` document to enable all users to read and execute the document, while also giving the owner write privileges.

```
chmod 755 hello.htm
```

7. The document is now accessible through your NCSA HTTPD server. If your site is running a server that, by default, denies access to documents, configure the proper access control for the document. This step enables your server to service requests for the document.

How It Works

Servers provide the World Wide Web community with access to documents on your machine. For the server to find these documents, the documents must be located in a limited number of predefined locations. The two most common locations are a specified document directory and a specific subdirectory of each user's home directory.

The root of the document hierarchy is specified in the server resource map file. The `DocumentRoot` directive specifies this location. Documents installed in this directory or its subdirectories are visible to the server and can be requested by appropriate clients. The documents in this hierarchy must have protections set so that the server has read and execute permission on the file.

Documents are also commonly installed in users' home directories. The `UserDir` directive can be used in the NCSA HTTPD server resource map file to designate the particular subdirectory in the home directory where the server looks for documents. After you place documents in this subdirectory, they will be available for access over the World Wide Web. Set the permissions on these files so that the server can access them and provide them to requesting clients. The documents you place in this directory are subject to the limitations imposed by your Web site administrator.

Use caution when installing documents. After the document has been made available, anyone with the proper access can request and view the file. You should review each document before you install it on your server. Check for both correctness of the document and suitability of the material. Documents that are improperly formatted or badly designed reflect on your site as a whole. Furthermore, be wary of installing published materials on the Web that might violate copyright laws.

Comments

If you are a Web site administrator, you should develop rules and procedures for developing and submitting documents for installation on your server. To help prevent future problems, these rules should be cleared through the appropriate publications and legal offices of your business. In addition, you should give your users a clear policy for publishing Web-based materials on your site.

If you are a document developer, you should ask your Web site administrator to provide you with a copy of your site's publication policies. This will give you some guidelines to follow when publishing information over your Web site.

Chapter 13, "Handling Server Security," provides more information about document access control and security configuration.

12.8 How do I... Start or stop the server?

COMPATIBILITY: UNIX SERVERS, NETSCAPE FASTTRACK SERVERS

Problem

I have installed my server software and am ready to begin making HTML documents available to the World Wide Web community. How do I start my server?

I need to perform some maintenance or reconfiguration of my server. How do I start and stop the server to accomplish my task?

Technique

Maintenance of a server requires you to start, stop, and restart the server. This is true for most servers. How you start the server depends on the specific parameters that your server accepts and whether the server is run as a standalone server or by the Internet services manager process, `inetd`. Stopping the server entails determining the process ID for the server process and terminating it. To stop and restart the server, you can either do a manual stop and start of the server or use a command that will do both.

This How-To describes these three tasks in detail, with specific examples for the NCSA HTTPD server.

Steps

This section provides instructions for starting and stopping UNIX servers. The examples given use the NCSA HTTPD server as a typical UNIX server.

Starting the Standalone Server

You can usually start a standalone server manually from a command prompt. If you are running the server through the `inetd` process, see "Starting the `inetd` Server."

1. To start the server from a command prompt, run the server program with appropriate parameters for your configuration. Table 12-1 presents the arguments supported by the HTTPD application.

Table 12-1 Command-line options for HTTPD

ARGUMENT	EXPLANATION
`-d path`	Specifies where the server looks for its configuration files. It should match the location specified using the `ServerRoot` directive in the server configuration file.
`-f file`	Tells the server which server configuration file to use.
`-v`	Prints the version number of the server you are running.

If you want to run an HTTPD server with the configuration information in the default directory and default files, issue the following command at a UNIX prompt:

```
/usr/local/etc/httpd/httpd
```

If you want to run another server with configuration files in the `conf` subdirectory of `/usr/local/httpd2`, issue the following command:

```
/usr/local/etc/httpd/httpd -d /usr/local/httpd2
```

2. If you want the server to run whenever the system reboots, you must modify the system's automated startup files. You must access the system through a privileged user account to perform this task. After you have logged in to the system as the `superuser`, open the appropriate startup file in your favorite text editor. This file is called `/etc/rc.local` on many versions of the UNIX operating system.

3. Add the following lines of code at the end of this file:

```
if [ -f /usr/local/etc/httpd/httpd ]; then
   /usr/local/etc/httpd/httpd -d /usr/local/httpd2
fi
```

Change the second line to reflect the command you would have used from a UNIX prompt.

4. Save this file. The next time the system reboots, the server will start automatically. If you are starting a server with the `inetd` process, you should proceed to the next set of steps; otherwise, you are finished.

Starting the `inetd` Server

If you are starting an `inetd`-controlled server, you must verify or modify several files to make sure they are configured properly.

1. The first file you must examine is the `/etc/services` file. This file lists many Internet services such as Telnet and FTP. Log in as `superuser` and open the file in your favorite text editor.

2. Add a line for your server. This line should consist of the service name `http`, followed by a specification of the port and protocol. The following line adds the HTTP service to port 8080 using TCP:

```
http          8080/tcp
```

3. Save the `/etc/services` file.

4. Open the `/etc/inetd.conf` file.

5. Add the following line:

```
http stream tcp nowait nobody /usr/local/etc/httpd httpd
```

6. Append to this line any arguments that are suitable for your configuration. For example, if the server root for this server is `/usr/local/httpd2`, use the following line:

```
http stream tcp nowait nobody /usr/local/etc/httpd httpd -d ⇐
/usr/local/httpd2
```

   Refer to Table 12-1 for applicable command line options.

7. Save the file. You are now ready to start the server.

8. The server is controlled by the `inetd` process; therefore, to start the server, stop and restart the `inetd` process. Anytime the system reboots, furthermore, the server starts automatically when the `inetd` process starts.

Stopping the Server

The UNIX operating system assigns a process ID to each running process. You use the process ID to terminate a running process.

1. Identify the process ID for the server application. This process ID can be found in one of two ways. If your server provides this information, you can retrieve it from the server log files. For example, an NCSA HTTPD server logs its process ID in the file specified with the `PidFile` directive in the server configuration file. So if this file were specified as `log/httpd.pid` in the `/usr/local/httpd2` directory, you would issue the following `cat` command to retrieve the process ID for the server:

```
cat /usr/local/httpd2/log/httpd.pid
```

   The other approach is to list the running processes using the `ps` command and identify the process ID for the server from this list. Use a filtering program such as `grep` to narrow the list of potential processes. For example, to list all HTTPD processes, use the following command:

```
ps -aux | grep httpd
```

   Then choose the appropriate process ID from the list.

2. After you have determined the process ID for the server process, you must terminate the process using the **kill** command. For example, if you have determined that the process ID of the server is **4099**, issue the following command at the UNIX prompt:

```
kill 4099
```

Stopping and Restarting the Server

You have two choices. You can either follow the two separate procedures for stopping the server and then restarting it or follow the instructions here for stopping and restarting the server in one step.

1. To stop the server and automatically restart it, follow step 1 above to stop the server.

2. Then, instead of using the **kill** command by itself, add the option **-1** to it. For example, if you have determined that the process ID of the server is **4099**, issue the following command at the UNIX prompt:

```
kill -1 4099
```

How It Works

Start your server after the initial installation. The server must also be started after your system has rebooted, which can occur for reasons ranging from a software upgrade to a power failure. The server can either be started manually or through an automatic start procedure, depending on the server type.

Start a standalone server manually by executing the appropriate server command at the UNIX prompt. This starts the process. If you are running the server as a user other than yourself as you are specified in the server configuration file, run the server as **superuser**. If the server is run automatically, a suitable command must be added to the system startup files. This command tells the system to run the server whenever the system is started. In any case, the first time you run a standalone server, it will have to be from the command line, unless you want to reboot your system.

If the server is controlled by the **inetd** process, you must register the server with this process. This involves modifying several static configuration files that the **inetd** process uses when starting. These files tell **inetd** about the processes it will control. After you have modified these files appropriately, you can stop and restart **inetd**. This causes the configuration files to be read and your server to be started. You will also have configured the server to start whenever the system starts because **inetd** is automatically run when the system starts.

You must shut down the server when you want to perform extended maintenance on your site or server configuration. You must also bring the server down when you want to upgrade or change your server software. Shutting down involves identifying the server process ID and having the operating system terminate that process.

Finally, you will stop and restart the server when configuration changes are necessary. Stopping and restarting the server causes the server to initialize itself using the new values stored in the configuration files. Changes made to the configuration files will not take effect until the server has been restarted.

Comments

Configuration alterations in the **access.conf**, **httpd.conf**, **mime.types**, and **srm.conf** files necessitate a server stop and restart to apply the changes. You can modify these files while the server is running in its previous configuration, and then use the Stopping and Restarting the Server procedure described earlier to stop and immediately restart the server.

Starting and stopping a Netscape FastTrack server is a significantly more automated task. This software provides several means of starting and stopping the server.

- ✔ Netscape Server Management control panel: Selecting a server and then clicking the Start or Stop button manually starts and stops the selected server. This control panel also allows the configuration of a server to start with Windows automatically. Figure 12-17 displays this control panel.

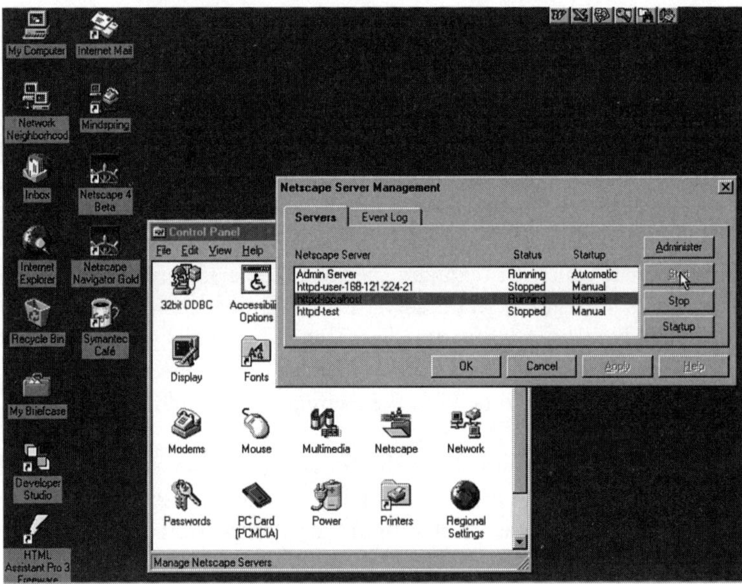

Figure 12-17 Starting/stopping the server through the Server Management control panel

- ✔ Administration server main access page: The administration server triggers the start or stop of a particular Web server running on the host machine when the switch next to the identifier for that server is flipped on the administration server main access page. In Figure 12-18, three servers run on the particular host machine. One of these servers is on, whereas the other two are off. Selecting the switch associated with a particular server toggles its current status.
- ✔ Particular server administration page: A server's administration page allows the toggling of its on/off status. Figure 12-19 shows the initial appearance of a server's administration page; the page displays the current status, as well as providing buttons for starting and stopping the server.

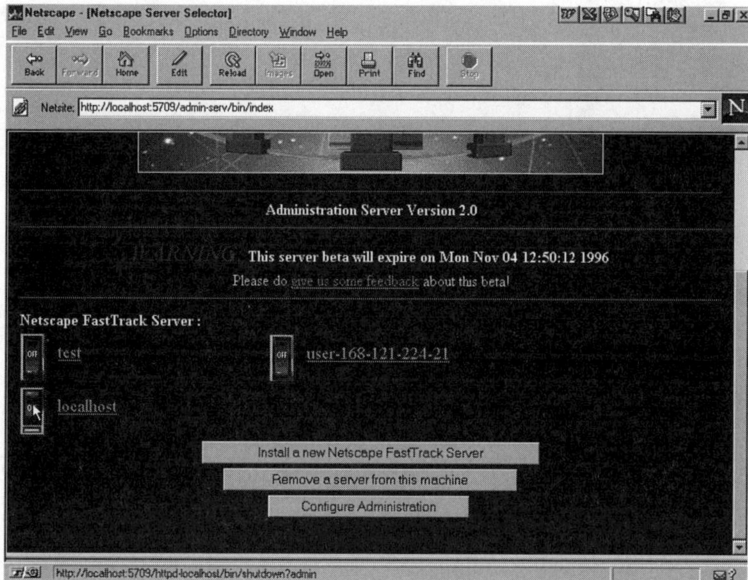

Figure 12-18 Starting/stopping a server through the administration server main access page

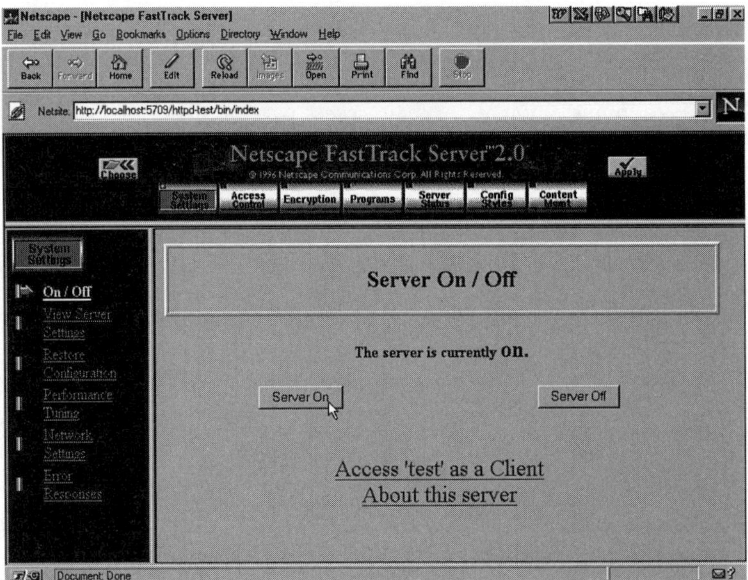

Figure 12-19 Starting/stopping a server through its administration page

COMPLEXITY
BEGINNING

12.9 How do I... Register my server?

COMPATIBILITY: ANY SERVER

Problem

My server is running, and I have installed several documents. However, I am finding that few people are connecting to my server. How do I let people know that my server is active and what type of information I am providing?

Technique

After you have created your site, you can register it in appropriate locations to attract the interest of people likely to use your Web site. Do this by registering your site through other Web sites and newsgroups.

This How-To provides step-by-step instructions for publicizing your Web site throughout the world by using several available forums.

Steps

Three primary methods are used to announce your server to the world. The following instructions provide a stepwise guide to the registration procedure:

1. Register your server with appropriate Web sites. Registrations are often categorized by location of site or subject. The following list provides URL references to selected sites suitable for the registration of your site:

- ✔ `http://www.yahoo.com/bin/add`
- ✔ `http://altavista.digital.com/`
- ✔ `http://www.infoseek.com/`
- ✔ `http://www.excite.com/`
- ✔ `http://www.lycos.com/`
- ✔ `http://www.infospace.com/submit.html`
- ✔ `http://web.nexor.co.uk/aliweb/doc/aliweb.html`

In addition to using to these Web sites, you should try to publicize your Web site through other Web sites at your facility or in your community by contacting the appropriate Web administrator.

2. Submit news of your server site to the Usenet newsgroup `comp.infosystems.www.announce`. You can access this group through the newsreader program with which you are most familiar. If your server is of particular interest to a particular domain, you might want to announce its location in other suitable newsgroups. Before taking such an action, consider that you are likely to generate a considerable increase in access volume through such an announcement. Therefore, you should be sure that the information you provide is both interesting and relevant to the newsgroup where you advertise. Usenet News is an extremely large forum, and by selectively choosing the newsgroups to which you announce your Web site, you will attract only those individuals most likely to use and benefit from your site.

3. Finally, you might want to announce your site through mailing lists. Send announcements to mailing lists related to the information at your site. Because mailing lists distribute to a limited number of subscribed members, this type of an announcement might serve as a test for your decision to announce your site to a general newsgroup. You might want to announce to a relevant mailing list and wait for feedback from the list membership before placing an item in a newsgroup distributed worldwide. In addition, you will probably want to send a message to a mailing list devoted to listing such announcements, such as `net-happenings@is.internic.net`.

How It Works

Unless you publicize the existence of your site, very few members of the World Wide Web community will access your server.

The methods just described publicize your site to users who might be interested in the information you are providing. You can announce your site's existence through appropriate newsgroups.

In addition, many existing sites will list new Web sites in a special area of their own site. This provides some additional publicity as well as providing users with access points to your server. When you first create your Web site, no other site links to information on your server. This situation will change when people know that your site exists. Registering your site at other locations provides people with initial access to your Web site, and after your site has been found, others will begin to provide links within their own information to relevant documents on your server.

Comments

Keep in mind that you can cross-list with other Web sites in your area or at your facility. Many site administrators will provide a link to your site if they feel it is appropriate. You may in turn provide a link back to their sites.

CHAPTER 13
HANDLING SERVER SECURITY

13

HANDLING SERVER SECURITY

How do I...

After you have announced the existence of your Web server, people—many people—will try to access your site. You have no control over who will try to view your material, so you must decide whether to establish security for your site. If you are distributing sensitive or restricted information, then security constraints are a necessity.

The two most commonly used forms of security provided by server software are *domain restrictions* and *browser authentication*. Domain restrictions enable you to specify which machines on the Internet can or cannot access your Web site. Browser authentication restricts access by requiring a valid username and password. These two mechanisms can be combined for even stronger security.

The various server software packages provide a variety of security features and hazards. This chapter examines the security capabilities of the following server software packages:

- ✔ NCSA HTTPD (UNIX), also derivatives such as Apache
- ✔ WinHTTPD (Windows 3.1)
- ✔ CERN HTTP (UNIX, VMS)
- ✔ MacHTTP and WebSTAR (Mac)
- ✔ Netscape FastTrack server (Windows 95)

13.1 Specify Allowable Features on an HTTPD Server

You might not want to allow certain features to be used in particular portions of your document tree on your HTTPD server. This How-To shows how to specify the features you want to support in each directory of your document tree.

13.2 Establish Domain and Address Security on an HTTPD Server

HTTPD domain-based security enables you to place restrictions on parts of your document tree based on the domain or machine making a request. This How-To describes how to use this feature on an HTTPD server.

13.3 Set Up User and Password Security on an HTTPD Server

HTTPD supports user authentication security, which requires the user to enter a username and password before accessing restricted information. In this How-To, you will learn how to configure password security on an HTTPD server.

13.4 Use HTTPD Server-Side Includes

HTTPD and Netscape's FastTrack support a feature known as *server-side includes*, which allows inclusion of server-generated, dynamic information in HTML documents. Because server resources are used, this feature represents a potential security hazard; however, with careful supervision, you can minimize this risk while retaining the convenience and usefulness of this feature. In this How-To, you will learn how to use HTTPD server-side includes.

13.5 Establish Directory-Level Security on a CERN HTTP Server

You can set access restrictions on a CERN HTTP server to limit actions in specified directories of the document tree through a combination of host filtering and user authentication. These restrictions, unlike those in HTTPD, can be set to allow only access selectively; no means of selectively denying access is supported. This How-To describes how you can set up directory-level security on a CERN HTTP server.

13.6 Set Up File-Level Security on a CERN HTTP Server

In addition to directory-level security, as supported in HTTPD, the CERN package provides a way to specify access restrictions at the file level. With the CERN server, individual files within the same directory can be configured with different security constraints. In this How-To, you will learn how to configure file-level security on a CERN server.

13.7 Install a CERN Proxy Server

The CERN HTTP server software can be run as a proxy server, allowing communication from behind an Internet firewall. The information in this How-To shows how you can configure your CERN server to act as such a proxy.

13.8 Establish Domain and Address Security and Password Authentication on MacHTTP and WebSTAR Servers

This How-To describes the basic forms of server-level security available with the MacHTTP and WebSTAR servers. As the other major Web server packages do, MacHTTP and WebSTAR allow domain name and machine name specification as well as user authentication. Methods are covered for securing a server and the individual documents and directories it serves, along with the method for entering usernames and passwords.

13.9 Configure SSL Security on a FastTrack Server

The Netscape FastTrack server provides mechanisms for security at several levels. The first level of security involves the encryption level of the connection between Web browsers and the server. This How-To details how to configure this security measure through the FastTrack administration server.

13.10 Set Up User and Password Security on a FastTrack Server

The Netscape FastTrack server also supports username/password and Internet domain security. This How-To walks you through the configuration of username/password security and Internet domain restrictions.

13.11 Use Public Key Encryption

Web servers and browsers communicate in the open. Servers transmit Web pages in an unsecured fashion using standard HTTP. In this How-To, you will learn how Web servers and browsers can use public key encryption techniques to provide secure transmission of HTML documents.

COMPLEXITY
INTERMEDIATE

13.1 How do I... Specify allowable features on an HTTPD server?

COMPATIBILITY: HTTPD-BASED SERVERS

Problem

The HTTPD server offers a wide range of features, which is what makes it so versatile. However, some of these features can cause security risks in certain areas. Furthermore, not all features are necessary in all areas of the document tree.

How can I selectively choose which features to allow in which areas of my document tree?

Technique

The HTTPD server software, and derivatives such as Apache and WinHTTPD, enable you to specify which server features to support in each directory of the document tree. The server finds these specifications in two locations:

- ✔ The global access configuration file
- ✔ Per directory access control files

You can edit the appropriate files to specify the features you want to support in each directory. If you are not the site administrator, you will likely find it easier to create per-directory access control files in those directories for which you are responsible. The following steps walk you through this process. The available features are described in the "How It Works" section that follows.

Steps

These steps show how to specify the features to be supported in a given directory. You may specify this information in either the global access configuration file for the server or in a per-directory access control file located in the directory.

1. To edit a per-directory access control file, begin with step 4. Otherwise, change directories to the configuration directory for the server. Usually this

is the **conf** subdirectory of the **ServerRoot**, for example, **/usr/local/etc/httpd/conf**.

2. Open the global access control file in your favorite text editor. By default, this file is called **access.conf** (**access.cnf** in WinHTTPD). If this file is not present, check the server resource map file (**srm.conf** or **srm.cnf**) and look for the **AccessConfig** directive, which should tell you the location and filename of the correct file.

3. At the end of the file, create a directory-sectioning directive to store your feature specifications. A directory-sectioning directive has an opening tag composed of the **<Directory>** label, followed by the path to the directory for which you are creating the sectioning directive. The closing tag is composed of the **</Directory>** label. For example, to create a directory-sectioning directive for the **/usr/local/mydocs** directory, insert the following lines in the file:

```
<Directory /usr/local/mydocs>

</Directory>
```

All feature directives for this directory should be contained between the opening and closing tags for this directory-sectioning directive. You should now proceed with step 5.

4. Change to the directory where you want to specify features. In this directory, edit (or create, if necessary) a per-directory access control file. The default name for such a file is **.htaccess** (**#haccess.ctl** in WinHTTPD). This name can be changed with the **AccessFileName** directive in the server resource map file, usually **srm.conf** or **srm.cnf**. Open the appropriate file in your text editor. Your insertion point should not be within the boundaries of an existing sectioning directive (unless you are editing the contents of that particular directive). The beginning or the end of the file is a good place to enter a new directive.

5. Insert the directive for the feature you want to support in this directory. Directives can either be sectioning or single line directives. For example, to insert a directive that associates the description **My Family Picture** with the file **fam1999.gif**, insert the following directive:

```
AddDescription 'My Family Picture' fam1999.gif
```

The acceptable feature directives are listed in the "How It Works" section.

6. Save the file. If you have made changes to the global configuration files, you must stop and restart the server for your changes to take effect, as described in How-To 12.8.

How It Works

Each feature that you want to support in a directory is specified with a directive. HTTPD supports two types of directives in access files. The standard directive is specified in a single line. The first string in the line is the directive command; the remainder of the line can contain any necessary data associated with the particular command. The `AddDescription` directive, shown in step 5, is an example of this type of directive.

The second type of directive is the sectioning directive. A sectioning directive has similar syntax to an HTML element: It begins with an opening tag and ends with a closing tag. Directives can be specified within the scope of a sectioning directive. The `<Directory>` directive used in step 3 is an example of a sectioning directive. This How-To and the following two cover the current comprehensive set of access file directives. The ones in this How-To determine features allowed in a particular directory or set of directories. Following is a list of these directives and their functions:

- ✔ `AddDescription`: Use this directive to associate a description with a particular file. This description is used when an automatic index of the directory is generated. A description is often much more helpful than a filename. This directive can be used in either the global access file or a per-directory access file. For example, to associate the phrase "Hang 10" with the file `surf.htm`, issue the following directive:

```
AddDescription 'Hang 10' surf.htm
```

Descriptions can also contain links; therefore, if a brief description is not sufficient, you can link a portion of the description to a Web document.

```
AddDescription 'My <A HREF="http://www.mysite.edu/~me/fam.htm">Family</A>⇐
 Picture' fam1999.gif
```

The preceding line associates the description `My Family Picture` with the file `fam1999.gif`; the word `Family` is a hypertext link to the document `http://www.mysite.edu/~me/fam.htm`.

- ✔ `AddEncoding`: Use this directive to associate a particular filename extension with an appropriate encoding mechanism. Browsers requesting encoded documents must have local capability to decode that particular type of encoding, as well as to support the HTTP encoding header elements. For example, to specify that the `.gz` filename extension should indicate gzip compression, issue the following directive:

```
AddEncoding x-gzip gz
```

This directive can be used in either type of access file.

- ✔ **AddIcon**: You can use the **AddIcon** directive in both the global access configuration file and per-directory access control files. Use this directive to associate a particular icon with a particular file type. If the server performs automatic indexing, this icon is presented with any file meeting the established filename extension criteria. The arguments to this directive are the path to the icon along with a list of filenames, wildcards, filename extensions, or one of two special names: **^^DIRECTORY^^** or **^^BLANK_ICON^^**.

  Several examples of this directive follow:

```
AddIcon /icons/image.gif .gif .jpeg .fif .xbm
```

When the server automatically generates an index for this directory and finds a file with the extension **.gif**, **.jpeg**, **.fif**, or **.xbm**, it references the **/icons/image.gif** image to display next to the filename.

```
AddIcon /icons/dir.xbm ^^DIRECTORY^^
```

If a subdirectory is found during automatic indexing, then the **/icons/dir.xbm** image displays with that index entry.

```
AddIcon (SND,/icons/sound.gif) *.au
```

This example specifies both an icon and an alternative textual message that can be used by browsers that do not support inline images. This directive causes the **/icons/sound.gif** image to display next to any AU sound file. If the browser does not support inline images, then the text message **SND** displays instead of the icon.

- ✔ **AddType**: The **AddType** directive provides Multipurpose Internet Mail Extensions (MIME)-type information for special document types found in a particular directory. This directive contains three parts: the command, the MIME type, and a list of recognized filename extensions. Use this directive in either the global access file or a per-directory access file.

  For example, if you want the server to run Common Gateway Interface (CGI) executables outside the script directory, issue the following directive:

```
AddType application/x-httpd-cgi .cgi
```

- ✔ **AllowOverride**: Use of this directive is limited to the global access configuration file. The **AllowOverride** directive specifies which features can be overridden by a per-directory access control file. The directive is followed by a list of options that can be overridden by the local access control.

  Table 13-1 summarizes the available arguments for this directive.

Table 13-1 `AllowOverride` **arguments**

ARGUMENT	FEATURE
`All`	Local access control can override any features.
`AuthConfig`	Accesses security information (see How-To's 13.2 and 13.3).
`FileInfo`	`AddType` and `AddEncoding` directives.
`Limit`	Limit sectioning directive (see How-To's 13.2 and 13.3).
`None`	Local access control cannot override any global specified features.
`Options`	Options directives.

- `DefaultIcon`: This directive specifies an icon for the server to use if a specific icon cannot be associated with the desired file. This directive can be used in either the per-directory or the global access control files. If you want to use the icon `unknown.xbm` when an icon is required but the actual icon is unknown, issue the following directive:

```
DefaultIcon /icon/unknown.xbm
```

  A server-wide default icon is usually defined in the server resource map file. The access control directive overrides the server default for a specific directory.

- `DefaultType`: This directive can be used in either the global access file or a per-directory access control file. The data supplied with the directive specifies the default MIME type for files in the directory. If the server is unable to determine the type of a file in the directory based on filename extension, it uses this default type.

  A server-wide default type is specified in the server resource map file; however, you can override this default with an access file default type. The most commonly used default type specified in the server resource file is `text/plain`, which tells the server to treat a data object as a straight ASCII text file if the type of the object cannot be determined.

  If you create a directory that contains only GIF files, you might want to issue the following directive:

```
DefaultType image/gif
```

  This directive is required if any of the GIF files in the directory do not have the `.gif` filename extension.

- `<Directory>`: Use this directive only in the global access configuration file to specify the directory affected by the enclosed directives. For example, to create a directory-sectioning directive for the `/htdocs/private/mydocs` directory, use the following directive:

```
<Directory /htdocs/private/mydocs>

</Directory>
```

You can use the asterisk as a wildcard character to create a directory directive that affects multiple similarly named document directories. For example, to refer to all the document directories in user home directories (usually in a subdirectory called `public_html`), use the following directive:

```
<Directory /*/public_html*>

</Directory>
```

- ✔ `IndexIgnore`: Use this directive in either access file to specify filename patterns that should be ignored by server automatic indexing. Follow the directive command with a list of the filenames (possibly using wildcards) to be ignored by indexing. For example, to ignore all files with the `.bak` extension, issue the following directive:

```
IndexIgnore *.bak
```

- ✔ `Options`: Use the `Options` directive in either the global or a per-directory access file. This directive tells the server which server options are available in a particular directory. Follow the directive with a list of those options that you want to be available. Table 13-2 indicates the options available on the HTTPD server (with the third column indicating whether you can use the argument with WinHTTPD).

Table 13-2 `Options` **arguments**

ARGUMENT	FEATURE	WINHTTPD
`All`	Makes all options available.	Yes
`ExecCGI`	Allows execution of CGI applications.	No
`FollowSymLinks`	Allows following of symbolic links.	No
`Includes`	Allows use of server-side includes.	No
`IncludesNoExec`	Allows use of server-side includes, except `exec`.	No
`Indexes`	Generates index file automatically.	Yes
`None`	Makes no options available.	Yes
`SymLinksIfOwnerMatch`	Allows symbolic links only if owner of link and source are the same.	No

- ✔ `ReadmeName`: Use this directive in either the global access configuration file or a per-directory access control file. A server-wide `readme` filename can be established in the server resource map file. The filename specified in this directive is used when automatic indexing occurs. This file is presented to the user at the top of the directory listing.

Comments

If you have modified the global access configuration file, you must stop and restart the server for the changes to take place.

For better security, the site administrator might want to use the following access practices:

- ✔ When possible, issue an `AllowOverride None` directive for directories in the global access configuration file.
- ✔ Do not allow server-side includes. At a minimum, restrict the use of the `exec` server-side command with the `Options` directive.
- ✔ Because the site administrator does not have complete control over the content of the directory trees, protect users' home directories. You can do this by inserting the following directory-sectioning directive into your global access configuration file:

```
<Directory /*/public_html*>
AllowOverride None
Options Indexes SymLinksIfOwnerMatch
</Directory>
```

Modify the argument in the opening tag to reflect the locations of your user document trees.

COMPLEXITY
INTERMEDIATE

13.2 How do I... Establish domain and address security on an HTTPD server?

COMPATIBILITY: HTTPD-BASED SERVER

Problem

I do not want people outside my business to access some critical documents that I want to make available to employees within the business. I have some even more sensitive documents that I want to make accessible only to people on a particular computer at my site. How can I attain this kind of security?

Technique

You can restrict access to portions of your server by either allowing or denying access to particular computers or domains on the Internet. This type of security is referred to as *domain/address security* or *host filtering*.

You can achieve this level of security by using a `<Limit>` sectioning directive to modify the access control files of your server either at the global level, in the server access configuration file, or at the local level in the per-directory access control files.

Steps

The following instructions show you how to establish host filtering security for particular portions of your document tree:

1. To establish host filtering using a per-directory access control file, skip to step 4. Otherwise, log in as the Web site administrator and change directories to the configuration directory for the server. Usually this is the `conf` subdirectory of the `ServerRoot`.

2. Open the global access control file with your text editor. By default, this file is called `access.conf` (`access.cnf` in WinHTTPD). If this file is not present, check the server resource map file and look for the `AccessConfig` directive, which should tell you the location of the correct file.

3. Locate the directory-sectioning directive associated with the document tree that you want to protect. If a `<Directory>` directive does not exist, go to the end of the file and add it. (Refer to How-To 13.1 for more information on creating a directory-sectioning directive.) Your insertion point should be between the opening and closing tags of this directive. Then skip to step 5.

4. Change to the directory in which you want to specify features. In this directory, edit (or create, if necessary) a per-directory access control file. The default name for such a file is `.htaccess` (`#haccess.ctl` in WinHTTPD). This name can be changed with the `AccessFileName` directive in the server resource map file. Open the appropriate file in your text editor. Your insertion point should not be within the boundaries of an existing sectioning directive (unless you are editing the contents of that particular directive); the beginning or the end of the file is a good place to add it.

5. If a `<Limit>` sectioning directive already exists, modify this directive to suit your new security needs. If not, you can create such a directive by inserting the appropriate opening and closing tags in your access file. The `<Limit>` opening tag is composed of the command followed by a list of HTTP methods that you want to restrict. Insert the following lines of code to create a directive to restrict `GET` method transactions:

```
<Limit GET>

</Limit>
```

The code within the `<Limit>` directive establishes the host filtering that occurs when a client requests a transaction of a specified method type in the protected directory.

6. Use a combination of three subdirectives to achieve this protection: **order**, **allow**, and **deny**. The **order** directive defines the order of evaluation for **allow** or **deny** directives. The **allow** and **deny** directives, respectively, permit and restrict access to the machines or domains specified as arguments for the directive. For example, to allow clients running on the machine **mysite.edu** access to the directory, you could use the following `<Limit>` sectioning directive:

```
<Limit GET>
order deny,allow
deny from all
allow from mysite.edu
</Limit>
```

More details on these subdirectives and further examples can be found in the "How It Works" section.

7. Save the file. If you have made changes to the global configuration files, you must stop and restart the server for your changes to take effect, as described in How-To 12.8.

How It Works

You can support host filtering by the `<Limit>` sectioning directive in either a server's global access configuration file or a per-directory access control file. This directive begins with an opening tag containing the `<Limit>` command, followed by a list of HTTP methods to which you want this directive to apply. The methods that are currently understood are **GET**, **PUT**, and **POST**; however, the **PUT** method is not currently implemented by HTTPD.

Specify the host restrictions you want to make, using one of the following subdirectives:

- ✔ **Order**: This subdirective specifies the order in which to evaluate **allow** and **deny** subdirectives in the `<Limit>` sectioning directive. The two possible values for the argument of this directive are **allow,deny** and **deny,allow**. Depending on which value you select, the server evaluates all **allow** subdirectives followed by all **deny** subdirectives, or all **deny** subdirectives followed by all **allow** subdirectives. The default order is **deny,allow**. Thus, the ordering determines whether **allow** will override **deny**, or vice versa.

- ✔ **allow from**: The **allow** subdirective specifies machines and domains allowed to access information in the protected directory. The arguments of this directive are those names, IP addresses, or partial names and addresses for which you want to allow access. Place a space between each such name or address.

- ✔ **deny from**: The **deny** subdirective specifies machines and domains not allowed to access information in the protected directory. The arguments of this directive are those names, IP addresses, or partial names and addresses for which you want to deny access. Place a space between each such name or address.

Figure 13-1 shows the results of an attempted access to a document in a directory protected with the following **<Limit>** directive:

```
<Limit GET>
order deny,allow
deny from all
allow from .ncsa.uiuc.edu
</Limit>
```

GET method access to the documents in this directory is denied to all browsers except those running on machines in the **.ncsa.uiuc.edu** domain. **GET** requests made from machines within this domain will receive the requested document.

NOTE

The special name `all` refers to requests from any site.

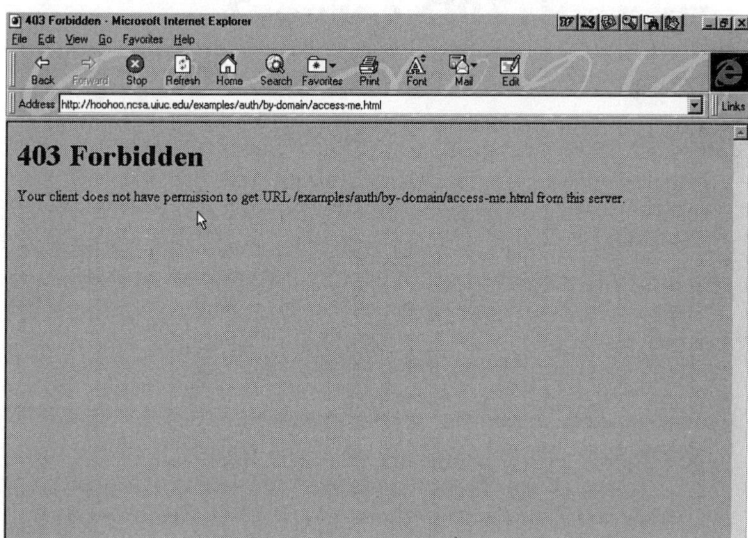

Figure 13-1 Attempting to access a domain-protected document

The following `<Limit>` directive will deny access to browsers run on the **mysite.edu** machine but allow access from anywhere else:

```
<Limit GET>
order allow,deny
allow from all
deny from mysite.edu
</Limit>
```

Thus, host filtering supported by HTTPD enables you to place access restrictions by allowing or denying access to a portion of the document tree by Internet machine name or address or by domain name or address.

Comments

`<Limit>` sectioning directives can be created for each specific HTTP method that might be used to access documents in the protected directory.

The **require** subdirective of the `<Limit>` directive is described fully in How-To 13.3, which describes user authentication protection. Furthermore, you can combine host filtering with user authentication to create multiple levels of security.

COMPLEXITY
INTERMEDIATE

13.3 How do I... Set up user and password security on an HTTPD server?

COMPATIBILITY: HTTPD-BASED SERVERS

Problem

Host filtering will not suffice for my security needs; the people who must access the sensitive information are at diverse locations and use a variety of machines in many different domains. Is there a way I can require user authentication with a password before allowing access to a private portion of my document tree?

Technique

The Basic authentication package is supported by a variety of server software packages, including HTTPD. This authentication package requires that a browser submit a username and password to authenticate itself. This information is checked against a list of acceptable users and passwords stored on the server. If the submitted username and password are authorized to access the requested document, the server provides the requested material; if not, access is denied.

HTTPD supports user authentication through the use of password files, group files, and access file directives. The following instructions lead you through the process of setting up user authentication-based security for specified portions of your document tree.

Steps

The following steps show how to configure the HTTPD server to provide password-based user authentication for access to portions of your document tree. Using these instructions, you can create password and group files and issue appropriate access file directives. These access file directives are explained in greater detail in the following "How It Works" section.

1. Create a password file. HTTPD includes the `htpasswd` program to aid you in this task (`htpasswd.exe` in WinHTTPD). Locate this program in the `support` subdirectory of the server. You should change directories to the location where you want to store a password file. If a password file already exists in this directory, proceed to step 2. Otherwise, create a new password file with this program. For example, to create a new password file called `newpass` in the current directory and add an entry for the user `duke`, issue the following command:

```
htpasswd -c newpass duke
```

2. Use the `htpasswd` application to add password file entries for any users you want to create. Because the password file already exists, do not use the `-c` parameter. For example, to add an entry for a user `harpo` in the `newpass` password file, use the following command:

```
htpasswd newpass harpo
```

3. If you want to establish groups of users who will share similar access privileges, create or edit a group file. If you do not want to create user groups, skip to step 6. Otherwise, you should change directories to the location where you want to store the group file.

4. Create a group file or open an existing one in your text editor. Add, delete, or alter entries as appropriate. Each entry is contained on a single line. The line begins with a group name followed by a colon (`:`). The remainder of the entry is a list of users in the group. For example, the following line designates the `tv` group, composed of users `duke` and `harpo`:

```
tv: duke harpo
```

5. After you make your edits, save this group file.

6. If you want to establish user authentication protection using a per-directory access control file, proceed with step 9. Otherwise, log in to your machine as the Web site administrator and change directories to the configuration directory for the server. Usually this is the `conf subdirectory` of the `ServerRoot`.

7. Open the global access control file in your text editor. By default, this file is called **access.conf** (**access.cnf** in WinHTTPD). If this file is not present, check the server resource map file and look for the **AccessConfig** directive, which should tell you the location of the correct file.

8. Locate the directory-sectioning directive associated with the document tree you want to protect. If a **<Directory>** directive does not exist, go to the end of the file and add such a directive. (See How-To 13.1 for more information on creating a directory-sectioning directive.) Place your insertion point between the opening and closing tags of this directive, but not within another sectioning directive, such as a **<Limit>** directive. Proceed with step 10.

9. Change directories to where you want to specify features. In this directory, edit (or create, if necessary) a per-directory access control file. The default name for the file is **.htaccess** (**#haccess.ctl** in WinHTTPD). This name can be changed with the **AccessFileName** directive in the server resource map file. Open the appropriate file in your text editor. Do not place your insertion point within the boundaries of an existing **<Limit>** directive. The beginning or end of the file is a good location.

10. Issue an **AuthType** directive to let the server know the type of authentication scheme to use when access attempts are made. In general, you will use the Basic protection scheme. Insert the following line in the access file:

```
AuthType Basic
```

11. Give the server a name for the security setup. This information is sent to the browser making an access attempt. The **AuthName** directive assigns this information. For example, you could use the following directive to assign the name **ProtectionExample** to the setup used to protect the documents in the current directory tree:

```
AuthName ProtectionExample
```

This name can appear as the title of the pop-up window requesting authentication information.

12. Specify the location of the password file that contains the username and password pairs for users who have access to the documents in this document tree. Use the **AuthUserFile** directive to designate the location of this file. For example, to specify **/usr/local/httpd/conf/newpass** as the password file, issue the following command in your access file:

```
AuthUserFile /usr/local/httpd/conf/newpass
```

13. Specify the location of a group file with the **AuthGroupFile** directive. For simple single-user security, specify a dummy file. If you use NCSA HTTPD, insert the following line in your access file:

```
AuthGroupFile /dev/null
```

If you use WinHTTPD, insert the following line in your access file:

```
AuthGroupFile c:/httpd/conf/empty.pwd
```

Or to specify an actual group file (such as **c:\httpd\conf\group.pwd**), use the following directive:

```
AuthGroupFile c:/httpd/conf/group.pwd
```

14. Finally, create or edit the **<Limit>** directive for this directory. If a **<Limit>** directive already exists, modify this directive to suit your new security needs. If not, create the directive by inserting the appropriate opening and closing tags in your access file. The **<Limit>** opening tag is composed of the command followed by a list of HTTP methods that you want to restrict. Insert the following lines to create a directive to restrict **GET** method transactions:

```
<Limit GET>

</Limit>
```

15. Use the **require** subdirective to specify the users who have access to the document tree. For example, if you want to allow users **duke** and **milo** and members of the **tv** group access to the directory, use the following **<Limit>** sectioning directive:

```
<Limit GET>
require user duke
require user milo
require group tv
</Limit>
```

The specified users and groups must appear as entries in the password and group files, respectively.

16. Save this file. If you have made changes to the global configuration files, you must stop and restart the server for your changes to take effect, as described in How-To 12.8.

How It Works

HTTPD allows the restriction of access to protected material by requiring that a user supply a valid username and password. Three key elements are necessary for this to work with HTTPD.

1. First, files containing valid username and password pairs must be stored on the server in a read-accessible location.

2. Next, group files must be created or modified as necessary.

3. Finally, access files, either global or local, must be configured to specify which users are eligible to access the protected files in a given manner.

Figure 13-2 shows the result of an attempt to access a document protected with user authentication. Many browsers remember the username and password that you have entered and supply this information the next time authentication is required. If a different username and password pair is required for other restricted documents, the browser prompts you for this new information.

Password Files

The **htpasswd** program (**htpasswd.exe** in WinHTTPD) is provided with the HTTPD software and is located in the **support** subdirectory. This application takes either two or three parameters. The format for such a command appears as follows:

```
htpasswd [-c] password_file user_name
```

You must use three parameters when you create the first username and password pair in a given password file. The **-c** parameter specifies that a new password file is being created. The other two parameters, the password filename and the username, are the same whether you are creating a new file or adding an entry to an existing file. For example, the following is the HTTPD procedure to create a new password file called **example.pwd** with two users, **bill** and **ted**:

```
glean dsk 151 >htpasswd -c example.pwd bill

Adding password for bill.
New password:
Re-type new password:
glean dsk 152 >htpasswd example.pwd ted
Adding user ted
New password:
Re-type new password:
```

The resulting password file might look like this:

```
bill:VCPfU..tx1IjY
ted:KAUrn7rvfOroM
```

Multiple password files can exist on a single server, with several stipulations. First, all password files must be stored in a location readable by the server application. Second, each directory can specify only a single password file; therefore, the password file must contain all users who must access the directory that references that password file.

Group Files

Specifying a list of individual users is often unwieldy. You might choose to create groups of users with similar access privileges. These groups are specified in a group file. The format of a group file is a series of entries, with each entry appearing on a single line.

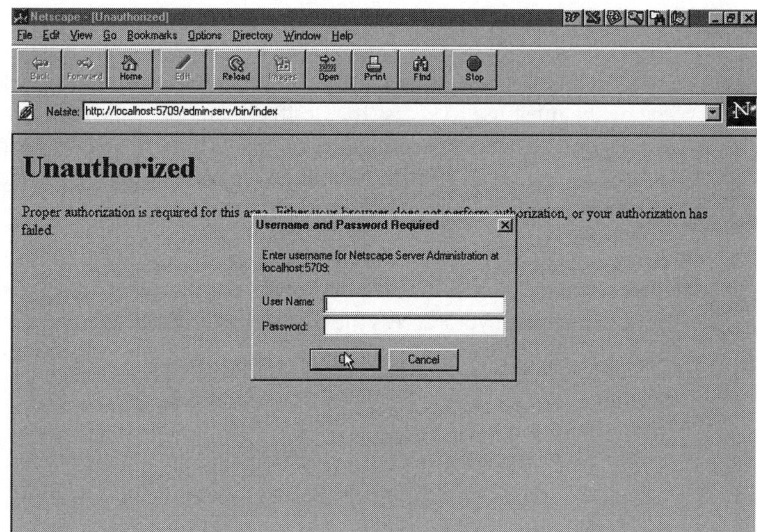

Figure 13-2 Attempting to access a document protected by Basic authentication

Each line is composed of a group name and a user list. These two elements are separated by a colon (`:`). For example, the following group file defines two groups, `friends` and `relatives`:

```
friends: paul jess steve jeanne
relatives: jenny elliot mom
```

The `friends` group consists of users `paul`, `jess`, `steve`, and `jeanne`. The `relatives` group consists of users `jenny`, `elliot`, and `mom`.

Access Files

The HTTPD user authentication feature also requires the configuration of access files to establish the particular authentication required for designated portions of the document tree. Several access file directives are required to support this security mechanism. These directives can be used in either the global access configuration file or the local per-directory access control files.

- ✔ `AuthGroupFile`: The `AuthGroupFile` directive specifies the location of the group file to be used in the user authentication protection of the current directory. For group-based access restriction, this file must be readable by the HTTPD server. The directive command is immediately followed by the file specification of the group file. For example, the following directive designates the file `c:\httpd\conf\group.pwd` as the group file for authentication:

```
AuthGroupFile c:/httpd/conf/group.pwd
```

- ✔ `AuthName`: This directive indicates the name of the authentication setup being used by the server. This information is passed to a browser making a request so that the end user can determine which username and password he or she must use to access the desired material. This name can be arbitrarily chosen by the person configuring the authentication security. The string immediately following the directive command is the name associated with the authentication setup.
- ✔ `AuthType`: The most common authentication type is Basic. However, limited alternatives exist for certain browsers and servers. In general, use the following line in your access file to specify the Basic authentication method:

```
AuthType Basic
```

Table 13-3 displays some other common authentication types. This table also provides pointers on where to find additional online information on these authentication types.

Table 13-3 Authentication types

TYPE (SERVER)	URL
Anonymous (Apache)	http://www.apache.org/docs/1.1/mod_auth_anon.html
DBM (HTTPD)	http://hoohoo.ncsa.uiuc.edu/docs/tutorials/howto/
	dbm_support.html
Berkeley DB (Apache)	http://www.apache.org/docs/mod_auth_db.html
Kerberos (HTTPD)	http://hoohoo.ncsa.uiuc.edu/docs/tutorials/howto/
	kerberos.html
MD5 (HTTPD)	http://hoohoo.ncsa.uiuc.edu/docs/tutorials/howto/
	md5_auth.html
MD5 (Apache)	http://www.apache.org/docs/mod_digest.html
mSQL (Apache)	http://www.apache.org/docs/1.1/mod_auth_msql.html

- ✔ `AuthUserFile`: This directive specifies the password file used in the authentication setup. The directive consists of the command, followed by the path of the password file to be used. Password files must be readable by the server software for user authentication protection to be handled properly. Furthermore, the specified password file should contain an entry for each user either directly specified in a `require` subdirective or indirectly included as a group member through a `require` subdirective. For example, the following directive indicates the use of `c:\httpd\conf\password.pwd` as the password file for the current authentication setup:

```
AuthUserFile c:/httpd/conf/password.pwd
```

✔ `require` (`<Limit>` subdirective): `require` subdirectives must occur within a `<Limit>` sectioning directive. (Other aspects of the `<Limit>` directive are covered more completely in How-To 13.2.) The `require` subdirective consists of a directive command, `require`; followed by a type, either `user` or `group`; and concluded by a username or group name, depending on the stated type. The server restricts transactions of the type specified by the `<Limit>` directive to only authenticated users specified with require subdirectives. For example, to restrict `GET` access of documents in a given directory to valid user `bill` and members of the `relatives` group, include the following `<Limit>` directive:

```
<Limit GET>
require user bill
require group relatives
</Limit>
```

Comments

`<Limit>` sectioning directives can be created for each specific HTTP method that can be used to access documents in the protected directory.

The `order`, `allow`, and `deny` subdirectives of the `<Limit>` directive are described fully in How-To 13.2. Furthermore, user authentication can be combined with the host filtering methods described in How-To 13.2 to create multiple levels of security.

In addition, the usernames and passwords used to support user authentication may or may not have any correlation to the usernames and passwords with which individuals log in to their system.

NOTE

In general, HTTP requests using Basic authentication send usernames and passwords as simple encoded text. Anyone with access to the packet transmissions between the browser and the server can easily retrieve this information. SSL or SHTTP provides a more secure method of transport. Check your particular server for this support. The SSLeay package is freely available for use with the NCSA HTTPD and Apache Web servers for the UNIX platform; see `http://www.psy.uq.oz.au/~ftp/Crypto/` for more information on this package. Also, see How-To 13.9 to configure SSL with a Netscape FastTrack server.

COMPLEXITY
ADVANCED

13.4 How do I... Use HTTPD server-side includes?

COMPATIBILITY: HTTPD-BASED, NETSCAPE FASTTRACK

Problem

I need to include dynamic information in my HTML document, but I don't want to write a small gateway application for each of these tasks. How can I incorporate on-the-fly information in a convenient way?

Technique

The NCSA HTTPD server and its derivatives provide a mechanism for placing dynamic information within HTML documents. This mechanism is referred to as *server-side includes*.

In an HTTP transaction, a user makes a request and the server responds with the requested item, with little regard for the actual content data. When an HTML document containing server-side includes is requested, the server reads the document, resolves server-side includes, and creates the resulting document.

The following procedure shows you how to use server-side includes.

Steps

Enabling server-side includes on your Web site involves two primary tasks. You must make several system configuration modifications, and you must add the server-side include commands to appropriate documents. An explanation of each of these tasks is presented below.

Configuration

HTTPD-Based Servers

This procedure describes the modifications you must make to your server configuration to allow the support of server-side includes.

1. If you want to configure server-side includes with a per-directory access control file, skip to step 4. Otherwise, log in to your machine as the Web site administrator and change directories to the configuration directory for the server. Usually this is the `conf` subdirectory of the `ServerRoot`.

2. Open the global access control file in your text editor. By default, this file is called `access.conf`. If this file is not present, check the server resource map file and look for the `AccessConfig` directive, which should tell you the location of the correct file.

3. Locate the directory-sectioning directive associated with the document tree in which you want to use server-side includes. If a **<Directory>** directive does not exist, go to the end of the file and add such a directive; refer to How-To 13.1 for more information on creating a directory-sectioning directive. Your insertion point is between the opening and closing tags of this directive. Then skip to step 5.

4. Change directories to the directory in which you want to allow HTML documents with server-side includes. In this directory, edit (or create, if necessary) a per-directory access control file. The default name for such a file is **.htaccess**. This name can be changed with the **AccessFileName** directive in the server resource map file. Open the appropriate file in your text editor. Your insertion point should not be within the boundaries of an existing sectioning directive; the beginning or the end of the file is a good location.

5. Insert the following **AddType** directive in this access file. The filename extension can be changed if you want to associate a different extension with documents that contain server-side includes. For example:

```
AddType text/x-server-parsed-html .shtml
```

6. Issue an **Options** directive to allow server-side includes. If no **Options** directive is present, the default value is **All**; in this case, you can either continue with step 7 or create an **Options** directive for this directory. The directive should, at a minimum, include the **Includes** or **IncludesNOEXEC** option. For example, the following directive specifies automatic indexing and server-side includes, with the exception of **execs** in the configured directory:

```
Options Indexes IncludesNOEXEC
```

7. Save the file. If you have made changes to the global configuration files, you must restart the server for your changes to take effect, as described in How-To 12.8.

Netscape FastTrack

This procedure describes the modifications you must make to your Netscape FastTrack server configuration to allow the support of server-side includes.

1. Access the FastTrack administration server.

2. Select the server that you want to configure for server-side includes. The server's administration page should appear.

3. Select the Content Management option from the top frame menu.

4. Select the Parse HTML option from the left frame menu. The Parse HTML configuration form should appear to the right. See Figure 13-3.

5. Select the location(s) for which you want to configure server-side includes. You can select an existing pattern from the menu, browse the document directory, or specify a wildcard pattern.

6. Choose the level of parsed HTML you want. Selecting No turns off this feature. The other choices both allow includes; however, the `no exec` option, the equivalent of the HTTPD `IncludesNoEXEC` option, supports all server-side include directives except `exec`.

7. Select the types of HTML files that the server should parse. Selecting all HTML files instructs the server to parse all files with the `text/html` MIME type (see Appendix C, "MIME," for more information). Selecting files with the extension `.shtml` instructs the server to parse only files ending with the `.shtml` filename extension.

8. Save the file. If you have completed all changes to the server, you must apply the changes by selecting the Apply button from the top frame menu of the particular server's administration page.

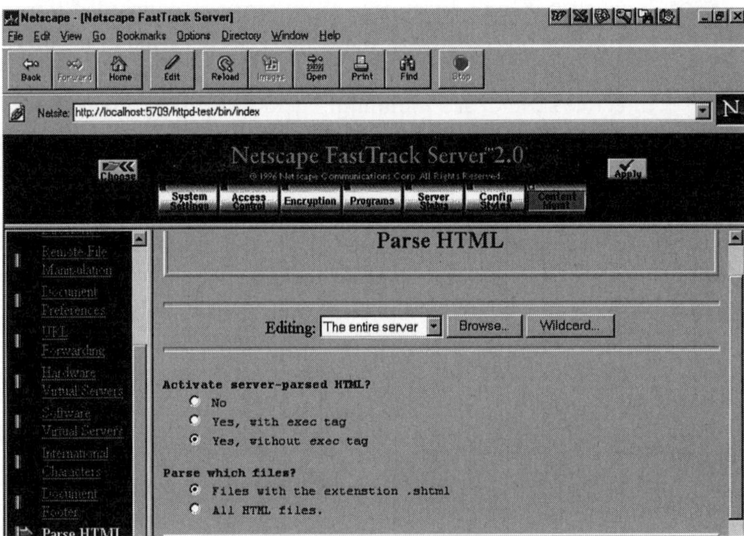

Figure 13-3 Configuring server-side includes through the Parse HTML configuration form

NOTE

Direct modification of the particular FastTrack server's `obj.conf` file provides an alternative means of configuring this feature. See the online documentation for additional information on this process.

Inserting Directives

After you have configured your server to allow server-side includes, you can begin using server-side include commands in your documents. The following steps walk you through the process of incorporating server-side include commands into your HTML documents.

1. Change directories to the location where the HTML documents in which you want to use server-side includes are stored.
2. Open the document in which you want to include server-side information in your text editor. Move the insertion point to the location in the document where you want to insert the dynamic information.
3. Issue a server-side **`include`** command within the context of an HTML comment. The text of the comment should begin with a pound symbol (**#**). For example:

```
<!--#command tag1="..." tag2="..." ... -->
```

So if you wanted to include the text of the file **`DocumentRoot/header.htm`** in your document, you would issue the following directive in your document:

```
<!--#include virtual="/header.htm" -->
```

4. When your edits are complete, save your document. The filename extension of your document should indicate the presence of server-side includes.
5. Check the document in your browser.

How It Works

Several popular server software packages provide server-side includes as a mechanism for incorporating dynamic information into static HTML documents. The server accomplishes this by parsing embedded commands within the text of the document, and then evaluating these commands to generate the final document sent to the client.

For the server to differentiate properly documents that have server-side includes from those that do not, the server must be configured to recognize objects of the **`text/x-server-parsed-html`** MIME type (**`magnus-internal/parsed-html`** with Netscape's FastTrack), created to support server-side includes. Add this type and associate it with an appropriate filename extension, usually `.shtml`. Unless you want to allow server-side includes in documents server-wide, issue the appropriate `AddType` directives in the HTTPD access files that control the specific directories in which you want to permit server-side includes. If you do want to support server-side includes globally, issue this directive in the HTTPD server resource map file. For FastTrack servers, establish directory restrictions through the Parse HTML configuration page.

In addition, for HTTPD-based servers, you must configure the options in the directories where you want to support server-side includes. By default, all options are available in all directories. However, if you must restrict some options while supporting server-side includes, issue an `Options` directive with either the `Includes` or the `IncludesNOEXEC` argument. The `Includes` option allows the use of all server-side commands; the `IncludesNOEXEC` argument allows the use of all server-side commands except `exec`. With Netscape FastTrack Server, you perform these same configuration tasks by selecting items through the Parse HTML configuration form. Use of `exec` might constitute a security risk, hence the need for two separate options.

The following is a list of supported server-side include commands, as well as a summary of how they work and the arguments they take. This discussion is followed by Table 13-5, which describes the environment variables visible to server-side include documents.

- ✔ `config`: This command defines several characteristics of file parsing. Table 13-4 shows the tags supported by this command.

Table 13-4 Tags in a `config` server-side include command

TAG	VALUE
`errmsg`	Specifies the error message sent to the client if an error occurs during the parsing process.
`timefmt`	Format to use when a date is requested. The string must conform to the specification of date format strings
	for the UNIX `strftime` library function.
`sizefmt`	Format to use when a file size is displayed. There are two acceptable values:
	`bytes`: Represents the straight byte count of the file.
	`abbrev`: Shows an abbreviated file size (for example, 1.2MB).

For example, the command

```
<!--#config errmsg="Error in parsed HTML" timefmt="%D" sizefmt="abbrev">
```

would set the error message to `"Error in parsed HTML"`; the time format to `"%D"`, so a date might appear as `1/1/99`; and the size format to `"abbreviated"`, so a file size of `9,876,543` displays as `9.9MB`.

- ✔ `echo`: The `echo` command can display any of the environment variables specified in Table 13-5. The single valid tag for this command is `var`. The value associated with this tag is the variable to be displayed.

For example, to display the current date in your document, use the following server-side include:

```
<!--#echo var="DATE_LOCAL">
```

- ✔ **exec**: This include puts the results of executing the command passed as a tag into the resulting document sent to the client. The valid tags for this command are **cmd** and **cgi**.

  The value of the **cmd** tag must be a string. This string is passed to **/bin/sh** for execution. The variables specified in Table 13-5 can be used by this command.

  The **cgi** tag is used to refer to a gateway application whose results will be included in the resultant document. The reference to the Common Gateway Interface (CGI) program should be a standard virtual path to a valid gateway program.

  The following include could be used if, for example, you wanted to include a listing of the people currently logged in to the server site within an HTML document:

```
<!--#exec cmd="/usr/ucb/finger">
```

- ✔ **fsize**: The **fsize** command has the same valid tags as **include**: **file** and **virtual**. It displays the size of the file referenced in the tag. This data is shown in the format specified with the **sizefmt** tag of the **config** command.

  If you want to track the size of a particular file, you can create an HTML document that displays this information whenever you access it. For example, the following include displays the size of the file **/export/home/00/ht1/logs/error_log**:

```
<!--#fsize virtual="/logs/error_log">
```

- ✔ **flastmod**: The **flastmod** command has the same valid tags as **include**: **file** and **virtual**. This command displays the date on which the target referenced by the tag was last modified. This date is printed in the format specified using the **timefmt** tag in the **config** command.

  Use this command to keep track of when a particular file was last modified. For example, if you always want to know when the last server error occurred, create an HTML document that dynamically determines when the server error log was last changed. Such a command might look like the following:

```
<!--#flastmod virtual="/logs/error_log">
```

✔ `include`: This command places the text of one document within another. Documents to be included are subject to the standard access control restrictions. This command uses one of two valid tags:

The `file` tag specifies the location of the file to be included relative to the current directory. The target can be another parsed HTML document, but not a CGI application.

The `virtual` tag references a document by way of the virtual path from the `DocumentRoot`. As with the target of a file tag, this file can be another parsed document, but cannot be a gateway application. You can find an example of this command in step 3 of "Inserting Directives," earlier in the chapter.

Several environment variables are set when server-side includes are evaluated. These variables appear in Table 13-5.

Table 13-5 Environment variables set while server-side includes are evaluated

VARIABLE	VALUE
DOCUMENT_NAME	Current filename
DOCUMENT_URL	Virtual path to the current document
QUERY_STRING_UNESCAPED	Any search query the client sent
DATE_LOCAL	Current date, local time zone
DATE_GMT	Current date, Greenwich mean time
LAST_MODIFIED	Date current document was last modified

Comments

Server-side includes provide a means of including dynamic information within HTML documents without resorting to gateway scripts, but there are significant drawbacks: inefficiency and lack of security.

Server-side includes decrease server efficiency. The server can no longer act strictly as a dispatcher because it must not only process the requests, but also read and comprehend the content of the response to generate the appropriate resulting HTML document. This inefficiency can be minimized by using server-side includes only in directories that require them. In other words, place the configuration information either in per-directory access control files or within a directory-sectioning directive in the global access configuration file in an HTTPD-based server; for Netscape's FastTrack server, limit your choice of directories using the location specification portion of the parsed HTML configuration form. If potential inefficiency is not an issue, much of the configuration information can be declared server-wide in the server resource map file (HTTPD) or Entire Server location selection (FastTrack).

In addition, server-side includes represent a security risk. The most flagrant potential risk is the `exec` command, which enables an HTML document to include the results of the execution of an application. This command could allow unauthorized access to the server machine. You can reduce this risk by using the `Options` directive to restrict either all server-side include commands or only `exec` commands.

13.5 How do I... Establish directory-level security on a CERN HTTP server?

COMPATIBILITY: CERN HTTP

Problem

I have sensitive data in certain areas of my document tree that I must distribute to a select audience via my CERN HTTP server software. How can I make sure that only the people I specify can access the protected documents?

Technique

The CERN server software uses a combination of host filtering and user authentication to provide directory-level server security. Establishing directory-level security entails the following tasks:

- ✔ Establishing the protection setup
- ✔ Associating these setups with portions of the document tree
- ✔ Generating any supporting password and group files

This How-To shows you how to accomplish these tasks, letting you establish directory-level security for your CERN server.

Steps

The directory-level security configuration process can be broken down into three broad categories:

- ✔ Protection setup definition
- ✔ Directory association
- ✔ Auxiliary file maintenance

These tasks are handled individually in the following procedures. In each category, several alternative approaches are described.

Examples of several directory-level protection configurations are provided in the "How It Works" section.

Protection Setup Definition

The CERN server software provides three methods for specifying protection setups. You can

- ✔ Define named setups in the global configuration file
- ✔ Define setups as separate external security setup files
- ✔ Define setups through inline specification

The following procedures cover the first two approaches. Later in this How-To, the "Association of Directories with Protection Setups" section describes the third method.

Defining Named Setups

If you want to define a setup in a separate file, use the procedure given under "Defining Setup Files." Otherwise, log in to the server machine as the site administrator.

1. Change directories to the location of your global server configuration file. This file is usually located in the `config` subdirectory of the server software.
2. Open the configuration file in your text editor.
3. Move the insertion point to a new line. You should define your protection setup object before you try to associate it with a particular directory. If you are editing an existing setup, move your insertion point to within the setup object and skip to step 7.
4. Insert the following lines of code, substituting whatever you choose for the object name represented by `PROTNAME` in the code:

```
Protection PROTNAME {
}
```

5. Place your insertion point between the opening curly brace and the closing curly brace.
6. Insert a `UserId` directive to indicate the user ID that the server must assume to access the protected directory. For example, if the server needs to run as user `me` to access directories owned by this user, issue the following directive:

```
UserId me
```

   The default user ID is `nobody`.

7. Insert a `GroupId` directive to indicate the group ID that the server must assume to access the protected directory. For example, if the server must

run as a group called **users** to access the desired directories, use the following directive:

```
GroupId users
```

The default group ID is **nogroup**.

8. Insert the following directive to specify the authentication type:

```
AuthType Basic
```

9. Use a **ServerId** directive to specify a name for the setup. For example, to name the setup **MySetup**, use the following directive:

```
ServerId MySetup
```

10. Specify the password file to use with this setup using the **PasswordFile** directive. To use the password file **/home/htpass**, include the following line:

```
PasswordFile /home/htpass
```

11. Specify the group file to use with this setup using the **GroupFile** directive. To use the group file **/home/htgroups**, include the following line:

```
GroupFile /home/htgroup
```

12. Specify the masks for the setup to indicate the types of transactions and the limitations on them. You can specify this as either a generic mask or a series of transaction-specific masks. The following is the syntax of a **mask** command:

```
mask_command group, user user@address, @address, ...
```

Table 13-6 specifies the valid **mask** commands.

Table 13-6 Mask directives

MASK COMMAND	TRANSACTIONS COVERED
delete-mask	Protects DELETE method requests.
Get-mask	Protects GET and HEAD method requests.
mask	Use this mask when method-specific mask is unavailable.
post-mask	Protects POST method requests.
put-mask	Protects PUT method requests.

The **mask** command itself is followed by a series of usernames, group names, and machine/domain addresses in any combination. Additional information on the syntax of this list can be found in the "How It Works" section. This syntax is referred to as a group definition; it is the same as the one used in group files described in the "Auxiliary File Maintenance" section. For example, to restrict **PUT** method requests to user **jenny**, use either of the following directives:

```
put-mask jenny
```

or

```
mask jenny
```

The second is more restrictive in that transactions of all methods are restricted to the user **jenny**. If a generic mask is defined, it serves as the default mask if a specific transaction mask is not defined.

13. You have now defined a protection setup. If you have no more protection setups to create at this time, save the current file.

14. Because you have modified the global configuration file, you must stop and restart the server process to put your configuration changes into effect.

Defining Setup Files

You can define security setups as external files. Except for limited exceptions, these files contain the same information as named setups. Files, however, contain neither the **UserId** nor the **GroupId** directives. This information is provided at the time the setup file is associated with a document tree.

1. Change directories to the location where you want to store the file that defines a protection setup. Each file defines a single protection setup.

2. Choose a name for your protection setup file and open this file in your text editor.

3. Insert the following directive to specify the authentication type:

```
AuthType Basic
```

4. Use a **ServerId** directive to specify a name for the setup. For example, to name the setup **MySetup**, use the following directive:

```
ServerId MySetup
```

5. Specify the password file to use with this setup using the **PasswordFile** directive. To use the password file **/home/htpass**, include the following line:

```
PasswordFile /home/htpass
```

6. Specify the group file to use with this setup using the **GroupFile** directive. To use the group file **/home/htgroups**, include the following line:

```
GroupFile /home/htgroup
```

7. Specify the masks for the setup to indicate the types of transactions and the limitations on them. You can specify this as either a generic mask or a series of transaction-specific masks. The following is the syntax of a **mask** command:

```
mask_command group, user user@address, @address, ...
```

Table 13-6, in the "Defining Named Setups" section earlier in the chapter, specifies the valid **mask** commands. The **mask** command itself is followed by a series of usernames, group names, and machine/domain addresses in any combination. Additional information on the syntax of this list can be found in the following "How It Works" section. This syntax is referred to as a *group definition*; it is the same as the one used in group files described in the "Auxiliary File Maintenance" section, later in the chapter. For example, to restrict **PUT** method requests to user **jenny**, use either of the following directives:

```
put-mask jenny
```

or

```
mask jenny
```

The second is more restrictive in that transactions of all methods are restricted to the user **jenny**. If a generic mask is defined, it serves as the default mask if a specific transaction mask is not defined.

8. You have now defined a protection setup. Save the current file.

Association of Directories with Protection Setups

Several methods exist for configuring a particular directory with a specific security setup. The following steps lead you through several variations of the **Protect** directive in the server configuration file to create these associations. Instructions for using the **DefProt** directive for this task can be found in the documentation for the CERN server software.

1. Associate a protection setup with a directory in the server configuration file. Change directories to the location of your global server configuration file; this file is usually located in the **config** subdirectory of the server software.

2. Open the configuration file in your text editor. Move the insertion point to a new line. If you have defined protection setups within your configuration file, this insertion point should be farther down in the file than the protection setup objects you want to use. If you are editing an existing directory-level protection association, move your insertion point to the desired **Protect** directive.

3. Insert (or modify) a **Protect** directive to associate a protection setup with a directory. If you plan to use a protection setup only once, consider associating the directory to an inline specification of a setup, as shown in step 5. If you want to associate a directory with a previously declared setup object in the configuration file, proceed with step 4. Otherwise, associate a directory with an external protection setup file using the following directive:

```
Protect template path user.group
```

In this directive, the template is the path to the tree of documents to be protected. This path is an absolute path to the protection setup file that specifies the desired protection for the document tree. Finally, the `user.group` field specifies the identity the server must assume to gain access to the document tree. So, for example, to protect the `/horses/mysystem` directory using the `/WWW/config/prot.setup1` protection setup file with the server running as user `me` in group `users`, issue the following directive:

```
Protect /horses/mysystem/* /WWW/config/prot.setup1 me.users
```

4. You have now protected the specified directory. Proceed with step 6.

5. Using a previously defined protection setup object, insert a `Protect` directive with the following syntax:

```
Protect template prot_obj
```

The template is a wildcard-capable specification of the directory to be protected, and `prot_obj` is the name used as the second parameter to the `Protection` directive when creating the object. A wildcard-capable directory specification can include an asterisk (*) to match multiple paths; for example, `/horse/*` refers to all subdirectories of the `/horse` directory. Use the following directive to protect the `/horses/mysystem` directory using the `PROTNAME` protection setup object:

```
Protect /horses/mysystem PROTNAME
```

You have now protected the specified directory. Proceed with step 6.

6. Associate an inline protection setup with a directory. You should create an inline protection setup only for one-time use. Be careful with the syntax of this usage of the `Protect` only directive. It should appear as follows:

```
Protect template {
        setup
        }
```

Be sure to place a space between the template and the opening brace, as well as to place the closing brace on a line by itself. In addition, comments are not permitted within the scope of an inline setup object. In the preceding syntax, `template` refers to the directory to be protected, whereas `setup` refers to a series of directives as defined in steps 6 through 12 of the

"Defining Named Setups" section, earlier in the chapter. The following is an example of this usage:

```
Protect /horses/mysystem {
    UserId me
    GroupId users
    AuthType Basic
    ServerId MySetup
    PasswordFile /home/htpass
    GroupFile /home/htgroup
    GetMask jenny elliot mom @(*.*.cau.edu)
}
```

This associates the inline setup provided with the specified directory.

7. When you are finished, save the server configuration file. You must now restart the server before your changes can take effect.

Auxiliary File Maintenance

CERN security requires the maintenance of two types of auxiliary files: password files and group files. These files serve the same purpose that they do in the HTTPD server. The formats and maintenance utilities, however, differ. The following steps take you through the creation and maintenance of CERN password and group files.

The CERN server package provides the **htadm** application to help maintain server password files. The following "How It Works" section explains how to use this application. However, the first three of the following steps show how to create and add user/password pairs with this program:

1. Change directories to the location where you want to store a password file.

2. Create a new password file using the following **htadm** application syntax:

```
htadm -create filename
```

For example, use the following command to create a password file called **.htpass** in the current directory:

```
htadm -create .htpass
```

3. Add users to the password by calling this application with the following syntax:

```
htadm -adduser filename username password realname
```

For example, the following command creates an entry in the **.htpass** password file for user **jenny** with password **math** and a real name of **Jenny Helen**:

```
htadm -adduser .htpass jenny math Jenny Helen
```

You can use this command to create as many users as required. Additional password maintenance functions are described in the "How It Works" section.

4. If you do not need to create a group file, you have completed setting up directory-level protection. Otherwise, change directories to the location where you want to store a group file. Either choose a name for this group file or edit an existing group file. In either case, open your chosen group file in your text editor.

5. A group file is a series of lines, each of which defines a group. The line begins with a group name, followed by a colon (`:`), followed by a list of items. The following is the syntax of an entry:

```
groupname: item, item, item, item, ...
```

6. An `item` can be a user, a group, a machine, a domain, or any combination of users or groups with machines or domains. The list defines the group. Create or edit any necessary groups.

7. Save the group file.

How It Works

Like HTTPD, the CERN HTTP server software supports security through host filtering and user authentication. Unlike HTTPD, the syntactic specification of both types of security is remarkably similar in the CERN package. The first component required to establish directory-level protection of a CERN server is the protection setup object or file. After that is located, you must know which directives to use. Table 13-7 summarizes the directives used in the specification of a protection setup.

Table 13-7 Protection directives

DIRECTIVE	PURPOSE	RESTRICTION
`AuthType`	Specifies authentication scheme to be used.	None
`GroupFile`	Specifies full path of the group file for this setup.	None
`GroupId`	Designates group server needs to run as `mask` commands (see Table 13-6).	Setup object
`PasswordFile`	Specifies full path of the password file for this setup.	None
`ServerId`	Name to differentiate among setups on a server.	None
`UserId`	Designates user that runs the server.	Setup object

The `mask` command takes a group definition as a parameter. A *group definition* is a comma-separated list of users, groups, potentially wildcarded Internet addresses, and combinations of users or groups with an address or addresses. Parentheses are used for logical groupings of users/groups or address templates. For example, the following are all valid group file entries, each composed of a group name, a colon, and a group definition.

The group **us** consists of users **you** and **me**:

```
us: you, me
```

The group **them** consists of users **he**, **she**, and **it**; however, **it** must be trying to access the server from a machine in the **auc.edu** domain (**144.125.*.*** is the **auc.edu** domain). This entry does not restrict users **he** and **she** to a particular machine or domain.

```
them: he, she, it@144.125.*.*
```

The group **us_and_them** consists of all users in the groups **us** and **them** plus users from the **CERN** domain (**128.141.*.*** is **CERN**).

```
us_and_them: us, them, @128.141.*.*
```

The group **some_of_them** consists of only those members of the group **them** accessing the server from machines in either the **auc.edu** or the **jpl.nasa.gov** domains (**128.149.*.*** is the **jpl.nasa.gov** domain).

```
some_of_them: them@(*.*.auc.edu, 128.149.*.*)
```

The group **we** consists of the users **me**, **myself**, and **i** when attempting to access the server from Internet address **144.125.96.233**.

```
we: (me, myself, i)@144.125.96.233
```

Two special predefined groups exist: **All** and **Anybody**. The **All** group consists of all valid users in the designated password file. The **Anybody** group represents protection without user authentication; this is the implied group when an item in a group definition is only an at sign (**@**), followed by a machine or domain address.

The **mask** commands specify individuals who may have a particular type of access to the protected portion of the server. Thus, with the capabilities of the **mask** directives, you could create protections to support strict host filtering or user authentication. For example, the following setup object performs host filtering that allows access only from machines in the **jpl.gov** domain (**128.149**):

```
Protection jplFilter {
    UserId me
    GroupId users
    AuthType Basic
    ServerId HostFilter
    PasswordFile /dev/null
    GroupFile /dev/null
    getmask @128.149.*.*
    }
```

Protection setups can also be defined to perform strictly user authentication. For example, the following object defines a protection allowing access for users **jenny** and **david**, regardless of what machine they use to access the server:

```
Protection authEx {
    UserId me
    GroupId users
    AuthType Basic
```

```
ServerId UserAuthenticate
PasswordFile /WWW/.htpass
GroupFile /dev/null
getmask jenny, david
}
```

Compared to NCSA HTTPD, the limitation of the protection setups is their incapability to deny access to specified users, groups, or machines. However, the trade-off is the capability to combine specific users and groups with specific machines or domains.

Protection setups are the first stage in establishing directory-level security. The second stage of this process is the association of protection setups with particular portions of the document tree. Use the **Protect** directive to accomplish this task. Several syntactic forms of this command, along with relevant examples, are provided in steps 3 through 5 of the "Association of Directories with Protection Setups" portion of the Steps section earlier in the chapter.

Finally, the users and groups specified in the protection setup masks must be defined in the designated password and group files, respectively. CERN password files are maintained using the **htadm** package distributed with the CERN software. Use this application to create, edit, and check password files. Table 13-8 summarizes the parameters and use of this application.

Table 13-8 htadm parameters

PARAMETERS	PURPOSE
`-adduser password_file`	Adds the specified user to the designated file.
`user password real_name`	
`-check password_file user password`	Checks the specified user's password.
`-create password_file`	Creates the designated password file.
`-deluser password_file user`	Deletes the user from the designated file.
`-password password_file user password`	Changes the specified user's password.

Group files are maintained with a standard text editor. Groups are specified one per line. Each line is composed of a group name, a colon, and a group definition. The group definition uses the same syntax as described in step 12 of the "Defining Named Setups" section, earlier in the chapter.

After protection setups have been defined and associated with relevant portions of the document tree and necessary auxiliary files have been created, directory-level security is configured for the specified directories. When a client requests a document in a protected directory, the protection setup associated with the directory is examined. If the type of access is restricted and the requester does not fit the appropriate mask criteria, then access is denied.

Comments

Directory-level security can be used in combination with file-level access control (see How-To 13.6) to achieve two levels of security. If both file and directory-level restrictions are imposed, then the conditions defined by both the mask and file-level access control list must be met for access to be granted.

Use of the `DefProt` directive establishes a default protection setup; however, without an access control list or a `Protect` directive, no documents are actually protected. If the setup file argument is missing from a `Protect` rule, this information is inherited from the most recently used `DefProt` directive. Further information on the `DefProt` directive can be found in the documentation for the CERN HTTP server at URL `http://www.w3.org/hypertext/WWW/Daemon/User/Config/Rules.html`.

COMPLEXITY
INTERMEDIATE

13.6 How do I... Set up file-level security on a CERN HTTP server?

COMPATIBILITY: CERN HTTP

Problem

I need more finely tuned control than directory-level protection. Most of the documents in my protected document tree can be safely viewed by a large group of valid users; however, I want to restrict the access of several particular documents to a few users out of that large group. Is there a way I can do that?

Technique

The CERN HTTP server lets you set up security on a file-by-file basis using access control list files that reside in directories in which file-level restrictions are desired. In the access control file, each individual file in the directory can be referenced with an allowable transaction method and associated with a group of valid users.

This access control list provides host filtering and user authentication requirements for the file in the protected directory. If directory-level protection is already in force, then the access control list serves as a second level of security.

Thus, the specification of file-level security involves the creation of an access control list file in the directory that is to be protected. The following steps show how to create a CERN access control list file.

Steps

You should be familiar with establishing directory-level security before configuring file-level protection. How-To 13.5 provides this information. You need not include a **mask** command if you do not want to require two levels of security.

After you have established directory-level security for the directory in which you want to install file-level security, you can proceed with the following steps:

1. To allow the file-level access control list to supersede any masks in the protection setup, insert the following directive in the protection setup associated with the directory protected:

```
ACLOverRide On
```

2. Change to the directory where you want to install file-level security.

3. Create a file named **.www_acl** in your text editor. If it already exists, you can edit the previously defined security constraints in the existing file.

4. Each line of this file represents the security configuration for a particular file or set of files. The following is the general syntax for the access control list file line:

```
file_specification: METHOD_LIST : group_definition
```

To add protection for a file, add a line to the access control list file. The **file_specification** is the name of a file in the current directory or a wildcard specification matching several local files. The **METHOD_LIST** determines which types of HTTP transactions are permitted. Finally, the **group_definition** is a list of items with the same syntax as either mask parameters or group definitions in group files. The following line allows **GET** method access to all files with the **.htm** file extension by group-list items **dsk** and **them**:

```
*.htm: GET : dsk, them
```

5. You can add additional lines to specify file-level security for additional files.

6. When you have completed your edits, save the file.

How It Works

CERN server file-level security is configured with access control files. These files are located within the directory where the protected files reside. The standard name used by the server package for these files is **.www_acl**.

This file is composed of entry lines, each of which is examined whenever a request is made for a document within the directory. Actually, unless an **ACLOverRide On** directive appears in the directory protection setup, the request transaction must meet the restriction specified with the **mask** directive, if such directives are present. If these directory-level restrictions have been met, the request is then checked against the file-level security in the access control file.

The entries in the access control file are composed of three colon-separated fields. The first field contains the specification of a file to be protected; this specification can potentially contain a wildcard to protect several similarly named files. The second field is a list of HTTP methods that are to be protected for the given file specification. Finally, the last field contains a group definition that has the same syntax as described for **mask** directives and group file entries, described in How-To 13.5.

Having passed the directory-level security, the file specification and request method are matched against entries in the access control list. Unlike the matching of rules in the configuration file, examination does not stop when a matching file specification and method are found, but continues until no more entries are found or a valid entry is found.

For example, given the following access control list file:

```
ping*: GET, POST: jim, alex, @(*.*.auc.edu)
*.htm: GET, POST, PUT: jenny@(*.*.jpl.nasa.gov)
```

a **GET** method request by authenticated user **jenny** on a machine in the ***.*.jpl.nasa.gov** domain for the **pingpong.htm** file would succeed. This is so even though an earlier file specification and method match had been identified, but with a failure for invalid authentication.

For an access control list to be useful, the directory must already be configured in the global configuration file for directory-level security. This is required primarily to establish the password and group files to be used in evaluating group definitions in the access control list file.

Comments

File-level access control requires the definition of directory-level access control within the server's configuration file, through either a **Protect** or a **DefProt** directive for the directory in question. This directory-level specification is necessary to specify the password and group files that must be referenced to verify valid users. If masks are defined in the directory access control, then both the masks as well as the restrictions in the access control list must be met to achieve access.

Inclusion of an **ACLOverRide On** directive in a protection setup for a directory enables a local access control list file to supersede the restriction specified in the setup. In effect, mask directives in the setup are ignored. Overriding the protection setup is a potential security risk and should be weighed by the site administrator before he or she includes the override directive in a protection setup.

13.7 How do I... Install a CERN proxy server?

COMPATIBILITY: CERN HTTP

Problem

For security reasons, my site is running behind an Internet firewall, but behind the firewall we still need access to Internet-based information. Can a CERN HTTP server provide proxy service to the machines within the firewall?

Technique

The CERN HTTP server can act as a proxy server. In fact, the server software can function as both a proxy server and a standard HTTP server at the same time.

To provide proxy service, the server's global configuration file must be set properly. You can specify various aspects of your proxy: what methods are supported, which sites can use your proxy, whether caching occurs, and even whether your proxy server actually uses another proxy server to fulfill requests. After your proxy is running on the firewall machine, requests from inside the firewall are filtered and serviced through the proxy server accessing information outside the confines of the firewall.

Clients also must be configured properly to recognize and use the proxy server. Environment variables must be set to designate a proxy server to use for the various supported Internet protocols. Many popular browsers support proxy access, including Lynx, Mosaic, and Netscape. Tips on configuring particular browsers are provided in the following "How It Works" section.

The following instructions provide an approach to configuring a CERN server to act as a proxy server.

Steps

Do not start the proxy configuration from scratch. The CERN server software comes with several sample configuration files. If you cannot find these files, they are available in the CERN server documentation and can be found at URL `http://www.w3.org/hypertext/WWW/Daemon/User/Config/Examples.html`. You should select the proxy configuration file that does or does not configure caching, whichever you require.

The following steps show you several ways to modify the available example configurations:

1. Change directories to the location of your global server configuration file; this file is usually located in the `config` subdirectory of the server software.

2. Open the configuration file in your text editor. Move your insertion point to the first instance of the **Pass** directive. Modify proxy parameters from this point forward.

3. Often file protocols and FTPs are used interchangeably. For your proxy to support this alias, insert or uncomment the following directive:

```
Map file:* ftp:*
```

4. Selectively comment or uncomment the **Pass** directives for the protocols you want your proxy to support. Comment lines in the configuration file begin with a pound sign (**#**). Configure a **Pass** directive for each protocol you want the proxy to service. For example, the following line supports HTTP protocol proxy support:

```
Pass http:*
```

5. By default, only **GET**, **POST**, and **HEAD** HTTP methods are enabled on your proxy server. To support other methods, issue an appropriate **Enable** directive in your configuration file. For example, to allow **PUT** method requests, add the following line:

```
Enable PUT
```

On the other hand, if you want to restrict already enabled methods, issue a suitable **Disable** directive. For example, the following line disables **POST** method requests on the proxy server:

```
Disable POST
```

6. Use host restrictions to designate particular domains and machines that can use your CERN server as a proxy. Define a protection to limit access according to the instructions in How-To 13.5. This definition must not contain a reference to any password or group files. Furthermore, use the **mask** directive to specify a generic mask for this protection. Finally, do not include references to specific users or groups in the mask you set in the protection setup. After you have created an appropriate protection setup, associate this setup with the particular proxy protocol you want to protect. Use a standard **Protect** directive to configure your host restrictions. For example, the following directive associates the **PROT1** setup with HTTP protocol proxy service:

```
Protect http:* PROT1
```

7. One of the features that a proxy server can provide is the caching of documents retrieved from external sites. This feature provides greater efficiency in situations in which particular outside resources are accessed on a regular basis. Selected directives used to configure a caching proxy server are discussed in the following “How It Works” section. In the configuration of a

caching proxy server, start with the caching proxy configuration file provided through either the CERN distribution directories or the URL **http://www.w3.org/hypertext/WWW/Daemon/User/Config/Examples.html**. If you intend for your server to act as a caching proxy, enable caching by specifying a directory to store cached documents. Use the **CacheRoot** directive for this task. For example, to enable caching with documents stored in the **/usr/local/cache** directory, issue the following directive:

```
CacheRoot /usr/local/cache
```

8. Skip to step 9 if you are not configuring your server to act as an inner proxy server accessing an outer proxy server that provides access to the Internet. To configure your CERN server as an inner proxy server, issue the following directives indicating the URL of the outer proxy server as the parameter of the directives:

```
ftp_proxy http://other.proxy.server.edu/
gopher_proxy http://other.proxy.server.edu/
http_proxy http://other.proxy.server.edu/
wais_proxy http://other.proxy.server.edu/
```

Choose only directives appropriate to the protocols for which you want the outer proxy consulted.

9. Save these changes. Stop and restart the server to see your changes.

How It Works

For security reasons, many businesses and institutions are placing firewall systems between their own internal networks and the rest of the Internet. This provides greater security against a variety of potential problems. However, the downside is that the firewall not only keeps people out, it keeps people in.

A proxy server acts as a bridge between those within the firewall and information residing on the Internet that can be accessed through several popular protocols. Figure 13-4 graphically demonstrates the job of a proxy server. Machines within the firewall, **in1**, **in2**, and **in3**, place HTTP requests with the proxy server running on the machine maintaining the firewall. The proxy server acts as the original requester's agent; it retrieves the desired information from sites outside the protected local network, **out1**, **out2**, **out3**, and **out4**. Then, the proxy passes the retrieved information to the requester.

Many clients support the use of a file proxy, which works the same as an FTP proxy. To support this use of the file proxy, add the line shown in step 3 earlier. This line tells the server to treat all file requests as FTP requests.

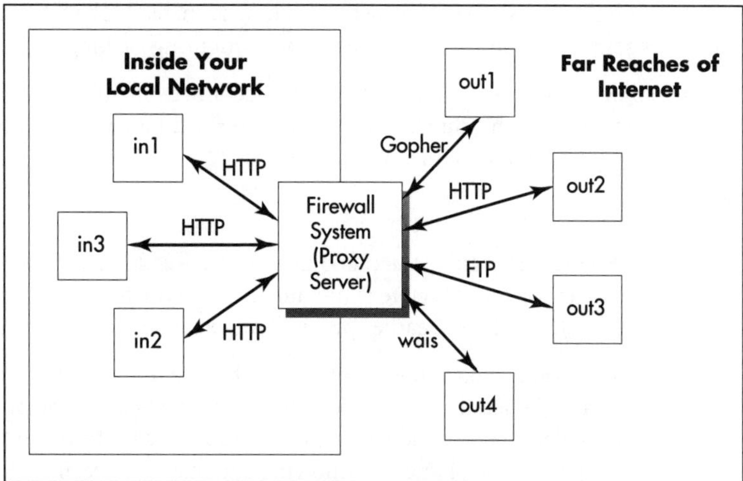

Figure 13-4 Providing proxy service through a firewall

The CERN server can act as a proxy server for a variety of Internet protocol requests. The CERN proxy server can support the following protocols:

- ✔ FTP
- ✔ Gopher
- ✔ HTTP
- ✔ News
- ✔ WAIS

Use a **Pass** directive, as described in step 4, to allow proxy access to any of these services.

You can configure the CERN proxy server to restrict access to particular proxy services. These restrictions are limited to host filtering. To establish this type of protection for a particular type of service, issue a **Protect** directive to associate a previously defined protection setup with a particular service. Step 6 includes an example of associating a protection setup with HTTP proxy service.

Caching enables a proxy server to retain documents retrieved beyond a single request. When caching is enabled, a proxy client requests a document from the proxy, and the proxy retrieves the file from the appropriate site as usual. Then, instead of just passing the document back to the requesting client, the proxy server also retains a copy of the document for possible future use.

You enable caching, either explicitly by issuing a **Caching** directive or implicitly by specifying a cache directory using the **CacheRoot** directive. Because a cache directory is necessary for caching documents, use of this directive serves as sufficient indication to the software that caching is enabled. The following list summarizes some of the directives available for configuring caching:

- ✔ `Caching`: Use this directive to enable caching explicitly. The two valid parameters of this directive are `On` and `Off`. Add the following line to your configuration file to turn on caching:

```
Caching On
```

- ✔ `CacheRoot`: Designate the cache directory using this directive. The single parameter for this directive is the directory in which you want cached documents stored. Step 7 earlier provides an example of this directive.

- ✔ `CacheSize`: Establish the maximum cache size in megabytes with this command. When the size of the cache reaches this limit, the proxy server begins deleting older and larger cached documents. The default size is 5MB. For example, issue the following command to specify a 40MB cache:

```
CacheSize 40 M
```

- ✔ `CacheUnused`: Use this directive to specify how long unused cached files stay in the cache. Multiple instances of this directive specify the time limit for different types of cached documents. If a document matches several of these directives, then the last `CacheUnused` directive appearing in the configuration file and matching the document applies. For example, if the following set of `CacheUnused` directives appears in the configuration file, the document `ftp://www.mysite.edu/README` remains in the cache seven days rather than four and a half days:

```
CacheUnused *                          4 days 12 hours
CacheUnused ftp:*                      5 days
CacheUnused ftp://www.mysite.edu/*    7 days
```

URL `http://www.w3.org/hypertext/WWW/Daemon/User/Config` provides information on additional directives for more fine-tuned control of proxy server caching.

A CERN proxy server can also act as client with reference to another proxy server. Step 8 earlier provides information on configuring this feature. This situation arises from a potential need to pass multiple levels of firewalls or to create multiple levels of document caches.

In the first case, security concerns lead to the creation of multiple levels of firewalls to protect more sensitive areas of the local network better. Examine Figure 13-4 again; picture `in1` not as a machine, but as a subnet protected by a firewall, with an inner proxy used by the systems inside the subnet to access both the machines in the local network and the outer proxy, which in turn can access the rest of the Internet.

In the second case, efficiency concerns lead to the creation of multiple levels of caching proxies. By caching often-used documents, the proxy server obviates the need to retrieve the document at each use; the proxy sends the previously retrieved copy to service new requests. Multiple levels of caches provide a storage hierarchy supporting the retention of the most frequently used documents at the closest location, and they provide a means of establishing priority of retained documents. The outer proxy has one set of criteria for retaining documents, whereas the inner proxy has a more specific set of criteria based on the requirements of clients serviced by the inner proxy. In this way, the outer proxy caches documents frequently accessed by all its clients, whereas the inner proxy provides access to documents cached in its own cache as well as those in the outer proxy's cache.

Comments

The steps provided above do not try to describe the entire server configuration process; they deal solely with the configuration of the proxy server. You should consult the CERN server documentation for instructions on adding or modifying appropriate directives within the configuration file. Online information is available at URL `http://www.w3.org/hypertext/WWW/Daemon/User/Config/`.

When configuring a proxy server, you must not try to establish user authentication on proxy services. The only security that functions properly for proxy service is host filtering.

A CERN server can act as both proxy server and HTTP server at the same time. To configure your server to perform in this way, configure your server as you would for a standard HTTP server, and then continue with the procedure defined in this How-To.

The latest release of the Apache Web server contains an experimental module that provides support for proxy service. See `http://www.apache.org/docs/1.1/mod_proxy.html` for additional information on installing and configuring an Apache server as a proxy server.

Browsers behind a firewall must also be configured for use with proxies. Netscape Navigator provides a dialog box from the Preferences menu that enables you to perform this configuration task. Figure 13-5 displays this dialog box.

Using this dialog box, specify the hostnames for the machines that serve as proxies for the desired protocol. The No Proxy portion of the dialog box enables the specification of Internet domains accessible directly without requiring a proxy.

Configuring other browsers to deal with proxies usually involves setting environment variables. Browsers such as Mosaic and Lynx use environment variables to set this information. In UNIX and VMS, the following environment variables configure the protocol-specific proxies:

- ✔ `ftp_proxy`
- ✔ `gopher_proxy`
- ✔ `http_proxy`
- ✔ `news_proxy`
- ✔ `wais_proxy`

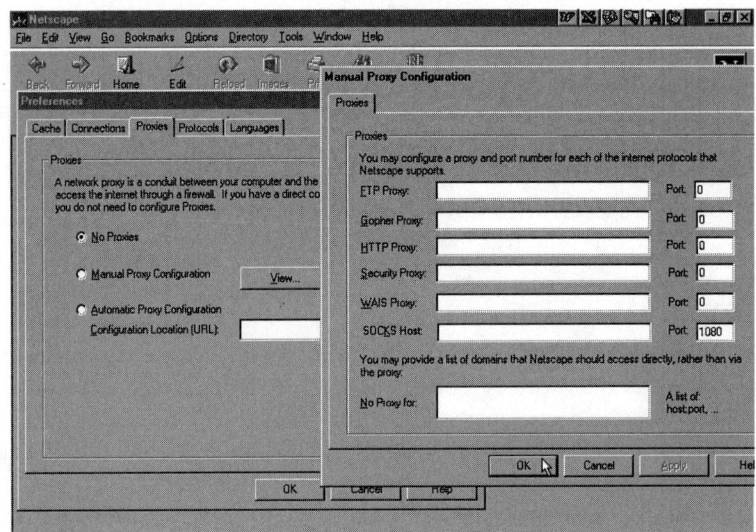

Figure 13-5 Configuring proxy service with Netscape Navigator

For example, to configure UNIX Mosaic to access **proxy.mysite.edu** for HTTP requests, issue the following C shell command before running Mosaic:

```
setenv http_proxy "http://proxy.mysite.edu/"
```

Consult the relevant portions of your browser documentation for other browsers.

COMPLEXITY
INTERMEDIATE

13.8 How do I... Establish domain and address security and password authentication on MacHTTP and WebSTAR servers?

COMPATIBILITY: MACHTTP, WEBSTAR

Problem

I want to allow and deny access to my server, MacHTTP or WebSTAR, based on the machine or network a user is trying to access from. I would also like to require passwords for certain documents and directories on my server. How can I do this?

Technique

You can restrict access to your server based on the user's machine name, domain name, or IP address by editing the **MacHTTP.config** file for your server. Two command keywords, **ALLOW** and **DENY**, enable you to limit the machines and networks that have access to your server.

User authentication handles file-level and directory-level security. User authentication is based on the notion of realms. A realm is a group of files or folders that contain a common substring in their names. A realm is specified in the **MacHTTP.config** file using the keyword **REALM**. The **REALM** keyword is followed by a name substring and a description. The specified substring is unique to all the names of the protected files or their parent directories. The description is effectively the name of the realm. No blank spaces are allowed in the realm name. (The entire description must be a contiguous string of characters.)

The following procedures show how to add server-wide host filtering and file-level and folder-level user authentication.

Steps

The first procedure here outlines the steps necessary to establish host filtering on your MacHTTP or WebSTAR server. These instructions are immediately followed by the process for installing user authentication at the file and folder levels. In both cases, make the necessary modifications to the **MacHTTP.config** file.

Host Filtering

The following procedure describes the necessary steps for configuring host filtering on your server. Host filtering works across all documents on your server.

1. Open the **MacHTTP.config** file in your text editor.

2. For each machine or network domain that you want to allow on your server, issue an **ALLOW** directive. The parameters of the **ALLOW** command are either names or appropriate IP addresses. For example, to allow access to the server from machine **foo.bar.com**, add the following directive:

```
ALLOW foo.bar.com.
```

Or to allow access to the server from all machines in the **bozo.net** network, add the following directive:

```
ALLOW bozo.net.
```

3. For each machine or network domain that you want to prevent from accessing your server, issue a **DENY** directive. The parameters of the **DENY** commands are either names or appropriate IP addresses. For example, to deny access to the server from machine **foo.bar.com**, add the following directive:

```
DENY foo.bar.com.
```

Or to deny access to the server from all machines in the **bozo.net** network, add the following directive:

```
DENY bozo.net.
```

4. Save this file and restart your server.

User Authentication and Password Creation

User authentication provides file-level and directory-level security on MacHTTP and WebSTAR servers. The following process describes the two components necessary to configure user authentication. The first component of configuration is the specification of files to be protected. The second is the specification of usernames and passwords that allow access to protected files.

1. Open the **MacHTTP.config** file in your text editor.

2. For each set of files or folders you want to protect, issue a **REALM** directive. The **REALM** command requires two parameters: a string that defines which files are in the realm and a description that serves as the name of the realm. For example, to create the realm **round** protecting files containing the string **cam** in their path, issue the following **REALM** directive:

```
REALM cam round
```

3. Save this file and restart your server.

4. Add users by selecting the Passwords interface found at the bottom of the Edit pull-down menu.

5. Select the realm you want this user to have access to in the pull-down menu found at the bottom of the Passwords interface. (All realms that have been declared in the **config** file should show up here.)

6. Enter a username and a password with which this user will access protected files in this realm.

7. If you want this user to have access to multiple realms, repeat steps 5 and 6 for every realm that you want to allow this user to access.

8. Exit this dialog box.

How It Works

MacHTTP and WebSTAR provide both host filtering and user authentication security. The host filtering facilities let machines and domains, specified by name or IP address, be allowed or denied access to the server as a whole. User authentication provides finer-tuned security by requiring a username and password to access any files or folders containing a specified string in their path.

Host filtering uses the **ALLOW** and **DENY** commands to specify access restrictions. The **ALLOW** and **DENY** keywords are followed by an explicit machine name followed by a period, or a substring of the machine or domain name without a period, specifying that every access from a machine or network that contains that substring should be either allowed or denied access. You specify machines and domains by either name or IP address.

For example, to allow access to all machines whose IP addresses start with **128.122.1**, and to deny access to all machines in the **bar.com** domain, enter the following statements:

```
ALLOW 128.122.1
DENY bar.com.
```

Notice that the **bar.com** entry is followed by a period. All domain names are case sensitive and must be followed by a period. Also notice that the IP address is not followed by a period. This allows machines with IP addresses starting with **128.122.1** to access the server; this specification includes machines such as **128.122.12.7**, **128.122.1.1**, and **128.122.193.74**. If you want to be specific, append a period to the end of the IP address. For example, to allow access from only the machine with IP address **128.122.1.1**, issue the following directive:

```
ALLOW 128.122.1.1.
```

MacHTTP and WebSTAR assume that you will specifically deny and allow all machines if you use the **DENY** or **ALLOW** statements. That is, there is an implicit **DENY** for all machines if you use the **ALLOW** command. This means that, if you want to allow access from all machines with the exception of a machine called, say **whoopy.fun.gov**, you must allow all machines before denying this last one with the following statements:

```
ALLOW 1
ALLOW 2
ALLOW 3
ALLOW 4
ALLOW 5
ALLOW 6
ALLOW 7
ALLOW 8
ALLOW 9

DENY whoopy.fun.gov.
```

Notice that there are no periods following the numbers. This means that any machines whose IP addresses start with the numbers 1 through 9 will be allowed access, with the exception of **whoopy.fun.gov**, which is specifically denied access.

In a similar fashion, if you want to deny access from all machines except machines in the **spew.org** domain, but you also want to deny access from one machine within this domain called **pooky**, you could take advantage of the explicit **DENY** and use the following statements:

```
ALLOW spew.org.
DENY pooky.spew.org.
```

MacHTTP and WebSTAR's user authentication facilities support security at the file and folder levels. Use the `REALM` directive to specify the protected files and folders. This command takes two parameters: a name substring and a description. The name substring determines which files are protected. The description serves as the name of the protected realm. (The description must not contain blank spaces.)

For example, to create a realm called `My_Friends` that controls all files and directories whose names contain the string `friend`, enter the following statement in your `config` file:

```
REALM friend My_Friends
```

Now you could create a folder on your server called `friend`, `friends`, `my_friend23`, or any other legal filename that contains the string `friend`. Only users associated with the `My_Friends` realm could access the files in this folder. Likewise, if you had a file on your server called `cool_friends.html`, this file would also be governed by the `My_Friends` realm.

Similarly, if you wanted to create realms for `Trusted_Users`, `Officers`, `Presidents`, and `Riff_Raff`, you could declare the following realms:

```
REALM trust     Trusted_Users
REALM office    Officers
REALM pres      Presidents
REALM rifraf    Riff_Raff
```

Any files that contained `trust` somewhere in their URL would be governed by the `Trusted_Users` realm; likewise, any URL on this server containing `office` would fall under `Officers`, a URL containing `pres` would fall under `Presidents`, and so on.

After you have set up your realms, you must create usernames and passwords for people who will be able to access these documents. This is a relatively easy task that can be done using the Passwords interface found at the bottom of the Edit pull-down menu when your MacHTTP or WebSTAR server is running. Figure 13-6 displays the dialog box you see when selecting this option on a MacHTTP server.

A user can be removed from a realm using this same interface. The interface lists the entries as `Username Realm`, so delete the entry for the realm(s) that you no longer want this user to access.

Comments

MacHTTP and WebSTAR's security features are similar to the features found in NCSA's HTTPD and the CERN server, if somewhat crude in comparison. MacHTTP and WebSTAR do not let you allow and deny machines and networks on a per-directory level as the NCSA server does. But user authentication is easy to set up and administer, and it provides an adequate level of security for most installations.

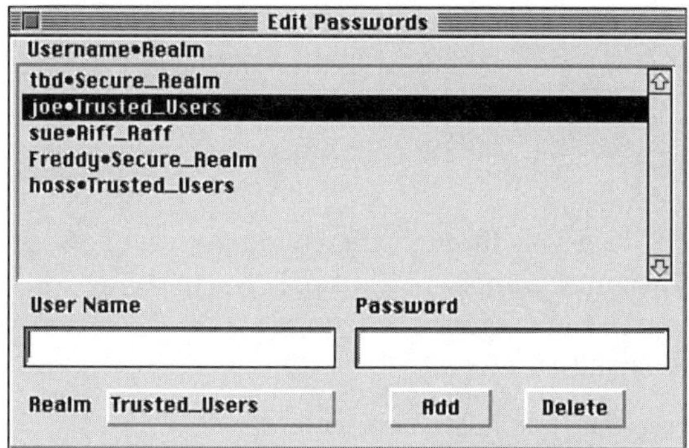

Figure 13-6 MacHTTP passwords interface

COMPLEXITY
INTERMEDIATE

13.9 How do I... Configure SSL security on a FastTrack server?

COMPATIBILITY: NETSCAPE FASTTRACK SERVER

Problem

Standard HTTP transmits information over the Internet in the clear. This method is vulnerable to interception by anyone with the proper know-how and access. I want to encrypt my HTTP transmissions. How do I configure this security using my Netscape FastTrack server?

Technique

The Netscape FastTrack server provides several levels of access security. The administration server provides the interface for configuring this security information.

The FastTrack server supports the following types of server security:

- ✔ SSL (Secure Sockets Layer): SSL provides encryption of the communications between the FastTrack server and SSL-compatible browsers.
- ✔ User and group access restrictions: User and group restrictions provide restricted access to specified users.
- ✔ Host machine and domain restrictions: This security measure restricts or allows access to or from particular Internet machines or domains.

These three levels of security provide an effective means of limiting access to restricted documents on your FastTrack server. The SSL level applies to the server as a whole;

user and group restrictions and host and domain restrictions apply on a per-directory or per-file basis. See How-To 13.10 for information on configuring username/password or domain restrictions on your FastTrack server.

Steps

The following steps lead you through the configuration of SSL security on a FastTrack server. This process applies only if you plan to register your server with a third-party certification authority such as Verisign (`http://www.verisign.com`); this process entails paying a fee.

1. Access the FastTrack administration server.

2. Select the server that you want to configure for SSL. The server's administration page should appear.

3. Select the Encryption option from the top frame menu. If you have generated a key pair, proceed with step 6.

4. Access the Generate Key option of the left frame menu. Follow the procedure outlined in the Netscape Info window, as displayed in Figure 13-7.

5. Enter the relative path of the key pair generated in step 4 in the `Key File Path` field of the Generate a Key Pair. Select OK, and from the confirmation screen, select the Save and Apply button.

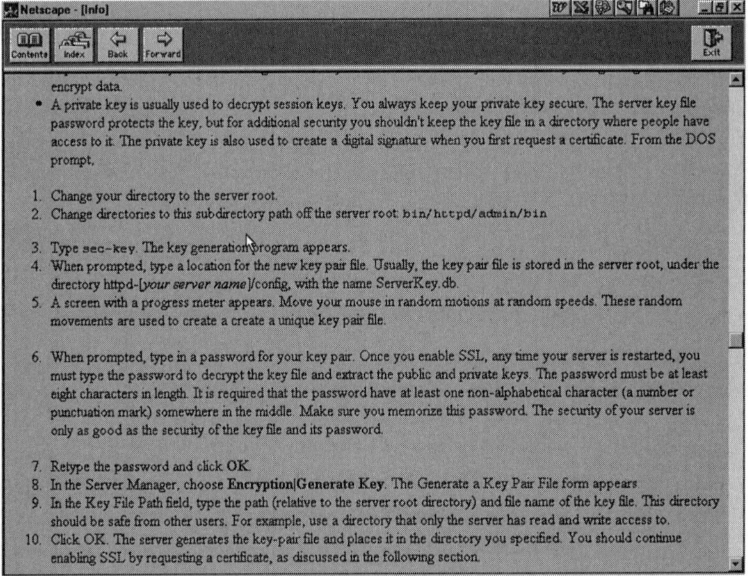

Figure 13-7 Netscape info for generating a key pair

6. Select the Request Certificate option from the left frame menu. If you have already requested a certificate, proceed to step 8.

7. Fill out the form provided in the right frame. The information entered is sent to the e-mail address of the Certificate Authority (CA) that you specified in the form. (See `http://www.verisign.com` for additional information on certificates.)

8. Install the certificate that you receive from your CA, using the Install Certificate option from the left frame menu.

9. Enable SSL from the Encryption On/Off form, using the On/Off option from the left frame menu. This form also allows the selection of port numbers for SSL communications. The default port for such communications is 443, just as the default port for standard Web servers is 80. Make your changes and then click the OK button.

10. Select Save and Apply for your changes to take effect.

How It Works

FastTrack supports encrypted communications channels between browsers and servers. The server uses SSL as the mechanism for supporting this communication. To differentiate this protocol from standard HTTP, URLs requested via a secure channel use HTTPS. (For more information on the standard HTTP communications process, see Appendix G, "HTML Hypertext Transfer Protocol (HTTP).") When a browser requests a secure channel from the server, the following conversation occurs:

- ✔ Connection: The browser successfully connects to the server via HTTPS.
- ✔ Server certificate response: The server responds with its digital certificate.
- ✔ Server certificate verification: The browser confirms the certificate with a third-party CA. If the certificate is not trustworthy, the browser can either reject the connection or warn the user about the situation.
- ✔ Master key generation and transmission: The browser uses the server's public key and a random number to generate a master key. The browser sends this key to the server.
- ✔ Master key decryption: The server uses its private key to decrypt the master key.
- ✔ Session key generation: The server and browser generate session keys using the master key.
- ✔ Encrypted transmissions: All further communications between the browser and server use the session key for encryption.

For this process to work, the server must have a digital certificate installed. Preferably, a recognized CA has signed this server certificate. FastTrack supports the acquisition and installation of signed digital certificates through the administration server.

The initial generation of a key pair occurs through a DOS window. The FastTrack distribution provides the sec-key program to generate the initial key pair. The process uses the motion of the mouse to generate a random number that is incorporated into the key pair. The program stores the key pair in the file requested at the outset. This filename should be entered into the Generate a Key Pair configuration form of the server so that the server knows where the keys are installed, as seen in Figure 13-8.

After you generate the key pair, you must request a certificate from a CA. The FastTrack server provides a form to facilitate the certificate request process, as shown in Figure 13-9. Verisign (`http://www.verisign.com`) is one of the most popular CAs. You must enter the e-mail address for a CA so that the administration server knows where to send the request. The CA will return a certificate to you via e-mail. The CA will usually charge a renewable fee for supplying its service. To install the certificate, enter the appropriate information in the Certificate Installation form of the administration server, as displayed in Figure 13-10.Enable SSL communications by turning on this feature in the Encryption On/Off form, as seen in Figure 13-11. You might also want to specify the port over which the server should listen for HTTPS requests; the default port is 443. Selecting any other port will require that users specify the port when requesting a document. After you have enabled SSL, you must save and apply the changes for them to take effect.

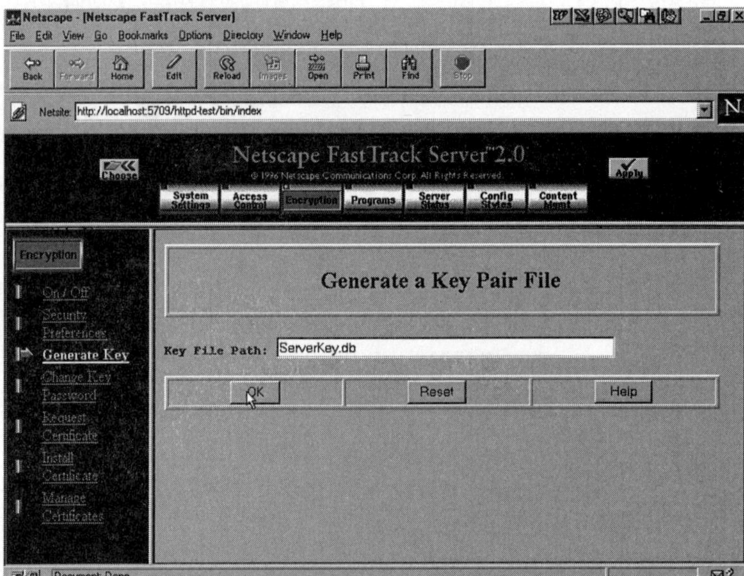

Figure 13-8 Generate a Key Pair configuration form

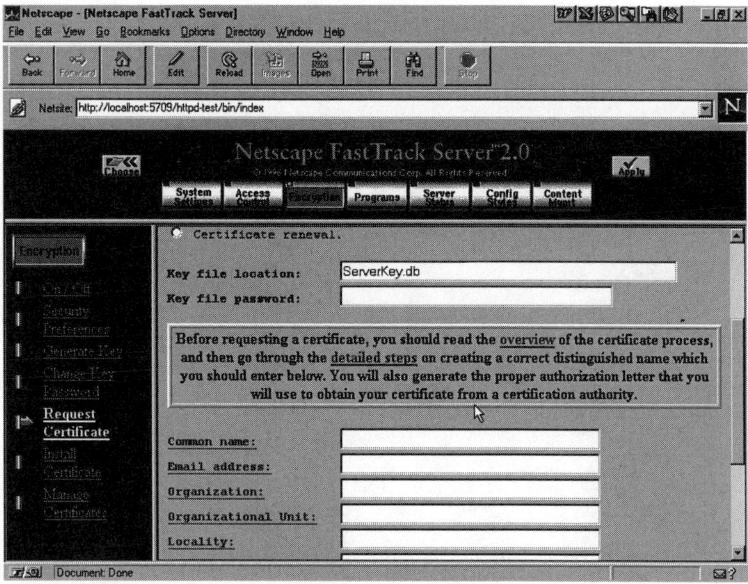

Figure 13-9 Requesting a certificate

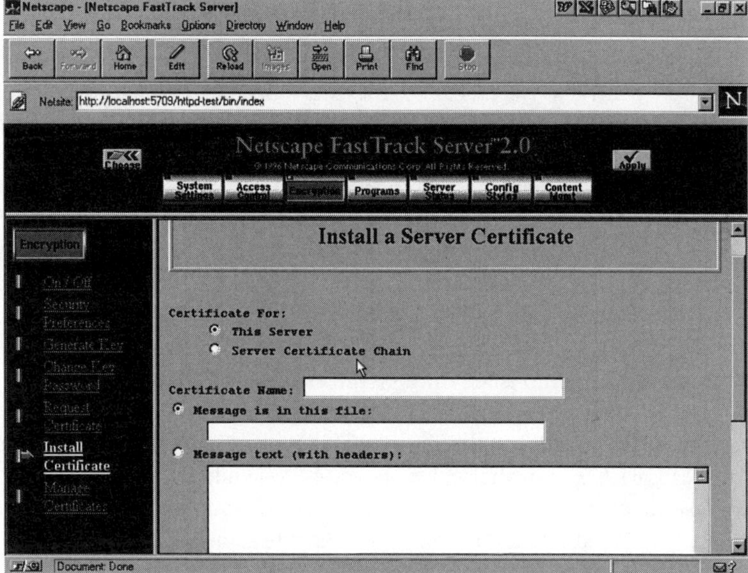

Figure 13-10 Installing a certificate

Figure 13-11 Encryption On/Off form

Comments

Configuring SSL does not require the configuration of user and group or host restrictions. (See How-To 13.10.) Using SSL alone provides secure communications channels between browsers and your server. Therefore, all transmissions over the secure channel will be encrypted. In this manner, you can protect the integrity of information sent from your server against prying eyes with access to the Internet packet communications. Viewers of information from your server know that the information originated from your server and that any attempt to insert substitute packets into the information stream will fail because an intruder will not have access to the proper session key.

In addition to the administration server interface, aspects of security configuration can be accomplished through direct editing of the proper server configuration file(s), usually **`obj.conf`**. See the online documentation for the FastTrack server for detailed information on this process. This method is not recommended for the novice or causal site administrator. Unless you have significant experience in the syntax for FastTrack server configuration files, or previous experience with configuring HTTPD-based or CERN servers, the benefits gained over using the administration server do not generally rise above the cost of the learning curve.

COMPLEXITY
INTERMEDIATE

13.10 How do I... Set up user and password security on a FastTrack server?

COMPATIBILITY: NETSCAPE FASTTRACK SERVER

Problem

Certain areas of my server contain sensitive information that I want available through my server; however, I want some control over who accesses these documents. Different documents on my server require different levels of access security. How do I configure this security using my Netscape FastTrack server?

Technique

The Netscape FastTrack server provides several levels of access security. The administration server provides the interface for configuring this security information.

The FastTrack server supports the following types of server security:

- ✔ SSL (Secure Sockets Layer): SSL provides encryption of the communications between the FastTrack server and SSL-compatible browsers. (See How-To 13.9.)
- ✔ User and group access restrictions: User and group restrictions provide restricted access to specified users.
- ✔ Host machine and domain restrictions: This security measure restricts or allows access to or from particular Internet machines or domains.

These three levels of security provide an effective means of limiting access to restricted documents on your FastTrack server. User and group restrictions and host and domain restrictions enable you to restrict access to your server on a per-directory or per-file basis.

Steps

The following sets of steps lead you through the configuration of username/password and domain security on a FastTrack server. This process steps you through the tasks of user management, group management, and restriction of particular documents based on users or groups or based on the Internet machine or domain.

User and Password Management

1. Access the FastTrack administration server.
2. Select the server that you want to configure for server-side includes. The server's administration page should appear.
3. Select the Access Control option from the top frame menu.
4. If you want to modify an existing user database, proceed to step 5. Otherwise, you must create a new database by selecting the Manage User Databases option from the left frame menu. The right frame that appears enables you to create or remove a user database.
5. Select the particular option from the left frame menu applicable to the task you want to perform. FastTrack supports the following permissible tasks:

   Create user: Create a new user with an associated password in a particular user database.

   Remove user: Select an existing user to remove from a particular user database.

   List users: Display the users in a particular user database.

   Edit user: Edit information concerning a specified user.
6. Fill out the forms associated with specific tasks, making sure to select the particular database(s) you want to affect.
7. Select OK to process the form information.

Group Management

1. Access the FastTrack administration server.
2. Select the server that you want to configure for server-side includes. The server's administration page should appear.
3. Select the Access Control option from the top frame menu.
4. If you want to modify an existing user database, proceed to step 5. Otherwise, you must create a new database by selecting the Manage User Databases option from the left frame menu. The right frame that appears enables you to create or remove a user database.
5. Select the particular option from the left frame menu applicable to the task you want to perform. FastTrack supports the following permissible tasks:

   Create group: Create a new group in a particular user database.

   Remove group: Select an existing group to remove from a particular user database.

   List group: Display the groups in a particular user database.

   Edit group: Edit the users and groups contained within a specified group.

6. Fill out the forms associated with specific tasks, making sure to select the particular database(s) you want to affect.
7. Select OK to process the form information.
8. Depending upon the task accomplished, you might have to select Save and Apply to affect the changes that you have entered.

Application of Restrictions

1. Access the FastTrack administration server.
2. Select the server that you want to configure for server-side includes. The server's administration page should appear.
3. Select the Access Control option from the top frame menu.
4. Select the Restrict Access option from the left frame menu.
5. Select the directories or files for which you want to enable access controls. You can select an existing pattern from the menu, browse the document directory, or specify a wildcard pattern.
6. Click the Turn On Access Control button. Additional options will become available in the right frame configuration form.
7. Choose the default accessibility of the chosen location, directories or files. The defaults may be set for both reads and writes to the specified location. The default accessibilities are `allow` or `deny`. Selecting `deny` denies all attempts to access the location; selecting `allow` allows all attempts to access the location.
8. Select the Edit Permissions button to restrict the defaults chosen.
9. Select the domain and host restrictions that you want established for the location.
10. If the default chosen is `deny`, select the user and groups allowed to access the location.
11. Select the Done button when you have finished entering information.
12. When you return to the Restrict Access form, select the OK button.
13. Select the Save and Apply button to affect the changes that you have made. The administration server makes appropriate changes to the configuration files, and then stops and restarts the server.

How It Works

User and Group Management

The first stage in establishing user or group restrictions for your server is to create the database of users who will be able to access the various parts of your server. How you organize these users will depend on your particular needs. FastTrack provides several levels of user data organization. The highest level of organization is the user database. Within a particular database, groups serve as a collection mechanism. Furthermore, not only do groups organize users, they can also organize other groups. These levels of organization are not necessary for the establishment of user restrictions; however, they ease the configuration of restrictions for blocks of users.

From an organizational standpoint, you might want to create distinct user databases for different divisions of users. All FastTrack servers running on the same host share access to all user databases created. Databases serve as the unit of user information, transportable to servers running on different host machines. If each division of a company runs its own internal server with a database of users, a company might incorporate each division's database to restrict access to the company's overall Web server. The server administration page of a particular server allows the creation of new databases through the Access Control|Manage User Databases options, as shown in Figure 13-12. User databases store both user and group information.

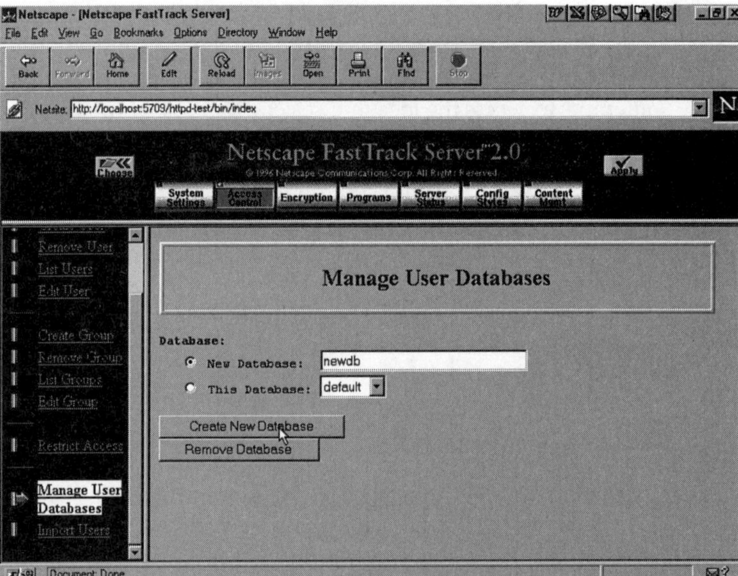

Figure 13-12 Managing user databases

Each user to whom you want to give access to a particular portion of the Web server requires an entry in a user database accessible to that server. The administration server provides several options for maintaining information in user databases:

✔ Create User: This option allows the creation of a new user within a specified user database. Figure 13-13 shows the administration server interface to this function. The database stores the username, real name, and password for the user. The user enters the specified username and password whenever accessing documents on the server, subject to this user entry.

✔ Remove User: This option removes a user from a specified database. The entry form requires the specification of the user name of the entry to remove and the menu selection of the database from which to make the removal.

✔ List Users: Initially, this option displays the usernames of all users in the currently selected database without any filtering of the usernames. When the interface appears, however, you may select a different database and provide a wildcard pattern limiting the search of usernames. Pressing the Show Users button displays the users, subject to the entered specifications.

✔ Edit User: The Edit User option allows the alteration of the data associated with a particular username so you can accomplish real name and password changes for a particular username through the provided form.

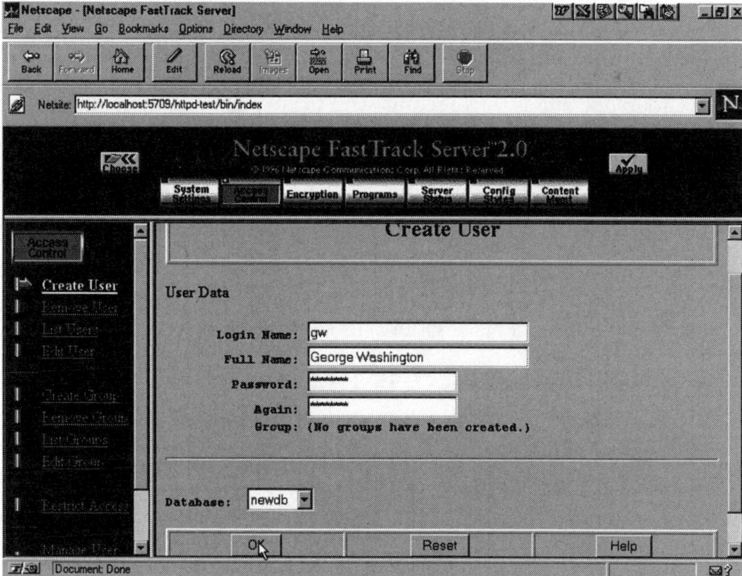

Figure 13-13 Creating a new user

Organize users, also previously created groups, within the context of a particular database. Groups provide a convenient mechanism for specifying blocks of users with similar access privileges. As with the user management functions, the administration server provides several form interfaces for group creation and management:

- ✔ Create Group: This option provides support for the creation of a new group. The interface provided by the administration server requires the selection of a database, the specification of a group name, and the selection of a parent group. If the new group is part of an existing group, you must select this existing group as the parent; otherwise, select NONE as the parent group. Figure 13-14 displays this interface.
- ✔ Remove Group: This option enables you to remove an existing group from a particular database. You must select the database and select the group that you want to remove. Selecting OK processes this selection.
- ✔ List Group: This option provides a list of all groups existing within the selected database. As with the list user option discussed under user management, the interface allows the selection of a database and the specification of a wildcard filter. This information constrains the search when you press the List Groups button.
- ✔ Edit Group: When a group exists, the Edit Group option supports the selection of users and groups that make up the selected group. The interface provides a selection list of users and other groups in the selected database. The highlighted items in the group and user selection lists are those groups and users that are, or are intended to be, part of the selected group. Figure 13-15 displays an example of this screen.

Group operations might require you to alter configuration information. Therefore, to effect such changes, the server might need to be stopped and restarted. If this is the case, the administration server will generally follow the configuration screen with a Save and Apply screen that automatically performs the requisite stop and restart. You can manually stop and restart the server using the procedures outlined in How-To 12.8.

After the necessary databases, users, and groups are created, you establish access privileges for users or groups through the Access Control|Restrict Access option.

Application of Access Restrictions

The FastTrack server enables the specification of user or group restrictions and host or domain access restrictions. The administration server provides the means for enabling both these security features. Figure 13-16 displays the Restrict Access form presented by the administration server. In this form, you enter the location(s) for which you want to enable access controls, and then you turn on or off the access controls as appropriate. If access controls are enabled, the form also lets you specify the default access modes for read and write operations to the specified location(s). In addition, you can specify an alternative message for when an unauthorized user attempts to access a protected document.

Figure 13-14 Creating a new group

Figure 13-15 Editing a group's members

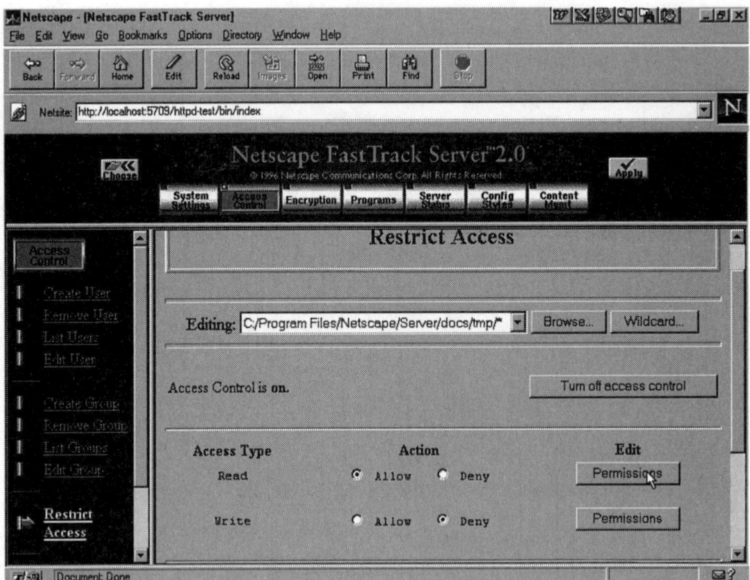

Figure 13-16 Applying access restrictions

The Permissions button appears next to the default access mode for reading and writing. The selection of this button enables the configuration of exceptions to the default access mode indicated. The form that appears depends on the default chosen. If the `allow` default is selected, the form appearing allows the specification of host machine and Internet domains that should be denied access; this configuration form appears in Figure 13-17. If the **deny** default is selected, the form appearing allows the specification of host machine and Internet domains that should be allowed access, as well as specific users and groups allowed access when making requests from specific machines; Figure 13-18 displays this configuration form. In either case, select the Done button after you enter all desired information.

Selecting the Done button returns you to the Restrict Access form. At this point, you are not completely finished: You will must stop and restart the server to effect your changes. The easiest way to do this is to select the OK button at the bottom of the Restrict Access form. This triggers the appearance of the familiar Save and Apply form, seen in Figure 13-19. Selecting the Save and Apply button automatically performs all the necessary steps to effect the specified change. If you are making other changes, you can select the Save button; and then after all configuration changes are done, select the Apply button from the top menu frame of the administration server.

Netscape - [Resource Access Control]
File Edit View Go Bookmarks Options Directory Window Help
Back Forward Home Edit Reload Images Open Print Find Stop
Netsite: http://localhost:5709/httpd-test/bin/accdeny?access_type=read&acl_name=httpd-test_formgen-READ-ACL_allow-1106
What's New? What's Cool? Destinations Net Search People Software
Deny Access to a Resource
Resource: C:/Program Files/Netscape/Server/docs/tmp/*
Access Method: Read
Hostname Processing
Include specified names only
Include aliases of specified names
Hosts Always Denied Access:
Hostnames: *.ncsa.uiuc.edu
IP Addresses:
Be sure to click OK in the Restrict Access window to make these changes!
Done
Cancel
Help
Document: Done

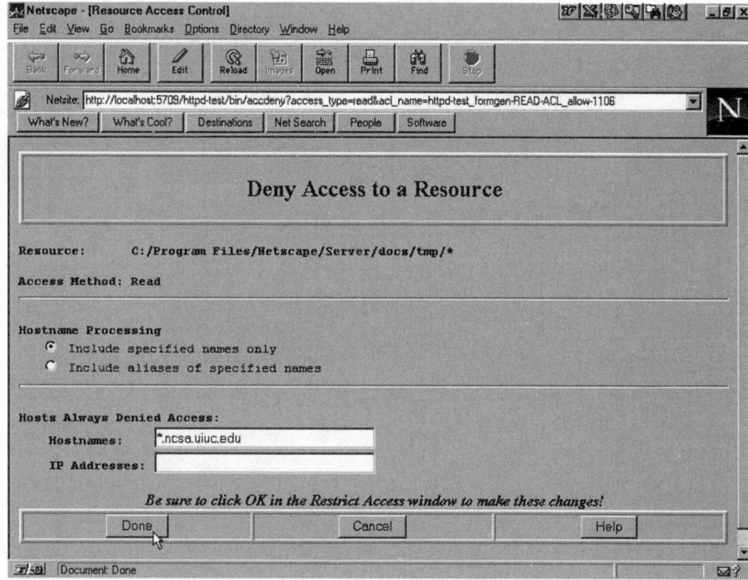

Figure 13-17 Editing `allow` permissions

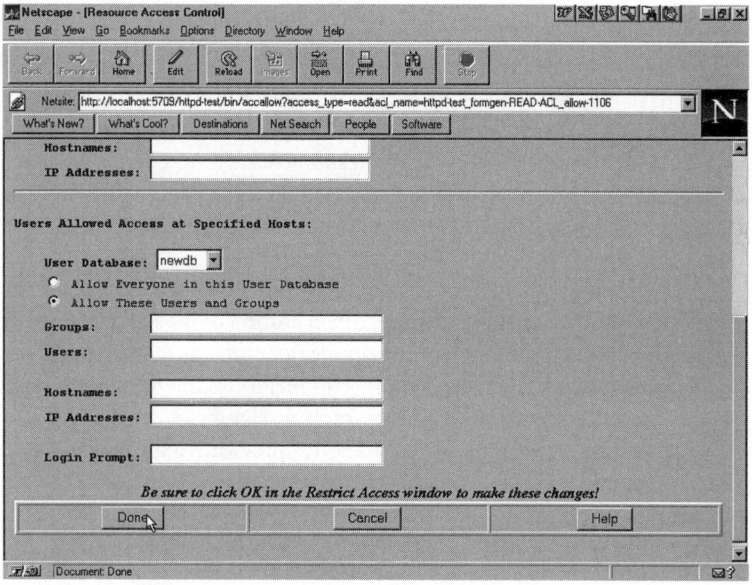

Netscape - [Resource Access Control]
File Edit View Go Bookmarks Options Directory Window Help
Back Forward Home Edit Reload Images Open Print Find Stop
Netsite: http://localhost:5709/httpd-test/bin/accallow?access_type=read&acl_name=httpd-test_formgen-READ-ACL_allow-1106
What's New? What's Cool? Destinations Net Search People Software
Hostnames:
IP Addresses:
Users Allowed Access at Specified Hosts:
User Database: newdb
Allow Everyone in this User Database
Allow These Users and Groups
Groups:
Users:
Hostnames:
IP Addresses:
Login Prompt:
Be sure to click OK in the Restrict Access window to make these changes!
Done
Cancel
Help
Document: Done

Figure 13-18 Editing `deny` permissions

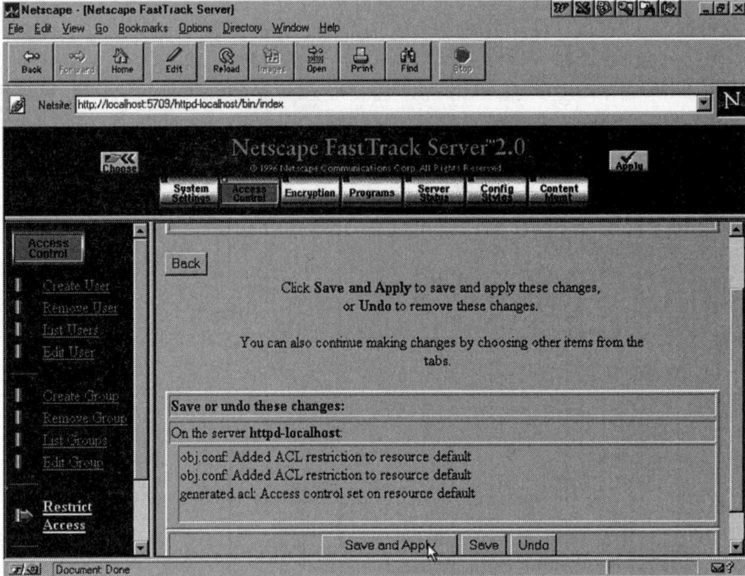

Figure 13-19 Saving and applying the changes

Comments

You can configure and use user and group or host restrictions regardless of whether you have enabled SSL. Without SSL, however, usernames and passwords get sent over an unencrypted communications channel. This is the common situation for most servers supporting the Basic authentication package. You derive the best security from use of both mechanisms; however, based on the sensitivity of information on your server and the cost, you might want to use just the username and group restriction mechanism.

In addition to the administration server interface, aspects of security configuration can be accomplished through direct editing of the proper server configuration file(s), usually **obj.conf**. See the online documentation of the FastTrack server for detailed information on this process. This method is not recommended for the novice or causal site administrator. Unless you have significant experience in the syntax for FastTrack server configuration files, or previous experience with configuring HTTPD-based or CERN servers, the benefits gained over use of the administration server do not generally rise above the cost of the learning curve.

COMPLEXITY
INTERMEDIATE

13.11 How do I... Use public key encryption?

COMPATIBILITY: PUBLIC KEY ENCRYPTION-CAPABLE SERVER AND BROWSER

Problem

I have confidential documents that I want to provide to select users in a secure fashion. The Basic authentication scheme will not suffice because under this scheme, servers transmit documents and browsers send requests in the open. Consequently, unauthorized individuals monitoring the network traffic might view my confidential pages.

Technique

Servers and browsers use encryption on documents and requests before transmission over an open connection. The recipient decrypts the transmission before presenting the document or servicing the request. Thus, diverting or examining transmissions yields only an encrypted transmission.

Steps

For a browser or server that has built-in encryption capabilities, the actual encryption process should be transparent and not require any additional work on your part. The only exception to this might be a requirement to acquire a certification of authenticity transported by a secure means, such as Secure Sockets Layer (SSL) or SHTTP (Secure HTTP). (See **http://www.verisign.com/netscape/index.html** and How-To 13.9 for additional information on receiving and using a digital ID with a Netscape FastTrack server.)

For browsers and servers requiring plug-in components, installation and configuration will vary. The following steps provide a generic approach for finding the appropriate encryption software.

1. Determine the type of public key encryption software necessary for you to communicate. Table 13-9 specifies the common public key encryption software.

Table 13-9 Common public key encryption software

ENCRYPTION SOFTWARE	LOCATION
PGP	http://www.efh.org/pgp/pgpwork.html
RIPEM	http://www.cs.indiana.edu/ripem/dir.html

2. Download a software package suitable for your hardware and software platform. Source and executable code for these packages can be accessed through the references provided in Table 13-9.

3. Examine the manual for the software package to determine how to generate, maintain, and publish public keys.

4. Configure your browser and server to call the plug-in package when receiving an encrypted transmission.

Configuring an NCSA HTTPD Server with PGP/PEM Hooks

The following procedure provides an approach for configuring an HTTPD server to serve encrypted HTML pages and respond to encrypted requests:

1. If you did not compile your server with the `-DPEM_AUTH` flag set, you must acquire such a server or recompile with this flag set. (This must be an export-controlled version of 1.5; only the export-controlled version contains the necessary hooks.)

2. Retrieve scripts that will call the encryption software to either decrypt requests or encrypt documents. (These scripts are available in distributions of HTTPD 1.3, and will likely be available through the export-controlled version of 1.5.)

3. Edit and install the scripts as necessary and described within the scripts.

4. Edit the server configuration file `httpd.conf`. Add the following directives to add pointers to the PGP and PEM scripts:

```
PGPEncryptCmd /usr/local/somewhere/pgp-enc
PGPDecryptCmd /usr/local/somewhere/pgp-dec
PEMEncryptCmd /usr/local/somewhere/ripem-enc
PEMDecryptCmd /usr/local/somewhere/ripem-dec
```

   The paths should specify where these scripts are located on your server site.

5. Add the following two lines to indicate the name of the server entity used to identify the server's public key:

```
PGPServerEntity webmaster@mysite.edu
PEMServerEntity webmaster@mysite.edu
```

   This entity should be the same one you place on the public/private keys that you generate for your server.

6. To protect desired HTML pages with encryption, open the local or global access file in an editor.

7. Within the file or within the proper **<DIRECTORY>** element in the global file, change or add an **AuthType** directive with a value of **PEM** or **PGP** as desired.

```
AuthType PEM
```

The remainder of the access file can be modified, as described in How-To's 13.1, 13.2, and 13.3.

8. Close the file or edit another **<DIRECTORY>** element.

Configuring an NCSA X-Mosaic Browser with PGP/PEM Hooks

The following steps guide you through configuring NCSA's X-Mosaic browser to use a plug-in PGP- or PEM-based package to encrypt or decrypt HTTP requests and responses:

1. If you did not compile your Mosaic browser with the **-DPEM_AUTH** flag set, you must acquire such a browser or recompile with this flag set.

2. Open your X resources file and add the following resources. Modify the data values to correspond to appropriate information for your system.

```
Mosaic*pemEncrypt: /usr/local/somewhere/ripem-enc
Mosaic*pemDecrypt: /usr/local/somewhere/ripem-dec
Mosaic*pemEntity: me@mysite.edu
Mosaic*pgpEncrypt: /usr/local/somewhere/pgp-enc
Mosaic*pgpDecrypt: /usr/local/somewhere/pgp-dec
Mosaic*pgpEntity: me@mysite.edu
```

The entity value should correspond to the key name that you previously sent to the server administrator.

3. Save the resource file and restart your X environment.

How It Works

Transferring encrypted transmissions over the Web requires the use of several HTTP header elements and compatible encryption/decryption software supported by both the browser and the server. The actual encryption/decryption software may be supplied as part of the browser or server, as it is with Netscape's Navigator and Commerce Server, or as external plug-in components, as it is with NCSA's HTTPD and Mosaic. After you add the plug-in components or acquire a package with included software, the actual encryption/decryption process is transparent.

The benefit of plug-in encryption is that you are not limited to encryption technologies supplied with your browser or server. The primary disadvantage is that you are required to acquire, install, and configure the plug-in encryption modules to meet your needs. On the other hand, the benefit of built-in encryption is that your use of it is transparent from the start. The disadvantage is that you are limited to the encryption technologies supplied with your browser or server.

The proposed public key protection differs slightly from the prototype scheme implemented by NCSA. The following discussion examines the proposed scheme. (See the following "Comments" section for an examination of NCSA's prototype implementation.) If you are unfamiliar with HTTP, consult Appendix G, "HTML Hypertext Transfer Protocol (HTTP)," as a reference.

First, the browser requests a file protected by encryption.

```
GET /protected/mydoc.htm HTTP/1.0
UserAgent: MyBrowser/1.0
```

The server denies this initial request for the document unless the request includes required authentication information. This denial includes a copy of the server's public key in the **WWW-Authenticate** HTTP response header field. For example, such a response might look like the following:

```
HTTP/1.0 401 Unauthorized -- authentication failed
WWW-Authenticate: Pubkey realm="RealmName", key="EncodedServerPublicKey"
```

When the browser determines that the server denied an unauthorized request, the browser prompts the user for an authorized username and password. The browser concatenates this username and password with the IP address of your machine, a time stamp, and the browser's public key. A colon separates each of these fields. The browser encrypts this string using the server's public key and generates a new request.

```
GET /protected/mydoc.htm HTTP/1.0
UserAgent: MyBrowser/1.0
Authorization: Pubkey EncodedEncryptedString
```

The server unencodes and decrypts the authorization data. The server checks the structure of the data to confirm that it contains five colon-separated fields. Next, the IP address contained in the string is matched against the IP address of the machine making the request. The server then compares the time stamp to the current server time. If any of these checks fails, authorization is denied. When these checks succeed, a process similar to the Basic authentication scheme is used to check the validity of the specified username and password for the requested document.

When the server completes these checks, it generates a response. This response uses the browser's public key to transfer the information necessary for the browser to decrypt the requested document securely. The server encrypts the document itself, using a single-key encryption method such as **DES** or **IDEA**; for large documents, public-key encryption methods require significantly more time than single-key encryption systems. The response body contains this encrypted document. The response header includes fields that, in conjunction with the browser private key, allow decryption of the response body. These fields include **DEK-Info**, **Key-Info**, and **MIC-Info**. Such a response might appear as follows:

```
HTTP/1.0 200 OK
DEK-Info: DES-CBD,...
Key-Info: DES_ECB,...
MIC-Info: MD5,...
Content-length: ...

Encrypted Document
```

The browser uses its private key and the information in the header to decrypt the transmitted document, which it presents to the user. (For more information on these additional header fields, see Request for Comments number 1421, available at URL `http://www.w3.org/hypertext/WWW/AccessAuthorization/rfc1421.html`.)

Comments

NCSA implemented a prototype of this scheme using either PGP or RIPEM for HTTPD 1.3 and Mosaic (X Window version); however, because of legal restrictions, it removed the hooks for this scheme. Current documentation indicates that encryption mechanisms might be added to HTTPD in an export-controlled version of 1.5.

The SSLeay package is a free product that supports SSL for HTTPD and Apache servers. You should read the documentation carefully before installing this package with your server. Several legal issues exist concerning retaining proper software necessary licenses for SSL to work properly. These issues differ depending on whether you are within or outside the United States. See `http://www.psy.uq.oz.au/~ftp/Crypto/` for a more detailed discussion of both how to configure an HTTPD or Apache server with SSLeay and the legal ramifications and requirements.

Netscape's Navigator and FastTrack Server use RSA encryption technology. This encryption software is built in. Therefore, these packages will use this encryption software as necessary in a transparent manner.

The NCSA prototype implementation supports calls to external encryption software to encrypt/decrypt transmissions. An example transcript of the HTTP request process under this prototype appears as follows.

First, the browser requests a document.

```
GET /protected/mydoc.htm HTTP/1.0
UserAgent: Mosaic/X 2.2
```

The server denies access.

```
HTTP/1.0 401 Unauthorized
WWW-Authenticate: PEM entity="webmaster@mysite.edu"
Server: NCSA/1.3
```

The browser retrieves the public key for the specified entity, using the `finger` command, and sends an encrypted request as the body of an HTTP request using a proprietary content type. Table 13-10 shows the proprietary MIME types created to support this prototype.

Table 13-10 Proprietary MIME types to support encryption system prototype

MIME TYPE	PURPOSE
application/x-www-pem-request	Body contains a PEM-encrypted request.
application/x-www-pgp-request	Body contains a PGP-encrypted request.
application/x-www-pem-reply	Body contains a PEM-encrypted response.
application/x-www-pgp-reply	Body contains a PGP-encrypted response.

The browser generates an encrypted request by using the retrieved public key to encrypt the actual request. The browser places this encrypted request as the HTTP request body. The request header specifies both the browser's PEM or PGP entity and the content type, from among those mentioned in Table 13-10.

```
GET / HTTP/1.0
Authorization: PEM entity="me@mysite.edu"
Content-type: application/x-www-pem-request

--- BEGIN PRIVACY-ENHANCE MESSAGE ---
Encrypted request...
--- END PRIVACY-ENHANCE MESSAGE ---
```

The server generates a response in a similar fashion. The server retrieves the public key for the specified entity from a local key file and generates an encrypted response. This encrypted response becomes the body of the HTTP response sent. The header of the response uses one of the reply MIME types listed in Table 13-10.

```
HTTP/1.0 200 OK
Content-type: application/x-www-pem-reply

--- BEGIN PRIVACY-ENHANCE MESSAGE ---
Encrypted response...
--- END PRIVACY-ENHANCE MESSAGE ---
```

CHAPTER 14

THE COMMON GATEWAY INTERFACE (CGI)

14

THE COMMON GATEWAY INTERFACE (CGI)

How do I...

Common Gateway Interface (CGI) applications are the source of dynamic, interactive HTML documents. They can present snapshots of current server information. They can accept user-specified data, process it, and respond with ad hoc HTML 4.0 pages generated from the processed information.

CGI applications present changing data such as up-to-the-minute stock quotes. They can interpret and process input, such as sending an e-mail message, and they can provide a dynamic response to input data, such as presenting the results of a database query. This chapter discusses CGI issues, from the interaction between the server, browser, and CGI program to interpreting data passed to CGI programs. Finally, this chapter describes the development of CGI programs by presenting and explaining how to enable people to send you e-mail through a Web page, whether or not their browsers support `mailto` resources.

CGI applications are often referred to as *gateway applications*, *programs*, or *scripts*. The name can vary, but the purpose of these programs remains the same: to generate dynamic World Wide Web documents.

The server executes gateway programs locally; therefore, these applications can access system resources beyond those commonly available through the server. Consequently, CGI applications represent a potential security risk for the server site, and the server administrator might restrict the development, installation, and maintenance of applications.

14.1 Pass Data to a CGI Application

When a user activates a link or a button triggering a CGI application, the server launches that program. First, the CGI application must acquire information. In this How-To, you will learn how the server receives information from an HTML page and sends it to CGI applications.

14.2 Send Information to a Browser from CGI Applications

After a CGI program has performed its appointed task, it sends the result to the server, which passes it on to a browser. In this How-To, you will learn how to use the two most common methods for transmitting information to a browser from a gateway application.

14.3 Create a Simple CGI Application

You want people to access up-to-date data through an HTML document, but you don't want to make an employee modify the document every 10 minutes. In this How-To, you will learn how to develop a CGI application to generate an HTML page from raw data whenever the page is accessed.

14.4 Install a CGI Application

You have created a CGI application to generate dynamic HTML documents. Now you want people to link and send data to your program. In this How-To, you will learn how to make your gateway program accessible from your servers.

14.5 Create a Query Document Using the `<ISINDEX>` Element

The HTML `<ISINDEX>` element enables users to input a single piece of data. In this How-To, you will learn how to use this element to provide data to gateway programs.

14.6 Access Client Data in sh CGI Scripts

If you are running a UNIX-based server or a server equipped with a Bourne shell script interpreter, your first CGI application is likely to be developed in this Bourne shell script language. In this How-To, you will learn how to access input data in a CGI Bourne shell script.

14.7 Parse Client Data in CGI Programs and Scripts

You develop gateway programs in many different languages. Acquiring user data from HTML forms is a common task, independent of the CGI programming language chosen. In this How-To, you will learn how to acquire data from HTML forms.

14.8 Process `FILE` Type Input from an HTML Form

The common method of entering gateway application data is through form input fields. HTML 3.2 added a `FILE` input type to these existing input types. This addition requires the modification of the standard method of parsing and retrieving data sent to gateway applications. In this How-To, you will learn how to parse HTML form data in a manner consistent with `FILE` type submissions.

14.9 Write a CGI Application to Send Me E-Mail

In this How-To, you will learn how to combine all the necessary elements of CGI application development to build a CGI e-mail support package.

COMPLEXITY
ADVANCED

14.1 How do I...
Pass data to a CGI application?

COMPATIBILITY: HTML, HTTP, CGI/1.1

Problem

When I create dynamic documents, I must send input data from my HTML page to the server. This data passes through many hands before my CGI application can process it and generate an HTML document. The HTML document that calls the CGI application directly affects how information is passed to my gateway program. What is this process, and how will the data eventually reach my application? How is the passing mechanism determined?

Technique

Your CGI application receives data from three sources: the server, a user, and the author of the HTML page triggering the application. Ultimately, all data passed to your gateway program is sent by the server. The data supplied by the server is available via special environment variables. This type of data is commonly available to gateway programs of all types. Details on these environment variables are in the "Comments" section.

Browsers transform user and author data and then send it to the server. The server, in turn, sends it to your CGI application in a manner prescribed by the CGI protocol. Both of these data types are sent in the form of attribute/value pairs. (For example, a pair might associate the value `red` with the attribute `color`.) User data is supplied by the reader, and author data is supplied by you or whoever is authoring the HTML page accessing your gateway program.

CGI provides several mechanisms for passing data to your applications. How data is sent depends on the input and the HTTP request method used. There are three common methods:

- ✔ Command-line arguments: The server starts your application and passes the data on the command line.
- ✔ Environment variables: The gateway program accesses data placed in specified environment variables. The server places this information in these locations before starting your application.
- ✔ Standard input data block: The server launches the gateway program and places a data block in an area accessible to your program. The gateway application then reads and interprets this data.

Figure 14-1 graphically displays these three methods.

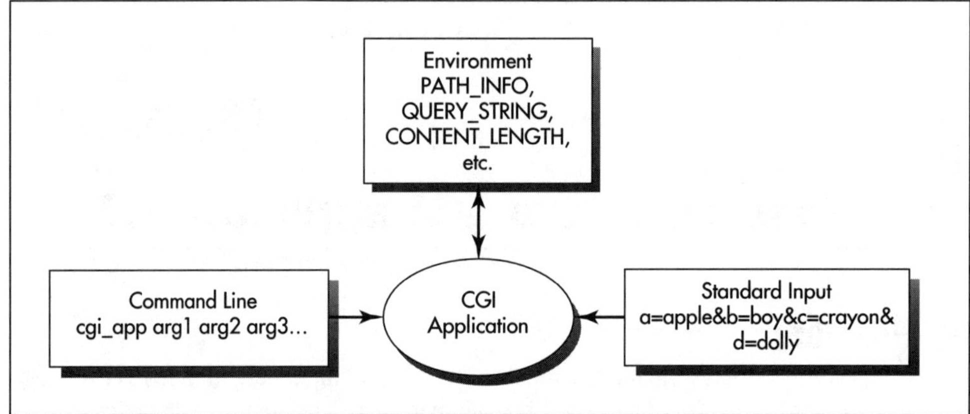

Figure 14-1 CGI provides three data-passing mechanisms

Steps

How the server passes data to your application is based on the way you gather your input data and how you send it. In addition to user input, the server places specific information in the execution environment of your CGI application, independent of how user data is passed.

This How-To demonstrates how to pass user and author data to gateway programs from your HTML documents.

Sending Command-Line Argument Input Data

`<ISINDEX>` user data generates command-line arguments. This is the only way a server passes command-line arguments to a gateway application. To generate CGI application input data as command-line arguments, use an `<ISINDEX>` element to request user data:

1. Open the searchable document in a text editor.
2. Include an `<ISINDEX>` element in the `<HEAD>` element of the document.
3. Save this document.

NOTE

`<ISINDEX>` elements can be used only in searchable documents. If your server does not support all HTML documents as searchable documents, this element can be used only in dynamically searchable documents generated by gateway applications.

Sending Input Data Through the Environment

Two types of data can be made available through environment variables. Server-specified data is available when any gateway application is started. This commonly available data is described in the "Comments" section.

This section describes how to send user-entered and author-entered data via the `QUERY_STRING` environment variables. This data is entered via an HTML interactive form. The following procedure describes how to create this embedded form:

1. Open the document from which data will be sent to your gateway application.
2. Move your insertion point to the location in the document where you want to request and specify data.
3. Insert a `<FORM>` element. This element should use the `GET` method. Enclose in the `<FORM>` element any elements necessary to request the desired data. For example, the following element transmits the user data via an environment variable to the `cgi_app` CGI application:

```
<!-- Appropriate HTML elements for document -->
<FORM METHOD="GET" ACTION="http://www.mysite.edu/cgi-bin/cgi_app"⇐
ENCTYPE="application/x-www-form-urlencoded">
...
<INPUT TYPE="submit" VALUE="Mail">
</FORM>
<!-- More HTML elements to conclude document -->
```

Chapter 11, "HTML Interactive Forms," provides more information on the creation of HTML forms.

4. Save this document.

Sending Additional Author Input Data Through the Environment

This section describes how you can specify author data to be passed to a gateway application via the **PATH_INFO** environment variables. This data is included as additional path information in a URL referring to the target gateway application. Therefore, you can send this type of information via either an **ACTION** attribute of a form when user input is also required or a standard link anchor when user input is not required. The following procedure describes how to send this type of author data:

1. Open the document from which additional author data will be sent to your gateway application.

2. Move your insertion point to the location in the document where you specify the URL of the gateway application.

3. If this is in a **<FORM>** element, include on the tail end of the form's **ACTION** URL the desired author data. Enclose in the **<FORM>** element any elements necessary to request the desired user input. (Chapter 11 provides more information on the creation of HTML forms.) For example, the following element transmits the user data via environment variable to the **cgi_app** CGI application. The **PATH_INFO** environment variable stores the author data **"author_data"**.

```
<!-- Appropriate HTML elements for document -->
<!-- The form's method may be either GET or POST -->
<FORM METHOD="GET" ACTION="http://www.mysite.edu/cgi-bin/cgi_app/⇐
author_data" ENCTYPE="application/x-www-form-urlencoded">
...
<INPUT TYPE="submit" VALUE="Mail">
</FORM>
<!-- More HTML elements to conclude document -->
```

Or, if in an anchor, include on the tail end of the anchor's **HREF** URL the desired author data. For example, the following element transmits the author data via the **PATH_INFO** environment variable to the **cgi_app** CGI application:

```
<!-- Appropriate HTML elements for document -->
A standard link can be used to pass
<A HREF="http://www.mysite.edu/cgi-bin/cgi-app/author_data">author data</A>
to a gateway application.
<!-- More HTML elements to conclude document -->
```

4. Save this document.

Sending Input Data Through Standard Input

This is the most common method of passing input data. Unlike the other methods, this approach is not hindered by the size restriction of a command line or environment variables.

This section describes how you can send data to your CGI application as a data block on the standard input stream. This data is entered through an HTML document with a form specifying the `POST` method. The following procedure describes how to pass data to CGI applications through the application's standard input:

1. Open the document from which data will be sent to your gateway application.

2. Move your insertion point to the location in the document where you want to request and specify data.

3. Insert a `<FORM>` element. This element should use the `POST` method. Enclose in the `<FORM>` element any elements necessary to request the desired data. For example, the following element transmits data by the standard input to the `cgi_app` CGI application:

```
<!-- Appropriate HTML elements for document -->
<FORM METHOD="POST" ACTION="http://www.mysite.edu/cgi-bin/cgi_app"⇐
ENCTYPE="application/x-www-form-urlencoded">
...
<INPUT TYPE="submit" VALUE="Mail">
</FORM>
<!-- More HTML elements to conclude document -->
```

How It Works

Your CGI application receives information by three means:

- ✔ Command-line arguments
- ✔ Environment variables
- ✔ Standard input

Sending Command-Line Argument Input Data

The server generates command-line inputs by interpreting the data entered into an `<ISINDEX>` element. For example, Figure 14-2 displays a sample document

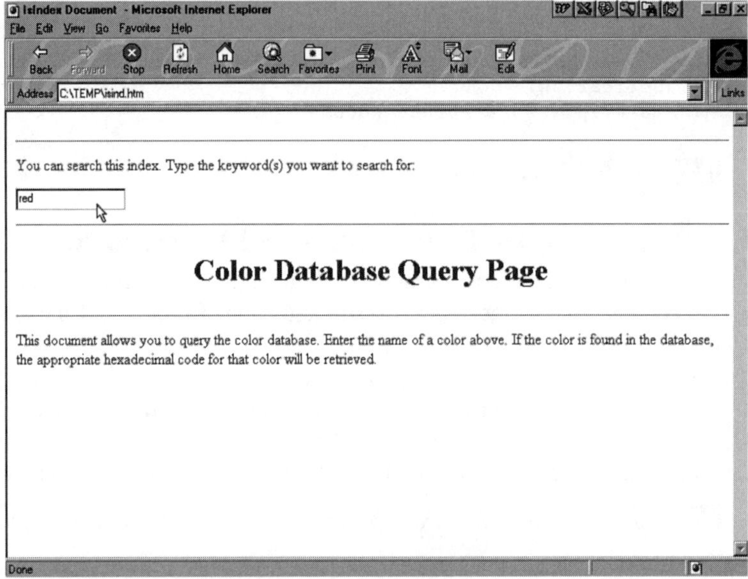

Figure 14-2 The `<ISINDEX>` tag causes the reader to be prompted for search terms

containing an `<ISINDEX>` element. The input field generated by the `<ISINDEX>` element prompts the user for information from an HTML document.

The reader enters data in the input field. After the data is entered, the browser generates a `GET` method HTTP request. The browser submits a query URL with the `GET` request. This URL is composed of the current URL with the input data appended as a query string. Each word in the input field is separated by a plus sign in the query URL:

```
URL?arg1+arg2+arg3+arg4...
```

This query URL is passed to the server, which starts the gateway program in the URL with the arguments on the command line.

```
cgi_app arg1 arg2 arg3 arg4...
```

NOTE

You can also pass author data by simulating the results of an `<ISINDEX>` input request. The query URL in this form would take the place of a standard URL when specifying a link anchor. Generally, an appended query string that does not contain an equal sign (=) is considered an `<ISINDEX>` type request—for example, `<A`

Sending Input Data Through the Environment

GET method HTML forms generate user data sent via environment variables. For example, the following elements transmit one piece of user data and two pieces of author data via environment variable to the specified CGI program. (Chapter 11 provides more information on the creation of HTML forms.)

```
<!-- Appropriate HTML elements for document -->
<FORM METHOD="GET" ACTION="http://www.mysite.edu/cgi-bin/cgi_app"
ENCTYPE="application/x-www-form-urlencoded">
Enter the Text of your message below:<BR>
<TEXTAREA NAME="arg1" ROWS=10 COLS=40></TEXTAREA>
<INPUT TYPE="hidden" NAME="arg2" VALUE="dsk@cau.auc.edu">
<INPUT TYPE="hidden" NAME="arg3" VALUE="Miscellaneous">
<INPUT TYPE="submit" VALUE="Mail">
</FORM>
<!-- More HTML elements to conclude document -->
```

The text area element in this form represents information entered by the reader that the gateway application accesses. The two hidden input elements contain information specified by the author of the HTML page calling the gateway application.

When the reader enters data in the input fields of the form and presses the Submit button, the browser generates a GET method HTTP request. The GET request includes a query URL composed of the gateway URL specified by the form's ACTION attribute, with the input data appended. Data is transformed to encode special characters and spaces before submission to the server. The appended query string contains attributes and values separated by equal (=) signs, with each attribute/value pair separated by an ampersand (&).

```
URL?arg1=val1&arg2=val2&arg3=val
```

This query URL is sent to the server, which runs the gateway program represented by the URL in the following environment:

```
QUERY_STRING="arg1=val1&arg2=val2&arg3=val3"
```

NOTE

A query URL in this format can replace a standard URL as the target of a link anchor in an HTML document. Use this method, as well as hidden form input fields, to send author data as attribute/value pair data to a gateway application—for example, `<AHREF="URL?arg1=val1&arg2=val2&arg3=val3...">...</A>`.

Sending Additional Author Input Data Through the Environment

The PATH_INFO environment variable stores data that is appended to a URL. Whether the URL is the target of a link, the action of a GET method form, or the action of a **POST** method form, you can send author data through this variable. For example, the **ACTION** URL and the link target URL both specify author data sent to the **cgi-app** gateway application.

```
<!-- Appropriate HTML elements for document -->
<FORM METHOD="GET" ACTION="http://www.mysite.edu/cgi-bin/cgi-app/⇐
author_data" ENCTYPE="application/x-www-form-urlencoded">
Enter the Text of your message below:<BR>
<TEXTAREA NAME="arg1" ROWS=10 COLS=40></TEXTAREA>
<INPUT TYPE="submit" VALUE="Mail">
</FORM>
<!-- More HTML elements to conclude document -->
A standard link can be used to pass
<A HREF="http://www.mysite.edu/cgi-bin/cgi-app/author_data">author data</A>
to a gateway application.
<!-- More HTML elements to conclude document -->
```

When a link or button is pressed, the reader triggers an appropriate HTTP request. The **METHOD** attribute of the form specifies the method to use if the results of a form are submitted. A standard **GET** method request is performed if a link is activated. The browser generates a URL to submit with the request. This URL is composed of the gateway application's URL, with the author-specified data appended. Table 14-1 displays the possible browser-generated URLs depending on the access method.

Table 14-1 URLs generated to send author data

ACCESS TYPE	URL GENERATED
Link	URL/author_data
GET method form	URL/author_data?user_data
POST method form	URL/author_data

This URL is passed to the server that runs the gateway program represented by the URL. The server places the author data in the **PATH_INFO** environment variable:

```
PATH_INFO="/author_data"
```

Sending Input Data Through Standard Input

Standard input passed data is generated through an HTML form with the **POST** method specified. For example, the following **<FORM>** element sends data to the **cgi_app** application's standard input:

```
<!-- Appropriate HTML elements for document -->
<FORM METHOD="POST" ACTION="http://www.mysite.edu/cgi-bin/cgi_app"⇐
ENCTYPE="application/x-www-form-urlencoded">
Enter the Text of your message below:<BR>
<TEXTAREA NAME="arg1" ROWS=10 COLS=40></TEXTAREA>
<INPUT TYPE="hidden" NAME="arg2" VALUE="dsk@cau.auc.edu">
<INPUT TYPE="hidden" NAME="arg3" VALUE="Miscellaneous">
<INPUT TYPE="submit" VALUE="Mail">
</FORM>
<!-- More HTML elements to conclude document -->
```

When this form is submitted, one piece of user data, "arg1", and two pieces of "author data", "arg2" and "arg3", are sent to the standard input of the cgi_app application.

The reader enters data in the form's input fields. After the Submit button is pressed, the browser generates a POST method HTTP request containing a gateway URL specified by the form's ACTION attribute. The input data from the form is transformed and sent to the server in the request body. (See Appendix G, "HTML Hypertext Transfer Protocol (HTTP)," for information on the format of an HTTP request.)

The server runs the gateway application specified by the URL in the request. The server sends the input data to this program's standard input. The environment variable CONTENT_LENGTH stores the number of characters sent by the server.

The data sent on the standard input is formatted as a series of attribute/value pairs. The attributes and values are separated by equal signs (=), and each pair is separated by an ampersand (&):

```
arg1=val1&arg2=val2&arg3=val3
```

General Information on Data Passing

The data-passing approach chosen is based on the request type (GET or POST) and nature (<ISINDEX>, form, or link) of the input being sent. Table 14-2 summarizes these options. The Input Provider column specifies where the input to the gateway application originates. Readers generate user data when they input information into the HTML document calling the gateway application. Authors specify author information when they append information to a target URL or when they include hidden input fields in a form. The URL shows the format of the URL generated by the browser and sent to the server as part of the HTTP request. The final column specifies the way the gateway application receives the input data.

Table 14-2 Data-passing methods for various interaction types

ACCESS TYPE	INPUT PROVIDER	URL PASSING METHOD
<ISINDEX>	User: URL?arg1+arg2...	Command line
Link	Author: URL?arg1+arg2...	Command line
GET form	User: URL?arg1=val1&arg2=val2...	Environment
Link	Author: URL?arg1=val1&arg2=val2...	Environment
GET form	User and author:	Environment
	URL/author_data?arg1=val1...	
POST form	User and author: URL/author_data	Env./standard input
Link	Author: URL/author_data	Environment
POST form	User: URL	Standard input

NOTE

When author data is passed through a query URL (`GET` method form style or `<ISINDEX>` style), the HTML document author is responsible for encoding the special characters in the query string (see Table 14-3).

When a client sends information from an HTML form, special characters in the data are transformed before transmission to the server. This is done so that the meanings of special characters are not misinterpreted. Table 14-3 shows the special characters and how they are transformed in a data block or a query string.

Table 14-3 Permuted characters and escaped values

CHARACTER NAME	CHARACTER	INPUT VALUE
Tab	\ t	%09
Carriage return	\ n	%0A
Exclamation point	!	%21
Double quote	"	%22
Pound	#	%23
Dollar sign	$	%24
Percent sign	%	%25
Single quote	'	%27
Open parenthesis	(	%28
Close parenthesis	)	%29
Plus sign	+	%2B
Comma	,	%2C
Slash	/	%2F
Colon	:	%3A
Semicolon	;	%3B
Less than	<	%3C
Greater than	>	%3E
Question mark	?	%3F
Open bracket	[	%5B
Back slash	\	%5C
Close bracket	]	%5D
Caret	^	%5E
Back quote	`	%60
Open brace	{	%7B

CHARACTER NAME	CHARACTER	INPUT VALUE
Pipe	|	%7C
Close brace	}	%7D
Tilde	~	%7E

How-To's 14.6, 14.7, and 14.8 discuss procedures for accessing the input data and transforming it into a usable format.

Comments

Information is placed in the environment by the server and is made available when a gateway application is launched. Table 14-4 explains commonly accessed environment variables and the values they hold. This information will help you develop your own CGI applications.

Table 14-4 Commonly accessed environment variables

ENVIRONMENT VARIABLE	VALUE
`CONTENT_LENGTH`	Length of data block on standard input for `POST` or `PUT` method requests.
`CONTENT_TYPE`	MIME type of the information being sent via the `POST` or `PUT` method.
`PATH_INFO`	String containing the additional information appended to the application path.
`QUERY_STRING`	Contains the information appended to the URL passed to the server. This information follows the question mark. `<ISINDEX>` data is available both through command-line arguments and through this variable.
`REMOTE_ADDR`	IP address of the remote machine accessing the server.
`REMOTE_HOST`	Name corresponding to the remote machine accessing the server. If this information is unavailable, this entry is left blank.
`REMOTE_IDENT`	Contains the unauthenticated ID of the user requesting the CGI application.
`REQUEST_METHOD`	Specifies the HTTP method sent to the server by the client (`GET`, `POST`, and so on).
`SCRIPT_NAME`	Contains the name of the script being called as it would appear in a URL.
`SERVER_NAME`	Specifies the name of the server being accessed.
`SERVER_SOFTWARE`	Contains the name and version of the server software being run.

A full specification of environment variables available to CGI applications can be found via the CGI specification at `http://hoohoo.ncsa.uiuc.edu/cgi/overview.html`. Furthermore, additional environment variable information is usually available. These variables have the `HTTP_` prefix. The information contained in these variables is directly incorporated from the client's HTTP request header (as described in Appendix G). So, for example, `HTTP_USER_AGENT` would contain the data passed to the server in the `User-Agent` field of the HTTP request header.

14.2 How do I...
Send information to a browser from CGI applications?

COMPATIBILITY: HTML, HTTP, CGI/1.1

Problem

I want to send my results from a gateway application to the server and then to a browser. How does the server get the information, and what does it do with it? I need to know the details of this process to build my CGI programs properly.

Technique

The browser receives gateway-generated information via the server in two ways:

- ✔ Parsed header: Gateway application results are placed on standard output. The server takes this information, manipulates it, and sends it to the client.
- ✔ Nonparsed header. A gateway program beginning with the `nph-` prefix indicates that the CGI application is a nonparsed header (`nph`) program. This means that results sent to the standard output by this type of application are not processed by the server, but passed directly to the client through the server.

Information is passed to the server through these two methods. Figure 14-3 shows the relationship between these two methods in relation to the browser, the server, and your CGI application. The upper arrow represents the path of the parsed header method. The lower arrow represents the passthrough using a nonparsed header program. In either case, the result is an HTTP response sent to the browser. (See Appendix G, "HTML Hypertext Transfer Protocol (HTTP)," for information on HTTP responses.)

Steps

The following step-by-step procedures show how to pass information to the browser via the parsed and nonparsed header methods.

WARNING

It is imperative that server directives from parsed header applications and response headers from nonparsed header applications terminate with a blank line. This blank line indicates the end of the header and the beginning of any attached object.

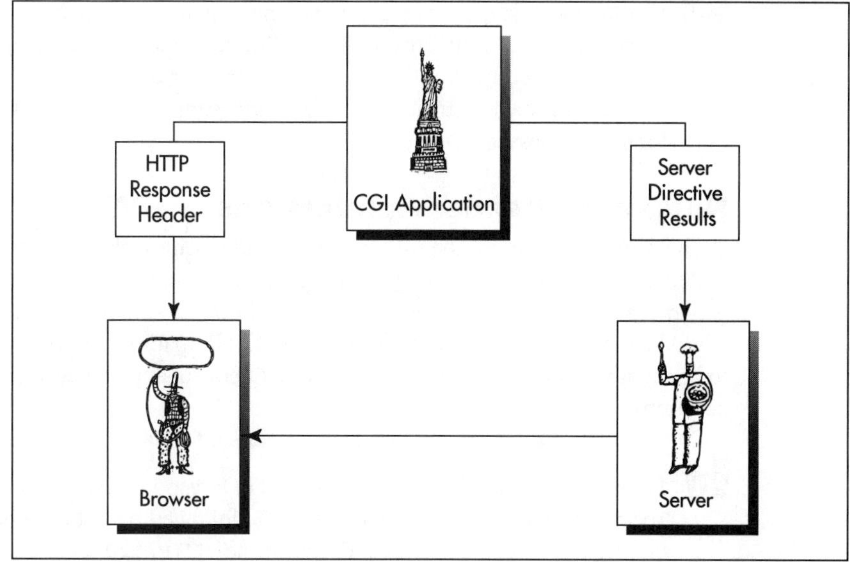

Figure 14-3 Passing of information from a gateway application to the browser

Parsed Header

If the results generated by a CGI application are relatively simple, you don't need to fine-tune the response header that will be eventually passed to the browser. Use the following procedure to pass CGI information to the browser via the server:

1. Issue a server directive as the first line of your gateway application output. Servers currently support three allowable server directives:

```
Content-type: type/subtype
Location: URL
Status: code message
```

The "How It Works" section describes these three server directives.

For example, the following line might be used in a Bourne shell script. Substitute corresponding statements used in other development languages.

```
echo Content-type:  text/html
```

2. Follow the server directive with a blank line. For example, in a Bourne shell script, issue the following command. In other development languages, use corresponding commands.

```
echo
```

3. In a **Content-type** server directive, the remainder of the output is the object returned to the browser (an HTML document, a GIF image, and so on). In a **Status** server directive, the remainder of the output is the text of the error message returned to the browser; simple text is the safest format for such a message.

Nonparsed Header Applications

With an **nph** application, the full response header sent to the client must be generated and returned by your gateway program. Use the following process to generate a minimal HTTP response header. Additional response header fields that could be included are discussed in Appendix G. Nonparsed header programs tend to be slightly faster because the server need not perform any processing or make any additions.

Many browsers, but not all, can deal with less information than this minimum.

1. Issue a status line. The first line of an HTTP response header contains a specification of the protocol and version, followed by a status code, and ending with a status message. For example, **HTTP/1.0 200 OK** would be an appropriate first line. This should be the first line placed on standard output by your application. In a Bourne shell script, you could enter

```
echo "$SERVER_PROTOCOL 200 OK"
```

2. In the next line, specify the date that the current document was put together. Your gateway application should calculate this information and place it on the standard output—for example, **Date: Sat, 25-Dec-99 14:24:32 GMT**. Because all servers work according to Greenwich mean time (GMT), make sure that the times you generate are for this time zone. The following code segment is appropriate for generating this information in a Bourne shell script:

```
echo -n "Date: "

/usr/bin/date -u -'+%a, %d-%h-%y %T GMT'
```

3. Specify the server software and version being used. This information is found in the **SERVER_SOFTWARE** environment variable. For example, if you're using NCSA version 1.3 server software, send the line **Server: NCSA/1.3** to the standard output next. You could use the following code in a Bourne shell script:

```
echo "Server: $SERVER_SOFTWARE"
```

4. Include a MIME version field. The current version is 1.0. Therefore, a line such as **MIME-version: 1.0** should appear next. You could use the following code in a Bourne shell script:

```
echo "MIME-version: 1.0"
```

5. Add other header fields as required by the status code and the resultant data being transmitted back to the browser. (See the "Comments" section and Appendix G.)

6. Terminate the HTTP response header with a blank line. For example, use the following code in a Bourne shell script:

```
echo
```

7. If a `Content-type` field appears in the response header, the remainder of the output after the blank line is the object returned to the browser (an HTML document, a GIF image, and so on).

How It Works

Your application sends its results to the standard output. If the name of your gateway program does not begin with the `nph-` prefix, the server parses and interprets the results your application places on the standard output. If your application name starts with the `nph-` prefix, the server assumes that the program is a nonparsed header program and retransmits the results from the gateway application without modification.

In the case of a parsed header application, the server reads and interprets the server directive. The remaining results placed on the standard output are interpreted based on the server directive. Unless the `Content-type` directive is used, additional results passed to the standard output might cause problems. The server then generates an appropriate HTTP response header and attaches any associated data to it. Figure 14-4 displays this process for the three accepted server directives, which are as follows:

- ✔ `Content-type: type/subtype`: Indicates that the object in the HTTP response body is of the specified MIME type.
- ✔ `Location: URL comment`: Indicates that the requested file is in a different location. The URL specifies where the desired information is located.
- ✔ `Status: code message`: Enables you to specify an exit status for your CGI application.

With respect to `nph` gateway applications, the data placed on the standard output by your application is passed directly back to the client. Therefore, your application generates a complete HTTP response header, with associated data.

In either case, the browser receives an HTTP response header and any relevant data objects.

Comments

Both methods rely on passing information to the server via the standard output. The difference is that nonparsed header gateway applications are responsible for generating an entire HTTP response header, plus any generated results from execution. CGI programs with parsed headers provide just a server directive, however, and enable the server to construct an appropriate HTTP response header. Appendix G provides information on HTTP response header fields you can use in your nonparsed header CGI applications.

Status codes and status messages tell the browser the status of its request. Status codes range from 200 to 599. A code within the 200 to 299 range indicates a successful transaction.

A code from 300 to 399 specifies some manner of redirection. This usually implies that a `Location` field will appear later in the response header, defining the URL to use in lieu of the requested one.

Status codes between 400 and 599 indicate errors. The nature of the error is often explained in a small HTML or text document in the HTTP response body.

When using a nonparsed header application, you are responsible for generating the complete response header and any attached object. Using particular status codes suggests the inclusion of specific header fields and attached objects. Table 14-5 maps status codes to suggested header fields beyond the minimum suggested in the nonparsed header procedure given in the "Steps" section.

Table 14-5 Suggested header fields for response status categories

STATUS CODE	SUGGESTED RESPONSE INFORMATION	ATTACHED OBJECT?
200-299	`Content-type, Content-Length` (if known)	Yes
300-399	`Location`	No
400-599	`Content-type, Content-Length`	Yes (error message)

Table 14-6 specifies many commonly used status codes, along with an explanation of their meaning.

Table 14-6 Commonly used status codes

STATUS CODE	EXPLANATION
200	Completed successfully.
201	`POST` method request completed successfully.
202	Request has been queued, but results are unknown.
203	Completed, but all information was not returned.
204	No operation. Completed successfully.
301	Requested data moved permanently to another location.
302	Request completed, but desired data is at another location.
400	Syntax error in request.
403	Access to requested resource is forbidden.
404	Requested URL not found.
500	Internal server error.
501	Server does not support requested method.

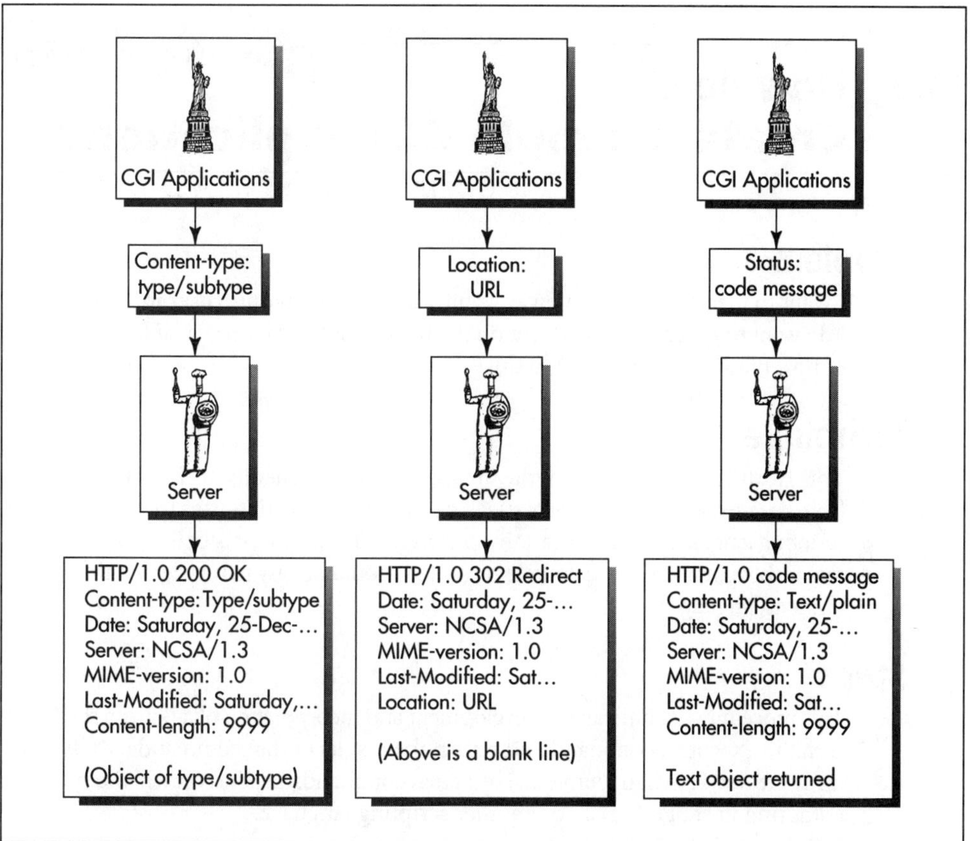

Figure 14-4 Transformation of parsed header CGI output to an HTTP response message

Aside from error codes and complete success, the status code you are most likely to use is code 204. This code indicates no response but successful completion. An HTTP response using this code results in no change to the document currently seen in the browser. This code is handy for specifying the default action to be taken in an imagemap, or to demonstrate how a particular browser displays a link. In either case, you can specify the following gateway application as the target URL:

```
#!/bin/sh

# Indicate status followed by a blank line
echo Status:  204 No response, but successful
echo
```

14.3 How do I... Create a simple CGI application?

COMPATIBILITY: HTML, HTTP, CGI

Problem

I want to create a simple gateway application. I don't require user input data, but I do want to generate a document on the fly from information available on the server host machine. How can I do this?

Technique

This How-To shows how to write an application to generate an HTML document from data existing at the server site. The sample application uses the Bourne shell scripting language for demonstrative purposes. This language is both easy to use and reasonably portable. The technique presented should be easy to transfer to other development languages.

Steps

This procedure documents the development and incorporation of a Bourne shell CGI script to execute a command and return the results of that command as a dynamically created HTML document. The actual commands depend on whether you are authoring in sh, Perl, TCL, or another scripting language.

1. In a text editor, create a file called `first.cgi`.

2. The script must begin with the following line specifying the execution environment:

```
#!/bin/sh
```

3. Issue a server directive to the standard output. In the case of a script written to process a command and report the output, the most likely directive you will use is `Content-type`. The actual type you specify should correspond to whatever type of file your application will send back to the browser.

```
echo Content-type: text/html
```

This code segment indicates that the attached file is an HTML document.

NOTE

How-To 14.2 goes into detail on the use of the three valid server directives.

4. Terminate the server directive with a blank line indicating that the attached object follows. Use a single **echo** statement to generate this blank line:

```
echo
```

5. Set the **PROG** variable to the program you want to run. For example, if you want the script to generate the local date and time on the server, use the following line:

```
PROG=/usr/bin/date
```

6. Because the server directive you used indicates that an HTML document is attached, generate the HTML-formatted output of your specified command. The following segment of code generates the beginning of an HTML document to be returned to the browser:

```
cat << EOF
<!DOCTYPE HTML PUBLIC "-//W3C//DTD HTML 3.2//EN">
<HTML>
<HEAD>
<TITLE>
EOF

echo "$PROG Response Page"

cat << EOF
</TITLE>
</HEAD>
<BODY>
<H1>
EOF

echo "$PROG Response Page"

cat << EOF
</H1>
<HR>
EOF
```

The **cat << EOF** commands cause the script to output the proceeding text until an **EOF** is reached.

7. Run the specified program on the server. You must format the results for presentation by the browser. The following code executes the program and formats the results as the content of a **<PRE>** element:

```
echo \<PRE\>
$PROG
echo \</PRE\>
```

8. End the document by closing the `<BODY>` and `<HTML>` elements:

```
cat << EOF
</BODY></HTML>
EOF
```

9. Save this script file and exit the editor.

10. Change permissions on the script file, if necessary, to make it executable.

11. Test the application. The results seen should start with a server directive, followed by a blank line. The blank line is followed by an attached document. The results that should appear from the execution of the script developed in this How-To should look like this:

```
Content-type: text/html

<!DOCTYPE HTML PUBLIC "-//W3C//DTD HTML 3.2//EN">
<HTML>
<HEAD>
<TITLE>
/usr/bin/date Response Page
</TITLE>
</HEAD>
<BODY>
<H1>
/usr/bin/date Response Page
</H1>
<HR>
<PRE>
Sat Dec 25 14:24:32 EDT 1999
</PRE>
</BODY></HTML>
```

12. Make the script available for use through your HTML documents. First, install the script and register it with your server. For servers such as NCSA or CERN, gateway applications should be placed in a `cgi-bin` directory by default.

13. Determine the URL of your installed CGI application.

14. Refer to your gateway script as the destination for HTML links.

How It Works

Gateway applications of this type process data and generate results that are sent back to the client in some specified format. Figure 14-5 diagrams the execution of such a CGI application. The application generates an appropriate server directive,

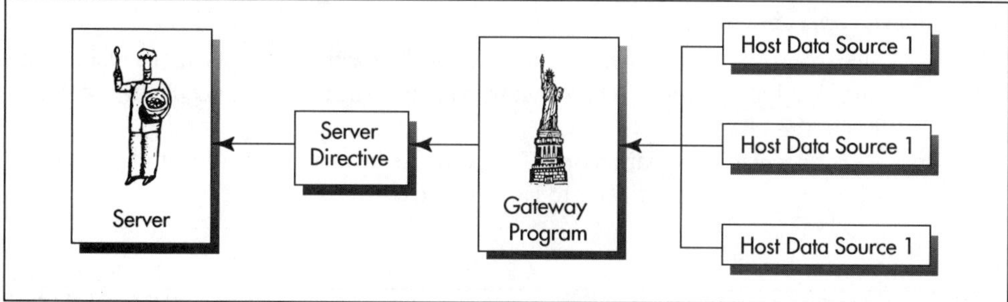

Figure 14-5 Transformation of parsed header CGI output to an HTTP response message

separated from the body of the message by a blank line. The object returned to the browser follows the blank line.

The script, using the program `/usr/bin/date` developed in this example, is on the CD-ROM, with the filename `FIRST.CGI`.

When a link specifies this gateway script as its destination, the application generates a parsed header and a message body, which are passed to the server. The server processes this information and generates a full HTTP response header to return to the client.

Figure 14-6 shows the page resulting from the activation of a link to the `first.cgi` script.

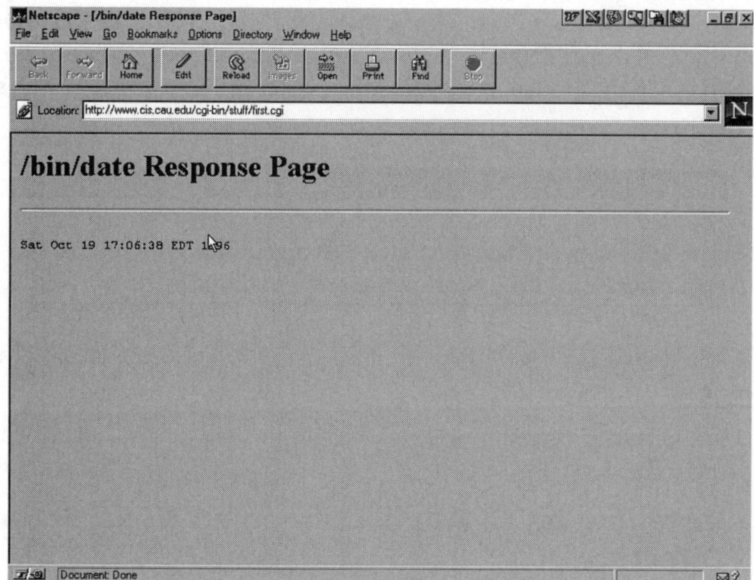

Figure 14-6 Results of activating a link to `first.cgi`

Comments

More complex methods are necessary for dealing with CGI applications that require some level of user input. These methods are investigated more deeply in later How-To's in this chapter.

For detailed information on HTTP response header information and parsed versus nonparsed headers, refer to How-To 14.2.

COMPLEXITY
BEGINNING

14.4 How do I... Install a CGI application?

COMPATIBILITY: NCSA HTTPD, CERN HTTP

Problem

After I've written my gateway application, I must make it available. Where do I need to place the application so that I can access it from an HTML document, and how do I create a reference to it?

Technique

This How-To describes standard procedures for installing CGI applications on NCSA or CERN servers. Other servers provide different means for registering allowable gateway applications. The "Comments" section provides useful references to information on installing gateway applications on several other servers.

NCSA and CERN servers use two installation methods: script directories and file types. NCSA allows for both types, whereas the CERN server allows only script directories.

NOTE

You might need to discuss the installation of any CGI application with your Web site administrator. CGI applications are run on the host machine and therefore represent a potential security risk.

Steps

The following sections provide detailed instructions for installing CGI applications on NCSA and CERN servers.

Installing a CGI Application in an NCSA Script Directory

You make script directory specifications in the server resource map file. The following steps describe how to install your CGI application using this method:

1. If you are installing your application to an existing script directory, skip to step 5. Otherwise, change to the directory containing the server resource map file and load the `srm.conf` file into your text editor.

> **NOTE**
>
> To specify new script directories, you must have server administrator privileges.

2. Append a `ScriptAlias` directive to the `srm.conf` file. The format for this command is as follows:

```
ScriptAlias virtual_directory physical_directory
```

`virtual directory` refers to the path you should put in a URL to reference this script directory. `physical directory` represents the actual directory located on the machine running the server; if a relative path is specified, `ServerRoot` is assumed to be the base path.

The following lines designate the `/usr/local/httpd/bin/` and `ServerRoot/my-cgi-bin/` directories as script directories. In URLs, refer to them as `/local/bin/` and `/mybin/`, respectively.

```
ScriptAlias     /local/bin/     /usr/local/httpd/bin/
ScriptAlias     /mybin/     my-cgi-bin/
```

Any URL specified for a link anchor or HTML form action referencing `http://www.mysite.edu/mybin/myscript` causes the server to execute `ServerRoot/my-cgi-bin/myscript`. You can have as many `ScriptAlias` directives in your configuration as you want.

3. Save the configuration file.

4. Stop the server and restart it. This causes the server to read the altered configuration file and treat your script directories properly.

5. Move or copy your executable CGI application to a script directory. In UNIX, use the `mv` or `cp` command. For example, to move the gateway program `first.cgi` to `/usr/local/httpd/bin`, issue the following command:

```
mv first.cgi /usr/local/httpd/bin
```

> **NOTE**
>
> To install applications in existing directories, you need write access to the script directory.

6. Make sure that the application is executable by all users because the user associated with the server needs execution access to your code. Use the following UNIX command to give read and execute privileges to all users:

```
chmod ugo+rx first.cgi
```

Installing a CGI Application in a CERN Script Directory

The CERN Web server provides a script directory mechanism for installing gateway programs. The following steps describe how to install your programs using this method:

1. If you are installing your application to an existing script directory, skip to step 5. Otherwise, change to the directory containing the server configuration file and load the **httpd.conf** file into your text editor.

NOTE

To specify new script directories, you must have server administrator privileges.

2. Add **exec** rules to this file. The format for this command is **Exec /virtual_directory/*/physical_directory/***. You may add as many script directories as you want with **exec** rules. The physical directory represents the location to which the server should map the virtual directory when seen in a URL. The following line designates the **/usr/local/httpd/bin/** directory as a script directory. In URLs, refer to this directory as **/local/bin/**.

```
Exec     /local/bin/*     /usr/local/httpd/bin/*
```

   Any URL specified as a link anchor or HTML form action referencing **http://www.mysite.edu/local/bin/myscript** causes the server to execute **/usr/local/httpd/bin/myscript**.

3. Save the configuration file.

4. Stop the server and restart it. This causes the server to read the altered configuration file and treat your script directories properly.

5. Move or copy your executable CGI application to a script directory. In UNIX, use the **mv** or **cp** command. For example, to move the gateway program **first.cgi** to **/usr/local/httpd/bin**, issue the following command:

```
mv first.cgi /usr/local/httpd/bin
```

NOTE

To install applications in existing directories, you need write access to the script directory.

6. Make sure that the application is executable by all users because the user associated with the server needs execution access to your code. Use the following UNIX command to give read and execute privileges to all users:

```
chmod ugo+rx first.cgi
```

Installing a CGI Application Using the NCSA File Type Mechanism

With this method, gateway programs can be placed anywhere. The server recognizes an application by an extension type. This type can be established across all documents on a particular server, or on an individual directory basis.

1. If you are installing your application to a directory with an access file set for CGI applications, or if your server has been configured to allow CGI applications anywhere, skip to step 4. If you are configuring the server to allow gateway applications anywhere, change to the directory containing the server resource map file, load the `srm.conf` file into your text editor, and skip to step 3. If you are configuring a single directory for gateway applications, change to the directory you are configuring and load the access control file (the default name is `.htaccess`) into your text editor. If an access file does not exist, create one using the filename specified in the server resource map file. The directive you are looking for is `AccessFileName`.

2. Insert the following line in the access control file. This line allows execution of gateway applications in this directory:

```
Options ExecCGI
```

NOTE

To specify execution of CGI applications in a particular directory, you must have read and write access to the directory-level access control file.

3. Insert an `AddType` directive. This directive tells the server how to interpret files with a given extension. For example, if you want all files with the extension `.cgi` to be treated as gateway programs, insert the following line into the access control file:

```
AddType     application/x-httpd-cgi     .cgi
```

NOTE

To specify the file type across a server, you must have server administrator privileges. For individual directories, you must have read and write access to the directory level access control file.

4. Move or copy your executable CGI application to the desired directory. If you have set the server so that gateway programs can reside anywhere, then the only restriction is that the chosen directory must be visible to the server. In UNIX, use the `mv` or `cp` command. For example, to move the gateway program `first.cgi` to `/usr/local/httpd/bin`, issue the command

```
mv first.cgi /usr/local/httpd/bin/first.cgi
```

NOTE

You must have read and write access to the directory where you want to place your application.

5. Make sure that the application is executable by all users because the user associated with the server needs execution access to your code. Use the following UNIX command to give read and execute privileges to all users:

```
chmod ugo+rx first.cgi
```

How It Works

Both NCSA and CERN servers enable you to configure directories so that the server treats your files in these directories as gateway programs. After you have configured directories as script directories, whenever the server sees a URL addressing the logical name for such a directory, it launches the filename attached to the URL as a CGI application. To install an application, move the executable code or script to the directory and make sure that it can be executed by the server. The procedures in this How-To show the steps required to establish script directories and install applications in them.

The other means provided by the NCSA server for installing gateway programs is by file type and modification of access control files. Access control files can appear anywhere visible to your server. They control how files in the current directory and its subdirectories are accessed. In the access control file, specify that the server treat all files ending with a particular file extension as CGI applications. Gateway applications can then be installed any place that is controlled by the modified access file. If the server resource map file is modified, then applications can appear wherever they are visible to the server, as long as they have the correct filename extension.

Comments

Documentation for CGI application installation for various servers can be found at the locations in Table 14-7.

Table 14-7 CGI documentation for various servers

SERVER	CGI INFORMATION LOCATION
NCSA	http://hoohoo.ncsa.uiuc.edu/docs/tutorials/cgi.html
CERN	http://www.w3.org/pub/WWW/Daemon/User/CGI/Overview.html
FastTrack	See online material distributed with the server
WN	http://hopf.math.nwu.edu/
MacHTTP/WebSTAR	http://www.starnine.com/development/extending.html
WinHTTPD	http://www.city.net/win-httpd/

Installing gateway applications for a FastTrack server is almost identical to the processes described for NCSA. The actual configuration file command syntax is slightly different. However, because the administration server provides a form-based interface for configuring appropriate directories, these differences are transparent unless you configure your FastTrack server by direct configuration file modification.

COMPLEXITY
INTERMEDIATE

14.5 How do I... Create a query document using the <ISINDEX> element?

COMPATIBILITY: CGI

Problem

I am interested in creating a searchable document. The search criterion is a simple list of terms. How do I place a query for the search terms and information on how to access this data from my CGI application into my document?

Technique

This How-To describes the process for developing a gateway program to manage an **<ISINDEX>** query document. Because **<ISINDEX>** documents generate query URLs by appending a query string to the current URL, CGI applications that generate and handle **<ISINDEX>** query documents must have two components: one to generate the query page and one to generate the response page.

When the URL is triggered, the application checks the number of command-line arguments to determine whether to generate the query page or the response page. **<ISINDEX>** query terms are sent to the application as command-line arguments. (Refer to How-To 14.1 for more information on how information is passed to gateway applications.) Figure 14-7 displays the approach taken with this technique.

Steps

The following procedure delineates the steps you should follow to develop your **<ISINDEX>** gateway applications. The example provided was developed using the Bourne shell script language to run the **finger** utility with any arguments specified in the **<ISINDEX>** field. When developing your applications, use the appropriate constructs in your development language to accomplish the tasks demonstrated in the steps. When you have completed the procedure, you can use the URL for your **<ISINDEX>** application as you would any other URL (for the target of a link, an open location, and so on).

1. Open a text editor and begin writing the source for your **<ISINDEX>** application. Place any necessary header information in your application (script to use, header files, helper functions, and so on). In the sample **finger** script, this step includes specifying the Bourne shell, as well as defining a variable pointing to the **finger** program.

```
#!/bin/sh
#Finger <ISINDEX> application
FINGER=/usr/ucb/finger
```

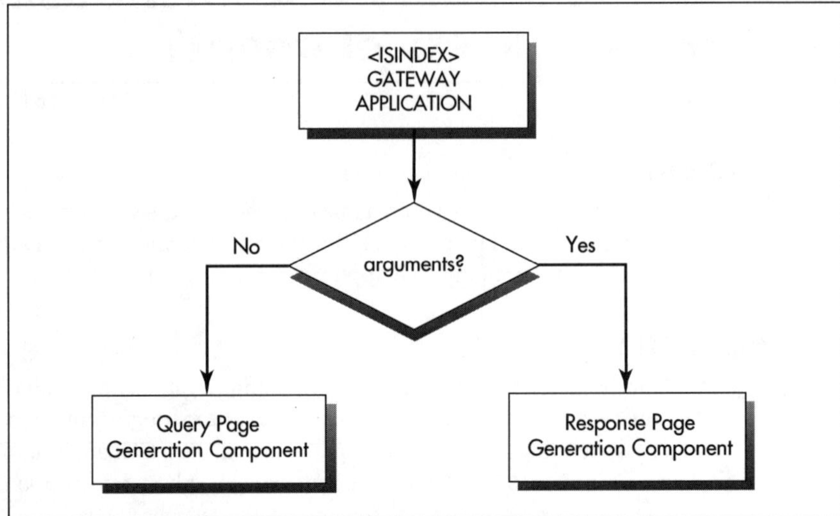

Figure 14-7 <ISINDEX> application architecture

2. Determine whether any command-line arguments have been passed to your application program. If no arguments are present, call the query generation component. If arguments are present, process them and call the response generation component. In the sample application, use an `if` statement to determine whether arguments are present. The `then` portion leads to the query generator, whereas the `else` (step 6) leads to the response generator.

```
# Determine if command line arguments are present.
if [ $# = 0 ]; then
```

3. Develop the query generation component. The first part of the query generation sends the `Content-type` server directive, followed by a blank line. Because you are using an `<ISINDEX>` element, specify `text/html` as the type. In the example, the `echo` command places this information on the standard output.

```
echo Content-type: text/html
echo
```

NOTE

If this `<ISINDEX>` application is a nonparsed header application (`nph-` prefix on the application filename), generate the full response header as described in How-To 14.2.

4. Attached to this response header, include an HTML document that has the `<ISINDEX>` element in the `<HEAD>` component. The `<HEAD>` component should also contain an appropriate title for the generated document. In the sample application, use the `cat` command to place this information on the standard output. (This particular `cat` command also places the body on the standard output in step 5.)

```
cat << EOF
<!DOCTYPE HTML PUBLIC "-//W3C//DTD HTML 3.2//EN">
<HTML>
<HEAD>
<TITLE>Finger Query</TITLE>
<<ISINDEX>>
</HEAD>
```

5. Add information relevant to the application and the proper format for submitting input text in the body of the document. In the Bourne shell file, a `cat` command places this information on the standard output (continued from the listing in step 4). The `EOF` command signals the end of the information.

```
<BODY>
<H1>Finger Query</H1>
<HR>
This is a "finger" query page. Enter a series of user@host entries in the
available search dialog.
<HR>
</BODY>
</HTML>
EOF
```

6. Develop a response to the query. The response to the query is like any other gateway application response. A server directive (or response header for `nph` applications) is sent, terminating with a blank line. The blank line is followed by an attached file, if required. The sample application signifies the response generation component with the `else` command from the `if` statement entered in step 2:

```
else
```

7. The response document is begun by sending the appropriate server directive on the standard output. As with the query component, the sample application uses the `echo` command to perform this task:

```
# Generate Response Document

echo Content-type: text/html
echo
```

8. Generate the attached file by processing and sending back an appropriately generated document. In the sh script example, this is done using a `cat` command. The processing of the arguments is embedded in the document generation process.

```
cat << EOF
<!DOCTYPE HTML PUBLIC "-//W3C//DTD HTML 3.2//EN">
<HTML>
<HEAD>
<TITLE>Finger Response</TITLE>
</HEAD>
<BODY>
<H1>Finger Response</H1>
<HR>
Input Terms Were: $*
<PRE>
EOF

$FINGER $*

cat << EOF
</PRE>
<HR>
</BODY>
</HTML>
EOF
```

9. Add any necessary closing information. In the sample application developed in this procedure, the closing information is simply the termination of the `if` statement that checked the argument count:

```
if
```

10. Save the application and compile it, if necessary.

11. If feasible, test your application. First, run it with no arguments to see that it generates a proper HTML document with `<ISINDEX>` in the `<HEAD>`. Then, if the response component generates a readable output (for example, text or HTML), run your application with command-line arguments.

12. Install your `<ISINDEX>` application as described for CGI application installation in How-To 14.4.

How It Works

When a browser first accesses the URL of your application through a link or an open location, your application launches without command-line arguments (unless the author or opener has appended a query string to the URL). Your application detects that no command-line arguments are present and executes the query generation component. When the user enters the desired input in the query page, the server launches the same application; however, the browser appends a query string composed of the user response to the URL. Therefore, the server converts the query string into command-line arguments and launches your application. This execution of your application receives command-line arguments and runs the response component of the application.

The sample application developed through this procedure can be found in file `SECOND.CGI` on the CD-ROM.

When a link to a URL without a query string attached associated with an `<ISINDEX>` gateway application is triggered, the server launches the application without command-line arguments; therefore, the query generation component executes. For the sample application, running the query generator component results in the HTML document seen in Figure 14-8.

If you enter data in the provided query field and submit the request, the browser generates a request with the inputs attached to the URL as a query string. This URL is submitted to the server, which launches the gateway application with the items in the query string passed as command-line arguments. If you launch the sample application with the query text `president@whitehouse.gov`, the result is a document like the one shown in Figure 14-9.

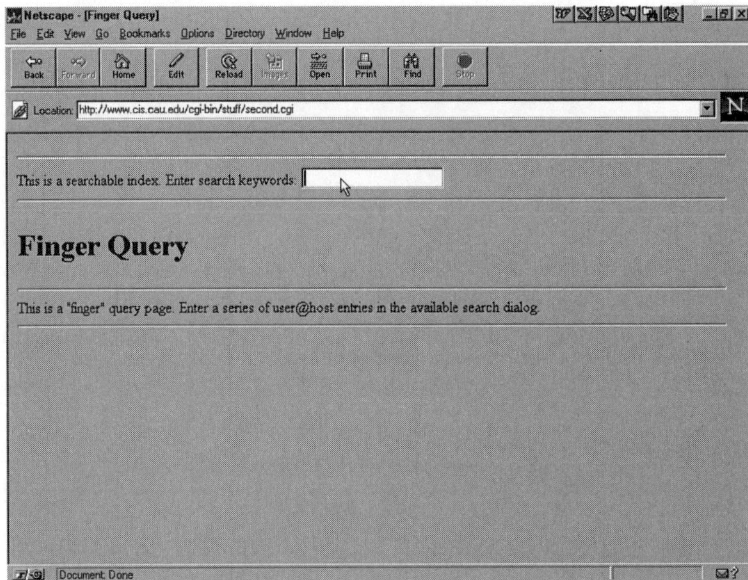

Figure 14-8 Execution of `second.cgi` without command-line arguments

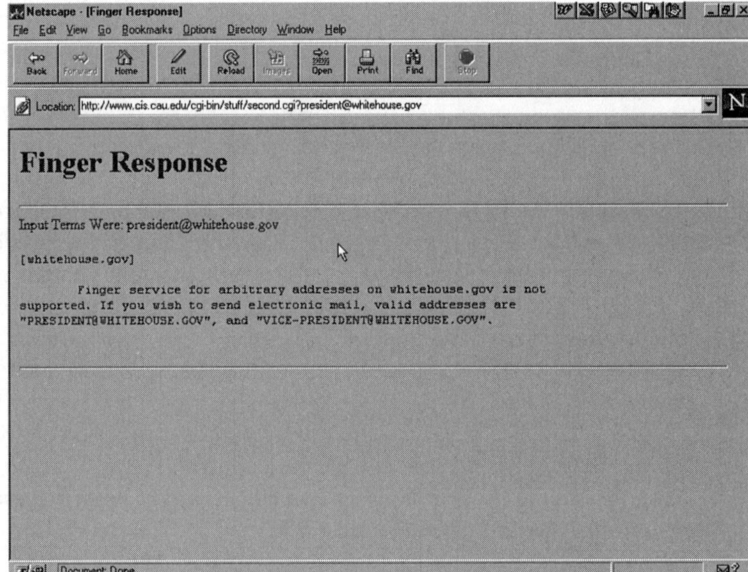

Figure 14-9 Execution of `second.cgi` with command-line arguments

Comments

Even though the sample application was developed using the Bourne shell language, the components represented in the code can be used for **<ISINDEX>** applications written in any development language. You must map your language's constructs into the three primary tasks specified:

- ✔ Decision
- ✔ Query generation
- ✔ Response generation

Steps 7 and 8 of the procedure can be modified if a different type of response is required, based on the processing of the data. In the sample script, the response from `finger` was presented, whether it generated a valid response or an error. In your application, you might want to send a different response message based on the results of processing the data. For example, if the input is processed correctly, you might send a TIFF file with a `Content-type: image/tiff`, a redirection command with a `Location:URL`, or a particular error with a `Status` directive. If an error is generated, you might want to respond with an HTML document describing the error that occurred.

The `finger` program is a UNIX utility that provides information about valid users on specified machines. The formats for acceptable command-line arguments are provided in Table 14-8. Multiple command-line arguments are acceptable.

Table 14-8 Information request arguments of `finger`

COMMAND-LINE ARGUMENT	INFORMATION REQUEST
`user`	Information for user on current machine
`user@host`	Information for user on host machine
`@host`	List users currently on host machine

14.6 How do I... Access client data in sh CGI scripts?

COMPATIBILITY: CGI, BOURNE SHELL

Problem

For reasons of portability, I've decided to write gateway applications using Bourne shell scripts. I must retrieve user-specified form data. The information is encoded and sent by several means. Is there an efficient mechanism for accessing the data that was originally entered?

Technique

Your first step in developing a Bourne shell application that requires user input data is the retrieval of the input data. This common task is performed by all CGI applications that require input data. This information can be in several forms:

- ✔ Query string from a **GET** method form
- ✔ Standard input from a **POST** method form
- ✔ Command-line arguments from an **<ISINDEX>** query

This How-To provides step-by-step instructions for retrieving and accessing input data from both **GET** and **POST** method forms. How-To 14.5 presents a way to retrieve **<ISINDEX>** data.

Steps

To access user input data from a Bourne shell script, you develop and install a helper application that parses the input data and places it in environment variables that can be accessed by your shell script.

The helper application called **shparse** was developed in the C language, and the first three steps involve the creation and installation of this program.

The remainder of the steps provide instructions on incorporating the helper function in your gateway scripts and offer a simple sample script. If the **shparse** program has already been compiled and installed in a location visible to your sh application, you should skip ahead to step 4.

1. Copy the following files from the CD-ROM to a local directory where you will build the **shparse** program:

parse.h: This file contains necessary header information.

parse.c: This file holds the helper function and declarations for reconstructing **POST** method form data.

parseget.c: This file holds the helper function and declarations for reconstructing **GET** method form data.

shparse.c: This file holds the main **shparse** application.

2. Using your C compiler, compile the three C files that you just copied in the previous step and rename the output **shparse**, for example:

```
gcc -o shparse parse.c parseget.c shparse.c
```

3. Move the **shparse** application to a location visible to your shell gateway programs. Make sure that the file security for the **shparse** application is set for execution by all individuals who need access to it.

4. Open your Bourne shell application in your text editor.

5. Insert the following lines to specify a Bourne shell script and to read the user input data into environment variables:

```
#!/bin/sh

eval `shparse`
```

6. Develop the rest of your application. All input data appears in environment variables with the **INPUT_** prefix. The remainder of each variable name is the attribute associated with the attribute/value pair. If multiple inputs have the same attribute, they are placed in the environment individually, as **INPUT_SUF**, **INPUT_SUF_D1**, **INPUT_SUF_D2**, and so on.

NOTE

If you want to change the default prefix from INPUT_ to something else, modify the shparse.c file before compilation.

7. Test your application by running it with suitable environment variables set and providing data on the standard input, if necessary. If the application works as you expect, proceed to the next step; otherwise, debug your sh script as necessary.

8. Install your application in a suitable location. Refer to How-To 14.4 for information on application installation.

How It Works

The first step in your CGI application is to call the **shparse** application in the manner just described. Figure 14-10 shows how your Bourne shell script and the **shparse** application interact with each other and with the server.

After the input data has been parsed, your script can access and process this data as necessary to generate the proper response. The response is passed back to the server, and from the server to the browser. The output of your gateway application should conform to the standard specifications, as described in How-To 14.2.

Next is a sample application written using the **shparse** application developed in this How-To.

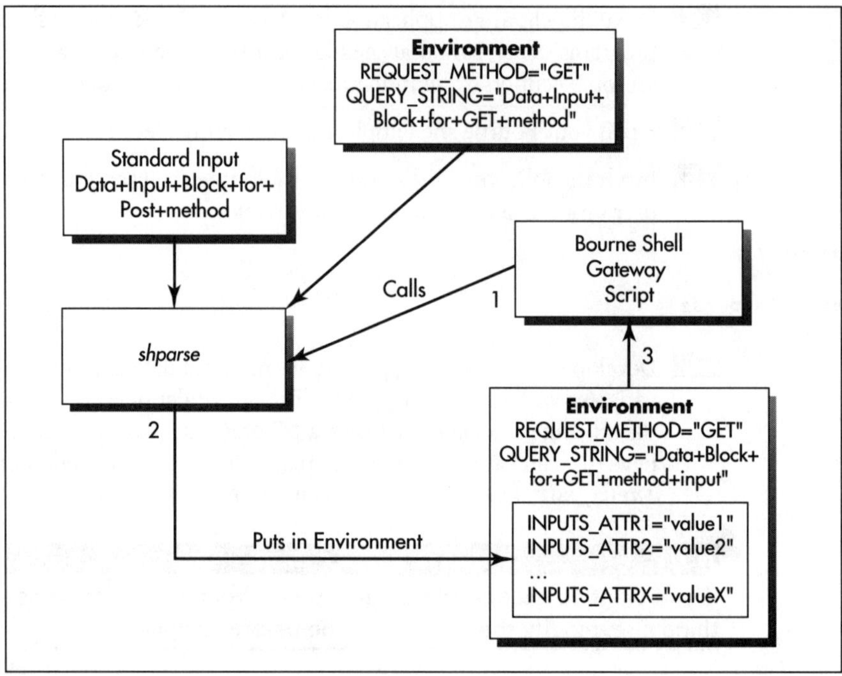

Figure 14-10 `shparse` and your Bourne shell gateway program

```
#!/bin/sh

eval `shparse`

echo Content-type: text/plain
echo

echo argc is $#. argv is "$*".
echo

echo Environment Variables
echo SERVER_SOFTWARE = $SERVER_SOFTWARE
echo SERVER_NAME = $SERVER_NAME
echo REQUEST_METHOD = $REQUEST_METHOD
echo HTTP_ACCEPT = "$HTTP_ACCEPT"
echo PATH_INFO = "$PATH_INFO"
echo PATH_TRANSLATED = "$PATH_TRANSLATED"
echo SCRIPT_NAME = "$SCRIPT_NAME"
echo QUERY_STRING = "$QUERY_STRING"
echo REMOTE_HOST = $REMOTE_HOST
echo REMOTE_ADDR = $REMOTE_ADDR
echo REMOTE_USER = $REMOTE_USER
echo AUTH_TYPE = $AUTH_TYPE
echo CONTENT_TYPE = $CONTENT_TYPE
echo CONTENT_LENGTH = $CONTENT_LENGTH
```

```
echo Form Inputs
echo INPUT_T1 = $INPUT_T1
echo INPUT_T2 = $INPUT_T2
echo INPUT_T3 = $INPUT_T3
```

This application displays generic environment variables, plus the environment variables `INPUT_T1`, `INPUT_T2`, and `INPUT_T3`. These three environment variables are assumed to have been generated by the evaluation of the results of **shparse**. The values associated with form input fields `T1`, `T2`, and `T3` are stored respectively in the previously mentioned environment variables.

Comments

These programs and scripts were developed and tested on a UNIX platform machine. Modification may be necessary, depending on the target platform.

Furthermore, complications will arise if an attribute name ends in the suffix `_DX` or if more than 10 values are associated with a particular attribute.

COMPLEXITY
ADVANCED

14.7 How do I... Parse client data in CGI programs and scripts?

COMPATIBILITY: CGI

Problem

The browser transforms HTML form data before submitting it to the appropriate server, and ultimately to my gateway application. How do I process this data to regenerate the original data submitted by the user?

Technique

You have created a form to query the reader for information necessary for the generation of a dynamic document. Each entry the user makes is associated with an attribute, or name, defined in your form. The form data is passed to your application through the server. However, this information is modified in the process. Because most CGI applications must transform and parse this data, a systematic approach to regenerating the input data is desirable.

This How-To presents a generic method suitable to break the data block passed to your gateway application into its original form. Figure 14-11 gives an overview of this processing technique.

The browser receives the data entered into HTML forms. For safety and security reasons, the browser transforms the special characters in this form data. The browser transmits this data to the server through either a `GET` or a `POST` method transaction.

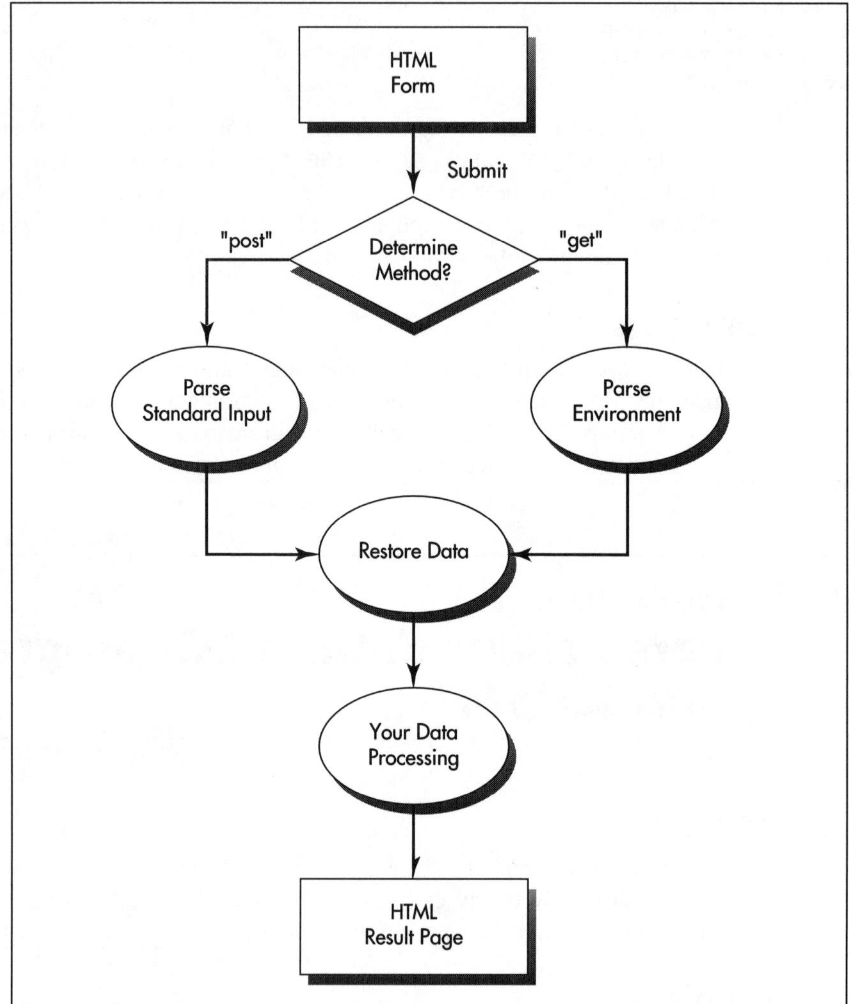

Figure 14-11 Regenerating HTML form data in gateway applications

Depending on the method, your gateway application retrieves the data from the environment or standard input, respectively. You must then transform the data to restore the special characters. Your application can now proceed to processing the data and generating an HTML results page.

Steps

The following steps enable you to parse and transform the modified data passed to your program. The original data will be placed in a specified location, with each of the attributes specified in your HTML form associated with the data the user entered.

The "Comments" section describes the use of this procedure with several common gateway application development languages.

1. Open the source code of your gateway application.

2. Determine the request method used to pass data to your application. This information is stored in the **REQUEST_METHOD** environment variable. In C, you retrieve this information using the **getenv** function; for example, the following line stores the method type in the **app_check** variable:

```
/* Check to determine what method was used to call this application.  */
app_check=getenv("REQUEST_METHOD");
```

3. Parse the data from the appropriate source depending upon the request method. If the request method is **GET**, parse the data from the **QUERY_STRING** environment variable. If the request method is **POST**, retrieve the data from the standard input. For example, in Perl, the following lines retrieve the data sent by a **GET** request:

```
#Read the form data from the environment
$data = $ENV{ QUERY_STRING };
```

For a **POST** request, the following lines retrieve the data:

```
#Determine the length of the POST'd data.
$len = $ENV{ CONTENT_LENGTH };
#Read the form data from the standard input
read(STDIN, $data, $len);
```

4. Separate the attribute/value pairs.

5. Break the pairs into attributes and values.

6. Restore the special characters. This process depends significantly on your implementation language. The "How It Works" section describes this process.

NOTE

You can combine steps 4 through 6 if this combination yields a more suitable implementation.

7. Implement the data processing and result generation components of your gateway application. (See How-To 14.6 for an example using a Bourne shell.)

8. Save your gateway application.

9. Compile your program, if necessary.

10. Test your application. You might need to set environment variables manually and supply standard input data to perform this task. Correct any errors.

11. Install your application in a suitable location. Refer to How-To 14.4 for information on application installation.

How It Works

Your CGI application must retrieve and restore form data before use. When a reader triggers the Submit button for your form, the browser packages and transmits the entered data. The HTTP request type specified in the form's `METHOD` attribute determines how the browser sends this data.

`POST` is the preferred transmission method because a `POST` data block does not have as many size constraints. The maximum size of the command line and maximum length of an environment variable both constrain a `GET` method data block. With the `GET` method, the browser transforms the form data and appends it to the URL submitted to the server. With the `POST` method, the browser composes the information entered in a form into a data block that it passes to the server as the attached object in the HTTP request.

The server passes the data to the CGI application either as an environment variable or as standard input, for `GET` and `POST` requests, respectively. You must transform this data back into standard ASCII and then resolve it back into attribute/value pairs. These attribute/value pairs can then be accessed by the CGI application.

The browser transforms the input data by stringing together attribute/value pairs. The browser places an equal sign (=) between each attribute and its value, and it places an ampersand (`&`) between each pair. It converts the spaces in any attribute or value to plus signs (+) and converts any special characters into an escaped value (as seen in Table 14-3 in How-To 14.1).

Therefore, breaking the data passed to the gateway program at ampersands reconstitutes the pairs, and breaking the pairs at equal signs separates the components of the pair. The restoration of each attribute or value to its original format is accomplished by examining each character and modifying it appropriately. Plus signs in the input are changed back to spaces. Escaped characters, when encountered, are converted back to their original ASCII form.

For example, the form shown next has three data fields named `"message"`, `"teacher"`, and `"topic"` that will be composed and sent to the CGI application `t2`. The `POST` method will be used to pass the data to the application.

```
<!DOCTYPE HTML PUBLIC "-//W3C//DTD HTML 3.2//EN">
<HTML>
<!-- Sample Data Entry Form - Calls CGI application t2 -->
<HEAD>
<TITLE>Sample Form</TITLE>
</HEAD>
```

```
<BODY>
<H1>Sample Form</H1>
<HR>
<FORM METHOD="POST" ACTION="http://www.mysite.edu/cgi-bin/t2"
ENCTYPE="application/x-www-form-urlencoded">
Enter the Text of your message below:<BR>
<TEXTAREA NAME="message" ROWS=10 COLS=40></TEXTAREA>
<INPUT TYPE="hidden" NAME="teacher" VALUE="dsk@cau.auc.edu">
<INPUT TYPE="hidden" NAME="topic" VALUE="Miscellaneous">
<INPUT TYPE="submit" VALUE="Mail">
</FORM>
<HR>
<H6>Last Modified: March 9, 1995 by dsk@cau.auc.edu</h6>
</BODY>
</HTML>
```

Figure 14-12 shows how Microsoft Internet Explorer presents this form. It has a single visible input field and a Submit-type button labeled Mail. Two hidden input fields are also present.

When the button is pressed, the browser composes an input block and passes the information to the specified CGI application via the server. The data block generated for this sample form looks like this:

```
message=This+is+a+sample+of+text+input.++This+might+have%0Abeen+entered+⇐
into+the+sample+form+whose%0Asource+appears+in+figure+5%2D8%2D1.++How+will+⇐
it%0Abe+processed%3F&teacher=dsk@cau.auc.edu&topic=Miscellaneous
```

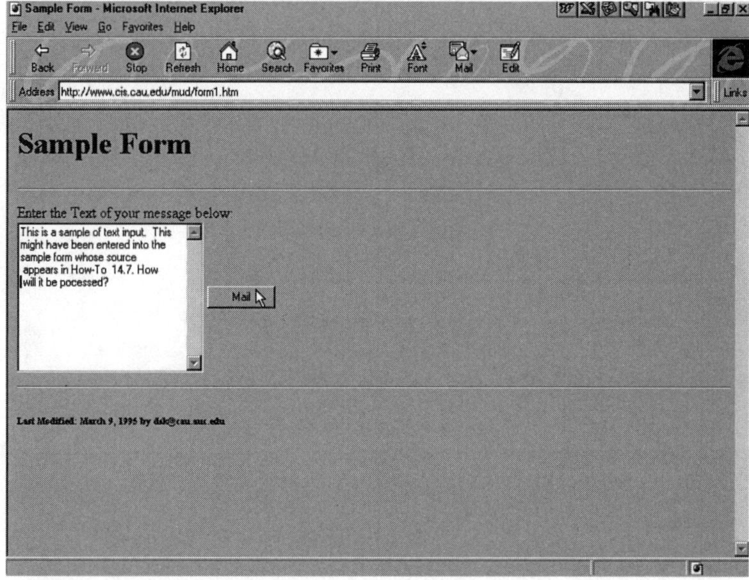

Figure 14-12 Sample form (as displayed) with input

Comments

The CD-ROM contains source code in several programming languages that accomplishes the tasks specified in the preceding steps. Following are specific instructions for each of these languages.

C Implementation

The C implementation of this process requires the files **parse.h**, **parse.c**, and **parseget.c**. The file **main.c** gives you a template to use for your C gateway program development.

To use these files, copy the file **main.c** to the filename that you want to use to store your main function. This file contains the C statements necessary to parse and restore HTML form data.

Edit this file to add any includes necessary to your application, any variables that must be declared, and the statements necessary to accomplish the remainder of your program. You access the form's data through the inputs array.

Compile **main.c**, **parse.c**, and **parseget.c**, together with any other required C files, to generate your executable application. You can test your application by simulating **GET** or **POST** requests by placing suitable information in the environment and on the standard input.

For the sample form shown in Figure 14-12, the inputs array after executing the supplied code contains the data (**input_count = 3**) shown in Table 14-9.

Table 14-9 Contents of input array for Figure 14-12

ENTRY	DATA
inputs[0].attribute	"message"
inputs[0].value	"This is a sample of text input. This might
	have\nbeen entered into the sample form
	whose\nsource appears in figure How-To 14.7. How will
	it\nbe processed?"
inputs[1].attribute	"teacher"
inputs[1].value	"dsk@cau.auc.edu"
inputs[2].attribute	"topic"
inputs[2].value	"Miscellaneous"

Multiple entries in the inputs array support multiple values for the same attribute. If the query string sent to your application were

```
t1=a1&t2=a2&t1=a3
```

the inputs array would store multiple entries for the same attributes. The values in the relevant variables for the query string are shown in Table 14-10. The attribute **"t1"** would have values of **"a1"** and **"a3"**.

Table 14-10 Duplicate values example under C

VARIABLE	VALUE
input_count	3
inputs[0].attribute	"t1"
inputs[0].value	"a1"
inputs[1].attribute	"t2"
inputs[1].value	"a2"
inputs[2].attribute	"t1"
inputs[2].value	"a3"

C++ Implementation

The C++ implementation uses the following files from the CD-ROM: **INPUTS.H**, **PARSE.H**, **PARSE.C**, **PARSEGET.C**, and **INPUTS.CPP**. When creating a C++ CGI program, add these files to the compile line. These files declare and define the **Inputs** class you will use to retrieve and restore form data.

The **Inputs** class is responsible for parsing and converting the form data. The public interface to the class provides the necessary access mechanism for the use of HTML form input. This class provides two methods: **count** and the indexing operator **[]**. The **count** method returns the number of attribute/value pairs that the browser sent. The indexing operator receives an attribute in the form of a string and returns a value associated with that attribute. In instances of multiple values, repeated use of the indexing operator with the same attribute index cycles through all values associated with the attribute. The return of a null pointer indicates the end of the cycle. If you must retrieve the first value instance for an attribute, you must reset the **Inputs** object; you do this by using an empty string (**""**) with the indexing operator.

NOTE

To guarantee finding all values, do not try to access the value of a second attribute until you have cycled through all values of the first.

When you declare an object of this class in your application, all the data management is performed for you. Plus signs in the input are changed back to spaces. Escaped characters (refer to Table 14-3 in How-To 14.1), when encountered, are converted back to their original ASCII form. The **Inputs** object will provide you with access to pass the data through the indexing operator.

In your application program, you must add the following line to include the declaration of the **Inputs** class:

```
#include "Inputs.h"
```

You perform the retrieve and restore functions by declaring an object of class **Input**. If you pass no parameters, the default values are assumed for the maximum number of pairs, length of attribute fields, and length of value fields. Specification of parameters will substitute the value given for the default. The following lines of code provide a few sample declarations of objects:

```
Inputs inputs;               // Take defaults
Inputs inputs(10);           // Only 10 input pairs maximum
Inputs inputs(10,64);        // Only 10 inputs and max attrib length of 64
Inputs inputs(10,64,128);    // Only 10 inputs, 64 max on attrib, 128 max
                             // On val
```

Access is provided to this data through the use of the indexing operator. The index used is the attribute for which you want to find the value. In the example shown in Figure 14-12, indexing the **Inputs** object would yield the results in Table 14-11. In this table, the ordering of accesses matters.

Table 14-11 Data access under C++ from the form in Figure 14-12

VARIABLE	VALUE
`inputs["message"]`	`"This is a sample of text input. This might have\nbeen entered into the sample form whose\nsource appears in How-To 14.7. How will it\nbe processed?"`
`inputs["teacher"]`	`"dsk@cau.auc.edu"`
`inputs["teacher"]`	`(char *)null`
`inputs["topic"]`	`"Miscellaneous"`
`inputs["teacher"]`	`"dsk@cau.auc.edu"`
`inputs[""]`	`(char *)null`
`inputs["teacher"]`	`"dsk@cau.auc.edu"`

The **Inputs** class provides a cycling method for accessing multiple values associated with an attribute. For example, the input string here would indicate that the attribute **"t1"** has values of **"a1"** and **"a3"**:

```
t1=a1&t2=a2&t1=a3
```

The resulting **Inputs** object would return the first value in the first access, the second value in the second access, and a null pointer on the third access attempt. The values in the relevant variables derived from the query string are shown in Table 14-12.

Table 14-12 C++ handling of duplicate values

VARIABLE	VALUE
`inputs["t1"]`	`"a1"`
`inputs["t2"]`	`"a2"`

VARIABLE	VALUE
inputs["t1"]	"a1"
inputs["t1"]	"a3"
inputs["t1"]	(char *)NULL

The order in which the accesses occur is significant. The cycle for the "t1" attribute resets at the access of the value of attribute "t2". The null pointer returned in the last line indicates a full cycle through the values of attribute "t1".

Perl Implementation

The Perl implementation of the data retrieval and restoration process uses the file `main.pl` from the CD-ROM. You can use this file as a template for your gateway scripts. Copy this file to whatever name you want for your Perl CGI application and add the commands necessary to implement the processing and result generation portions of your script.

The Perl commands in `main.pl` provide you with the necessary retrieval and restoration of the form data. The script first checks the HTTP method used in the request. Based on this information, the script determines the location of the input data block. The transformation of the data occurs in the following order:

- ✔ All spaces restored
- ✔ Attribute/value pairs separated
- ✔ All ampersands (&) restored
- ✔ Pairs separated into attributes and values
- ✔ Special characters restored for all attributes and values
- ✔ Array inputs defined

Your commands access the form data submitted through the inputs array. Use the attribute name as the index to access the value. For example, the form shown in Figure 14-12 fills the inputs array as shown in Table 14-13.

Table 14-13 Figure 14-12 data access from Perl

VARIABLE	VALUE
inputs{message}	"This is a sample of text input. This might
	have\nbeen entered into the sample form
	whose\nsource appears in How-To 14.7. How will
	it\nbe processed?"
inputs{teacher}	"dsk@cau.auc.edu"
inputs{topic}	"Miscellaneous"

14.8 How do I... Process FILE type input from an HTML form?

COMPATIBILITY: HTML 3.2+, CGI, NETSCAPE NAVIGATOR

Problem

The browser transforms HTML form data before submitting it to the appropriate server, and ultimately to my gateway application. I cannot use the standard approach because the form is sending a file as input. How do I access this form data?

Technique

You have created a form to query the reader for information necessary for the generation of a dynamic document. Each entry the user makes is associated with an attribute, or name, defined in your form. The form data is passed to your application through the server. However, this information is modified in the process. Because most CGI applications must transform and parse this data, a systematic approach to regenerating the input data is desirable.

This How-To presents a generic method suitable to break the data block passed to your gateway application into its original form. Figure 14-11 in How-To 14.7 gives an overview of the processing technique for standard gateway applications. Figure 14-13 extends this general approach to deal with HTML 4.0's `FILE` input type.

The browser receives the data entered into HTML forms and combines this with any files selected. The browser transmits this data to the server through a `POST` method transaction. Your gateway application retrieves the data from the standard input. You must parse the data to regenerate the attribute/value pairs. Your application can now proceed to processing the data and generating an HTML results page.

NOTE

Currently, only the Netscape Navigator browser supports this aspect of the HTML 4.0 standard. Other browser software that supports HTML forms will not allow the submission of `FILE` type input data. Furthermore, the submission process has not been formalized into the CGI/1.1 standard; therefore, the process described in this How-To examines the mechanism established by Netscape to convey `FILE` type information. Published specifications indicate Microsoft's intent to support `FILE` type input in the Internet Explorer browser.

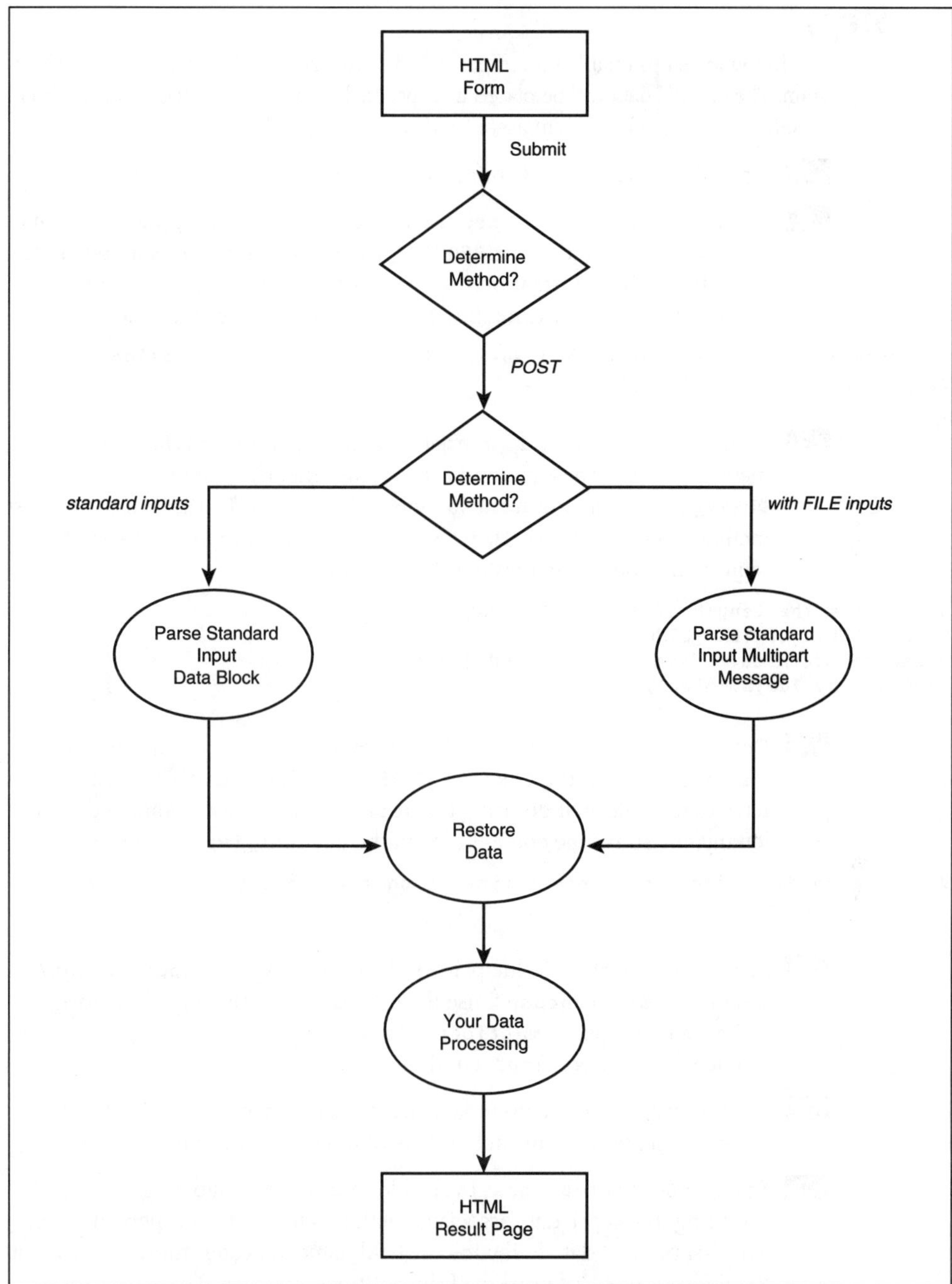

Figure 14-13 Regenerating HTML form data in gateway applications—revisited

Steps

The following steps enable you to parse and transform the data passed to your program. The original data will be placed in a specified location, with each of the attributes specified in your HTML form associated with the data the user entered.

1. Open the source code of your gateway application.

2. Determine the request method used to pass data to your application. This information is stored in the **REQUEST_METHOD** environment variable. In C, you retrieve this information using the **getenv** function; for example, the following line stores the method type in the **app_check** variable:

```
/* Check to determine what method was used to call this application.  */
app_check=getenv("REQUEST_METHOD");
```

3. Parse the data from the appropriate source, depending on the request method. If the request method is **GET**, parse the data from the **QUERY_STRING** environment variable (refer to How-To 14.7). If the request method is **POST**, retrieve the data from the standard input. For a **POST** request, the following lines retrieve the data:

```
#Determine the length of the POST'd data.
$len = $ENV{ CONTENT_LENGTH };
#Read the form data from the standard input
read(STDIN, $data, $len);
```

4. Determine the content type of the data on the standard input. This information is stored in the **CONTENT_TYPE** environment variable. In C, you retrieve this information using the **getenv** function; for example, the following line stores the content type in the **content_type** variable:

```
/* Check to determine what content type is on the standard input.  */
content_type=getenv("CONTENT_TYPE");
```

5. Separate the attribute/value pairs. If the content type is **"application/x-www-form-urlencode"**, use the procedure described in How-To 14.7. If the content type is **"multipart/form-data; boundary=some_string"**, continue with this process.

6. Find an instance of the boundary string. (See Appendix C, "MIME," for more information on the architecture of multipart MIME messages.)

7. Scan the **Content-Disposition** field immediately following the boundary string. Break the data associated with this field into component pieces. The first piece of data following the field name indicates information about the derivation of this portion of the multipart message. This data item should indicate that the component is **"form-data"**. The remaining data

items represent paired data. Among these data, a pair with the identifier **"name"** indicates the attribute name from the HTML form associated with the data in this portion of the multipart message. For example:

```
Content-Disposition: form-data; name="category"
```

This line indicates that the message body for this portion of the multipart message contains the value data associated with the **category** attribute, the data submitted by the user for the **INPUT** item in the HTML form with the **NAME="category"**.

8. In the situation where the **Content-Disposition** field contains filename paired data entry, the body in this portion of the message represents a file submitted through a **FILE** type input field. If this is not the case, proceed with step 9 to parse and store the data value. The message portion header of a file submission contains an additional field indicating the content type of the field submitted. Your gateway application will need to determine *a priori* whether or not it can deal with file data of this content type—for example,

```
Content-Disposition: form-data; name="stuff"; filename="C:\caulogo.gif"
Content-Type: image/gif
```

The first line indicates that the message body for this portion of the multipart message contains the value data associated with the **stuff** attribute. On the client machine running the browser, the file submitted is named **C:\caulogo.gif**. The second line indicates that the file submitted is a GIF image. (See Appendix C for additional information on potential MIME types.)

9. Read the blank line that separates the header portion of this part of the multipart message from the body portion.

10. Read the body portion and dispose of the data as required by your application. A usual disposition of standard form data might be in name/value paired character arrays. File data might require an indirect method of storage, such as storing the **INPUT** field name and the filename as a paired character array while caching the actual file on the server's hard disk.

11. The body portion terminates with another instance of the boundary string. If this is the end of the file, continue with step 12 to process the data; otherwise, return to step 7 to process the next portion of the message.

NOTE

The last instance of the boundary string usually has two additional dashes appended to it.

12. Implement the data processing and result generation components of your gateway application. (Refer to How-To 14.6 for an example using the Bourne shell.)

13. Save your gateway application.

14. Compile your program, if necessary.

15. Test your application. You might need to set environment variables manually and supply standard input data to perform this task. Correct any errors.

16. Install your application in a suitable location. Refer to How-To 14.4 for information on application installation.

How It Works

HTML form data that includes submitted files requires the use of the `ENCTYPE="multipart/form-data"` attribute in the `<FORM>` element. The use of this encoding type instructs Netscape Navigator (the only browser currently supporting `FILE` input types) to submit the HTML form data as a multipart MIME message (see Appendix C).

Figure 14-14 displays a form using this type of encoding; the complete HTML source for this form is in the `FILEDNLD.HTM` file on the CD-ROM. The `<FORM>` element that generates the input areas on this page appears here.

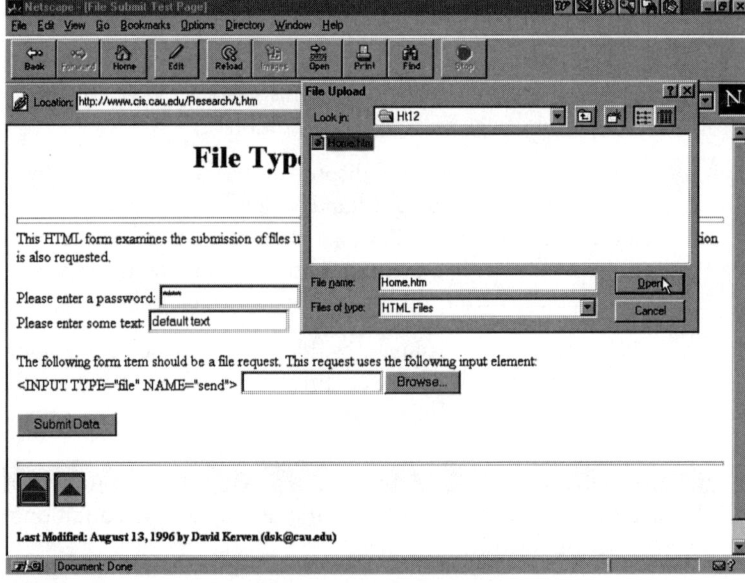

Figure 14-14 Sample file download form

```
<FORM ACTION="/cgi-bin/p" METHOD="POST" ENCTYPE="multipart/form-data">
<!-- Hidden Element -->
<INPUT TYPE="hidden" NAME="hide" VALUE="newstuff">
Please enter a password:
<INPUT TYPE="password" NAME="pw"><BR>
Please enter some text:
<INPUT TYPE="text" NAME="txt" VALUE="default text">
<P>
The following form item should be a file request.
This request uses the following input element:<BR>
&lt;INPUT TYPE=&quot;file&quot; NAME=&quot;send&quot;&gt;
<INPUT TYPE="file" NAME="send">
<P>
<INPUT TYPE="submit" VALUE="Submit Data">
</FORM>
```

Selecting the Submit Data button in Figure 14-14 generates the following multipart message sent to the standard input of the specified gateway application:

```
-----------------------------51412919431542
Content-Disposition: form-data; name="hide"

newstuff
-----------------------------51412919431542
Content-Disposition: form-data; name="pw"

adfa
-----------------------------51412919431542
Content-Disposition: form-data; name="txt"

default text
-----------------------------51412919431542
Content-Disposition: form-data; name="send";
filename="C:\MSOFFICE\WINWORD\HTML3HT\CHAP2\CD\HT12\Home.htm"
Content-Type: text/html
<HTML>
<HEAD>
<TITLE>Home Page of XXXXXXXXXX</TITLE>
</HEAD>
<BODY>

<!-- Mark the beginning of this portion with a horizontal rule. -->
<HR>
<!-- Center your name as a level 1 header. -->
<H1>XXXXXXXX</H1>
<!-- Provide any desirable contact information. -->
999 My Street<BR>
City, ST Postalcode<BR>
E-mail: my_id@mysite.edu

<!-- Mark the beginning of this portion with a horizontal rule. -->
<HR>
<!-- Choose the heading text that you feel appropriate. -->
<H1>About Me</H1>
```

continued on next page

continued from previous page

```
<!-- The formatting and information should be developed to suit your ⇐
needs -->
This is the first paragraph in this section about myself.
I have been at MY BUSINESS for the past X years.
<P>
I am currently working on several projects.
These projects include...

<!-- Mark the beginning of this portion with a horizontal rule. -->
<HR>
<!-- Substitute the appropriate information in your document. The date ⇐
should -->
<!-- appear in a long format with the mont name written out since the ⇐
 order -->
<!-- conventions for date abbreviations vary. -->
Last modified on CURRENT_DATE by YOUR_NAME (YOUR_E-MAIL)

</BODY>
</HTML>

-----------------------------51412919431542--
```

Your gateway application must parse this multipart message and extract the necessary HTML form data in the form of attribute/value data pairs and file data. The process works by repeatedly parsing the subcomponents of the message, where each subcomponent is demarked by an arbitrarily chosen boundary string, `---------------51412919431542` in the example.

Each subcomponent has a header portion and a body portion. The header portion contains any relevant meta-information about the body portion. The body portion contains the actual data submitted through the form. A blank line separates the header portion from the body portion.

Minimally, the header contains a disposition field that indicates how the gateway application should treat the body portion; currently, the only defined disposition is `form-data`. The remainder of the disposition field contains information about the HTML form input item that generated the particular subcomponent. In the case of any input type other than `FILE`, this usually simply contains the name of the input item from the form. In the case of the `FILE` input types, the disposition field also contains the filename representing the location of the submitted file on the client submitting the file. Use the presence of the filename data pair on the disposition line to clue your gateway application in to the fact that the body portion of this subcomponent contains file input data. The header portion can also contain a `Content-type` field specifying the type of data sent in the body portion; file submission will always include this field.

The body portion of the subcomponent contains the actual data submitted by the user. For HTML form input other than file type, the body portion contains the relevant value that the user entered. Unlike a data block, this textual information is not URL encoded. In the case of file type form input, the header contains a **Content-type** field describing the type of file sent; the body portion contains the data of the type specified. For information concerning the different types of data, see the information in Appendix C.

Comments

The file **P.C** on the CD-ROM contains the source code for the p application that processes the data from the form shown in Figure 14-14. This application simply generates a **text/plain Content-type** server directive (see How-To 14.2), calls a standard test application that displays the pertinent environment variables, and displays the multipart MIME message sent by the browser. Figure 14-15 displays the result of submitting the form shown in Figure 14-14.

This application does not separate the input data. It is a diagnostic application for viewing any **POST** method form submissions.

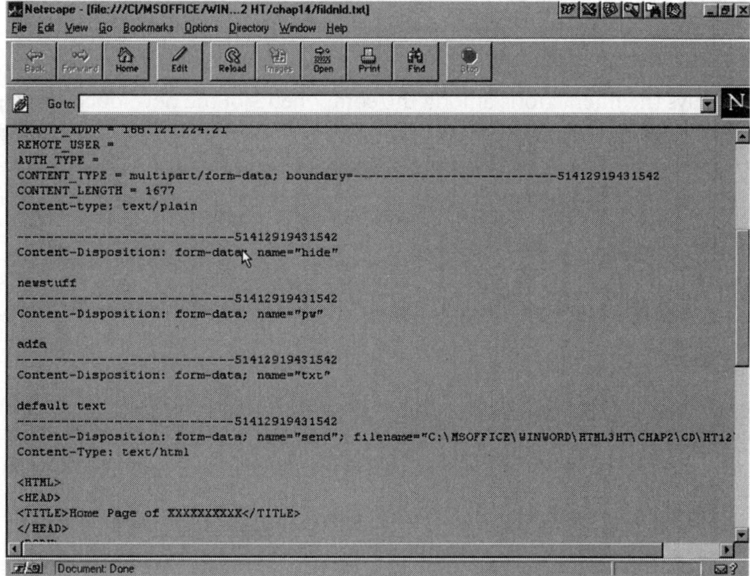

Figure 14-15 Environment variables and multipart MIME message generated

14.9 How do I... Write a CGI application to send me e-mail?

COMPATIBILITY: CGI; C; HTML 2, 3, 3.2

Problem

Some browsers support `mailto` resources, but not all. I want to let people send me e-mail through a Web page, whether their browser supports this or not. How can I generate an HTML form and gateway application to accomplish this task? What must I do to extend this capability to allow e-mail to be sent to other users?

Technique

Establishing e-mail Web pages for a specified group of users requires two gateway applications. The first generates an HTML form to gather the e-mail message to be sent. The second CGI program receives the input from this form, determines whether the target of the e-mail is in a defined set of allowed targets, sends the e-mail if appropriate, and generates a resultant HTML document. Figure 14-16 displays the interactions among the components of the developed package.

This How-To shows a step-by-step process for developing, installing, and maintaining a CGI e-mail handling package on your server.

Steps

The C source code for the e-mail package is available on the CD-ROM in files `mailgen.c` and `mailsend.c`; you also need helper files `parse.h` and `parse.c`.

1. Change directories to the location where you want to perform your development tasks.
2. Copy the `maitgen.c` file from the CD-ROM. This file contains the source code for the application that will generate an e-mail form for any target.
3. Choose a name for the `mailsend` component of this package.
4. Open the `mailgen.c` file in your text editor.
5. Identify the following line and modify it to specify the URL for the `mailsend` CGI application:

```
/* This should point to the URL of the application that will send the  *
 * mail to the designated recipient.                                   */
#define MAILSEND http://www.mysite.edu:8080/cgi-bin/mailsend
```

This URL reflects the name chosen in step 3.

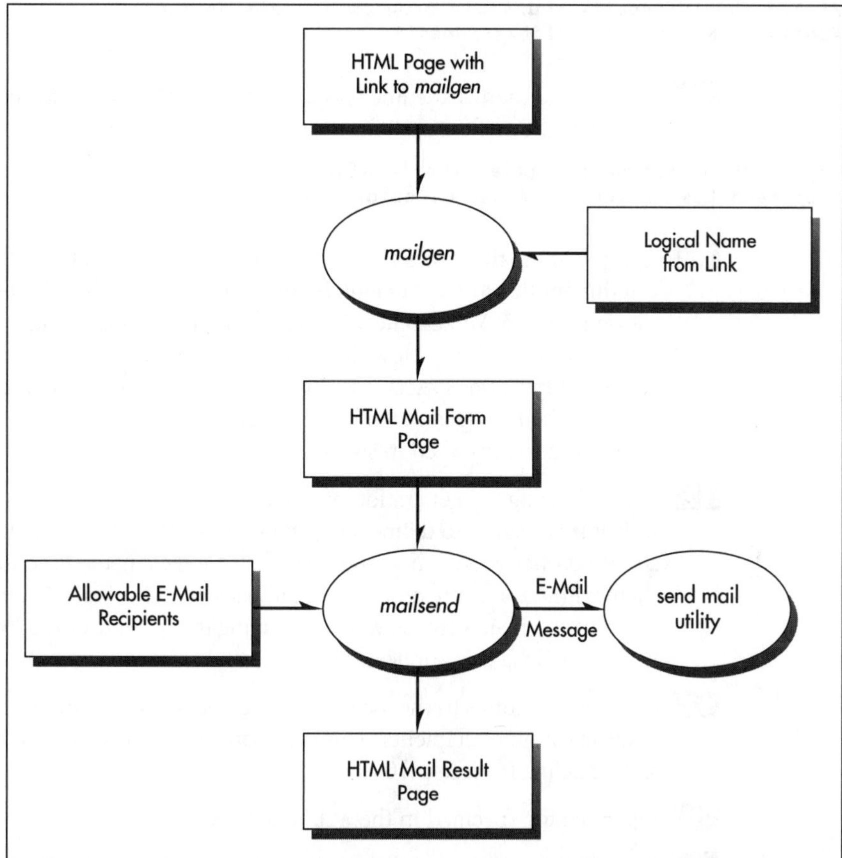

Figure 14-16 How the e-mail CGI package components interact

6. Compile `mailgen.c` and install the executable as you would any other gateway program. The default name for this executable is `mailgen`. Refer to How-To 14.4 for details on CGI application installation. Access this gateway application through a standard link with the logical name of the destination passed as additional path information.

7. Copy files `parse.h`, `parse.c`, and `mailsend.c` from the CD.

8. Open the `mailsend.c` file in your text editor. This file contains the source code for the application that sends the results of a form generated by `mailgen` to the appropriate recipient.

9. Identify and modify the line defining the location of your server system's `mailsend` utility. On UNIX systems, this utility is usually either `"sendmail"` or `"smail"`.

```
/* You should specify your mail program in this define.                */
#define SENDMAIL "/usr/lib/sendmail"
```

10. Identify and modify the line specifying the location of the file containing the list of allowable e-mail destinations.

```
/* The ALLOW define specifies the location of the allowable users file.*/
#define ALLOW "/usr/local/some_directory/.allow"
```

11. Compile these three files to create the **mailsend** application. If you do not call this application **mailsend**, be sure you specified the URL of this application in step 5. You can now install **mailsend** as you would any other CGI program. Refer to How-To 14.4 for more information on installing gateway applications. Access this gateway application through the specified action in the form generated by **mailgen**, or whatever you choose to call the application installed in step 6.

12. Begin allowing the generation of e-mail pages for selected users. Your first task at this stage is to define a group of users you want to provide with this service. Either you or they must establish a logical name used to refer to them within the context of this e-mail package. This logical name helps generate the mail form, as well as verifying that each user is allowed to receive mail via this application.

13. Change directories to the location where you want to store the file of allowable e-mail recipients. This is the directory you specified in the **ALLOW** define from step 10.

14. Open the file specified in the **ALLOW** define.

15. Add a line for each e-mail recipient. A line is composed of the logical name, followed by white space, followed by the e-mail address.

16. After entering all valid recipients, add a line containing the word **end**.

17. Generate e-mail forms for submitting mail to users specified in the **ALLOW** file by referencing the URL of the **mailgen** CGI application. Appended to this URL should be the logical name of the mail recipient in the form of path information. For example, if the **mailgen** program were located in the **/cgi-bin** directory and you wanted to create a link to a mail page for registered logical name **paul**, the requested URL would be **http://www.mysite.edu/cgi-bin/mailgen/paul**.

How It Works

The two programs, **mailgen** and **mailsend**, interact with each other and with the **ALLOW** file to provide a mechanism to support e-mail for a set of registered users.

The e-mail package is launched when a link referencing the URL of the **mailgen** application is triggered. For example, **http://www.mysite.edu/cgi-bin/mailgen/abner** specifies the e-mail entry page associated with the logical name **abner**.

NOTE

You can also enter the package by sending the proper data fields to the mailsend application via the POST HTTP method; however, in general, most users enter the package through mailgen.

When the link is triggered, a mail entry form is dynamically tailored to the specific logical name passed via additional path information. For example, the form displayed in Figure 14-16 was generated by a link designating logical name **dsk** as the target.

The user fills in the data fields with his or her name, return address, and the body of the message. When the Submit button is pressed, the input data is sent by **POST** method to the **mailsend** CGI application.

The **mailsend** application is responsible for processing and storing the data, as well as giving the user a response concerning the data items in question. The input data is passed to the application through an input data block on the standard input. Then **mailsend** calls the C build function to parse and convert the attribute/value pairs.

The **mailsend** application goes through the following steps in the process of delivering mail messages:

1. Retrieves the user input data from the form. This task is performed by the procedure in How-To 14.7 for parsing HTML **POST** method form data.
2. Opens the file of allowable mail recipients and checks for the specified logical name among those listed. If this is not present, **mailsend** returns an error document.
3. Opens a pipe to the **mailsend** utility.
4. Writes the mail message to this pipe.
5. Closes the pipe to the **mailsend** utility. This action in effect causes the e-mail to be sent to the specified recipient.
6. Begins generation of a response page.
7. Formats and presents the page to the user.
8. Closes the generated document.

If the data present in Figure 14-17 were submitted, then the resultant document would look like the one shown in Figure 14-18. The mail application on the server site would be responsible for handling the delivery of the mail to its destination.

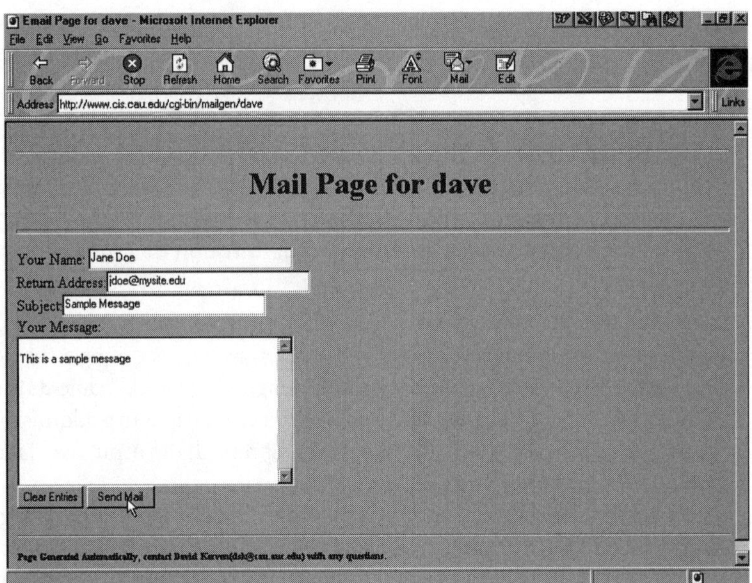

Figure 14-17 E-mail entry form

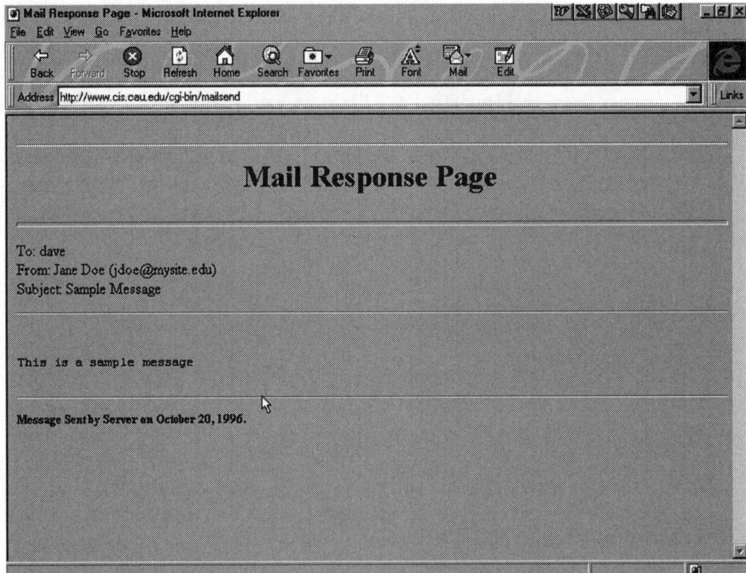

Figure 14-18 E-mail response page

Comments

The package developed in this How-To was compiled and tested in the UNIX environment. Porting the application to other environments will require some modification.

PART IV

DYNAMIC HTML AND OTHER ADVANCED TOPICS

CHAPTER 15

NAVIGATOR AND INTERNET EXPLORER HTML EXTENSIONS

15

NAVIGATOR AND INTERNET EXPLORER HTML EXTENSIONS

How do I...

The World Wide Web is changing at a remarkable rate. New browsers such as Microsoft Internet Explorer 3.0 and Netscape 4.0, with new HTML extensions, are unveiled all the time. New technologies such as Java and VRML have been introduced to the

World Wide Web. The range of capabilities available to Web page authors is growing every day. This chapter examines some of the new HTML extensions and new technologies. (Because some of the content of this chapter is based on beta versions of software and rapidly evolving languages and protocols, some of this information might be out of date by the time you read this.)

15.1 Add Marquees of Scrolling Text

Text scrolling across a page is a unique way to grab the attention of a reader. This How-To shows how to use an HTML extension in Microsoft Internet Explorer 3.0 to create marquees of text that can scroll across the screen in a variety of styles.

15.2 Use TrueType and Other Fonts

Now it is possible to exercise some control over the fonts in which a Web page is rendered. This How-To shows you how to set the fonts used.

15.3 Format My Web Page in Multiple Columns

You no longer need to use a table to create multiple-column Web pages. This How-To shows you an alternative way to create "newspaper"-style Web pages.

15.4 Insert Blank Space into My Web Page

There are times when you would like to have blank space (that is, nothing) on part of a Web page. This How-To shows you how to include blank space on a Web page.

15.5 Add Color to Tables

One way to make tables really stand out on a page is to include color cells and backgrounds. This How-To shows how easy it is to add colors to a table.

15.6 Add a Background Image to a Table

There are times when you might want to make a table a bit more exciting by adding a background image to it. This How-To shows you how to add background images to your tables.

15.7 Control Table Borders

There are times when you might want part of a table to have borders and another part either not to have borders or to have different borders. This How-To shows you how to control the borders of your tables.

15.8 Create New Windows for Linked Documents

Often it's useful to have a document that's referenced in a link in a Web page appear in a separate window so the reader can easily compare the two documents. This How-To shows how to use an HTML extension supported by Netscape 2.0 and above to open a separate window automatically and place the linked document there.

15.9 Use Netscape's Client Pull

The Netscape Client Pull feature provides a means for automatically loading new documents at specified time intervals. This capability provides support for slide shows as well as text-based animation. This How-To explains how to use the Netscape Client Pull feature in your documents.

15.10 Specify Netscape Server Push

With the Netscape viewer, you can develop gateway applications that provide automatically updating HTML pages. In this How-To, you will learn how to create Common Gateway Interface (CGI) applications to generate server-pushed HTML pages.

COMPLEXITY
INTERMEDIATE

15.1 How do I... Add marquees of scrolling text?

COMPATIBILITY: INTERNET EXPLORER 3.0

Problem

I would like to bring attention to some text on my Web page by scrolling it across the page. How can I easily create a marquee of scrolling text for my page?

Technique

Microsoft Internet Explorer 3.0 supports the HTML extension **<MARQUEE>**, which enables people using that browser to see marquees of text that scroll across the screen. Several attributes for the tag enable you to control the size, scrolling behavior, and color of the marquee.

Steps

1. Open your document and identify the text you want to use as the marquee and the location in the page for the marquee.

2. Place the **<MARQUEE>** tag at the beginning and the **</MARQUEE>** tag at the end of the text that will be in the marquee. This creates a default marquee that scrolls across the screen once—for example,

```
<MARQUEE>This is an example of a marquee</MARQUEE>
```

3. You can control the type of scrolling used with the **BEHAVIOR** attribute. The **BEHAVIOR** attribute supports three values, described in Table 15-1. The default value for **BEHAVIOR** is **SCROLL**.

Table 15-1 Values for the BEHAVIOR attribute in <MARQUEE>

VALUE	DESCRIPTION
ALTERNATE	Bounces the text back and forth between the two sides of the screen.
SCROLL	Starts the text all the way off the screen and moves it across the marquee all the way off the screen on the other side.
SLIDE	Starts the text all the way off the screen and moves it across the marquee until the text touches the margin on the other side of the screen.

To create a sliding marquee, use

```
<MARQUEE BEHAVIOR=SLIDE>This is an example of a sliding
marquee</MARQUEE>
```

To create a bouncing marquee, use

```
<MARQUEE BEHAVIOR=ALTERNATE>This is an example of a
bouncing marquee</MARQUEE>
```

4. The DIRECTION attribute controls the direction in which the text moves across the marquee. DIRECTION can have two values: LEFT (for text scrolling from right to left) and RIGHT (for text scrolling from left to right). The default value is LEFT. To create a scrolling marquee that goes from right to left, use

```
<MARQUEE DIRECTION=LEFT>This is an example of a marquee moving
 right to left</MARQUEE>
```

5. You can control the speed of the marquee with two attributes, SCROLLAMOUNT and SCROLLDELAY. SCROLLAMOUNT sets the number of pixels between each redraw of the marquee. That is, the next time the marquee is drawn, the contents of the marquee will be moved down by the number of pixels set by the SCROLLAMOUNT attribute. The SCROLLDELAY attribute sets the delay, in milliseconds, between redraws. A marquee can be speeded up by increasing the value of the SCROLLAMOUNT attribute (moving the text a greater distance between redraws), decreasing the value of the SCROLLDELAY attribute (shortening the time between redraws), or both. For example, to create a scrolling marquee that moves the text 25 pixels between redraws, you would use

```
<MARQUEE SCROLLAMOUNT=25>This is an example of a marquee</MARQUEE>
```

To create a marquee that waits 10 milliseconds between redraws, use

```
<MARQUEE SCROLLDELAY=10>This is an example of a marquee</MARQUEE>
```

To combine the two attributes in the same marquee, use

```
<MARQUEE SCROLLAMOUNT=25 SCROLLDELAY=10>This is an example of a marquee ⇐
</MARQUEE>
```

6. You can set the number of times the marquee scrolls across the page with the **LOOP** attribute. To create a continuously scrolling marquee, set **LOOP** equal to **-1** or **INFINITE**. To create a marquee that will scroll across the screen five times, use

```
<MARQUEE LOOP=5>This is an example of a marquee that scrolls 5 times ⇐
</MARQUEE>
```

To create a marquee that scrolls continuously, use

```
<MARQUEE LOOP=INFINITE>This is an example of a continuously scrolling ⇐
marquee</MARQUEE>
```

7. The **BGCOLOR** attribute sets the background color of the marquee. The attribute can be set to a hexadecimal set of red, green, and blue intensities (known as an *RGB triplet*) or to one of a set of special color names supported by Internet Explorer. For example, each of the following two lines creates a marquee with a red background:

```
<MARQUEE BGCOLOR="#FF0000">This is an example of a marquee with a
red background</MARQUEE>
<MARQUEE BGCOLOR="Red">This is an example of a marquee with a red
background</MARQUEE>
```

8. The **HEIGHT** and **WIDTH** attributes adjust the height and the width of the marquee. They can be set equal to a specific distance in pixels or to a percentage of the width or height of the screen. To create a marquee that is 300 pixels wide and 50 pixels high, use

```
<MARQUEE WIDTH=300 HEIGHT=50>This is an example of a marquee</MARQUEE>
```

To create a marquee that is 20 percent of the height of the screen and 75 percent of the width of the screen, use

```
<MARQUEE WIDTH=75% HEIGHT=20%>This is an example of a marquee</MARQUEE>
```

9. The **ALIGN** attribute sets the alignment of the text around the marquee. **ALIGN** can have three values: **TOP** (for text aligned with the top of the marquee), **MIDDLE** (for text aligned with the middle of the marquee), and **BOTTOM** (for text aligned with the bottom of the marquee). The **ALIGN** attribute does not control the alignment of text within the marquee. For example, to align text that follows the marquee with the top of the marquee, use

```
<MARQUEE ALIGN=TOP>The text that follows this marquee will be aligned with
the top of the marquee</MARQUEE> Some text that follows the marquee.
```

10. The **HSPACE** and **VSPACE** attributes adjust the horizontal and vertical margins, respectively, of the marquee. These attributes are set equal to the size, in pixels, of the margin. For example, to create a marquee with a 10-pixel margin on the top and bottom and a 15-pixel margin on the left and right, use

Scrolling Text
This is normal text.
This is a sample Marquee -- wee
This Marquee will scroll forever!

Figure 15-1 An example of <MARQUEE>

```
<MARQUEE VSPACE=10 HSPACE=15>This is an example of a marquee with
horizontal and vertical margins</MARQUEE>
```

An example of the **<MARQUEE>** tag is shown in Figure 15-1. The HTML code used to create the figure can be found on the CD-ROM as file **15-1.HTML**.

How It Works

When Internet Explorer recognizes the **<MARQUEE>** tag in a file, it creates a marquee on the page, using values from any attributes in the **<MARQUEE>** tag. The text moves across the marquee in the style defined by the attributes or by using the default values if no attribute values are specified.

Comments

The **<MARQUEE>** tag currently is supported only by Internet Explorer. Users with other browsers, such as Netscape and Mosaic, will be unable to see the marquee; the text will appear normally on the page. The use of long text strings in marquees and short values for the **SCROLLDELAY** attribute might slow down the user's computer, particularly a slower machine or one running other applications at the same time. You can find updated information about **<MARQUEE>** on the Web at the URL **http://www.microsoft.com/windows/ie/IE20HTML.htm**.

COMPLEXITY
INTERMEDIATE

15.2 How do I... Use TrueType and other fonts?

COMPATIBILITY: INTERNET EXPLORER, NETSCAPE 3+

Problem

I'm tired of always having the same font on all my Web pages. How can I use different fonts?

Technique

Netscape 3.0 and later and Internet Explorer both recognize a **FACE** attribute in the **<FONT>...</FONT>** tag. When you set the **FACE** attribute to a desired font, all the following text will be rendered in either the set font or a default font if the desired font isn't available on the user's system. The form of the **<FONT>** tag is

```
<FONT FACE="font name for first choice, 2nd choice, 3rd choice">...</FONT>
```

You can also add the size and color attributes to alter the appearance of your text. A complete tag would look like this:

```
<FONT FACE="arial" SIZE=5 COLOR="FF0000">This is big Arial
 if you are on a PC</FONT>
```

Steps

The following steps show how to use different fonts in your Web documents.

1. Create a new document or open an existing document where you want to format text in a different font.

2. Place the **<FONT>...<FONT>** tags around the text you want to render differently. Include the **FACE** attribute and set it to the font you want to use. It is best to set at least one alternative font, in case the font you want to use isn't available on a user's system. You can also include **SIZE** and **COLOR** attributes, for example:

```
<FONT FACE="Comic Sans MS, Courier NEW>This is my text</FONT>
```

3. View your document to make sure everything looks like you think it should. Experiment some.

How It Works

When the browser encounters the **<FONT>** tag, it will try to render the text between the tags in the first font listed in the **FACE** attribute; if that font is not found, the browser will try to use the second font, and so on. If no font is found that matches the one in the **FACE** attribute, the browser will use the default font.

Comments

Remember that Macs and PCs use different basis system fonts. Microsoft has TrueType fonts available on its Web site for people to download. Still, you cannot assume that everybody will have this TrueType available. You can find more information on fonts at **http://www.microsoft.com/truetype/**. Figure 15-2 shows some examples of rendered fonts.

Font Face Demo

This is the default.

This is arial on a PC, Helvetica on a Mac!

ABCDEFGHIJKLMNOPQRSTUVWXYZ!

This is comic sans or NY on the Mac.

ABCDEFGHIJKLMNOPQRSTUVWXYZ!

Figure 15-2 Rendered fonts

COMPLEXITY
INTERMEDIATE

15.3 How do I... Format my Web page in multiple columns?

COMPATIBILITY: NETSCAPE 3+

Problem

I want to have more than one column on my Web page, and I would like another way of doing this besides using tables. What can I do?

Technique

You can create multiple column Web pages by using the **<MULTICOL>... </MULTICOL>** tags. Any text between these tags will be rendered in the number of columns you specify. It is even possible to nest **<MULTICOL>** tags inside other **<MULTICOL>** tags, which creates a "newspaper" effect. The format of the **<MULTICOL>** tag is as follows:

```
<MULTICOL COL="number of columns" GUTTER="number" WIDTH="number"
```

To break down these attributes:

- ✔ `COL`: The number of columns you want to render, which can be any number
- ✔ `GUTTER`: The space between columns, where the default value is 10 pixels
- ✔ `WIDTH`: The width of all the columns associated with the tag, where the width can be given in pixels or as a percentage of the screen (if no width is given, the columns will take up all the available screen)

Steps

The following steps show how to create documents with multiple columns:

1. Either open an existing document or create a new document.

2. Place **<MULTICOL>...</MULTICOL>** tags at the beginning and the end of the selected text. Set the **COLUMN**, **GUTTER**, and **WIDTH** attributes, for example:

```
<HTML><HEAD><TITLE>Multiple Column Example</TITLE></HEAD>
<BODY>
<H2>Newspaper like</H2>
<MULTICOL COLS=2 GUTTER=10 WIDTH="100%">
Today in the news, the President said that he is the president and he
doesn't care what congress says as well.  "He do what he pleases."<P>
Congress of course said, "well even if he is the president he still should
at least listen to us."  To which the president replied, "Leave me alone."
As you can plainly see it has been a slow news day.<P>
<H4>Sports</H4>
Scores: <BR>
8 -6 <BR>
9-5<BR>
4-3 (in 10 innings)<BR>
<P>
In other sports news. The international Olympic committee decided
against moving skiing to the summer games. Like a spokesman said,
"true the Summer games get better exposure but we think that skiing
really benefits from snow."

</MULTICOL>
</BODY>
</HTML>
```

3. View your document to make sure it looks like you want. Experiment with different values for the different attributes so you see how they affect the documents.

How It Works

When the browser encounters a **<MULTICOL>...</MULTICOL>** tag pair, all the text between these two tags is rendered in the number of columns the **COLUMN** attribute is set to.

Comments

By nesting **<MULTICOL>** tags inside each other, you can easily create a page that has a different number of columns throughout. Examples of this are shown on the book's sample Web page at **http://www.psnw.com/~jmz5/waite/columns.html**. Figure 15-3 shows how the preceding example looks when rendered with Netscape 3 or 4.

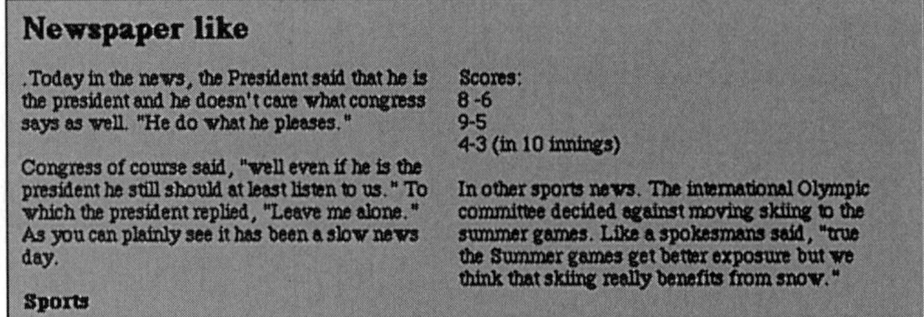
Newspaper like
.Today in the news, the President said that he is the president and he doesn't care what congress says as well. "He do what he pleases."
Congress of course said, "well even if he is the president he still should at least listen to us." To which the president replied, "Leave me alone." As you can plainly see it has been a slow news day.
Sports
Scores:
8 -6
9-5
4-3 (in 10 innings)
In other sports news. The international Olympic committee decided against moving skiing to the summer games. Like a spokesmans said, "true the Summer games get better exposure but we think that skiing really benefits from snow."

Figure 15-3 Multiple columns used on a Web page

COMPLEXITY
BEGINNING

15.4 How do I... Insert blank space into my Web page?

COMPATIBILITY: NETSCAPE 3+

Problem

I would like to be able to position text farther down or farther across the screen than my current position. How can I do this?

Technique

You can insert horizontal or vertical space with the **<SPACER>** tag. The **<SPACER>** tag looks like this:

```
<SPACER TYPE="horizontal | vertical" SIZE="a number">
```

The browser will insert either horizontal or vertical space equal to the amount set in **SIZE**.

Steps

The following steps show one way to insert blank space into a document:

1. Open or create a new document in which you want to include some blank space.

2. Place a **<SPACER>** tag wherever you want to have blank space. Set **TYPE** to either **HORIZONTAL** or **VERTICAL** and **SIZE** to the amount of space you would like, for example:

Spacer Demo

Printed after Horizontal Spacer 50.

Printer after Vertical Spacer 50.

Figure 15-4 Web page with blank space inserted

```
<HTML><HEAD><TITLE>Spacer Demo</TITLE></HEAD>
<BODY BGCOLOR="FFFFFF">
<SPACER TYPE="HORIZONTAL" SIZE="50">Printed after 50 horizontal spaces.
<SPACER TYPE="VERTICAL" SIZE="50">Printed after 50 vertical spaces.
</BODY>
</HTML>
```

3. View your document to make sure it looks like you want it to look. Feel free to experiment.

How It Works

When the browser encounters a **<SPACER>** tag, it inserts the amount of space as governed by the attributes.

Comments

There isn't a lot of documentation on **<SPACER>**. Still, it is a useful tag, especially because browsers ignore multiple spaces in a row. **<SPACER>** gives you finer control over where you position text and graphics. Figure 15-4 shows how the preceding example looks in Netscape 3.0.

15.5 How do I... Add color to tables?

COMPATIBILITY: NETSCAPE 3+, INTERNET EXPLORER 3+

Problem

I have a table on my page, but it is kind of boring. I would like to liven it up by adding some color to it. How do I do this?

Technique

Color is added to tables in the same manner that it is added to backgrounds. You can insert a **BGCOLOR** attribute in the **<TABLE>** tag to set the color of the entire table, or you can insert a **BGCOLOR** attribute in a **<TD>** or **<TH>** tag to set the color of a particular cell. The color is set to a six-digit hexadecimal number. Refer to the section on background colors (How-To 15.6).

Steps

The following steps show you how to add color to your tables:

1. Create a new document or open an existing one with a table.
2. If you want to give the table a background color, add the **BGCOLOR** attribute to the **<TABLE>** tag, for example:

```
<TABLE BGCOLOR="FF0000">
THE REST OF THE TABLE TAGS
</TABLE>
```

3. If you want to make any individual cells different colors, add the **BGCOLOR** attribute to the cells you want to change, for example:

```
<TD BGCOLOR="FFFF00">This cell is a different color</TD>
```

4. View your table to make sure it looks like you want it to. Experiment with color combinations until you get them just right.

How It Works

When Netscape or Internet Explorer encounters a **<TABLE>** tag, it will look for **BGCOLOR** attributes, either in the **<TABLE>** tag itself or in **<TD>** and **<TH>** tags found within. If any **BGCOLOR** tags are found, the table or the cell will be rendered in the appropriate color.

Comments

Color can make a nice addition in any table. Figure 15-5 shows an example of color being used in a table. To see some color examples of the table, check out `http://www.psnw.com/ ~jmz5/waite/tables.html`.

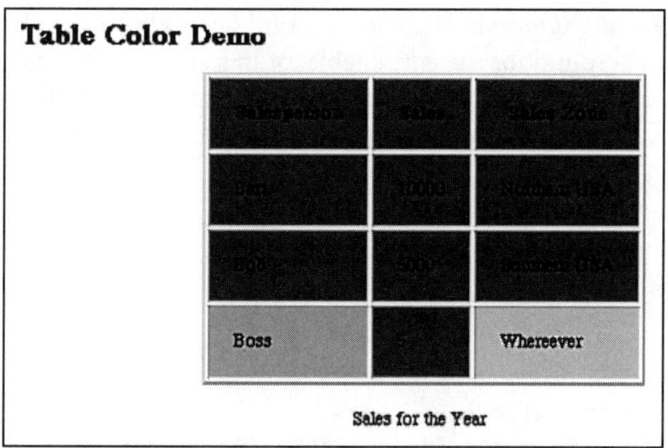

Figure 15-5 Color used in a table

15.6 How do I... Add a background image to a table?

COMPATIBILITY: INTERNET EXPLORER 3+

Problem

I have a table on my page. I would really like to liven it up by adding a background to it. How do I do this?

Technique

Backgrounds are added to tables much as they are to pages. You include a **BACKGROUND** attribute in either the **<TABLE>** or **<TD>** tag, setting the **BACKGROUND** to the URL of the image you would like to use as the background of either the entire table or a single cell.

Steps

The following steps show one way of adding a background to your table:

1. Create or obtain a suitable image to use as a background.

2. Open an existing document or create a new one that contains a table.

3. Include a **BACKGROUND** attribute either in the **<TABLE>** tag, if you want to use a background for the entire table, or in a specific **<TD>** tag, if you want only a certain cell to use a background. Remember to set the URL of **BACKGROUND** to the image you want to use. Here's an example:

```
<HTML><HEAD><TITLE>Table Width Demo</TITLE></HEAD>
<BODY BGCOLOR="FFFFFF">

<H2>Table Background Demo</H2>
<BIG>The following example shows how to add a background to
a table.</BIG>

<CENTER>
<TABLE BORDER=2 BACKGROUND="slow_back.gif">
<TR><TH>Salesperson</TH><TH>Sales</TH><TH>Sales Zone</TH></TR>
<TR><TD >Bart</TD><TD>10000</TD><TD>Northern USA</TD></TR>
<TR><TD>Bob</TD><TD>5000</TD><TD>Southern USA</TD></TR>
<TR><TD>Boss</TD><TD>5</TD><TD>Whereever</TD></TR>
...
<CAPTION ALIGN="BOTTOM">Sales for the Year </CAPTION>
</TABLE>
</CENTER>
</BODY>
```

4. View your document to make sure it looks like you want it to.

How It Works

When Internet Explorer encounters a **BACKGROUND** attribute in either a **<TABLE>** or **<TD>** tag, it uses the image pointed to by the attribute as the background for either the table or the cell in question.

Comments

This is a nice feature of Internet Explorer 3.0. Remember, though, that not all images make good backgrounds. Also, remember that putting an image in a table can be tricky; if the size of the table and the background image don't correspond, your page could look a little strange. Figure 15-6 shows an example of a background image in a table.

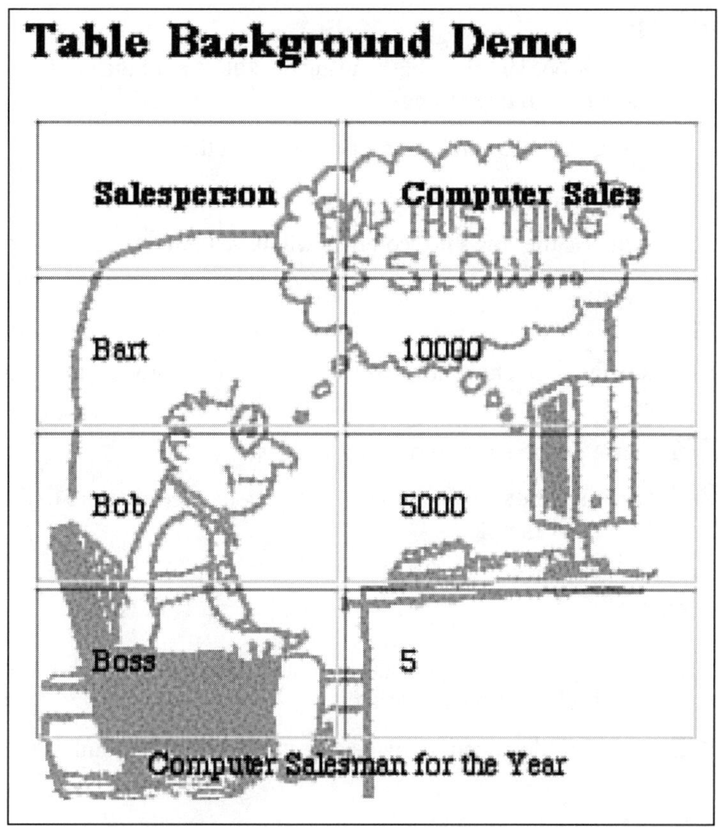

Figure 15-6 Background image in a table

COMPLEXITY
INTERMEDIATE

15.7 How do I... Control table borders?

COMPATIBILITY: INTERNET EXPLORER 3+

Problem

I have a table, but I don't want all my borders to be the same. How do I control table borders?

Technique

You can set the borders of a table by using the **RULES** attribute inside a **<TABLE>** tag. **RULES** can be set to three things:

- ✔ **ROW**: Only rows will have borders between them.
- ✔ **COLS**: Only columns will have borders between them.
- ✔ **NONE**: Neither rows nor columns will have borders.

Steps

The following steps show how easy it is to alter the borders of rows and columns in tables:

1. Create or open a document with tables.
2. Add the **RULES** attribute to the **<TABLE>** tag, setting rules to the desired value, for example:

```
<TABLE RULES=ROWS BORDER=2>
Other table tags and text
</TABLE>
```

The preceding tag will create a table where the rows, but not the individual columns, are bordered.

3. View your document to make sure it looks like you think it should.

How It Works

Before Internet Explorer 3.0 renders a table, it will check to see whether the **<TABLE>** tag has a **RULES** attribute associated with it; if it does, the browser will render the table accordingly.

Comments

Remember, so far this feature is available only with Internet Explorer. Figure 15-7 shows an example of different borders in a table.

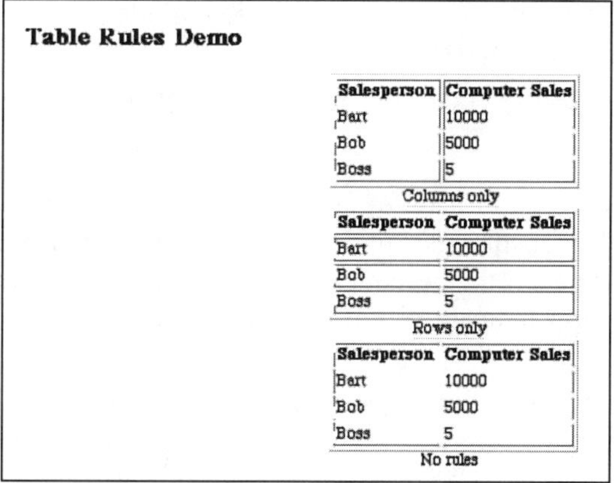

Figure 15-7 Tables with different borders

15.8 How do I... Create new windows for linked documents?

COMPATIBILITY: NETSCAPE 2+ AND INTERNET EXPLORER 3.02

Problem

I would like to include a link to a document in my Web page, but instead of loading that document in the same browser window, replacing the previous page, I would like the new document to go into a separate window. Is there a way to create new windows for linked documents?

Technique

Netscape 2+ supports the `TARGET` attribute of the anchor tag `<A>`, which identifies the name of a new window that opens containing the new document. The `TARGET` attribute can also be used with the `<BASE>` tag to identify a default target window name for all links in a document that do not include the `TARGET` attribute.

Steps

1. Open your document. Identify the links that you want to have go to separate windows.

2. To send the document referenced in a link to another window, add the `TARGET` attribute and set it equal to the name of the window. For example, to send the document referenced by a link to a window named The Widgets Page, you would enter

```
<A HREF="http://www.widgets.com/" TARGET="The Widgets Page">Go to the
 Widgets Page</A>
```

3. The **TARGET** attribute can also be used in the **<AREA>** element in client-side imagemaps. This enables the link for a specific area of an imagemap to appear in a separate window. For example, to send the document referenced by a link in an imagemap to another window named The Widgets Page, enter

```
<AREA SHAPE="RECT" COORD="90,90,120,95" HREF="http://www.widgets.com/"
 TARGET="The Widgets Page">
```

4. The **TARGET** attribute can also be used in the **<FORM>** element. This sends the output of a form submission to a separate page. For example, to send the results of a form to a page thanking the user for filling out the form, enter

```
<FORM ACTION="results.cgi" TARGET="Thanks!">
```

5. Netscape reserves certain "magic" target names for specific purposes. The "magic" names and their uses are described in Table 15-2.

Table 15-2 "Magic" values for TARGET

NAME	DESCRIPTION
"_blank"	Loads the referenced document into a blank window.
"_self"	Loads the referenced document into the same window where the anchor was selected.
"_parent"	Loads the referenced document into the parent frameset of the current document.
"_top"	Loads the referenced document into the full body of the window if frames are being used.

For example, to load a document to a new, blank window, use

```
<A HREF="http://www.widgets.com/" TARGET="_blank">Go to the
Widgets Page</A>
```

6. To send all the links on a page without the **TARGET** attribute to a specific window, add the **<BASE>** element to the header of the page (that is, within the **<HEAD>** and **</HEAD>** tags) and set the **TARGET** attribute equal to the name of the window. For example, to send all links without a **TARGET** attribute to a window named Default Window, enter

```
<BASE TARGET="Default Window">
```

How It Works

When Netscape encounters a URL, an imagemap listing, or a form with the **TARGET** attribute, it creates a new window with the title of the window set to the value of the **TARGET** attribute. However, if the **TARGET** attribute is set to one of the reserved "magic" names, the browser executes the specific task defined by that name.

Comments

A new window is created only if a window does not already exist with a particular name. If a named window does exist, the document displayed in that window is replaced with the one currently being referenced. Names for **TARGET** must begin with a letter or number, with the exception of the" magic" names listed in Table 15-2. Also, the **TARGET** attribute is currently supported by Netscape and Internet Explorer 3.02. Other browsers ignore the attribute and load the documents normally. For updated information about targeted windows in Netscape, check the URL **http://www.netscape.com/assist/net_sites/new_html3_prop.html#Target**.

15.9 How do I... Use Netscape's Client Pull?

COMPATIBILITY: HTTP/1, NETSCAPE NAVIGATOR

Problem

I would like to create an interactive slide presentation on the Web. I must be able to specify a default link to follow after a specified amount of time. How can I create this type of HTML document?

Technique

This facility is not supported directly by HTML. To create a document of this type, however, you can use the Client Pull feature of the Netscape Navigator browser.

The Client Pull feature works by allowing a special use of the **<META>** element within the head of a document. You can use this element to instruct the Netscape Navigator browser to load a new document in a specified amount of time. Through this mechanism, you can develop interactive slide presentations and guided tours.

Steps

The following procedure shows how to develop documents using the Client Pull feature of the Netscape Navigator browser:

1. Determine the document to which you want to add the Client Pull feature. This document could be the beginning of a slide show, the first frame of a character-based animation, or a document that gets updated periodically by the server system. In any case, you should open this document in your favorite text editor or HTML editor, even though most HTML editors do not support the particular element you are adding.

2. In the `<HEAD>` element of the document, add a `<META>` element. Add the following text within the `<HEAD>` element:

```
<META HTTP-EQUIV="Refresh" CONTENT=
```

3. Continue the previous line as appropriate for the situation. Table 15-3 displays the possible values for the `CONTENT` attribute.

Table 15-3 `CONTENT` attribute values for `Refresh`

VALUE	USE
`number`	Specifies delay for the current document to refresh.
`number; URL=URL`	Specifies a URL to load after a delay.

For example, if you want to reload the same document after 20 seconds, add the following text in the `CONTENT` field:

```
20
```

If you want the document `http://www.mysite.edu/next.htm` to load after a 30-second delay, include the following text in the `CONTENT` field:

```
"30; URL=http://www.mysite.edu/next.htm"
```

4. Terminate the `<META>` element with a greater than sign (>).

5. Save the altered document. This document is now set to tell a client to pull a new document after the specified delay.

How It Works

The Client Pull feature of Netscape Navigator enables a document to specify that another document be loaded in a defined amount of time. This is supported through the use of a `Refresh` directive built into the head portion of an HTML document with the use of the `<META>` element.

The directive includes both the new document to load and the time to wait. Figure 15-8 shows how the HTML document in the following code is displayed using Netscape Navigator.

```
<HTML>
<HEAD>
<META HTTP-EQUIV="Refresh"
CONTENT="5; URL=http://jasper.cau.auc.edu:8080/dsk/push-pull/doc2.htm">
<TITLE>Sample Client Pull Document 1</TITLE>
<LINK REV="made" HREF="mailto:me@mysite.edu">
</HEAD>
<BODY>
<H1>Sample Looping Document</H1>

<P>
This is a simple looping example of the Client Pull feature of Netscape.
<P>
This is document 1 of 2.  The other document will be loaded in 5 seconds.
Wait for it...  Follow the bouncing A.
<PRE>
A
</PRE>
Either hit the stop key or go back to the <A HREF="/index.htm">experimental
 server</A> to stop looping.
<HR>
<H6>Last Modified: April 12, 1995 by Me</H6>
</BODY>
</HTML>
```

The document appearing in Figure 15-9 is loaded five seconds after the one that appears in Figure 15-8. These two documents loop back and forth to create the effect of a bouncing letter `A`. The HTML code for this second document appears next:

```
<HTML>
<HEAD>
<META HTTP-EQUIV="Refresh"
CONTENT="1; URL=http://jasper.cau.auc.edu:8080/dsk/push-pull/doc1.htm">
<TITLE>Sample Client Pull Document 2</TITLE>
<LINK REV="made" HREF="mailto:me@mysite.edu">
</HEAD>
<BODY>
<H1>Sample Looping Document</H1>

<P>
This is a simple looping example of the Client Pull feature of Netscape.
<P>
This is document 2 of 2.  The other document will be loaded in 1 second.
Wait for it...  Follow the bouncing A.
<PRE>
     A
</PRE>
Either hit the stop key or go back to the
<A HREF="//www.cis.cau.auc.edu/index.htm"> server</A> to stop looping.
<HR>
<H6>Last Modified: April 12, 1995 by Me</H6>
</BODY>
</HTML>
```

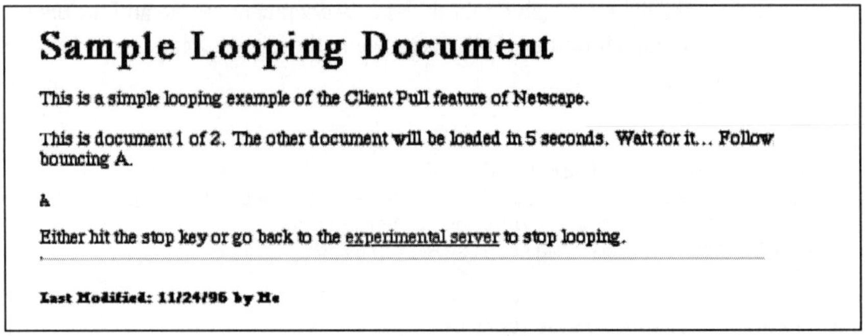

Sample Looping Document

This is a simple looping example of the Client Pull feature of Netscape.

This is document 1 of 2. The other document will be loaded in 5 seconds. Wait for it... Follow bouncing A.

A

Either hit the stop key or go back to the experimental server to stop looping.

Last Modified: 11/24/96 by Me

Figure 15-8 First document of the Client Pull example

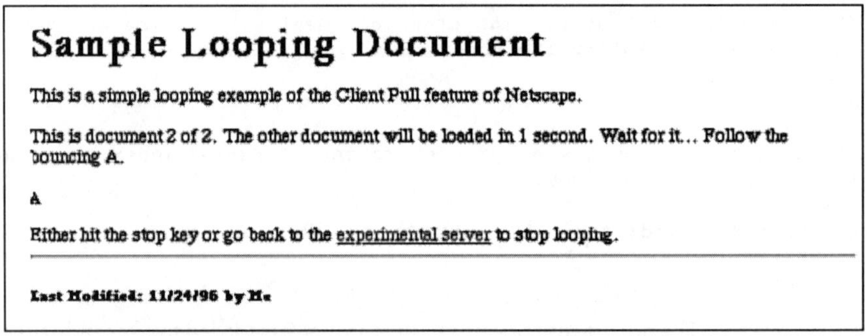

Sample Looping Document

This is a simple looping example of the Client Pull feature of Netscape.

This is document 2 of 2. The other document will be loaded in 1 second. Wait for it... Follow the bouncing A.

A

Either hit the stop key or go back to the experimental server to stop looping.

Last Modified: 11/24/96 by Me

Figure 15-9 Second document of Client Pull example

The only ways to stop the infinite looping are to press the Stop button on the Netscape Navigator menu bar or to activate a link within one of the two documents.

The Client Pull feature is supported by allowing documents to send a **Refresh** directive in the HTTP response; however, they do not necessarily refresh themselves. They might refresh with some other document. The use of the **<META>** element with an **HTTP-EQUIV** attribute tells the server to add the information provided in the response header that is sent back to the client when this particular document is retrieved. (See Appendix G, "HTML Hypertext Transfer Protocol (HTTP)," for more information on HTTP responses.) For example, the document appearing in Figure 15-8 would have the following line in the response header sent with the document:

```
Refresh 5; URL=http://jasper.cau.auc.edu:8080/dsk/push-pull/doc2.htm
```

This line instructs the Netscape Navigator client to refresh the current document with the one specified in the given URL. Similarly, the response header sent along with the document appearing in Figure 15-9 would include a **Refresh** directive as follows:

```
Refresh 1; URL=http://jasper.cau.auc.edu:8080/dsk/push-pull/doc1.htm
```

This in turn causes the browser to go back to the first document after one second has elapsed. These directives in the response header tell the client when and what to reload.

Comments

This feature is currently supported only by Netscape Navigator browsers. Whether other browser applications will support this feature in the future is unknown. Most other browsers currently ignore the **Refresh** directive sent in the response header and, consequently, do not refresh after the specified delay.

You can also use the **Refresh** directive in response headers generated through gateway applications. This enables your CGI program to generate a response page and load a URL after a suitable delay. (See Chapter 14, "The Common Gateway Interface (CGI)," for more information on CGI applications.)

COMPLEXITY
ADVANCED

15.10 How do I... Specify Netscape Server Push?

COMPATIBILITY: CGI, NETSCAPE NAVIGATOR

Problem

The information in my document changes frequently. I would like to update my HTML document as new information arrives. How can I create such a document?

Technique

Netscape Navigator supports a mechanism called Server Push to provide this capability. Instead of a standard HTTP access as described in Appendix G, "HTML Hypertext Transfer Protocol (HTTP)," a Server Push keeps the connection between client and server open. When a request from the client is serviced, an initial response is made. The client/server connection is not closed until the server drops the connection. While connected, the server sends updated documents, which the browser displays as they arrive.

The Server Push capability is supported through the use of CGI applications that repeatedly generate and send new documents to the browser at intervals specified by the application. The initial response generated by the gateway program indicates that the response is composed of multiple documents, each of which replaces the previous one. A step-by-step process for developing such an application is given next.

Steps

You can change directories to a location where you want to build your Server Push gateway program and begin the development process. The following method deals with the response generation portion of your application. The tasks performed should be accomplished using the commands in your chosen programming language.

1. Start your application by retrieving any data that the user has submitted to your gateway application. You will find a procedure for accomplishing this task in How-To's 14.6 and 14.7.

2. Decide whether the input data, if any, will be processed before, during, or after the generation of your response document. If your response depends on the results of processing, then processing, or at least partial processing, must occur before response generation. If the results are directly embedded in the response, then the processing must occur during response generation. Finally, if the response is independent of the processed data, processing can occur after the response is generated. The decision on when and how processing is performed needs to be decided on an application-by-application basis. Based on this decision, intersperse the processing as appropriate among the following steps.

3. Generate the response header indicating that the document will be updated. This response uses the standard **Content-type** server directive. However, the type specified should be a **multipart/x-mixed replace; boundary=boundary_string**, where **boundary_string** is replaced by some boundary string indicator of your choice. For example, in Perl you could use the **print** command as shown here:

```
print "Content-type: multipart/x-mixed-replace;boundary=WhyNot\n\n";
```

4. Send the boundary string, preceded by two dashes to signal the beginning of a response document. To begin a response document, place **--boundary_string** on the standard output. In C, you might use the **printf** command.

```
printf("--WhyNot\n");
```

5. Place the **Content-type** server directive appropriate for the document type you will be attaching on the standard output, followed by a blank line. In Perl, you could use the **puts** command to accomplish this task.

```
print "Content-type: text/plain\n";
```

6. Output your attached document in the format specified in step 5.

7. Perform whatever processing tasks are required (waiting for new data from an outside source, waiting a specified amount of time, processing the next data set). When you have performed these tasks and are ready to generate an update to the current document, return to step 4; the new document will replace the currently viewed one. If you are not going to generate any more updates, continue with step 8.

8. Send the boundary string surrounded by pairs of dashes, `--boundary_string--`, to the standard output. In Perl, you would use the `print` command for this task.

```
print "--WhyNot--\n";
```

9. After your application has been developed and, if required, compiled, you can install this gateway application.

10. Reference the URL for this gateway application as you would any other CGI program.

How It Works

The use of this procedure is shown through the development of a sample Server Push gateway application. This sample application is written in the Perl scripting language. Furthermore, this sample Server Push application requires no input from the user. The purpose of this program is to provide a snapshot of the individuals logged in to the server when the document is first retrieved (see Figure 15-10) and then again 30 seconds later through the use of the `finger` network utility. The source for this application appears on the CD-ROM in file **NPH-PUSH.CGI**.

When this script is initially accessed, the document provides information about who is currently logged in to the server system, as shown in Figure 15-10. Figure 15-11 shows what is displayed 30 seconds later. If you wanted to perform a more systematic monitoring, you could have placed the `finger` document generation phase in a loop.

This application follows the procedure just described. There is no input to deal with, and processing occurs during response generation. The initial response header is sent, signaling that the following response messages will successively replace the previous message. The boundary string is sent to signal the first document. The first message is the immediate result of the `finger` command, with some HTML formatting around it. To make sure the output buffer is flushed, the signal for the second document is sent. When this document is complete, some internal processing occurs; namely, the application sleeps for 30 seconds. Finally, the second document, another HTML-formatted `finger` result, is sent. The overall message concludes with the boundary string, surrounded by dashes, being sent to the standard output.

Comments

When using the Server Push capability and buffered output, you must make sure to flush your output buffer when a particular component message is complete. If you do not, your component objects may simply appear one after the other after several have been generated. In the Perl script example described in this How-To, `(STDOUT); $|=1;` flushes the standard output after the completion of the first HTML document.

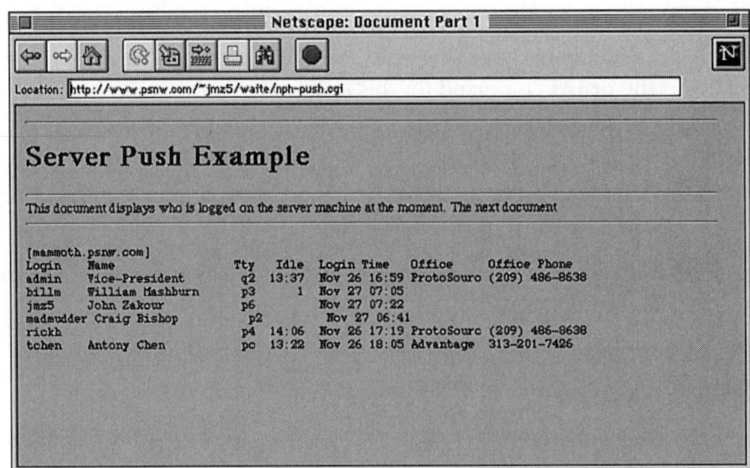

Figure 15-10 First results from Server Push

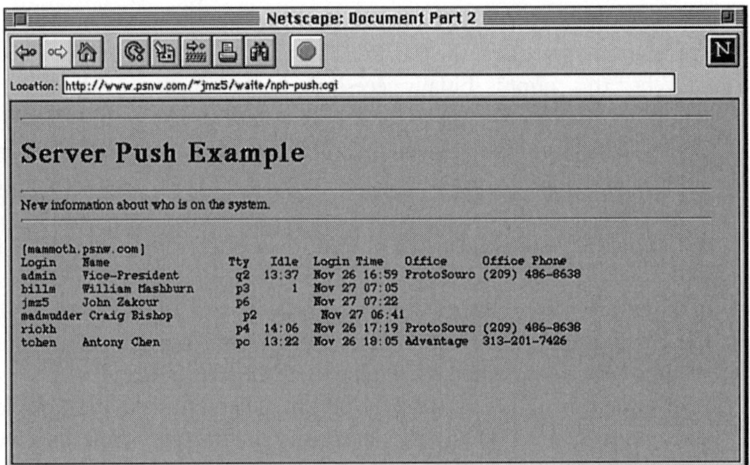

Figure 15-11 System status 30 seconds after first results

If you do not provide a termination for the multipart document response by including a final boundary string (`--boundary_string--`), the only way to stop updating the document is to activate a link in the document or to use a stop facility provided by your browser.

Finally, implementation of a Server Push gateway application should be done in a language that terminates the application when the user interrupts the request, with the stop facility, for example. Applications written in the Bourne shell scripting language might not terminate when an interrupt occurs, which means that server resources continue to be used even though the browser no longer requests them.

CHAPTER 16

CASCADING STYLE SHEETS

16

CASCADING STYLE SHEETS

How do I...

HTML is in a continuous state of evolution. New features and elements are proposed and discussed daily. Style sheets are one such proposed addition. From a historical perspective, HTML style sheets are not particularly new conceptually. They were first introduced as a potential enhancement of HTML 2.0 and were later included in the draft specification of HTML 3.0. HTML 4.0 allows users to include style sheets in several ways. Currently, the Amaya browser for the UNIX/X11 platform and its precursor Arena, Microsoft Internet Explorer 3.0 and later, and Netscape Navigator 4.0 are the only browsers that provide some support for style sheets. (Netscape Navigator 4.0 also provides support for dynamic style sheets, which are described in Chapter 21, "Dynamic Style Sheets and Fonts.")

Style sheets serve a variety of purposes. You can attach them to Web pages to create a consistent look for a group of documents. As a Web surfer, you can create a style sheet that your browser will apply to all incoming documents. The style sheet mechanism provides a versatile means of extending, enhancing, and modifying the way browsers present Web pages.

For the remainder of this chapter, refer to Table 16-1 for units of length applicable to various aspects of the HTML style sheets that you develop.

Table 16-1 Style sheet units of length

ABBREVIATION	UNIT TYPE	DESCRIPTION
`cm`	centimeters	
`em`	ems	Width of the character m
`ex`	exes	Height of the character x
`in`	inches	
`mm`	millimeters	
`pc`	picas	1 pica = 12 points
`pt`	points	1 point = 1/72 inch
`px`	pixels	Single cell on display

NOTE

Microsoft Internet Explorer 3 does not support the length units ems (`em`) and exes (`ex`). Netscape Navigator 4.0 does not support the length unit picas (`pc`).

The How-To's in this chapter introduce the use of this exciting HTML feature.

16.1 Create a Style Sheet to Alter an HTML Element

Style sheets provide a mechanism for supporting consistent styles across multiple Web pages. Style sheets enable you to extend and enhance HTML elements in significant ways. This How-To shows you how to build style sheets conforming to the Cascading Style Sheets standard, level 1 (CSS 1 standard).

16.2 Alter an Element's Font Characteristics

Style sheets allow greater flexibility and control with respect to the size and types of fonts used to display Web pages. This How-To demonstrates the various font-related properties that you can specify using HTML 4.0 style sheets.

16.3 Alter an Element's Color

Style sheets support a significant enhancement in your ability to control the color of text displayed in your Web page. With style sheets, you can selectively choose the text color within any HTML element. This How-To provides a practical guide to using the style sheet color property.

16.4 Alter an Element's Background

HTML 4.0 allows only a single background specification for an entire page. With style sheets, you can add different backgrounds to different elements within your Web page. In this How-To, you will learn how to use style sheet background properties.

16.5 Alter an Element's Text Properties

Text properties give you greater control over the presentation of a textual element. In this How-To, you will learn how to use the various text properties available through style sheets.

16.6 Alter the Borders of an Element

Style sheets allow the specification of borders around any HTML 4.0 element. You can configure a variety of aspects of the borders, including style, color, and width. This How-To provides an introduction to the use of the various border-related style sheet properties.

NOTE

Internet Explorer 3.0 does not support border properties.

16.7 Specify Layout Constraints of an Element

One of the biggest shortfalls of HTML 4.0 is the lack of flexible layout controls. Current "fixes" resort to the use of tables or lists to manage margins and spacing. Style sheets provide an effective means for specifying page layout. This How-To introduces you to the style sheet properties that support page layout.

16.8 Indicate Style Information for List Elements

HTML 4.0 supports the use of different list styles using the `TYPE` attributes of ordered and unordered lists (see How-To's 6.2 and 6.4 in Chapter 6, "Lists"). Style sheets also provide another means of specifying this list style information. In this How-To, you will learn how to specify the style of lists using style sheet properties.

NOTE

Internet Explorer 3.0 does not support list style properties.

16.9 Cascade HTML Style Sheets

You can combine style sheets with other style sheets as well as with HTML `<STYLE>` elements. This combination leads to aggregate style sheets and alternative style sheets. This How-To explains how to attach style sheets to Web pages to provide alternative and aggregate presentation styles for the page.

16.10 Add Cascading Style Information Directly to a Web Page

Besides attaching style sheets to pages, style information can be embedded directly into a Web page. This How-To details how to add style information to specific Web pages, or even a specific element within a page.

16.11 Include Style Elements and Protect Browsers Without Style Support

The information in `<STYLE>` elements might be misinterpreted by older browsers. In this How-To, you will learn how to reduce the potential misinterpretation of style information by browsers that do not support `<STYLE>` elements.

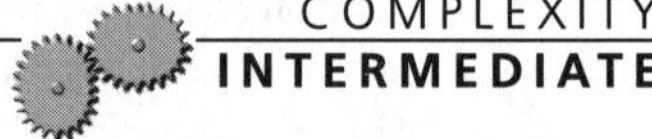

COMPLEXITY
INTERMEDIATE

16.1 How do I... Create a style sheet to alter an HTML element?

COMPATIBILITY: HTML 3+, INTERNET EXPLORER 3.0+, NETSCAPE NAVIGATOR 4.0+

Problem

I want to establish standard styles for use in many of my Web pages. I want to enhance Web pages that I retrieve to maximize the capabilities of my browser. For legal reasons, a section of all my Web pages must appear the same. How can I create a style sheet for my documents?

Technique

You create style sheets through a standard text editor. You specify a set of parameters and values that you want to associate with HTML elements of a particular type, such as `<P>` elements, or a particular class within an element, such as `<P CLASS="red">`. Each style sheet can define properties for any number of elements. Each entry in a style sheet is composed of a selector indicating the HTML 4.0 element that is modified and one or more declarations indicating properties to set or modify.

Style-sheet–capable browsers read the style sheets associated with a Web page and those designated by the reader and try to apply the styles to the page. A cascading mechanism helps resolve conflict among multiple applicable styles. (See How-To 16.9 for information on how to cascade style information.)

Steps

The following steps take you through the style sheet creation process. You should select the elements and properties that you want to include. A full list of properties that can modify HTML 4.0 elements is provided in the "How It Works" section, with additional details and specific examples provided in subsequent How-To's.

1. Open the style sheet in a text editor.

2. Use the `@import` command to import and combine existing style sheets with the current style sheet. Conflicts in declarations are resolved in favor of the declarations of the importer. Thus, to include the entries from `sheet1.css`, issue the following command:

```
@import sheet1.css -- Use entries from sheet1, but override as follows --
```

NOTE

Internet Explorer 3.0, 4.0, and Netscape Navigator 4.0 do not support imported style sheets.

3. If you are modifying or adding a property to an existing entry, move to that entry in the sheet and proceed with step 4. Otherwise, specify the selector for the HTML 4.0 element that you want to modify. The following examples represent possible selectors.

The following selector indicates the modification of `<H1>` elements:

```
H1
```

The following selector indicates the modification of `<H1>` and `<H2>` elements:

```
H1,H2
```

The following selector indicates the modification of `red` class, `<P>` elements:

```
P.red
```

The following selector indicates the modification of **red** class elements:

```
.red
```

The following selector indicates the modification of **<H2>** elements that follow **<P>** elements:

```
P H2
```

4. Include the declaration(s) for the selector within opening and closing curly braces ({ and }). For example, the following declaration indicates that the browser should draw the selected element using the color red. See How-To's 16.2 through 16.8 for information on the particular declaration types.

```
{ color: red }
```

5. Return to step 2 to continue editing; otherwise, save your style sheet.
6. Proceed to How-To 16.9 for a discussion on including the style sheet in your Web page.

How It Works

Style sheets are composed of standard text. A style sheet consists of a series of entries, each composed of a selector and a declaration. The selector indicates the HTML 4.0 element(s) affected by the properties in the declaration. A declaration can end with either a **!legal** or **!important** designation, indicating an imperative for using the particular declaration.

You can specify a selector in several forms. Selectors can specify a very narrow or very broad portion of a Web page, ranging from a particular class of an HTML element preceded by some other element to the entire page. In addition, the declarations for a selected element are inherited by elements contained within the selected elements. For example, using HTML as the selector indicates that the declaration applies to all elements contained within the **<HTML>** element, namely, the entire document. Generally, the selector falls into the following categories (brackets indicate optional user additions):

- **element**: You can select a single HTML element for which the declaration applies. For example, you might use the following selector to indicate application to **<H1>** elements:

```
H1
```

- **element1,element2,[element3,...]**: Use this form to apply the same declaration to several HTML elements. The following selector indicates application of the declaration to **<H1>** and **<H2>** elements:

```
H1,H2
```

- `element.class`: Use this form to specify a declaration that applies only to a particular class of a particular HTML element. Thus, the following selector specifies the application of the selector to `<P>` elements with `red` class designation:

```
P.red
```

- `class`: Use this form to apply the same declaration to all HTML elements with the specified class. The following selector indicates that the declarations apply to all HTML elements of the `red` class:

```
.red
```

- `preceding_element1 [preceding_element2...] element`: Use this form to indicate that a declaration applies only when the last HTML element is contained within the specified preceding HTML elements. The following selector applies to all `<STRONG>` elements within `<P CLASS="red">` elements:

```
P.red STRONG
```

Declarations specify the properties of the selector set by the style sheet entry. Style sheets allow modification of a large variety of properties. The current HTML 4.0 style sheet specifies level 1 properties. (See `http://www.w3.org/pub/WWW/Style/` for the current status of style sheets.)

Each declaration is composed of a property and a value. The property indicates what to modify, and the value indicates the value(s) of the modification. The level 1 properties are, for the most part, stable. (For additional level 1 properties and other information, see URL `http://www.w3.org/pub/WWW/TR/REC-CSS1.html`.) Table 16-2 lists the categories of declarations and the How-To's that explain these categories.

Table 16-2 Using different types of declarations

DECLARATION TYPE	HOW-TO
Font related	16.2
Foreground color	16.3
Background characteristics	16.4
Text properties	16.5
Border properties	16.6
Layout constraints	16.7
List style constraints	16.8

Web pages appear different depending on the style sheets associated with them. In Figures 16-1 and 16-2, a different style sheet is attached to the same Web page. The following is the source code for this page:

```
<HTML>
<HEAD>
<TITLE>Style is Everything</TITLE>
<LINK TITLE="Style Sheet 1" REL=stylesheet HREF="style1.css">
</HEAD>
<BODY>
<H1>Going in Style</H1>
<P>
Putting on the Ritz
</BODY>
</HTML>
```

Figure 16-1 shows how this page appears with the following style sheet. The HTML source for this appears on the CD-ROM in file **STYLE1.HTM**, with the style sheet stored in **STYLE1.CSS**.

```
H1 { color: #F00 }
P { font-size: 16pt, color: #00F }
```

Changing the **<LINK>** element to attach the style sheet below results in the Web page seen in Figure 16-2. The HTML source for this appears on the CD-ROM in file **STYLE2.HTM**, with the style sheet stored in **STYLE2.CSS**.

```
H1 { color: #00F, background: #FFF }
P { font-size: 8pt, color: #0F0 }
```

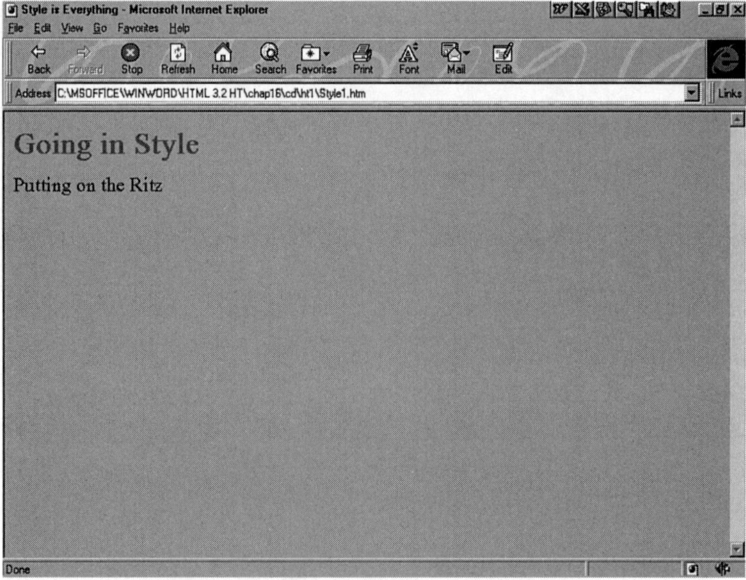

Figure 16-1 Paragraph with large font and red level 1 header

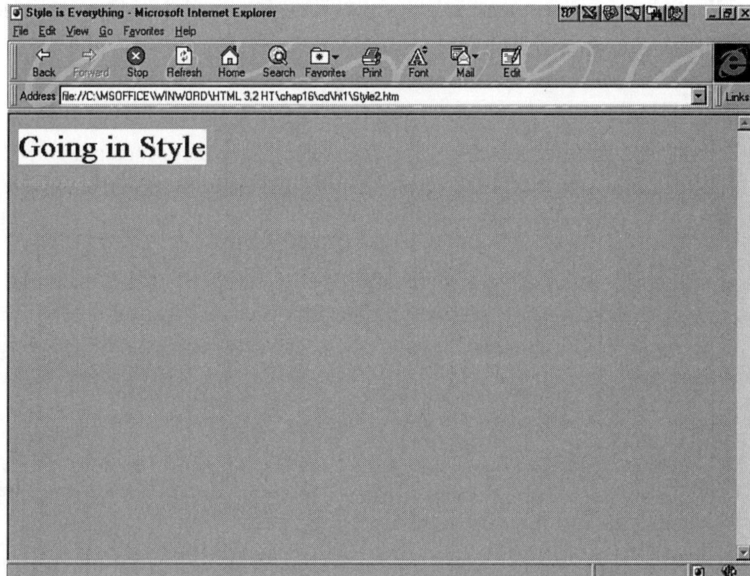

Figure 16-2 Paragraph with small font and blue level 1 header on white background

Comments

The cascading style sheet standard is still in the draft stages. The elements described in this How-To are fairly stable; however, they might be subject to change. For up-to-the-minute information on style sheet development, you might want to consult the evolution of the style sheet standard at `http://www.w3.org/pub/WWW/Style/`.

The only browsers currently supporting cascading style sheets are Arena for the X Window environment, recently superseded by the Amaya browser; Microsoft Internet Explorer 3.0 and above; and Netscape Navigator 4.0 and above.

COMPLEXITY
INTERMEDIATE

16.2 How do I... Alter an element's font characteristics?

COMPATIBILITY: HTML 3+, INTERNET EXPLORER 3.0+, NETSCAPE NAVIGATOR 4.0+

Problem

HTML 4.0 goes farther than previous HTML standards in allowing me to control the fonts used to display my page; however, this standard falls far short of the flexibility I can get with a high-powered desktop publishing environment. Is there anything I can do to close the gap?

Technique

Style sheets provide control of a variety of properties associated with the font used to display a specified HTML 4.0 element. These font choices can cover as broad a span of a page as the entire `<BODY>` element or as restricted as a single class of a narrower element type, such as all `<ADDRESS CLASS="dsk">` elements.

To specify font constraints on HTML 4.0 elements, you must select the element(s) you want to configure and select the properties you want to alter. You will associate this style information with your Web page using the methods discussed in How-To's 16.9 and 16.10.

Steps

The following procedure walks you through the process of associating font-related style information with your Web page:

1. Select the HTML 4.0 element in your Web page, or in the broad set of documents, using the style sheet you are modifying and to which you want to apply stylistic constraints. Create an appropriate selector as described in How-To 16.1.
2. Select the font-related property that you want to alter from Table 16-3.

Table 16-3 Font-related properties

DECLARATION	DESCRIPTION
`font-family`	Delineates a prioritized list of fonts to use.
`font-style`	Specifies the style of the font selected.
`font-variant`	Selects normal or small caps variations.
`font-weight`	Indicates the weight of the font to use.
`font-size`	Specifies the size of the font to use.
`font`	Provides support for combination of multiple font properties.

3. Use How-To's 16.9 and 16.10 to select and create the appropriate mechanism for adding this style information to the Web page(s) of your choice.

How It Works

Using style sheets, you can choose to alter any of the following font-related properties:

- ✔ `font-family`: Value: `family-name1|generic-family1 [family-name2|generic-family2...`

The browser generally determines the default font family used to present Web pages. This property allows the specification of a prioritized list of font families to use. Replace spaces in font family names with dashes (for example, `new century schoolbook` becomes `new-century-schoolbook`) or place quotes around the font name (`"new century schoolbook"`). CSS level 1 defines the following generic family names: cursive, fantasy, monospace, serif, and sans-serif. You should generally include a generic font family at the end of your font family list. For example, use the following to establish a font list for paragraphs (`<P>` elements):

```
P { font-family: helvetica, new-century-schoolbook, cursive }
```

- ✔ `font-style`: Value: `italic | oblique | normal`

  This property determines the style of font that a browser uses to display the elements specified by the selector. The default value is `normal`. You can use this property to alter the style. For example, use the following to designate that browsers should display `<H4>` elements as italic:

```
H4 { font-style: italic }
```

- ✔ `font-variant`: Value: `small-caps | normal`

  This property determines the variant of font that a browser uses to display the elements specified by the selector. The default value is `normal`. You can use this property to switch between the current two allowable variants: `normal` and `small caps`. For example, use the following to designate that browsers should display `<H4>` elements as small caps:

```
H4 { font-variant: small-caps }
```

NOTE

Neither Internet Explorer 3.0 nor Netscape Navigator 4.0 support `font-variant`. Preview versions of Internet Explorer 4.0 do support it, though.

- ✔ `font-weight`: Value: `normal | light | demi-light | light | medium | demi-bold | bold | extra-bold | bolder | lighter | 100 | 200 | 300 | 400 | 500 | 600 | 700 | 800 | 900`

  The default font-weight is `normal`. You set the weight with either a number or a relative modifier (such as `bolder`). The number should range from 100 to 900, corresponding to the lightest weight through the darkest. On this scale, `normal` corresponds to 400 and `bold` corresponds to 700. The lighter and bolder terms instruct the browser to lighten or darken with respect to the weight inherited from the surrounding HTML element. For example, use the following to present an entire Web page as bold:

```
HTML { font-weight: bold }
```

NOTE

Not all options for `font-weight` will be available for all fonts or will be supported by the browser.

- ✔ `font-size`: Value: `length | percent | # | xx-small | x-small | small | medium | large | x-large | xx-large | smaller | larger`

  The browser usually determines the default font size. You can specify a size, a percentage of the font size in the parent element, or a relative size using either a number or one of the descriptive literals above (such as `smaller` or `larger`). For example, use the following to set the font sizes of `<H5>` and `<H6>` elements, respectively:

```
H5 { font-size: 12pt }
H6 { font-size: small }
```

- ✔ `font`: Value: `<font-size> [ / <line-height> ] <font-family>`

  Use this property as a shorthand for setting various font attributes at once. Setting a font property by itself overrides the shorthand value. For example, use the following to set the font of `<STRONG>` elements that follow `<P CLASS="script">` paragraphs:

```
(P.script) STRONG { font: 16pt/20pt cursive }
```

For more information on the font-related property of CSS 1, see the current Internet draft at `http://www.w3.org/pub/WWW/TR/WD-css1.html#font-properties`.

Figure 16-3 displays the `FONTS.HTM` file from the CD-ROM. Figure 16-4 shows this same document in a browser without style sheet capability.

The following style sheet, `FONTS.CSS` on the CD-ROM, is linked to the page using the mechanism described in How-To 16.9:

```
H1 {     font-family: Braggadocio, "Comic Sans MS", sans-serif;
     font-size: 32pt;
     font-weight: extra-bold
     }
P.italics {      font-style: italic;
         font-weight: light}
```

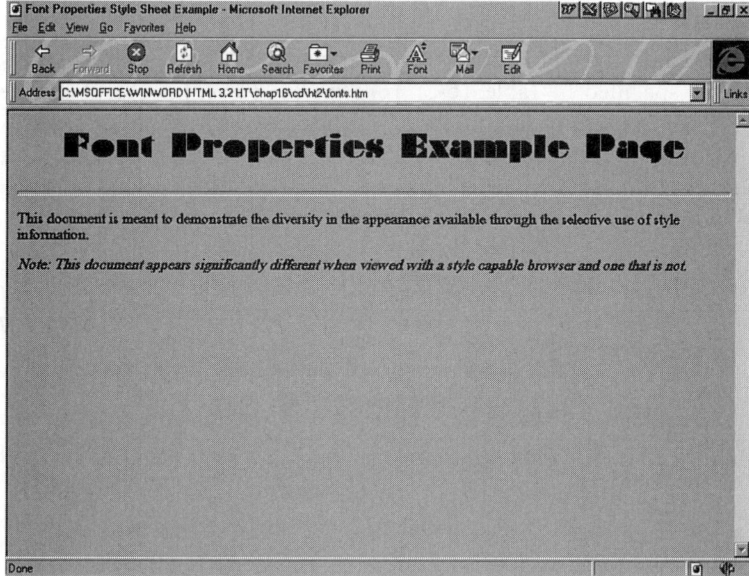

Figure 16-3 Font properties example page in a style sheet–capable browser

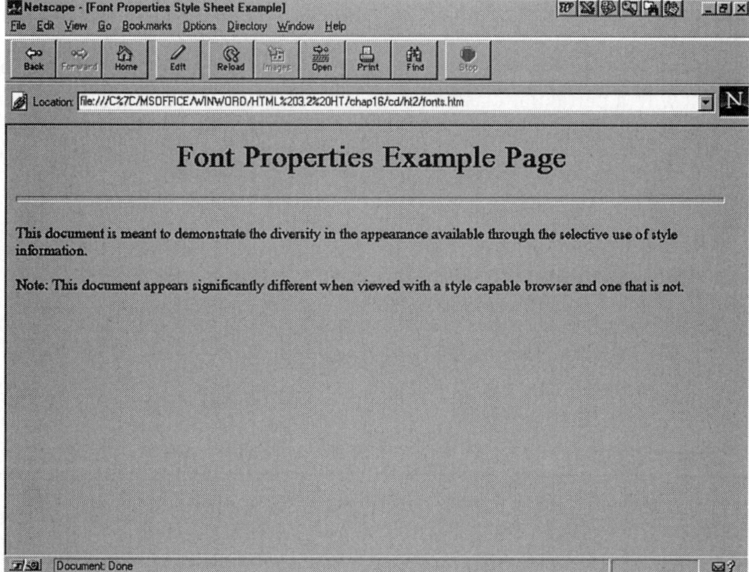

Figure 16-4 Font properties example page in a browser without style sheet capability

Comments

Microsoft Internet Explorer 3.0 supports the following subset of the font properties specified in Table 16-3: `font-size`, `font-family`, `font-weight`, and `font-style`. In addition, the values associated with these properties do not conform in all cases to the CSS 1 standard. Consult Microsoft's style sheet guide for specific information on Internet Explorer support (`http://www.microsoft.com/workshop/author/howto/css-f.htm`).

COMPLEXITY
INTERMEDIATE

16.3 How do I... Alter an element's color?

COMPATIBILITY: HTML 3+, INTERNET EXPLORER 3.0+, NETSCAPE NAVIGATOR 4.0+

Problem

I would like the browser to display different portions of the text of my Web page using different colors. How can I specify the color for text within particular HTML 4.0 elements?

Technique

Style sheets provide the `color` property to associate a foreground color used to draw text with a particular class, a particular HTML 4.0 element, or a particular class of a particular element.

Steps

The following procedure walks you through the process of altering the color of particular elements within your Web pages:

1. Select the HTML 4.0 element in your Web page, or in the broad set of documents using the style sheet you are modifying, to which you want to apply stylistic constraints. Create an appropriate selector as described in How-To 16.1.

2. Select the color to which you want to change this element. Table 16-4 provides the named colors supported by the CSS level 1 standard.

Table 16-4 Supported named colors

COLOR	HEXADECIMAL TRIPLET	COLOR	HEXADECIMAL TRIPLET
Black	#000000	Green	#008000
Silver	#C0C0C0	Lime	#00FF00

COLOR	HEXADECIMAL TRIPLET	COLOR	HEXADECIMAL TRIPLET
Gray	#808080	Olive	#808000
White	#FFFFFF	Yellow	#FFFF00
Maroon	#800000	Navy	#000080
Red	#FF0000	Blue	#0000FF
Purple	#800080	Teal	#008080
Fuchsia	#FF00FF	Aqua	#00FFFF

3. Use How-To's 16.9 and 16.10 to select and create the appropriate mechanism for adding this style information to the Web page(s) of your choice.

How It Works

You alter the color used to display the text within a particular HTML 4.0 element using the **color** property. Use this property to set the color for the selector; see How-To 16.1 for the different definitions of selectors. You can specify the color value in several ways. These methods include by name, by 3-tuple (three numbers corresponding to the red, green, and blue components of the desired color), or by hexadecimal value. The list of supported colors appears in Table 16-4. The proposal calls for the acceptance of RGB values as either 3-tuples or hexadecimal. For example, use any one of the following to set a red color for **<H1 CLASS="red">**:

```
H1.red { color: red }
H1.red { color: 1.0 0.0 0.0 }      /* Floating point 3-tuple */
H1.red { color: 255 0 0 }          /* One byte value 3-tuple */
H1.red { color: #F00 }           /* Single digit hexadecimal */
H1.red { color: #FF0000 }          /* Double digit hexadecimal */
```

For more information on the **color** property of CSS 1, see the current Internet draft at URL **http://www.w3.org/pub/WWW/TR/WD-css1.html#color**.

Figure 16-5 displays a document with the following **<STYLE>** element in its **<HEAD>** element:

```
<STYLE>
<!--
BODY { color: teal }
.red { color: red }
-->
</STYLE>
```

This style element instructs the browser to display the text within any HTML 4.0 element that has a **CLASS** attribute with a value of **red** in the color red and all other text within the **<BODY>** element of the Web page in teal. A paragraph element and a level 2 header element use this style information. The file **RED.HTM** on the CD-ROM contains complete HTML 4.0 source for the document appearing in Figure 16-5.

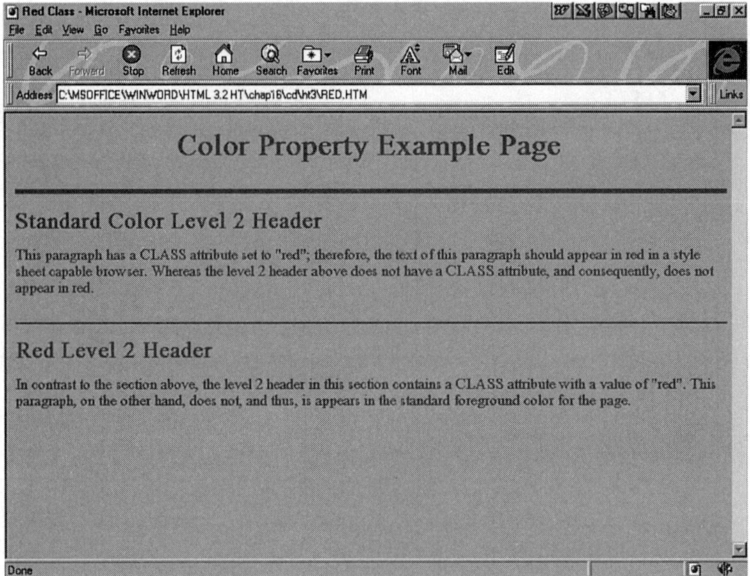

Figure 16-5 Red class

Comments

Appendix H, "HTML Color Table," provides a table of hexadecimal triplet values and the color that these values represent. Consult this table for helpful hints for coming up with appropriate color values.

Not all forms for specifying colors are supported by Microsoft Internet Explorer and Netscape Navigator. Neither supports the floating-point 3-tuple or the 1-byte value 3-tuple described earlier.

You can use the `color` property, along with a special style sheet class, `A:visited`, to implement the same tricks discussed in How-To 2.11 with respect to blending and vanishing visited links. The files `BLEND.HTM` and `VANISH.HTM` on the CD-ROM implement these tricks. The style information in these Web pages is defined within the body of the document as discussed in How-To 16.10 and the cross-browser protection mechanism from How-To 16.11 to incorporate the necessary information. However, for best cross-browser performance, you are better off using the methods for these tricks from How-To 2.11 because those methods hinge on HTML 4.0 standard features rather than style sheet capability. Figure 16-6 shows the use of the `ALINK` method for blending in a browser without style sheet support; Figure 16-7 displays the style sheet method for blending in a browser without style sheet support.

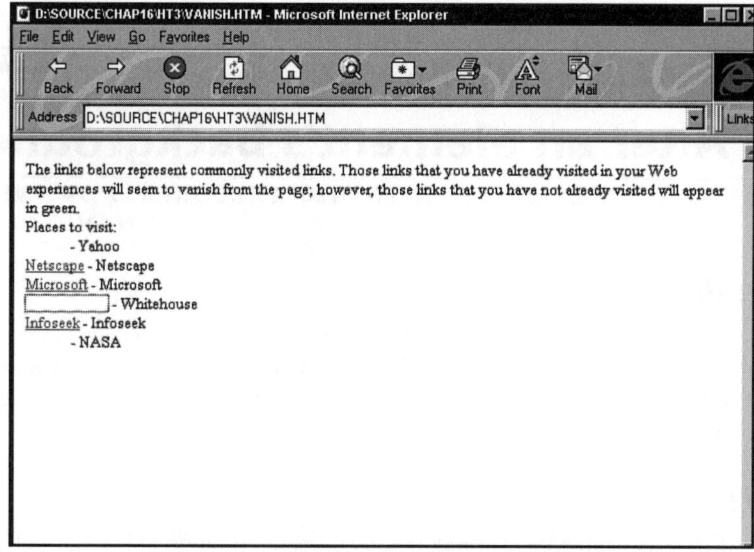

Figure 16-6 Vanishing links using the `ALINK` attribute of the `<BODY>` element

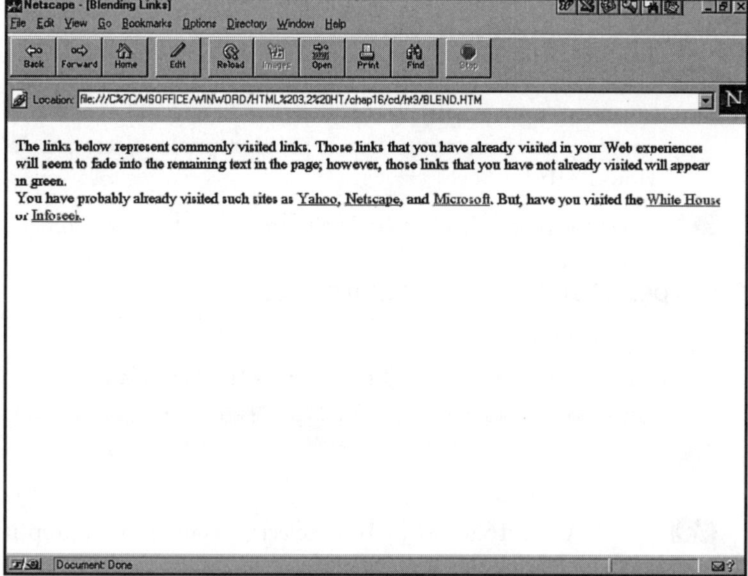

Figure 16-7 Vanishing links using the style sheet method

16.4 How do I...
Alter an element's background?

COMPATIBILITY: HTML 3+, INTERNET EXPLORER 3.0+, NETSCAPE NAVIGATOR 4.0+

Problem

HTML 4.0 enables me to alter the background of my Web page; however, I would like more control over the background than HTML 4.0 permits. I want to specify different backgrounds for different portions of my Web page. How can I selectively modify the backgrounds of particular HTML 4.0 elements?

Technique

CSS level 1 provides the **background** property to support alterations of background for elements covered by selectors (as described in How-To 16.1).

Steps

The following procedure steps you through the process of altering the background of selected portions of your Web page:

1. Select the HTML 4.0 element in your Web page or in the broad set of documents using the style sheet you are modifying and to which you want to apply stylistic constraints. Create an appropriate selector, as described in How-To 16.1.

2. Select the type of background value you want to select from Table 16-5.

Table 16-5 Types of style sheet backgrounds

VALUE	DESCRIPTION
color	Color value for the background—either by name (see Table 16-6) or by value.
URL	Specify a background image. See the "How It Works" section for additional modifiers for this value type.

3. Use How-To's 16.9 and 16.10 to select and create the appropriate mechanism for adding this style information to the Web page(s) of your choice.

How It Works

You use the **background** property to associate a particular background with an HTML 4.0 element. The **background** property has the following syntax:

```
background: transparent | <color> || <url> || <repeat> || <scroll>
|| <position>
```

Set the background of an element as either a particular color, a background pattern, or transparent. The default value is **transparent**. You indicate a color value as described for the **color** property in How-To 16.3. Use a URL to indicate a background pattern; the URL should be placed within parentheses. For example, use the following to set the background of unordered lists (**<UL>**) and list elements (**<LI>**), respectively:

```
UL { background: #F00 }
LI { background: url(http://www.mysite.edu/pix/checker.gif) }
```

The **background** property is not inherited by contained elements per se; however, because the default background is transparent, the designated background might still apply.

If you have opted to use a background image specified by a URL, several optional modifiers can be used. These modifiers represent the following:

- ✔ **<repeat>**: This optional modifier can be one of the following literals: **repeat**, **repeat-x**, **repeat-y**, or **no-repeat**. If no **<repeat>** modifier is chosen, the browser will assume the default of **repeat**. The literals designate whether the background image is repeated horizontally and vertically, just horizontally, just vertically, or not at all.
- ✔ **<scrolling>**: This optional modifier can be either **fixed** or **scroll**. **scroll** is the default value if a scrolling modifier is not specified. This modifier indicates whether the background image should remain fixed with respect to page motion or scroll with the page, respectively. Selecting **fixed** is analogous to the fixed background image discussed in How-To 2.12.

NOTE

<scrolling> is not supported in Netscape Navigator 4.0.

- ✔ **<position>**: This optional modifier lets you specify the position of the background image relative to the modified element. Consult **http://www.w3.org/pub/WWW/TR/REC-CSS1.html#background** for examples and details of specifying the image position.

For more information on the **background** property of CSS 1, see the current Internet draft at **http://www.w3.org/pub/WWW/TR/REC-CSS1.html#background**.

Figure 16-8 displays a document with the following **<STYLE>** element in its **<HEAD>** element:

```
<STYLE TYPE="text/css">
<!--
BODY { color: teal ;
     background: yellow}
.red { color: red }
H2 { background: black}
-->
</STYLE>
```

This style element instructs the browser to display the text within any HTML 4.0 element that has a **CLASS** attribute with a value of **red** in the color red, and all other text within the **<BODY>** element of the Web page in teal. (See How-To 16.3 for information on the use of the **color** property.) A paragraph element and a level 2 header element use this style information. The background of the **<BODY>** element for this page is set to yellow, whereas the background for level 2 header elements is set to black. The file **BACKGRND.HTM** on the CD-ROM contains complete HTML 4.0 source for the document appearing in Figure 16-8. For an example using an image as the background for an element, see the discussion of the button trick in the "Comments" section.

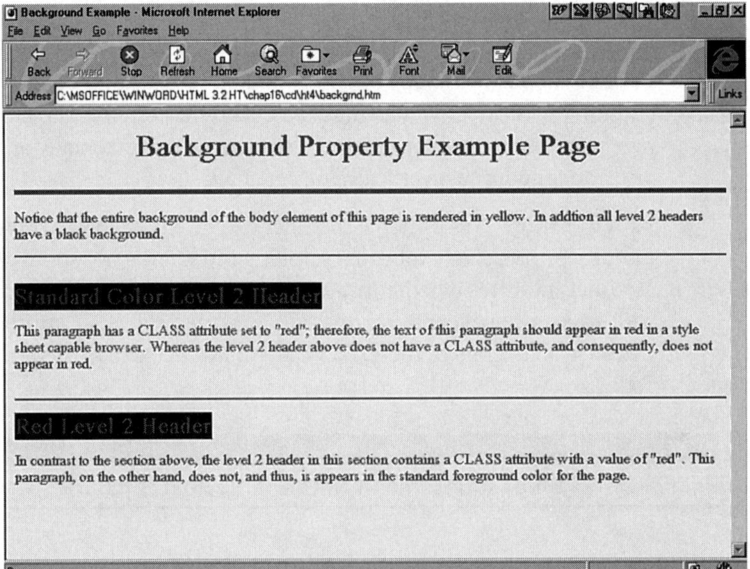

Figure 16-8 Yellow background of the body element and black background of level 2 headers

Comments

One neat trick that you can do with selective backgrounds is to simulate textured buttons. The usual method for including buttons on a page requires a separate image for each button. With style sheets, however, you can simulate a set of buttons with similar texture by creating a list or table, depending on your desired layout for the buttons. You configure the elements of the list or cells of the table to use the same texture as a background image. This improves performance by requiring the reader to download a single image for all the buttons rather than one image per button.

The **BUTTONS.HTM** file on the CD-ROM contains an example of this usage. Figures 16-9 and 16-10 show this page in a style-sheet–capable browser and a style-sheet–incapable browser, respectively. You should note that, even in the style-sheet-incapable browser, the page still appears fine with a list or table of links rather than buttons.

NOTE

Internet Explorer 3.0 has a slight problem with this trick with respect to previously visited links using the list format; the problem does not seem to occur with the table implementation.

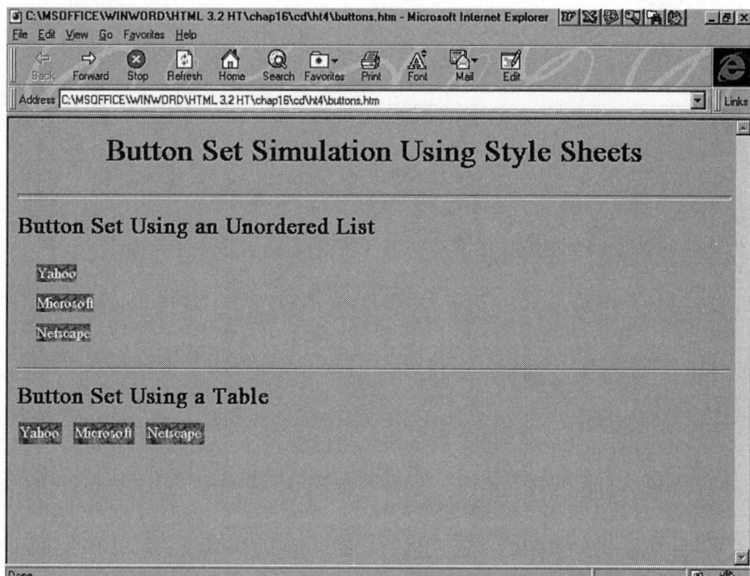

Figure 16-9 Buttons trick in a style-sheet–capable browser

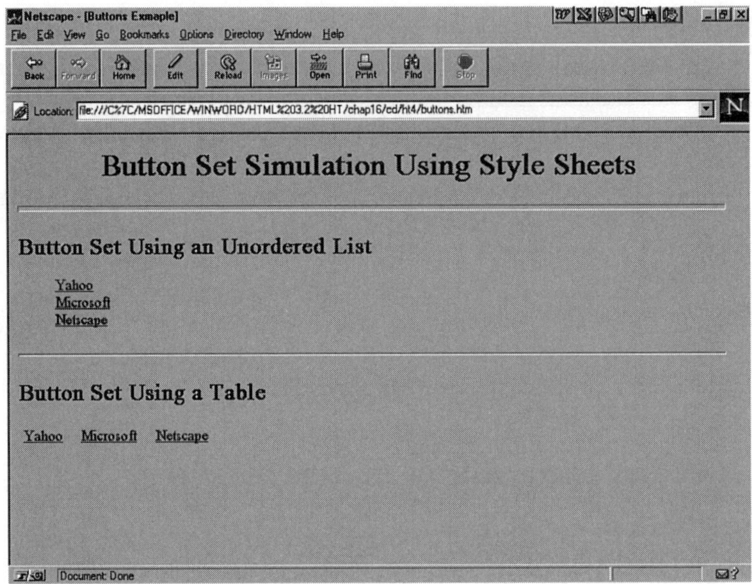

Figure 16-10 Buttons trick in a browser without style sheet capability

COMPLEXITY
INTERMEDIATE

16.5 How do I... Alter an element's text properties?

COMPATIBILITY: HTML 3+, INTERNET EXPLORER 3.0+, NETSCAPE NAVIGATOR 4.0+

Problem

I would like to modify the alignment of the text associated with a particular HTML element. I want to turn off the underlining of links within my Web page. I want to configure a special class of indentations to associate with several different HTML elements in my page. How do I provide this text-related style information?

Technique

The CSS level 1 standard supports a variety of properties for specifying the style of the text associated with particular HTML elements. Use the appropriate property from those listed in Table 16-6.

Table 16-6 CSS 1 text-related properties

PROPERTY	DESCRIPTION
`letter-spacing`	Adds space between letters of text.
`line-height`	Specifies the height of a line of text within the targeted selector.
`text-align`	Selects the alignment style for the text within the targeted selector.
`text-decoration`	Places decorative effect on the text.
`text-indent`	Indents the text a specified amount.
`text-transform`	Performs case transformation on text.
`vertical-align`	Positions the selected element vertically.
`word-spacing`	Provides additional space between words.

The "How It Works" section provides detailed information on the use of these properties.

Steps

The following procedure walks you through the process of associating text properties with HTML elements in your Web page:

1. Select the HTML 4.0 element in your Web page, or in the broad set of documents using the style sheet you are modifying, to which you want to apply stylistic constraints. Create an appropriate selector, as described in How-To 16.1.
2. Select the text property that you want to use from Table 16-6.
3. Use How-To's 16.9 and 16.10 to select and create the appropriate mechanism for adding this style information to the Web page(s) of your choice.

How It Works

You can select to modify the style information represented by the following text-related properties defined for CSS level 1:

- ✔ `letter-spacing`: Value: `normal | <length>`

  The default value for this property is `normal`. The length should be specified in terms of the units shown in Table 16-1. The actual value specified determines the space between characters in addition to the default distance. Negative values are allowable, subject to browser constraints. In addition, if the letter spacing is specifically set to `zero`, the browser should refrain from attempting to justify text on a line.

NOTE

`letter-spacing` is not supported in either Internet Explorer 3.0 or Netscape Navigator 4.0. It is supported by Internet Explorer 4.0, though.

- ✔ `line-height`: Value: `<number> | <length> | <percentage>`

  This property determines the distance between two adjacent baselines. The default value for this property varies among browsers. When a number is specified as the value, this number serves as a multiplier with respect to the current font height. You can also specify this distance using a length in one of the unit types presented in Table 16-1. Finally, you can indicate the distance as a percentage of the current font height. For example, the following `<STYLE>` element defines that `<P>` elements should render text with a line height equal to 150 percent of the font height:

```
<STYLE TYPE="text/css">
<!--
P { line-height: 150% }
-->
</STYLE>
```

- ✔ `text-align`: Value: `left | right | center | justify`

  This property specifies the proper alignment for the selected element. The default value varies depending on your browser. For example, the following would specify an inline indication of right alignment for the indicated address:

```
<P STYLE="text-align: right">
John Q. Public
9999 Oakmore St.
Atlanta, GA 30333
<P><!-- Next Paragraph>
```

NOTE

Internet Explorer 3.0 does not support the `justify` values, and the default alignment is left. Internet Explorer 4.0 adds support for `justify`.

- ✔ `text-indent`: Value: `<length> | <percentage>`

  Use this property to indent text associated with a particular selector. The amount of indentation can be specified as an absolute amount in one of the unit types recognized in Table 16-1 or as a percentage of the enclosing element's width. The default value of this property is `zero`.

✔ `text-decoration`: Value: `none | [underline | overline | line-through | blink ] +`

Use this property to associate a decoration with a particular selector. For example, to create an underlined **<H2 CLASS="under">** element, use the following:

```
H2.under { text-decoration: underline }
```

NOTE

Internet Explorer 3.0 and 4.0 support only the values `none`, `underline`, and `line-through`. Netscape Navigator 4.0 supports those as well as `blink`, but not `overline`.

✔ `text-transform`: Value: `capitalize | uppercase | lowercase | none`

The default value of this property is **none**. The literal values above indicate their respective purposes. A **capitalize** value indicates that the first letter of each word of text in the selected element should be uppercase. The **uppercase** value specifies that all text should be uppercase, and the **lowercase** value instructs the browser to render all text in lowercase.

NOTE

`text-transform` is not supported by Internet Explorer 3.0.

✔ `vertical-align`: Value: `baseline | sub | super | top | text-top | middle | bottom | text-bottom | <percentage>`

Most of the potential values for **vertical-align** are self-explanatory. Six of these values (**baseline**, **middle**, **sub**, **super**, **text-bottom**, and **text-top**) represent vertical alignment with respect to the parent element of the selector modified. The **top** and **bottom** values represent vertical alignment with respect to the tallest and lowest elements, respectively, on the same line with the modified element. The percentage represents a percentage of the value of the line height of the element itself.

NOTE

`vertical-align` is not supported by Internet Explorer 3.0 or Netscape Navigator 4.0. Preview releases of Internet Explorer 4.0 support only the `super` and `sub` attributes of `vertical-align`.

✔ `word-spacing`: Value: `normal | <length>`

As with letter spacing, the default value of this property is `normal`. By specifying an explicit value, you instruct the browser to add the specified amount of space in addition to the default. The actual word spacing is also influenced by the justification of the text.

NOTE

`word-spacing` is not supported by Internet Explorer 3.0, 4.0, or Netscape Navigator 4.0.

For more information on the text-related properties of CSS 1, see the current Internet draft at **`http://www.w3.org/pub/WWW/TR/WD-css1.html#text-properties`**.

Figure 16-11 displays a document using several of the text-related properties discussed earlier. The address appearing immediately following the first horizontal rule uses the following `<P>` element to right-align the text:

```
<P STYLE="text-align: right; color: green; background: white">
John Q. Public<BR>
9999 Oakmore St.<BR>
Atlanta, GA 30333
```

The strikethrough of the word **`black`** in the first paragraph uses a **`text-decoration`** property defined in the Web page's `<STYLE>` element. The `<STYLE>` element contains the following line responsible for the strikethrough in this case:

```
FONT.del { text-decoration: line-through; color: black }
```

The use of the following `<P>` element generates the double-spaced second paragraph of this page:

```
<P CLASS="red" STYLE="line-height: 20pt">
```

NOTE

This element uses a specified `<STYLE>` element constraint and an inline `<STYLE>` attribute.

The following specification for indented paragraphs is used to indent the first paragraph 1/4 of the width of the `<BODY>` element of this page:

```
P.indent { text-indent: 25% }
```

The file `TEXT.HTM` on the CD-ROM contains the complete HTML 4.0 source for the document appearing in Figure 16-11.

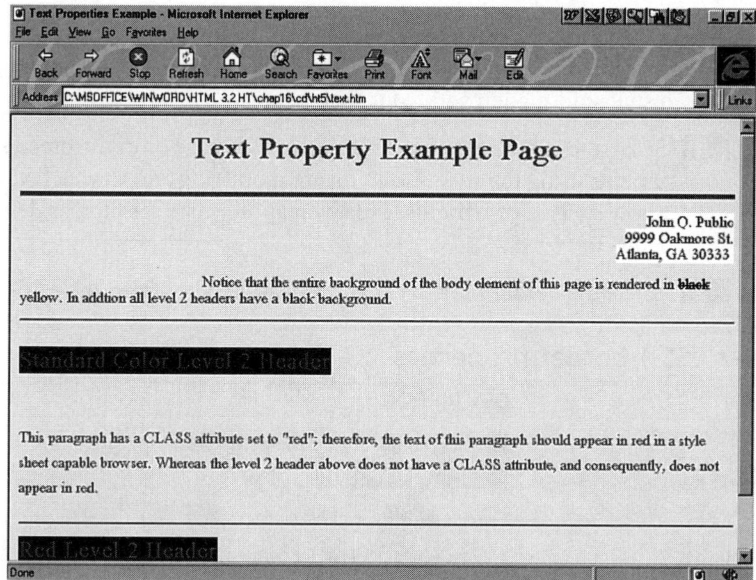

Figure 16-11 Text-related properties document

Comments

Microsoft Internet Explorer supports a limited set of the text-related properties. Release 3.0 supports `line-height`, `text-align`, `text-decoration`, and `text-indent` properties. Further restrictions with respect to these properties are identified earlier.

COMPLEXITY
INTERMEDIATE

16.6 How do I... Alter the borders of an element?

COMPATIBILITY: HTML 3+, NETSCAPE NAVIGATOR 4.0+, INTERNET EXPLORER 4.0+

Problem

I would like to add borders around certain elements in my Web page. How do I indicate the size, style, and location of such borders using CSS level 1?

Technique

Use the various border properties listed in Table 16-7 to indicate borders around specific HTML 4.0 elements in your Web pages.

Steps

The following procedure walks you through the process of associating border-related style information with your Web page:

1. Select the HTML 4.0 element in your Web page or in the broad set of documents using the style sheet you are modifying and to which you want to apply stylistic constraints. Create an appropriate selector, as described in How-To 16.1.

2. Select the border property that you want to alter from Table 16-7.

Table 16-7 CSS 1 border properties

PROPERTY	DESCRIPTION
`border`	Shorthand for specifying padding constraints.
`border-bottom`	Specifies the border bottom.
`border-left`	Specifies the left side of the border.
`border-right`	Specifies the right side of the border.
`border-top`	Specifies the border top.
`border-bottom-width`	Sets the width of the top border.
`border-left-width`	Sets the width of the left border.
`border-right-width`	Sets the width of the right border.
`border-top-width`	Sets the width of the top border.
`border-width`	Sets the width of the entire border.
`border-color`	Sets the color of the border.
`border-style`	Sets the style of the border.

NOTE

`border-left`, `border-right`, `border-top`, and `border-bottom` are not supported by Netscape Navigator 4.0.

3. Select the border width using one of the following: `thin | medium | thick | <length>`. A `<length>` is some value in one of the units specified in Table 16-1. The width of the entire border can be selected with `border-width` or each side of the border can be set with `border-left-width`, `border-right-width`, `border-top-width`, and `border-bottom-width`.

4. Choose a border style from the following: `none | dotted | dashed | solid | double | groove | ridge | inset | outset`.

5. Specify the color for the border, using a color value as described in How-To 16.3.

6. Use How-To's 16.9 and 16.10 to select and create the appropriate mechanism for adding this style information to the Web page(s) of your choice.

How It Works

All the border properties work in a similar manner. After choosing the HTML 4.0 elements through selectors, you specify the particular border to alter with any necessary additional data. A border is a potentially visible band of space surrounding an element.

No matter which border property you modify, you can specify the following three types of additional data: a border width, a border style, and a color.

- `border width`: Value: `thin | medium | thick | <length>`

  The `border width` value is the first of a border property's parameters. This first value can be one of the literals (`thin`, `medium`, and `thick`) or a length in one of the unit types detailed in Table 16-1.

- `border style`: Value: `none | dotted | dashed | solid | double | groove | ridge | inset | outset`

  The `border style` value is the second border property parameter. The value in the property specification should be a literal describing how the border of the element should look. `none` designates no border even if a border width had been set for this element. `dotted` signifies the use of a dotted line to draw the border. A `dashed` value requests the use of a dashed line. `solid` suggests the use of a solid line as the border; `double` indicates the use of a double line around the specified element. The `groove` and `ridge` values connote the use of a 3D effect drawn using the element's color property value. Similarly, `inset` and `outset` paint their respective effects using the color value associated with the element modified.

NOTE

Netscape Navigator 4.0 and Internet Explorer 4.0 do not support the border styles `dashed` and `dotted`.

- `border color`: `<color>`

  The third parameter of a border property is the color value for the element modified. The color chosen must conform to the methods of color specification discussed in How-To 16.2.

The **border** property alone is shorthand for the specification of equivalently constrained borders on all sides of an element. For more information on the border properties of CSS 1, see the current Internet draft at **http://www.w3.org/pub/WWW/TR/WD-css1.html#border-top-border-right-border-bottom-border-left-border**.

The following is an example of including borders of different types in documents using style sheets:

```
<HTML>
<HEAD>
<TITLE>Style Sheet Tests</TITLE>
<STYLE TYPE="text/css">
<!--
P      {font-family: arial;
       color: #008080;
       font-size: 18pt}

P.border1      {border: inset green 10pt}

P.border2      {border-style: groove;
      border-left-width: 18pt;
      border-right-width: 27pt;
      border-top-width: 9pt;
      border-bottom-width: 36pt;
      border-color: teal;}

-->
</STYLE>
</HEAD>

<BODY>

<P CLASS=border1>Here is an example of one kind of table border,
which should appear as an inset with 10-point green lines.</P>

<P CLASS=border2>Here is another example, which shows how one
can change the thickness of each side of the border.</P>



</BODY>
</HTML>
```

See Figure 16-12 to find how this is displayed in Netscape Navigator 4.0. The HTML used to create this, which includes the style sheet, is on the CD-ROM as file **BORDER.HTM**.

Comments

Microsoft Internet Explorer 3.0 does not support the border properties.

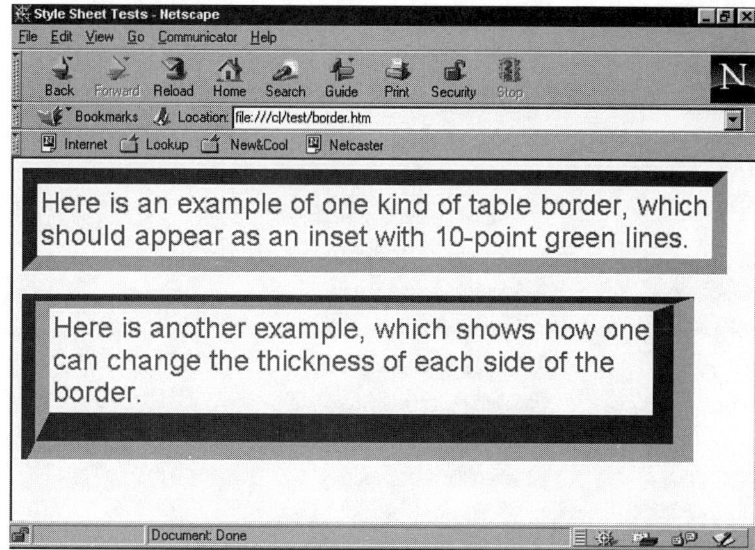

Figure 16-12 Examples of borders created using style sheets

COMPLEXITY
ADVANCED

16.7 How do I... Specify layout constraints of an element?

COMPATIBILITY: HTML 3+, INTERNET EXPLORER 3.0+, NETSCAPE NAVIGATOR 4.0+

Problem

HTML 4.0 provides extremely limited means of controlling the layout of its elements; either I need to "misuse" elements or lay out all my elements using tables. How can I specify layout constraints for elements using the CSS level 1 standard?

Technique

CSS level 1 provides a large number of layout support properties that you can use to control the layout of HTML 4.0 elements in your Web pages. Table 16-8 lists and briefly describes these layout properties.

The "How It Works" section provides detailed information on the detailed syntax of these layout properties.

Table 16-8 CSS 1 layout constraints

PROPERTY	DESCRIPTION
`border properties`	See How-To 16.6.
`clear`	Specifies the clearance requirements of an element.
`float`	Indicates where the element should float.
`height`	Specifies the height of an element.
`margin`	Shorthand for specifying margin constraints.
`margin-bottom`	Selects the bottom margin.
`margin-left`	Sets the left margin.
`margin-right`	Specifies the right margin.
`margin-top`	Selects the top margin.
`padding`	Shorthand for specifying padding constraints.
`padding-bottom`	Selects the bottom padding.
`padding-left`	Sets the left padding.
`padding-right`	Specifies the right padding.
`padding-top`	Selects the top padding.
`width`	Specifies the width of an element.

Steps

The following procedure walks you through the process of specifying layout constraints for your Web page:

1. Select the HTML 4.0 element in your Web page or in the broad set of documents using the style sheet you are modifying and to which you want to apply stylistic constraints. Create an appropriate selector as described in How-To 16.1.
2. Select the layout constraints that you want to set from Table 16-8.
3. Choose any values required by the chosen layout constraint. See detailed descriptions in the following "How It Works" section.
4. Use How-To's 16.9 and 16.10 to select and create the appropriate mechanism for adding this style information to the Web page(s) of your choice.

How It Works

The CSS level 1 standard provides several style properties that enable you to control the layout of HTML 4.0 elements in your Web pages. You can select to modify the style information represented by the following layout properties defined for CSS level 1:

- ✔ `clear`: Value: `none | left | right | both`

This value specifies the layout of an element with respect to floating elements that can occupy either side of the displayed Web page. The default value for this property is **none**; thus, the browser should render the element next to any element floating to the left and consider any right-floating elements the right boundary. Specifying any of the other values indicates that the browser should not display the configured element until it is beyond the floating object conforming to the specified value (**left**, **right**, or **both**).

NOTE

Internet Explorer 3.0 and 4.0 do not support this layout property.

✔ **Float**: Value: **none | left | right**

This property enables you to configure an element so that browsers float the element to either the right or left margin of the page. The default value for this property is **none**, indicating that an element should not float to either margin.

NOTE

Internet Explorer 3.0 and 4.0 do not support this layout property.

✔ **Height**: Value: **<length> | auto**

Use this property to set the height of an element. You can specify the height as either **auto**; the default, which enables the element to size itself as required; or a specific length in a unit mentioned in Table 16-1.

NOTE

Neither Internet Explorer 3.0, 4.0, nor Netscape Navigator 4.0 support this layout property.

✔ **margin**, **margin-bottom**, **margin-left**, **margin-right**, **margin-top**: Value: **<length> | <percent> | auto**

Use these properties to set the appropriate margins of the selector. The value can be either a length, a percentage of the parent element's width, or an automatic setting. Margin values can be negative. For example, to set the left margin of a list element (**<LI>**) to be 20 percent of its parent's width and the right margin to 25 percent, and to set the top margin of paragraph (**<P>**) element to 12 points, use the following:

```
LI { margin-left: 20%; margin-right: 25% }
P.double { margin-top: 12pt }
```

The `margin` property is shorthand for the other four. `margin property` requires between one and four values representing the top, right, bottom, and left margins, respectively. If only one value is given, the value is applied to all margins. If two or three values are given, the browser should use the values specified for the opposite sides.

Figure 16-13 displays a page with the preceding margin constraints in a style-sheet–capable browser; Figure 16-14 shows the same page in a browser without this capability. The CD-ROM contains the complete style sheet and HTML sources for these pages in the `MARGINS.CSS` and `MARGINS.HTM` files, respectively.

Use these properties to set the appropriate padding of the selector. The padding represents the distance between the border of the element and the element content. The value can be a length, a percentage of the parent element's width, or an automatic setting. Padding values cannot be negative. In all other respects, these properties are configured in the same way as margins.

NOTE

Internet Explorer 3.0 does not support these layout properties.

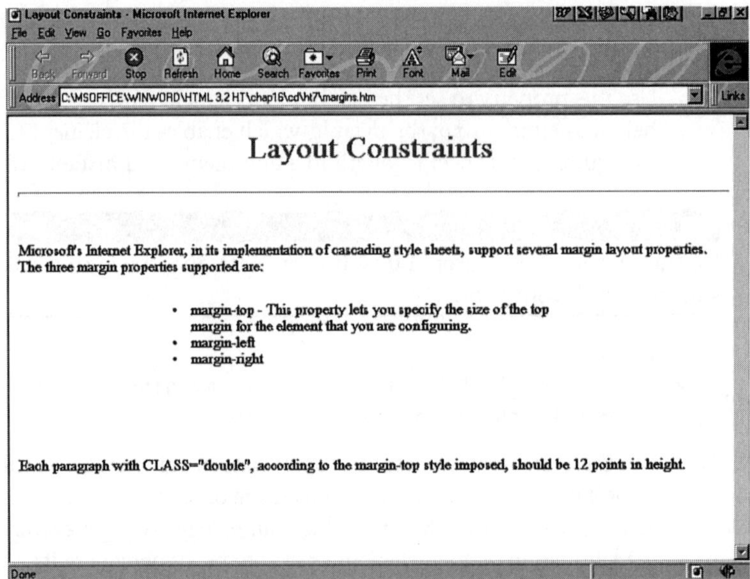

Figure 16-13 Layout constraint page in a style-sheet–capable browser

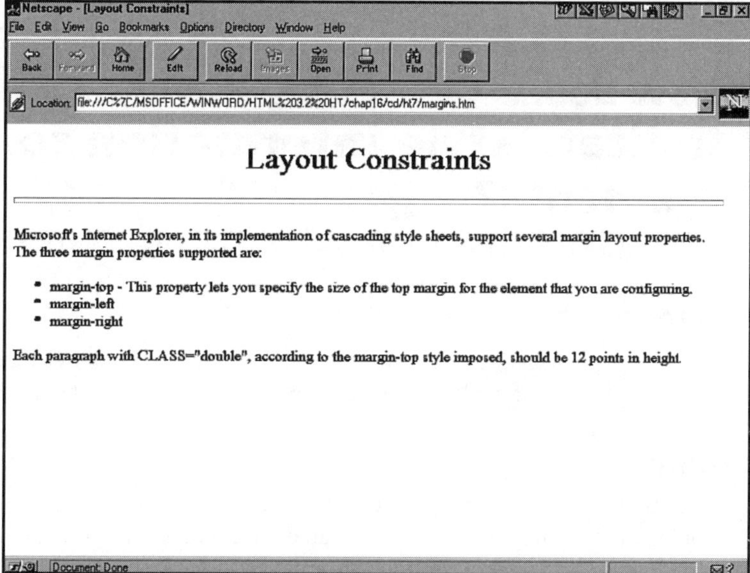

Figure 16-14 Layout constraint page in a browser without style sheet capability

- ✔ `Width`: Value: `<length> | <percent> | auto`

  Use this property to specify the width of an element as either a specific width in a recognized unit from Table 16-1 or a percentage of the parent element's width. The default value enables the element to size itself. If applied to an inserted media type, the element should scale the object as appropriate; if this element's `height` property is set to `auto`, the default, the aspect ratio should remain the same.

NOTE

Internet Explorer 3.0 and 4.0 do not support this layout property.

For more information on the layout properties of CSS 1, see the current Internet draft at `http://www.w3.org/pub/WWW/TR/WD-css1.html#box-properties`.

Comments

Of the preceding layout constraints, Microsoft Internet Explorer 3.0 supports only the `margin-left`, `margin-right`, and `margin-top` properties.

16.8 How do I... Indicate style information for list elements?

COMPATIBILITY: HTML 3+, NETSCAPE NAVIGATOR 4.0+

Problem

CSS level 1 provides more fine-grained control of the style of list elements. How do I control the style of my list elements using the CSS 1 `list-style` property?

Technique

The CSS 1 `list-style` property enables you to control both the style and the positioning of the bullet or number associated with individual list items. To constrain a particular list element, choose an appropriate selector and specify the style desired for this selector.

Steps

The following procedure walks you through the process of indicating list elements in style information for your Web page:

1. Select the HTML 4.0 element in your Web page or in the broad set of documents using the style sheet you are modifying and to which you want to apply stylistic constraints. Create an appropriate selector as described in How-To 16.1.

2. Select the style of the list element marker from Table 16-9.

Table 16-9 CSS 1 list styles

STYLE	DESCRIPTION
`disc`	Default value; filled bullet
`circle`	Open circle
`square`	Square bullet
`decimal`	Decimal number (1, 2, 3, 4, and so on)
`lower-roman`	Lowercase Roman numerals (i, ii, iii, iv, and so on)
`upper-roman`	Uppercase Roman numerals (I, II, III, IV, and so on)
`lower-alpha`	Lowercase alphabetic (a, b, c, d, and so on)
`upper-alpha`	Uppercase alphabetic (A, B, C, D, and so on)
`none`	No marker

NOTE

Netscape Navigator 4.0 does not support the list style `none`.

3. Select the desired positioning of the list element marker with `list-style-position`. You can choose either `inside` or `outside`. The default positioning is `outside`.

NOTE

Netscape Navigator 4.0 does not support `list-style-position`.

4. Use How-To's 16.9 and 16.10 to select and create the appropriate mechanism for adding this style information to the Web page(s) of your choice.

How It Works

CSS level 1 provides the `list-style` property to constrain the presentation of elements within ordered and unordered HTML 4.0 lists. `list-style` attaches to `<LI>` HTML 4.0 elements within `<OL>` and `<UL>` elements.

This constraint can be imposed at a higher level than directly associated with `<LI>` elements. If an HTML 4.0 element has this property set, elements contained within that element are similarly subject to the imposed setting. For example, the following `<DIV>` element standardizes all list elements used within its context, unless subjected to an overriding `list-style` property:

```
DIV.nomark { list-style: none}
```

All list elements that would have a mark no longer have one within division elements constrained by this selector. However, more localized `list-style` property constraints could override this inherited style.

In addition to the type of mark used, the `list-style` property allows the specification of the default positioning of the indicated mark. The two potential values are `inside` and `outside`, with `outside` being the default value. This positioning value indicates the positioning of the mark with respect to the remainder of the text within the list element. With selection of the outside positioning, the mark appears outside all portions of the list elements, subject to the constraint. In the case of `inside`, the mark appears within the text of the list elements. For example, a browser might display an outside lowercase Roman numeral list as follows:

```
i.     The mark appears outside the entire
          text of the list element.
    ii.     Second such list element.
```

On the other hand, a browser might display an inside lowercase Roman numeral list as follows:

```
i.    The mark appears outside the entire
   text of the list element.
   ii.    Second such list element.
```

For more information on the `list-style` property of CSS 1, see the current Internet draft at `http://www.w3.org/pub/WWW/TR/WD-css1.html#list-style`.

The following is an example of how these list styles could be used in a document:

```
<HTML>
<HEAD>
<TITLE>Style Sheet Tests</TITLE>
<STYLE TYPE="text/css">
<!--
UL LI      {list-style: square}

OL LI      {list-style: lower-roman}

-->
</STYLE>
</HEAD>

<BODY>

<OL>
<LI>uno
<LI>dos
<LI>tres
</OL>

<UL>
<LI>uno
<LI>dos
<LI>tres
</UL>

</BODY>
</HTML>
```

See Figure 16-15 to see how this is displayed in Netscape Navigator 4.0. The HTML file used to create this, which includes the style sheet, is available on the CD-ROM as file `LISTS.HTM`.

Comments

Microsoft Internet Explorer does not yet support this property. Use of the `TYPE` attribute of `<LI>` elements as described in How-To 6.4 allows for similar control of list style.

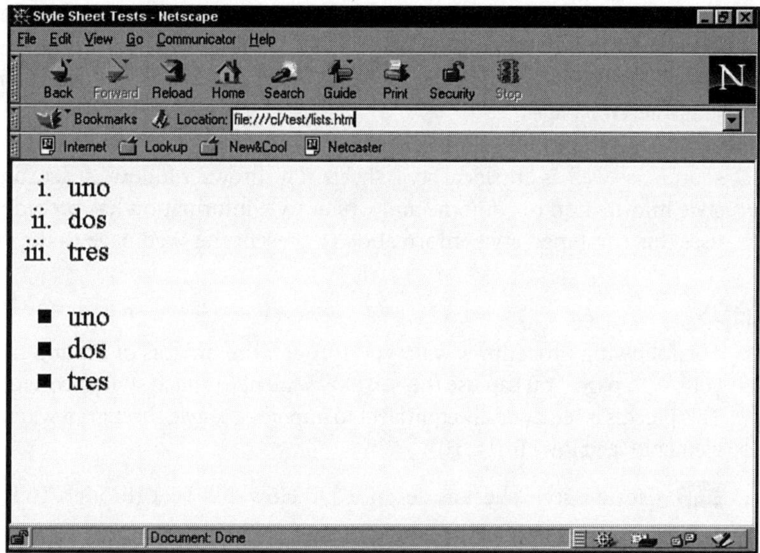

Figure 16-15 Changing list styles for numbers and bullets using style sheets

COMPLEXITY
ADVANCED

16.9 How do I... Cascade HTML style sheets?

COMPATIBILITY: HTML 3+, INTERNET EXPLORER 3.0+, NETSCAPE NAVIGATOR 4.0+

Problem

I need to associate style sheets with my Web pages. How can I do that, and how do the attached style sheets interact among themselves to resolve conflicting property specifications?

Technique

You can associate style information with your Web page in several ways:

- ✔ You can embed the style information directly through a **STYLE** attribute.
- ✔ You can embed the style information directly through a **<STYLE>** header element.
- ✔ You can attach style sheets directly through **<LINK>** elements.

The first two methods involve inserting style information directly into a Web page; How-To 16.10 discusses the methods for accomplishing this. The third method, discussed in this How-To, involves creating a separate style sheet that can be linked to multiple Web pages.

Browsers combine and integrate style information determined from these sources, as well as any local style sheets. The browser follows strict rules on which style information to combine and which style information has precedence. It then uses this combined style information to present the Web page to the viewer.

Steps

The following procedures walk you through the process of linking style sheets to your Web page. You can use the `<LINK>` element to attach style sheets to a Web page. This process is semantically equivalent to importing a style sheet from within a `<STYLE>` element (see How-To 16.10).

1. Create a style sheet as described in How-To's 16.1 through 16.8.
2. In a text editor, open the Web page to which you want to add a style sheet.
3. Find the `<HEAD>` element of your Web page.
4. Add a `<LINK>` element, with the `HREF` attribute set to the URL of the style sheet you want to attach. The `TITLE` attribute serves as the combination mechanism; all style sheets attached by `<LINK>` with the same title are combined. Therefore, set the `TITLE` attribute to indicate which group of style sheets the one you want to add should combine with. For example, to attach `sheet1.css` to the `"Company"` group of style sheets, you would add the following `<LINK>` element:

```
<LINK REL=stylesheet TITLE="Company" HREF="sheet1.css" TYPE="text/css">
```

   The `REL` attribute should be set to `"stylesheet"`. The `TYPE` attribute should be set to `"text/css"` to distinguish it from dynamic (JavaScript) style sheets (see Chapter 21, "Dynamic Style Sheets and Fonts").

5. Perform step 4 for each style sheet you want to attach.
6. Save your Web page.
7. Test your Web page.

How It Works

The cascading style sheet model lets you associate stylistic information with presented Web pages. A browser generally can receive stylistic information from three sources:

- ✔ Reader style information: A particular reader has created a style sheet (as described in How-To's 16.1 through 16.8), or the browser has built-in style constraints. In either case, the browser combines this information with incoming style information.

NOTE

Neither Internet Explorer 3.0, 4.0, nor Netscape Navigator 4.0 supports local style sheets.

- ✔ External style sheets: External style sheets are linked to a Web page via `<LINK>` elements. Each such style sheet is separately requested by the browser.
- ✔ Internal style information: Web pages contain internal style information in `<STYLE>` elements and `STYLE` attributes (see How-To 16.10).

The browser accumulates style information from these three sources to derive a single set of style constraints. The first possible conflict that might arise in this process is the potential multiplicity of grouped external style sheets. This situation arises when `<LINK>` elements with different `TITLE` attributes occur in the same Web page. All external style sheets with the same `TITLE` are combined; however, the choice of which combined style sheet to use rests with the reader. The model suggests that the reader should be able to choose among the `TITLE` attributes for the desired combined style.

The model suggests the following steps in resolving conflicts whenever stylistic information is combined and applied to a particular element:

1. Remove declarations for the same property for the same selector by removing the more imported, least local declaration. Thus, if a color declaration for the `<H1>` element appears in both the `<STYLE>` element for a page and an imported style sheet, then the declaration from the `<STYLE>` element remains.
2. If rules for the same selector and property still exist, remove all but the declaration specified last.
3. Determine all declarations applicable to a particular element.
4. Applicable declarations are sorted by weight, with `!important` or `!legal` declarations being heavier than normal declarations.
5. Sort the applicable declarations by information origin, with incoming style information overriding reader style information.
6. Sort the applicable declarations by the detail of the selector specification. For example, a `<STRONG>` element appearing within an `<LI>` element is more specific than a `<STRONG>` element alone.

7. Allow specific property declarations to override a generic property. For example, specification of a **font-size** property would override the value from a **font** property.

8. If a conflict still remains, resolve the conflict in favor of the declaration declared last.

After proceeding through this resolution scheme, the browser applies the remaining declarations to the element in question.

Comments

Style sheets are currently supported only by a limited number of browsers: Arena browser for the X Window environment (**http://www.w3.org/pub/WWW/Arena/**), Amaya (**http://www.w3.org/**), Microsoft Internet Explorer 3.0 and later (**http://www.microsoft.com/ie**), and Netscape Navigator 4.0 and later (**http://www.netscape.com/**). Even these browsers do not support selection among titled combined style sheets. Adding style sheet capability to existing browsers might lead to some discrepancies between the proposed model and the implemented solution.

You should examine **http://www.w3.org/pub/WWW/Style/** for the latest information on style sheets. The CSS level 1 specification seems relatively stable at this point. The working draft for this standard is located at **http://www.w3.org/pub/WWW/TR/WD-css1.html**.

COMPLEXITY
INTERMEDIATE

16.10 How do I... Add cascading style information directly to a Web page?

COMPATIBILITY: HTML 3+, INTERNET EXPLORER 3.0+, NETSCAPE NAVIGATOR 4.0+

Problem

I would like to specify stylistic constraints peculiar to an individual Web page. It seems pointless for me to create an entire style sheet for use with only a single page. How can I provide style information specific to a single page within that page?

Technique

You can associate style information with your Web page in several ways:

- ✔ You can embed the style information directly through a **STYLE** attribute.
- ✔ You can embed the style information directly through a **<STYLE>** header element.

✔ You can attach style sheets directly through `<LINK>` elements. See How-To 16.9.

Browsers combine and integrate style information determined from these sources as well as any local style sheets. The browser follows strict rules on which style information to combine and which style information has precedence. It then uses this combined style information to present the Web page to the viewer.

NOTE

Neither Internet Explorer 3.0, 4.0, nor Netscape Navigator 4.0 supports local style sheets.

Steps

The following procedures walk you through configuring style information specific to a single Web page or to a specific element within a page.

<STYLE> Element Process

You can use the `<STYLE>` element to mix and match existing style sheets with local overrides to develop a combined set of stylistic information for use with a particular Web page.

1. Open your HTML page in a text editor.
2. Locate the `<HEAD>` portion of the document.
3. If a `<STYLE>` element does not exist, create one using the following lines:

```
<STYLE TYPE="text/css">
</STYLE>
```

   You will add style information between the opening and closing tags of this element.

4. Use the `@import` command to import any standalone style sheets. For example, to include the `sheet1.css` and `sheet2.css` style sheets, insert the following two lines in the `<STYLE>` element:

```
@import sheet1.css
    @import sheet2.css
```

NOTE

Neither Internet Explorer 3.0 nor Netscape Navigator 4.0 supports the importation of style sheets.

5. Add declarations that you want to override the declarations in the imported style sheets.

NOTE

Internet Explorer 3.0 does not support overriding linked style sheets by a <STYLE> element; if you must override a linked style sheet or a <STYLE> element, use the inline <STYLE> attribute discussed later in the chapter.

6. Save the Web page.
7. Test your Web page.

STYLE Attribute Process

The **STYLE** attribute can be used to configure style information specific to a single element within a Web page.

1. Open your HTML page in a text editor.
2. Locate the element within the page for which you want to define style constraints.
3. If a **STYLE** attribute does not exist, create one. For example, you might use the following modified **<H1>** element to indicate a red, 32-point level 1 header:

```
<H1 STYLE ="color: red; font-size: 32pt">Red, 32 Pt Level 1 Header</H1>
```

   You will add style information between the quotation marks that delimit the value of this attribute.

4. Add declarations that you want to override the declarations in the imported style sheets or **<STYLE>** element declarations. Separate each declaration with a semicolon.
5. Save the Web page.
6. Test your Web page.

How It Works

Embedded **<STYLE>** elements work in an identical fashion to attached style sheets. In fact, the style information from the **<STYLE>** element is combined with style information from one or more attached style sheets. The "How It Works" section in How-To 16.9 outlines the conflict resolution process to resolve conflicting style information.

<STYLE> elements provide a finer grain of control than an attached style sheet. The particular styles chosen can be more tuned to the particular page. In fact, this is the very purpose of the **<STYLE>** element. Whereas attached style sheets can provide generic style information across a broad spectrum of Web pages, the information provided in the **<STYLE>** element can provide page-specific guidance for displaying particular HTML 4.0 elements or classes of elements.

STYLE attributes establish the finest granularity. With the **STYLE** attribute, you can individually control the style information with respect to a single HTML 4.0 element within a single Web page. The style information specified in this attribute applies only to the element in which the attribute is defined.

Comments

Internet Explorer 3.0's implementation of cascading style information is slightly non-standard. Microsoft's implementation places any style information provided with the following precedence, from highest to lowest:

- ✔ **STYLE** attribute
- ✔ Attached style sheets through **<LINK>** elements
- ✔ Embed the style information through a **<STYLE>** header element

The CSS 1 standard actually calls for **<STYLE>** element information to override conflicting attached style sheet information.

COMPLEXITY
BEGINNING

16.11 How do I... Include style elements and protect browsers without style support?

COMPATIBILITY: HTML 3+, INTERNET EXPLORER 3.0+, NETSCAPE NAVIGATOR 4.0+

Problem

Most browsers do not support style elements in the **<HEAD>** tag of an HTML document. In fact, several of them even misinterpret and attempt to display this information as page content. How do I include style information while maintaining cross-browser support?

Technique

Browsers that understand the **<STYLE>** element have no problem parsing and using information found within this element; however, older browsers and browsers that lack style support sometimes try to display the content of the **<STYLE>** element as Web page content.

Steps

Use the following process to modify your **<STYLE>** element to protect browsers that do not support this element:

1. Open your HTML page in a text editor.
2. Locate the **<HEAD>** portion of the document.
3. Locate the **<STYLE>** element within the **<HEAD>** element.

```
<STYLE TYPE="text/css">
/* Your Declarations */
</STYLE>
```

4. Insert comment tags around the declarations within your style element.

```
<STYLE TYPE="text/css">
<!--
/* Your Declarations */
-->
</STYLE>
```

5. Save the Web page.
6. Test your Web page.

How It Works

By surrounding the style information with an opening and closing comment tag, you can ensure that browsers that do not support **<STYLE>** elements will simply ignore the content as if it were a comment. **<STYLE>** enabled browsers, however, will parse and apply the stylistic constraints specified to the appropriate Web page content.

Comments

Even if your readers will be using only **<STYLE>** enabled browsers, you should still consider the use of the comment tags. This mechanism entails minimal additional work while protecting against future potential problems.

CHAPTER 17

WEB PROGRAMMING WITH JAVA AND JAVASCRIPT

17

WEB PROGRAMMING WITH JAVA AND JAVASCRIPT

How do I...

Many of the first generation of Web pages were static pages, using just basic HTML tags to provide information. Some pages utilized CGI scripts, which allowed some interactivity but required everything to run on the server, which could slow down performance at busy times. In the last two years, though, two innovative new technologies have enabled people to create dynamic, interactive Web pages without loading down a Web server with CGI scripts.

One new tool for Web page designers is the Java programming language. The language can be used to write small programs named applets, which can be incorporated into Web pages to provide a wide variety of effects and applications. These Java applets are downloaded from the server and run on the browser's computer using a special program called a "virtual machine," which enables the same Java applet to run on Macintosh, Windows, and UNIX machines. This cross-platform support has made Java quite popular among Web designers.

The other tool is a scripting language called JavaScript, developed by Netscape. Despite the name, this language has little in common with Java. JavaScript scripts are incorporated directly into Web pages and can provide several features useful for interactive Web pages. JavaScript scripts can verify information submitted in forms, provide dynamic content, and even manipulate images on the page. JavaScript is supported by both Netscape and Microsoft, although most of the new features in the language have been added by Netscape.

This chapter provides an introduction to Java and JavaScript and their use in Web pages. Each of these languages is complicated and advanced enough to merit separate books, so it's not possible to go into great detail on these languages. However, these How-To's provide the basics for using Java and JavaScript on the Web.

17.1 Write a Basic Java Applet

Java is an object-oriented programming language that enables designers of Web pages to create highly interactive pages. This How-To shows how to write a basic Java applet, or application, for use in a Web page.

17.2 Include a Java Applet in an HTML Document

After a Java applet is written, code must be included in the Web page so that the page can access the applet. This How-To shows how to include tags so that the page can access and run the appropriate Java applet.

17.3 Pass Variables from a Web Page to an Applet

There are cases in which you will want to provide a Java applet with a set of initial values based on user input or other criteria to get the desired result. This How-To shows how to use the `<PARAM>` element in HTML 4.0 to send a set of initial values to an applet.

17.4 Find More Information About Java

There is far more to Java than can be presented in a few How-To's. This How-To lists resources that any aspiring Java programmer will find useful.

17.5 Improve Java Applet Download Time

A problem with Java applets is that complex applets can require a large number of calls to the server to download different classes used by the applet, slowing them down. This How-To shows two methods, one used by Netscape and the other by Internet Explorer, to improve Java applet downloading time by bundling together the classes used by the applet.

17.6 Include a Script Element

JavaScript is a powerful but simple scripting language that can be incorporated into Web pages, even with small snippets. This How-To shows how to include elements of JavaScript into Web pages to enhance their functionality.

17.7 Write a Basic JavaScript Script

JavaScript can be used to create detailed, highly interactive pages. Although JavaScript is a topic suitable for an entire book, this How-To will show the basics of writing a JavaScript script.

17.8 Include a Script in a Web Page

JavaScript, developed by Netscape, enables users to create scripts without delving into complex languages such as Perl or Java. The scripts can be included in the same document as the rest of the Web page. This How-To shows how to use the `<SCRIPT>` tag in Netscape to run JavaScript scripts.

17.9 Generate a Pop-Up Dialog Box Using JavaScript

One of the useful applications of JavaScript is the capability to write small scripts that generate dialog boxes that pop up on the screen with advice, warnings, or other special information. This How-To shows you how to write a JavaScript script that can generate a pop-up dialog box on the user's screen.

17.10 Check an HTML Form for Required Input Fields

Another useful application of JavaScript is to create scripts that can check HTML forms and see whether all the required fields have been filled out before the form is sent to the server for processing. This How-To shows how to write a script that can check to see whether certain fields in a form have been filled out.

17.11 Create Image Rollover Effects with JavaScript

A popular JavaScript trick is a set of functions that replace an image with another image when the mouse passes over the image on the screen. This is very useful for creating highlighted menus and other types of interactivity in a Web page. This How-To shows how to use JavaScript to created image rollover effects on Web pages.

17.12 Find More Information on JavaScript

Like Java, there is much more to JavaScript than can be crammed into a few How-To's. This How-To provides information on resources that will help anyone trying to learn this new scripting language.

17.13 Provide an Alternative If Scripting Is Not Supported

Many browsers in use on the Web do not support JavaScript or do not have JavaScript enabled. These users need alternatives to scripts used on Web pages. This How-To shows how to provide alternative HTML code or Common Gateway Interface (CGI) scripts to these users.

17.1 How do I... Write a basic Java applet?

COMPATIBILITY: NETSCAPE 2+, INTERNET EXPLORER 3

Problem

I'm interested in making my page more interactive by adding Java applets, programs that can be run from my page. However, I don't know anything about the language and don't know where to begin. How do I write a simple Java applet?

Technique

A full description of Java is beyond the scope of this book. Those who have written programs in C++ will find Java familiar, but others might have difficulty trying to learn the language. However, most applets have a similar structure that can be briefly described and then duplicated for other applets. This How-To shows how to create a basic but useful applet that displays the current time. How-To 17.2 shows how to incorporate the applet into an HTML document.

Steps

1. Open a file in a text editor. Name the file whatever you want to name the applet, appended with the suffix `.java`, such as `MyApplet.java`.

2. Specify any libraries of routines that must be included for the applet to run correctly. Applets in general require a library named `java.applet.Applet`. For this applet, you will need two other libraries: `java.util.Date` (which will provide a command to obtain the current time) and `java.awt.Graphics` (which includes graphics routines for displaying the results of the date on the page). Add libraries using the `import` command:

```
import java.util.Date;
import java.applet.Applet;
import java.awt.Graphics;
```

Be sure to add a semicolon (`;`) after each line, because this is the method Java uses to indicate the end of a line.

3. Java is based on creating program classes based on previous classes. This enables a program to call on several higher-level classes without explicitly referencing them in the code. The class to extend on here is called `Applet` (which you have included by importing the `browser.Applet` library). Use the `public class` command and the name of the current applet to define a new class based on the `Applet` class:

```
public class CurrentDate extends Applet {
```

Note the open brace used at the end of the line instead of a semicolon. This indicates that the lines that follow it all belong to the class `CurrentDate`.

4. Define the current date by creating a new variable, `d`, of the class `Date`, and setting it equal to the current date, as follows:

```
Date d = new Date();
```

5. The applet now needs an initialization routine that defines an area on the page where the date is displayed. This is done with a routine called `init()`, which is public and returns no data (`void`). In the routine, a `resize` command defines the area, in pixels, of the page section reserved for displaying the date—for example,

```
public void init() {
resize(300,25);
}
```

6. Next, include a routine to display the date on the page. Create a graphics routine called `paint` that contains the necessary commands:

```
public void paint(Graphics g) {
```

7. To display the date, the applet must convert the information stored in the date variable into a string that can be drawn on the page. Run a function called `toString()` that converts the date variable `d` into a string and sets it equal to a new variable `s` of class `String`:

```
String s = d.toString();
```

8. The final part of the applet is the command that prints the string containing the current date on the page. The routine `g.drawString()`, part of the `java.awt.Graphics` package imported at the beginning of the applet, does this. The command needs three values: the string, the x pixel location of the beginning of the string, and the y pixel location for the bottom of the string. For example, to print the time after the string `"Current time: "` and place it near the top of the window, use

```
    g.drawString("Current time: "+s, 5, 25);
    }
}
```

Note that because this is the last command of the applet, you must include the closing braces for the **paint** routine and the overall class.

9. Finally, run the applet through the Java compiler. If the compiler doesn't find any errors, it produces another file that contains the executable code for the applet. The filename is the name of the applet, plus the file suffix **.class**. In this case, it creates a file named **CurrentDate.class**. The exact method of submitting the applet to the compiler varies from system to system. For example, if you use a UNIX system, at the prompt enter the command

```
javac CurrentDate.java
```

The full code of the document is included on the CD-ROM as file **CURRENTDATE.JAVA**.

How It Works

First, the browser loads any libraries of routines that might be necessary for the browser to work. A new applet is created by extending an existing **Applet** class, thereby calling on all the parent routines to the applet. This particular applet uses a command to find the current date on the machine, converts it to a string, and then invokes a display routine to print it on the screen.

Comments

The Java language is still under development. To keep up with the current status of the language, check the Java home page at Sun Microsystems, **http://java.sun.com**.

COMPLEXITY
INTERMEDIATE

17.2 How do I... Include a Java applet in an HTML document?

COMPATIBILITY: HTML 3.2+

Problem

I have written a Java applet and I'd like to include that applet in my Web page. How can I add a Java applet to an HTML document?

Technique

The **<APPLET>** tag, added in HTML 3.2, enables you to include a Java applet in a Web page. This element lets you specify the path to the applet, the amount of space on the screen the applet will occupy, and alternative code for browsers that don't support Java. The **<APPLET>** tag can be used in conjunction with the **<PARAM>** tag (see How-To 17.3) to pass variable names and values to Java applets.

Steps

1. Open your HTML document and locate the section of document where you want to add the applet.

2. Place the **<APPLET>** and **</APPLET>** tags where you want the applet to be in your document. Set the **CODE** attribute equal to the name of the applet. For example, to insert the applet **CurrentDate.class** into a Web page, enter

```
<APPLET CODE="CurrentDate"></APPLET>
```

3. If the applet is not located in the same directory as the HTML document, use the **CODEBASE** attribute to provide the location of the applet. **CODEBASE** can be a pathname or a URL. If the applet in the last step is located in the directory **applets/new**, use

```
<APPLET CODE="CurrentDate" CODEBASE="applets/new"></APPLET>
```

4. The **WIDTH** and **HEIGHT** attributes are required for the **<APPLET>** element. They give the width and height of the applet display area in pixels. To create a display area 300 pixels wide and 75 pixels high for the applet, use

```
<APPLET CODE="CurrentDate" WIDTH=300 HEIGHT=75></APPLET>
```

5. Similar to **WIDTH** and **HEIGHT**, **VSPACE** and **HSPACE** set the vertical and horizontal margins, respectively. Set the attributes equal to the size of the margin in pixels. To insert an applet with a vertical margin of 20 pixels and a horizontal margin of 10 pixels, enter

```
<APPLET CODE="CurrentDate" WIDTH=300 HEIGHT=75 VSPACE=20 HSPACE=10>⇐
</APPLET>
```

6. The **ALIGN** attribute controls the alignment of the applet. The **<APPLET>** tag's **ALIGN** supports many of the values used by the **<IMG>** element (see Chapter 8, "Establishing Links"). The valid values for **ALIGN** include the following:

   - ✔ **left** (left side of the screen)
   - ✔ **right** (right side of the screen)
   - ✔ **top** (aligns with the top of the tallest item on the line)
   - ✔ **texttop** (aligns with the top of text on that line)
   - ✔ **middle** (aligns the baseline of the line with the middle of the applet display)

- ✔ **absmiddle** (aligns the middle of the line with the middle of the applet display)
- ✔ **baseline** (aligns the baseline of the line with the bottom of the applet display)
- ✔ **bottom** (same as **baseline**)
- ✔ **absbottom** (aligns the bottom of the line with the bottom of the image)

For example, to align the line that follows the applet with the top of the applet display, enter

```
<APPLET CODE="CurrentDate" WIDTH=300 HEIGHT=75 ALIGN=TOP></APPLET>
```

7. The **NAME** attribute gives the applet instance a specific name for potential future reference. This is a more advanced feature that enables applets on the same page to communicate with each other. For example, to give an applet instance the name **"current"**, enter

```
<APPLET CODE="CurrentDate" WIDTH=300 HEIGHT=75 NAME="current"></APPLET>
```

8. There are two ways you can insert text that browsers which don't support Java applets can display. One way is to use the **ALT** attribute and set it equal to a text string that explains what the applet is. For example, to include the **ALT** attribute in the preceding applet, enter

```
<APPLET CODE="CurrentDate" WIDTH=300 HEIGHT=75 ALT="This is a Java applet ⇐
that displays the current time."></APPLET>
```

Another way to do this is to place the text between the **<APPLET>** and **</APPLET>** tags. This text displays in browsers that don't support Java applets, but is ignored by those that do run applets. To revise this example using this method, enter

```
<APPLET CODE="CurrentDate" WIDTH=300 HEIGHT=75>This is a Java applet that ⇐
displays the current time.</APPLET>
```

A sample output of the **CurrentDate** applet (described in How-To 17.1) as seen in Netscape 3.0 is shown in Figure 17-1. The HTML code used to create the output is on the CD-ROM as file **17-1.HTML**.

How It Works

For the **<APPLET>** element, the tag instructs the browser to load and run the Java applet named in the tag. The browser creates a display area for the applet on the page based on the size of the display area and the alignment of the display as specified by attributes in the tag. The browser also passes values for any applet-specific variables that the applet requires to run correctly.

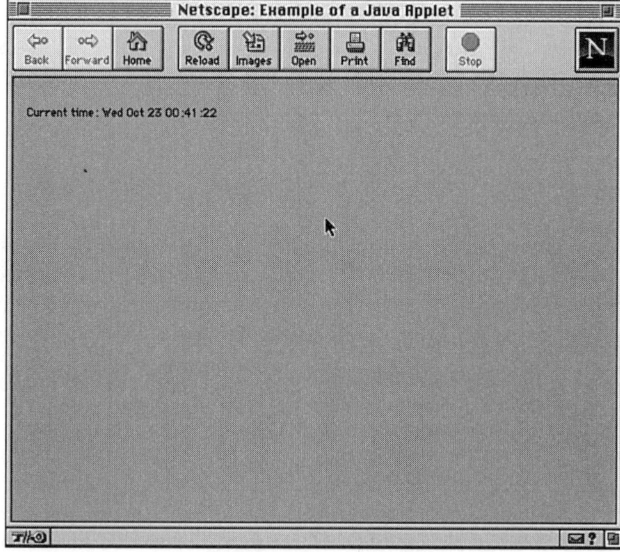

Figure 17-1 An example of a Java applet

Comments

Because not all browsers support Java (particularly Microsoft Internet Explorer before version 3.0 and Netscape Navigator before 2.0, on most platforms), and not all users of Java-capable browsers have Java enabled for security reasons, it's important to include some kind of alternative for those users. You can put any text, image, or other markup between the **<APPLET>** and **</APPLET>** tags, so you can be very flexible in the content you provide for the Java-disabled.

COMPLEXITY
INTERMEDIATE

17.3 How do I... Pass variables from a Web page to an applet?

COMPATIBILITY: HTML 3.2+

Problem

I need to give an applet a set of starting values for it to run properly, and those values can be different at the different times I run the applet. How can I pass a variable and its value from a Web page to the applet?

Technique

HTML 4.0 includes the **<PARAM>** tag, which, in conjunction with the **<APPLET>** tag (refer to How-To 17.2), can be used to send a value for a named variable from the page to the applet.

Steps

1. Open your HTML document and locate the parts of the document that contain references to Java applets that need variable values passed to them. This example uses a hypothetical applet, **CurrentDateTwo**, which can take parameters named **TimeZone** and **Size**.

2. Between the **<APPLET>** and **</APPLET>** tags, enter the **<PARAM>** tag.

```
<APPLET CODE="CurrentDateTwo" WIDTH=50 HEIGHT=75>
<PARAM>
</APPLET>
```

3. Add the **NAME** attribute to the **<PARAM>** tag and set it equal to the name of the variable in the Java applet that will receive the value.

```
<APPLET CODE="CurrentDateTwo" WIDTH=50 HEIGHT=75>
<PARAM NAME="TimeZone">
</APPLET>
```

4. Add the **VALUE** attribute to the **<PARAM>** tag and set it equal to the value that will be passed on to the named variable in the Java applet.

```
<APPLET CODE="CurrentDateTwo" WIDTH=50 HEIGHT=75>
<PARAM NAME="TimeZone" VALUE="Eastern">
</APPLET>
```

5. Repeat the process for any additional variables you want to pass on to the applet.

```
<APPLET CODE="CurrentDateTwo" WIDTH=50 HEIGHT=75>
<PARAM NAME="TimeZone" VALUE="Eastern">
<PARAM NAME="Size" VALUE="5">
</APPLET>
```

How It Works

When a browser encounters the **<PARAM>** tag within the **<APPLET>** tag, it reads in the variable name and value specified and passes that value to the named variable in the current applet.

Comments

The **<PARAM>** tag must be placed within the **<APPLET>** and **</APPLET>** tags so that the variable names and values are linked to the appropriate applet. Other information, such as alternative text, can still be included in between the **<APPLET>** and **</APPLET>** tags.

17.4 How do I... Find more information about Java?

COMPATIBILITY: NETSCAPE 2+, INTERNET EXPLORER 3

Problem

I'm very interested in learning more about the Java language and writing applets for my Web pages. How do I find more information about Java?

Technique

Because Java is a complete programming language, we can only touch on a few key issues of the language and its use in Web applets in this book. As one might expect, though, a wide range of Java resources is available on the Web that you can use to expand your knowledge of Java.

Steps

You might want to open your Web browser so you can look at the Java resources discussed next.

1. The first stop in any exploration of Java on the Web should be Sun's Java home page at **http://www.javasoft.com/**. Sun developed the Java language long before the language was applied to the Web, and Sun has the most authoritative resources on the language and its application to Web applets.

2. If your interest is limited to finding an interesting applet for your page, one of the largest collections of applets can be found at Gamelan, **http://www.gamelan.com/**. This site has a wide variety of applets and applications, from business to entertainment. This site also lists full-fledged Java applications and links to resources to learn more about Java.

3. There are several sites with tutorials about Java and extensive links to other Java resources on the Web. A few of the best sites are

- ✔ **http://www.sover.net/~manx/java.html**
- ✔ **http://www.progsource.com/java.html**
- ✔ **http://www.digitalfocus.com/digitalfocus/faq/**

- ✔ `http://www.javashareware.com`
- ✔ `http://www.java.co.uk/javacentre.html`

4. The more experienced Java programmer will likely find *JavaWorld* magazine, **`http://www.javaworld.com/`**, a useful resource. This online publication includes the latest Java news and articles to increase one's knowledge of some more advanced aspects of the language.

How It Works

These Web sites provide information, sample applets, and other documentation that you can use to build your knowledge of Java. Most of these resources include samples of Java applets online so you can see the code in action.

Comments

The Web is changing very rapidly, so some of the resources described here might no longer exist by the time you read this. You might want to supplement these resources with others on the Web (many more Java-related Web sites can be found using one of the popular search engines) or with a book or other documentation.

COMPLEXITY
ADVANCED

17.5 How do I... Improve Java applet download time?

COMPATIBILITY: NETSCAPE 2+, INTERNET EXPLORER 3

Problem

I have some complex applets that call on several different Java classes. When I include these applets in my Web page, the applets download and run slowly because each class must download separately. How can I improve the loading time of my applets?

Technique

Netscape and Microsoft have developed their own methods of downloading a single object with all the classes required for that applet. Only a single connection is needed to download the package, allowing the applet to run faster. Unfortunately, the two methods described here are not compatible with each other. The following steps show how to use this technique with Netscape's **`ARCHIVE`** attribute and Microsoft's **`CAB`** architecture.

Steps

Open the HTML document that includes references to Java applets.

Netscape Navigator

1. Place all the `.class` files needed for your applet into a single `.zip` file, using a Java development tool or other application.

2. Place this `.zip` file in the same directory as the applet that will use the classes in the `.zip` file.

3. Use the `APPLET` tag to place the applet in the appropriate location on the page. Include a new attribute called `ARCHIVE` and set it equal to the filename of the `.zip` file.

```
<APPLET CODE="MyApplet.class" ARCHIVE="MyApplet.zip" WIDTH=200 HEIGHT=200>
If you're reading this text, you don't have a Java-enabled browser.
</APPLET>
```

Microsoft Internet Explorer

1. Use an application to create a CAB file. Microsoft offers the Cabinate Software Development Kit and CABView, which allows the drag-and-drop creation of CAB files, for this. More information about Microsoft CAB tools is available at `http://www.microsoft.com/workshop/prog/cab`.

2. After the CAB file (which usually has the filename extension `.cab`) has been created, it can be referenced by a Java applet in a Web page. One way is to use the `<PARAM>` tag (see How-To 17.3). The `NAME` attribute is set to `"cabbase"` and the `VALUE` attribute is set equal to the filename of the CAB file:

```
<APPLET CODE="MyApplet.class" WIDTH=200 HEIGHT=200>
<PARAM NAME="cabbase" VALUE="MyApplet.cab">
</APPLET>
```

3. For larger Java libraries, you can use the `<OBJECT>` element in a Web page to refer to CAB files. This requires using the Microsoft Java development tools to create a unique class identifier (CLSID) for the library. An example of this in a Web page is

```
<OBJECT
    CLASSID="clsid:12345678-9abc-def1-1234567890ab"
    CODEDBASE="cabs/MyApplet.cab#Version=1,0,0,12">
</OBJECT>
```

How It Works

With either the **ARCHIVE** or **CABBASE** techniques, the browser is prompted to download a single file containing all the `.class` files needed by a particular browser. This file is then uncompressed and the files are stored in memory or on the disk for access by the applet.

Comments

This is a very new area, which is only starting to be supported by browsers and Java development tools. **ARCHIVE** and **CABBASE** are not recognized by versions of Netscape and Internet Explorer before 3.0. Moreover, Netscape does not yet support the **CABBASE** technique, and Internet Explorer does not yet support the **ARCHIVE** technique, reducing their usability in Web pages. Sun introduced a competing format named JAR (Java Archive), similar to the ZIP format used by Netscape Navigator. Information about this format is available at `http://www.javasoft.com/products/JDK/1.1/docs/guide/jar/jarGuide.html`.

17.6 How do I... Include a script element?

COMPATIBILITY: NETSCAPE 2+, INTERNET EXPLORER 3

Problem

I want to be able to do more with my pages than simple HTML enables me to do. I have heard about JavaScript, and it sounds easier to use than other scripting languages. How do I go about adding a JavaScript script element in my HTML documents?

Technique

JavaScript is a powerful, fairly easy-to-use addition to the Netscape and Internet Explorer browsers. According to the Netscape press release, it "allows cross-platform scripting of events, objects and actions." You can use JavaScript to accomplish many tasks that you would have previously needed Java or Perl to perform. JavaScript is an object-based scripting language like the Java language, except that JavaScript is less extendible and simpler to use.

Although JavaScript can be used to create sophisticated scripts (see How-To 17.8), elements of JavaScript can be included within HTML elements to perform specific, simple tasks, such as displaying a message in a window or displaying text when a user passes over a link. This How-To provides examples of how to include JavaScript elements in a Web page.

Steps

1. Open the HTML document in which you want to include JavaScript elements.

2. One way to include JavaScript elements in a Web page is to include an element that would cause the browser to go back to the previous page in the browser's history, like the Back button. First, create a button similar to those used with forms in Chapter 11, "HTML Interactive Forms."

```
<FORM><INPUT TYPE="button" VALUE="Go to previous page"></FORM>
```

3. Now add the JavaScript element to the `<INPUT>` tag so that it will perform the function described.

```
<FORM><INPUT TYPE="button" VALUE="Go to previous page" ⇐
onClick="history.back()"></FORM>
```

Don't worry about the exact syntax used here; it will become familiar to you as you learn JavaScript. Instead, concentrate on how the JavaScript element is used in an HTML element.

4. Another example of including a JavaScript element in a Web page is the ability to use JavaScript to display alternative information whenever a user passes over a link. For example, create a link on a page

```
<A HREF="otherpage.html">Link to another page</A>
```

5. To display something other than the URL of the link when the cursor passes over the link, you can enter something like

```
<A HREF="otherpage.html" onMouseOver="window.status='This is a link ⇐
to my other page'; return true">Link to another page</A>
```

Again, don't worry about the exact syntax of the JavaScript used here, but instead focus on how it is included in the HTML tags.

An example of the use of JavaScript elements in a page is shown in Figure 17-2. The HTML code used for that figure is included on the CD-ROM as file `17-2.HTML`.

How It Works

A browser that supports JavaScript will interpret JavaScript elements contained within the body of an HTML document. For these elements to be used, they must be set equal to some JavaScript attribute that signals to the browser when the JavaScript code should be executed. Some examples of these attributes are shown in How-To 17.7.

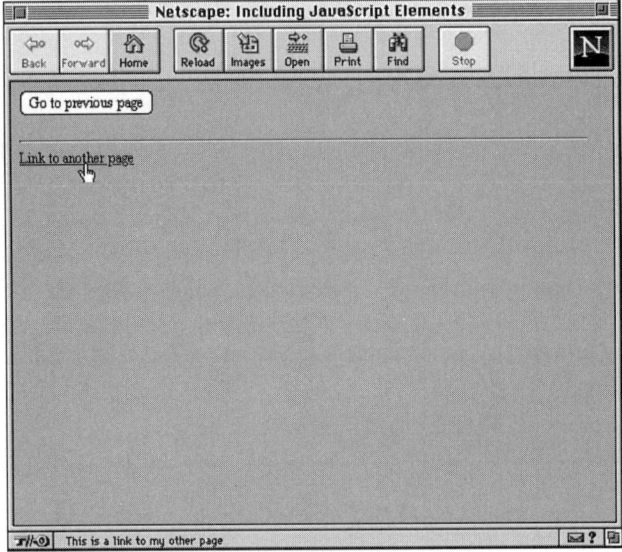

Figure 17-2 Examples of JavaScript elements in a page

Comments

Including JavaScript elements directly into an HTML tag in a Web page is the best solution when something simple is being done, such as brief messages or basic actions. Anything that requires more JavaScript markup to be accomplished would probably be better off in its own script, which will be described in How-To 17.8.

COMPLEXITY
ADVANCED

17.7 How do I... Write a basic JavaScript script?

COMPATIBILITY: NETSCAPE 2+, INTERNET EXPLORER 3

Problem

I want to do more things with my pages than simple HTML lets me. I know I could use Java or Perl, but I am looking for something a bit simpler to learn. I have heard about JavaScript, and it sounds like it will meet most of my needs. How do I go about writing a basic JavaScript script?

Technique

JavaScript is a property-based scripting language that uses objects. It is a small but complete, fully functional language. JavaScript does not enable you to create new objects as you can with Java. Instead, you use a group of predefined objects to accomplish your tasks.

The object hierarchy is as follows. The document object and all objects above the document are always available. All the objects below the document object are created on the fly, depending on the HTML code in the document.

For example, the following sample script has a form that contains a text field called `"name"`:

```
<INPUT TYPE="text" NAME="name" SIZE=20>
```

To refer to that text field, you must use the object name, complete with all its ancestors.

```
document.forms[0].name
```

To use the value of that text field, use

```
document.forms[0].name.value
```

As of this writing, all forms in a document are stored in a forms array. To refer to the forms, you use `"forms[0]"` for the first form, `"forms[1]"` for the second form, and so on.

Now that you have objects to use, you must know when to use them. This is where event handlers come into play. Event handlers are the result of certain user actions, such as clicking on a button or check box or selecting certain text.

For example, the following code causes the JavaScript function `doform()` to execute when the button defined by this tag is clicked on:

```
<INPUT TYPE="button" VALUE="Go for it" onClick="doform(this.form)">
```

The function uses the items created by `<INPUT TYPE>` tags in the current form as parameters.

The types of event handlers currently supported are

- ✔ `onFocus`: Script to run when the form element is the focus of input
- ✔ `onBlur`: Script to run on loss of input focus
- ✔ `onChange`: Script to run when a field's value is changed
- ✔ `onSelect`: Script to run when a text field is selected
- ✔ `onSubmit`: Script to run when a form is submitted
- ✔ `onClick`: Script to run when a button is clicked

Outside of objects and event handlers, JavaScript greatly resembles other programming languages you are probably already familiar with.

JavaScript has variables. To create a variable, name the variable with the **var** statement or simply use it. For example:

```
var score
score = 0
```

Both of the these statements create a variable named **score**.

JavaScript has a set of built-in functions. It also allows the declaration of user-defined functions (brackets indicate optional user additions):

```
function name ([parameter] [, parameter] [, ..., parameter] ) {
    statements }
return
```

JavaScript has complete sets of assignment (=), arithmetic (+, –, *, /), logical (&&, ||, !), and comparison (==, >, >=, <, <=, !=) operators.

JavaScript also supports many types of control structures, such as

```
if (condition) {
    statements
} [else {
    else statements} ]
```

and

```
while (condition) {
    statements}
```

and

```
for ([initial expression;] [condition;] [update expression]) {
    statements
}
initial expression = statement | variable declaration
```

As you can see, JavaScript is a complete language. You can use different combinations of objects and event handlers along with all or some of the other features of JavaScript to create JavaScript scripts.

The keywords currently used and reserved by JavaScript are

break	continue	else	false
for	function	if	in
null	return	this	true
var	while	with	

For the latest list of all the items and features, refer to the Netscape home page at **http://home.netscape.com/**.

Steps

The following steps show one way you can create and use a JavaScript script. This is a basic script, yet it takes advantage of many of the nicer features of JavaScript. There are, of course, many other ways to create JavaScript scripts.

1. Decide what you want to do, and then decide whether JavaScript really is the best way to do it. This example uses forms to make a simple test for a user to take, and you'll need an application to test the answers sent by a form and to grade the results. This is a fine application for JavaScript.

2. Create a base HTML document for your JavaScript script. For this example, use

```
<HTML>
<HEAD>
<TITLE>JavaScript Example</TITLE>
</HEAD>
<BODY>
<H2>Knowledge Tester</H2>
<HR>
<HR>
</BODY>
</HTML>
```

There's not much here yet, but it's a good start.

3. Add the form that contains the questions for the user to answer and for JavaScript to process.

```
<FORM>
Enter your name please:
<INPUT TYPE="text" NAME="yourname" SIZE=20><P>
Who's buried in Washington's grave?
<INPUT TYPE="text" NAME="question1" SIZE=15 ><P>
Roosters lay eggs (true or false)?
<INPUT TYPE="text" NAME="question2" SIZE=5 ><P>
<INPUT TYPE="button" VALUE="Go for it" onClick="doform(this.form)">
<HR>
<BR>
Result:
<INPUT TYPE="text" NAME="score" SIZE=15 >
<BR>
</FORM>
```

When viewed through a browser, this form looks like Figure 17-3.

This is a pretty typical form, except for the `onClick` event handler, which is the JavaScript extension. This causes the JavaScript `doform()` to execute when the user clicks on the button.

4. Now that you have the form to interact with, you need JavaScript to process this form. To start the script, place the `<SCRIPT>...</SCRIPT>` tags in the header of your document.

```
<SCRIPT LANGUAGE="JavaScript">
</SCRIPT>
```

You are placing this script in the header. Also, you want the script to contain a function that executes when the user clicks on the Forms button.

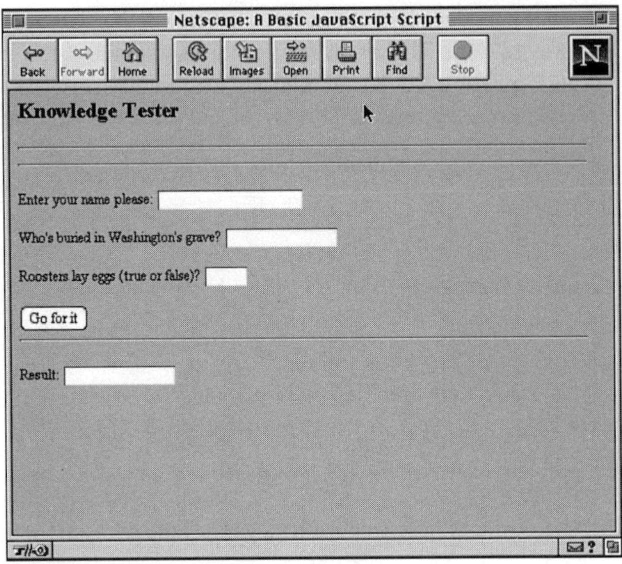

Figure 17-3 A form in JavaScript

5. Define and insert the JavaScript function. Make sure that the function name is the same used when the function is called in the `<INPUT TYPE="button"...>` tag. The function used in this example is

```
function doform(form) {
   if (confirm("Are you sure "+document.forms[0].yourname.value+"?")){
      score=0
      if (document.forms[0].question1.value=="Washington"){
               score=score+1; }
            if (document.forms[0].question2.value=="false"){
             score=score+1; }
      form.score.value = (score / 2)*100
  }
 else
      alert("Please come back again.")
}
```

6. Save and name the HTML document with the JavaScript script in it. The entire document and script will look like this:

```
<HTML>
<HEAD>
<TITLE>JavaScript Demo</TITLE>
<SCRIPT LANGUAGE="JavaScript">
function doform(form) {
   if (confirm("Are you sure "+document.forms[0].yourname.value+"?")){
      score=0
      if (document.forms[0].question1.value=="Washington"){
               score=score+1; }
```

```
            if (document.forms[0].question2.value=="false"){
              score=score+1; }
        form.score.value = (score / 2)*100
  }
  else
        alert("Please come back again.")
}
</SCRIPT>
</HEAD>

<BODY>
<H2>Knowledge tester</H2>
<HR>
<FORM>
Enter your name please:
<INPUT TYPE="text" NAME="yourname" SIZE=20><P>
Who's buried in Washington's grave?
<INPUT TYPE="text" NAME="question1" SIZE=15 ><P>
Roosters lay eggs (true or false)?
<INPUT TYPE="text" NAME="question2" SIZE=5 ><P>
<INPUT TYPE="button" VALUE="Go for it" onClick="doform(this.form)">
<HR>
<BR>
Result:
<INPUT TYPE="text" NAME="score" SIZE=15 >
<BR>
</FORM>
</BODY>
</HTML>
```

7. View the document with the latest version of Netscape to make sure everything is working properly. When first executed, the screen should look like Figure 17-4. After the user answers the questions and clicks the Go for it button, the screen should resemble Figure 17-5.

8. Experiment! The best way to learn JavaScript is to change this example and see what effects your changes have. When you are comfortable with this script, start writing your own scripts.

How It Works

When the user clicks on the Go for it button, the information in the form is sent to the `doform()` function named in the `<INPUT TYPE>` tags and defined in the header of the document.

Four fields of information are sent to the function:

- ✔ `yourname`: Named by the first `<INPUT TYPE>` tag and referenced by `document.forms[0].yourname`
- ✔ `question1`: Named by the second `<INPUT TYPE>` tag and referenced by `document.forms[0].question1`

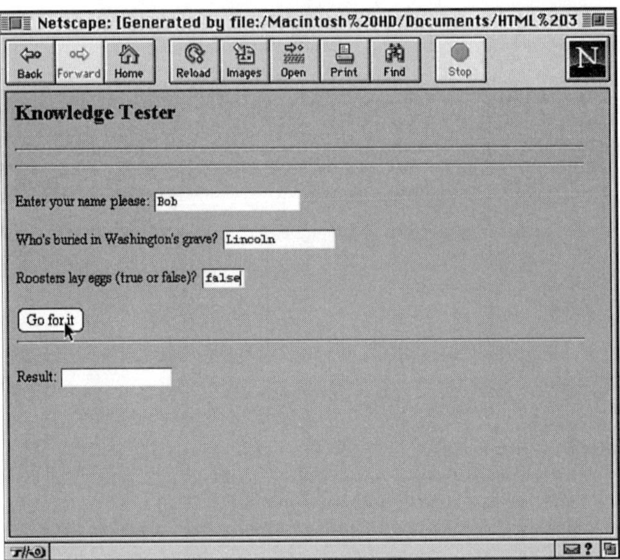

Figure 17-4 Starting the JavaScript script on the page

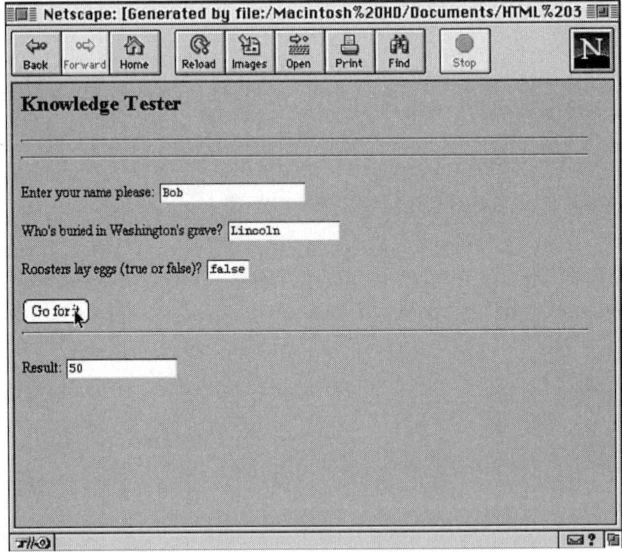

Figure 17-5 Output from the JavaScript script

- ✔ `question2`: Named by the third `<INPUT TYPE>` tag and referenced by `document.forms[0].question2`
- ✔ `score`: Named by the fifth `<INPUT TYPE>` tag and referenced by `document.forms[0].score`

The value of any of these fields can be found by appending **.value** to the reference for that field, such as

```
document.forms[0].name.value
```

The first statement in the function

```
if (confirm("Are you sure "+document.forms[0].yourname.value+"?")){
```

sets up a control structure and gives the user a chance to back out. It uses the **confirm** method to display a dialog box, such as the one shown later in the chapter in Figure 17-8, in the user's window.

The results from the dialog box are then processed by the **if** statement. If the user responds negatively (clicks No), the function executes the **else** block. In this case, that puts up a **Please come back again.** message in an Alert box. The function then exits, returning control to the form.

If the user responds positively, the function executes the statements under the **if** statement. These statements work as follows:

```
score=0
```

This creates a variable to calculate the user's score.

The following statements compare the value of the information entered in the form with the correct answer. If the value equals the correct answer, then the user's score is incremented.

```
if (document.forms[0].question.1.value=="Washington"){
     score = score + 1; }
if (document.forms[0].question.2.value=="false"){
     score=score+1;}
```

Finally, the user's final score is calculated by

```
document.forms[0].score.value= (score /2)*100
```

This value is placed into the score field created with the form. When the function exits, the updated score value is shown in the field.

Comments

In the old days (a few years ago), you would have used Perl to do something like this example. Although this example is rudimentary because it contains no error checking and is case sensitive, you can still see how easy JavaScript makes certain tasks, such as validating forms input.

Please note: JavaScript is a vast enough topic that it could easily be the subject of a book. This section did not even go into such matters as methods or object properties. For more information on these, consult the latest Netscape documentation.

17.8 How do I...
Include a script in a Web page?

COMPATIBILITY: NETSCAPE 2+, INTERNET EXPLORER 3

Problem

I want to be able to do more with my pages than simple HTML enables me to do. I have heard about JavaScript, and it sounds easier to use than other scripting languages. How do I go about adding a JavaScript script in my HTML documents?

Technique

You can use JavaScript to accomplish many tasks that you would have previously needed Java or Perl to perform. JavaScript is an object-based scripting language like the Java language, only JavaScript is less extendible and easier to use.

To include a JavaScript script in an HTML document, use the **<SCRIPT>** tag. The **<SCRIPT>** tag's format is

```
<SCRIPT LANGUAGE="language.name" [SRC="a URL for the script"]>
a JavaScript script
</SCRIPT>
```

In this format, **LANGUAGE** is the language the script is written in, and **SRC** is an optional attribute that gives the URL of the script to be loaded. **LANGUAGE** is mandatory unless the **SRC** attribute gives the scripting language.

Steps

The following steps give a rudimentary introduction to how you can add JavaScript scripts (see How-To 17.7) to your Web pages.

1. Create a basic HTML document using any text editor. For this example, use the very basic document that follows:

```
<HTML>
<HEAD>
<TITLE>JavaScript Demo</TITLE>
</HEAD>
<BODY>
The above line was written from a JavaScript script. And so is the ⇐
following line.
<P>
</BODY>
</HTML>
```

2. Enter the **<SCRIPT>** tags.

3. Enter the JavaScript script between the two tags. This example uses two very simple scripts that write to the screen. The script lines are

```
<SCRIPT LANGUAGE="JavaScript">
document.write("Simple demo...")
document.write("<P>")
</SCRIPT>
```

and

```
<!-- Second Script -->
<SCRIPT LANGUAGE="JavaScript">
document.write("<P>THE END...")
</SCRIPT>
```

Notice the HTML tags embedded in `write`. These function just as they would normally in HTML.

4. Save and name the document.

5. View the document to make sure it works the way you think it should. For example, look at the following:

```
<HTML>
<HEAD>
<TITLE>JavaScript Demo</TITLE>
</HEAD>
<BODY>
<!-- First Script -->
<SCRIPT LANGUAGE="JavaScript">
document.write("Simple demo...")
document.write("<P>")
</SCRIPT>
The above line was written from a JavaScript script. And so is the ⇐
following line.
<P>

<!-- Second Script -->
<SCRIPT LANGUAGE="JavaScript">
document.write("<P>THE END...")
</SCRIPT>

<!-- It may not seem like much now, as you do this without using
JavaScript, but in the next section you will see some of the power ⇐
of JavaScript. -->

</BODY>
</HTML>
```

When viewed by a browser that supports JavaScript, the example looks like Figure 17-6. A browser that does not support JavaScript displays `The above line was written from a JavaScript script. And so is the following line.`

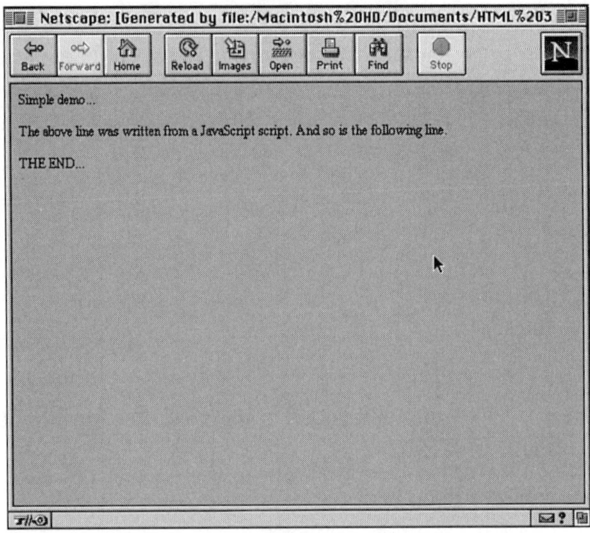

Figure 17-6 A script as seen in a JavaScript-aware browser

How It Works

A browser that supports JavaScript reads and evaluates the scripts embedded between the `<SCRIPT>` tags. JavaScript functions are stored but not evaluated until they are executed by events in the page.

Comments

It is possible to do a lot with JavaScript. JavaScript can be a very helpful tool when it comes to event-handling tasks such as reading and validating information from forms and responding to other types of user actions, such as clicks. Although not as powerful as Java or Perl, JavaScript is less cumbersome and therefore easier to learn and use than the other two.

COMPLEXITY
ADVANCED

17.9 How do I... Generate a pop-up dialog box using JavaScript?

COMPATIBILITY: NETSCAPE 2+, INTERNET EXPLORER 3

Problem

I would like to create a simple dialog box that appears with a brief message at certain points in my Web page. How do I generate pop-up dialog boxes in JavaScript?

Technique

JavaScript provides the programmer with several simple ways to include dialog boxes that pop up when needed. These boxes can provide a warning, a chance for the user to confirm his or her choice, or a way for the user to enter specific data.

Steps

1. Open the HTML document in which you want to add a JavaScript dialog box.

2. Identify the portion of the document in which you want to generate a dialog box. For this example, we'll create a button similar to that used in How-To 17.6:

```
<INPUT TYPE="button" NAME="Press Me">
```

3. One kind of dialog box is the alert box, which is used to provide a warning or other notice to the user. The `alert()` element in JavaScript is used to create an alert box, with the text to be displayed in the box placed within the parentheses. Use the example started in the previous step.

```
<INPUT TYPE="button" VALUE="Press Me" onClick="alert('This is the wrong ⇐
button to push!')">
```

4. Another kind of dialog box is the confirmation box. This is used to give the user the chance to confirm a task before it is executed, with the option to cancel. The JavaScript element `confirm()` works like `alert()`, described in the previous step.

```
<INPUT TYPE="button" VALUE="Press Me" onClick="confirm('Are you sure?')">
```

This is usually used as part of a larger script, where the value returned by the `confirm()` element (`True` or `False`) is used to direct the future action of a script.

5. A third option for a dialog box is the prompt box, which enables the user to enter a certain value that will be given to a variable in a script. The JavaScript `prompt()` element is used to create this. It takes on two values: the message displayed in the box and the default value. Use the example from step 1.

```
<INPUT TYPE="button" VALUE="Press Me" ⇐
onClick="prompt('Enter your favorite number,'')">
```

As with the `confirm()` option, `prompt()` is usually used with a script to process the value entered by the user.

Examples of JavaScript dialog boxes are shown in Figures 17-7 (alert), 17-8 (confirm), and 17-9 (prompt). The HTML and JavaScript used to create these can be found on the CD-ROM as file `17-4.HTML`.

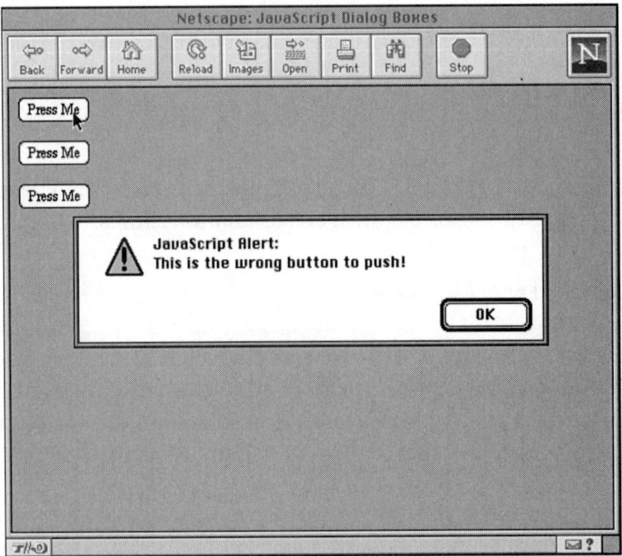

Figure 17-7 An alert dialog box in JavaScript

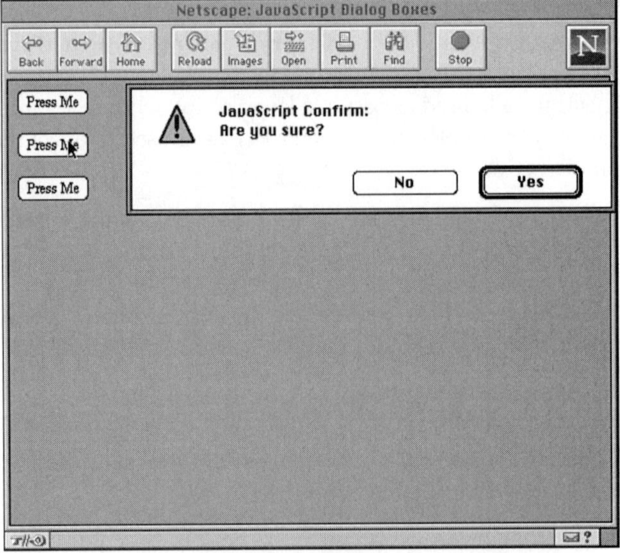

Figure 17-8 A confirm dialog box in JavaScript

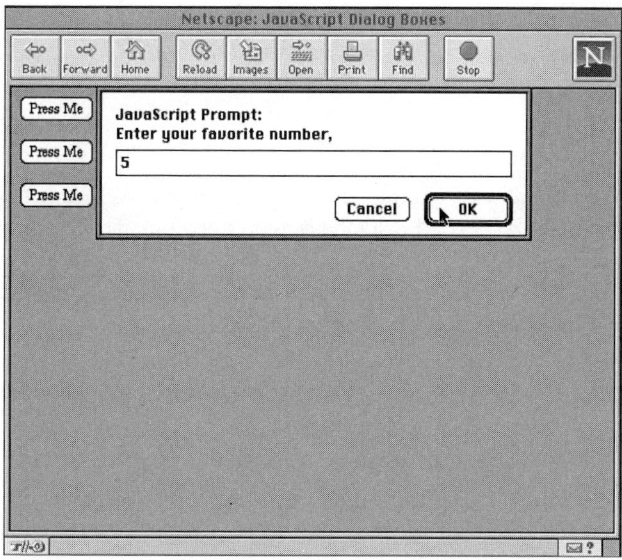

Figure 17-9 A prompt dialog box in JavaScript

How It Works

When a JavaScript-aware browser receives a JavaScript command to generate a dialog box, it will create the box depending on the type of box requested. The contents of the box depend on the data passed to the JavaScript routine, and the action taken depends on the type of dialog box generated and the option the user chooses.

Comments

Most of the examples shown are very simplistic. In a real JavaScript routine, the dialog boxes shown here would have been included as part of a larger function called somewhere on a Web page. The next section shows a slightly more sophisticated routine that does use dialog boxes as part of its operation.

COMPLEXITY
ADVANCED

17.10 How do I... Check an HTML form for required input fields?

COMPATIBILITY: NETSCAPE 2+, INTERNET EXPLORER 3

Problem

My Web page includes a form that sends data to a Common Gateway Interface (CGI) script on my server. To decrease the workload on my server, I would like to use JavaScript in some way to make sure the forms are completely filled out before sending them to the server. How do I have JavaScript verify that the form has been filled out before proceeding?

Technique

There is a way to include a simple JavaScript script in a Web page that can verify whether or not all the desired fields have been filled out. The script will keep the form from being sent to a CGI script if the data is not filled out, or else allow it to proceed if it is. This is a good example of a simple script that brings together some of the JavaScript aspects described earlier in this chapter.

Steps

1. Open an HTML document.

2. Create a simple form. For this example, the form will have only two fields, a name and an e-mail address.

```
<FORM METHOD="POST" ACTION="myscript.cgi">
Name: <INPUT TYPE="text" NAME="yourname"><BR>
E-Mail: <INPUT TYPE="text" NAME="email"><BR>
<INPUT TYPE=SUBMIT VALUE="Enter!">
</FORM>
```

3. Now add a JavaScript attribute to the `<FORM>` tag so that when the form is submitted, the contents of the form are first passed to a JavaScript routine that will verify that all the fields in the form are filled. Also give the form a name, which you will need for the script.

```
<FORM METHOD="POST" ACTION="myscript.cgi" NAME="theform" ⇐
onSubmit="return formCheck()">
Name: <INPUT TYPE="text" NAME="yourname"><BR>
E-Mail: <INPUT TYPE="text" NAME="email"><BR>
<INPUT TYPE=SUBMIT VALUE="Enter!">
</FORM>
```

4. Now you can set up the script in the header of the document.

```
<SCRIPT LANGUAGE="JavaScript">
</SCRIPT>
```

5. The script will have one function, called `formCheck()`, which will check the contents of the submitted forms.

```
<SCRIPT LANGUAGE="JavaScript">
function formCheck()
{
}
</SCRIPT>
```

6. For the form to be valid, both the name and e-mail address fields must have some content in them. You can test for this by seeing whether first one field, and then the other, is empty.

```
<SCRIPT LANGUAGE="JavaScript">
function formCheck()
{
     if (document.theform.yourname.value == " ")
     {
     }

     if (document.theform.email.value == " ")
     {
     }
}
</SCRIPT>
```

7. Now you must include some action if either field is empty. One possibility is an alert dialog box that warns the user. You can also include a `return false` statement, which quits the script and keeps the form from being submitted.

```
<SCRIPT LANGUAGE="JavaScript">
function formCheck()
{
     if (document.theform.yourname.value == " ")
     {
     alert("You did not include your name. Please try again.");
     return false;
     }

     if (document.theform.email.value == " ")
     {
     alert("You did not include your e-mail address. Please try again.");
     return false;
     }
}
</SCRIPT>
```

An example of this form is shown in Figure 17-10. The HTML and JavaScript code used to generate this can be found on the CD-ROM as file **17-5.HTML**.

How It Works

When the user fills out and submits the form, the browser first calls on the JavaScript function listed in the `<FORM>` tag. The form runs through a series of `if` statements, checking to see whether each field has a value entered. If a field turns up empty, then a warning message is displayed by the browser and the form submission is canceled.

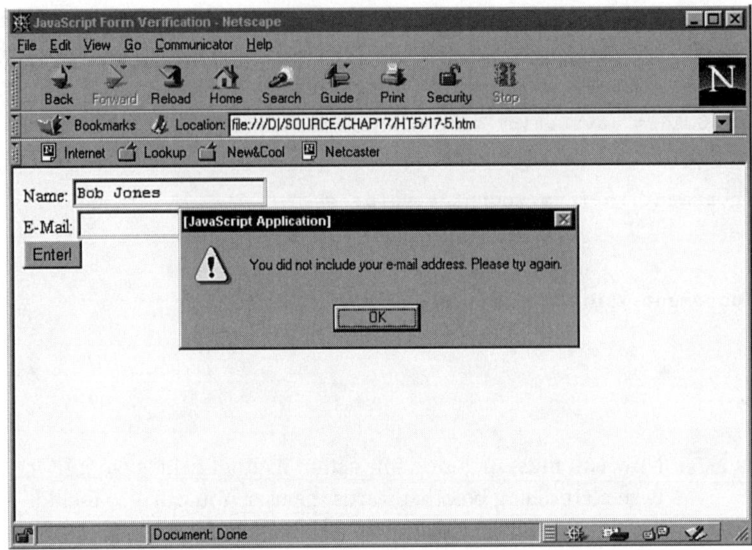

Figure 17-10 A JavaScript script checking an HTML form

Comments

This form can be expanded from the simple two-field version to one with as many fields as needed. It's also possible to parse the values submitted to look for specific things, such as whether the e-mail address submitted is of proper form.

17.11 How do I... Create image rollover effects with JavaScript?

COMPATIBILITY: NETSCAPE 3+, INTERNET EXPLORER 4

Problem

I've seen Web pages where the images displayed change when the mouse is moved over them. I understand that one popular way of making these changes is with JavaScript, but I don't know how it's done. How can I create an image rollover script in JavaScript?

Technique

JavaScript 1.1, the version of JavaScript that came with Netscape Navigator 3.0, included a new JavaScript object called **`Image`**. This object enables scripts to manipulate images displayed on the page, including replacing one image with another. This has become a popular technique for including interactivity on Web pages, buttons that can "light up" when the mouse passes over them.

This script usually works by using two sets of images, an "on" set and a "off" set. The script will display the on image when the mouse passes over the appropriate area, and will reset to the off image when the mouse leaves the area.

Steps

You will need two sets of images, the on and off sets, to use this script. You can use already-created images or make your own in the graphics program of your choice.

1. First, add the **<SCRIPT>** tags in the header of the document, where the image rollover script will go.

```
<SCRIPT LANGUAGE="JavaScript">
<!--

// -->
</SCRIPT>
```

2. Because the **Image** object is a fairly recent addition to JavaScript and thus is supported only in certain browsers, you will need to test to make sure the user's browser supports the **Image** object. If not and the script tries to access the **Image** object, the browser will generate an error message. To test for this, look to see whether the browser recognizes the **Image** object and set the value of a variable accordingly.

```
<SCRIPT LANGUAGE="JavaScript">
<!--

if (document.images) rollover = "yes";
      else rollover = "no";

// -->
</SCRIPT>
```

3. To make sure the image rollover effects are instantaneous, without any delays as new images are loaded, all the images should be preloaded. This can be done with a set of JavaScript commands using the **Image** object, after checking to make sure the browser uses rollovers. If you're using three images in your rollover setup, with the on images named **img1on.gif**, **imf2on.gif**, and **img3on.gif** and the off images named **img1off.gif**, **img2off.gif**, and **img3off.gif**, you would use

```
<SCRIPT LANGUAGE="JavaScript">
<!--

if (document.images) rollover = "yes";
      else rollover = "no";

if (rollover = "yes") {
```

```
        img1on = new Image();
        img2on = new Image();
        img3on = new Image();
        img1off = new Image();
        img2off = new Image();
        img3off = new Image();

        img1on.src = "img1on.gif";
        img2on.src = "img2on.gif";
        img3on.src = "img3on.gif";
        img1off.src = "img1off.gif";
        img2off.src = "img2off.gif";
        img3off.src = "img3off.gif";
}
// -->
</SCRIPT>
```

4. To switch the images, a function must identify the image to be displayed.

```
<SCRIPT LANGUAGE="JavaScript">
<!--

if (document.images) rollover = "yes";
        else rollover = "no";

if (rollover == "yes") {
        img1on = new Image();
        img2on = new Image();
        img3on = new Image();
        img1off = new Image();
        img2off = new Image();
        img3off = new Image();

        img1on.src = "img1on.gif";
        img2on.src = "img2on.gif";
        img3on.src = "img3on.gif";
        img1off.src = "img1off.gif";
        img2off.src = "img2off.gif";
        img3off.src = "img3off.gif";
}

function imageSwitchOn(imageName) {
        if (rollover == "yes") {
                imageOn = eval(imageName + "on.src");
                document [imageName].src = imageOn;
        }
}

// -->
</SCRIPT>
```

5. Similarly, another function is necessary to switch the image back to the off version when the mouse moves off the image.

```
<SCRIPT LANGUAGE="JavaScript">
<!--
```

```
if (document.images) rollover = "yes";
     else rollover = "no";

if (rollover == "yes") {
     img1on = new Image();
     img2on = new Image();
     img3on = new Image();
     img1off = new Image();
     img2off = new Image();
     img3off = new Image();

     img1on.src = "img1on.gif";
     img2on.src = "img2on.gif";
     img3on.src = "img3on.gif";
     img1off.src = "img1off.gif";
     img2off.src = "img2off.gif";
     img3off.src = "img3off.gif";
}

function imageSwitchOn(imageName) {
     if (rollover == "yes") {
          imageOn = eval(imageName + "on.src");
          document [imageName].src = imageOn;
     }
}

function imageSwitchOff(imageName) {
     if (rollover == "yes") {
          imageOff = eval(imageName + "off.src");
          document [imageName].src = imageOff;
     }
}

// -->
</SCRIPT>
```

6. In the body of the document, include the **<IMG>** tags for the images that will be used for the image rollover trick. In each image tag include a new attribute, **NAME**, that will be used by the script for the rollover. The value of **NAME** should be the "root" name of the image, that is, **img1**, **img2**, and so on.

```
<IMG SRC="img1off.gif" HEIGHT=100 WIDTH=100 ALT="image 1" NAME="img1">
<IMG SRC="img2off.gif" HEIGHT=100 WIDTH=100 ALT="image 2" NAME="img2">
<IMG SRC="img3off.gif" HEIGHT=100 WIDTH=100 ALT="image 3" NAME="img3">
```

7. For the rollover to work, the images must be linked to other pages. With the **<A>** tags for the link, two JavaScript events, **onMouseOver** and **onMouseOut**, are use to signal when the mouse passes over or leaves the image and calls the **imageOn** and **imageOff** functions described in the header, respectively.

```
<A HREF="page1.html" onMouseOver="imageSwitchOn('img1')" ⇐
onMouseOut="imageSwitchOff('img1')">
<IMG SRC="img1off.gif" HEIGHT=100 WIDTH=100 ALT="image 1" NAME="img1">
</A>
<A HREF="page1.html" onMouseOver="imageSwitchOn('img2')" ⇐
onMouseOut="imageSwitchOff('img2')">
<IMG SRC="img2off.gif" HEIGHT=100 WIDTH=100 ALT="image 2" NAME="img2">
</A>
<A HREF="page1.html" onMouseOver="imageSwitchOn('img3')" ⇐
onMouseOut="imageSwitchOff('img3')">
<IMG SRC="img3off.gif" HEIGHT=100 WIDTH=100 ALT="image 3" NAME="img3">
</A>
```

An example of an image rollover routine at work is shown in Figure 17-11. The HTML and JavaScript code used is on the CD-ROM as file **17-5A.HTML**.

How It Works

The script in the header of the document includes a function to test to make sure the browser supports the **Image** object and, if it does, loads a set of images and defines two functions for switching images. When the mouse cursor passes over an image defined as such in the document, an **onMouseOver** event is triggered in JavaScript. This calls a function that displays the on image in place of the default off image on the screen. Similarly, when the mouse cursor moves off the image, an **onMouseOut** event is triggered, which calls a function that changes the on image back to the off image.

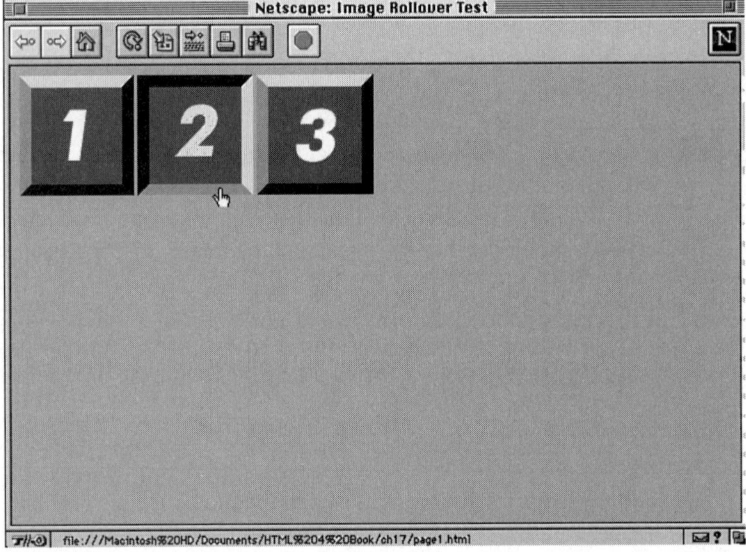

Figure 17-11 An example of an image rollover effect

Comments

The `Image` object in JavaScript is supported only in some browsers that include JavaScript support. The `Image` object was introduced in Netscape Navigator 3.0 and is included in later versions, but Navigator 2.0, which has JavaScript support, does not understand the `Image` object. Microsoft Internet Explorer will include the `Image` object in version 4.0, although the Macintosh version on Internet Explorer 3.01 already includes the `Image` object.

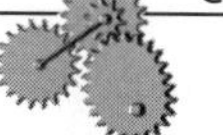

COMPLEXITY
ADVANCED

17.12 How do I... Find more information on JavaScript?

COMPATIBILITY: NETSCAPE 2+, INTERNET EXPLORER 3+

Problem

I would like to learn more about JavaScript to see how I can implement my own scripts for my Web pages. How do I find out more information on JavaScript?

Technique

Because JavaScript is much like a complete programming language, we can touch on only a few key issues of the language and its use in Web applets in this book. As one might expect, though, a wide range of JavaScript resources is available on the Web that you can use to expand your knowledge of JavaScript.

Steps

You might want to open your Web browser to explore some of these resources.

1. Because Netscape introduced JavaScript to the Web, you might expect good JavaScript resources from the company. In fact, there is detailed information on the language and its applications in Web pages at `http://home.netscape.com/eng/mozilla/Gold/handbook/javascript/`.

2. If you're looking for JavaScript scripts to add to your pages, you can go to the same place you could go to for Java applets: Gamelan, at `http://www.gamelan.com/`. Gamelan has links to a wide variety of JavaScript scripts and general JavaScript resources.

3. Another resource for JavaScript scripts on the Web can be found at `http://www.geocities.com/SiliconValley/9000/`. A variety of different scripts, all written by the same authors, can be found here.

4. For tips on writing your own JavaScript scripts, the JavaScript Tip of the Week site at `http://webreference.com/javascript/` has several useful tips. You can learn script techniques like the form verification routine found in How-To 17.10.

How It Works

These Web sites provide information, sample applets, and other documentation that you can use to build your knowledge of JavaScript. Most of these resources include samples of JavaScript scripts online so you can see the code in action.

Comments

The Web is changing very rapidly; some of the resources described here might no longer exist by the time you read this. You might want to supplement these resources with others on the Web (many more JavaScript-related Web sites can be found using one of the popular search engines) or with a book or other documentation.

17.13 How do I... Provide an alternative if scripting is not supported?

COMPATIBILITY: NETSCAPE 2+, INTERNET EXPLORER 3+

Problem

I'm using several JavaScript scripts in my Web pages, but I realize that some people do not use browsers that support it or have turned off JavaScript. How do I provide an alternative if JavaScript is not supported on the browser?

Technique

Although JavaScript can do many things, not all people are able to or want to take advantage of it. Therefore, it is important to provide alternatives to scripting so that information on the Web page is still available to those users. There are several ways to do this.

Steps

1. Open an HTML document that contains JavaScript scripts.

2. Because browsers that don't support JavaScript won't recognize that the items contained within the **<SCRIPT>** and **</SCRIPT>** tags are part of a script and not markup, they will try to print these items on the screen. To avoid this, you can use a trick to make them invisible:

```
<SCRIPT LANGUAGE="JavaScript">
<!--
document.write("This will appear only on a JavaScript-enabled browser");
//-->
</SCRIPT>
```

Because HTML browsers recognize **<!--** as the beginning of a comment and **-->** as the end, they will not print what is between them. JavaScript, however, will see and process the contents of the script between the **<!--** and **-->** tags because it defines comments differently.

3. Another trick exists for displaying alternative text for JavaScript-disabled browsers. JavaScript recognizes any single line that begins with **<!--** as a comment, so it will ignore anything else on that line as a comment. Combining that with the closing HTML comment symbol, you can provide alternative text for other browsers.

```
<SCRIPT LANGUAGE="JavaScript">
<!--> <H1>This is visible only to JavaScript-disabled browsers</H1>
document.write("This will appear only on a JavaScript-enabled browser");
//-->
</SCRIPT>
```

4. Netscape introduced the **<NOSCRIPT>** tag in version 3. Designed to work analogously to **<NOFRAMES>** for framed pages, it provides alternative content for browsers not using JavaScript.

```
<SCRIPT LANGUAGE="JavaScript">
<!--
document.write("This will appear only on a JavaScript-enabled browser");
//-->
</SCRIPT>
<NOSCRIPT>
<H1>This is visible only to JavaScript-disabled browsers</H1>
</NOSCRIPT>
```

An example of how these techniques work on browsers with JavaScript support turned on and off are shown in Figures 17-12 and 17-13, respectively. The HTML code used for both can be found on the CD-ROM as file **17-6.HTML**.

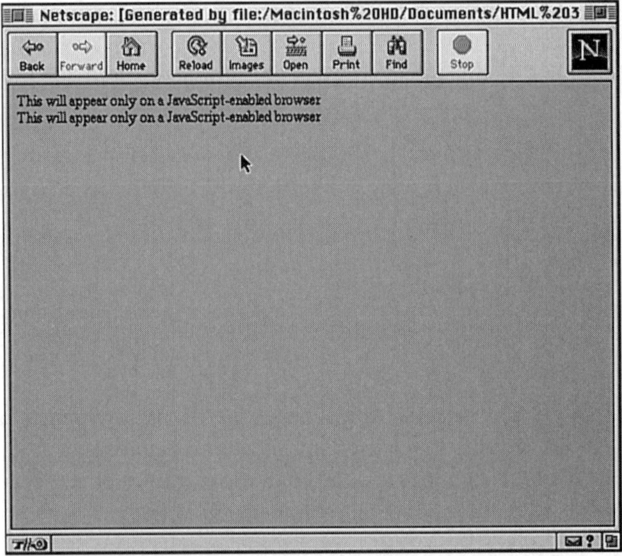

Figure 17-12 Hidden JavaScript in a JavaScript-enabled browser

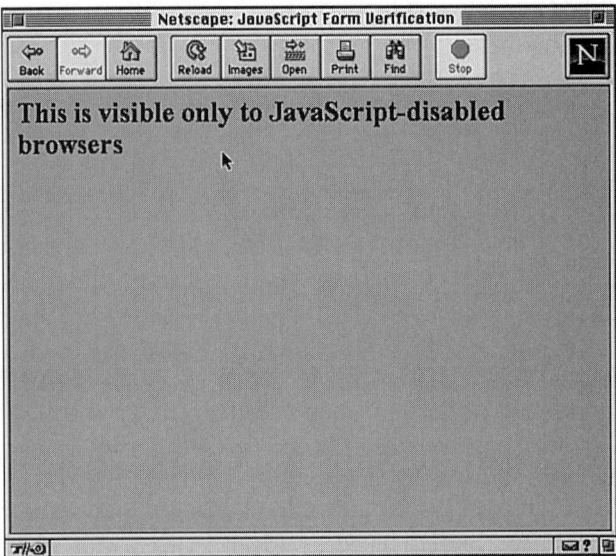

Figure 17-13 Hidden JavaScript in a JavaScript-disabled browser

How It Works

Because HTML and JavaScript use different definitions of comment beginnings and endings, it is possible to "hide" content from JavaScript-enabled or -disabled browsers by carefully applying the comment marks described here. The `<NOSCRIPT>` tag promises to make it easier to separate content between the two sets of users.

Comments

The `<NOSCRIPT>` tag was introduced in Netscape Navigator 3, so previous versions support JavaScript but not the `<NOSCRIPT>` tag. In these cases, the browsers will not know what the `<NOSCRIPT>` tags mean and will display the markup inside them, even though the JavaScript scripts are running!

CHAPTER 18

DIRECT INCLUSION OF MULTIMEDIA OBJECTS

18

DIRECT INCLUSION OF MULTIMEDIA OBJECTS

How do I...

When the Web was first developed several years ago, it was a text-only medium: No pictures, no sounds, and no animations were available. The Web first started to become popular when browsers such as Mosaic allowed people to view graphics embedded in pages. Since then the number of multimedia types supported by Web browsers has exploded. It's now possible to include interactive animations, high-quality music, and three-dimensional worlds in Web pages—as long as users are patient enough to wait for them to download! This chapter looks at some of the ways you can include multimedia in your Web pages. It's not possible to discuss in detail all the different ways, but after going through this chapter, you'll understand the basics of adding multimedia to the Web.

18.1 Embed Objects Supported by Plug-ins

Plug-ins are a way to add functionality to your Web browser by enabling it to interpret and display different types of files, including sounds and videos. This How-To shows how to reference a multimedia file in a Web page so that a user with the appropriate plug-in will be able to view it.

18.2 Directly Incorporate Windows-Supported Information Types into a Web Page

Microsoft Internet Explorer supports an expanded version of embedding multimedia objects that includes Windows-supported information types and Java applets. This How-To shows how to use the `<OBJECT>` tag to include these elements in a Web page.

18.3 Include a Video in My Web Page

Animations can make a Web page more entertaining or useful. However, they require the use of an external application that can display animations, which not all Web users might have. This How-To shows how to use an HTML extension in Microsoft Internet Explorer 3 to add an inline video in AVI format to your Web page and how to embed other types of videos into pages that can be viewed by Internet Explorer or Netscape Navigator.

18.4 Add Sound Tracks to My Web Page

A sound track can add to the multimedia experience of viewing a page. However, there is no standard way to have a sound play in the background while the user is reading a Web page. This How-To shows how you can use an HTML extension in Microsoft Internet Explorer 2 and later to play sound tracks in the background and how to embed into a page a sound that can be interpreted by Netscape and Microsoft.

18.5 Include a Director Application

Macromedia Director is a multimedia authoring application used by many designers. Macromedia has released Shockwave, a plug-in for Web browsers that enables users to view specially prepared Director movies in Web pages. This How-To shows how to convert a Director movie in the correct format and how to include it on a Web page.

18.6 Communicate Between a Web Page and a Shockwave Movie

One advantage of Shockwave movies is that you can include links to other Web pages within them, adding an additional degree of interactivity. You can also pass information from a Web page to a Shockwave movie. This How-To shows how to communicate between a Web page and a Shockwave movie.

18.7 Include a Shockwave Flash Movie in a Web Page

Another version of Shockwave, Shockwave Flash, enables designers to include interactive vector graphics in pages that can be viewed with a Shockwave Flash plug-in. This How-To shows how to include Shockwave Flash graphics on a Web page.

18.8 Embed a VRML Space

Virtual Reality Modeling Language (VRML) is a popular way of creating three-dimensional spaces, or worlds, on the Web. Both Microsoft Internet Explorer and Netscape Navigator support several methods for including these spaces on a Web page. This How-To shows how to include a VRML space on a Web page.

18.9 Include a Multimedia Object to Maximize Cross-Browser Support

Both Microsoft and Netscape have developed their own ways of including multimedia objects on Web pages, and these methods are not always compatible with each other or with other Web browsers. This How-To looks at ways to include multimedia objects supported by the widest variety of browsers.

18.1 How do I... Embed objects supported by plug-ins?

COMPATIBILITY: INTERNET EXPLORER, NETSCAPE NAVIGATOR

Problem

I have a multimedia file that I want to include on a Web page. It is supported by a browser plug-in. How do I write the HTML so that the browser will load the file and display it on the screen with the plug-in?

Technique

Both Microsoft Internet Explorer and Netscape Navigator support the `<EMBED>` tag, which enables multimedia applications supported by plug-ins to be downloaded and displayed by the user. The syntax of the `<EMBED>` tag is very similar to the `<IMG>` tag discussed in Chapter 9, "Using Images in Your Documents."

Steps

1. Open the HTML document to which you want to add the multimedia objects. Identify the objects you want to add and the locations on the page to add them.

2. At the location of the HTML document where you want to place the object, add the `<EMBED>` tag.

```
<P> My multimedia object is below:</P>
<EMBED>
```

3. Include the `SRC` attribute and set it equal to the URL of the object. The URL can be a local reference or a full URL to an object on another site.

```
<P> My multimedia objects are below:</P>
<EMBED SRC="widget.mov">
<EMBED SRC="http://www.widgets.com/widget.mov">
```

4. As with images, you can use the `HEIGHT` and `WIDTH` attributes to set the height and width of the image in pixels.

```
<P> My multimedia objects are below:</P>
<EMBED SRC="widget.mov" HEIGHT="50" WIDTH="50">
<EMBED SRC="http://www.widgets.com/widget.mov" HEIGHT="100" WIDTH="175">
```

5. For browsers that don't support plug-ins, or for users who don't have the appropriate plug-in installed, the `ALT` attribute can be used to display alternative text.

```
<P> My multimedia objects are below:</P>
<EMBED SRC="widget.mov" HEIGHT="50" WIDTH="50" ALT="My widget movie">
<EMBED SRC="http://www.widgets.com/widget.mov" HEIGHT="100" WIDTH="175" _
ALT="Their widget movie">
```

6. In addition to these attributes, several other attributes specific to the object and the plug-in can be added. These attributes provide additional information on how the file should be displayed, such as whether and how many times it should loop and how the file should be started. Some of the additional attributes are discussed in How-To's elsewhere in the chapter.

How It Works

When a browser encounters an `<EMBED>` tag, it loads the file and determines the MIME type it has. The MIME information explains to the browser what kind of file is being downloaded. The browser then checks for the plug-in that corresponds with that MIME type and uses that plug-in, if available. If no corresponding plug-in exists, an error message is usually displayed and the multimedia file is not displayed on the screen. The user then has the option of finding and downloading the appropriate plug-in, if one exists for that browser and operating system.

Comments

Embedded files can't be displayed unless the appropriate plug-in exists on the user's system. This places the burden of finding and maintaining a collection of plug-ins on the browser user, who will often have the time, disk space, or general inclination to keep plug-ins only for major file formats (such as sounds, videos, and Shockwave). Keep this in mind if you're planning to use a more obscure file format that requires a specialized plug-in that many users might not have.

COMPLEXITY
INTERMEDIATE

18.2 How do I... Directly incorporate Windows-supported information types into a Web page?

COMPATIBILITY: INTERNET EXPLORER

Problem

I would like to include a file in a Windows-specific format into my Web page. How can I write the HTML so the file can be included and viewed by people using specific browsers?

Technique

Internet Explorer supports the `<OBJECT>` element, which enables Web page designers to include a variety of multimedia and other files, including Java applets. `<OBJECT>` was designed to replace `<EMBED>` and `<APPLET>` eventually and to become the primary way to include multimedia files and applications in Web pages.

Steps

1. Open your HTML document. Locate the files you want to include as multimedia objects in the page and their location in the page.

2. Enter the `<OBJECT>` tag where you want to locate the object on the page. A closing tag, `</OBJECT>`, is required, although no content needs to exist between the two tags.

```
<P>Here is my multimedia object:</P>
<OBJECT></OBJECT>
```

3. The `CODEBASE` attribute is used to define the codebase, or location, of the object. The attribute is set equal to the URL of the file.

```
<P>Here is my multimedia object:</P>
<OBJECT CODEBASE="myfile.class"></OBJECT>
```

4. Similarly, the **DATA** attribute is set equal to the URL that defines the data for the object.

```
<P>Here is my multimedia object:</P>
<OBJECT CODEBASE="myfile.class" DATA="data.class"></OBJECT>
```

5. Like the **<IMG>** tag, **<OBJECT>** accepts attributes such as **ALIGN**, **HEIGHT**, **WIDTH**, **HSPACE**, **VSPACE**, **BORDER**, and **USEMAP**.

```
<P>Here is my multimedia object:</P>
<OBJECT CODEBASE="myfile.class" DATA="data.class" HEIGHT=100 WIDTH=75 _
ALIGN=CENTER></OBJECT>
```

6. The **STANDBY** attribute can be included and set equal to a text message to be displayed by the browser while waiting for the object to load.

```
<P>Here is my multimedia object:</P>
<OBJECT CODEBASE="myfile.class" DATA="data.class" HEIGHT=100 WIDTH=75 _
ALIGN=CENTER STANDBY="Object loading...please wait"></OBJECT>
```

7. Although there doesn't need to be any content between the **<OBJECT>** and **</OBJECT>** tags, you can place any valid HTML markup there to be displayed by a browser that does not support the **<OBJECT>** tag.

```
<P>Here is my multimedia object:</P>
<OBJECT CODEBASE="myfile.class" DATA="data.class" HEIGHT=100 WIDTH=75 _
ALIGN=CENTER STANDBY="Object loading...please wait">You need to_
use a browser that supports OBJECT to see this file</OBJECT>
```

How It Works

If a browser supports the **<OBJECT>** tag, it will load the corresponding file and display it according to the values set in the attributes contained within the **<OBJECT>** tag. If a browser doesn't support the **<OBJECT>** tag, it will display whatever markup is contained between the **<OBJECT>** and **</OBJECT>** tags.

Comments

Currently only Internet Explorer supports the **<OBJECT>** tag, which limits the tag's usefulness on the Web. The tag might be more widely supported down the road, though, and might even become a part of a future HTML standard. Until that time, you will need to look into workarounds for other browsers. How-To 18.9 will help you do this.

18.3 How do I... Include a video in my Web page?

COMPATIBILITY: INTERNET EXPLORER, NETSCAPE NAVIGATOR

Problem

I have a video clip that I would like to include in my Web page so that the video displays on the screen as the user reads the page. Is there a way to include a video on my Web page?

Technique

Both Netscape Navigator and Microsoft Internet Explorer support embedded video, using the appropriate plug-ins. In addition, Internet Explorer supports inline AVI videos natively, which enables them to be played on the page instead of by an external application or with a plug-in. The browser supports attributes that let you control the size of the video display, the number of times it plays, and when to start the video.

Steps

Find the video clip you want to include in the page. Open your document and find the location where you want to add the video clip.

Embedded Video for Plug-ins (Netscape and Internet Explorer)

1. Insert the **<EMBED>** tag in the area of the document where you want to place the video. Set the **SRC** attribute equal to the URL of the video file.

```
<P>Here is an animation of the planet Mars:</P>
<EMBED SRC="mars.mov">
```

2. To reserve an area of the window for the video, include the **HEIGHT** and **WIDTH** attributes and set them equal to the size of the video image, in pixels.

```
<P>Here is an animation of the planet Mars:</P>
<EMBED SRC="mars.mov" HEIGHT="150" WIDTH="150">
```

3. For people unable to load or view the video, include the **ALT** tag and set it equal to some text describing the video.

```
<P>Here is an animation of the planet Mars:</P>
<EMBED SRC="mars.mov" HEIGHT="150" WIDTH="150" ALT="Video of Mars">
```

4. If the video you are using is a QuickTime video, there are several other attributes you can include in the `<EMBED>` tag. If you want the video to loop around and play again after finishing, set the `LOOP` attribute equal to `TRUE`.

```
<P>Here is an animation of the planet Mars:</P>
<EMBED SRC="mars.mov" HEIGHT="150" WIDTH="150" ALT="Video of Mars" _
LOOP=TRUE>
```

Otherwise you can set `LOOP` equal to `FALSE`.

5. For the video to play automatically when loaded, include the `AUTOPLAY` attribute equal to `TRUE`. As with the `LOOP` attribute, this also can be set to `FALSE` if you don't want the video to start automatically.

```
<P>Here is an animation of the planet Mars:</P>
<EMBED SRC="mars.mov" HEIGHT="150" WIDTH="150" ALT="Video of Mars" _
LOOP=TRUE AUTOPLAY=TRUE>
```

6. If you want a control panel to appear so users can stop, start, and scan through the video, set the `CONTROLLER` attribute equal to `TRUE`. Otherwise, this can be set to `FALSE`.

```
<P>Here is an animation of the planet Mars:</P>
<EMBED SRC="mars.mov" HEIGHT="150" WIDTH="150" ALT="Video of Mars" _
LOOP=TRUE AUTOPLAY=TRUE CONTROLLER=TRUE>
```

7. If you are using an AVI video and a plug-in such as ClearVideo (formerly CoolFusion), you can add other attributes to the `<EMBED>` element. The equivalent of `CONTROLLER` is `SHOWCONTROLS`, which can be set to `TRUE` (to display a control panel) or `FALSE`.

```
<P>Here is an animation of the planet Mars:</P>
<EMBED SRC="mars.avi" HEIGHT="150" WIDTH="150" SHOWCONTROLS=TRUE>
```

8. You can assign specific commands to the video based on mouse clicks within the image. `ONLBUTTONDOWN` enables you to assign a command, such as pause or play, to the left mouse button, whereas `ONLDOUBLECLK` does the same when the left mouse button is double-clicked. For example, to assign a single left button click to pause the video and a double-click to start the video over, enter

```
<P>Here is an animation of the planet Mars:</P>
<EMBED SRC="mars.avi" HEIGHT="150" WIDTH="150" SHOWCONTROLS=TRUE _
ONLBUTTONDOWN="pause" ONLDOUBLECLK="play repeat">
```

Inline AVI Video (Internet Explorer)

1. Use the `<IMG>` tag (see Chapter 9, "Using Images in Your Documents") to insert the video. Set the attribute `DYNSRC` (for "dynamic source") equal to

the name of the video. **DYNSRC** can be a filename, a full path, or a URL to the video file. For example, to include a video with the filename **mars.avi**, enter

```
<IMG DYNSRC="mars.avi">
```

2. If the video is accessible by HTTP from **www.widgets.com** in the directory **videos/mars.avi**, enter

```
<IMG DYNSRC="http://www.widgets.com/videos/mars.avi">
```

3. For browsers that don't support AVI videos, you can specify an image to be shown in its place. To do this, set the **SRC** attribute equal to the filename of the image. In the example from the last step, to add a reference to an image called **mars.gif**, you would enter

```
<IMG DYNSRC="mars.avi" SRC="mars.gif">
```

4. Use the **START** attribute to tell the browser when to start playing the video. **START** can have two values, **fileopen** and **mouseover**. If **START** is set equal to **fileopen**, the video starts playing as soon as the file has finished loading. If **START** is set equal to **mouseover**, the video will not start playing until the user moves the mouse cursor over the animation. The default value is **fileopen**. To insert a video that doesn't start playing until the user moves the cursor over the video, use

```
<IMG DYNSRC="mars.avi" SRC="mars.gif" START=MOUSEOVER>
```

5. It's possible to use both **FILEOPEN** and **MOUSEOVER** for the **START** attribute. In this case, the video will play as soon as the file loads, and again each time the cursor passes over the video. To do this, enter

```
<IMG DYNSRC="mars.avi" SRC="mars.gif" START=FILEOPEN,MOUSEOVER>
```

6. You can add a set of video controls beneath the video clip with the **CONTROLS** attribute. For example, to add a set of video controls to a clip, use

```
<IMG DYNSRC="mars.avi" SRC="mars.gif" CONTROLS>
```

7. The number of times the video displays can be set with the **LOOP** attribute. The **LOOP** attribute can be set to the number of times the video is played. Setting **LOOP** equal to **INFINITE** or **-1** plays the video continuously. To play a video clip five times, use

```
<IMG DYNSRC="mars.avi" SRC="mars.gif" LOOP=5>
```

To play the video continuously, use

```
<IMG DYNSRC="mars.avi" SRC="mars.gif" LOOP=INFINITE>
```

A sample of a movie included in a Web page (in this case, a QuickTime movie embedded into Netscape) is shown in Figure 18-1.

How It Works

When an **<EMBED>** element is encountered on a Web page, the browser checks the MIME type of the file referenced in the element. If the file is of a type supported by plug-ins installed with the browser, the file is downloaded and displayed, and the browser passes on the values of any attributes to the plug-in. If the file format is not supported by any plug-ins on the user's computer, an error message is displayed and video is not shown.

When Internet Explorer identifies the **DYNSRC** attribute in the **<IMG>** tag, it loads the video file specified by that attribute. The browser then displays the video, using the values provided by any attributes or the default values.

Comments

If you use the **<EMBED>** method, note that a typical user will likely have only a few plug-ins of the most common type installed on his or her computer, so the user might not be able to view videos not in common formats (such as AVI, MPEG, and QuickTime). You might want to convert your video to one of these formats to maximize the number of people able to view your work.

Besides the attributes just mentioned, you can use other **<IMG>** attributes. See Chapter 9 for a full discussion of the attributes supported by **<IMG>**. Currently, only Internet Explorer 2 and later support inline AVI video, so users with other browsers

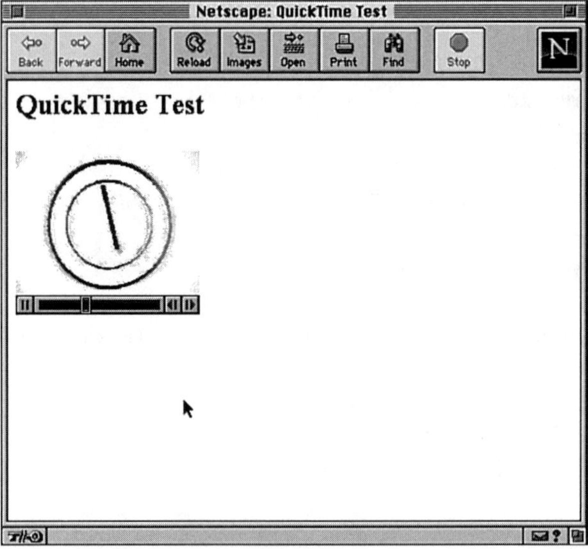

Figure 18-1 A QuickTime movie in a Web page

will be able to see only the image referenced in the **SRC** attribute. You can provide a link to the animation (in AVI or another format) that people with other browsers can see with an external application. For example, to include a link to an MPEG version of an animation, enter

```
<A HREF="mars.mpg"><IMG DYNSRC="mars.avi" SRC="mars.gif"></A>
```

You can find updated information about including AVI videos on the Web at the URL `http://www.microsoft.com/workshop/author/newhtml/default.htm`.

COMPLEXITY
INTERMEDIATE

18.4 How do I...
Add sound tracks to my Web page?

COMPATIBILITY: INTERNET EXPLORER, NETSCAPE NAVIGATOR

Problem

I would like to include some music that will play on the user's computer when he or she reads my page. How can I include a sound track on my Web page?

Technique

Both Microsoft Internet Explorer and Netscape Navigator support the use of the **<EMBED>** tag to include sound files. This method relies on plug-ins to play the sound file. Microsoft's Internet Explorer 2 and above also support the HTML extension **<BGSOUND>**, which enables users to add sounds that will play in the background. Other browsers can treat this like any other unsupported HTML element. The browser supports several different sound formats and enables you to control the number of times the sound is played.

Steps

Identify the appropriate sound for your page and open the document that contains the HTML code for the page.

Embedded Sound for Plug-ins (Netscape and Internet Explorer)

1. Insert the **<EMBED>** tag in the page. Set the **SRC** attribute to the URL of the sound file.

```
<BODY>
<EMBED SRC="sound.mid">
</BODY>
```

2. There are other attributes you can add to the **<EMBED>** tag that are relevant to sound files and are supported by many audio plug-ins, such as LiveAudio, which comes with Netscape Navigator. To have the sound start automatically when loaded, include the **AUTOSTART** attribute and set it equal to **TRUE**. **AUTOSTART** can also be set to **FALSE** in the opposite case.

```
<BODY>
<EMBED SRC="sound.mid" AUTOSTART=TRUE>
</BODY>
```

3. You can control the number of times the sound is played with the **LOOP** attribute. When **LOOP** is set to **TRUE**, the sound will loop continuously; when **LOOP** is set to **FALSE**, the sound will play only once; and when **LOOP** is set to an integer, the sound will play that number of times before stopping. For example, to tell the sound plug-in to play the sound five times, use the following:

```
<BODY>
<EMBED SRC="sound.mid" LOOP=5>
</BODY>
```

4. You can control where in the sound the plug-in should start or stop with the **STARTTIME** and **ENDTIME** attributes. Both take a pair of numbers, separated by a colon, that tell how many minutes and seconds into the music the plug-in should start or stop playing. To start 15 seconds into the sound and end 1 minute 30 seconds into the sound, use

```
<BODY>
<EMBED SRC="sound.mid" STARTTIME="00:15" ENDTIME="01:30">
</BODY>
```

5. You can control the volume at which the sound is played with the **VOLUME** attribute set to **<EMBED>**. The **VOLUME** attribute takes a number between 0 and 100, which represents the percentage of the maximum volume on the browser's computer system. To play a sound at 75 percent of the maximum volume, use

```
<BODY>
<EMBED SRC="sound.mid" VOLUME=75>
</BODY>
```

6. You can also define what sort of control, if any, the user can have with the sound. To display a console with Play, Pause, and Stop buttons and a volume controller, set the **CONTROLS** attribute to **CONSOLE** in the **<EMBED>** tag (this is the default). To provide a smaller version on the controller, you can set **CONTROLS** to **SMALLCONSOLE** instead. To keep any console from appearing and have the sound in the background, replace the **CONTROLS** attribute with **HIDDEN** and set it equal to **TRUE**. For example, to include a console for a user to control the sound explicitly, use

```
<BODY>
<EMBED SRC="sound.mid" CONTROLS=CONSOLE>
</BODY>
```

However, to keep any console hidden and have the sound play in the background, use

```
<BODY>
<EMBED SRC="sound.mid" HIDDEN=TRUE>
</BODY>
```

<BGSOUND> Tag (Internet Explorer)

1. Insert the `<BGSOUND>` tag in the body of the page. The location of the tag within the body is not important; the sound will be played as soon as the page is loaded, regardless of where the tag is located. No closing tag is required.

```
<BODY>
<BGSOUND>
</BODY>
```

2. To identify the name of the sound file, include the attribute `SRC` and set it equal to the name of the file. For example, to include a file named `bam.wav`, use

```
<BODY>
<BGSOUND SRC="bam.wav">
</BODY>
```

3. Like with many other HTML tags, you can specify the full pathname of the file or include a URL that goes to a sound file on another computer. For example, if the sound file is located in the directory `sounds/loud`, use

```
<BODY>
<BGSOUND SRC="sounds/loud/bam.wav">
</BODY>
```

4. If the file is accessible by HTTP from the computer `www.widgets.com` in the same directory as this example, you would enter

```
<BODY>
<BGSOUND SRC="http://www.widgets.com/sounds/loud/bam.wav">
</BODY>
```

5. To play the sound more than once, you can use the `LOOP` attribute. Set the attribute equal to the number of times you want the sound played. To play the sound from the last step three times, enter

```
<BODY>
<BGSOUND SRC="sounds/loud/bam.wav" LOOP=3>
</BODY>
```

6. To play a sound in the background continuously, set the LOOP attribute equal to infinite. Setting LOOP equal to -1 has the same effect. To make the sound in the last example play continuously, enter

```
<BODY>
<BGSOUND SRC="sounds/loud/bam.wav" LOOP=INFINITE>
</BODY>
```

How It Works

When an <EMBED> element is encountered on a Web page, the browser checks the MIME type of the file referenced in the element. If the file is of a type supported by plug-ins installed with the browser, the file is downloaded and played, and the browser passes on the values of any attributes to the plug-in. If the file format is not supported by any plug-ins on the user's computer, an error message is displayed and the sound is not played.

When Internet Explorer loads a page that contains the <BGSOUND> tag, it loads the sound file specified by the SRC attribute. The browser then plays the sound the number of times indicated by the LOOP attribute. The browser will play the sound once if the LOOP attribute is missing.

Comments

If you use the <EMBED> method, note that a typical user will likely have only a few plug-ins of the most common type installed on his or her computer, so the user might not be able to play sound files that are not in common formats. LiveAudio, for example, supports WAV, AIFF, AU, and MIDI formats. For more advanced information on including sounds in pages using <EMBED>, with an emphasis on LiveAudio, visit http://www.goodnet.com/~jeriii/info/embed.htm.

As of this writing, Internet Explorer supports three sound formats: WAV, AU, and MID (MIDI). Sound files in other formats will not be played by Internet Explorer. Note that <BGSOUND> is an HTML extension supported only by Internet Explorer. Other browsers, such as Netscape and Mosaic, will skip over the tag and not load or play the specified sound. You can find updated information about <BGSOUND> on the Web at the URL http://www.microsoft.com/ie/.

COMPLEXITY
INTERMEDIATE

18.5 How do I...
Include a Director application?

COMPATIBILITY: INTERNET EXPLORER, NETSCAPE NAVIGATOR, DIRECTOR

Problem

I have a multimedia presentation I have created using Macromedia Director. I want to include this on my Web site and have people view it, even if they don't have a copy of Director. How can I include a Director application in my Web page and make it visible to as many people as possible?

Technique

Macromedia has introduced Shockwave, a method of including Director movies on a Web page. Shockwave consists of two parts: an application called Afterburner that compresses Director movies into a special format, and a browser plug-in called Shockwave that can read the Afterburner-compressed files and display them in the browser. This method enables designers to create high-quality interactive multimedia applications that include sound and video and can react to user input.

Steps

1. Within Director, create a standard Director movie for your specific project and save it as a Director file.
2. Drag the icon for the Director movie onto the icon for Afterburner, or start up Afterburner and use it to locate the Director movie you want to convert. In Director 5, choose Afterburner from the `Xtras` directory.
3. When prompted, give the filename for the compressed file. This filename should end in `.dcr` (as in `movie.dcr`) to help identify the file as a Shockwave file.
4. Place the converted file into the appropriate directory on your Web server.
5. Now open the HTML document in which you want to include the Shockwave movie.
6. At the appropriate location in the file, insert the `<EMBED>` tag and include the `SRC` attribute, setting it equal to the URL of the Shockwave movie.

```
<P>Here is a Shockwave movie:</P>
<EMBED SRC="movie.dcr">
```

7. You can also include the **HEIGHT** and **WIDTH** attributes to reserve space in the browser window for the movie.

```
<P>Here is a Shockwave movie:</P>
<EMBED SRC="movie.dcr" HEIGHT=150 WIDTH=275>
```

8. The **ALT** attribute can also be included to display alternative text if the browser can't show the Shockwave movie (if, for example, a user has a text-only browser or does not have the Shockwave plug-in).

```
<P>Here is a Shockwave movie:</P>
<EMBED SRC="movie.dcr" HEIGHT=150 WIDTH=275 ALT="My shockwave movie!">
```

9. The **ALIGN** attribute can also be used to align the Shockwave movie onto a particular side of the browser window, taking as its values the same values as the **<IMG>** element.

```
<P>Here is a Shockwave movie:</P>
<EMBED SRC="movie.dcr" HEIGHT=150 WIDTH=275 ALT="My shockwave movie!" _
ALIGN=LEFT>
```

10. The **PLUGINSPAGE** attribute enables some browsers (including Netscape Navigator) to load a page if the browser does not have the appropriate plug-in for the specified file. For Shockwave files, you will want to reference Macromedia's Shockwave page at **http://www.macromedia.com/shockwave/**.

```
<P>Here is a Shockwave movie:</P>
<EMBED SRC="movie.dcr" HEIGHT=150 WIDTH=275 ALT="My shockwave movie!" _
ALIGN=LEFT PLUGINSPAGE="http://www.macromedia.com/shockwave/">
```

11. To control what color palette is used to display Shockwave movies, use the **PALETTE** attribute. When this attribute is set to **BACKGROUND** (the default) the Shockwave movie uses the current system color palette. When this attribute is set to **FOREGROUND**, the movie's own color palette takes over. This can affect the appearance of other movies and graphics on the page, so use it with caution. To set the palette to the movie's own palette, use

```
<P>Here is a Shockwave movie:</P>
<EMBED SRC="movie.dcr" HEIGHT=150 WIDTH=275 ALT="My shockwave movie!"
ALIGN=LEFT PALETTE=FOREGROUND>
```

12. You can also set the value for the color of the rectangle that appears as the movie loads but has not yet begin to play. The **BGCOLOR** attribute works like the **BGCOLOR** attribute to **<BODY>** (see How-To 2.9), including the use of hexadecimal values to describe the color. To set the color of the movie rectangle to white (**FFFFFF**), use

```
<P>Here is a Shockwave movie:</P>
<EMBED SRC="movie.dcr" HEIGHT=150 WIDTH=275 ALT="My shockwave movie!" _
ALIGN=LEFT BGCOLOR="#FFFFFF">
```

13. Shockwave movies can also be embedded using the **<OBJECT>** element. **OBJECT** requires specific values for two attributes, **CLASSID** and **CODEBASE**, which are given below:

```
<P>Here is a Shockwave movie:</P>
<OBJECT CLASSID="clsid:166B1BCA-3F9C-11CF-8075-444553540000"_
CODEBASE="http://active.macromedia.com/director/cabs/_
sw.cab#version=6,0,0,0">
</OBJECT>
```

14. The **<OBJECT>** tag accepts **HEIGHT**, **WIDTH**, and **BGCOLOR**, as described earlier. To specify the location of the Shockwave movie, though, use the **<PARAM>** tag within the **<OBJECT>...</OBJECT>** tag. The **NAME** attribute should be set to **SRC**, whereas the **VALUE** attribute should be set to the URL for the movie.

```
<P>Here is a Shockwave movie:</P>
<OBJECT CLASSID="clsid:166B1BCA-3F9C-11CF-8075-444553540000"_
CODEBASE="http://active.macromedia.com/director/cabs/_
sw.cab#version=6,0,0,0">
<PARAM NAME="SRC" VALUE="movie.dcr">
</OBJECT>
```

A screen shot of the process of "burning" a Director movie into a Shockwave file is shown in Figure 18-2.

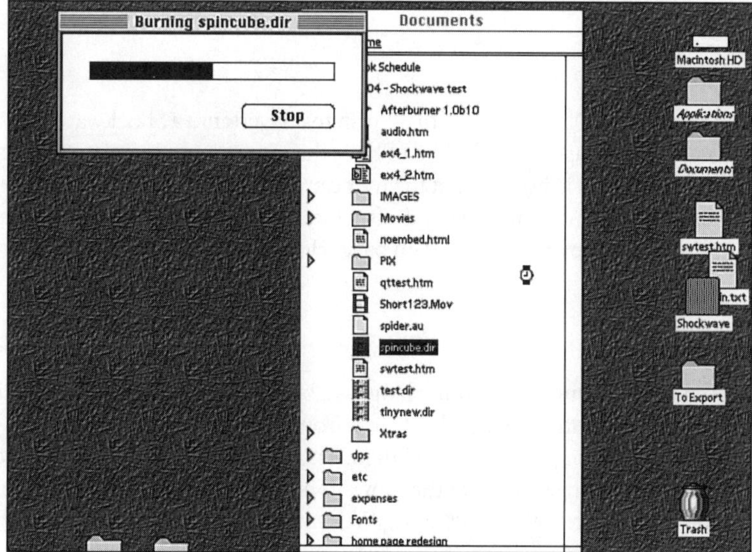

Figure 18-2 "Burning" a Director movie into a Shockwave file

How It Works

The Afterburner application reads in a Director movie and then compresses it to create a smaller file that takes less time to transfer across the Net. On the user's end, when he or she encounters a page with a Shockwave movie referenced in an `<EMBED>` tag, the browser checks to see whether the Shockwave plug-in is available. If the plug-in is available, the movie is downloaded and the plug-in is used to uncompress the movie and display it within the browser window. If the plug-in is not available, an error message is displayed and the movie is not shown.

Comments

The only current way to create Shockwave movies is through Director, a powerful but rather expensive multimedia application. If you don't have Director, you can still include Shockwave movies created elsewhere, but you cannot create your own. Also, although Afterburner does a good job compressing Director movies, the files can still be rather large and take considerable time to download, especially for people with slower modems. Keep file size in mind when creating Shockwave movies.

COMPLEXITY
ADVANCED

18.6 How do I... Communicate between a Web page and a Shockwave movie?

COMPATIBILITY: INTERNET EXPLORER, NETSCAPE NAVIGATOR, DIRECTOR

Problem

I've created a Director movie that I plan to convert into a Shockwave movie to include on my Web page. I would like to have the movie include links to other Web pages within the movie itself so that the user can click on something in the movie and automatically go to that page. I'd also like to be able to send information to the Shockwave movie from the Web page. How do I add Web links to a Director application?

Technique

You can use Lingo, a scripting language built into Director, to include links to Web pages for specific parts of the movie. You can also pass information from the Web page to specific parameters in Lingo. This can become quite complicated depending on the sophistication of the movie. This How-To provides a simple example that shows the essentials of including Web links in a Director/Shockwave movie.

Steps

Open your Director movie in Director. (This How-To assumes you have Director, which is essential in the creation of Shockwave movies.)

Adding Links to Web Pages in Shockwave

1. Select the cast member (portion of the movie, such as a graphic element) to serve as the link. The element you choose depends on the type and number of links you plan to include in your movie.
2. Double-click on that cast member to open it in the Paint window.
3. Select the Script button, in the menu bar in the top center of the Paint window. This opens a new script window that you can edit.
4. In the Script window, enter

```
on mouseUp
    goToNetPage("test.html")
end
```

   where `"test.html"` is replaced with the URL of the page you want to link.

5. Close the Script window, and then close the Paint window. Save the movie in Director format and, if you are finished with any other modifications to the movie, quit Director.
6. You can now convert the Director movie into Shockwave format using the process described in How-To 18.5. The completed Shockwave file will have the link to the page embedded in it, which will be activated when the user clicks on that element of the movie.

Passing Information into a Shockwave Movie

1. Decide what information you want to send into the Shockwave movie. Table 18-1 shows a list of available parameters you can use.

Table 18-1 Parameters available in a Web page for Lingo

PARAMETER	DESCRIPTION
`swURL`	URL to access
`swText`	Text to include in movie
`swForeColor`	Modifies the foreground color of an object
`swBackColor`	Modifies the background color of an object
`swFrame`	Targets a specific frame

continued on next page

continued from previous page

PARAMETER	DESCRIPTION
swColor	Modifies the color of an object
swName	Specifies a name to use or display in a movie
swPassword	Specifies a password to use in a movie
swBanner	Specifies text to appear as a banner in a movie
swSound	Names a specific sound to play in the movie
swVolume	Sets the volume of the sound in the movie
swPreloadTime	Sets the number of seconds of a sound file that will be loaded before play begins
swAudio	Specifies the URL of an audio file for the movie
swList	Specifies a comma-delimited list of values for use by the movie
sw1 - sw9	User-defined values

2. If you reference the Shockwave movie in the page with the **<EMBED>** tag, add the parameters listed above directly into the tag, setting each equal to the appropriate value. For example, to pass a URL into a Shockwave movie, use

```
<EMBED SRC="widgets.dcr" HEIGHT=100 WIDTH=100 _
swURL="http://www.widgets.com">
```

3. If you use the **<OBJECT>** tag to reference the movie, the Lingo parameters go into the **<PARAM>** tags listed between **<OBJECT>** and **</OBJECT>**. The **NAME** attribute is set to the Lingo parameter and **VALUE** is set to the value of the parameter. For example, to pass a URL into a Shockwave movie, use

```
<OBJECT CLASSID="clsid:166B1BCA-3F9C-11CF-8075-444553540000"_
CODEBASE="http://active.macromedia.com/director/cabs/_
sw.cab#version=6,0,0,0">
<PARAM NAME="SRC" VALUE="widgets.dcr">
<PARAM NAME="swURL" VALUE="http://www.widgets.com/">
</OBJECT>
```

A screen shot of the process of including the script in the Director movie is shown in Figure 18-3.

How It Works

When a user clicks in a linked portion of a Shockwave movie, the Shockwave plug-in looks up the URL referenced in the script for that element. The plug-in then passes the URL on to the browser, which will leave the current page for the new page. The Shockwave movie can also recognize specific parameters in **<EMBED>** or **<OBJECT>** tags and then apply them to the appropriate places in the Lingo code for the movie.

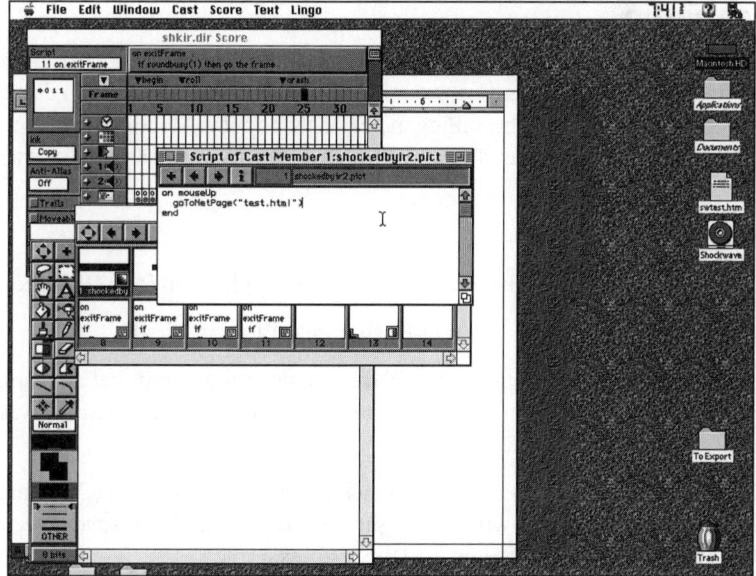

Figure 18-3 Including a Web script in a Director movie

Comments

Links in a Shockwave movie are relative to the location of the movie, not to the page itself. Thus, when using links, the Shockwave creator must be careful to specify the path to the desired document relative to the location of the movie, not the page where the movie was shown.

COMPLEXITY
ADVANCED

18.7 How do I... Include a Shockwave Flash movie in a Web page?

COMPATIBILITY: INTERNET EXPLORER, NETSCAPE NAVIGATOR, MACROMEDIA FLASH 2

Problem

I'm interested in adding some interactive graphics to a Web page, but don't need the level of sophistication offered by Director. Macromedia's Flash 2 application seems to provide what I need. How do I include Flash movies in a Web page?

Technique

Macromedia Flash enables users to create interactive presentations using vector graphics. This format makes the movies highly compressible and quick to download, which is why this format is becoming increasingly popular. Macromedia has made the use of Flash in Web pages similar to the use of Shockwave Director movies.

Steps

1. Use Macromedia Flash 2 to create an application for a Web site.
2. Under the File menu in Flash 2, select Export Movie.
3. Choose the option Flash Player Movie in the menu that appears. Use a filename ending in **.swf** so that it can be recognized as a Shockwave Flash movie.
4. Add the HTML markup to include the Flash movie in a Web page. Using **<EMBED>**, you will use the same syntax as for Shockwave Director movies, as described in How-To 18-5—for example,

```
<EMBED SRC="movie.swf" HEIGHT=100 WIDTH=100></EMBED>
```

5. The procedure for using **<OBJECT>** is also similar to that used for Director, described in How-To 18.5. The **<OBJECT>** tag requires specific values for **CODEBASE** and **CLASSID**.

```
<OBJECT CLASSID="clsid:D27CDB6E-AE6D-11cf-96B8-444553540000"_
CODEBASE="http://active.macromedia.com/flash2/cabs/_
swflash.cab#version=2,0,0,0">
</OBJECT>
```

6. Specify the name of the Flash movie in **<OBJECT>** with the **<PARAM>** tag within **<OBJECT>...</OBJECT>**. The **NAME** attribute should be set to **Movie** and the **VALUE** set to the URL for the Flash movie.

```
<OBJECT CLASSID="clsid:D27CDB6E-AE6D-11cf-96B8-444553540000"_
CODEBASE="http://active.macromedia.com/flash2/cabs/_
swflash.cab#version=2,0,0,0">
<PARAM NAME="Movie" VALUE="movie.swf">
</OBJECT>
```

How It Works

The Flash application creates an animation, with options for interactivity, that is then saved to a specific format for inclusion in a Web page. The **<EMBED>** and **<OBJECT>** tags specify the location and type of file being referenced so that the appropriate plug-in can be used to view the file.

Comments

For a user to see a Shockwave Flash movie, he or she must have the Shockwave plug-in. The latest versions of the Shockwave plug-in support movies made in Director and Flash. The MIME type for Flash on the server that hosts the Shockwave application must be set for the movie to be transferred correctly. The MIME type must be set to `application/x-shockwave-flash` and the suffix set to `.swf`. See How-To 12.6 for more information on setting MIME types on a server.

COMPLEXITY
ADVANCED

18.8 How do I... Embed a VRML space?

COMPATIBILITY: INTERNET EXPLORER, NETSCAPE NAVIGATOR

Problem

I have created a three-dimensional world using VRML that I would like to share with people on the Web. I would prefer to have them be able to view it directly from their Web browsers and not have to start a separate VRML browser to view it. How do I embed a VRML space into a Web page?

Technique

Several different methods exist for embedding VRML (Virtual Reality Modeling Language) spaces, or worlds, into Web pages. Most require that some kind of plug-in be installed on the user's machine, although Internet Explorer provides a more seamless approach to including VRML spaces within Web pages.

Steps

1. Create a VRML space in the application of your choice and place it on your Web server in the appropriate location. Open an HTML document in which you want to include the VRML space and locate the portion of the document where the VRML space will go.

2. Netscape Navigator 3 comes with the Live3D plug-in, which can be used to display VRML spaces embedded in documents. To embed a VRML space in a document that can be read by Live3D, use the `<EMBED>` tag and set the `SRC` attribute equal to the URL of the VRML file.

```
Here is a VRML space:
<EMBED SRC="myspace.wrl">
```

3. You can reserve space for the VRML display on the screen by including the **HEIGHT** and **WIDTH** attributes and setting them equal to the size of the VRML display area, in pixels.

```
Here is a VRML space:
<EMBED SRC="myspace.wrl" HIGHT=300 WIDTH=400>
```

4. Several other VRML plug-ins will work with Netscape and Internet Explorer, including Cosmo Player, CyberHub Client, Topper, VR Scout, Vrealm, and WIRL. Most of these plug-ins are supported for Windows 95 and Windows NT only, although there is increasing support for the Macintosh and UNIX systems. All these use similar **<EMBED>** commands to support displaying VRML spaces, but some may use proprietary attributes that might be of interest. Check out these plug-ins. The Netscape site has a detailed, updated list of VRML and other plug-ins, with links to sites for more information. How-To 10.10 also has additional information.

5. Internet Explorer 3 supports a more seamless approach to including VRML spaces in Web sites. Simply use the **<IMG>** tag and set the VRML attribute equal to the location of the VRML space.

```
Here is a VRML space:
<IMG VRML="myspace.wrl">
```

6. You can still use the **SRC** attribute and set it equal to a regular image. The normal image will appear on browsers that don't support the **VRML** attribute in the **<IMG>** tag (that is, most browsers except Internet Explorer 3 and later versions).

```
Here is a VRML space:
<IMG VRML="myspace.wrl" SRC="stillpic.gif>
```

7. As with any other case of the **<IMG>** tag, you can include **WIDTH** and **HEIGHT** attributes and include alternative text in the **ALT** attribute for browsers that don't support or aren't loading images of any kind.

```
Here is a VRML space:
<IMG VRML="myspace.wrl" SRC="stillpic.gif" HEIGHT=300 WIDTH=400 _
ALT="VRML space">
```

How It Works

As with other instances of **<EMBED>**, when the browser encounters an **<EMBED>** tag, it checks the MIME type of the file being requested with the available plug-ins installed with the browser. If a suitable plug-in exists, the VRML space is downloaded and displayed in the browser window. If no plug-in that supports VRML can be found, an error message is shown by the browser and the VRML space is not displayed.

Internet Explorer has built-in support for VRML spaces. If the VRML attribute is found in an <IMG> tag, that VRML space is loaded and displayed instead of a normal image. For other browsers, the VRML attribute is ignored and the normal image, as specified by the SRC attribute, or the ALT text, if no other image is available, is shown in its place.

Comments

VRML spaces can become very complex and large, so the files can take some time to download. Take this into account when designing Web pages: People might not have the patience to wait several minutes for a VRML space to download.

COMPLEXITY
ADVANCED

18.9 How do I... Include a multimedia object to maximize cross-browser support?

COMPATIBILITY: INTERNET EXPLORER, NETSCAPE NAVIGATOR

Problem

I have a multimedia file that I want to include in a Web page. How can I write the HTML for the file so that it can be viewed in the largest possible number of browsers?

Technique

Because different browsers support different tags for multimedia files, it takes a little effort to write HTML so that the file can be viewed in several different browsers. One important trick is the <NOEMBED> tag, which can be used to designate HTML markup to be displayed if the file requested in the <EMBED> tag cannot be used.

Steps

1. Open your HTML document and locate the areas where files are embedded or otherwise included.

2. After an <EMBED> tag, you can place a <NOEMBED>...</NOEMBED> pair of tags and place HTML markup to display if the file requested in the <EMBED> file cannot be displayed. For example, to display alternative markup if a browser does not support <EMBED>, the following:

```
<EMBED SRC="myspace.wrl" HIGHT=300 WIDTH=400>
<NOEMBED>
<EM>You need a VRML plug-in to view this</EM>
</NOEMBED>
```

3. If the browser does not support an inline version of a particular file using the <EMBED> command, you can add a link to a version of the file within the <NOEMBED> content and allow the user to view the file using an outside helper application, if any.

```
<EMBED SRC="myspace.wrl" HIGHT=300 WIDTH=400>
<NOEMBED>
<EM><A HREF="myspace.wrl">Check out my VRML space</A></EM>
</NOEMBED>
```

4. You can maximize support for Navigator and Internet Explorer by placing the <EMBED> tag within <OBJECT>. Because Netscape does not support <OBJECT>, it will ignore the <OBJECT> markup and use the <EMBED> tag instead. Because Internet Explorer has better support for the <OBJECT> tag than for <EMBED>, it will use the <OBJECT> markup instead because it comes first.

```
<OBJECT CODEBASE="test.class" CLASSID="12345-ABCDE" HEIGHT=100 WIDTH=80>
<PARAM NAME="SRC" VALUE="test.file">
<EMBED SRC="test.file" HEIGHT=100 WIDTH=80>
</EMBED>
<NOEMBED>
Sorry, you don't seem to be able to support this file.
</NOEMBED
</OBJECT>
```

5. Figure 18-4 shows an example of a Web browser that shows the text in the <NOEMBED> tag because it doesn't support <EMBED>. In this particular case, the browser is from America Online for the Macintosh.

How It Works

If a browser supports the <EMBED> command, it will ignore the content contained between the <NOEMBED> and </NOEMBED> tags. However, browsers that do not support <EMBED> will ignore it and the <NOEMBED> commands, enabling the content between the <NOEMBED> and the </NOEMBED> tags to be displayed. This content can include text, images, other embedded files, and any other valid HTML markup.

Comments

If a browser supports the <EMBED> command but not the type of file requested, it should not display what is contained between the <NOEMBED> and </NOEMBED> tags. In that case, nothing will be displayed. Thus, it's useful to describe any embedded files in "plain view" in the document, not hidden in a <NOEMBED> region that might not be displayed.

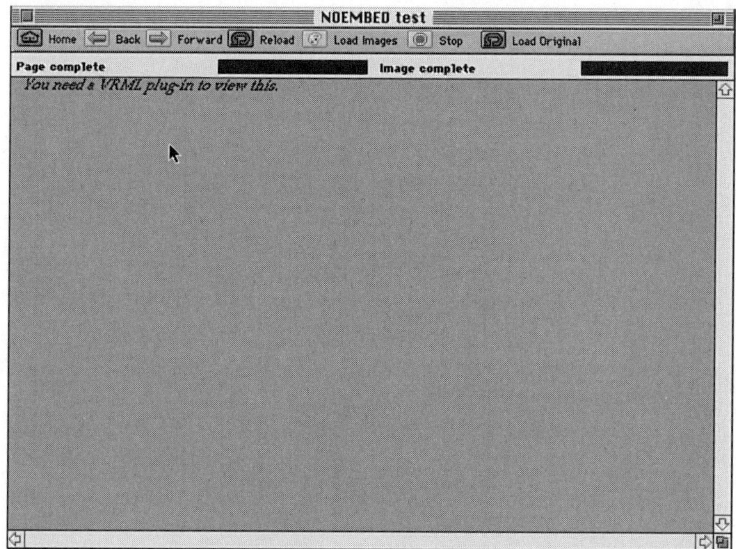

Figure 18-4 An example of the use of `<NOEMBED>`

CHAPTER 19

FRAMES

19

FRAMES

How do I...

Frames are nonstandard additions to HTML, added to Netscape's browser and then adopted by Internet Explorer. They are powerful features that enable a page to be broken into many different sections that, although related, operate independently of each other.

19.1 Include Frames in My Web Page

Frames are a way in Netscape and Explorer to divide the browser window into several independent sections, each displaying a separate document. A link in a document in one frame can load a document in another frame. This How-To discusses how to create frames in a Web page and link documents to different frames.

19.2 Make Frames Go Away

Many times, frames are fine for some information but limit the view for other information. This How-To shows how to link from a page in a frame to a page without a frame.

19.3 Use One Frame to Index Another That Will Display the Contents

One of the most common uses for frames is to split the screen into two columns. One column is a table of contents or an index. The other column is content based on what the user selects in the first column. This How-To shows one way to accomplish this.

19.4 Add a Floating Frame to My Web Page

Internet Explorer allows the creation of inline frames—frames that float on a Web page just as an image does. This How-To shows how you can create inline frames.

19.5 Create a Borderless Frame

There are times when you want a frame on a page but you don't want that frame to have a border. This How-To shows you how to create frames without borders.

19.6 Create Frames with Borders Between Them

You might want to separate frames with a color border now and then. This How-To shows you how to create frames with a color border between them.

19.7 Minimize Work When Maintaining Frame and Nonframe Versions of My Pages

You are creating pages for browsers that support frames, yet because you don't want to ignore people on older browsers, you are also maintaining nonframe versions of your pages. This How-To will help you minimize the work.

19.1 How do I... Include frames in my Web page?

COMPATIBILITY: NETSCAPE 2, INTERNET EXPLORER 2

Problem

I see many pages around the Web where the screen is broken into separate windows or frames. How can I add frames to my documents?

Technique

Frames are created through the use of frame documents, which in turn are created by using <FRAMESET> tags and <FRAME> tags. Frame documents are not all that different from regular HTML documents. In frame documents, the <FRAMESET> container is used in place of a <BODY> container. The <FRAMESET> container describes the different HTML "sub" documents that will make up the frames on the page.

The basic structure of a frame document is

```
<HTML>
<HEAD>
</HEAD>
<FRAMESET>
other FRAMESETS or FRAME tags or NOFRAME tags
</FRAMESET>
</HTML>
```

The <FRAMESET>...</FRAMESET> tags are used as the container of the frame document and to define the size of the frames. The tag has two attributes, **ROWS** and **COLS**. **ROWS** describes the numbers of rows of the screen allocated to each frame. **COLS** describes the number of columns of the screen in which each frame in the document will be allocated. These numbers can be given as an absolute number or a percentage value, or a * can be used to indicate that the corresponding frame should receive all the remaining space. For example,

```
<FRAMESET ROWS="50%, 25%,25%>
```

creates three frames. The first frame is twice as long as the other two frames.

```
<FRAMESET COLS=150,*>
```

creates two frames. The first has a fixed column width of 150 pixels; the second receives the remaining part of the screen.

It is possible to nest <FRAMESET>...</FRAMESET> tags inside other <FRAMESET>...</FRAMESET> tags to create all sorts of effects.

The second tag used to create frames is the <FRAME> tag. It defines a frame within a frameset and has six possible attributes. The <FRAME> tag syntax is

```
<FRAME SRC="url" NAME="window_name" MARGINWIDTH="value"
MARGINHEIGHT= "value" SCROLLING="yes|no|auto" {NORESIZE}>
```

SRC is the URL of the source document to be displayed in this frame.

NAME is an optional attribute that assigns a name to a frame so that the frame can be used by links in other documents or by JavaScript scripts. All names must begin with an alphanumeric character. The following names are reserved, though, because they have special meanings:

- ✔ **_blank**: Always load this link into a new, unnamed window.
- ✔ **_self**: Always load this link over itself.
- ✔ **_parent**: Always load this link into its parent or itself if it has no parent.
- ✔ **_top**: Always load this link at the top level or itself if it is at the top level.

MARGINWIDTH is an optional attribute used to set the width of the margins of the frame. If this attribute is used, the value is in pixels.

MARGINHEIGHT is the same as **MARGINWIDTH**, except that it controls the upper and lower margins of the frame.

SCROLLING is used to describe whether the frame should have a scrollbar. Setting this attribute to **yes** means the frame always has a scrollbar. Setting the attribute to **no** means the frame never has a scrollbar. Use of the **auto** setting displays a scrollbar when needed. This is an optional attribute, with **auto** being the default.

NORESIZE is an optional attribute. If **NORESIZE** appears in the tag, the user will not be able to change the size of the frame. By default, all frames can be resized.

For example,

```
<FRAME SRC="http://www.myserver.com/title.html" NORESIZE>
```

loads the document retrieved at **www.myserver.com/title.html** into the defined frame. Because of the **NORESIZE** attribute, the user will not be able to change the size of this frame.

Finally, the **<NOFRAME>...</NOFRAME>** tags can be used in conjunction with the other frame tags. Use the **<NOFRAME>** tag to provide alternative information to browsers that are non-frame-capable (or -friendly) clients. A frame-capable client ignores all items found inside the **<NOFRAME>** tags—for example,

```
<NOFRAME>
The information on the page makes use of frame technology. For best
results, use the latest version of Netscape.
</NOFRAME>
```

This code causes the message between the tags to be displayed by any browser that cannot render frames.

Steps

The following steps show one way that you can add frames to your documents:

1. Think about the number of frames you want to use in your document and the screen layout. It might help to design the initial screen layout on paper. This example contains three documents in three frames: a header in a top frame and two equally sized frames underneath on left and right parts of the screen. These frames contain a graphic and a description, respectively.

Here's a quick sketch of the layout:

```
|       Header                          |
|    Graphic  |     Description         |
|    frame    |     frame               |
```

2. Compose the individual documents that will make up the individual frames. This example has three frames and, therefore, three separate documents. Each document is as follows.

There is a very simple header document, **header.html**:

```
<HTML>
<!-- header.html -->
<!-- This document is used as the header frame for the frameset -->
<HEAD><TITLE>Cartoons</TITLE></HEAD>
<BODY>
<center>
<H1>A Cartoon</H1>
Enhanced with Netscape 2.0 Frames
</center>
</BODY>
</HTML>
```

The document **picture.html** contains the graphic you want to show in the second (left side) frame.

```
<HTML>
<HEAD><TITLE>A toon</TITLE></HEAD>
<!-- picture.html -->
<!-- this document simply loads a picture -->
<BODY>
<IMG ALIGN=CENTER SRC="slow.GIF">
<P><small>My favorite cartoon<Sup>1
<P>
1</SUP>By Jz</small>
</BODY>
</HTML>
```

Finally, **facts.html** contains the information you want to show in the third (right side) frame.

```
<HTML>
<!-- facts.html -->
<!-- simple document that contains information to be shown in a frame -->
<HEAD><TITLE>Facts</TITLE></HEAD>
<BODY>
<H2>Some notes about cartoons</H2>
Cartoons have been around for a long time.  Almost as soon as papers
first came into existence, cartoons started popping up in them.  Today
comics can be found in almost any language known to man.
<P>
Cartoons serve many functions:
<UL><LI>To entertain
<LI>To enlighten
<LI>To inform
</UL>
Or some combination of all three.
<P>
A good source of cartoons on the web is
<A HREF="http://www.phlab.missouri.edu/~c617145/comix.html">
Comics 'n Stuff</A>
<P>
<P>
</BODY>
</HTML>
```

These three documents are all quite simple, but when combined into frames on a screen, they can be quite effective.

3. Create the document that will hold the three frames. This can be done with any text editor. This document will begin and end like any other HTML document, with the **<HTML>** tags.

4. Define the first frameset by using the **<FRAMESET>** tag.

```
<FRAMESET ROWS="70,*">
```

This tag, in effect, splits the screen into two horizontal sections. The first section is 70 rows long. The remaining section occupies the rest of the screen.

5. Add the first frame with the **<FRAME>** tag:

```
<FRAME SRC="header.html" NORESIZE>
```

This tag causes the document **header.html** to display in the first frame, the one designated to be 70 rows long. The user cannot resize this frame.

6. Add a second frameset that will be nested into the first frameset. This is done with

```
<FRAMESET COLS="50%,*">
```

This tag creates another frameset in the area of the screen not occupied by the **header.html** frame. This new frameset consists of two frames of equal size.

7. Add the second and third documents to their respective frames.

```
<FRAME SRC="picture.html" MARGINHEIGHT=0 MARGINWIDTH=4 SCROLLING=no ⇐
NAME="toon">
<FRAME SRC="facts.html" NAME="story" NORESIZE>
```

This works just as the **<FRAME>** tag did in step 5, only these frames are included in the second frameset.

8. Close the two framesets.

```
</FRAMESET>
</FRAMESET>
```

9. Include some information for browsers that do not support frames. This is done by inserting information between **<NOFRAME>...</NOFRAME>** tags. The information included here can be anything from a simple message to a nonframe version of your document. For a sample of this, you can view the entire document, shown at the end of this section.

10. Save and name the document. For this example, use **toon_dem.html**. The entire document is shown below.

```
<HTML>
<TITLE>About Cartoons</TITLE>

<!-- Create the first frameset and load the first frame -->

<FRAMESET ROWS="70,*">
<FRAME SRC="header.html" MARGINHEIGHT=0 MARGINWIDTH=0
SCROLLING="no" NORESIZE>

<!-- Create the second frameset and load the second and third frames -->

<FRAMESET COLS="50%,*">
<FRAME SRC="picture.html" MARGINHEIGHT=0 MARGINWIDTH=4 SCROLLING=no ⇐
NAME="toon">
<FRAME SRC="facts.html" NAME="story" NORESIZE>

</FRAMESET>
</FRAMESET>
<NOFRAME>

<!-- The following is used by non-frame-aware browsers -->

<H2>Cartoons</H2>
<IMG ALIGN=LEFT SRC="slow.GIF">
Cartoons have been around for a long time.  Almost as soon as papers
first came into existence cartoons started popping up in them.  Today
comics can be found in almost any language known to man.
<P>
Cartoons serve many functions:
<UL><LI>To entertain
<LI>To enlighten
<LI>To inform
</UL>
Or some combination of all three.
<P>
A good source of cartoons on the web is
<A HREF="http://www.phlab.missouri.edu/~c617145/comix.html">
Comics 'n Stuff</A>
<HR>
Note:this is one of my favorite cartoons<P>
</NOFRAME>
</HTML>
```

11. View the document to make sure it looks the way you think it should. Figure 19-1 shows how the sample document looks when viewed by a browser that supports frames.

12. Just to be cautious, view your document with a browser that does not support frames to see if it looks okay. Figure 19-2 shows what the sample document looks like when seen through an older version of Netscape.

13. Experiment with different frame settings.

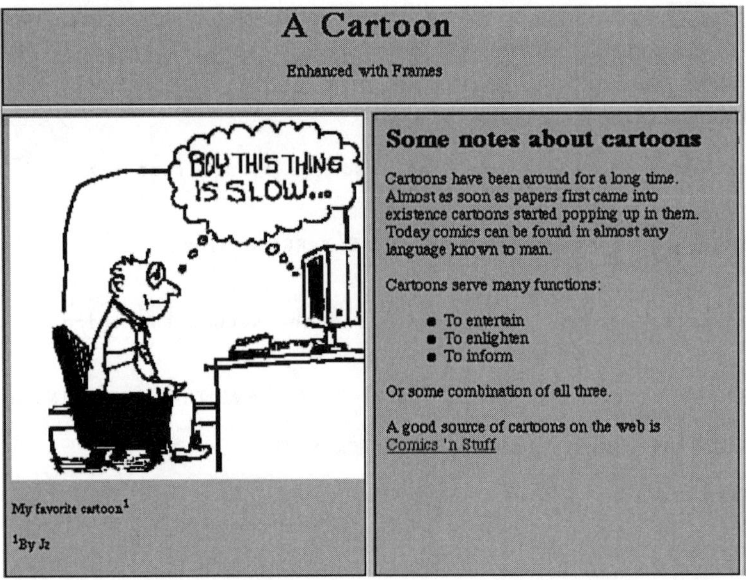

Figure 19-1 A frames demonstration

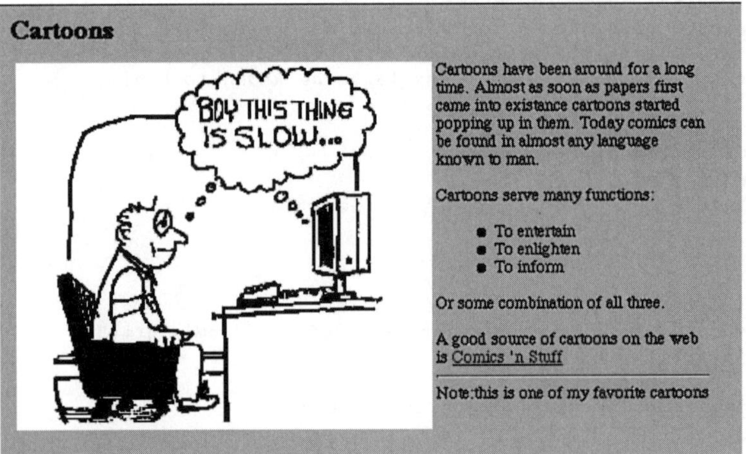

Figure 19-2 The sample document when viewed with Netscape 1.1

How It Works

The first `<FRAMESET>` tag splits the screen into two parts: a top section with a length of 70 pixels and a bottom section that occupies the remaining portion of the screen. The first `<FRAME SRC>` tag loads the `header.html` document into the top frame. The next <FRAMESET> tag splits the remaining section of the screen into two equal frames. The next two <FRAME SRC> tags load the **picture.html** and the **facts.html** documents into these frames. When a frames-aware browser encounters these tags, it renders the documents in three separate frames.

The <NOFRAME> tags render information on browsers that do not support frames.

Comments

Frames are one of the newer, more dynamic, and powerful additions to HTML. This example gives a general overview of frames. It covers only the basics. More examples will follow. If you are interested in finding the latest information on frames, check the latest online documentation at the Netscape home page: **http://home.netscape.com/**.

19.2 How do I... Make frames go away?

COMPATIBILITY: NETSCAPE 2, INTERNET EXPLORER

Problem

Frames are great for some things, but they really limit what my readers can see for other things. Can I make a page in a frame link to another page that is not in a frame?

Technique

To create a link from a frame to a page that is not in a frame, you use the TARGET attribute. The TARGET attribute is attached to the <A HREF>...</A> tag with the form

```
<A HREF="URL"TARGET="name">
```

where TARGET is the name of a frame (as assigned in a <FRAME> tag) or can be set to one of the special values shown in Table 19-1.

Table 19-1 Special values for TARGET attributes

VALUE	DESCRIPTION
_top	This will cause the URL specified in HREF to load into the entire browser window, thus removing any frames.
_blank	This will cause the URL specified in HREF to load into a new unnamed browser.
_self	This will cause the URL specified in HREF to load over the current window.
_parent	This will cause the URL specified in HREF to load into the frameset's parent window.

For this example, you will be using the **_top** setting.

Steps

The following steps show one way to create links from frames to documents not in frames:

1. Create a document that contains frames.

2. In one of the frames, include an `<A HREF>` tag with a `TARGET` attribute set to `_top`—for example,

```
<A HREF="index.html" target=_top>Home</A>
```

3. Check your document to make sure it works the way you think it should.

How It Works

When the browser references a link with the `TARGET` set to `_top`, it places the contents of that link in a new window. Thus, any frames you might have had on the referring page are not used.

Comments

The next section shows this tag at work. Note that, although the use of frames might be a more advanced concept, removing frames is actually quite simple.

COMPLEXITY
INTERMEDIATE

19.3 How do I... Use one frame to index another that will display the contents?

COMPATIBILITY: NETSCAPE 2, INTERNET EXPLORER

Problem

One thing I see a lot of people doing with frames is splitting the browser window into two sections. One section contains an index or table of contents. The second section contains corresponding information that will pop up after the user selects something from the first window. How can I do this?

Technique

To create an index or a table of contents that gives users a choice of options and then updates or displays whatever the users choose in another corresponding window, use the `<FRAMESET>` element to split the screen into two separate frames. Create one frame that will contain the specified information and label this frame with the `NAME` attribute in the `<FRAME>` tag—for example,

```
<FRAME  SRC="info.html" NAME="info">
```

Create another frame. This frame will contain links to the first frame. To make sure this information loads in the first frame, specify the frame's name in the `<A HREF>` tag—for example,

```
<A  HREF="links.html" TARGET="info">Information</A>
```

Steps

The following steps show one way to create an index that displays information in another frame:

1. Decide on the layout you want to use. For this example, we will be using a very simple two-frame structure. The frame on the left will hold an index—in this case, cartoons from which to choose. The frame on the right will contain the results of the selection.

2. Decide on a name for the frame in which you want the information to appear when something is selected in the index. For this example, use the name `toon`.

3. Create the base document that will hold the `<FRAMESET>` and `<FRAME>` tags. The document will look like the following:

```
<HTML>
<TITLE>Frames</TITLE>
<FRAMESET COLS="25%,*">
<FRAME SRC="toon_list.html"  MARGINHEIGHT=0 MARGINWIDTH=0 SCROLLING="yes"
NORESIZE>
<FRAME SRC="slow.gif" NAME="toon">
</FRAMESET>
<NOFRAMES>
You need frames for this example
</NOFRAMES>

</HTML>
```

4. Create the HTML document that will act as the index. Make sure each of the links that should display its information in the `"toon"` frame includes `toon` in the target—for example,

```
<HTML> <TITLE>Choices</TITLE> <BODY BGCOLOR="FFFFFF">
<H3>Pick a toon</H3>
<UL>
<A Href="cc/cc1001.GIF" target="toon">October 1st</A><P>
<A Href="cc/cc1002.GIF" target="toon">October 2nd</A><P>
<A Href="cc/cc1003.GIF" target="toon">October 3rd</A><P>
<A Href="cc/cc1004.GIF" target="toon">October 4th</A><P>
<A Href="cc/cc1007.GIF" target="toon">October 7th</A><P>
<A Href="cc/cc1008.GIF" target="toon">October 8th</A><P>
<A Href="cc/cc1009.GIF" target="toon">October 9th</A><P>
```

continued on next page

continued from previous page

```
<A Href="cc/cc1010.GIF" target="toon">October 10th</A><P>
<A Href="cc/cc1011.GIF" target="toon">October 11th</A><P>
<A Href="cc/cc1012.GIF" target="toon">October 12th</A><P>
</UL>
<A Href="index.html" target="_top">Home</A>
</HTML>
```

5. View the document to make sure it looks and acts like you think it should. Figure 19-3 shows a two-frame example.

How It Works

When the browser encounters an **<A HREF>...</A>** tag in a frame, if that tag contains a target that is a different frame, the results of the **<A HREF>...</A>** tag will display in the targeted frame.

Comments

This example could have been smoother if, instead of displaying only the GIF in the **toon** frame, we had created an HTML file for each **toon** pointed to by the **TOON_LIST** frame. This way it would have been possible to add background colors and links.

This How-To has Intermediate complexity because, when you understand the concept of frames, creating this sort of display is not all that complex.

Figure 19-3 Two frames: one that is an index and the other that shows results of that index

19.4 How do I... Add a floating frame to my Web page?

COMPATIBILITY: INTERNET EXPLORER 3

Problem

When I'm using Internet Explorer, I notice that sometimes I come across frames that seem to be in the middle of nonframed documents. How can I add these "floating" frames to my pages?

Technique

Internet Explorer enables you to treat frames of HTML code much like you would an image, by letting you insert the frame into a document and align text to it. The tag used for this is **<IFRAME>...</IFRAME>**. The attributes for **<IFRAME>** are

```
ALIGN=LEFT|CENTER|RIGHT
FRAMEBORDER=1|0 (1 for border)
HEIGHT
WIDTH
MARGINHEIGHT
MARGINWIDTH
NAME="name to use in TARGET"
SRC="URL"
SCROLLING="yes|no"
```

All the size attributes are in pixels.

Steps

Follow these steps to add inline (floating) frames to your Internet Explorer documents:

1. Decide on the layout of the document. For this example, we will be using a document that contains a list of links to cartoons. When the user selects a cartoon from this list, it is displayed in an inline frame.

2. Create the document that will hold the inline frame.

3. Add the **<IFRAME>...<IFRAME>** tag. Make sure to set the **NAME**, **HEIGHT**, and **WIDTH** attributes—for example,

```
<IFRAME SRC="slow.gif" Name="itoon" Align="right" Width=384 Height=288>
</IFRAME>
```

4. Add the appropriate links to the document, making sure that the **TARGET** attribute is set to the name of the **IFRAME**—for example,

```
<A Href="cc/cc1001.GIF" target="itoon">October 1st</A>
```

5. Check the documents to make sure everything looks and works like you think it should. Figure 19-4 shows one example.

How It Works

When Internet Explorer encounters an **<IFRAME>...</IFRAME>** tag, it creates a frame in the document and places whatever is pointed to by the **SRC** attribute into that frame. The whole process works very much like loading an image or graphic into a document.

Comments

Notice that the **<IFRAME>...</IFRAME>** tags must be closed. In the future, there might be a difference between inline and floating frames, but as of this writing, they seem to be one and the same. Our guess is that the **<IFRAME>** tag is an open tag because it is meant to allow Web designers to build frames on the fly someday by entering tags and text between the **<IFRAME>** tags, much like forms work.

It would be nice if Netscape had the capability to recognize inline frames.

Figure 19-4 An inline frame

19.5 How do I... Create a borderless frame?

COMPATIBILITY: INTERNET EXPLORER, NETSCAPE 4.0

Problem

I would like to use frames, but I don't want them to have any borders. How do I accomplish this?

Technique

To create frames without borders, use the **FRAMEBORDER** attribute in a **<FRAME>** or **<IFRAME>...</IFRAME>** tag, and set it to **0**.

Steps

Follow these simple steps to create a frame without a border:

1. Find or create a document with frames.
2. Decide which frames you want to make borderless.
3. Set the **FRAMEBORDER** attribute to **0** in the **<FRAME>** tag.

```
<FRAME SRC="slow.gif" NAME="toon" FRAMEBORDER=0>
```

4. View the document to make sure it works and looks like you think it should. Figure 19-5 shows a document with frames without borders.

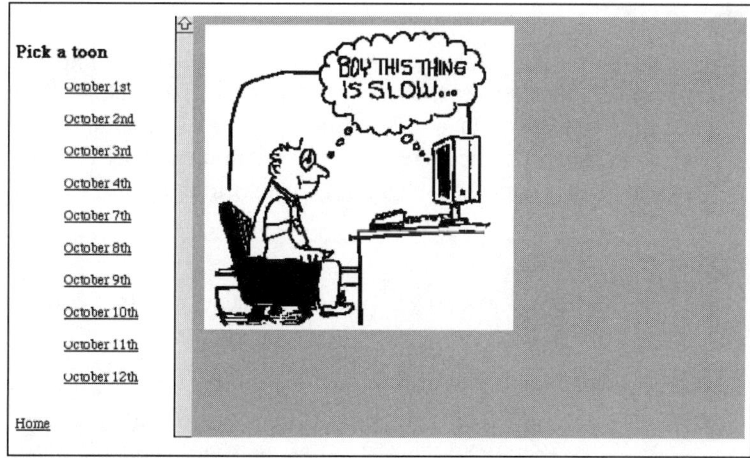

Figure 19-5 Document with a borderless frame

How It Works

When Internet Explorer encounters a <FRAME> or <IFRAME> tag, it checks to see whether that tag contains a FRAMEBORDER attribute. If it does and if the attribute is set to 0, then no border is displayed for that frame.

Comments

The <FRAMEBORDER> tag can help create seamless pages with frames. Notice that, although frames are a more advanced concept, removing their borders is quite simple.

NOTE

Netscape 4.0 supports borderless frames by setting FRAMEBORDER to NO.

COMPLEXITY
INTERMEDIATE

19.6 How do I... Create frames with borders between them?

COMPATIBILITY: INTERNET EXPLORER

Problem

I would like to separate my frames with a color border. How do I accomplish this?

Technique

To create frames with a color border between them in Internet Explorer, you use the combination of FRAMESPACING and FRAME BORDER in the <FRAMESET> tag. You also use either BACKGROUND or BGCOLOR attributes in the <BODY> tag. Setting FRAMESPACING to a number greater than 0 will result in space between frames. This allows any background or background color set in the <BODY> tag to display.

Steps

The following steps show how to create documents with frames that have colored borders between them:

1. Decide on the layout of your document.
2. Create the document that will hold the frames. Make sure that you include a <BODY> tag and set the BGCOLOR to the color of the border you want to place between the frames—for example,

```
<BODY BGCOLOR="0000FF">
```

3. Add the `<FRAMESET>` tag to the document. Make sure to include the **FRAMESPACING** attribute and set it to a significant number of pixels—for example,

```
<FRAMESET COLS="25%,*" FRAMEBORDER=0 FRAMESPACING=20>
```

4. Add the `<FRAME>` tags to the document. The final document will now resemble the following, at least in structure:

```
<HTML>
<TITLE>Frames</TITLE>
<BODY BGCOLOR="0000FF">
<FRAMESET COLS="25%,*" FRAMEBORDER=0 FRAMESPACING=20>
<FRAME SRC="toon_list.html"  MARGINHEIGHT=0
MARGINWIDTH=0 SCROLLING="yes" BORDERCOLOR="FF00FF" NORESIZE>
<FRAME SRC="slow.gif" NAME="toon" FRAMEBORDER=0>
</FRAMESET>
</BODY>
</HTML>
```

5. View the document to make sure it looks and acts the way you intended. Figure 19-6 shows a sample document with a colored border between frames.

How It Works

By setting **FRAMESPACING** to a significant number of pixels, you create space between frames, thereby letting the background color set in the **<BODY>** tag be seen.

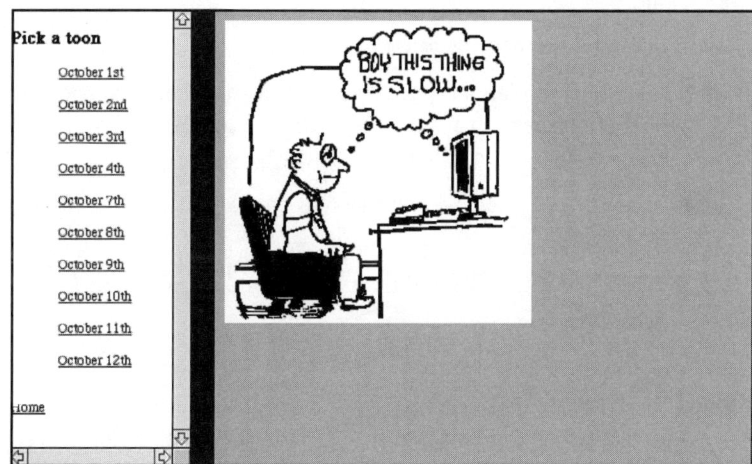

Figure 19-6 Frames with a colored border between them

Comments

By using `FRAMESPACING` and `FRAMEBORDER`, you can create some neat effects. The document used in this example will display only a blank blue background when viewed with Netscape because Netscape ignores `<BODY>` tags in frames.

COMPLEXITY
INTERMEDIATE

19.7 How do I... Minimize work when maintaining frame and nonframe versions of my pages?

COMPATIBILITY: NETSCAPE 2, INTERNET EXPLORER

Problem

My pages use frames, but I am also using the `<NOFRAMES>` tag to display versions of my pages without frames. I find this is a lot of work. What can I do to minimize this work?

Technique

Creating framed and nonframed versions of your pages can be quite time-consuming, but with a little planning, you can minimize the work.

Steps

The following steps show some techniques you can use when working with both framed and nonframed versions of your pages:

1. Take time to plan out your design so the nonframed version is as close to the framed version as possible. With a little forethought, you can copy and paste changes from one to the other.
2. Record somewhere what frame files correspond to what nonframed versions.
3. Give the framed files and their corresponding nonframe files similar names.

How It Works

A little planning, design work, and record keeping in the beginning stages can save a lot of time in the later updating stages.

Comments

Other techniques that might be possible are to use **INCLUDE** files to hold your text in both the frame and nonframe files. This would allow you to update the **INCLUDE** file. The downside to this is that many servers do not support **INCLUDE** files. Even if a server does support **INCLUDE** files, these files can put an added drain on the system, so this might be an extravagant use of **INCLUDE** files.

Perl programmers might be able to create scripts that enable them to update a series of related framed and nonframed files easily.

A final note on frames: Many of these examples can be found on the accompanying Web page at **http://www.psnw.com/~jmz5/waite/frames**.

CHAPTER 20

DYNAMIC HTML

20

DYNAMIC HTML

How do I...

Layers are a new addition to HTML, added to Netscape 4.0 with the `<LAYER>` tag and available through Internet Explorer 4.0 by defining them with cascading style sheets. Layers are a powerful addition to HTML. They give page designers a host of new abilities, such as the ability to position content at an exact position on a page, the ability to overlay content, the ability to hide or show content or portions of content, and the ability to create animation and movement without using Java.

Layers do have certain drawbacks, though. Although they have great potential, to make the most out of this potential, you must use a scripting language such as JavaScript to create scripts or functions to modify layer attributes and reposition layers. Also, as of this writing, only Netscape 4.0 has full support of layers via the `<LAYER>` tag. Internet Explorer supports layers but not as completely as Netscape. Other browsers may or may not include support for layers. It should also be noted that Netscape

4.0 is a powerful but HUGE browser. Many Netscape fans might opt to keep using Netscape 3.0. So although layers are very powerful, a page designer must be aware that a fair number of people might be surfing the Web with a browser that does not support layers. Still, if you are willing to take the risks, layers can add a lot to a page.

To get the most out of layers, you must use JavaScript (or another scripting language) and have at least a basic understanding of certain programming concepts such as the use of variables, functions, and flow control structures and statements. Although JavaScript and scripting or programming are beyond the scope of this book, Chapter 17, "Web Programming with Java and JavaScript," gives a good general introduction to JavaScript. The examples used throughout this chapter strive to be as simple as possible. You can make layers and a little JavaScript go a long way. For those who really want to dive deep into JavaScript, many books are available.

20.1 Create a Layer

Layers enable you to position content at an exact location on the screen. This simple How-To shows you how to use the `<LAYER>` tag to create layers.

20.2 Create an Inflow Layer

Besides creating layers at an exact (or absolute) location in a document, you can also create an inflow layer—one that flows naturally in a document. This How-To shows how to use the `<ILAYER>` tag to create inflow (or relative) layers.

20.3 Create a Layer Using Style Sheet Syntax

Besides using the `<LAYER>` and `<ILAYER>` tags to create layers, you can create layers by using cascading style sheets syntax. This How-To shows the use of style sheet syntax to define layers.

20.4 Hide and Show Layers

Each layer has a visibility assigned to it. A layer can be either shown or hidden. This How-To shows how to set and change a layer's visibility using the `VISIBILITY` attribute and JavaScript.

20.5 Change the Stacking Order of Layers

Each layer has a stacking order called `Z-INDEX` assigned to it. A layer can appear either above or below another layer. This How-To shows how to set and change this stacking order using `Z-INDEX` and JavaScript.

20.6 Dynamically Move Layers to Create Animation

Layers are dynamic: They can move from one part of the screen to another. This How-To shows one way to move or create animation with a layer by changing a layer position with the JavaScript function `MoveBy`.

20.7 Set and Change the Clipping Area of a Layer

Each layer is assigned a "clip area," or a rectangle of visible area. This clip area can be changed on the fly. This How-To shows how to use the `CLIP` attributes and JavaScript to set and change a layer's clip area.

20.8 Protect Browsers That Don't Support Layers

Because not all browsers support layers, you might want to alert readers with nonlayer browsers that your page uses layers. This How-To shows use of the `<NOLAYER>` tag for displaying messages on older browsers.

20.1 How do I... Create a layer?

COMPATIBILITY: NETSCAPE 4.0

Problem

I've heard a lot about layers and "dynamic HTML" that lets me position objects precisely on the screen. How do I create a layer?

Technique

The easiest way to create a layer is by use of the `<LAYER>...</LAYER>` tags. You can place any valid HTML tag, element, or content inside the `<LAYER>...</LAYER>` tags. The `<LAYER>` tag has the following attributes (these are taken directly from Netscape's site and are subject to change):

- ✔ **ID**: The name of the layer to be used by other layers or by JavaScript.
- ✔ **LEFT** and **TOP**: The horizontal and vertical positions of the layer in pixels, with the top-left corner of the screen being (0,0).
- ✔ **PAGEX** and **PAGEY**: The horizontal and vertical positions of the layer relative to the document's window.
- ✔ **SRC** and **source-include**: The pathname of a file that contains HTML formatted content.
- ✔ **Z-INDEX**, **ABOVE**, and **BELOW**: The stacking order of a layer. These three parameters are mutually exclusive. Only one is valid at any given time.
- ✔ **WIDTH**: The width of the layer's content. It controls the right margin for wrapping.
- ✔ **HEIGHT**: The height of a layer's clipping region.
- ✔ **CLIP**: The viewable area of a layer. This can be less than the **WIDTH** and the **HEIGHT**, enabling you to create some advanced affects.
- ✔ **VISIBILITY**: Whether a layer is visible or not. Valid values are **SHOW** and **HIDE**.

- **BGCOLOR**: The background color to be used by the layer. (Works just like the **BGCOLOR** attribute in the **<BODY>** tag.)
- **BACKGROUND**: An image to be used as the background for the layer. (Works just like **BACKGROUND** in the **<BODY>** tag.)
- **OnMouseOver**, **OnMouseOut**: JavaScript routine (event handler) to use when the mouse enters or leaves the layer.
- **OnFocus**, **OnBlur**: JavaScript routine to use when the layer receives or loses keyboard focus.
- **OnLoad**: JavaScript routine to use when the layer is first loaded.

All these attributes are "reflected" in JavaScript. This means that a page designer can use a layer's ID to modify the layer's content either directly or with a JavaScript method (function). For example, use `layerName.propertyName` to access a property:

```
document.layers["layerName"].visibility="SHOW" or
```

Use `layerName.methodName(parameters)` to have a JavaScript method (or function) act on the named layer:

```
document.layers["layername"].moveBY(10,0);
```

These subjects are dealt with later in the chapter. For now, we'll concentrate on defining a layer.

Steps

The following steps show one way to create a layer:

1. Create a document that contains the layer. For experimental purposes, it might be best to start with a simple document.
2. Insert the **<LAYER>** tags into the document, setting any attributes you want to use. A few of the more basic attributes include **ID**, **LEFT**, **TOP**, and **VISIBILITY**—for example,

```
<LAYER ID="Layer1" TOP=50 LEFT=100">Layer content</LAYER>
```

3. Insert the layer's content between the **<LAYER>** tags. This content can be any valid HTML content. In other words, anything you can put in an HTML document can be included in a layer: text, graphics, other tags.
4. Experiment with the layer's attributes to see how changing the attributes affects the layer and the document.

How It Works

When the Netscape 4.0 browser encounters the **<LAYER>...</LAYER>** tags, it treats the content between the tags as a single entity. The user is given precise control over the placement of those objects. A change to one of the layer's attributes affects all the content in the layer. The following document shows very basic use of layers. Two simple boxes are placed on the screen. Figure 20-1 displays how this document looks when viewed with the latest version of Netscape.

```
<HTML>
<HEAD>
<TITLE>Layers Demo 20-1</TITLE>
</HEAD>
<BODY>
<H1>Layers</H1>
<LAYER ID="one" LEFT=80 TOP=120>
<IMG SRC="red.gif">Layer one 80*120
</LAYER>
<LAYER ID="two" LEFT=50 TOP=140>
<IMG SRC="green.gif">Layer two 50*140
</LAYER>
<HR>
This text is outside the layers. Notice how the layers are positioned
absolutely, independent of the order they appear in the document.
</BODY>
</HTML>
```

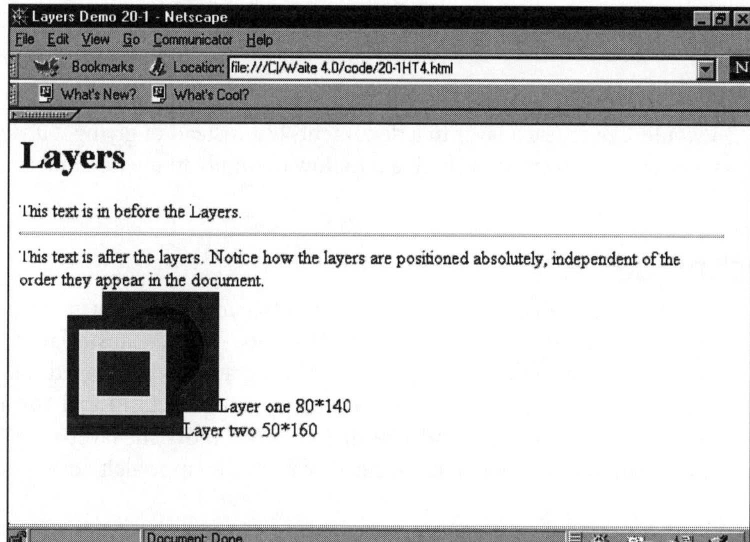

Figure 20-1 A simple use of layers

Comments

Layers are an exciting addition to HTML. They give Web page designers something they have craved since the conception of the Web: a way to put content exactly where they want to.

It is entirely legal to nest layers inside of layers. This gives you precise control of the placement of objects within a layer. When you move or modify a layer, all the layers nested within will be affected.

We should note that although layers are exciting and powerful, they are also new and, as of this writing, still evolving. The `<LAYERS>` tag is supported only by Netscape 4.0. (Layers can be implemented in Internet Explorer using style sheet syntax—see How-To 20.3.) We also should stress that, to get the full functionality from layers, an author must at least be familiar with using JavaScript.

NOTE

In early versions of layers, the `ID` attribute was called `NAME`.

COMPLEXITY
INTERMEDIATE

20.2 How do I... Create an inflow layer?

COMPATIBILITY: NETSCAPE 4.0

Problem

I would like to use a layer in a document, but instead of giving it absolute coordinates on the screen, I would like it to flow naturally in my document. How do I do this?

Technique

To create a layer that occurs in its "natural" place in a document, you create an inflow layer with the `<ILAYER>...</ILAYER>` tags. This creates a layer that is positioned relatively in the document, much like a graphic is positioned using the `<SRC>` tag. You can nudge the layer into position by using the `LEFT` and `TOP` attributes. In an inflow layer, the `LEFT` and `TOP` attributes will move the layer away from its natural position in the document instead of from the upper-left corner of the screen.

Steps

The following steps show one way to create an inflow layer:

1. Create a document that contains the inflow layer. For experimental purposes, it might be best to start with a simple document.

2. Insert the `<ILAYER>` tags into the document, setting any attributes you want to use. A few of the more basic attributes include **ID**, **LEFT**, and **TOP**. Remember, though, the **LEFT** and **TOP** attributes will be used to position the layer relatively from its natural spot, so the values will probably be much less than they would be for a regular layer—for example,

```
<ILAYER ID="Layer1" LEFT=5 TOP=5">Layer content</ILAYER>
```

3. Insert the layer's content between the `<ILAYER>` tags. Just as with the `<LAYER>` tags, this content can be any valid HTML content. In other words, anything you can put in an HTML document can be included in a layer: text, graphics, other tags.

4. Experiment with the layer's attributes to see how changing the attributes affects the layer and the document.

How It Works

When the Netscape browser sees the `<ILAYER>` tags, it treats the content between the tags as a single entity. The user can then position this layer away from its natural position. A change to one of the layer's attributes affects all the content in the layer. The following document shows a very basic use of inflow layers. The example is very similar to the one used in How-To 20.1. Figure 20-2 displays what this document looks like when viewed with Netscape 4.0. Notice the differences between how these inflow layers are rendered compared to the previous example.

```
<HTML>
<HEAD>
<TITLE>Layers Demo 20-2</TITLE>
</HEAD>
<BODY>
<H1>Inflow Layers</H1>
Inflow layers appear where they naturally fall within a document.
Notice how the two tags produce dramatically different results from their
non-inflow counterparts. This text is in before the Layers.<BR>
<ILAYER ID="one" LEFT=5 TOP=5>
<IMG SRC="red.gif">This layer is positioned 5 pixels left and
5 down from its natural position.
</LAYER>
<ILAYER ID="two" LEFT=10 TOP=2>
<IMG SRC="green.gif">This layer is positioned 10 pixels left and 2
 down from its. Natural position.
</LAYER>
<HR>
This text is after the layers. Notice how the layers flow naturally within
the document, thus you can subtly nudge layers where you would like them.
</BODY>
</HTML>
```

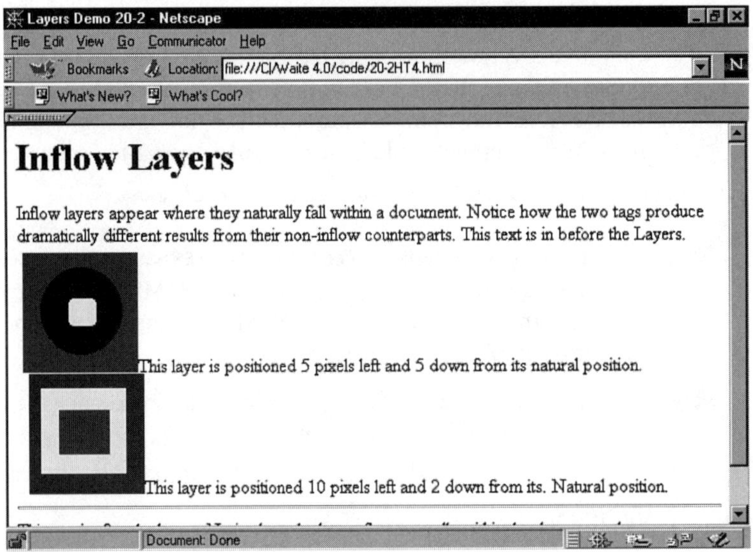

Figure 20-2 A simple inflow layer

Comments

Inflow layers are another useful addition to HTML. They give a Web page designer the ability to finely position a block of elements in a document.

20.3 How do I...
Create a layer using style sheet syntax?

COMPATIBILITY: NETSCAPE 4.0, INTERNET EXPLORER 4.0

Problem

I would like to use a layer in a document, but I would like both Netscape and Internet Explorer to be able to render this layer. How do I do this?

Technique

To create a layer that can be viewed with either Netscape or Internet Explorer, use `<STYLE>...</STYLE>` tags that contain cascading style sheet syntax that defines a layer. The layer can then be displayed in a document by placing its content between either `<SPAN>...</SPAN>` or `<DIV>...</DIV>` tags and setting the **ID** in the tag to the corresponding **ID** named in the `<STYLE>` definition.

Steps

The following steps show one way to create a layer using style sheet syntax:

1. Create a document that contains the layers. For experimental purposes, it might be best to start with a simple document.

2. In the **<HEAD>** portion of the document, insert the **<STYLE>...</STYLE>** tags, setting the type to **"text/css"**—for example,

```
<HEAD>
<STYLE TYPE="text/css">
<!-- Definitions go here →
</STYLE>
</HEAD>
```

3. Name and declare each layer's attributes between the **<STYLE>... </STYLE>** tags—for example,

```
#mylayer {position:absolute; left:10px top:20px;}
```

4. Use **<SPAN>...</SPAN>** tags to enter the layer's content and place it in the document. Set the **ID** attribute in the tag to its corresponding name defined in the **<STYLE>...</STYLE>** tags—for example,

```
<SPAN id=mylayer>
My layers content goes here.
</SPAN>
```

5. Add corresponding **<SPAN>** tags for each layer you want to use.

6. Experiment with your document.

How It Works

Defining the layers in the **<STYLE>** tags and then displaying them and their content with **<SPAN>** (or **<DIV>**) tags works much like using the **<LAYER>** tag. The layer defined in the **<STYLE>** tags is displayed by the **<SPAN>** tags and rendered accordingly, based on its assigned attributes. The following document shows a simple example:

```
<HTML>
<HEAD>
<STYLE TYPE="text/css">
#green {position:absolute; left:100px; top:150px;}
#red {position:absolute; left:50px; top:200px;}
</STYLE>
<TITLE>Layers Demo 20-3</TITLE>
</HEAD>
<BODY>
<H1>Layers with style sheet syntax</H1>
This text is in before the Layers.<BR>
<SPAN id="red">
```

continued on next page

continued from previous page

```
<IMG SRC="red.gif">left 50 px top 200 px
</SPAN>
<SPAN id="green">
<IMG SRC="green.gif"> left 100 px top 150 px
</SPAN>
<HR>
This text is after the layers.
</BODY>
</HTML>
```

The example is very similar to the one used in How-To 20.1, but now the layers are being defined differently. Figure 20-3 displays what this document looks like when viewed with the latest version of Netscape.

Comments

Although using style sheet syntax to create layers might not be as easy as using the `<LAYER>` tags, it has the advantage of being the one way you can create layers that both Netscape and Internet Explorer are able to render. We should mention, though, that the following attributes available to `<LAYER>` are currently not available when defining layers using style sheet syntax:

- ✔ `PAGEX` and `PAGEY`
- ✔ `ABOVE` and `BELOW` (from the `Z-INDEX`)
- ✔ `CLIP`
- ✔ `OnMouseOver`, `OnMouseOut`, `OnFocus`, `OnBlur`, `Onload`

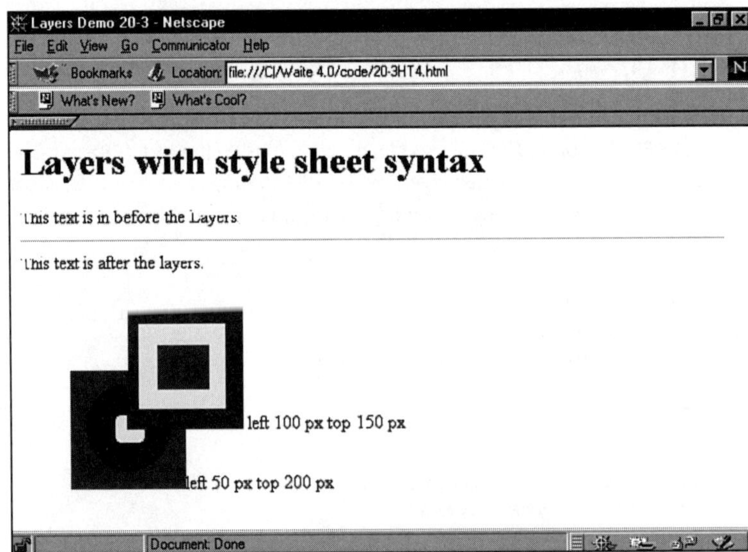

Figure 20-3 A couple of layers created with style sheets

We should also note that you can create inflow layers with style sheet syntax simply by substituting `relative` for `absolute` in the `position` attribute when defining the layer. For the W3C specification on defining layers with style sheets, check out the latest documentation at

```
http://www.w3.org/pub/WWW/TR/WD-positioning
```

Although the following examples in this chapter define layers with the `<LAYER>` tag, the JavaScript routines should work for layers defined with style sheets. For the most part, it should be a simple matter to convert the layers from one way of defining them to another. (As of this writing, defining layers with style sheets is just being implemented.)

COMPLEXITY
ADVANCED

20.4 How do I... Hide and show layers?

COMPATIBILITY: NETSCAPE 4.0

Problem

I would like to have a document with several different layers, yet I want to control which layers are seen and which layers are not. How do I accomplish this?

Technique

The visibility of a layer is controlled by the `VISIBILITY` attribute in the `<LAYER>` tag. If the layer's `VISIBILITY` is set to `SHOW`, that layer will be displayed by the browser. If `VISIBILITY` is set to `HIDE`, then the layer will be invisible. You can use a scripting language such as JavaScript to change the value of `VISIBILITY` based on certain events such as `MouseOver`, `MouseOut`, `OnLoad`, `OnFocus`, and `OnBlur`. The event to trigger and the script to run in case of this event are included in the `<LAYER>` tag. A very general tag follows:

```
<LAYER ID="name" LEFT="number" TOP="number" VISIBILITY="SHOW|HIDE|INHERIT"
OnEvent(parameter)="script_name">
```

In the preceding example, `OnEvent` would be replaced by any of the events named previously. `parameter` is an optional list of a value or values that can be sent to the script (method/function). In this case, `parameter` holds the number of the layer to act on. The script named in the `OnEvent` attribute would then handle the tasks of changing the `VISIBILITY` of the layer specified by the parameter—for example,

```
document.layers["name"].visibility="hide";
```

Steps

The following steps show one way to create show and hide layers:

1. Create a document that contains the layers. For experimental purposes, it might be best to start with a simple document.
2. Insert **<LAYER>** tags for each layer you want to have in the document.
3. Set the attributes for each layer. Important attributes in this case are **VISIBILITY**, the event to trigger changing the visibility, and the name of the script that actually changes the visibility. Remember to include (as the parameter for the script) the identifier of the layer that "called" this script. In this example, you will use

```
<LAYER id="one" LEFT=50 TOP=100 VISIBILITY="SHOW"
OnMouseOver="hideit(1); return false;">
```

4. Create the script named in the event attribute to handle changing the visibility. The script is placed between **<SCRIPT>** tags. The script can appear anywhere in the document. For this example, we are using a very simple script called **hideit()** and placing it at the beginning of the document. If a user positions the mouse over the visible layer, the script is activated. A basic outline of the script would be something like this:

```
<script>
function hideit(n)
//
// note this function could be slicker
//
{
      return;
}

</SCRIPT>>
```

5. Enter the JavaScript code into the script. In this case, the code is very simple. If the layer that calls the script sends a **1** in the event handler parameter, hide the first layer and show the second. If the layer that calls the script sends a **2** (or anything else), hide the second layer and show the first—for example,

```
if (n==1){
          document.layers["one"].visibility="hide";
          document.layers["two"].visibility="show";}
     else
          {
          document.layers["two"].visibility="hide";
          document.layers["one"].visibility="show";}
          }
```

6. Experiment with your document and script to see how different changes affect it.

How It Works

Each layer is assigned a **VISIBILITY** that, when set to **SHOW**, causes the layer to be visible; when set to **HIDE**, the layer is not. JavaScript gives us the ability to access and modify these values.

When a layer is created, it is possible to declare that certain events such as moving the mouse over it, page loading, or receiving keyboard focus will cause certain actions to happen. When one of these specified events occurs, the script named by the event attribute takes action accordingly, based on the parameter it was sent. In this simple example, if the parameter is **1**, then the first layer's visibility is set to **HIDE** and the second layer's is set to **SHOW**. If the parameter sent is not **1**, then the first layer is shown and the second is hidden. The complete example follows:

```
<HTML>
<HEAD>
<TITLE>Hiding 20-4</TITLE>
</HEAD>
<SCRIPT>

function hideit(n)
//
// note this function could be slicker
//
{
      if (n==1){
            document.layers["one"].visibility="hide";
            document.layers["two"].visibility="show";}
      else
            {
            document.layers["two"].visibility="hide";
            document.layers["one"].visibility="show";
            }

      return;
}

</SCRIPT>

<BODY>
<H1>Hide and Show</H1>
Move the mouse over an image. It disappears and the other appears
<LAYER id="one" LEFT=50 TOP=100 VISIBILITY="SHOW"
OnMouseOver="hideit(1);return false;">
<IMG SRC="red.gif">
</LAYER>
<LAYER id="two" LEFT=50 TOP=200 VISIBILITY="HIDE"
 OnMouseOver="hideit(2);return false;">
<IMG SRC="green.gif">
</LAYER>
</BODY>
</HTML>
```

Figure 20-4 shows what happens when this document is loaded. Figure 20-5 shows the result after the cursor moves over the first layer.

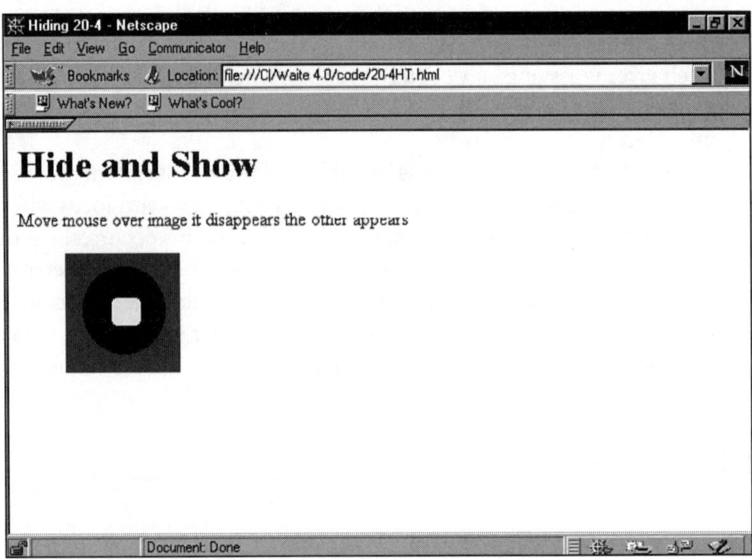

Figure 20-4 An example of hiding and showing layers

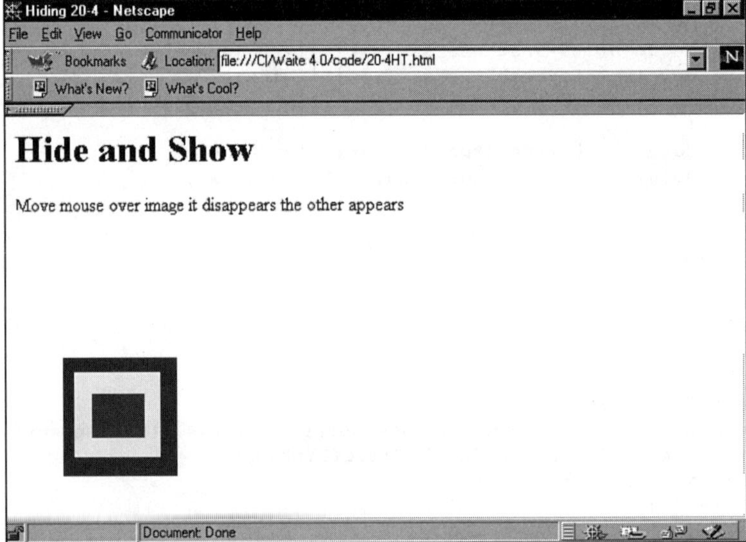

Figure 20-5 The example after the cursor has passed over the first layer

Comments

It is possible to hide and show layers without using a script, but their functionality really increases when you add a little JavaScript. A few comments:

- ✔ For layers nested inside of layers, you can set **VISIBILITY** to **INHERIT** so that the nested layer will automatically have the same **VISIBILITY** as its parent.
- ✔ Layers are assigned numeric IDs based on the order they are declared, with the first layer being layer 0, the second being layer 1, and so on. This example used a separate variable to decide whether we should change the first or second layer. It could have just as easily (but not quite as clearly) sent a 0 or 1.

This example and the others in this chapter are very simple examples of layers and JavaScript interacting.

COMPLEXITY
ADVANCED

20.5 How do I... Switch the stacking order of layers?

COMPATIBILITY: NETSCAPE 4.0

Problem

I would like to have a document with two different layers. Sometimes I would like the first layer to be on top of the second and other times I would like the second to be on top of the first. How do I do this?

Technique

The stacking order of a layer is controlled by the **Z-INDEX** attribute in the **<LAYER>** tag. The higher the **Z-INDEX**, the higher the layer will be stacked. The **Z-INDEX** can also be set to **ABOVE** and **BELOW**. You can use a scripting language such as JavaScript to change the value of **Z-INDEX** based on certain events such as **MouseOver**, **MouseOut**, **OnLoad**, **OnFocus**, and **OnBlur**. The event to trigger and the script to run in case of this event are included in the **<LAYER>** tag. A very general tag follows:

```
<LAYER ID="name" LEFT="number" TOP="number" Z-INDEX=1
OnEvent(parameter)="script_name">
```

In the preceding example, **OnEvent** would be replaced by any of the events named previously. **parameter** is an optional list of values you can send to the script. The script named in the **OnEvent** attribute would then handle the task of changing the **Z-INDEX**—for example,

```
red.zIndex=2;
```

Steps

The following steps show one way to change the **Z-INDEX** of layers:

1. Create a document that contains the layers. For experimental purposes, it might be best to start with a simple document.

2. Insert **<LAYER>** tags for each layer you want to have in the document.

3. Set the attributes for each layer. Important attributes in this case are **Z-INDEX**—for example,

```
<LAYER id="red" LEFT=10 TOP=100 Z-INDEX=2> Layer content</LAYER>
<LAYER id="green" LEFT=15 TOP=120 Z-INDEX=1>Layer Content</LAYER>
```

In this case, the layer called **"red"** would be on top of the layer called **"green"**.

4. Because layers are "event oriented," you must give the users some sort of event they can cause to change the **Z-INDEX**. In this case, build a simple button for them to click.

```
<INPUT TYPE=button VALUE="change stacking"
 OnClick="switchit(); return false;">
```

When a user clicks on this button, the **switchit()** script will be run.

5. Create the **switchit()** script named in the button's event handler. The script is placed between **<SCRIPT>** tags. The script can appear anywhere in the document. A basic outline of the script would be something like

```
<script>
function switchit()
////
{
return;
}
</SCRIPT>>
```

6. Enter the JavaScript code into the script. In this case, the code is very simple. If the layer named **"red"** has a **Z-INDEX** of **1**, then its **Z-INDEX** is changed to **2** and the **"green"** layer's **Z-INDEX** is set to **1**. If the **"red"** layer's **Z-INDEX** isn't **1**, then it is moved below **"green"**. **MoveBelow** is used here just to illustrate its use—for example,

```
var red = document.layers["red"];
var green = document.layers["green"];
if (red.zIndex == 1) {
// put red on top
      red.zIndex=2;
      green.zIndex=1;
}
else {
```

```
// put red below
      red.moveBelow(green);
}
```

7. Experiment with your document and script to see how different changes affect it.

How It Works

Each layer is assigned a **Z-INDEX**; the higher that **Z-INDEX**, the higher a layer is stacked. This **Z-INDEX** is accessible and changeable with JavaScript. The complete example follows:

```
<HTML>
<HEAD>
<TITLE>Switching HT20-5</TITLE>
</HEAD>
<BODY>
<SCRIPT>
function switchit(){
//
// there are two ways to change stacking order
// either directly change the Z-INDEX value or
// by moving a layer above or below another layer - both are shown here
//
      var red = document.layers["red"];
      var green = document.layers["green"];
      if (red.zIndex == 1) {
            // put red on top
            red.zIndex=2;
            green.zIndex=1;
      }
      else {
            // put red below
            red.moveBelow(green);
      }
      return;
}

</SCRIPT>
<H1>Switching Stacking Order</H1>
<LAYER id="red" LEFT=10 TOP=100 Z-INDEX=2>
<IMG SRC="red.gif">
</LAYER>
<LAYER id="green" LEFT=15 TOP=120 Z-INDEX=1>
<IMG SRC="green.gif">
</LAYER>
<FORM>
        <INPUT type=button value="Change stacking" OnClick="
switchit(); return false;">
        </FORM>
</BODY>
</HTML>
```

If you are not used to working with variable names, then this example might seem a bit more complex than it really is. The first two `var` statements declare two variables, one for the layer named `"red"` and one for the layer named `"green"`. This enables you to access and change those layers' attributes easily by using the dot (`.`) method—`layer_name.attribute`.

The `if` block checks to see whether the red layer's `Z-INDEX` is `1`. If so, the top part of the block sets the red `Z-INDEX` to `2` and the green `Z-INDEX` to `1`. If not, the bottom part of the block simply moves the red layer below the green. (In effect, setting its `Z-INDEX` to a lower number than the green's.)

Figure 20-6 shows this document when it is loaded. Figure 20-7 shows the change in the document after a user clicks the button.

Comments

It is possible to set the `Z-INDEX` of layers without using a script, but their functionality really increases when you add a little JavaScript.

Remember, the higher the `Z-INDEX`, the higher the layer's priority will be.

This example and the others in this chapter are very simple examples of layers and JavaScript interacting.

It is possible to make a layer transparent by setting its background color to `null`: `layer.bgcolor = null;`.

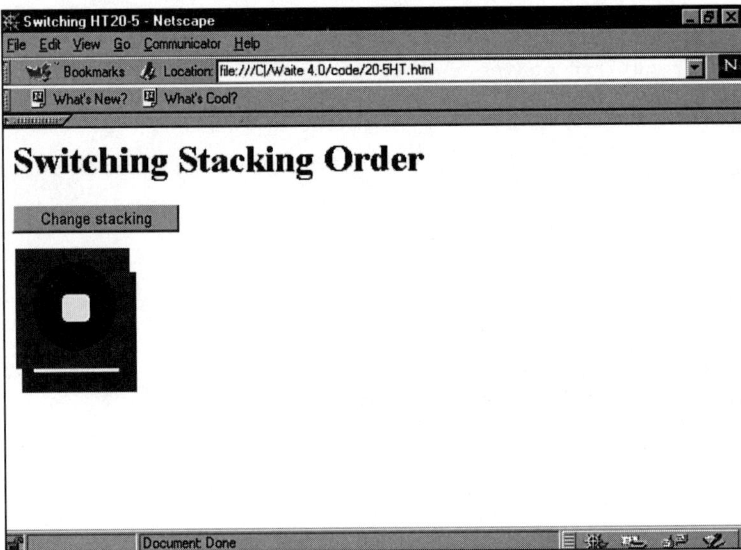

Figure 20-6 The initial stacking order

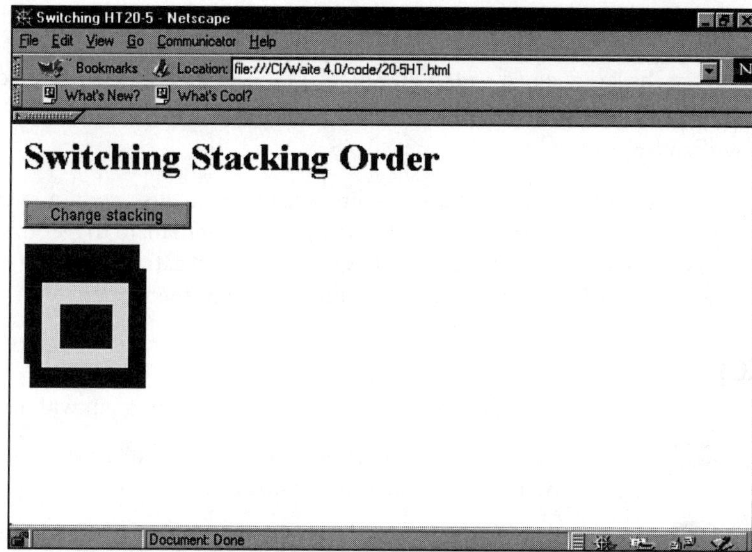

Figure 20-7 The new stacking order

COMPLEXITY
ADVANCED

20.6 How do I... Dynamically move layers to create animation?

COMPATIBILITY: NETSCAPE 4.0

Problem

I have a layer, but it's kind of boring just sitting there on the screen. I would like to have it move around some. How do I do this?

Technique

When layers are declared with the `<LAYER>` tag, they are assigned values for their left and top corners. These values can be changed by the JavaScript function `moveBy(x,y)` or `moveTo(x,y)`. `moveBy(x,y)` works by adding the x and y to the specified layer's coordinates. `moveTo(x,y)` moves the layer to the specified x and y coordinates. For example, the following would move the layer named `red` over 10 horizontal pixels:

```
red.moveBy(10,0);
```

(The layer's left coordinate would have 10 added to it. Remember that this left coordinate is actually the distance from the left corner.) The following function would move the layer named **red** to a position 100 pixels to the left of the top of the screen and 100 pixels down:

```
red.moveTo(100,100);
```

It is possible, as in the preceding examples, to use certain events such as **MouseOver**, **MouseOut**, **OnLoad**, **OnFocus**, and **OnBlur** to trigger the movement. These events can be keyed to the layer itself or to an external piece of content such as a button. This example will use a button to start the motion.

Steps

The following steps show one way to create simple animation with layers:

1. Create a document that contains the layers. For experimental purposes, it might be best to start with a simple document.
2. Insert **<LAYER>** tags for each layer you want to have in the document. For this example, use only one.
3. Set the attributes for the layer. Important attributes in this case are **ID**, **LEFT**, and **TOP**—for example,

```
<LAYER id="red" LEFT=10 TOP=130> Layer content</LAYER>
```

In this case, the layer called **"red"** would be positioned 10 pixels from the left corner of the screen and 130 from the top.

4. Because layers are event oriented, you must give the user some sort of event he or she can use to change the layer's position. To make things simple, build a simple button for users to click.

```
<INPUT TYPE=button VALUE="Move the box" OnClick="moveit(); return false;">
```

When a user clicks on this button, the **moveit()** script will run.

5. Create the **moveit()** script named in the button's event handler. The script is placed between **<SCRIPT>** tags. The script can appear anywhere in the document. A basic outline of the script would be something like this:

```
<script>
function moveit(){
{
      return;
}
</SCRIPT>
```

6. Enter the JavaScript code into the script. In this case, the code is simple. If the layer's left coordinate (distance from the left corner) is less than 400 pixels, then 10 pixels are added to the left coordinate—for example,

```
var red = document.layers["red"];
if (red.left<400){
        red.moveBy(10,0);}
else { red.left=10;}
return;
}
```

7. Because you are doing a repetitive task (something you want repeated over and over) you must tell the browser how often you want to repeat the function. To do that, use the **setTimeout** function.

```
setTimeout(moveit,10);
```

This function call will be placed right before the **return;** statement. It will automatically call the **moveit** function every 10/1000 of a second.

8. Experiment with your document and script to see how different values affect it.

How It Works

Every layer has certain x (**LEFT**) and y (**TOP**) coordinates. These coordinates are accessible and changeable with JavaScript. The complete example follows:

```
<HTML>
<HEAD>
<TITLE>Moving HT 20-6</TITLE>
<BODY>
<H1>Moving</H1>
<LAYER id="red" LEFT=10 TOP=130>
<IMG SRC="red.gif">
</LAYER>

<SCRIPT>
//
// simple move function
// note moveBy was once called offset
//
function moveit(){
var red = document.layers["red"];
if (red.left<400){
      red.moveBy(10,0);}
else { red.left=10;}
setTimeout(moveit,10);
return;
}
</SCRIPT>
<FORM>
         <INPUT type=button value="Move the box"
         OnClick="moveit(); return false;">
         </FORM>
</BODY>
</HTML>
```

If you are not used to working with variable names, then this example might also seem a bit more complex than it really is. The `var` statement declares a variable for the layer `"red"`. This enables you to access and change that layer's position easily.

The `if` block checks the red layer's horizontal position. If the position is less than 400 pixels, the position is increased by 10 pixels. If the position is greater than 400 pixels, the position is set back to 10 pixels. The effect is that the content of the layer (a red box) moves across the screen.

The **`setTimeout`** function is a built-in JavaScript function with the basic format of

```
setTimeOut("code executed, delay)
```

The code named in **`code executed`** will be repeated every **`delay`** milliseconds. Here the function causes the entire **`moveit`** function to be repeated every 10/1000 of a second.

Figure 20-8 shows this document when it is loaded. Figure 20-9 shows the change in the document after a user clicks the button.

Comments

It is possible to set the left and top coordinates of layers without using a script, but their functionality really increases when you add a little JavaScript.

To move a layer to an exact coordinate on the screen, you can use the JavaScript function **`moveTo(x,y)`**.

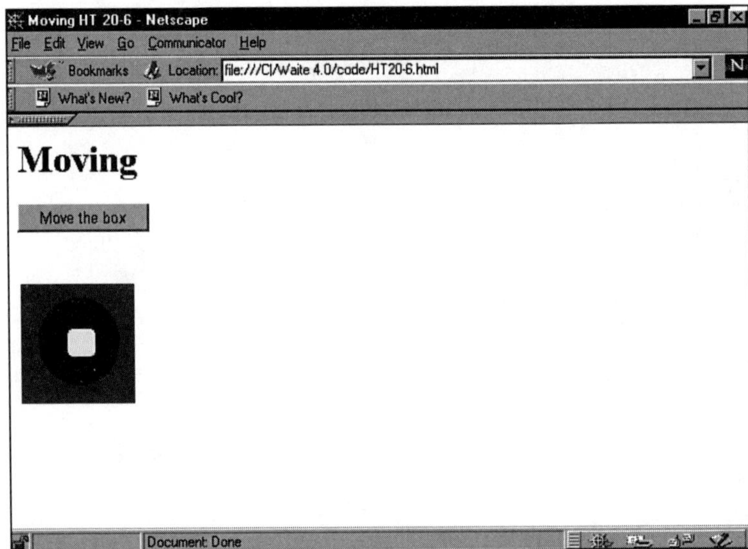

Figure 20-8 The initial box

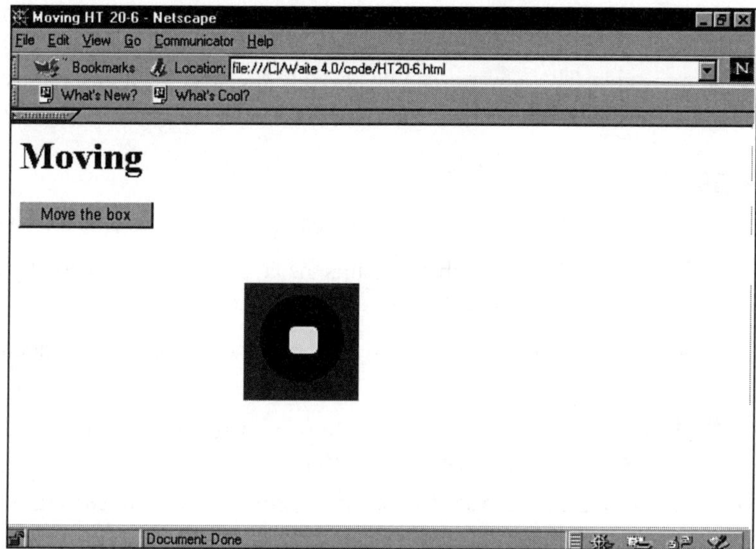

Figure 20-9 The moving box

COMPLEXITY
ADVANCED

20.7 How do I... Set and change the clipping area of a layer?

COMPATIBILITY: NETSCAPE 4.0

Problem

I have a layer that I would like to show different parts of at different times. How do I do this?

Technique

When layers are declared with the `<LAYER>` tag, they can be assigned values for a clip rectangle or the area of the layer that can be viewed. The values can be any of four numbers: left value, top value, right value, or bottom value. Or these values can be two numbers, right and bottom, in which case the top and left are assumed to be zero. These values are called `clip.top`, `clip.left`, `clip.right`, and `clip.bottom`. These can be accessed and changed via JavaScript. Two other values, `clip.width` and `clip.height`, are also available. If no clip area is set in the `<LAYER>` tag, the entire layer is viewable.

It is possible, as in the preceding examples, to use certain events such as **MouseOver**, **MouseOut**, **OnLoad**, **OnFocus**, and **OnBlur** to trigger the change in the clipping area. These events can be keyed to the layer itself or to an external piece of content such as a button. This example will use a button to start the motion.

Steps

The following steps show one way to change the clipping area of a layer:

1. Create a document that contains the layers. For experimental purposes, it might be best to start with a simple document.

2. Insert **<LAYER>** tags for each layer you want to have in the document. For this example, use only one.

3. Set the attributes for the layer. Important attributes in this case are **ID**, **LEFT**, **TOP**, and **CLIP**—for example,

```
<LAYER id="mylayer" LEFT=10 TOP=130 CLIP=10,20> Layer content</LAYER>
```

In this case, the layer called **mylayer** would be positioned 10 pixels from the left of the screen and 130 from the top. Only the first 10 horizontal and 20 vertical pixels will be viewable.

4. Because layers are event oriented, you must give users some sort of event they can trigger to change the layer's position. To make things simple, build a simple button for them to click.

```
<INPUT TYPE=button VALUE="Increase the Clip Area"
 OnClick="clipit(); return false;">
```

When a user clicks on this button, the **clipit()** script will run.

5. Create the **clipit()** script named in the button's event handler. The script is placed between **<SCRIPT>** tags. The script can appear anywhere in the document. A basic outline of the script would be something like this:

```
<script>
function clipit(){
{
      return;
}
</SCRIPT>
```

6. Enter the JavaScript code into the script. In this case, the code is simple. If the layer's left coordinate is less than 510 pixels, then 1 pixel is added to the left coordinate—for example,

```
var mylayer = document.layers["mylayer"];
if (mylayer.clip.right<510){
      mylayer.clip.right++;}
```

```
else { mylayer.clip.right=10;}
return;
}
```

7. Because you are doing a repetitive task (something you want repeated over and over), you must tell the browser how often you want to repeat the function. To do that, use the **setTimeout** function.

```
setTimeout(clipit,10);
```

This function call would be placed right before the **return;** statement. It will automatically recall the function every 10/1000 of a second.

8. Experiment with your document and script to see how different changes affect it.

How It Works

Every layer has clip coordinates. These coordinates are accessible and changeable with JavaScript. The complete example follows:

```
<HTML>
<HEAD>
<TITLE>Clipping HT20-7</TITLE>
<BODY>
<H1>Clipping</H1>
<LAYER id="mylayer" LEFT=10 TOP=130 CLIP=10,20>
<BIG><P>This is line 1. Experiment with the clip parameters
to see what happens!
<P>This is line 2</BIG>
</LAYER>

<SCRIPT>
//
// simple function
//
function clipit(){
      var mylayer = document.layers["mylayer"];
      if (mylayer.clip.right<510){
             mylayer.clip.right++;}
       else {mylayer.clip.right=10;}
      setTimeout(clipit,10);
return;
}
</SCRIPT>
<FORM>
         <INPUT type=button value="Increase the clip area"
 OnClick="clipit(); return false;">
</FORM>
</BODY>
</HTML>
```

If you are not used to working with variable names, then this example might seem a bit more complex than it really is. The `var` statement declares a variable for the layer `"mylayer"`. This enables you to access and change that layer's clip variables easily.

The `if` block checks to see whether the layer's `right.clip` position is less than 510 pixels. If so, the position is increased by 1 pixel. If not, the position is set back 10 pixels. The effect is that more and more of the content of the layer becomes visible.

The `setTimeout` function causes the entire `clipit` function to be repeated every 10/1000 of a second.

Figure 20-10 shows this document when it is loaded. Figure 20-11 shows the change in the document after a user clicks the button.

Comments

You can create some pretty nifty effects with layers, clipping, and a little JavaScript.

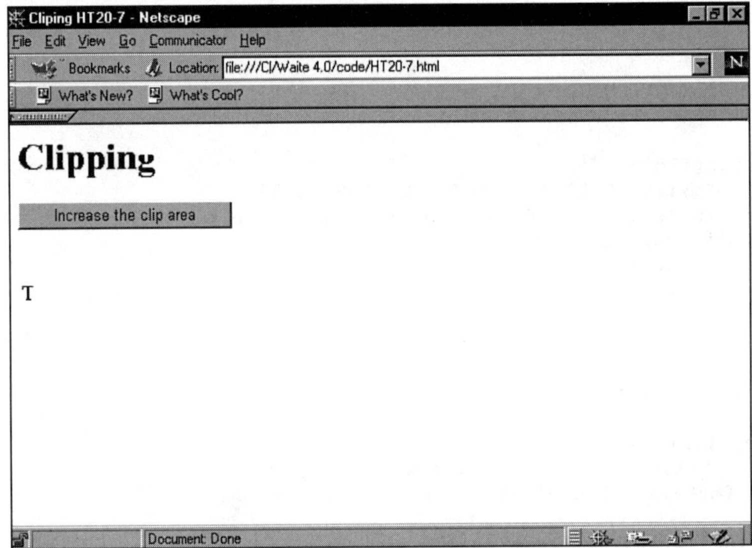

Figure 20-10 The initial clipping area

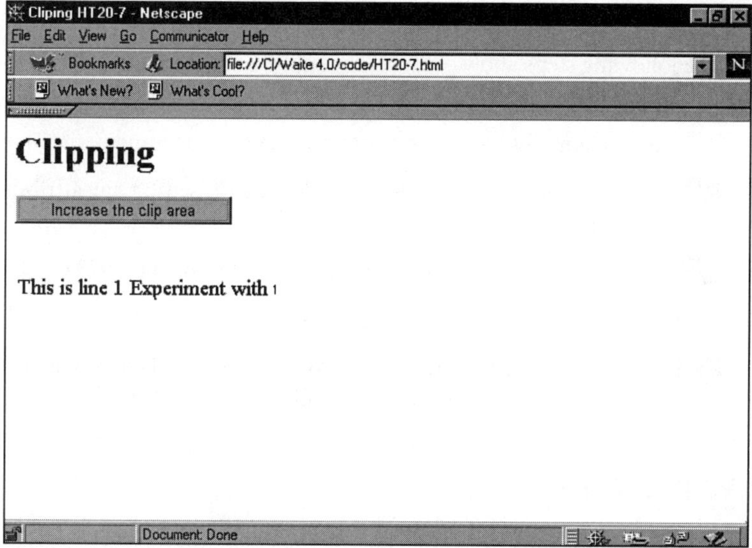

Figure 20-11 The view after a few seconds

COMPLEXITY
INTERMEDIATE

20.8 How do I... Protect browsers that don't support layers?

COMPATIBILITY: NETSCAPE 4.0

Problem

I would like to use layers in a document, but I would like to warn people with browsers that don't support layers. How do I do this?

Technique

You can use the **<NOLAYER>...</NOLAYER>** tags to surround content that will be ignored by Netscape 4.0. This lets you tell folks using other browsers what they are missing.

Steps

The following steps show one way to handle browsers that don't support layers:

1. Create a document that contains the inflow layer. For experimental purposes, it might be best to start with a simple document.
2. Insert any **<LAYER>** tags into the document, setting any attributes you want to use.
3. Insert the layer's content between the **<LAYER>** tags.
4. Insert **<NOLAYER>...</NOLAYER>** tags.
5. Enter the content between the **<NOLAYER>** tags. This is what browsers that do not support Netscape layers will see.

How It Works

When the Netscape 4.0 browser spots **<NOLAYER>** tags, it ignores the content between them. All other browsers will display the content between these tags instead of the layers.

Comments

As of this writing, the **<NOLAYER>** tags are not very well documented.

The following example is a little added extra to the chapter. It's a complete "game" written entirely in HTML with layers and JavaScript. This is just to show that a little layers can go a long way. Listing 20-1 is a clip from the game. You might want to examine this code to see a "complete" JavaScript layers application in action.

Listing 20-1 A simple JavaScript and layers game

```
<HTML>
<HEAD>
<TITLE>Mouse'm</TITLE>
<SCRIPT>
//
// set global variables
//
var timeId;
var c;
var sc;
var high=3;

//
// tell the user what's going on
//
function greet(){
     alert("Click Start, then move the mouse over anything that appears
below the line. The faster you do the more you score.  You have 30 seconds.
This is a simple game that uses Layers just to show some of the cool
things you can do. (Check out the source to see how easy it is to do
```

```
stuff like this with Layers!  I did this within a day of discovering
Layers.)");
      return;
}
//
// pick a random number
//
function picknum(h){
      num=parseInt(Math.random()*h+1);
return(num);
}
//
// initial house cleaning
//
function init(){
      c=0;
      sc=0;
      document.layers["over"].visibility="hide"; //just in case
      showTime();
      for (x=0; x<=high; x++){
            putit(x);}
return;
}
//
// this function runs every second --
//  if time is up it stops -- else it updates the timer
//
function showTime() {
      document.myform.tme.value = c;
      c++;
      if (c < 30) {
            timerId=setTimeout("showTime();",1000)
      }
      else {
            document.myform.tme.value="game over";
            for (x=0; x<=high; x++) {
                  document.layers[x].visibility="hide";
            }
            document.layers["over"].visibility="show";

      }
      return;
}
//
// the currently visible layer has been clicked on -- hide it and ⇐
show another
//
function putit(n)
{

      document.layers[n].visibility="hide";
      document.layers[n].moveTo(picknum(550),(picknum(145)+56))
      document.layers[n].visibility="show";
      sc++;
      document.myform.score.value = sc;
```

continued on next page

continued from previous page

```
      return;
}

</SCRIPT>

<BODY onLoad="greet();">

<TABLE align="center">
<FORM Name="myform">
<TR>
<TD bgcolor="00FFFF"><BIG>Mouse'm Game</BIG></TD>
<TD><INPUT TYPE="button" NAME="startButton" VALUE="start"
 onClick="init();"></TD>
<TD>Time: <INPUT TYPE="text" NAME="tme" SIZE="10"></TD>
<TD>Score: <INPUT TYPE="text" NAME="score" SIZE="10"></TD>
</FORM>
</TR>
</TABLE>

<HR>
<LAYER ID="zero" LEFT=50 TOP=100 VISIBILITY="HIDE"
 OnMouseOver ="putit(0);return false;">
<IMG SRC="green.gif" width=50 height=50>
</LAYER>
<LAYER ID="one" LEFT=50 TOP=300 VISIBILITY="HIDE"
OnMouseOver ="putit(1);return false;">
<FONT color="FF0000"><H3>Netscape</H3></FONT>
</LAYER>
<LAYER ID="two" LEFT=50 TOP=300 VISIBILITY="HIDE"
 OnMouseOver ="putit(2);return false;">
<FONT color="0000FF"><H3>Cool!</H3></FONT></LAYER>
<LAYER ID="three" LEFT=50 TOP=300 VISIBILITY="HIDE"
 OnMouseOver ="putit(3);return false;">
<FONT color="FF00FF"><H3>Layers</H3></FONT>
</LAYER>
<LAYER ID="over" LEFT=200 TOP=100 VISIBILITY="HIDE">
<TABLE><TR><TD bgcolor="FFFF00"><H1>Game Over</H1></TD></TR>
<TR><TD><A Href="http://www.psnw.com/~jmz5/jgames/">Back to Menu</A>⇐
</TD></TR>
</TABLE>
</LAYER>

</BODY>
</HTML>
```

CHAPTER 21

DYNAMIC STYLE SHEETS AND FONTS

21

DYNAMIC STYLE SHEETS AND FONTS

How do I...

In Chapter 16, "Cascading Style Sheets," we talked about cascading style sheets (CSS), a technology that gives Web page designers the power to define the layout of a Web page in ways not possible using simple HTML. These style sheets give page designers the ability to define colors, font characteristics, margins, and other aspects of page layout without resorting to browser-specific tricks or other techniques that do not render well on older browsers.

Cascading style sheets are not the only way to do this, however. Netscape has introduced a similar, but somewhat different, technology called dynamic style sheets (sometimes called JavaScript style sheets) in version 4.0 of Netscape Navigator. Dynamic style sheets are a combination of CSS and JavaScript: They use a syntax like that used in JavaScript, but offer most of the same features as CSS. The advantage of dynamic style sheets over CSS is that dynamic sheets can be altered by JavaScript routines (as the name suggests). The disadvantage is that they are supported only in the latest version of Netscape Navigator, with no guarantees of support in future versions of other browsers such as Microsoft Internet Explorer.

This chapter provides a basic introduction to dynamic style sheets and their use in Web pages. The full syntax used by dynamic style sheets is too comprehensive to be explained fully in this chapter, although Netscape maintains a complete reference to the features of dynamic style sheets on its Web site (`http://developer.netscape.com/library/documentation/communicator/dynhtml/index.htm`). Refer there for the full list of keywords and methods supported by dynamic style sheets.

21.1 Learn the Basics of Dynamic Style Sheets

If you're familiar with CSS and know at least a little bit about JavaScript, then the syntax used by dynamic style sheets will be easy to learn. This How-To introduces the basic syntax of dynamic style sheets and their capabilities to improve Web pages.

21.2 Define Styles in the Document Header

As with CSS, you can define styles for a Web page using dynamic style sheets in the header of the document. This How-To shows how to include the style information in the document header.

21.3 Specify a Style for a Particular Element

Although you can define a style that will be used throughout an entire document, there might be situations in which you want a style used just for a single element or section of a page. This How-To shows how to define a style for a particular element on a Web page.

21.4 Define a Class of Styles

If you have a set of style commands commonly used in different sections of a document, it might be more convenient to define those style commands as a single class and then to just refer to that class when it is needed in your page. This How-To explores how to define a class of style statements that can be used throughout a Web page.

21.5 Identify a Unique Style

There might be situations in which you need an exception to the styles used in your document and want a separate style defined instead. If there are several similar cases like this in a document, it might be more efficient to identify that particular circumstance and the style to be used there. This How-To explains how to identify unique styles that can be used and reused on a Web page.

21.6 Define a Style in a Particular Context

It can be useful to change the definition of the style of an element based on its context or where in a document it is located relative to other tags. This How-To explains how to use the JavaScript `contextual()` method to define styles for elements based on where specific page elements are located in a document.

21.7 Specify an External Style Sheet

If you're using the same style definitions over a set of documents, it is more efficient to define the styles in a separate document and then include a reference to those styles in each page rather than duplicating the entire set of style definition in each page. This How-To shows how to create external style sheet definitions and include them in your Web pages.

21.8 Include a Dynamic Font in a Page

Netscape Navigator 4.0 enables document authors not only to specify the font to use to display text but, with new TrueDoc technology, to provide the fonts that the browser will automatically download and display on the screen, even if the user doesn't have the specified font on his or her system. This How-To shows how to include such dynamic fonts on a page.

21.9 Specify the Size and Weight of a Dynamic Font

With dynamic fonts, you can specify the exact point size and weight of the font. This How-To shows how to include information about point size and weight of a font on a Web page.

21.10 Use JavaScript to Manipulate Dynamic Style Sheets

As the name suggests, dynamic style sheets are not static definitions of styles but can be modified using JavaScript routines. Although the degree to which you can modify style sheets on the fly is still limited, it can be a useful way to modify the appearance of a Web page without extensive editing of the style sheets. This How-To goes over the basics of using JavaScript to modify style sheets.

COMPLEXITY
ADVANCED

21.1 How do I... Learn the basics of dynamic style sheets?

COMPATIBILITY: NETSCAPE 4.0

Problem

I'm familiar with cascading style sheets and would like to start experimenting with dynamic style sheets. I have some knowledge of JavaScript, but I'm not an expert in it. What are the basics of dynamic style sheets that I must know to be able to start using them?

Technique

If you're familiar with CSS (refer to Chapter 16, "Cascading Style Sheets") and have some basic knowledge of JavaScript (refer to Chapter 17, "Web Programming with Java and JavaScript"), then the transition to dynamic style sheets will be simple and straightforward. Even if you're not familiar with one or both, you'll find that it will take only a little effort to start creating and using dynamic style sheets in your documents.

Dynamic style sheets combine the general definitions of CSS with the basic syntax used by JavaScript. Both cascading and dynamic versions of style sheets use the **<STYLE>** tag to define styles and can use the **CLASS** and **ID** attributes of other tags to define styles.

There are some differences between the two style sheet methods, though. The steps in this How-To cover some of the basics of dynamic style sheets and how they differ from CSS; other How-To's in this chapter go into more detail on specific ways to implement dynamic style sheets in your documents.

Steps

You need a copy of Netscape Navigator 4.0 on your computer system to be able to see the results of any dynamic style sheets you create because it is the only browser that currently supports dynamic style sheets. It will be very helpful to review Chapter 16 first, because many of the style definitions used there are applied here as well.

1. The biggest difference between cascading and dynamic style sheets is the syntax used to define the styles. Dynamic style sheets use a JavaScript-like syntax for definitions of style elements in a page instead of the CSS format. Fortunately, though, most of the definitions of terms are the same. As a rule,

- ✔ Names of single-word style properties, such as **color** and **align**, are the same in both style sheets.
- ✔ Two-word style properties that are in all lowercase with the words separated by a hyphen in CSS are used in dynamic style sheets without the hyphen and with the first letter of the second word capitalized. For example, **font-family** in CSS becomes **fontFamily** in dynamic style sheets and **text-decoration** becomes **textDecoration**.

2. This change in syntax reflects differences in how the styles are defined in the two style sheet methods. If you wanted the text of all the level 1 headings (**<H1>**) in a document to be green, you would use the following style in header of the document:

```
<STYLE TYPE="text/css">
     H1 {color: green;}
</STYLE>
```

However, using dynamic style sheets, the definition is somewhat different:

```
<STYLE TYPE="text/javascript">
     tags.H1.color = "green";
</STYLE>
```

More information on defining styles in dynamic style sheets is discussed starting in How-To 21.2.

3. Both cascading and dynamic style sheets support several different style properties that page designers can use. These properties are divided into several different groups that modify different aspects of the page:

- ✔ Font properties, which modify the font face, size, style, and weight
- ✔ Text properties, which modify the line height, alignment, decoration, and case of the displayed text
- ✔ "Block-level" formatting, which adjusts the margins, borders, padding, and alignment for elements such as paragraphs and headings
- ✔ Color properties, which modify the color of the text or background or add a background image
- ✔ Classification properties, which modify the style of lists and the use of white space

As discussed in step 1, the names of these style properties are slightly different in cascading and dynamic style sheets due to differences in the syntax of the two style sheet definitions.

Figure 21-1 shows an example of a dynamic style sheet in use.

Figure 21-2 shows what the same document looks like in a browser that doesn't support dynamic style sheets.

How It Works

Both cascading and dynamic style sheets require browsers to be able to parse the definitions of the styles as listed in the document and then render the document on the screen as defined. Both style sheets have similar capabilities and definitions, but their syntax is somewhat different.

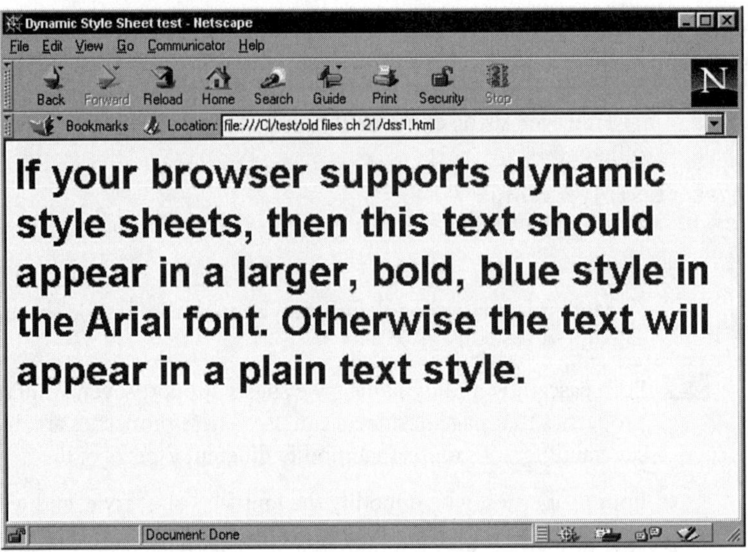

Figure 21-1 A dynamic style sheet in use in Netscape

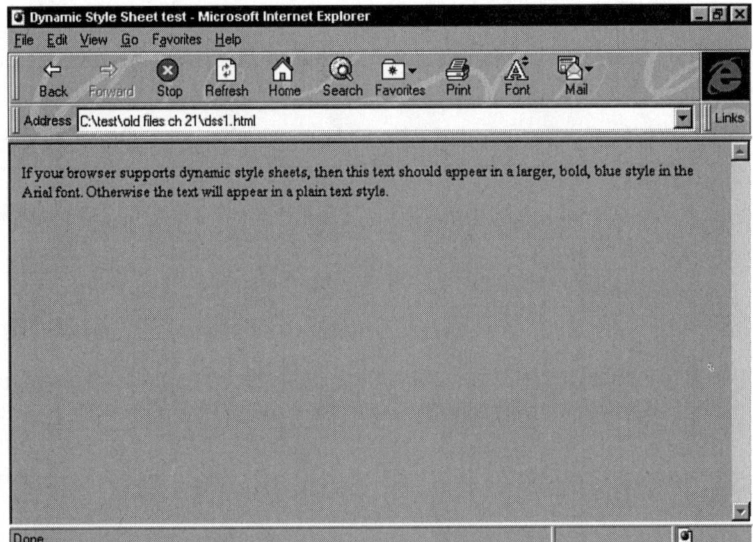

Figure 21-2 The same document as it appears in a browser that doesn't support dynamic style sheets

Comments

As of this writing, only Netscape Navigator 4.0 can support dynamic style sheets. It's not certain whether other browser makers will support dynamic style sheets in the future; Microsoft, for example, has its own plans for dynamic HTML that differ from Netscape's. The World Wide Web Consortium (W3C) has yet to weigh in on dynamic style sheets, although it wholeheartedly supports CSS. Thus, you'll want to consider carefully whether you want to use dynamic style sheets on the open Web, where perhaps only a minority of visitors will be using the appropriate browser. However, if you're willing to make that trade-off or you are designing pages in a closed environment such an intranet where all users will be using the same browser, dynamic style sheets can be a good method to use to modify the styles of documents.

COMPLEXITY
ADVANCED

21.2 How do I... Define styles in the document header?

COMPATIBILITY: NETSCAPE 4.0

Problem

I would like to use dynamic style sheets to define a set of styles for my document in the header of the document. These styles would be applied throughout the document. How can I define these styles?

Technique

As briefly discussed in How-To 21.1, styles can be defined in a document in a similar manner for both cascading and dynamic style sheets, although there are important differences in syntax. These style definitions can be placed in the header of the document and are applied throughout the document unless overridden by style markup for a specific section of a page.

Steps

1. Open the document to which you would like to add styles in your preferred editor. You need a copy of Netscape Navigator 4.0 to preview the results because that is the only browser that supports dynamic style sheets.

2. Like cascading style sheets, dynamic style sheets use the **<STYLE>** tag to define a set of styles in the document. However, the **TYPE** attribute for dynamic style sheets is different: **"text/javascript"** instead of **"text/css"**. Thus, in the header of your document, you can enter

```
<STYLE TYPE="text/javascript">

</STYLE>
```

3. Older browsers that don't support style sheets ignore the **<STYLE>** tags; however, they might try to display the text contained within the **<STYLE>** tags. To prevent this from happening, place HTML comment tags just after the **<STYLE>** tag and just before the **</STYLE>** tag. Comments are used as in JavaScript, so a JavaScript comment tag (**//**) will be needed before the closing comment tag.

```
<STYLE TYPE="text/javascript">
<!--

// -->
</STYLE>
```

4. Now you can start defining the styles for the document. The format for style sheet definitions in dynamic style sheets follows this format: **tags.ELEMENT.property**, where

- ✔ **tags** is the JavaScript object used for all definitions of styles for a particular HTML element.
- ✔ **ELEMENT** is the name of the HTML element, or tag, that will be modified by the style. Elements are written in uppercase, such as **H1** and **P**, not **h1** and **p**.
- ✔ **property** is the style sheet property used to modify the appearance of the specified HTML element throughout the document.

For example, to change the style of a level 2 heading (**<H2>**) so that it appears in a sans-serif font, enter

```
<STYLE TYPE="text/javascript">
<!--
    tags.H2.fontFamily = "sans-serif"
// -->
</STYLE>
```

5. Although each line of a style sheet can define only one property of a style sheet, you can include several different definitions for each element and for several different elements within the <STYLE> tags by placing each on a separate line. To add to the preceding example by making level 2 headings orange and defining the left and right margins of paragraphs to be 20 pixels wide, enter

```
<STYLE TYPE="text/javascript">
<!--
      tags.H2.fontFamily = "sans-serif"
      tags.H2.color = "orange"
      tags.P.marginLeft = 20
      tags.P.marginRight = 20
// -->
</STYLE>
```

Figure 21-3 shows an example of how the style sheet defined above would display text in Netscape.

How It Works

When a document is loaded into a browser that supports dynamic style sheets, the browser reads the definitions listed in the document for the style properties of the tags defined there. The browser then uses those properties to render the document on the page.

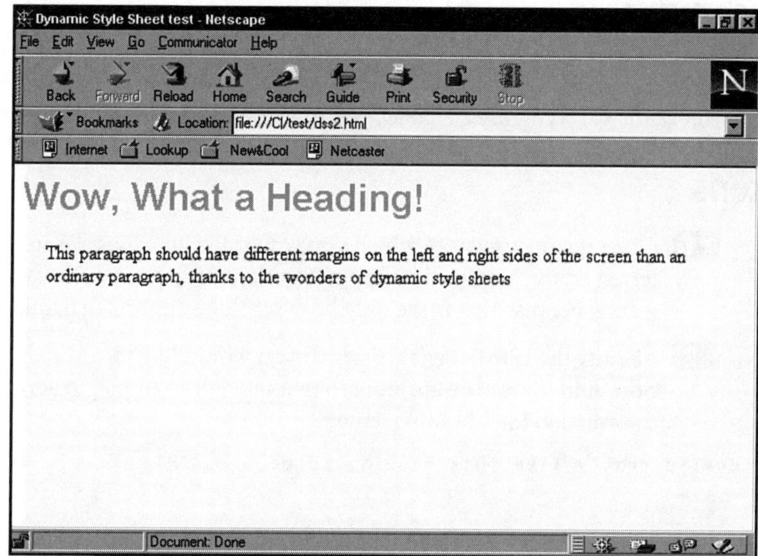

Figure 21-3 Using styles defined in the header of a document in a dynamic style sheet

Comments

If two or more different definitions are given for the same style for the same HTML element, the browser uses the last version defined. For example, if the style definition first sets the color of paragraphs to green and then later sets it to blue, the paragraphs will appear blue because that was the later definition. Although it's unlikely that you would give different definitions for the same style, this knowledge can help you debug any problems you notice with your style sheets.

COMPLEXITY
ADVANCED

21.3 How do I... Specify a style for a particular element?

COMPATIBILITY: NETSCAPE 4.0

Problem

Rather than define a style that will appear throughout a document, I want to alter the style of a particular element on my page. How can I do this using dynamic style sheets as simply as possible?

Technique

For special cases when you want to modify the style of a single element on the page, you can apply the **STYLE** attribute to that tag. This attribute, which Netscape Navigator 4.0 recognizes, enables you to enter style information directly.

Steps

1. Open the document to which you would like to add styles in your preferred editor. You need a copy of Netscape Navigator 4.0 to preview the results because that is the only browser that supports dynamic style sheets.

2. Identify the HTML tag(s) to which you would like to add style information. Add the **STYLE** attribute to that tag. For example, to add style information for a heading, enter

```
<H1 STYLE=>I'd really like this heading to be blue</H1>
```

3. Within the set of double quotes, you can now enter style information. Include the style property (color, margin, alignment, and so on) and the value you want to change it to. In the preceding example, to make the heading blue, enter

```
<H1 STYLE="color = 'blue'">I'd really like this heading to be blue</H1>
```

4. You can also apply style information directly to a document with the **<SPAN>** tag. Place the **<SPAN>** tag at the beginning of the text whose style you'd like to change and the **</SPAN>** tag at the end of the text.

```
<P>This is normal text, <SPAN>but I'd like this to be bold,</SPAN> and
back to normal again.
```

5. Now add the **STYLE** attribute to the **<SPAN>** tag and set it equal to the style changes you want to make to the text, as described in step 2:

```
<P>This is normal text, <SPAN STYLE="fontWeight = 'bold'">but I'd like
this to be bold,</SPAN> and back to normal again.
```

How It Works

A browser that supports dynamic style sheets will go through the document and look for any style definitions embedded within the HTML tags themselves, in addition to style sheet information located in the header, and take the appropriate action to modify the document.

Comments

If you define styles in the document header and define them in the body of the document as outlined in this How-To, the styles in the body of the document will override the styles in the header. This method is not suggested for anything more than minor style changes. Later How-To's show other methods of changing the style of specific elements in the body of a document that are more flexible and easier to implement.

COMPLEXITY
ADVANCED

21.4 How do I... Define a class of styles?

COMPATIBILITY: NETSCAPE 4.0

Problem

I'd like to make some basic changes in the style of my document in specific places but do not want to define the style for each case manually. Is there a way to define a certain set of style changes that can easily be applied to the elements I want to change?

Technique

Like cascading style sheets, dynamic style sheets support *classes*, or sets of style changes for a document. A class can be defined to change the style in a specific way for any element it is applied to, and classes can be used to identify logical sets of style changes that might be different for different HTML elements. The style changes can be applied directly to each HTML element or applied to part of a document with the **<SPAN>** tag.

Steps

1. Open the document to which you would like to add styles in your preferred editor. You need a copy of Netscape Navigator 4.0 to preview the results because that is the only browser that supports dynamic style sheets.

2. Classes of styles are defined within the **<STYLE>...</STYLE>** markup in the header of a document, so set the **<STYLE>** markup as described in How-To 21.2.

```
<STYLE TYPE="text/javascript">
<!--

// -->
</STYLE>
```

3. The syntax for defining classes in dynamic style sheets is ***classes.classname.element.property***, where

- ***classes*** is a JavaScript object used to define classes.
- ***classname*** is the name you give to this particular class.
- ***element*** is the HTML element whose style is being defined in this class.
- ***property*** is the style property to be applied to this element in this class.

For example, you can define a class called **bigred** that will increase the font size and change the color of paragraphs.

```
<STYLE TYPE="text/javascript">
<!--
      classes.bigred.P.color = "red"
      classes.bigred.P.fontSize = "large"
// -->
</STYLE>
```

4. To apply this style to specific paragraphs, you must add a new attribute, **CLASS**, to the HTML tag and set it equal to the style class defined in the header.

```
<P>This is an ordinary paragraph.</P>

<P CLASS="bigred">Look at me! I'm big and red!</P>
```

5. Classes work only for the HTML elements for which they're defined. If you try to apply the class to a different tag, you won't see any changes in the style because no style changes have been defined for that tag in the class definition. For example, if you tried to apply the class **bigred**, defined earlier, to a header, the style would not change.

```
<H1 CLASS="bigred">You'd think I'd be big and red, but I'm not.</H1>
```

6. You can avoid this problem by defining the style to be valid for all HTML elements. To do this, simply use the word **all** in place of a specific HTML element in the class definition in the header.

```
<STYLE TYPE="text/javascript">
<!--
      classes.bigred.all.color = "red"
      classes.bigred.all.fontSize = "large"
// -->
</STYLE>
```

Now the style will be applied to any HTML tag that references this class.

```
<H1 CLASS="bigred">Now I'm big and red!</H1>
<P CLASS="bigred">And so am I!</P>
```

7. You can also use the same class name to make different definitions for different HTML tags. This allows for logical grouping of style classes in documents. For example, we could define a class **QandA** that defines headings as bold, blue text and paragraphs as indented, italic text.

```
<STYLE TYPE="text/javascript">
<!--
      classes.QandA.H3.color = "blue"
      classes.QandA.H3.fontWeight = "bold"
      classes.QandA.P.marginLeft = 20
      classes.QandA.P.fontStyle = "italic"
// -->
</STYLE>
```

8. This new class can now be applied to the document in the same way described above.

```
<H3 CLASS="QandA">So what do you think of this new style?</H3>
<P CLASS="QandA">I think it's rather striking, if I do say so myself.</P>
```

Another way to apply this style would be to use the <SPAN> tag. Place the <SPAN> tag, with the attribute CLASS set equal to the class, at the beginning of the markup to define as a specific class, and the </SPAN> tag at the end of the markup that uses that class. Applied to this earlier example, the code looks like this:

```
<SPAN CLASS="QandA">
<H3>So what do you think of this new style?</H3>
<P>I think it's rather striking, if I do say so myself.</P>
</SPAN>
```

Some examples of the use of classes in dynamic style sheets are shown in Figure 21-4.

How It Works

Browsers that support dynamic style sheets read the class definitions in the header of the document. The browser then applies those styles to specified sections of the document, provided a style has been defined for the HTML element using that class. Classes can be specified in the body of the document either with the CLASS attribute of the tag or within the <SPAN> markup.

Comments

If a style is defined for a tag for the entire document and a separate style is defined for that element in the class, the style in the class overrides the style for the whole document in portions of the document where the style class is being used.

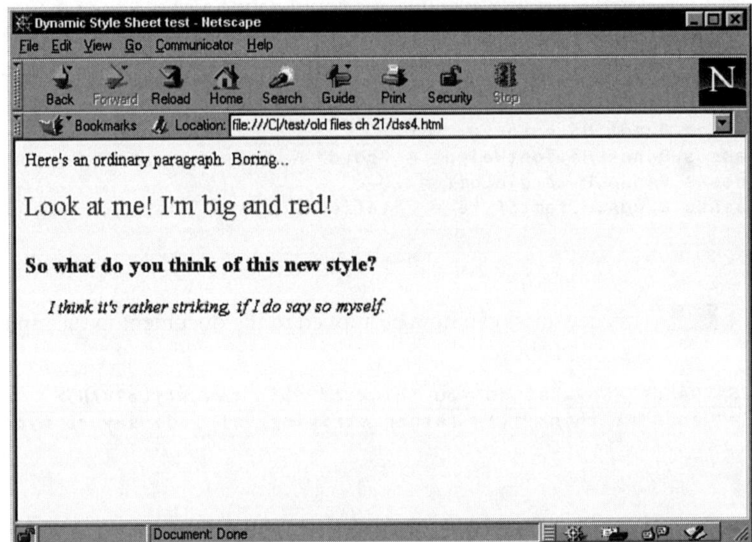

Figure 21-4 Examples of the use of classes in dynamic style sheets

21.5 How do I... Identify a unique style?

COMPATIBILITY: NETSCAPE 4.0

Problem

I'd like to make a slight change to an existing style to be used in a few limited places. Is there a way to do this short of manually defining the style in each place I want to make the change?

Technique

Dynamic style sheets support the **ID** attribute to HTML tags, which enables users to identify locations in the document where the style is changed. The definition of the changes is located, like regular style and class definitions, within the **<STYLE>** tags in the header of the document.

Steps

1. Open the document to which you would like to add styles in your preferred editor. You need a copy of Netscape Navigator 4.0 to preview the results because that is the only browser that supports dynamic style sheets.

2. Identified changes to styles are defined within the **<STYLE>...</STYLE>** markup in the header of a document, so set up the **<STYLE>** markup as described in How-To 21.2.

```
<STYLE TYPE="text/javascript">
<!--

// -->
</STYLE>
```

3. The syntax for defining identified changes to styles in dynamic style sheets is ***ids.name.property***, where

- ✔ ***ids*** is a JavaScript object used to identify style changes.
- ✔ ***name*** is the name you give to this particular style change.
- ✔ ***property*** is the style property to be applied to this element in this class.

For example, you can define an identity called **myblue** that will change the color to blue.

```
<STYLE TYPE="text/javascript">
<!--
     ids.myblue.color = "blue"
// -->
</STYLE>
```

4. To apply this style to specific paragraphs, you must add a new attribute, **ID**, to the HTML tag and set it equal to the style identity defined in the header. For example, you can combine the identity defined earlier with the **bigred** class defined in How-To 21.4.

```
<P CLASS="bigred">Look at me! I'm big and red!</P>
<P CLASS="bigred" ID="myblue">Wait, I'm blue!</P>
```

An example of the use of identities in style sheets is shown in Figure 21-5.

How It Works

A browser that supports dynamic style sheets locates any parts of a document that have been identified with a special style and then changes the style of the document there using the definition for the style ID contained in the header of the document.

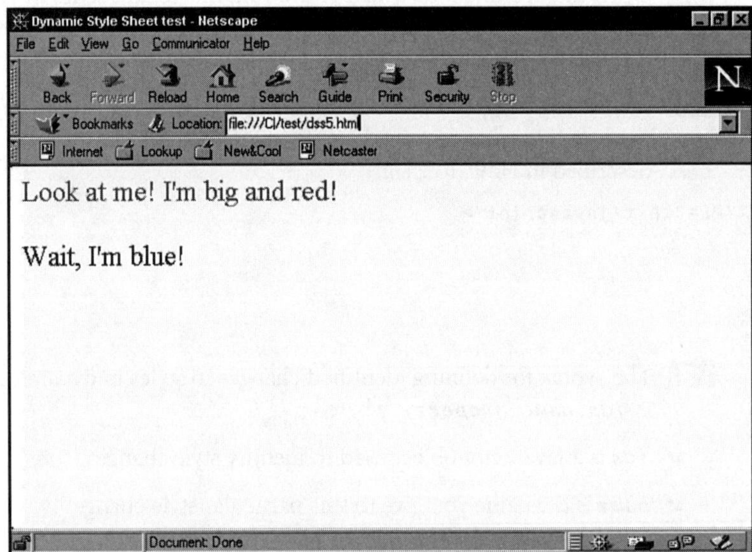

Figure 21-5 Using an identity to change the font color in a style sheet

Comments

Style identities override any changes in the overall style of the document defined in the header or any changes in style defined by classes. Note that there is nothing in the definition of style identities that ties them to a particular class or HTML tag, so they can be used in different places throughout a document as needed. If you're using IDs a lot, though, you might want to reconsider your overall style and class definitions to see if there is an easier way to make the style changes in your document.

COMPLEXITY
ADVANCED

21.6 How do I... Define a style in a particular context?

COMPATIBILITY: NETSCAPE 4.0

Problem

I would like to define the style for a particular element of a document based on the location of the element of the document, such as defining the style of list entries depending on the type of list they are in. I could do this with a set of style classes, but is there a simpler way to accomplish this?

Technique

Netscape's dynamic style sheet definition includes a JavaScript method called `contextual()`, which enables a page designer to define the style for an HTML element based on its context—that is, where in the document relative to other tags it is located.

Steps

1. Open the document to which you would like to add styles in your preferred editor. You need a copy of Netscape Navigator 4.0 to preview the results because that is the only browser that supports dynamic style sheets.

2. Identified changes to styles are defined within the `<STYLE>...</STYLE>` markup in the header of a document, so set up the `<STYLE>` markup as described in How-To 21.2.

```
<STYLE TYPE="text/javascript">
<!--

// -->
</STYLE>
```

3. To define a style based on context, use the `contextual()` method in the style sheet definition, and within the parentheses define the tags for this particular context. For example, if you want to define a style for list entries contained within bulleted lists, you would enter

```
<STYLE TYPE="text/javascript">
<!--
      contextual(tags.UL, tags.LI)
// -->
</STYLE>
```

Alternatively, to define the case of emphasized text located within a level 1 heading, enter

```
<STYLE TYPE="text/javascript">
<!--
      contextual(tags.EM, tags.H1)
// -->
</STYLE>
```

4. You can now apply style information to these contexts in the same way regular styles are defined. To make the list entries within bulleted lists blue, for example, enter

```
<STYLE TYPE="text/javascript">
<!--
      contextual(tags.UL, tags.LI).color = "blue"
// -->
</STYLE>
```

Or to make emphasized text within level 1 headings bold and green, enter

```
<STYLE TYPE="text/javascript">
<!--
      contextual(tags.H1, tags.EM).color = "green"
      contextual(tags.H1, tags.EM).fontFamily = "monospace"
// -->
</STYLE>
```

5. Contextual style definitions can also be tied to style classes and identities. For example, if you defined a class `bigred` for all HTML tags but wanted to change the font size for text located in lists, you would use

```
<STYLE TYPE="text/javascript">
<!--
      classes.bigred.all.color = "red"
      classes.bigred.all.fontSize = "large"
      contextual(classes.bigred.all, tags.UL).fontSize = "smaller"
// -->
</STYLE>
```

You could then apply the style sheet as follows:

```
<P>This is an ordinary paragraph.</P>

<DIV CLASS="bigred">
<P>This is a big red paragraph!</P>

<UL>
<LI>This should also be red
<LI>but smaller
</UL>
</DIV>
```

An example of the use of contextual markup in style sheets is shown in Figure 21-6.

How It Works

Browsers that support dynamic style sheets interpret the `contextual()` definitions in the style sheet definitions in the header to mean that a specific style will be applied any place in the document where the tags, classes, or identities are nested in that way.

Comments

Contextual definitions override any previous style definitions for that document, including main style sheet definitions, classes, and identities. Also note that Netscape Navigator 4.01 does not properly change colors for list entries, as attempted in step 3; the bullet will be colored, but the item associated with the bullet will not.

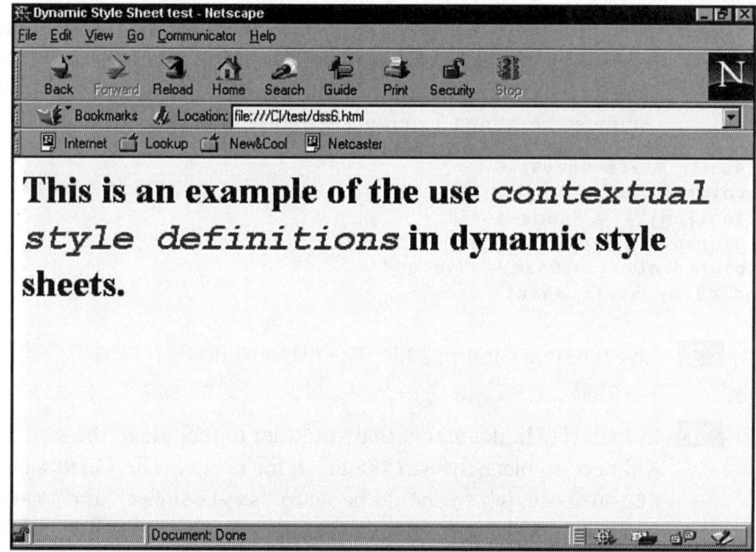

Figure 21-6 Changing styles using contextual style definitions

21.7 How do I... Specify an external style sheet?

COMPATIBILITY: NETSCAPE 4.0

Problem

I have a set of style definitions that I would like to use in a set of documents on my site. How can I set up the style sheets and definitions so I don't have to duplicate the style definitions in each document?

Technique

Netscape supports the use of external style sheets, separate files that contain style sheet information. These style sheets are referenced by HTML documents through the `<LINK>` tag in the header of the document.

Steps

1. Open the document to which you would like to add styles in your preferred editor. Also, open a separate document that will contain the styles for your external style sheet. You need a copy of Netscape Navigator 4.0 to preview the results because that is the only browser that supports dynamic style sheets.

2. Open the document that will contain the style sheet information. Enter the style sheet definitions into the document. Do not enter any HTML markup, including `<STYLE>`. You can use the JavaScript `//` markup for comments. A sample external style sheet could be

```
// this is my style sheet
tags.H1.color = "blue"
tags.H1.fontFamily = "sans-serif"
classes.bigred.all.color = "red"
classes.bigred.all.fontSize = "large"
//the end of my style sheet
```

3. Save the style sheet to a file. The filename needs no special extension, such as `.html`.

4. In each HTML document that you want to include in the style sheet, you will need to place the `<LINK>` tag in the header. The `<LINK>` tag needs the `REL` attribute, which should be set to `"stylesheet"`; the `TYPE` attribute, which should be set to `"text/JavaScript"` for dynamic style sheets; the `HREF` attribute, which is set to the URL for the style sheet; and an optional

TITLE. For example, if the external style sheet defined above is located in the same directory as your HTML document with the filename **mystyles**, use

```
<LINK REL="stylesheet" TYPE="text/JavaScript" HREF="mystyles" TITLE="my ⇐
style sheet!">
```

Alternatively, if the style sheet is located at **www.widgets.com** in the directory styles as filename **styles1**, use

```
<LINK REL="stylesheet" TYPE="text/JavaScript" ⇐
HREF="http://www.widgets.com/styles/styles1" TITLE="my style sheet!">
```

How It Works

When an HTML document is loaded, the browser finds the **<LINK>** tag and loads the file referenced there. The browser then applies to the HTML document the styles referenced in that file.

Comments

Although the style sheets defined in the external file sheet will be applied to the document, they can be overridden by styles defined locally in the header of the document or style definitions made elsewhere in the document for specific sections.

COMPLEXITY
ADVANCED

21.8 How do I... Include a dynamic font in a page?

COMPATIBILITY: NETSCAPE 4.0

Problem

I have some fonts I would like to use to display text on my Web pages. However, these fonts are uncommon and therefore unlikely to be on the typical user's computer system. How can I include these fonts on a Web page without requiring users to download and install a new font?

Technique

An adjunct to the dynamic style sheets supported in Netscape Navigator 4.0 is *dynamic fonts*. These fonts are based on a new technology called *TrueDoc* by Bitstream. They can be referenced on Web pages; if a font is not already installed on the browser's system, the browser will download a special file that contains information needed to display text on the Web page in that font, without downloading a whole new font and installing it into the system.

To display new fonts without downloading entire font files, TrueDoc technology uses Portable Font Resource (PFR) files. These files contain information about the size and shape of the characters in the font and the spacing between characters in a highly compressed format that can be quickly downloaded with the rest of the HTML document. To create PFR files, you need an authoring program that supports TrueDoc technology. Netscape promises to support the creation of PFR files as part of its Composer HTML authoring program. Some Web sites, including Netscape's, offer sample PFR files for people to use to try out dynamic fonts.

Steps

Open the document to which you would like to add styles in your preferred editor. Also, open a separate document that will contain the styles for your external style sheet. You need a copy of Netscape Navigator 4.0 to preview the results because that is the only browser that supports dynamic style sheets. You also need a PFR file containing the font definitions necessary for the font or fonts you plan to add to your document.

Netscape supports the inclusion of dynamic fonts in two manners: through the use of the `<LINK>` and `<FONT FACE>` tags or through the use of cascading style sheets. Both methods are explained next.

<LINK> and <FONT FACE>

1. In the header of the document, insert the `<LINK>` tag with two attributes: `REL`, which is set equal to `fontdef`, and `SRC`, which is set equal to the URL for the font definition file. For example, to reference a font definition file named `myfont.pfr` at `www.widgets.com`, use

```
<LINK REL=fontdef SRC="http://www.widgets.com/myfont.pfr">
```

2. In the body of the document, use the `<FONT>` tag with the attribute `FACE` set to the name of the font in those places where you want to use the font. This works just the same as if you were using an ordinary font, as described in How-To 15.2.

```
<FONT FACE="My Font">This is text using my special font!</FONT>
```

Style Sheets

1. To use a dynamic font in a style sheet, you must define the font in the style sheet definition in the header of the document using the `fontdef` command, giving the URL for the font definition file.

```
<STYLE TYPE="text/css">
<!--
     @fontdef url(http://www.wwidgets.com/myfont.pfr);
-->
</STYLE>
```

2. You can now use the font name in definitions of font families for HTML elements. For example, you could define that all level 1 headings be rendered in this font using

```
H1 {font-family: My Font}
```

An example of dynamic fonts from the Netscape site is shown in Figure 21-7.

How It Works

A browser that is TrueDoc-enabled recognizes the font definition files (`*.pfr`) and downloads them with the rest of the page. The browser uses the PFR file to render specific text on the page in that font. This works identically whether the PFR file is requested through style sheets or through the `<LINK>` and `<FONT FACE>` tags.

Comments

Unless you are using a PFR file provided by someone else (Netscape does provide a few such fonts), you need an application that can create PFR fonts from fonts on your own system. One of the first programs to do this is HexWeb Typograph from HexMac (`http://www.hexmac.com/`). Other programs, including Netscape's own Composer authoring program, will support the creation of PFR files in the future.

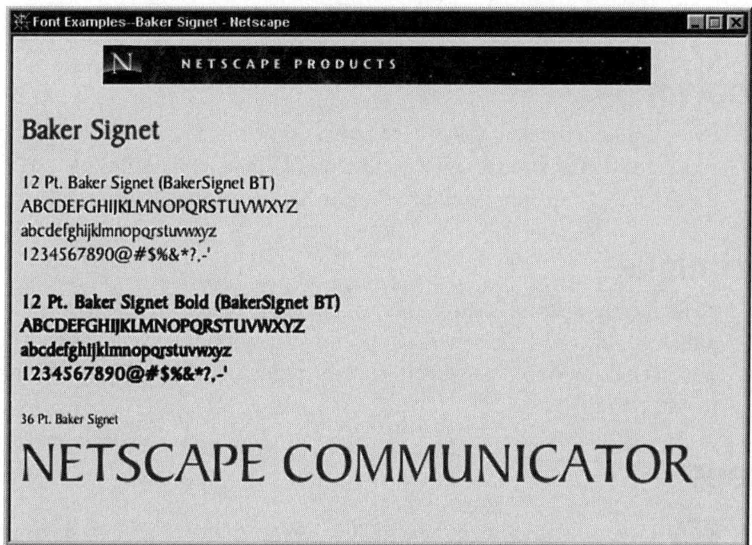

Figure 21-7 Dynamic fonts from Netscape's site

For PFR files to be downloaded from a server correctly, the server needs the correct MIME-type information for the PFR file. The MIME type for PFR files is `application/font-tfpfr` with a `.pfr` file extension. In the future, the MIME type might change to `font/truedoc`. Refer to How-To 12.6 for information about registering additional MIME types on your server.

Currently Netscape Navigator 4.0 is the only browser to support TrueDoc fonts embedded in Web pages. It is not certain that this will become the standard method for including fonts in pages in the future; Microsoft is investigating different methods for including fonts. You will want to pay attention to developments in this field and be prepared to make changes to how you use dynamic fonts in your pages in the future.

More information about dynamic fonts is available from Netscape online at `http://developer.netscape.com/library/documentation/communicator/dynhtml/webfont3.htm`.

COMPLEXITY
ADVANCED

21.9 How do I... Specify the size and weight of a dynamic font?

COMPATIBILITY: NETSCAPE 4.0

Problem

I would like to specify that a font appear on the screen in a specific point size and weight, rather than use vague commands such as `<B>` and `<FONT SIZE="+1">`. Is there a way to specify point sizes and weights for fonts?

Technique

Netscape Navigator 4.0 supports two new attributes to the `<FONT>` tag: `POINT-SIZE`, which enables Web designers to specify an exact point size for a font, and `WEIGHT`, which enables Web designers to specify a specific weight for a font, from very light to extra bold.

Steps

1. Open the document to which you would like to add styles in your preferred editor. Also, open a separate document that will contain the styles for your external style sheet. You need a copy of Netscape Navigator 4.0 to preview the results because that is the only browser that supports the `POINT-SIZE` and `WEIGHT` attributes to `<FONT>`.

2. To specify a specific point size for a specific section of text, place the **<FONT>** tag at the beginning of the section and **</FONT>** at the end.

```
<FONT>This text should be in a specific point size</FONT>
```

3. To set the point size, include the **POINT-SIZE** attribute in the **<FONT>** tag and set it equal to the desired size, in points, of the text. To create a 24-point section of font, for example, use

```
<FONT POINT-SIZE=24>This text should be in a specific point size</FONT>
```

4. To set the weight of the font, include the **WEIGHT** attribute of the font. **WEIGHT** can range from 100 (very light) to 900 (extra bold), in steps of 100. To make the sample text medium bold, try

```
<FONT WEIGHT=500>This text should be in a specific weight.</FONT>
```

5. You can combine the **POINT-SIZE** and **WEIGHT** attributes with other **<FONT>** attributes to create a specific text style for a section of a document. To create 18-point Arial text that is medium bold, for example, you would use

```
<FONT FACE="Arial" POINT-SIZE=18 WEIGHT=500>This text should be in a
medium-bold 18-point Arial.</FONT>
```

A sample of how some of the different point sizes appear in Netscape is shown in Figure 21-8.

How It Works

A browser that recognizes the **POINT-SIZE** and **WEIGHT** attributes to **<FONT>** changes the appearance of the sections of text so specified by changing the size and boldness of the displayed text.

Comments

In typography, a point is 1/72 of an inch. On computer screens, though, point size is much less exact, given the differences in monitor sizes and resolutions. Thus, text can appear in different sizes in different displays even though the font size has been set to a specific point size. Make sure to keep this in mind when you are designing Web pages.

Although **WEIGHT** is mentioned in Netscape's documentation online, it is not supported in Navigator 4.01.

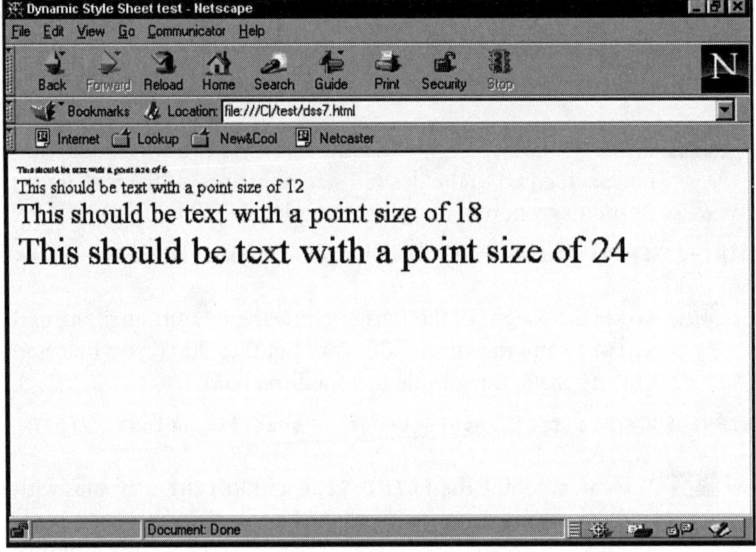

Figure 21-8 A sample of text in four point sizes using the `<FONT POINT-SIZE>` tag

COMPLEXITY
ADVANCED

21.10 How do I... Use JavaScript to manipulate dynamic style sheets?

COMPATIBILITY: NETSCAPE 4.0

Problem

I would like the browser to be able to change aspects of the appearance of the page based on things such as the time the user accesses the page, the type of computer he or she is using, and so on. I'd like to make changes in the style sheets rather than creating whole new versions of the page for each circumstance. Is there a way to manipulate the appearance of the page using dynamic style sheets and JavaScript?

Technique

Dynamic style sheets, as the name suggests, can be changed. The simplest way to do this, short of creating a separate version of the page with different style definitions, is to combine style sheets with JavaScript and use JavaScript functions to modify the values given to certain style attributes.

This How-To includes a specific, simple example of doing this that shows how to create a page that uses JavaScript to change the font color on a page depending on the time. It might not be a very useful application of dynamic style sheets in and of itself, but it shows how to make changes to dynamic style sheets. You can make these changes as complex as you want, but they will be built on the basics shown here.

Steps

1. Open the document to which you would like to add styles in your preferred editor. Also, open a separate document that will contain the styles for your external style sheet. You need a copy of Netscape Navigator 4.0 to preview the results because that is the only browser that supports dynamic style sheets.

2. This example uses a JavaScript script in the document header to get the time and to change the font color based on the time. Start by setting up the script and creating a function called **colorSelect()**.

```
<SCRIPT LANGUAGE="JavaScript">
<!--
function colorSelect() {

}
// -->
</SCRIPT>
```

3. The first part of the script gets the current time on the user's system, using JavaScript's **Date()** object.

```
<SCRIPT LANGUAGE="JavaScript">
<!--
function colorSelect() {
      time = new Date()
}
// -->
</SCRIPT>
```

4. For this example, you will do something very straightforward and simple, if not terribly useful: Get the number of seconds in the current time. If that value is less than 30 seconds, make the text color blue; if it is 30 seconds or more, make it green.

```
<SCRIPT LANGUAGE="JavaScript">
<!--
function colorSelect() {
      time = new Date()
      if (time.getSeconds() < 30) {
            theColor = "blue" }
      else {
```

continued on next page

continued from previous page

```
            theColor = "green" }
}
// -->
</SCRIPT>
```

5. To finish the script, have the function return the color name it chose.

```
<SCRIPT LANGUAGE="JavaScript">
<!--
function colorSelect() {
      time = new Date()
      if (time.getSeconds() < 30) {
            theColor = "blue" }
      else {
            theColor = "green" }

      return theColor
}
// -->
</SCRIPT>
```

6. Now set up a dynamic style sheet definition in the header, just after the JavaScript script.

```
<STYLE TYPE="text/javascript">
<!--

// -->
</STYLE>
```

7. In the style sheet, set the value of the colors for specific page elements to the script itself. The browser will then run the script to get the specific color.

```
<STYLE TYPE="text/javascript">
<!--
      tags.P.color = colorSelect()
      tags.H1.color = colorSelect()
// -->
</STYLE>
```

8. Enter standard HTML markup in the body of the document. Its color will be controlled by the style sheet, which gets its information from the JavaScript script.

```
<H1>A test of dynamic style sheets</H1>

<P>This is a test of dynamic style sheets. Depending on the time on your
 system, this text will be blue or green. Try reloading this page in
 about half a minute to see if the colors change</P>
```

9. Load the page into Netscape Navigator 4.0. Depending on the time on your system when you loaded the page, the text on the screen will be blue or green. To change the colors, reload the page about half a minute later; the text should change from blue to green, or vice versa. You've just created a truly dynamic style sheet!

The page is shown in Figure 21-9. The text is rendered in blue between seconds 0 and 29 and in green between seconds 30 and 59.

How It Works

Dynamic style sheets can accept JavaScript functions as values for style attributes. In those cases, the script runs when the page is loaded and the value from the script is used as the value for that style attribute. JavaScript functions can be used to provide values for essentially any JavaScript function.

Comments

When combining style sheets with JavaScript functions, the style sheet definition must come after the script because the script will be read and interpreted first when the page is loaded. If the style sheet includes a reference to a JavaScript function that hasn't been defined yet, the browser generates an error message.

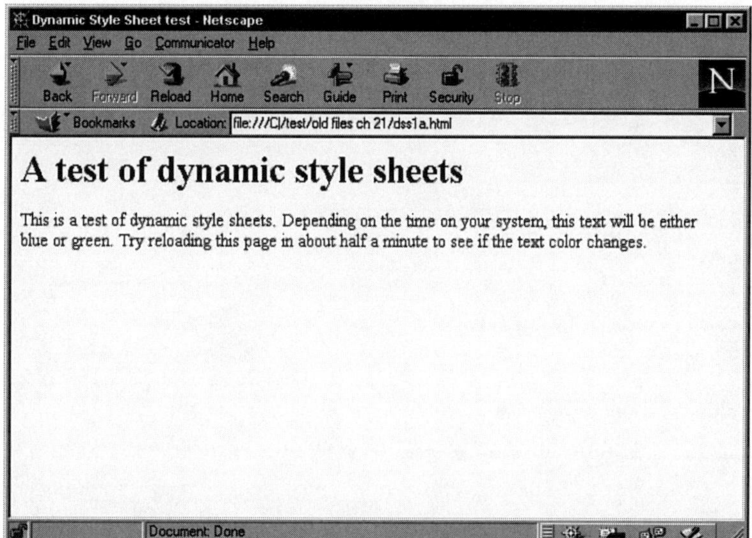

Figure 21-9 The result of the dynamic style sheet with text that changes from blue to green

After the page has been loaded, you can't use a JavaScript function to change the value of style sheet attributes and have that change displayed on the page. Changes in the style sheet definition must be made as the style sheet is loaded with the full document. You can get around this to some degree with some more JavaScript that writes to the page, incorporating style information.

The example in this How-To is deliberately simple to illustrate the basics of how to incorporate JavaScript and dynamic style sheets. You can use this to create more advanced, useful changes to pages, such as changes in text style depending on time of day or type of computer the browser is running on.

CHAPTER 22

UNSUPPORTED, PROPOSED HTML FEATURES

22

UNSUPPORTED, PROPOSED HTML FEATURES

How do I...

The HTML standard has evolved over time. This evolution has led to the proposal and development of a myriad of possible HTML elements. Despite the development of an HTML 4.0 proposed standard, individuals and software manufacturers are constantly proposing or incorporating modifications to the proposed standard.

Chapters 15 through 21 address many elements of these types, particularly those that popular browsers implement. This chapter discusses many additional elements that are implemented only, if at all, in an exceedingly limited manner. The HTML 3.0 standard defined most of these elements; however, most do not appear in the HTML 4.0 proposed standard. Even so, with the way HTML evolves, these elements could potentially be resurrected, either by a future HTML standard or by the incorporation of support for the element into a popular browser. The fact that a particular element is not part of the "standard" has not seemed to discourage browser developers from creating their own browser-specific extended dialects.

With this in mind, you should be wary of using these features in your Web pages and expecting generic browsers to display them in any particular manner. Most browsers simply ignore unrecognized HTML elements, so in general, their inclusion should not adversely affect the presentation of your Web page. The How-To's in this chapter examine these elements, providing step-by-step instructions for using them within your Web pages. However, considering the nature of these elements, each How-To attempts to present alternatives that conform to the proposed HTML 4.0 standard.

22.1 Mark an Abbreviation or Acronym

In your document, you can refer to several abbreviations or acronyms that might require special formatting. This simple How-To explains how to use HTML tags to mark these items.

22.2 Tag Computer Commands and Arguments

In the course of writing your page, you might want to insert brief sections of computer commands or arguments. This How-To explains how you can format these text elements in HTML.

22.3 Identify a Proper Name

You might want to identify proper names in your document, either for formatting purposes or to make the names easily extractable by indexing programs. This simple How-To explains how to identify proper names using HTML tags.

22.4 Denote Inserted or Deleted Text

Bills, contracts, and other legal documents often include sections that have been inserted or deleted since they were originally drawn up. This How-To explains how to include references to inserted or deleted sections of text easily.

22.5 Create a Multicolumn List

You might have information you would like to display in a series of lists side by side, such as a comparison of the characteristics of different items. This How-To will explain how to use the `WRAP` attribute for bulleted lists in HTML 3.0 to create multicolumn lists.

22.6 Specify the Language Context for the Remainder of a Web Page

The WWW, as the name implies, is worldwide in scope. Developing multilingual documents is a growing concern in HTML. Several proposed mechanisms provide support for specifying the language of a particular Web page. In this How-To, you will learn how to use these mechanisms to select a language for a Web page.

22.7 Place an Embedded Quotation

Often you have a quotation you would like to insert into a document. This is very simple to do manually, but HTML provides more sophisticated ways to insert quotations in pages, including using different quotation marks for different languages. This simple How-To explains how to add an embedded quotation to your page.

22.8 Align Text with Tabs

HTML provides elements to support the alignment of the textual content of your HTML documents. This How-To describes these elements, explains their use, and provides concrete examples. In this How-To, you will learn how to add horizontal alignment elements to your HTML pages.

22.9 Insert Cautionary Notes

The HTML 3.0 standard introduced a mechanism for incorporating admonishments, such as warnings, cautions, and notes, into your Web page. This How-To details this process.

22.10 Add a Footnote

Scholarly works require that an author designate the source of an original idea or quotation. HTML 3.0 provided a means of specifying such footnotes. Where feasible, HTML 3.0 suggested such footnotes use pop-up windows to display the relevant information. In this How-To, you will learn how to add pop-up footnotes within your Web pages.

22.11 Place a Mathematical Equation in My Web Page

If your page covers topics in math, science, or engineering, you might need to display special mathematical symbols not available in normal ASCII text. This How-To explains how to insert various types of mathematical symbols, including characters, vectors, and matrices, in your page, and how to format complex mathematical equations properly.

22.12 Insert an Array into a `<MATH>` Element

If your page covers topics in math, science, or engineering, you might run across the need to display mathematical arrays. This How-To explains how to insert arrays into your Web pages.

22.13 Change the Shape of a Link

Links have been limited to text and other objects, but HTML 3.0 provides a way to create a link within a part of an image by specifying the location and shape of the area in an image to serve as a link. This How-To shows how to create links of different shapes and embed them in images using HTML 3.0.

COMPLEXITY
BEGINNING

22.1 How do I... Mark an abbreviation or acronym?

COMPATIBILITY: HTML 3.0, 4.0

Problem

I have a page that includes several abbreviations and acronyms. I would like to call attention to them, but I don't require a specific physical style. Is there a generic way to call attention to these items in HTML?

Technique

HTML 3.0 supports two tags, **<ABBREV>** and **<ACRONYM>**, that can be used to mark abbreviations and acronyms, respectively. The physical style used for these items varies from browser to browser.

Steps

1. Open your document and locate the text you want to identify as an abbreviation or an acronym.

2. To identify an abbreviation, place the **<ABBREV>** tag at the beginning of the abbreviation and **</ABBREV>** at the end of the abbreviation.

```
The paper by Smith <ABBREV>et al.</ABBREV> shows how this can be done.
```

3. To identify an acronym, place the **<ACRONYM>** tag at the beginning of the acronym and **</ACRONYM>** at the end of the acronym.

```
The National Aeronautics and Space Administration, or ⇐
<ACRONYM>NASA</ACRONYM>, was founded in 1958.
```

How It Works

When a browser encounters either an <ABBREV> or an <ACRONYM> element, it formats the text contained between the opening and closing tags accordingly. The actual physical style applied to the text contained within these tags is controlled by the browser viewing the document. Neither element creates a visual effect in Netscape Navigator or Microsoft Internet Explorer.

Comments

Because formatting applied to the <ABBREV> and <ACRONYM> tags will vary from browser to browser, it might be bold, italic, or something else entirely. Thus, it's better to refer to acronyms or abbreviations by content rather than by style. Because they were additions to HTML 3.0, neither <ABBREV> nor <ACRONYM> is supported by older browsers. Furthermore, these elements do not appear in the HTML 3.2 or 4.0 standard, but browsers can choose to support them as nonstandard elements.

The original intent of these elements was to provide a logical character effect without necessarily any visual effect. For this purpose, no easy alternative is available in the current standard, but because no visual effect is intended, the nonconforming use of these elements will not hurt the appearance of your Web page in most browsers.

The first draft of the HTML 4.0 standard includes the <ACRONYM> element. However, this tag is not supported yet by the major browsers, and there is no guarantee the tag will stay in later drafts of the proposed standard.

22.2 How do I... Tag computer commands and arguments?

COMPATIBILITY: HTML 1, 2

Problem

On my page I would like to highlight names of computer programs and their arguments. I would like to format these samples differently than the standard text is formatted. How can I do this in HTML?

Technique

The HTML example style element <XMP> enables you to mark sample text. Use it to display computer commands and arguments. The text tagged by <XMP> is usually shown in a fixed-width font.

NOTE

The `<XMP>` element is not recommended for current use. Refer to Chapter 3, "Adding HTML Physical Character Effects," and Chapter 4, "Adding HTML Logical Character Effects," for potentially more appropriate HTML 4.0 elements.

Steps

To specify sample text, place the **<XMP>** tag at the beginning of the text and the **</XMP>** tag at the end of the text—for example,

```
At the prompt enter the command <XMP>lpr output.txt</XMP>.
```

How It Works

When a browser encounters an **<XMP>** element, it places everything between the opening and closing tags in sample style. Such text is usually rendered in a fixed-width font, but font style can vary among browsers. Both Netscape Navigator and Microsoft Internet Explorer currently support this element. Figure 22-1 displays the following document as rendered by Internet Explorer:

```
<HTML>
<HEAD>
<TITLE>Sample Stop/Restart Server</TITLE>
</HEAD>
<BODY>
Stop and restart the server by entering:<BR>
<XMP>
kill -1 SERVER_PROCESS_ID
</XMP>
</BODY>
</HTML>
```

The HTML source for this document also appears on the CD-ROM in the **XMP.HTM** file.

Comments

The specification of HTML 2 deprecated the use of this element. This deprecated specification also appeared in the HTML 3.0 and 3.2 specifications. Some older browsers and HTML documents can use this element. However, in general, you should select a more appropriate element from those discussed in Chapters 3 and 4. For the particular task of computer commands and arguments, consider the elements described in How-To 4.5.

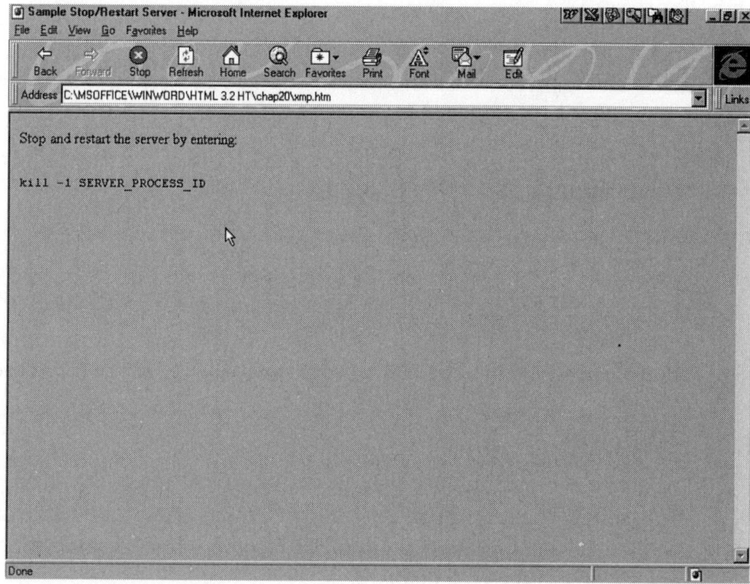

Figure 22-1 Sample element displaying a command and its arguments

22.3 How do I... Identify a proper name?

COMPATIBILITY: HTML 3.0

Problem

I would like to call attention to the names of people and to other proper names in my pages. The names do not necessarily have to be highlighted, but someone running an indexing program through my pages should be able to pull out the names easily. How can I do this in HTML?

Technique

HTML 3.0 provided two new tags, **<AU>** and **<PERSON>**, that can be used to identify the names of people as well as other proper names. **<AU>** identifies an author, whereas **<PERSON>** identifies any person (or other proper name).

Steps

1. Open your document and locate the text you want to identify as a proper name.

2. To identify the name of an author, place **<AU>** at the beginning of the name and **</AU>** at the end of the name.

```
<AU>William Faulkner</AU> wrote many novels set in Mississippi.
```

3. To identify the name of a person, place **<PERSON>** at the beginning of the name and **</PERSON>** at the end of the name.

```
<PERSON>Ronald Reagan</PERSON> was the 40th president of the United States.
```

How It Works

When a browser encounters either an **<AU>** or a **<PERSON>** tag, it does nothing to alter the style of the text; these tags simply identify names for outside indexing programs. Neither Netscape Navigator nor Microsoft Internet Explorer supports a visual effect for either of these elements.

Comments

The **<AU>** and **<PERSON>** tags are only supported by HTML 3.0, so neither the older, pre-HTML 3.0 browsers nor the post-HTML 3.0 browsers can take advantage of them. These tags are primarily used by programs that scan HTML files and index their contents. These elements do not appear in the HTML 3.2 or 4.0 standard, but certain browsers and applications use them.

The original intent of these elements was to provide a logical character effect without necessarily any visual effect. For this purpose, no easy alternative is available in the current standard, but because no visual effect is intended, the nonconforming use of these elements will not hurt the appearance of your Web page in most browsers.

22.4 How do I... Denote inserted or deleted text?

COMPATIBILITY: HTML 3.0, 4.0

Problem

I'm putting some legal documents on my Web page, and I would like to point out where sections of the text have been amended, either by additions of new sections or by deletions of old sections. Is there a way I can easily mark this in HTML?

Technique

HTML 3.0 provided two tags, **<INS>** and **<DEL>**, that enable you to mark sections of text that have been inserted or deleted from the original version of a document. As with other content styles, the physical rendering of the text depends on the browser.

Steps

1. Open your document and locate the text you would like to display as inserted or deleted text.

2. To mark text that has been inserted, place **<INS>** at the beginning of the inserted text and **</INS>** at the end of the inserted text.

```
His latest contract called for $3.5 million a year <INS>and a beachfront ⇐
condo</INS>.
```

3. To mark text that has been deleted, place **<DEL>** at the beginning of the section that has been deleted and **</DEL>** at the end of the text.

```
The people on the team now include John, Jane, <DEL>Bob,</DEL> and Arnold.
```

The first draft of HTML 4.0 includes the **CITE** attribute, which can be set equal to the URL for a document that explains the insertion or deletion.

```
The people on the team now include John, Jane, <DEL ⇐
CITE="http://www.mysite.edu/changes.html">Bob,</DEL> and Arnold.
```

The first draft of HTML 4.0 includes the **DATETIME** attribute, which can be used to provide the date and time of the insertion or deletion. The **DATETIME** attribute uses dates and times in the ISO 8601 standard format.

```
His latest contract called for $3.5 million a year <INS ⇐
DATETIME="1999-03-04T12:17:20">and a beachfront condo</INS>.
```

More information on ISO date and time formats is on the Web at **http://www.mcs.vuw.ac.nz/comp/Technical/SGML/doc/iso8601/ISO8601.html**.

How It Works

When a browser encounters an **<INS>** or a **<DEL>** element, it formats the text contained within the tags according to the style programmed into the browser. This style can vary from browser to browser. Neither Netscape Navigator nor Microsoft Internet Explorer supports a visual effect for either of these elements.

Comments

The <INS> and <DEL> elements don't actually insert or delete text; instead, they point out where text has been added to or removed from a document. These features were added only to HTML 3.0, so pre-HTML 3.0 and post-HTML 3.0 browsers do not support these tags. These elements do not appear in the HTML 3.2 standard.

The original intent of these elements was to provide a logical character effect without necessarily any visual effect. You could, however, use some standard physical effects to indicate insertions or deletions. Deletions can be addressed using the strikethrough element discussed in How-To 3.7. A physical effect for insertions is not so directly apparent. As a convention within an authoring group, insertions might be tagged as bold (How-To 3.1), italic (How-To 3.2), colored with a specific color (How-To 3.5), or underlined (How-To 3.6). Such a decision should reflect the needs of the organization adopting the change (for example, if color changes are standard in documents developed, then some other option might be a better choice to indicate insertions). A style sheet (see Chapter 16, "Cascading Style Sheets") could also be used to provide effects for insertions and deletions. Figure 22-2 displays several of these potential alternatives. The HTML code for this document appears in the INSDEL.HTM file on the CD-ROM.

The <INS> and <DEL> elements have returned in the first draft of the proposed HTML 4.0 standard, with the added CITE and DATETIME attributes described earlier. These tags are not supported by major browsers yet, though, and there is no guarantee these tags will appear in future drafts of HTML 4.0.

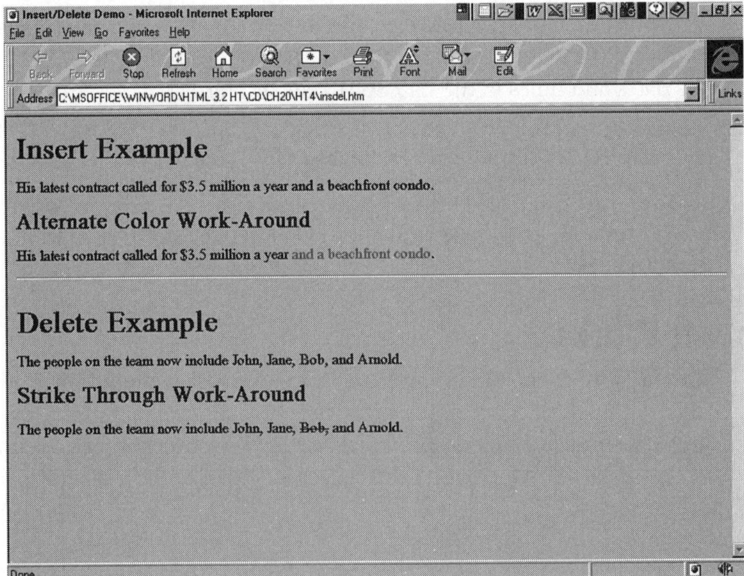

Figure 22-2 Insertion and deletion alternatives

COMPLEXITY
INTERMEDIATE

22.5 How do I... Create a multicolumn list?

COMPATIBILITY: HTML 3.0

Problem

I have a set of data I would like to display as a list. The data includes several different quantities, and I would like to display them side by side to make it easier for the reader to compare them. I don't want this to look like a table, though. How can I do this in HTML?

Technique

In HTML 3.0, the **WRAP** attribute added to a bulleted list will wrap list items across the screen into a set of columns. You can combine this with other attributes, such as **BLANK**, to create unmarked multicolumn lists.

Steps

1. Open your document. Identify the locations in your document where you want to include a list.

2. Place the items you want to include in the list in your document, using carriage returns to separate the items for clarity.

```
Red Sox
Cubs
Royals
Dodgers
Indians
Angels
White Sox
```

3. Place an **<LI>** tag in front of each list item.

```
<LI>Red Sox
<LI>Cubs
<LI>Royals
<LI>Dodgers
<LI>Indians
<LI>Angels
<LI>White Sox
```

4. To create a list in which the items go across the screen and then down, use the `<UL>` and `</UL>` tags with the attribute `WRAP="horiz"`.

```
<UL WRAP=HORIZ>
<LI>Red Sox
<LI>Cubs
<LI>Royals
<LI>Dodgers
<LI>Indians
<LI>Angels
<LI>White Sox
</UL>
```

5. To create a list in which the items go down the page before starting a new column, use the attribute `WRAP="vert"`.

```
<UL WRAP=VERT>
<LI>Red Sox
<LI>Cubs
<LI>Royals
<LI>Dodgers
<LI>Indians
<LI>Angels
<LI>White Sox
</UL>
```

How It Works

When an HTML 3.0-compliant browser reads the `WRAP` attribute, it formats the list items that follow it according to the attribute's value. If the `WRAP` attribute is set to `"horiz"`, it places the list items across the screen in a row until the end of the window is reached, and then it starts a new row. When the `WRAP` attribute is set to `"vert"`, it places list items down the screen until it reaches the bottom of the window, and then it starts a new column.

Comments

In a multicolumn list, the number of columns and the contents of each are controlled solely by the browser, not by the text. If you want explicit control over the layout of a multicolumn list, it would be better to set it up as a table, which provides explicit control over layout. Chapter 5, "Tables," discusses tables in detail. The `WRAP` attribute of the `<UL>` element does not appear in the HTML 3.2 or 4.0 standard.

As previously mentioned, the clearest alternative to creating the desired effect of this attribute is to format the list data as an HTML `<TABLE>` element rather than as a list. See Chapter 5 for further information on the creation and organization of HTML tables. Figure 22-3 displays several of these potential alternatives. The HTML code for this document appears in the `WRAP.HTM` file on the CD-ROM.

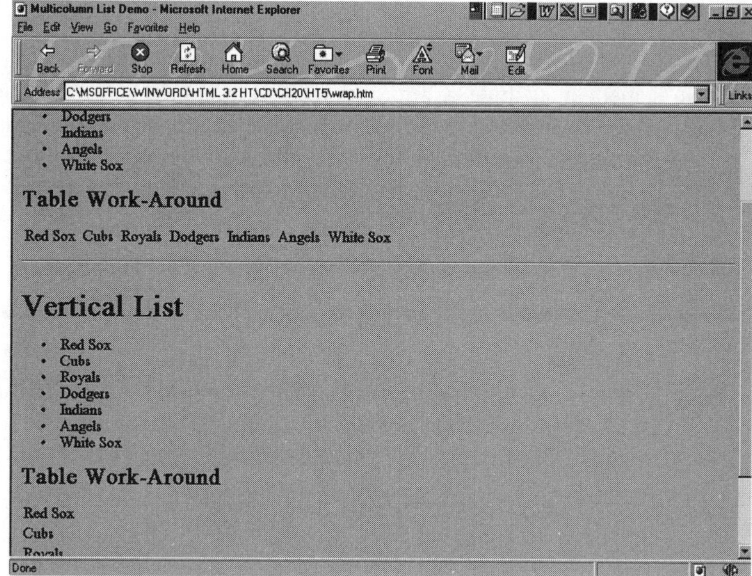

Figure 22-3 Multicolumn list alternatives

COMPLEXITY
BEGINNING

22.6 How do I... Specify the language context for the remainder of a Web page?

COMPATIBILITY: HTML 3.0, NETSCAPE, INTERNET EXPLORER

Problem

I am developing Web pages for an international audience, and I must provide multiple languages in my pages. How do I specify the appropriate character set to display the information in a particular language?

Technique

A proposed addition to the HTML 4.0 standard is the inclusion of the **LANG** element and attribute. Most other HTML 4.0 elements would support the use of **LANG** as an attribute.

Using the **LANG** attribute, you can select the appropriate language to use within the current HTML element. Using the **LANG** element, you can select the appropriate language to use over a specified range of your Web page.

Steps

The following steps walk you through the process of specifying a language using the **LANG** element or attribute, as appropriate. If you want to change the language of an existing Web page element only, use the **LANG** attribute. If you want to alter the language specification for a larger portion of the document, use the **LANG** element.

Adding a LANG Attribute

1. Open the Web page that you want to modify in a text editor.
2. Move the cursor to the end of the opening tag of the element that you want to modify.
3. Add the **LANG** attribute to this tag. The values associated with this attribute are the class and subclass strings that represent the desired language. Examine, for example, this level 1 header element: **<H1> å "   </H1>**.

   For display in Hebrew, you might add the following **LANG** attribute: `<H1 LANG="ISO8859-8"> å "    </H1>`.

> **NOTE**
>
> **HTML documents will appear in the appropriate language only in an application properly configured to deal with the alternative language. If the application is not properly configured, the page displayed will likely appear meaningless.**

4. Save the document.

Adding a LANG Element

1. Open the Web page that you want to modify in a text editor.
2. Move the cursor to the point just before where you want to specify the language change.
3. Insert a **<LANG>** element opening tag with a **LANG** attribute, as described in step 3 of the preceding procedure. For example, an opening tag to indicate the choice of the Cyrillic character set might appear as

```
<LANG LANG="KI08-R">
```

> **NOTE**
>
> **HTML documents will appear in the appropriate language only in an application properly configured to deal with the alternative language. If the application is not properly configured, the page displayed will likely appear meaningless.**

4. Move the cursor to the point where you want the language change to end and insert a `</LANG>` element closing tag.

```
</LANG>
```

5. Save the document.

How It Works

Browser applications display Web pages according to the character set specified in their configurations. Viewers can alter this default manually in most browsers. However, the LANG element and attribute assume that browsers eventually might support dynamic selection of character sets relevant to portions of a Web page.

An author specifies this linguistic shift as appropriate to the particular page authored. The specification may be at several levels of granularity: a single element, a portion of the page, or the entire Web page.

NOTE

A limited number of current browsers support the entire Web page level of granularity.

The two finer grains of specification are the province of the LANG attribute and element. Specifying a language with respect to an entire page is briefly discussed in the "Comments" section. In general, browsers should select the rendering language based on the proximity of the language specification to the text. The closest LANG attribute, whether in a LANG element or in another enclosing element, takes precedence. If the particular language is not supported by the browser, the browser should use the next closest. This selection process continues outward from the current element until the author-defined document-level language selection; this language serves as a default when no other language selection applies. If the browser does not support this default language, the browser should use the default language configured by the reader.

In the case of the LANG element, a LANG attribute of this element is also required. Whenever you use a LANG attribute, the value associated with the attribute is the name of the desired language. The current proposal for language naming is RFC 1766. Feel free to consult this reference; check a Web search tool for a current location. Under this standard, you compose a language name of a base type, optionally followed by a dash and a subtype. For example, EN represents the English language base type. From this base type, EN-US and EN-UK might, respectively, represent the United States and United Kingdom variants of the English language.

Some browsers, however, may opt for the use of particular character set designations as the appropriate value. IANA maintains a listing of currently registered character sets in a subdirectory of URL `ftp://ftp.isi.edu/in-notes/iana/assignments/`.

Comments

Currently, the `LANG` attribute is only a proposed addition to the standard. The WWW Consortium maintains current information on this developing standard, and additional information on the further internationalization of HTML and the Web, at `http://www.w3.org/pub/WWW/International/`.

Currently, neither Netscape Navigator nor Microsoft Internet Explorer supports this attribute. However, both browsers do support limited selection of character sets through the inclusion of a character-set parameter in the `Content-type` field in the response header returning a document. Authors may selectively add such a field using the `<META>` element. For example, the following `<META>` element would indicate use of the ISO8859-8 character set (Hebrew), as shown in Figure 22-4:

```
<META HTTP-EQUIV="Content-Type" CONTENT="text/html; charset=iso-8859-8">
```

Depending on the particular language, a browser may require manual adjustment of the character set encoding and font choice. For additional information on internationalization using Netscape, see URL `http://home.netscape.com/people/ftang/i18n.html`. For additional information on internationalization using Internet Explorer, see URL `http://www.microsoft.com/ie/most/howto/multi.htm`.

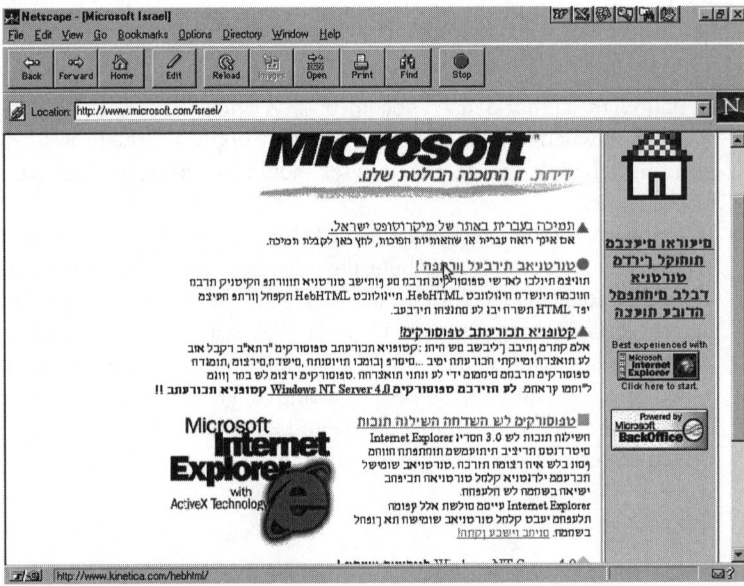

Figure 22-4 Use of the Hebrew character set

COMPLEXITY
INTERMEDIATE

22.7 How do I... Place an embedded quotation?

COMPATIBILITY: HTML 3.0, 4.0

Problem

I want to include a quotation in my page. However, I would like the browser to do the work of including the appropriate quotation marks for a given language. How can I embed this quotation using HTML?

Technique

HTML 3.0 introduced the **<Q>** tag, which places quotation marks around the tagged text. By adding the **LANG** attribute, you can tell the browser to use the quotation marks specific to a certain language.

Steps

1. To insert an embedded quotation, place the **<Q>** tag at the beginning of the text and **</Q>** at the end of the text.

```
Hamlet said, <Q>To be, or not to be, that is the question.</Q>
```

2. To use the quotation marks from a specific language, insert the **LANG** attribute in the **<Q>** tag and set it equal to a language. Languages are usually referred to by a two-letter abbreviation, such as **EN** for English, **FR** for French, and **DE** for German. The following line of code calls for the use of English (specifically, American English, which is represented by **EN-US**) quotation marks:

```
Hamlet said, <Q LANG="EN-US">To be, or not to be, that is the question.</Q>
```

To render the quotes as used in German, the code would look like this:

```
Hamlet said, <Q LANG="DE">To be, or not to be, that is the question.</Q>
```

The first draft of HTML 4.0 includes the **CITE** attribute of **<Q>**, which can be set to the URL of the document from which the quotation comes.

```
Hamlet said, <Q CITE="http://www.mysite.edu/shakespeare/hamlet.html">To ⇐
 be, or not to be, that is the question.</Q>
```

How It Works

When a browser encounters a **<Q>** tag, it replaces the **<Q>** and **</Q>** tags with opening and closing quotes, respectively. The text and the quotes are also rendered in italics. It uses the quotes for the language specified by the **LANG** attribute, or the default quotes if none is given.

Comments

The **<Q>** tag was introduced in HTML 3.0 and removed from HTML 3.2, so it is not supported by many browsers. Although the **<Q>** tag can be useful for rendering quotation symbols, especially for other languages, it might be simpler just to add the quote symbols manually, if they are available. As of this writing, neither Navigator nor Internet Explorer supports quotation symbols used in non-English languages. Furthermore, this element generates no visual effect in either browser.

This element does not appear in the HTML 3.2 standard. The **<BLOCKQUOTE>** element described in How-To 7.8 provides a potential alternative. Figure 22-5 displays several of these potential alternatives. The HTML code for this document appears in the **QUOTE.HTM** file on the CD-ROM.

The first draft of the HTML 4.0 proposal does include the **<Q>** tag and the new **CITE** attribute. However, this tag is not yet supported by the major browsers and is not guaranteed to appear in future drafts of the proposal.

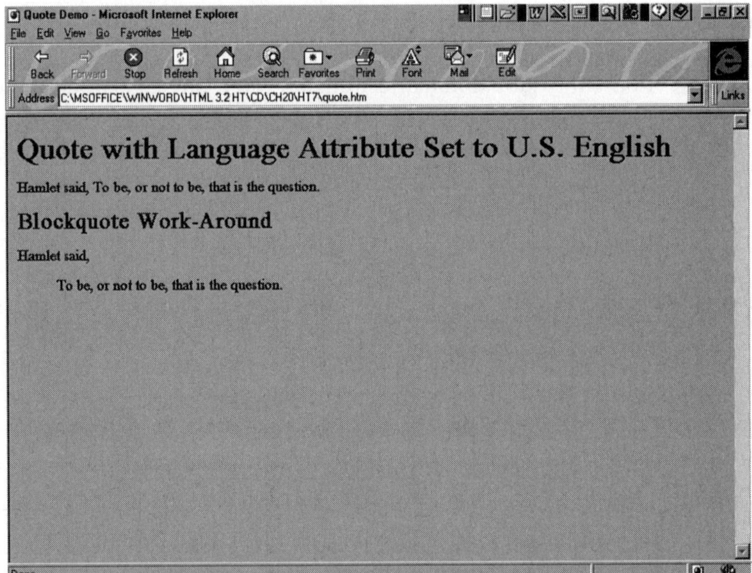

Figure 22-5 Quotation alternative

22.8 How do I... Align text with tabs?

COMPATIBILITY: HTML 3.0

Problem

I would like to control the horizontal spacing in my document. I want to be able to specify where I want items to appear and whether the items are centered, left-justified, or right-justified. How can I specify this type of formatting information with HTML 3.0?

Technique

There are several ways to specify horizontal alignment of text.

- ✔ Center element: This element began as a Netscape Navigator extension, but the HTML 3.2 standard adopted it. A center element is added like any other element. Use the procedure defined in How-To 7.3.
- ✔ Table element: This element allows for the fine control of the horizontal and vertical positioning of information and data. Use the procedures described in Chapter 5, "Tables," and Chapter 7, "Managing Document Spacing," to align text and data using tables.
- ✔ Tab elements: Tab elements are used to establish horizontal tabs in your HTML document. Because tabs were part of the HTML 3.0 specification, they are more likely to be understood and rendered than a center element.

Steps

Use the following steps to set and use tabs within an HTML 3.0 document. These tabs enable you to align text within the body of your HTML documents.

1. Open the HTML document you want to edit in your favorite text editor. (See How-To 2.4 on editing environments.) If your HTML editor enables you to create `<TAB>` elements with macro or menu options, follow the instructions for the editor.

2. Place the insertion point where you want to place the `<TAB>` element within your document.

3. Insert the appropriate `<TAB>` element in your document. `<TAB>` elements are empty and therefore do not require a closing tag. Use Table 22-1 to select the proper `<TAB>` element for your use.

Table 22-1 Attributes for the <TAB> element

TAB ELEMENT FORMAT	PURPOSE
`<TAB ID="name">`	Sets a tab at the current location default aligned left.
`<TAB ID="name" ALIGN="alignment">`	Sets a tab with a particular alignment.
`<TAB TO="name">`	Jumps to the specified tab location.
`<TAB INDENT=x>`	Indents x en spaces.
`<TAB ALIGN="right">`	Places remainder of the line flush right.
`<TAB ALIGN="center">`	Centers text between margins.
`<TAB ALIGN="left">`	Places text flush to the left.

4. Save your document, or continue editing. If you want to add additional `<TAB>` elements, return to step 2.

How It Works

You can align text horizontally with tabs. The `<TAB>` element supports the following attributes:

- `ALIGN="alignment"`: This specifies the alignment of the tab. This attribute has one of four values: `"left"`, `"right"`, `"center"`, and `"decimal"`. These values determine how text is situated with respect to the tab.
- `DP="c"`: This attribute specifies the character to be used by a decimal tab to align text. The default value is the period. However, if you want to align a tab with another character, include this attribute with the desired tab character as a value. For example, if you include `DP="$"` in the `<TAB>` opening tag, the tab will align along the dollar sign.
- `ID="name"`: This associates a name with a specific horizontal tab location. You can use the value associated with `ID` as the value of a `TO` attribute. In effect, using the `ID` attribute sets a tab at the named location. See the examples provided next.
- `INDENT="x"`: This allows the specification of a leading indent. The integer value associated with this attribute specifies the number of en spaces to indent a particular line. This attribute should not be used in conjunction with a `TO` attribute.
- `TO="name"`: Like `ID`, this takes a name as a value. The value indicates the horizontal position for the browser to tab forward to before rendering the text.

To indent several lines of text, use a `<TAB>` element with the `INDENT` attribute set. For example, the following code indents the specified line five en spaces. The `<BR>` element is used to force a line break at the location where the element appears. (Refer to How-To 7.4 for further information on the line break element.)

```
This line has no indentation.<BR>
<TAB INDENT=5>This line is indented 5 en spaces.
```

The resulting text looks like this:

```
This line has no indentation.
     This line is indented 5 en spaces.
```

Use a **<TAB>** element with an **ID** attribute to set tab locations. If you want a tab stop with other than left alignment, use the **ALIGN** attribute to specify the alignment. For example, use the following code to specify a left-aligned tab after the word **"bear"**. The second line represents a line indented right below the first.

```
We will watch the bear <TAB ID="bear"> walk through<BR>
<TAB TO="bear> the woods and take joy in this delight.
```

This would be rendered by browsers as follows:

```
We will watch the bear walk through
                       the woods and take joy in this delight.
```

If you use the **ALIGN** attribute without a **TO** attribute, the tab overrides the default alignment with respect to the margins of the page. If no paragraph elements are used, then this default alignment is left. If paragraph elements are used, you can set a default alignment for a particular paragraph using the same **ALIGN** attribute values as specified for a tab. (Refer to How-To 7.4 for further information on the paragraph element.)

```
<P ALIGN="center">
This line is centered.<BR>
So is this one.<BR>
<TAB ALIGN="left">This one is left justified.<BR>
Back to center.
```

This would appear in a browser as

```
                         This line is centered.
                            So is this one.
This one is left justified.
                            Back to center.
```

If you use a **<TAB>** element with both an **ALIGN** attribute and a **TO** attribute, the text following the tab is placed at the tab stop identified as the **TO** value and aligned as specified in the **ALIGN** value. The **DP** attribute enables you to define the character to align around. The default is the decimal point.

```
I will set my <TAB ID="here"> at this point.<BR>
<TAB ALIGN="decimal" TO="here">$500.00<BR>
<TAB ALIGN="decimal" TO="here">$1000.00<BR>
<TAB ALIGN="decimal" TO="here">approx $50.00
```

These lines appear as

```
I will set my at this point.
         $500.00
        $1000.00
  approx $50.00
```

The tab in this case is aligned around the decimal point.

Comments

A more complete discussion of the paragraph element is provided in How-To 7.4. This element can be used to establish the default horizontal alignment for a block of lines. The **<TAB>** element is not currently supported by any popular browsers. Furthermore, it does not appear in the HTML 4.0 standard. Unless use of the **<TAB>** element is mandatory, strongly consider using a **<TABLE>** element as a more powerful alternative.

22.9 How do I... Insert cautionary notes?

COMPATIBILITY: HTML 3.0

Problem

I want to deliver a warning to readers of my Web page. The message must stick out somehow and grab the reader's attention.

Technique

HTML 3.0 provides the **<NOTE>** element to support the specification of messages admonishing the reader of a page. You use this element by including it and the appropriate note text within the context of the Web page.

Steps

The following procedure provides step-by-step instructions for including a note as an admonishment within a Web page:

1. Open your Web page in a text editor.
2. Move your cursor to the position where you want the note to appear.
3. Insert a note element opening tag. The key attribute that should also appear in this tag is the **CLASS** element. The value of this attribute represents the type of note desired by the author. Table 22-2 summarizes these potential values and their respective purposes.

Table 22-2 Values for the `CLASS` attribute of `<NOTE>`

CLASS VALUE	NOTE TYPE
`note`	General purpose note.
`warning`	Provides the reader with a warning.
`caution`	Cautions the user against inappropriate actions.

4. Optionally, add an **SRC** attribute and value. Add this attribute if you want an image displayed as part of the note or if you want to override the browser's default image associated with a message of a given **CLASS**. The actual use of the **SRC** attribute may vary among different browsers.
5. Type the text of the note.
6. Insert a closing note tag.
7. Save the document.

How It Works

When a browser encounters a **<NOTE>** element, the browser should set the note off from the remainder of the page in such a way as to draw the reader's attention to the warning provided. The Arena browser associates a particular image with each of the potential note classes.

Comments

This element did not appear in the HTML 3.2 standard. Furthermore, this element is not directly supported by either Netscape Navigator or Microsoft Internet Explorer.

As an alternative, an author could use the indentation created through the "misuse" of a definition list or a block quote. (Refer to How-To 6.8 for more information on the proper use of a definition list or How-To 7.8 on block quotations.) This definition list mimics the appropriate indentation for a note. However, in this situation, the author would need to include an indicative image explicitly rather than count on an appropriate default image associated with the note's **CLASS** attribute. So for a warning note, the following might be an appropriate HTML 4.0-supported alternative:

```
<DL>
<DD>
<!-- An appropriate image inclusion using the IMG or OBJECT element as
 appropriate -->
Warning: You are entering a restricted area. If you are seeing this
message, you have gone too far.
Please report yourself to the nearest re-education center. War is peace.
</DL>

<BLOCKQUOTE>
<!-- An appropriate image inclusion using the IMG or OBJECT element as
appropriate -->
Warning: You are entering a restricted area. If you are seeing this
message, you have gone too far.
Please report yourself to the nearest re-education center. War is peace.
</BLOCKQUOTE>
```

The file **NOTE.HTM** on the CD-ROM contains the complete source for a simple Web page including this note. Figure 22-6 displays this document.

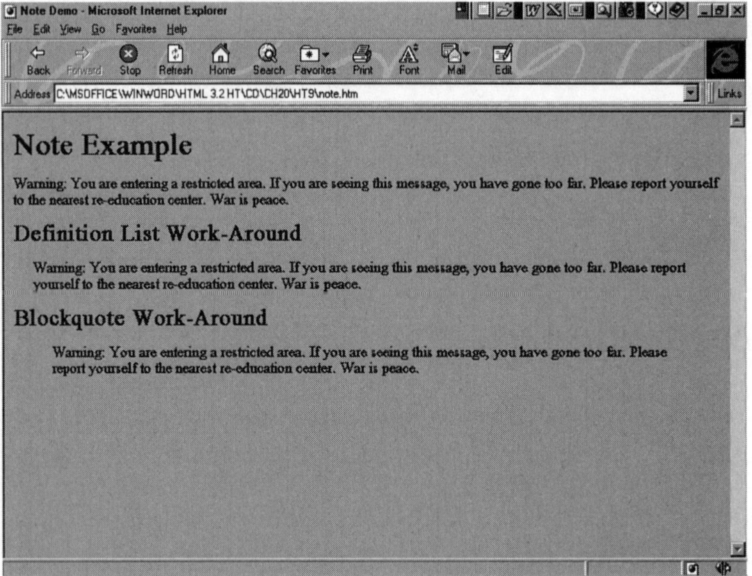

Figure 22-6 Mimicking a <NOTE> element with a definition list

22.10 How do I... Add a footnote?

COMPATIBILITY: HTML 3.0

Problem

Often scholarly works require the use of footnotes to credit original ideas and quotes properly. Authors also use footnotes to clarify cryptic portions of a literary work. How do I add a footnote to a Web page?

Technique

The HTML 3.0 standard provided the **<FN>** element to support the inclusion of footnotes in Web page. You place the footnote material within the bounds of the opening and closing tag of the element. The intent in the specification of this element is that the material should appear as a pop-up window when the reader triggers a link referencing the particular footnote. The target of the link is a named location within the current Web document. The named location is a specific **<FN>** element.

Steps

The following procedure provides a stepwise approach to the inclusion of footnotes within your Web page.

1. Open your Web page in a text editor.
2. Move to the end of the body portion of your Web page.
3. Insert an `<FN>` element opening tag. Choose a value for the `ID` attribute of this tag that is unique within the scope of this Web page.
4. Add the text of the footnote.
5. End the footnote text with an `<FN>` element closing tag.
6. Locate the text in your page that will reference a footnote and move the insertion point to just before this location. For example, you could create a footnote text referencing William Shakespeare with the following footnote element:

```
<FN ID="fn1">William Shakespeare</FN >
```

7. Insert an anchor around this text. The target (`HREF` attribute) of this anchor should name a location within the current document (a value beginning with a pound [#] sign). For example, if you want to link the phrase `To be, or not to be...` to a footnote, you might use the following anchor attribute around the phrase:

```
<A HREF="#fn1">To be, or not to be ... </A>
```

   This would link the quote to the footnote with an `ID` of `fn1`.

8. Save the document.

How It Works

The footnote element provides you with a mechanism to specify text that should appear in a pop-up window when a reader triggers the link attached to that footnote. The `<FN>` element delimits the text that appears in the pop-up window. The link locates the footnote text in the same manner that a named location within a document is found. When the location is found, the browser determines that the target of the link is a footnote rather than a named document location. After the browser makes this determination, it can display the footnote contents appropriately.

Comments

Because this element did not appear in the HTML 3.2 standard and neither Navigator nor Internet Explorer supports this element, you should seriously consider the available alternatives to this element. HTML 3.2 and 4.0 provide several alternative approaches to this task:

✔ Use anchor elements rather than footnote elements.

✔ Use a scripted procedure to produce the desired footnote.

✔ Use a Java application to support a pop-up message.

See Chapter 17, "Web Programming with Java and JavaScript," for some of the basics of Java and JavaScript programming. The first alternative uses anchors rather than the footnote element. The references within the document do not change, but instead of `<FN>` tags, use `<A>` tags around the intended footnote. Where the footnote element used an `ID` attribute in the opening tag, the anchor opening tag should use a `NAME` attribute.

COMPLEXITY
INTERMEDIATE

22.11 How do I... Place a mathematical equation in my Web page?

COMPATIBILITY: HTML 3.0

Problem

The material I want to include on my page contains several mathematical formulas that are difficult to show using normal text characters. I would like to show these equations as text, without having to resort to graphics. How can I format mathematical equations in HTML?

Technique

HTML 3.0 included several elements that can be used to format mathematical equations in the text of a page. The `<MATH>` element is used to identify equations, and tags contained within the `<MATH>` tag are used to format the equation. With these tags, you can display complicated equations with subscripts and superscripts, square roots, vectors, and other special symbols. You can use other tags to display integrals, summation symbols, and other mathematical symbols. Unfortunately, these commands do not exist in HTML 2.0 (or HTML 3.2 or 4.0), so older and newer browsers can't recognize them and, therefore, can't format the text correctly.

Steps

1. Open your document and locate the areas in the document where you would like to place mathematical formulas. Type plain-text versions of the formulas now to guide you later, when you add the HTML `<MATH>` tags.

2. To identify any equation, place the $tag at the beginning of the function and the$ tag at the end of the function.

```
The equation for kinetic energy is <MATH>E = 1/2mv2</MATH>
The function of the curve is <MATH>y = (3 + x)/(5 - 2x)</MATH>
```

3. As discussed in Chapter 3, "Adding HTML Physical Character Effects," you can use the <SUP> and <SUB> tags for superscripts and subscripts, respectively. However, within the and tags, you can use shortcuts for those tags: ^ for ^{and}, and _ for _{and}.

```
The equation for kinetic energy is <MATH>E = 1/2mv^2^</MATH>
The line can be represented by the equation <MATH>y = c_0_ + c_1_*x</MATH>
```

4. To express fractions, you can use the <BOX> and <OVER> tags. Place <BOX> at the beginning of the fraction, </BOX> at the end of the fraction, and <OVER> where the division between the numerator and denominator occurs. Within the <MATH> tag, you can substitute { (the left brace) for <BOX> and } (the right brace) for </BOX>.

```
The equation for kinetic energy is <MATH>E = <BOX>1<OVER>2</BOX> ⇐
mv^2^</MATH>
The equation for kinetic energy is <MATH>E = {1<OVER>2}mv^2^</MATH>
```

5. To place fractions and other mathematical equations in parentheses, brackets, braces, or horizontal lines, use the <BOX> tag and the desired symbol. Use the <LEFT> tag at the beginning of the expression, just after the symbol, and the <RIGHT> tag at the end of the expression, just before the closing symbol.

```
<MATH>{(<LEFT>3+x<OVER>5-2x<RIGHT>)}</MATH>
<MATH>{[<LEFT>3+2x<OVER>5-2x<RIGHT>]}</MATH>
<MATH>{|<LEFT>3+2x<OVER>5-2x<RIGHT>|}</MATH>
<MATH>{&ltbrace;<LEFT>3+2x<OVER>5-2x<RIGHT>&rtbrace;}</MATH>
```

Note that to display something within braces, you must use the special characters <brace; and &rtbrace; for the left brace and right brace symbols, respectively.

6. HTML 3.0 also provides several tags you can use within the <MATH> element to display special modified characters such as vectors, dots, and bars, shown in Table 22-3.

Table 22-3 Special mathematical symbols in HTML

TAG	DEFINITION
<VEC>	Displays a vector over a character.
<BAR>	Displays a horizontal bar over a character.
<DOT>	Displays a single dot over a character.
<DDOT>	Displays a double dot over a character.
<HAT>	Displays a hat (carat) (^) over a character.
<TILDE>	Displays a tilde (~) over a character.

For example:

```
The equation for kinetic energy is <MATH><VEC>E</VEC> = 1/2m<VEC>v</VEC> ⇐
^2^</MATH>

The average value of x, <MATH><BAR>x</BAR></MATH>, was 42.
```

7. The **<SQRT>** tag places the text found between it and the **</SQRT>** tag inside the square root symbol. A more general form is the **<ROOT>** tag, which, along with the **<OF>** tag, places the text between the **<OF>** and **</ROOT>** tags inside the root symbol and places the text located between the **<ROOT>** and **<OF>** in the area of the root symbol used to designate the power of the root (**2** for square root, **3** for cube root, and so on):

```
The Pythagorean theorem states that <MATH>c = <SQRT>a^2^ + Ü b^2^</SQRT> ⇐
</MATH>

The radius of a sphere with volume V is <MATH><ROOT>3<OF>{3V<OVER>4pi} ⇐
</ROOT></MATH>
```

Examples of the various mathematical styles are shown in Figure 22-7. The code is also available on the CD-ROM as file **MATH.HTM**.

How It Works

The **<MATH>** tag alerts the browser that the text contained within the **$** and **$** tags requires special formatting, including symbols that have different meanings within the **<MATH>** tags than they have in normal text. The special tags encountered within the **<MATH>** tags are then converted into appropriate graphics and spacing, according to the specifications of the browser.

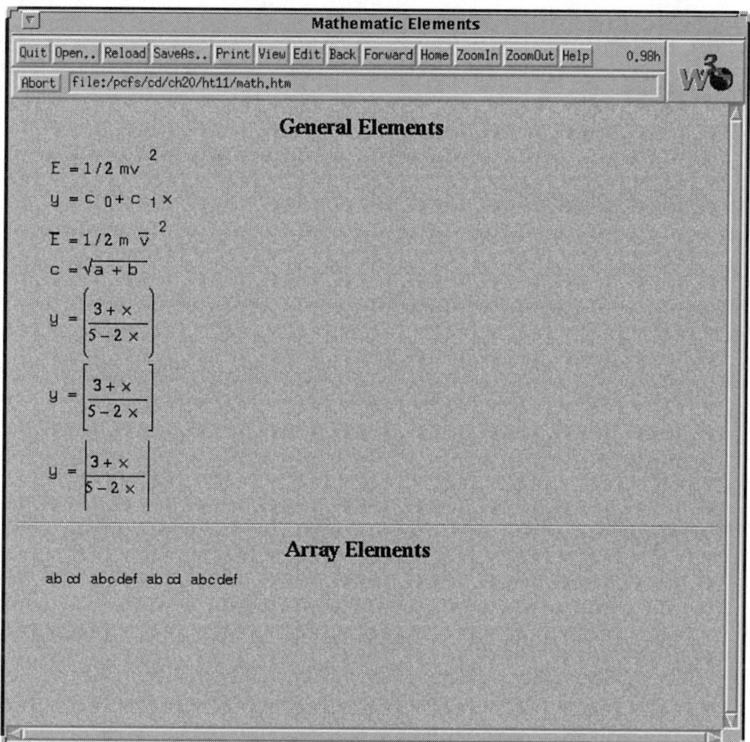

Figure 22-7 Use of math elements in a Web page

Comments

Because this mathematical notation is available only in HTML 3.0, people using pre-HTML 3.0 or post-HTML 3.0 browsers will not be able to see the appropriate graphics and spacing, which may render some equations more confusing than if they had been left as plain text. Keep this in mind when creating your documents. Also, not all the mathematical elements had been incorporated into Arena, the HTML 3.0 testbed browser; the browser did not yet support roots and some special characters. Neither Netscape Navigator nor Microsoft Internet Explorer supports mathematical symbols of any kind at this time. Work in the area of supporting mathematical symbols through HTML is continuing. The World Wide Web Consortium provides the most current information on work in this area.

22.12 How do I... Insert an array into a <MATH> element?

COMPATIBILITY: HTML 3.0

Problem

The material I want to include on my page contains mathematical matrices that are difficult to show using normal text characters. I would like to show these matrices as text, without having to resort to graphics. How can I format mathematical matrices in HTML?

Technique

HTML 3.0 includes several elements that can be used to support the inclusion of matrices within the context of a **<MATH>** element. The **<MATH>** element is used to identify and to format the mathematical constructs within a Web page. Within the **<MATH>** element, HTML 3.0 provides the **<ARRAY>**, **<ROW>**, and **<ITEM>** elements to create and manage matrices. Unfortunately, these commands do not exist in other versions of HTML, including 3.2 and 4.0, so most browsers don't recognize them and thus can't format the text correctly.

Steps

1. Open your document and locate the areas in the document where you would like to place your array.

2. To identify any matrix/array, place the **$** tag at the beginning of the matrix and the **$** tag at the end.

3. To create an array, use the **<ARRAY>** tag to define the beginning of an array and **</ARRAY>** to mark the end of the array. Within these tags, the **<ROW>** tag marks the beginning of a new row in the array and **<ITEM>** marks a new entry in the array.

```
<ARRAY>
    <ROW><ITEM>a<ITEM>b
    <ROW><ITEM>c<ITEM>d
</ARRAY>

<ARRAY>
    <ROW><ITEM>a<ITEM>b<ITEM>c
    <ROW><ITEM>d<ITEM>e<ITEM>f
</ARRAY>
```

4. To align the array within the window, use the **ALIGN** attribute within the **<ARRAY>** tag.

```
<ARRAY ALIGN=CENTER>
     <ROW><ITEM>a<ITEM>b
     <ROW><ITEM>c<ITEM>d
</ARRAY>
```

5. To align columns in the array, use the **COLDEF** attribute within the **<ARRAY>** tag. This attribute uses a capital letter to signify the alignment for each column in the array: **L** for left, **C** for center, **R** for right. For example, to align the first two columns in the center, but align the third column on the right, enter

```
<ARRAY COLDEF="CCR">
     <ROW><ITEM>a<ITEM>b
     <ROW><ITEM>c<ITEM>d
</ARRAY>
```

Examples of the various mathematical styles are shown in Figure 22-7. The code is also available on the CD-ROM as file **MATH.HTM**. The Arena browser displayed used in Figure 22-7 does not support **<ARRAY>** elements.

How It Works

The **<MATH>** tag alerts the browser that the text contained within the **$** and **$** tags requires special formatting, including symbols that have different meanings within the **<MATH>** tags than they have in normal text. The special tags encountered within the **<MATH>** tags are then converted into appropriate graphics and spacing according to the specifications of the browser.

Specifically, the **<ARRAY>**, **<ROW>**, and **<ITEM>** elements enable you to control the specific layout of a desired matrix. Each row of the intended matrix starts with a **<ROW>** element open tag; by default, the next **<ROW>** open tag ends the current row. Use the **<ITEM>** element to delimit the individual items within a row of the matrix. All **<ROW>** elements are within the scope of the enclosing **<ARRAY>** element. The array element supports several attributes within its opening tag:

- ✔ **ALIGN**: The **ALIGN** attribute describes the placement of the matrix with respect to the text immediately preceding or following it. The acceptable values for this attribute are **top**, **bottom**, and **middle**. These values hold the same meanings that they do in the context of embedded image alignment as described in How-To 9.3.

- ✔ **COLDEF**: The **COLDEF** attribute takes a string as its value. This string can contain the following characters: **+**, **–**, **=**, **C**, **L**, and **R**. The combination of such characters determines the formatting of the columns in the matrix. The **+**, **–**, and **=** signs instruct the browser to place the sign used between columns of the matrix. The **C**, **L**, and **R** values indicate that a particular column of the matrix should be center-, left-, and right-aligned, respectively.

NOTE

An ALIGN attribute used for a particular <ITEM> element will override the alignment suggested in the COLDEF string.

- ✔ LABELS: This attribute requires no value. It indicates to the browser that the first column and the first row of data represent header information rather than actual data. When you use this tag, the first <ITEM> in the first <ROW> element is ignored; however, this item must be present and not empty for proper management.

Comments

Current browsers do not support the <MATH> element; consequently, the <ARRAY> element and its subelements are also not supported. Research continues into the development of suitable elements to include mathematics within Web pages. For current information on this topic, refer to the HTML Activity Statement at URL http://www.w3.org/.

22.13 How do I... Change the shape of a link?

COMPATIBILITY: HTML 3.0, 4.0

Problem

I would like to define a certain area of a figure on my page as a link to a specific document. I don't want to go though the hassle of creating an imagemap, though. Is there a way to accomplish this using HTML 3.0?

Technique

The HTML 3.0 SHAPE attribute permits links of different shapes and sizes to be included in figures (using the HTML 3.0 <FIG> tag). SHAPE lets you do many of the same things an imagemap (see Chapter 9, "Using Images in Your Documents") does, but without the need to create a separate map file or deal with Common Gateway Interface (CGI) scripts.

Steps

1. Open your document. Also, load an image with a viewer that enables you to get the pixel locations on the image so that you can specify image locations in the links.

2. Decide what areas on the image will serve as links. These areas can be circles, rectangles, or even complex polygons. Note the pixel locations of the areas: the x coordinate increases to the right, and the y coordinate increases downward.

3. Create a list of links, as described in How-To 8.16. For each link, include the `SHAPE` attribute. The `SHAPE` attribute can take on the forms shown in Table 22-4.

Table 22-4 `SHAPE` **attribute types**

ATTRIBUTE	DESCRIPTION
`circle x,y,r`	A circle centered at the point (`x,y`) with radius `r`.
`rect x,y,w,h`	A rectangle of width `w` and height `h` with its upper-left corner at (`x,y`).
`polygon x1,y1,x2,y2,...`	A polygon that consists of lines linking the points (`x1,y1`), (`x2,y2`), and so on. The polygon is closed by a line linking the last set of points to the first set.
`default`	The background of the figure, which includes those points not inside a circle, rectangle, or polygon.

For example, a simple list consisting of a circle, rectangle, and triangle (three-point polygon), as well as a default link for the rest of the figure, might look like this:

```
<UL>
    <LI><A SHAPE="circle 10,10,5" HREF="page1.html">Page 1</A>
    <LI><A SHAPE="rect 30,20,10,5" HREF="page2.html">Page 2</A>
    <LI><A SHAPE="polygon 50,40,40,40,40,30" HREF="page3.html">Page 3</A>
</UL>
```

See Figure 22-8 for an example of how this would look.

4. This list of shaped links is then incorporated into a figure, using the HTML 3.0 `<FIG>` tag. An example using the list might look like this:

```
<FIG SRC="book.gif">
    <UL>
        <LI><A SHAPE="circle 10,10,5" HREF="page1.html">Page 1</A>
        <LI><A SHAPE="rect 30,20,10,5" HREF="page2.html">Page 2</A>
        <LI><A SHAPE="polygon 50,40,40,40,40,30" HREF="page3.html">Page ⇐
3</A>
</UL>
</FIG>
```

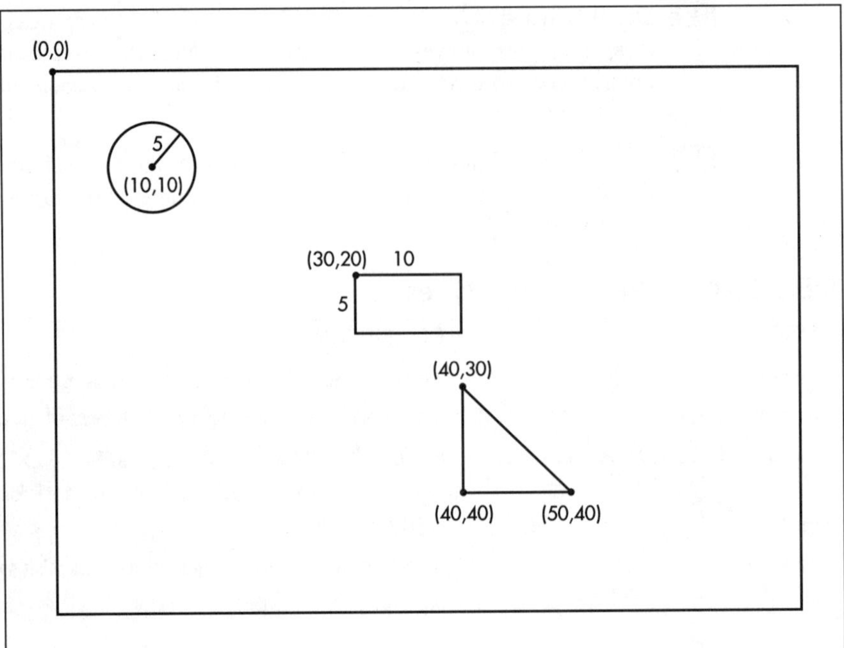

Figure 22-8 A sample imagemap for the SHAPE attribute

How It Works

The **SHAPE** attribute defines an area on the image as a link. If a reader selects that part of the image, the link is activated the way any other link would be. This works just as an imagemap would, but without the need to create a separate map file of the image or write a script to interpret the imagemap.

Comments

If a person selects an area of an image where two or more links overlap, the browser finds the link whose center is closest to the selected point and chooses it. If the default link is not created in the figure, any part of the figure outside the linked areas is not active and is not linked to other documents.

The **SHAPE** attribute was designed to be used in conjunction with the **<FIG>** element, which was proposed in HTML 3.0 as a more advanced version of **<IMG>**. However, **<FIG>** was not included in the HTML 3.2 or 4.0 specification and will likely not be found in future HTML versions. See How-To's 9.10 and 9.11 for ways to incorporate standard server-side and client-side imagemaps.

The first draft of the HTML 4.0 proposal includes the **SHAPE** attribute of **<A>**, designed to be used in conjunction with the **<OBJECT>** tag. However, this attribute is not yet widely supported and is not guaranteed to appear in future drafts of the HTML 4.0 proposal.

CHAPTER 23

SOME OF THE BEST SITES ON THE WEB

23

SOME OF THE BEST SITES ON THE WEB

A book on HTML isn't complete without some reference to pages on the Web that are cool. The following, although by no means all-encompassing, is a list of some of the best, coolest, and most useful spots on the Web. The criteria for inclusion were

- ✔ Visual interface
- ✔ Behind-the-scenes HTML
- ✔ Usefulness

The description of each Web page listed here includes a discussion of why its visual interface deserves mention and what HTML feature was used to make the page truly outstanding. We hope that perusing the pages in this chapter will give you inspiration for your own Web pages.

The Dominion

URL: `http://www.scifi.com/`
Owner: The SciFi Channel
Webmaster: Jamie Biggar
Purpose: Entertainment
The Dominion, the SciFi Channel's Web site, is one of the older but cooler sites on the Web. It is the place to go for all the latest info on what's happening in the world of sci-fi. Figure 23-1 shows The Dominion.

From the opening page on, you are greeted with simple yet smart backgrounds, animated icons, and a nice Java script that tells you the number of days you have left until the millennium.

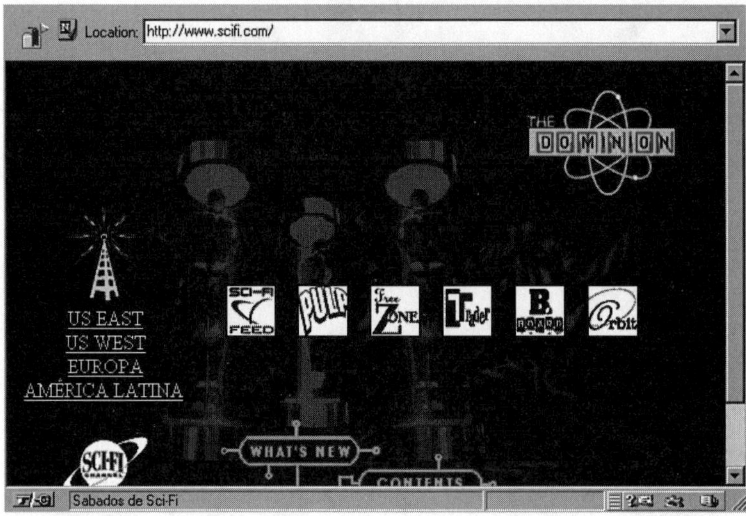

Figure 23-1 The Dominion

The Dominion uses almost every HTML trick in the book: backgrounds, tables, imagemaps, the works. You can maneuver successfully throughout its vast pages with menu bars. The site offers chat bulletin boards and has even hosted an online conference. This is truly a great Web site.

This site was nominated for the 1996 Still Cool Site of the Year. Check it out and you will see why.

People On-Line

URL: `http://pathfinder.com/people/toc.html`
Owner: *People* magazine (Time-Life)
Webmaster: `74774.1513@compuserve.com`
Purpose: Infotainment
This is the online version of the very popular *People* magazine. All the glitz and glamour of the magazine translates well to the Web. Figure 23-2 shows a sample "cover."

This page has a very nice look and feel. Many of the same images from the paper magazine make their way to the electronic version, and for some reason the look and feel of the electronic version is better. A part of the site is updated daily with all the latest celeb and entertainment news.

This page makes great use of graphics and imagemaps. The screens are well laid out and condensed. There is also a nice built-in keyword search that lets you find related articles.

A great mix of information, slick presentation, and smooth layout makes this one of the best conversions from paper to electronics on the Web.

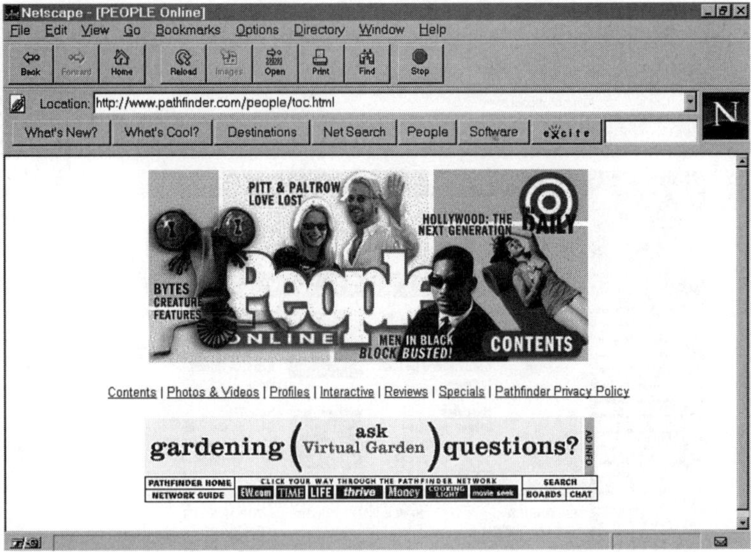

Figure 23-2 The cover of People On-Line

The Point

URL: `http://www.pointcom.com/`
Owner: Lycos
Webmaster: `webmasters@lycos.com`
Purpose: Index of leading sites on the Web
The Point is one of the premier index sites on the Web. Whereas other index sites tend to list many sites, The Point lists reviews of only the sites it considers to be in the top 5 percent of all Web sites. It is a well-executed and valuable reference. Figure 23-3 shows the Point's reviews menu.

The Point is one of the best-looking and easiest-to-navigate index sites. The writing makes many of the listings more fun to read than your average index.

In addition to the visual interface, it's also obvious that lots of thought went into the layout and design of this. The Top 5% lists can be displayed in several ways. Plus, now that it is owned by Lycos, besides featuring original site reviews, this ever-evolving site now gives easy access to the Lycos search engine and has news features. The Point is no longer alone in rating Web sites, but it still does an outstanding job.

ESPN SportsZone

URL: `http://ESPN.SportsZone.com/`
Owner: ESPN
Webmaster: Starware
Purpose: Complete sports updates and information
If you want to know anything about sports, this is the place to check first. All major sports are covered, with standings, scores, and articles. There is even a section

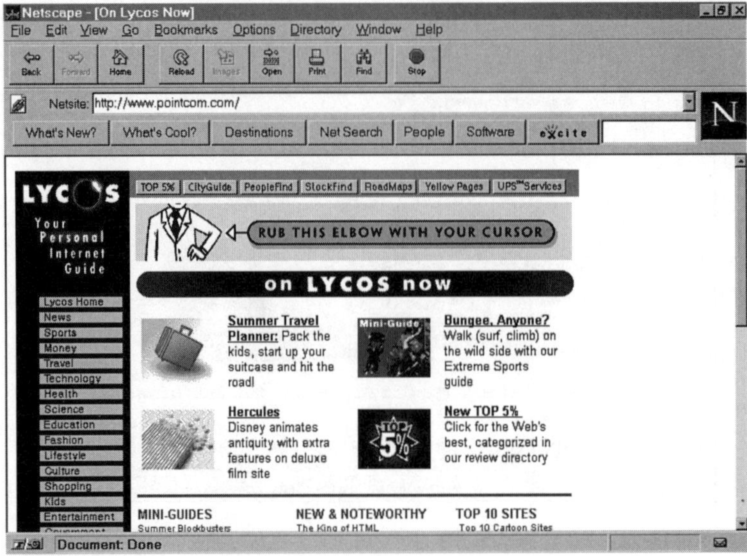

Figure 23-3 The Point

devoted to some of the less major sports. This is a fine sports reference. Figure 23-4 shows the ESPN SportsZone's home page.

SportsZone has a nice design and layout, is easy to look at, and is easy to navigate. Even the ads look cool.

Figure 23-4 The ESPN SportsZone home page

Notice the great use of tables and imagemaps in the various tables of contents and menu bars. The scripting is also impressive: The "up-to-the-minute" scores really are pretty much up to the minute.

One of the finest sites on the Web, this is a great blend of information and presentation and is what all sites should strive for.

WebComics Daily

URL: `http://www.webcomics.com/`
Owner: David de Vitry
Webmaster: David de Vitry
Purpose: Entertainment for comics lovers
If you are interested in seeing the comics that appear on the Web, WebComics Daily is a good, graphics-intensive alternative to lists of links. WebComics inlines the various daily comics from all over the Web into five easy-to-read pages. Figure 23-5 shows a typical page from WebComics Daily.

This page has a great design with a simple, yet effective, graphical toolbar. The choice of comics is nicely laid out on the top of each page. Each tool is labeled clearly.

This is no easy task, collecting the URLs of all the daily strips on the Web and then inlining them all in one well-organized, easy-to-read "magazine." This site also makes fine use of backgrounds to give it a really cool feel.

Creating such a fine Web resource must be a labor of love on Mr. de Vitry's part. Be forewarned, though; this is not a stop for someone with a slow connection.

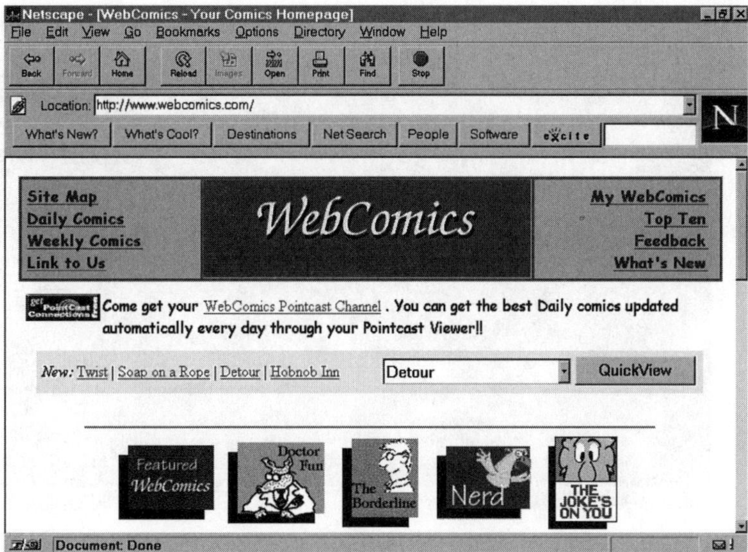

Figure 23-5 A typical page from WebComics Daily

SEDS Internet Space Warehouse

URL: `http://www.seds.org/`
Owner: Students for the Exploration and Development of Space (SEDS), University of Arizona Chapter
Webmaster: Chris Lewicki at `<webmaster@seds.org>`
Purpose: Information about and images of astronomy and space exploration

If you are interested in learning about astronomy and seeing some intergalactic images, check out SEDS. Figure 23-6 shows the SEDS home page.

Visitors to the SEDS home page are greeted with a view of the planet Earth taken from a hypothetical camera on the surface of the moon. Above it, a list of links enables users to learn more about the organization, study the planets, or look up images of planets, stars, and spacecraft.

The page uses an ingenious combination of normal links and imagemaps. A list of links is grouped together in the center of the page. Above and below the links are imagemaps that provide access to some of the same resources listed in the text links, as well as to new links. The designers also spent a great deal of time organizing the comprehensive archive of space images and providing a graphical interface that enables users to see thumbnails of the full images, as well as a search index for finding a particular image.

If you're accessing the Web through a slow connection, the use of a lot of images might make accessing the site frustrating. However, if you have any interest in space, or in a well-designed, graphics-rich Web page, the SEDS Internet Space Warehouse is a must-see.

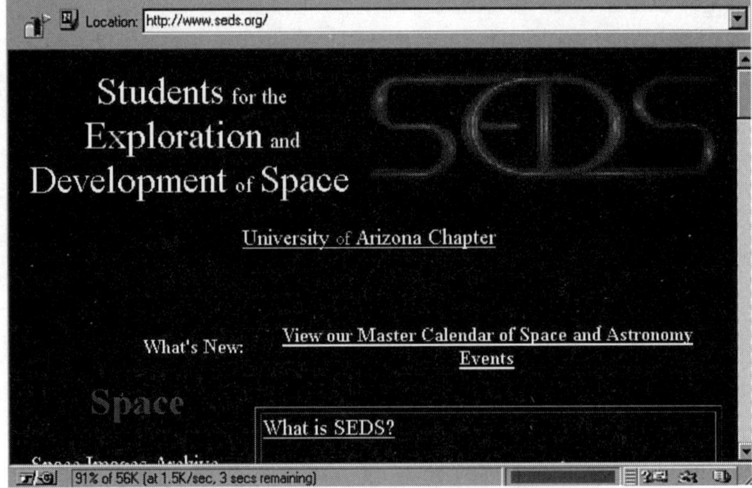

Figure 23-6 The SEDS home page

boston.com

URL: `http://www.boston.com/`
Owner: The *Boston Globe*
Webmaster: Dave Margulius at `<margulius@globe.com>`
Purpose: Information about Boston

Planning a trip to Boston? If so, make sure you visit boston.com before you leave. Figure 23-7 shows the boston.com home page.

A very basic page greets visitors to boston.com, with a handful of links to different resources. The information on the other side of those links, though, is enough to answer anyone's questions about Boston. Visitors can read the current issue of the *Boston Globe*, check out restaurant reviews, search classified ads, and take part in online discussions.

Load the boston.com page. Now reload it. If everything's working, the featured links you saw the first time should have been replaced with a different set. The site uses a CGI script to generate the HTML code for the home page on the fly, randomly selecting the featured links from a list. The site has power: Redundant Sun SPARCstation 20 servers run the Netsite commerce server from Netscape and access 40-gigabyte RAID disks. The site has a T3 connection to the Internet so it can handle heavy traffic with ease.

The boston.com site provides one-stop shopping for information about the Boston area. The site emphasizes information and keeps graphics and imagemaps to a minimum so that those using text-based browsers or who have turned off image loading can still make good use of the pages.

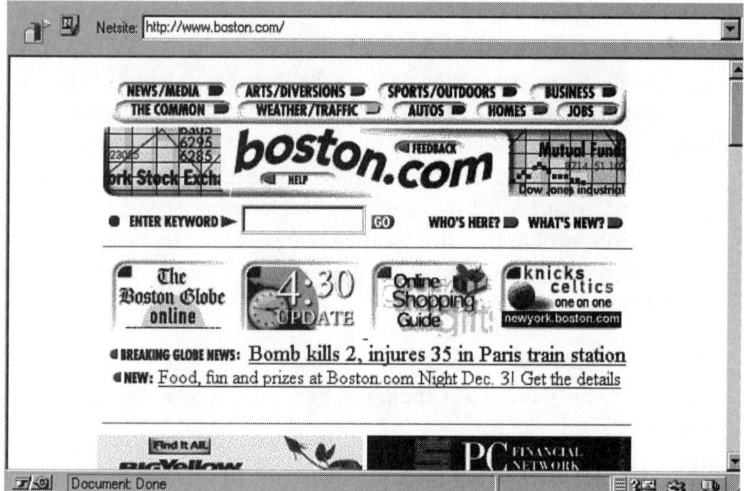

Figure 23-7 The boston.com home page

Amazon.com Books

URL: `http://www.amazon.com`
Owner: Amazon.com Books
Webmaster: `webmaster@amazon.com`
Purpose: Selling books
Looking for a book to buy? Try Amazon.com books. Figure 23-8 shows the Amazon.com home page.

Amazon.com, which modestly bills itself as "Earth's biggest bookstore," offers a catalog of 1 million titles. A search engine enables users to search the catalog by title, author, subject, or keyword. You can add (and remove) books from a shopping basket and arrange for payment when you're ready to buy them.

CGI scripts generate dynamic HTML documents so that when you return to the home page, a different book might be advertised than on your original visit. The search engine for the book catalog is very efficient; it can scan through the contents of the catalog and return an HTML document with the results of the search in only a few seconds.

Amazon.com shows how to combine a large catalog of information with a Web page and search engine to let visitors find the information they need quickly.

Red Dirt Shirt

URL: `https://hoohana.aloha.net/~reddirt/`
Owner: Red Dirt Shirts
Webmaster: `reddirt@aloha.net`
Purpose: T-shirt catalog
Looking for a T-shirt? Red Dirt Shirts has its catalog online. Figure 23-9 shows the Red Dirt Shirt home page.

The home page itself is not remarkable, but the list of "cool shirts" for sale shows a good way to create a catalog page on the Web. Small graphical images of the shirts are combined in a form so that people can see the variety of shirts available and immediately select those they want to buy.

The site uses a secure server from Netscape to provide safer transaction of credit card information for those using the Netscape Navigator browser (note the different protocol in the URL for the secure site: `https` instead of `http`).

The Red Dirt Shirts page shows how a catalog of merchandise can be simply and effectively created on the Web.

Switchboard

URL: `http://www2.switchboard.com/`
Owner: Coordinate.com
Webmaster: `webmaster@switchboard.com`
Purpose: Information
Looking for a somebody or some business? If they have a phone number listed in their name, you can find them here. Figure 23-10 shows the Switchboard home page.

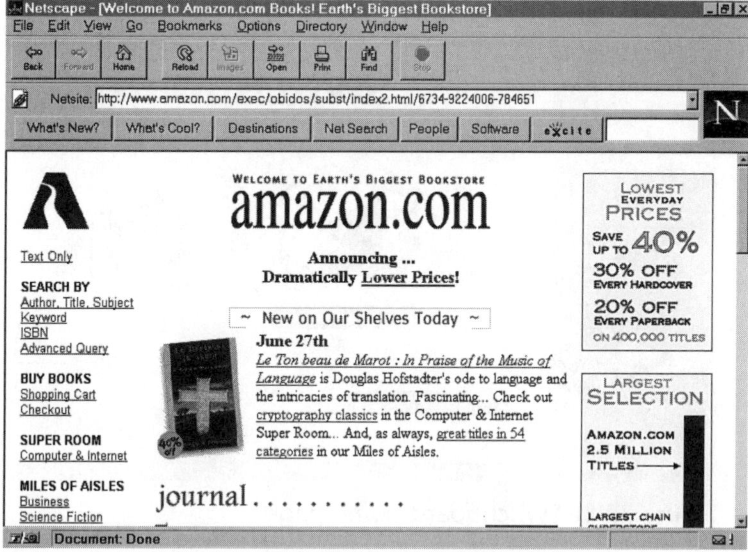

Figure 23-8 The Amazon.com home page

Graphically, Switchboard is nothing out of the ordinary; it has a nice, well-done home page. It has a simple but tasteful design. Some nice clean icons on the top of the page serve as a menu. There are also text versions of the icons until the graphical menu loads. It is all clean and simple, but nothing to make you say, "Wow!" It is the interface that makes this site so good.

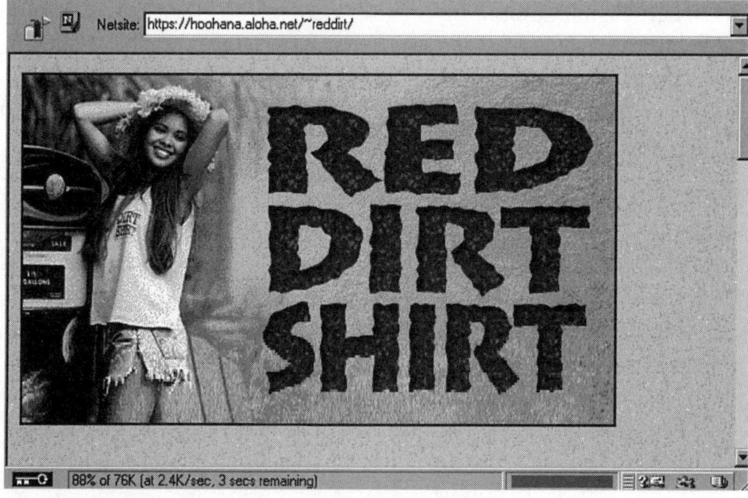

Figure 23-9 The Red Dirt Shirt home page

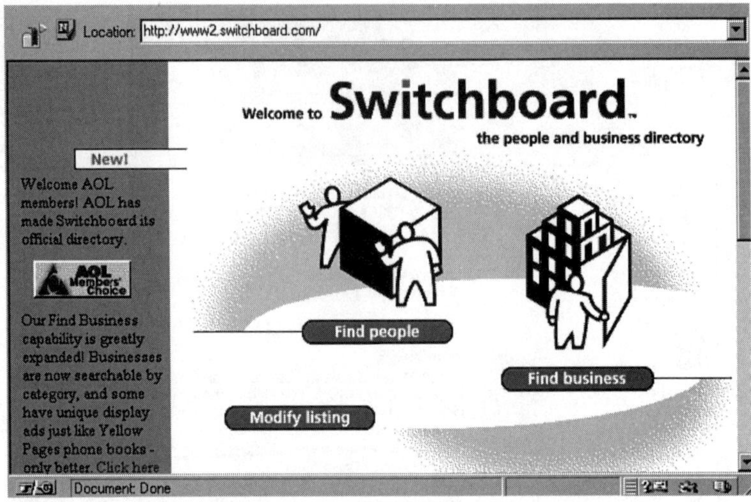

Figure 23-10 Switchboard home page

The site uses forms interacting through CGI with a very extensive database. The database contains the names of just about everybody in the United States who has a listed phone number. You enter the information about the person or persons you are looking for by filling in the proper fields of the form. Switchboard then gives you a list of all the people who match your criteria.

Switchboard is one of the more useful sites on the Web.

AltaVista

URL: `http://altavista.digital.com/`
Owner: Digital Computing
Webmaster: `suggestions.altavista@pa.dec.com`
Purpose: Searching
Looking for a Web site on, well, anything? If so, AltaVista should be the first place you look. Figure 23-11 shows the AltaVista home page.

The home page is very simple. It basically consists of a form in which you enter a phrase to search for. The phrase can be text or even a specific URL or part of a URL (which is really useful if you are trying to find sites that link to you).

The home page may be simple; the results aren't. After you enter the phrase you are looking for, AltaVista will search its extensive database and return any Web pages that have content that matches the phrase you entered. The matching pages are returned to you in groups of 10 or so, with the URL and some text from the page where a match is found. Clicking on the URL or the title will bring you to the page.

AltaVista is, if not the best, then one of the best searching mechanisms on the Web.

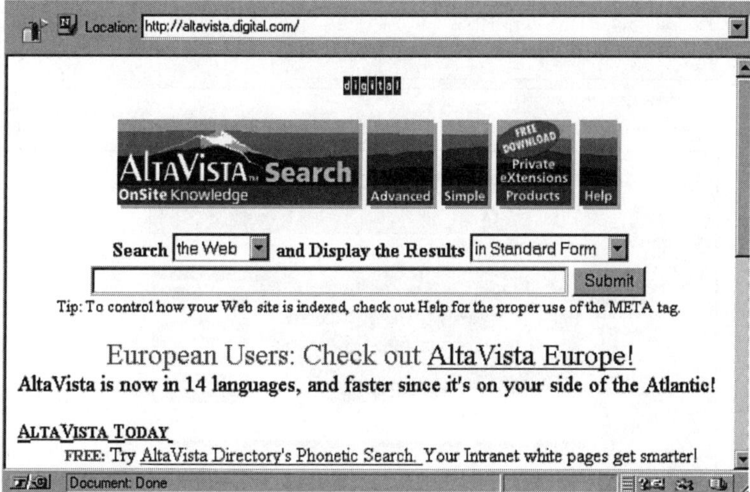

Figure 23-11 The AltaVista home page

GeoCities

URL: `http://www.geocities.com/`
Owner: David Bonner
Webmaster: `feedback@geocities.com`
Purpose: Web page hosting

GeoCities is a home page hosting site. It is one of the fastest-growing, most popular, and most useful sites on the Web. If you need a home page (or a second home page), GeoCities will give you disk space and a place to build your home page for free.

GeoCities is neatly organized into a growing number of expanding communities or neighborhoods. Each community is organized by interests (arts, technology, kids), so each user builds his or her home page in a neighborhood that suits his or her particular interests.

GeoCities is well organized and easy to look at. The icons used are colorful and interesting but not overwhelming. It's easy to surf around some of the more interesting places in GeoCities or to start picking out a spot for your home page. There is also plenty of online help available.

GeoCities makes extensive use of CGI scripts. Everything you need to do to build and maintain a home page can be done directly via the GeoCities Web site. It has scripts that let you choose your home page location, edit your page, and FTP files into your assigned directory. The whole system is quite well thought out and organized, making the entire process pretty much intuitive.

If you are looking for a place to house your home page, GeoCities is an excellent choice. Figure 23-12 shows the GeoCities home page.

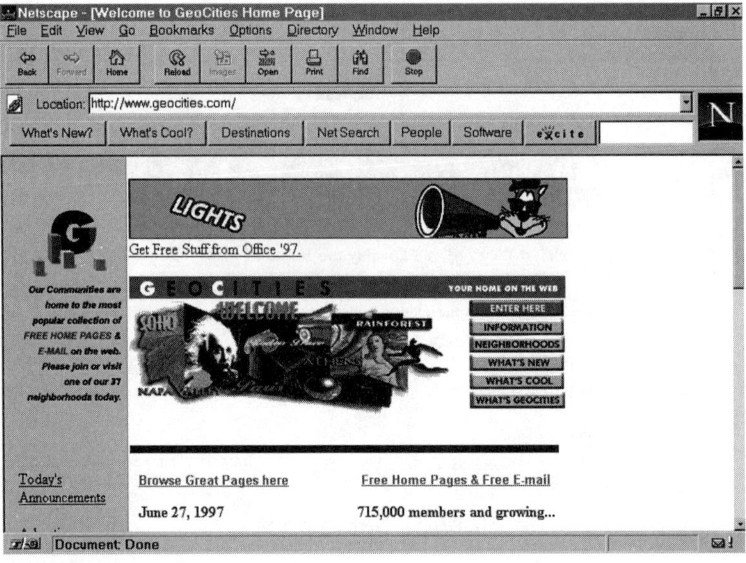

Figure 23-12 The GeoCities home page

CNN Interactive

URL: `http://www.cnn.com/`
Owner: Turner Broadcasting
Webmaster: `feedback@cnn.com`
Purpose: Information

This is certainly one of the most hyped sites on the Web. Its TV commercial boasts of being the "most informative site on the Internet." This is one of those cases where the performance matches the hype. If you are looking for information or news on current affairs, this is one of the first places you should stop.

CNN Interactive contains stories and information about current events from a wide range of different topics. Often the information presented is far more complete than on TV or in a standard newspaper. Related articles are grouped together so it is easy to research a topic in as much depth as you like. For people with fast connections, video clips are available.

CNN Interactive makes very good use of tables, inline images, and imagemaps. It is well laid out and spaced, allowing the reader to take in a lot of information on one screen without that screen being cluttered. The site also uses a Java applet at the top of the page to "scroll" through the latest headlines or show what's happening on CNN. It's not the trickiest bit of Java ever, but it's a nice touch. The site also makes good use of scripts to update stories constantly with the latest information.

CNN Interactive is one of the best-thought-out, most informative sites on the Web. Figure 23-13 shows the CNN Interactive home page.

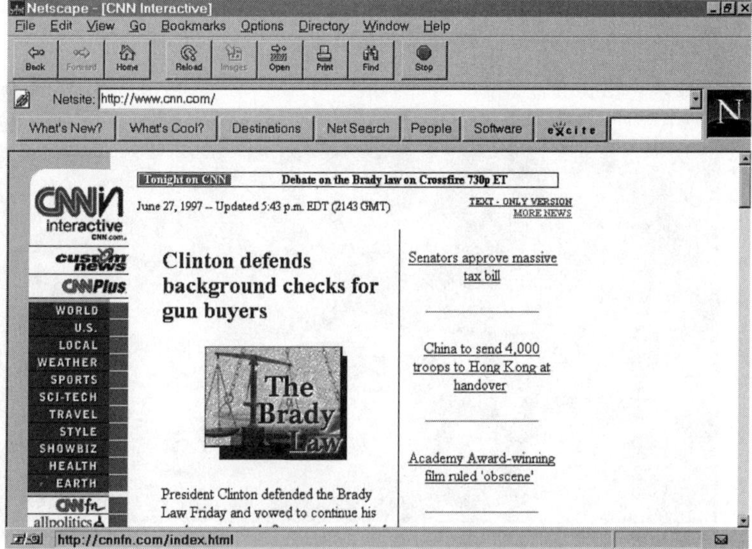

Figure 23-13 The CNN Interactive home page

GIF WIZARD

URL: `http://www.gifwizard.com/`
Owner: Raspberry Hill Publishing
Webmaster: `gifwizard@raspberryhill.com`
Purpose: Graphics utility

GIF WIZARD might not be one of the flashiest sites on the Web, but if you do a lot of work with GIF files, it certainly is one of the most useful. GIF WIZARD is an online utility that takes GIF files that are either online or on your local disk and enables you to compress and even resize them. It can be a big help to sites trying to optimize their images.

The interface to GIF WIZARD is nothing fancy, just a rather simple form. The form lets you enter the URL of the graphic to be optimized, while also providing the options of setting a background color and entering new width, height, and focus coordinates. After you enter these, a nifty compression routine optimizes the specified GIF file. Optimized files may be up to 90 percent smaller.

You should really try GIF WIZARD for yourself. The site might not have a lot of bells and whistles, but if you are looking to make your GIF files as small as possible (and who isn't?), this is a handy place to visit. Figure 23-14 shows the GIF WIZARD home page.

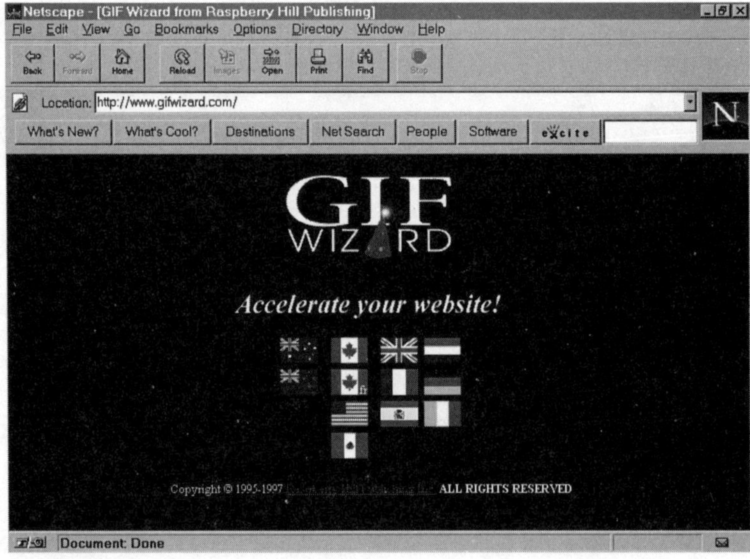

Figure 23-14 The GIF WIZARD home page

The Banner Generator

URL: `http://coder.com/creations/banner/`
Owner: Prescient Code Solutions
Webmaster: `info@coder.com`
Purpose: Banner creation
Need to a make a banner or a fancy text graphic for your Web site? If so, check out The Banner Generator. This useful Web site lets users create an endless variety of banners that they can download and use on their own home pages.

The Banner Generator, like GIF WIZARD, is not a heavily graphics-driven site. It uses a form on which users type the text of the banner they want to create. The form is also used to select and set a generous number of options. The form makes good use of pop-up menus to set options such as font style, image format, foreground and background color, and many advanced algorithms for special effects. The site then uses a script to create and display the banner. After you create the banner, you are pointed to your new banner's URL. Here you can examine the banner and then download it to your local machine. Nothing fancy, but the entire process is smooth, intuitive, and fun.

If you need to make banners for your Web site and don't have access to many software packages, The Banner Generator makes a great tool. Even if you do have access to a number of software packages, you still might want to check out this site because it is hard to beat when it comes to generating quick and painless banners. Figure 23-15 shows The Banner Generator's initial form.

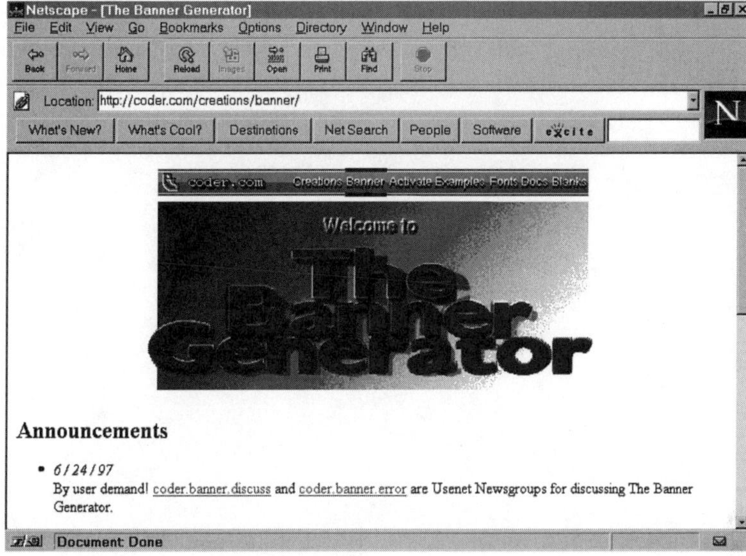

Figure 23-15 The Banner Generator form

PART V

APPENDIXES

HTML QUICK REFERENCE

This appendix lists the tags used in various versions of HTML, divided by subject, for quick reference when you're working on a page. References to the How-To's that describe the tags in greater detail are included. Tags that are available only in HTML 3.0 and above, Microsoft Internet Explorer, and Netscape are noted in the definition; otherwise, the tag is from HTML 2.0. If a tag has an attribute that can be included in the tag, it is shown in a list below the tag. An ellipsis (`...`) is used to indicate where text can be placed between tags. Text in italics indicates a variable that should be replaced with the appropriate filename, keyword, or number.

Generic Attributes and Events

HTML 4.0 includes a set of generic attributes used by most HTML tags. The following attributes are used by all tags except the following: **APPLET**, **AREA**, **BASE**, **BASEFONT**, **FONT**, **FRAME**, **FRAMESET**, **HEAD**, **IFRAME**, **LEGEND**, **META**, **PARAM**, **SCRIPT**, **STYLE**, and **TITLE**.

ATTRIBUTE	DEFINITION
`ID`	Identifies a particular tag for reference by style sheets and scripts.
`CLASS`	Identifies the class of a particular tag for use by style sheets and scripts.
`STYLE`	The style to be applied to the part of the document marked up by that tag,
	using Cascading Style Sheet format (or Dynamic Style Sheet format in Netscape 4.0).
`TITLE`	An advisory title that can be used to provide more information.

HTML 4.0 also supports a set of events than can be used to run scripts (written in JavaScript, VBScript, or other languages) when specific actions are performed by the user to that markup. These events are supported by all HTML 4.0 tags except the ones just listed, as well as the following: **BR**, **HR**, **ISINDEX**, and **MAP**.

EVENT	DEFINITION
onClick	Used when the mouse button is pressed.
onDblClick	Used when the mouse button is pressed twice.
onMouseDown	Used when the mouse button is pressed down and held.
onMouseUp	Used when the mouse button is released.
onMouseOver	Used when the cursor is moved over the object.
onMouseOut	Used when the cursor is moved off the object.
onMouseMove	Used when the cursor is moved.
onKeyPress	Used when a key is pressed and released.
onKeyDown	Used when a key is pressed down and held.
onKeyUp	Used when a key is released.

Document Basics

These tags provide the basic structure for an HTML document.

ELEMENT	HOW-TO	DEFINITION
<BODY>...</BODY>	2.7	Marks the beginning and end of the body of an HTML document.
BACKGROUND = *URL*	2.11	Specifies the image to be used as the background. (HTML 3.2+)
BGCOLOR = *color*	2.8	Specifies color for background (*color* can be a name or a hexadecimal number). (HTML 3.2+)
TEXT = *color*	2.9	Specifies color for the text. (HTML 3.2+)
LINK = *color*	2.10	Specifies color for links on a page. (HTML 3.2+)
ALINK = *color*	2.10	Specifies color for active links on a page. (HTML 3.2+)
VLINK = *color*	2.10	Specifies color for visited links on a page. (HTML 3.2+)
LEFTMARGIN = *n*		Specifies the distance between the left side of the document and the left edge of the browser window. (Microsoft)
TOPMARGIN = *n*		Specifies the distance between the top of the document and the top of the browser window. (Microsoft)
RIGHTMARGIN = *n*		Specifies the distance between the right side of the document and the right edge of the browser window. (MSIE 4.0)

ELEMENT	HOW-TO	DEFINITION
BOTTOMMARGIN = *n*		Specifies the distance between the bottom of the document and the bottom edge of the browser window. (MSIE 4.0)
BGPROPERTIES = FIXED		Fixes the location of the background image (that is, doesn't let it scroll). (Microsoft)
SCROLL = YES|NO		Turns the scrollbars on or off. (MSIE 4.0)
onLoad = *script*		Event that starts a script when the body has been loaded.
onUnload = *script*		Event that starts a script when the body has been removed.
<HEAD>...</HEAD>	2.5	Marks the beginning and end of the header of an HTML document.
<HTML>...</HTML>	2.5	Marks the beginning and end of an HTML document.
<TITLE>...</TITLE>	2.5	Identifies the title of an HTML document (used in the heading).
<!--...-->	2.6	Makes a comment in an HTML document.
<!DOCTYPE *HTML info*>		Defines the DTD used for this document (*HTML info* is the name of the DTD).
<META>		Provides meta-information about a document.
HTTP-EQUIV = *name*		The header of the HTTP file relevant to the data in the <META> document.
CONTENT = *name*		The data associated with the named HTTP header.
NAME = *name*		A description of the document.
URL = *URL*		A URL associated with the meta-information.

Physical Text Styles

These tags enable you to change the physical style of text in your document—that is, change how the text is displayed for the user.

ELEMENT	HOW-TO	DEFINITION
<B>...</B>	3.1	Makes text bold.
<BIG>...</BIG>	3.4	Puts text in a large-print font (usually one font size larger). (HTML 3.2+)
<BASEFONT>	3.4	Sets the default font qualities for the document. (HTML 3.2+)
SIZE = *n*		Sets the size of the default font (*n* is between 1 and 7). (HTML 3.2+)
COLOR = *color*		Sets the default color of the font (*color* can be a name or a hexadecimal number). (HTML 4.0)

continued on next page

continued from previous page

ELEMENT	HOW-TO	DEFINITION
FACE = *font name*		Sets the default font face. (HTML 4.0)
<BLINK>...</BLINK>		Makes blinking text. (Netscape)
<FONT>...</FONT>	3.4	
SIZE = *n*		Changes the font size by a value *n* (*n* can be any number from 1 to 7 or a positive or negative number to indicate an offset from the base font size). (HTML 3.2+)
COLOR = *color*		Changes the font color (*color* can be a name or a hexadecimal number). (HTML 3.2+)
FACE = *font name*		Changes the font style to the font(s) named, provided the fonts exist on the local system. (HTML 4.0)
<I>...</I>	3.2	Italicizes text.
<MARQUEE>...</MARQUEE>	15.1	Inserts a marquee of moving text. (Microsoft)
BEHAVIOR = *behavior*		How the text moves (SCROLL, SLIDE ALTERNATE).
BGCOLOR = *color*		Background color of the marquee (*color* can be a name or a hexadecimal value).
DIRECTION = *direction*		Direction the text scrolls (LEFT or RIGHT).
HEIGHT = *n*		Height of the marquee in pixels.
WIDTH = *n*		Width of the marquee in pixels.
HSPACE = *n*		Amount of horizontal space around the marquee.
VSPACE = *n*		Amount of vertical space around the marquee.
LOOP = *n*		Scrolls the marquee *n* times.
SCROLLDELAY = *n*		Number of milliseconds between each update.
SCROLLAMOUNT = *n*		Amount text has moved in one update.
TRUESPEED		Uses the exact scroll delay value specified to move the text. (MSIE 4.0)
<S>...</S>	3.7	Puts text in a strikethrough font. (HTML 3.2+, also </STRIKE>...</STRIKE> in Netscape)
<SMALL>...</SMALL>	3.4	Puts text in a small-print font. (HTML 3.2+)
_{...}	3.8	Puts text in subscript. (HTML 3.2+)
^{...}	3.8	Puts text in superscript. (HTML 3.2+)
<TT>...</TT>	3.3	Puts text in a teletype (fixed-width) font.
<U>...</U>	3.6	Underlines text.

Content Text Styles

These tags enable you to change the content style of the text in your document—that is, change the implied meaning of the text.

ELEMENT	HOW-TO	DEFINITION
`<ADDRESS>...</ADDRESS>`	4.8	Specifies the author, contact information, and so on, of the page.
`<CITE>...</CITE>`	4.3	Specifies a citation.
`<CODE>...</CODE>`	4.5	Includes code (from a computer program).
`<DEL>...</DEL>`	22.4	Specifies text that has been deleted from an earlier version of a document. (HTML 3.0, 4.0)
CITE = *URL*		Location of a document that refers to the change. (HTML 4.0)
DATETIME = *datetime*		Date and time of the change (*datetime* is in standard ISO format). (HTML 4.0)
`<DFN>...</DFN>`	4.4	Specifies a definition.
`<EM>...</EM>`	4.2	Emphasizes text.
`<Hn>...</Hn>`	4.1	Identifies the heading for a document (*n* can be a whole number between 1 [largest heading] and 6 [smallest heading]).
ALIGN = *alignment*		Sets the alignment of the heading (*alignment* can be LEFT, CENTER, or RIGHT [HTML 3.2+] or JUSTIFY [HTML 4.0]).
`<INS>...</INS>`	22.4	Specifies text that has been added to an earlier version of a document. (HTML 3.0, 4.0)
CITE = *URL*		Location of a document that refers to the change. (HTML 4.0)
DATETIME = *datetime*		Date and time of the change (*datetime* is in standard ISO format). (HTML 4.0)
`<KBD>...</KBD>`	4.7	Identifies input or output from a computer.
`<Q>...</Q>`	22.7	Identifies a quotation from another source. (HTML 3.0, 4.0)
CITE = *URL*		Specifies the document that is the source of the quotation. (HTML 4.0)
`<SAMP>...</SAMP>`	4.6	Specifies a sample of literal characters.
`<STRONG>...</STRONG>`	4.2	Strongly emphasizes text.
`<VAR>...</VAR>`	4.5	Specifies a variable.

Document Spacing

These tags control the spacing in your document.

ELEMENT	HOW-TO	DEFINITION
<BLOCKQUOTE>...	7.7	Creates a quotation block.
</BLOCKQUOTE>		
CITE = *URL*		Specifies the source document of the quotation. (HTML 4.0)
 	7.4	Inserts a line break.
CLEAR = *alignment*		Clears text wrap (*alignment* can be LEFT, RIGHT,
		NONE, or ALL). (HTML 3.2+)
<CENTER>...</CENTER>	7.3	Centers text (same as <DIV ALIGN=CENTER>).
		(HTML 3.2+)
<DIV>...</DIV>	7.8	Marks a division in a Web page. (HTML 3.2+)
ALIGN = *alignment*		Alignment of division (LEFT, CENTER, or RIGHT
		[HTML 3.2+] or JUSTIFY [HTML 4.0]).
<HR>	7.1	Adds a horizontal line.
ALIGN = *alignment*		Alignment of the line (*alignment* can be LEFT,
		RIGHT, or CENTER). (HTML 3.2+)
SIZE = *n*		Specifies the thickness of the line. (HTML 3.2+)
NOSHADE		Makes the line black. (HTML 3.2+)
WIDTH = *n%*		Specifies the width of the line (*n* can be any number from 0
		to 100). (HTML 3.2+)
COLOR = *color*		Color of the line (*color* can be a name or a
		hexadecimal number). (Microsoft)
<MULTICOL>...</MULTICOL>	15.3	Creates multicolumn text. (Netscape 3+)
COLS = *n*		Number of columns.
GUTTER = *n*		Number of pixels between columns.
WIDTH = *n*		Width of each column.
<NOBR>...</NOBR>	7.5	Marks text that should not have a line break included.
		(Microsoft/Netscape)
<P>...</P>	7.4	Creates a paragraph.
ALIGN = *alignment*		Alignment of the paragraph (*alignment* can be LEFT,
		CENTER, or RIGHT [HTML 3.2+] or JUSTIFY
		[HTML 4.0]).
<PRE>...</PRE>	7.6	Identifies preformatted text.
WIDTH = *n*		Width of text in characters. (HTML 3.2+)
<SPACER>	15.4	Creates horizontal or vertical space. (Netscape 3+)

ELEMENT	HOW-TO	DEFINITION
TYPE = *type*		Type of spacer to use (*type* can be HORIZONTAL,
		VERTICAL, or BLOCK).
SIZE = *n*		Size of horizontal or vertical spacer.
WIDTH = *n*		Width of block spacer.
HEIGHT = *n*		Height of block spacer.
ALIGN = *alignment*		Alignment of block spacer (*alignment* can be LEFT,
		CENTER, or RIGHT).
<WBR>		Includes a soft line break within a nonbreaking line.
		(Microsoft)

Tables

These tags enable you to create tables in HTML 3.2 and above.

ELEMENT	HOW-TO	DEFINITION
<CAPTION>...</CAPTION>	5.2	Identifies the table caption.
ALIGN = *alignment*		Alignment of the caption (*alignment* can be TOP or
		BOTTOM [HTML 3.2+] or LEFT or RIGHT [HTML 4.0]).
<COL>		Defines column-based default properties for tables. (HTML 4.0)
ALIGN = *alignment*		Alignment of entries in a row (*alignment* can be
		LEFT,CENTER, RIGHT, JUSTIFY, or CHAR).
VALIGN = *alignment*		Vertical alignment of table row entries (*alignment* can
		be TOP, MIDDLE, BOTTOM, or BASELINE).
SPAN = *n*		Number of columns spanned by the group.
WIDTH = *n*		Width of the column (*n* is pixels or a percentage).
<COLGROUP>		A container for a group of columns. (HTML 4.0)
ALIGN = *alignment*		Alignment of entries in a row (*alignment* can be
		LEFT,CENTER, RIGHT, JUSTIFY, or CHAR).
VALIGN = *alignment*		Vertical alignment of table row entries (*alignment* can
		be TOP, MIDDLE, BOTTOM, or BASELINE).
SPAN = *n*		Number of columns spanned by the group.
WIDTH = *n*		Width of the column (*n* is pixels or a percentage).
<TABLE>...</TABLE>	5.1	Defines a table.
BORDER = *n*		Shows the lines of the table to the specified thickness.

continued on next page

continued from previous page

ELEMENT	HOW-TO	DEFINITION
ALIGN = *alignment*		Alignment of the table (*alignment* can be LEFT, CENTER, or RIGHT [HTML 3.2+] or BLEEDLEFT or BLEEDRIGHT [Netscape]).
WIDTH = *n*		Fixed width of the entire table (*n* is any number and can be pixels or a percentage).
BGCOLOR = *color*	15.5	Defines the color of the background of the table (*color* can be a name or a hexadecimal number. (HTML 4.0)
BORDERCOLOR = *color*	15.5	Defines the color of a table border. (Microsoft)
BORDERCOLORLIGHT = *color*	15.5	Defines the color of the light portion of a 3D table border. (Microsoft)
BORDERCOLORDARK = *color*	15.5	Defines the color of the dark portion of a 3D table border. (Microsoft)
BACKGROUND = *URL*	15.6	Defines the location of the background image for a table. (Microsoft)
CELLSPACING = *n*	5.8	Sets the spacing between cells in a table.
CELLPADDING = *n*	5.9	Sets the spacing between cell contents and borders.
COLS = *n*	5.10	Sets the number of columns in a table. (HTML 4.0)
FRAME = *frame*	15.7	Defines the type of outside table border to show (*frame* can be VOID, ABOVE, BELOW, HSIDES, LHS, RHS, VSIDES, BOX, or BORDER. (HTML 4.0)
HEIGHT = *n*		Height of the table (*n* can be pixels or a percentage value). (Microsoft/Netscape)
RULES = *rule*	15.7	Defines the type of inside table border to show (rule can be NONE, GROUPS, ROWS, COLS, ALL). (HTML 4.0)
<TH>...</TH>, <TD>...</TD>	5.3, 5.4	Defines a table heading <TH> or a data table entry <TD>.
ALIGN = *alignment*		Alignment of entries in a row (*alignment* can be LEFT,CENTER, or RIGHT [HTML 3.2+] or JUSTIFY or CHAR [HTML 4.0]).
VALIGN = *alignment*		Vertical alignment of table row entries (*alignment* can be TOP, MIDDLE, BOTTOM, or BASELINE).
BGCOLOR = *color*		Defines the color of the background of the table (*color* can be a name or a hexadecimal number). (HTML 4.0)
BORDERCOLOR = *color*		Defines the color of a table border. (Microsoft)
BORDERCOLORLIGHT = *color*		Defines the color of the light portion of a 3D table border. (Microsoft)

ELEMENT	HOW-TO	DEFINITION
BORDERCOLORDARK = *color*		Defines the color of the dark portion of a 3D table border. (Microsoft)
BACKGROUND = *URL*		Defines the location of the background image for a table. (Microsoft)
ROWSPAN = *n*		Number of table rows the cell should cover.
COLSPAN = *n*		Number of table columns the cell should cover.
NOWRAP		Turns off word wrapping in the table cell.
WIDTH = *n*		Width of the cell, in pixels. (HTML 3.2 only)
HEIGHT = *n*		Height of the cell, in pixels. (HTML 3.2 only)
<TR>...</TR>	5.6	Starts a new row in the table.
ALIGN = *alignment*		Alignment of entries in a row (*alignment* can be LEFT,CENTER, or RIGHT [HTML 3.2+] or JUSTIFY or CHAR [HTML 4.0]).
VALIGN = *alignment*		Vertical alignment of table row entries (*alignment* can be TOP, MIDDLE, BOTTOM, or BASELINE).
BGCOLOR = *color*		Defines the color of the background of the table (*color* can be a name or a hexadecimal number). (HTML 4.0)
<TBODY>...</TBODY>		Defines the table body. (Microsoft)
ALIGN = *alignment*		Alignment of entries in a row (*alignment* can be LEFT,CENTER, or RIGHT [HTML 3.2+] or JUSTIFY or CHAR [HTML 4.0]).
VALIGN = *alignment*		Vertical alignment of table row entries (*alignment* can be TOP, MIDDLE, BOTTOM, or BASELINE).
BGCOLOR = *color*		Defines the color of the background of the table (*color* can be a name or a hexadecimal number). (MSIE 4.0)
<THEAD>...</THEAD>		Defines the table head. (Microsoft)
ALIGN = *alignment*		Alignment of entries in a row (*alignment* can be LEFT, CENTER, or RIGHT [HTML 3.2+] or JUSTIFY or CHAR [HTML 4.0]).
VALIGN = *alignment*		Vertical alignment of table row entries (*alignment* can be TOP, MIDDLE, BOTTOM, or BASELINE).
BGCOLOR = *color*		Defines the color of the background of the table (*color* can be a name or a hexadecimal number). (MSIE 4.0)
<TFOOT>...</TFOOT>		Defines the table foot. (Microsoft)
ALIGN = *alignment*		Alignment of entries in a row (*alignment* can be LEFT, CENTER, or RIGHT [HTML 3.2+] or JUSTIFY orCHAR [HTML 4.0]).

continued on next page

continued from previous page

ELEMENT	HOW-TO	DEFINITION
VALIGN = *alignment*		Vertical alignment of table row entries (*alignment* can be TOP, MIDDLE, BOTTOM, or BASELINE).
BGCOLOR = *color*		Defines the color of the background of the table (*color* can be a name or a hexadecimal number. (MSIE 4.0)

Lists

These tags enable you to create a number of different types of lists in your document.

ELEMENT	HOW-TO	DEFINITION
<OL>...</OL>	6.1	Creates an ordered (numbered) list.
COMPACT		Displays a compacted version of the list.
TYPE = *type*	6.2	Specifies the type of numbering used (*type* can be A, a, I, i, or 1). (HTML 3.2+)
START = *n*	6.2	Starting number of the list. (HTML 3.2+)
<UL>...</UL>	6.3	Creates an unordered (bulleted) list.
COMPACT		Displays a compacted version of the list.
TYPE = *type*	6.4	Specifies the type of bullet to use (*type* can be CIRCLE, DISC, or SQUARE). (HTML 3.2+)
<DL>...</DL>	6.8	Creates a glossary list.
COMPACT		Displays a compacted version of the list.
<MENU>...</MENU>	6.6	Creates a menu list.
COMPACT		Displays a compacted version of the list.
<DIR>...</DIR>	6.7	Creates a directory list.
COMPACT		Displays a compacted version of the list.
<DT>	6.8	Identifies a defined term in a glossary list.
<DD>	6.8	Identifies a definition in a glossary list.
<LI>	6.1, 6.3, 6.6, 6.7	Identifies a list item in <OL>, <UL>, <MENU>, or <DIR>.
TYPE = *bullet type*		Specifies the type of bullet to use for this and subsequent list entries in a bulleted list (*bullet type* can be CIRCLE, DISC, or SQUARE). (HTML 3.2+)
TYPE = *number type*		Specifies the type of numbering used for this and subsequent list entries in an ordered list (*number type* can be A, a, I, i, or 1). (HTML 3.2+)
VALUE = *n*		Starting number of this and later entries in a numbered list (*n* is any integer). (HTML 3.2+)

Links

These tags enable you to create links to Web pages, FTP and Gopher sites, and other Internet resources.

ELEMENT	HOW-TO	DEFINITION
<A>...</A>	8.5–8.14	Defines an anchor for a link.
HREF = *URL*		Specifies the destination of the link, using its URL.
NAME = *name*		Specifies the name of a section of a document for later use in links.
SHAPE = *shape*	22.13	Shape of a link embedded in a figure (*shape* can be circle x,y,r; rect x,y,r,h; polygon x1,y1,x2,y2,...,xn,yn; or default). (HTML 3.0, 4.0)
COORDS = *n*		Coordinates of a shaped link. (HTML 4.0)
TARGET = *target*	19.1	Specifies the target window for a link. (HTML 4.0)
ACCESSKEY = *character*		Key used with control key as shortcut to the link. (HTML 4.0)
TABINDEX = *n*		Position of the link in the tabbing order. (HTML 4.0)
<BASE HREF=*URL*>	8.3	Defines the base URL of the relative links in a document (located in the header of the document).
TARGET = *target*		Specifies the target window for the linked resource. (HTML 4.0)
<LINK>	8.4	Defines the relationship between the current document and other documents.
REL		Type of relationship between the current document and other documents (can also be used to link a document to a script or a style sheet). (HTML 4.0)
REV		Reverse relationship between other documents and the current one.
HREF = *URL*		URL of the reference.
TYPE = *MIME type*		MIME type of the linked document. (HTML 4.0)
TARGET = *target*		Specifies the target window for the linked resource. (HTML 4.0)

Images

These tags enable you to incorporate images into your pages.

ELEMENT	HOW-TO	DEFINITION
<IMG>	9.2	Includes an inline image.
ALIGN = *alignment*	9.3	Alignment of the image (*alignment* can be TOP, MIDDLE, BOTTOM, LEFT, or RIGHT). (HTML 3.2+)
ALIGN = *alignment*	9.3	Alignment of the image (*alignment* can be ABSBOTTOM, ABSMIDDLE, BASELINE, or TEXTTOP). (Netscape/Microsoft)
ALT = "*text*"	9.4	Text description of the image.
BORDER = *n*		Size of the picture border, in pixels. (HTML 3.2+)
HEIGHT = *n*	9.13	Fixed height of the image. (HTML 3.2+)
WIDTH = *n*	9.13	Fixed width of the image. (HTML 3.2+)
HSPACE = *n*		Horizontal runaround space, in pixels. (HTML 3.2+)
VSPACE = *n*		Vertical runaround space, in pixels. (HTML 3.2+)
ISMAP	9.10	Declares the image to be an imagemap.
SRC = *graphic filename*		Filename of the image.
LOWSRC = *graphic filename*	9.15	Filename of a low-resolution version of the image. (Netscape)
USEMAP = *URL*	9.11	URL of a client-side imagemap for the image. (HTML 3.2+)
DYNSRC = *URL*		URL of a VRML world or video clip to be displayed. (Microsoft)
LOOP = *n*		The number of times the video clip will play. (Microsoft)
<MAP>...</MAP>	9.11	Collection of links for a client-side imagemap. (HTML 3.2+)
NAME = *name*		Name of the imagemap.
<AREA>	9.11	Link in a client-side imagemap. (HTML 3.2+)
COORDS = *coords*		Coordinates defining the location of the link.
HREF = *URL*		Destination of the link.
NOHREF		Makes the region inactive in the imagemap.
SHAPE = *shape*		Type of shape for the link (*shape* can be RECT, CIRC, POLY, or DEFAULT).
ALT = "*text*"		Alternative text for the link.
TABINDEX = *n*		Position in the tabbing order. (HTML 4.0)
TARGET = *target*		Destination window of the link. (HTML 4.0)

Forms

These tags enable you to create forms that include different types of inputs; they also specify what to do with the results of the form when submitted.

ELEMENT	HOW-TO	DEFINITION
<FORM>...</FORM>	11.1	Defines a form.
ACTION = *URL*		Location (*URL*) of the script that will process the form results.
METHOD = *method*		Method of sending the form input (*method* can be GET or POST).
ENCTYPE = *enctype*		Encoding type for the form data. (HTML 3.2+)
onSubmit = *script*		Event that starts a script when the form is submitted. (HTML 4.0)
onReset = *script*		Event that starts a script when the form is reset. (HTML 4.0)
TARGET = *target*		Specifies the target window for the linked resource. (HTML 4.0)
<INPUT>		Creates an input area of the form.
TYPE =		Type of form input, listed below.
CHECKBOX	11.3	Check box.
FILE	11.7	Allows user to attach a file. (HTML 3.2+)
ACCEPT = *MIME type*		Limits the range of acceptable files. (HTML 4.0)
HIDDEN		Invisible input.
IMAGE	11.9	Returns information on where the user clicked on the image. (HTML 3.2+)
RADIO	11.4	Radio button.
PASSWORD	11.5	Password.
TEXT	11.2	Single-line text input.
SUBMIT	11.1	Button to submit the form input.
RESET	11.1	Button to reset the form input.
BUTTON		A generic button on the form. (HTML 4.0)
NAME = *name*		Name of this input variable, as seen by the script (but not displayed in the form).
SIZE = *n*		Defines the size of the text display for a TEXT form.
MAXLENGTH = *n*		Maximum length of a TEXT input item.
VALUE = "*text*"		Value used to initialize HIDDEN and TEXT fields, also required for RADIO and CHECKBOX fields.

continued on next page

continued from previous page

ELEMENT	HOW-TO	DEFINITION
DISABLED		Disables the field to prevent text from being entered.
CHECKED		Initializes a field in a CHECKBOX or RADIO to be selected.
READONLY		Makes the field read-only for CHECKBOX, PASSWORD, RADIO, and TEXT. (HTML 4.0)
SRC = *graphic filename*		Specifies the image filename for IMAGE, SUBMIT, and RESET.
ALT = "*text*"		Alternative text for image fields. (HTML 4.0)
ALIGN = *align*		Alignment of form element (*align* can be TOP, MIDDLE, BOTTOM, LEFT, or RIGHT).
TABINDEX = *n*		Sets position in the tabbing order. (HTML 4.0)
USEMAP = *URL*		URL of a client-side imagemap for the image. (HTML 4.0)
onFocus = *script*		Event that starts a script when a form field is the active field. (HTML 4.0)
onBlur = *script*		Event that starts a script when a form field no longer is the active field. (HTML 4.0)
onSelect = *script*		Event that starts a script when a text element in a form is selected. (HTML 4.0)
onChange = *script*		Event that starts a script when the value of a form field is changed. (HTML 4.0)
ACCESSKEY = *character*		Key used with control key as shortcut to the link. (MSIE 4.0)
<ISINDEX>		Defines a searchable index.
ACTION = *URL*		Specifies the gateway program to be used. (Microsoft)
PROMPT = "*text*"		Specifies the text to be shown before the prompt. (HTML 3.2+)
<OPTION>	11.6	Specifies an option in a <SELECT> menu form.
DISABLED		Disables the entry to prevent its selection.
SELECTED		Initializes the entry to be selected.
VALUE = *value*		Indicates the value that will be returned if this item is chosen.
<SELECT>...</SELECT>	11.6	Creates a menu of selections.
NAME = *name*		Name of the input variable, as seen by the script (but not displayed in the form).
MULTIPLE		Permits multiple selections to be made from the menu.
DISABLED		Disables the menu to prevent selections.
WIDTH = *n*		Fixed width of the menu. (Netscape)
HEIGHT = *n*		Fixed height of the menu. (Netscape)

ELEMENT	HOW-TO	DEFINITION
SIZE = *n*		Height of the menu.
TABINDEX = *n*		Sets position in the tabbing order. (HTML 4.0)
onFocus = *script*		Event that starts a script when a form field is the active field. (HTML 4.0)
onBlur = *script*		Event that starts a script when a form field no longer is the active field. (HTML 4.0)
onSelect = *script*		Event that starts a script when a text element in a form is selected. (HTML 4.0)
onChange = *script*		Event that starts a script when the value of a form field is changed. (HTML 4.0)
ACCESSKEY = *character*		Key used with control key as shortcut to the link. (MSIE 4.0)
<TEXTAREA>...</TEXTAREA>		Creates a multiline text input area for a form (any text located between the tags becomes the initial value for the form).
NAME = *name*		Name of the input variable, as seen by the script (but not displayed in the form).
ROWS = *n*		Number of rows down the text area should be.
COLS = *n*		Number of columns across the text area should be.
DISABLED		Disables the menu to prevent input.
READONLY		Makes the field read-only for CHECKBOX, PASSWORD, RADIO, and TEXT. (HTML 4.0)
TABINDEX = *n*		Sets position in the tabbing order. (HTML 4.0)
USEMAP = *URL*		URL of a client-side imagemap for the image. (HTML 4.0)
onFocus = *script*		Event that starts a script when a form field is the active field. (HTML 4.0)
onBlur = *script*		Event that starts a script when a form field is no longer the active field. (HTML 4.0)
onSelect = *script*		Event that starts a script when a text element in a form is selected. (HTML 4.0)
onChange = *script*		Event that starts a script when the value of a form field is changed. (HTML 4.0)
ACCESSKEY = *character*		Key used with control key as shortcut to the link. (MSIE 4.0)
WRAP = *wrap*		The type of text wrapping to use within the field (*wrap* can be OFF, PHYSICAL, or VIRTUAL). (Microsoft/Netscape)
<FIELDSET>...</FIELDSET>		Group together a set of fields in a form. (HTML 4.0)
<LEGEND>...</LEGEND>		Specifies the legend, or title, of a fieldset in a form. (HTML 4.0)

continued on next page

continued from previous page

ELEMENT	HOW-TO	DEFINITION
ALIGN = *align*		Alignment of the legend (*align* can be BOTTOM, TOP, LEFT, or RIGHT [HTML 4.0], or CENTER [MSIE 4.0]).
<BUTTON>...</BUTTON>		Creates a button in a form, labeled using the text between the start and end tags. (HTML 4.0)
NAME = *name*		Name of button for scripting or as a Submit button.
VALUE = *value*		Value passed on when button is clicked.
DISABLED		Prevents the button from being clicked.
TYPE = *type*		Specific type of button (*type* can be SUBMIT or RESET).
TABINDEX = *n*		Sets position in the tabbing order. (HTML 4.0)
onFocus = *script*		Event that starts a script when a form field is the active field.
onBlur = *script*		Event that starts a script when a form field is no longer the active field.
ACCESSKEY = *character*		Key used with control key as shortcut to the link. (MSIE 4.0)
<LABEL>...</LABEL>		Label for a field in a form. (HTML 4.0)
FOR = *id*		Matches label with the value of the ID attribute for the field.
DISABLED		Disables the label.
ACCESSKEY = *character*		Key used with control key as shortcut to the link.
onFocus = *script*		Event that starts a script when a form field is the active field.
onBlur = *script*		Event that starts a script when a form field is no longer the active field.

Frames

These tags let you create a variety of different types of frames in a document.

ELEMENT	HOW-TO	DEFINITION
<FRAMESET>	19.1	Defines a set of frames in a document. (HTML 4.0)
COLS = *n*		Creates column-oriented frames (*n* is a set of pixel widths or percentages).
ROWS = *n*		Creates row-oriented frames (*n* is a set of pixel widths or percentages).
FRAMEBORDER = 0,1	19.5	Turns on (1) or off (0) frame borders. (Microsoft)
FRAMEBORDER = YES,NO	19.5	Turns on or off frame borders. (Netscape)
BORDER = *n*	19.5	Thickness of frame borders. (Netscape/Microsoft)
BORDERCOLOR = *color*	19.5	Color of border (*color* can be a name or hexadecimal number). (Netscape/Microsoft)

ELEMENT	HOW-TO	DEFINITION
FRAMESPACING = *n*		Defines space between frames. (Microsoft)
onLoad = *script*		Event that starts a script when all the frames have been loaded.
onUnload = *script*		Event that starts a script when all the frames have been removed.
<FRAME>	19.1	Defines a frame. (HTML 4.0)
ALIGN = *align*		Alignment of frame or surrounding text (*align* can be LEFT, CENTER, RIGHT, TOP, or BOTTOM). (Microsoft)
BORDERCOLOR = *color*	19.5	Color of border (*color* can be a name or hexadecimal number). (Netscape/Microsoft)
FRAMEBORDER = 0,1	19.5	Turns on (1) or off (0) frame borders.
FRAMEBORDER = YES,NO	19.5	Turns on or off frame borders. (Netscape)
MARGINHEIGHT = *n*		Defines the margin height of frame, in pixels.
MARGINWIDTH = *n*		Defines the margin width of frame, in pixels.
NAME = *name*		Defines target name for the frame.
NORESIZE		Fixes the size of the frame so it cannot be adjusted by the user.
SCROLLING = YES,NO,AUTO		Turns scrolling on or off.
SRC = *URL*		Defines the URL for the frame.
HEIGHT = *n*		Height of frame (*n* is in pixels or percentages).
WIDTH = *n*		Width of frame (*n* is in pixels of percentages).
<IFRAME>...</IFRAME>	19.4	Defines a floating frame. (HTML 4.0)
ALIGN = *align*		Aligns a frame or surrounding text (*align* can be LEFT, CENTER, RIGHT, TOP, or BOTTOM).
BORDER = *n*		Thickness of frame borders. (Microsoft)
BORDERCOLOR = *color*		Color of border (*color* can be a name or hexadecimal number). (Microsoft)
FRAMEBORDER = 0,1	19.5	Turns on (1) or off (0) frame borders.
FRAMESPACING = *n*		Defines space between frames. (Microsoft)
MARGINHEIGHT = *n*		Defines the margin height of the frame, in pixels.
MARGINWIDTH = *n*		Defines the margin width of the frame, in pixels.
NAME = *name*		Defines target name for the frame.
NORESIZE		Fixes the size of the frame so it cannot be adjusted by the user. (Microsoft)
SCROLLING = YES,NO,AUTO		Turns scrolling on or off.

continued on next page

continued from previous page

ELEMENT	HOW-TO	DEFINITION
SRC = *URL*		Defines the URL for the frame.
HEIGHT = *n*		Defines the height of a floating frame.
WIDTH = *n*		Defines the width of a floating frame.
HSPACE = *n*		Horizontal margins around the frame. (Microsoft)
VSPACE = *n*		Vertical margins around the frame. (Microsoft)
<NOFRAMES>...</NOFRAMES>	19.7	Defines alternative text for those not using frames-enabled
		browsers. (HTML 4.0)

Multimedia

These tags enable you to include Java applets, JavaScript scripts, and other multimedia elements in your Web pages.

ELEMENT	HOW-TO	DEFINITION
<APPLET>...</APPLET>	17.2	Includes a Java applet. (HTML 3.2+)
ALIGN = *align*		Defines the alignment of the applet (*align* can be TOP,
		LEFT, MIDDLE, BOTTOM, or RIGHT). (HTML 4.0)
ALIGN = *align*		Defines the alignment of the applet (*align* can be
		ABSBOTTOM, ABSMIDDLE, BASELINE, or
		TEXTTOP). (Microsoft/Netscape)
CODE = *file*		Defines the filename of the applet.
CODEBASE = *URL*		Defines the URL to the applet.
ARCHIVE = *archives*		Comma-separated list of archive files. (HTML 4.0)
OBJECT = *object*		Serialized applet file. (HTML 4.0)
HEIGHT = *n*		Defines the height of the applet.
WIDTH = *n*		Defines the width of the applet.
HSPACE = *n*		Defines the horizontal space around the applet.
VSPACE = *n*		Defines the vertical space around the applet.
NAME = *name*		Defines the name of the applet to identify it to other applets
		on the page.
ALT = "*text*"		Alternative text to display in place of applet.
<EMBED>	18.1	Includes a multimedia object. (Microsoft/Netscape)
ALIGN = *align*		Defines the alignment of the applet (*align* can be TOP,
		LEFT, MIDDLE, BOTTOM, RIGHT, ABSBOTTOM,
		ABSMIDDLE, BASELINE, or TEXTTOP).
ALT = "*text*"		Alternative text to display in place of applet.

ELEMENT	HOW-TO	DEFINITION
HEIGHT = *n*		Defines the height of the object.
WIDTH = *n*		Defines the width of the object.
HSPACE = *n*		Defines the horizontal space around the object.
VSPACE = *n*		Defines the vertical space around the object.
NAME = *name*		Defines the name of the object to identify it to other objects
		on the page.
SRC = *URL*		Defines the URL of the object.
CODEBASE = *URL*		Defines the base URL for the object. (Microsoft)
<NOEMBED>...</NOEMBED>	18.9	Defines alternative text for browsers that don't support
		embedded objects. (Netscape/Microsoft)
<OBJECT>...</OBJECT>	18.2	Includes a multimedia object. (HTML 4.0)
ALIGN = *align*		Defines the alignment of the object (*align* can be
		BASELINE, CENTER, LEFT, MIDDLE, RIGHT,
		TEXTBOTTOM, TEXTMIDDLE, or TEXTTOP).
BORDER = *n*		Defines the width of the object border.
CLASSID = *URL*		Defines the class ID for object controls.
CODEBASE = *URL*		Defines the URL for the codebase of the object.
CODETYPE = *type*		Defines the media type of the object.
DATA = *URL*		Defines the location of data for the object.
DECLARE		Declares an object without starting it.
HEIGHT = *n*		Defines the height of the object.
HSPACE = *n*		Defines the horizontal space around the object.
NAME = *URL*		Defines the name of the object if submitted in a form.
SHAPES		Specifies that the object has shaped hyperlinks.
STANDBY = "*Message*"		Defines a message to display while the object is loading.
TYPE = *type*		Defines the media type for the object data.
USEMAP = *URL*		Defines a client-side imagemap to be used.
VSPACE = *n*		Defines the vertical space around the object.
WIDTH = *n*		Defines the width of the object.
TABINDEX = *n*		Sets position in the tabbing order
<PARAM>	17.3	Defines parameters to pass to a Java applet.
NAME = *name*		Defines the name of the variable.
VALUE = *value*		Defines the value to pass to the applet.
VALUETYPE = *type*		Specifies how to interpret the data (*type* can be DATE,
		REF, or OBJECT). (HTML 4.0)
TYPE = *type*		Defines the media type. (HTML 4.0)

continued on next page

continued from previous page

ELEMENT	HOW-TO	DEFINITION
<BGSOUND>		Includes a sound to play in the background. (Microsoft)
SRC = *URL*		Defines the URL of the sound file.
LOOP = *n*		Defines the number of times to play the sound.
BALANCE = *n*		Defines the balance between the left and right speakers (*n* is a number from –10,000 to +10,000).
VOLUME = *n*		Defines the volume of the sound (*n* is a number from –10,000 to 0).
<STYLE>...</STYLE>	16.10	Includes a style sheet. (HTML 4.0)
TYPE = *MIME type*		MIME type of the style sheet.
TITLE = "*text*"		Advisory information about the style sheet.
<SPAN>...</SPAN>		Applies style information to part of a document. (HTML 4.0)
<SCRIPT>...</SCRIPT>	17.8	Includes a script. (HTML 4.0)
TYPE = *MIME type*		MIME type of the script.
LANGUAGE = *language*		Defines the language of the script.
SRC = *URL*		Defines the URL of the script.
<NOSCRIPT>...</NOSCRIPT>	17.12	Defines alternative markup for browsers that don't support the script. (HTML 4.0)

B

WWW RESOURCES

This book can't go into full detail on every WWW and HTML topic, nor can it provide information on every WWW browser, server, or related application. This appendix is a brief list of information available on the Web and elsewhere on the Internet that will allow you to study in greater detail some of the topics addressed in the book, and also allow you to find Web-related software for your use.

NOTE

The following URLs were accurate when this appendix was written. However, URLs often change and Web sites sometimes disappear, so some of the sites listed may no longer be valid.

Basic Information on WWW and HTML

The World Wide Web (W3) Consortium

`http://www.w3.org/`

Home to general information on the World Wide Web and links to all areas of WWW and HTML.

The WWW Section of Yahoo!

`http://www.yahoo.com/Computers/World_Wide_Web`

Links to hundreds of pages regarding WWW and HTML.

Indexes

ALIWEB

`http://web.nexor.co.uk/public/aliweb/aliweb.html`

A searchable database of Web pages based on descriptions of sites by their creators.

AltaVista

`http://altavista.digital.com/`

A powerful search engine for finding Web pages and Usenet postings.

HotBot

`http://www.hotbot.com/`

A Web search engine sponsored by *HotWired*.

InfoSeek

`http://www.infoseek.com/`

Another good search engine for scanning the Web.

Lycos

`http://www.lycos.com/`

An extensive database of Web pages with sophisticated search tools.

OpenText

`http://www.opentext.com/`

An extensive database of Web sites.

TradeWave Galaxy

`http://www.einet.net/`

A subject-based guide to Web pages (formerly EINet Galaxy).

W3 Search Engines

`http://cuiwww.unige.ch/meta-index.html`

A page with links to a number of WWW search engines.

WebCrawler

`http://webcrawler.com/`

A search engine that uses its own index or checks the Web in real time to answer queries.

World Wide Web Worm (WWWW)

`http://wwww.cs.colorado.edu/wwww/`

A searchable database that can find Web pages by title or URL.

Yahoo!

`http://www.yahoo.com/`

A popular, extensive database of Web pages.

Browsers

Text-Based

Agora

`http://www.w3.org/hypertext/WWW/Agora/Overview.html`

A browser that uses e-mail to transfer pages, for those without full Internet access.

Emacs W3

`http://www.cs.indiana.edu/elisp/w3/docs.html`

An Emacs subsystem that can run WWW documents.

Line Mode Browser

`http://www.w3.org/hypertext/WWW/LineMode/`

A line-based (as opposed to screen-based) browser for dumb terminals.

Lynx

`http://www.cc.ukans.edu/about_lynx/about_lynx.html`

A screen-based text browser for UNIX, VMS, and DOS systems.

Macintosh

Cyberdog

`http://cyberdog.apple.com/`

A multifaceted Internet tool, including Web browser, that uses Apple's OpenDoc technology.

Enhanced Mosaic (Spyglass)

`http://www.spyglass.com/products/browser.html`

An enhanced version of NCSA's Mosaic, marketed solely to other companies.

Microsoft Internet Explorer

`http://www.microsoft.com/ie/`

Microsoft's powerful and increasingly popular Web browser.

Mosaic for Macintosh

`http://www.ncsa.uiuc.edu/SDG/Software/MacMosaic/MacMosaicHome.html`

The Macintosh version of the Mosaic browser.

Netscape Navigator

`http://home.netscape.com/`

The Macintosh version of the very popular Netscape Navigator browser.

NeXTSTEP

OmniWeb

`http://www.omnigroup.com/Software/OmniWeb/`

A Web browser marketed by Omni Development, Inc.

UNIX (X Window)

Amaya

`http://www.w3.org/hypertext/WWW/Amaya`

A combination browser and editor from the World Wide Web Consortium.

Arena

`http://www.w3.org/hypertext/WWW/Arena/`

A prototype HTML 3 Web browser developed by the World Wide Web Consortium.

Chimera

`http://www.unlv.edu/chimera/`

A small Web browser whose capabilities can be extended by users.

Enhanced Mosaic (Spyglass)

`http://www.spyglass.com/products/browser.html`

An enhanced version of NCSA's Mosaic, marketed solely to other companies.

Mosaic for X Window

`http://www.ncsa.uiuc.edu/SDG/Software/XMosaic/`

The X Window version of the Mosaic browser.

Netscape

`http://home.netscape.com/`

The X Window version of the very popular Netscape Navigator browser.

Viola

`http://marble.ebay.gnn.com/proj/viola/violaHome.html`

A Web browser created using the Viola hypermedia language.

Windows

Cello

`http://www.law.cornell.edu/cello/cellotop.html`

An old but once-popular Web browser.

Enhanced Mosaic (Spyglass)

`http://www.spyglass.com/products/browser.html`

An enhanced version of NCSA's Mosaic, marketed solely to other companies.

Galahad

`http://www.mcs.com/~jvwater/main.html`

An off-line Web browser.

Microsoft Internet Explorer

`http://www.microsoft.com/ie/`

Microsoft's powerful and increasingly popular Web browser.

Mosaic for Windows

`http://www.ncsa.uiuc.edu/SDG/Software/WinMosaic/HomePage.html`

The Windows version of the Mosaic browser.

Netscape

`http://home.netscape.com/`

The Windows version of the very popular Netscape Navigator browser.

SlipKnot

`http://www.interport.net/slipknot/slipknot.html`

A graphical Web browser that does not require a SLIP or PPP connection or TCP/IP.

Servers

Macintosh

MacHTTP

`http://www.biap.com/machttp_info.html`

A Web server program now superseded by WebSTAR.

WebSTAR

`http://mac-1.qdeck.com/webstar/`

An enhanced, commercial version of MacHTTP.

OS/2

GoServe

`http://www2.hursley.ibm.com/goserve/`

A server program that supports the Web and Gopher protocols.

UNIX

CERN/W3C HTTPD

`http://www.w3.org/hypertext/WWW/Daemon/Status.html`

A server program developed at CERN and available for most versions of UNIX.

Jungle

`http://catless.ncl.ac.uk/Programs/Jungle/`

A server written using the tcl/tk programming toolkit.

NCSA HTTPD

`http://hoohoo.ncsa.uiuc.edu/docs/Overview.html`

A server program written at NCSA.

Netscape Servers

`http://home.netscape.com/comprod/mirror/server_download.html`

A suite of commercial server programs created by Netscape.

PHTTPD

`http://www.signum.se/phttpd/`

A free, fast Web server program for computers running the Solaris (SunOS) operating system.

Plexus

`http://www.bsdi.com/server/doc/plexus.html`

A public domain Web server written in Perl.

WN

`http://hopf.math.nwu.edu/`

A Web server that incorporates navigation features and conditionally served files.

VAX/VMS

VAX/VMS Server

`http://kcgl1.eng.ohio-state.edu/www/doc/serverinfo.html`

A Web server program created at Ohio State.

Windows

HTTPS (Windows NT)

`http://www.w3.org/hypertext/WWW/HTTPS/Status.html`

A Web server program available for Intel-based systems and the DEC/Alpha.

WebSite (NT and Windows 95)

`http://website.ora.com/`

A Web server, with an included Enhanced Mosaic browser, that runs on 386 and higher machines.

Windows HTTPD (Windows 3.1)

`http://www.city.net/win-httpd/`

A small and very fast Web server based on NCSA HTTPD.

HTML Editors

Macintosh

Arachnid

`http://sec-look.uiowa.edu/about/projects/arachnid-page.html`

An HTML editor that won a 1995 Apple Enterprise Award.

BBEdit

`http://www.barebones.com/bbedit.html`

A popular, powerful Macintosh text editor with HTML capabilities.

Claris Home Page

`http://www.claris.com/products/clarispage/`

A WYSIWYG Web page tool that allows you to create pages without having to manually edit HTML.

GNNPress

`http://www.tools.gnn.com/press/index.html`

A multiplatform Web page design tool.

HoTMetaL PRO

`http://www.sq.com/products/hotmetal/hmp-org.htm`

A commercial HTML editor, with a less powerful but free version also available.

HTML Editor

`http://dragon.acadiau.ca/~giles/HTML_Editor/Documentation.html`

A semi-WYSIWYG HTML editor.

HTML Grinder

`http://www.matterform.com/grinder/`

An HTML editor that uses special plug-in modules to handle sophisticated tasks.

HTML-HyperEditor

`http://www.lu.se/info/Editor/`

An HTML editor written as a HyperCard stack that supports special characters used in other languages.

PageMill

`http://www.adobe.com/prodindex/pagemill/overview.html`

A powerful WYSIWYG editor that creates Web pages without requiring manual HTML editing.

PageSpinner

`http://www.algonet.se/~optima/pagespinner.html`

An HTML editor that supports many of the newest HTML extensions.

World Wide Web Weaver/HTML Web Weaver

`http://www.miracleinc.com`

A set of commercial and shareware HTML editors.

UNIX

A Simple HTML Editor (ASHE)

`ftp://ftp.cs.rpi.edu/pub/puninj/ASHE/README.html`

An HTML editor written in C using Motif and the NCSA HTML Widget.

City University HTML Editor

`http://web.cs.city.ac.uk/homes/njw/htmltext/htmltext.html`

A free, easily configurable HTML editor written using the Andrew toolkit.

GNNPress

`http://www.tools.gnn.com/press/index.html`

A multiplatform Web page design tool.

Symposia

`http://www.grif.fr/prod/sympro.html`

A Web design application for UNIX and Windows.

tkHTML

`http://www.cobaltgroup.com/~roland/tkHTML/tkHTML.html`

An HTML editor written using the tcl/tk toolkit.

Web Magic

`http://www.sgi.com/Products/WebFORCE/WebMagic/index.html`

A powerful Web page creation tool for users of SGI machines.

Windows

FrontPage

`http://www.microsoft.com/msoffice/frontpage/default.htm`

Microsoft's Web page and site development application.

GNNPress

`http://www.tools.gnn.com/press/index.html`

A multiplatform Web page design tool.

HomeSite

`http://www.dexnet.com/homesite.html`

A full-featured shareware Web page designer.

HotDog

`http://www.sausage.com/`

An HTML editor with a Windows 95–style interface that supports HTML 3 tags and Netscape extensions.

HoTMetaL PRO

`http://www.sq.com/products/hotmetal/hmp-org.htm`

A commercial HTML editor, with a less powerful but free version also available.

HTML Assistant Pro

`http://www.brooknorth.com/istar.html`

A commercial HTML editor based on a popular shareware editor.

HTML Writer

`http://lal.cs.byu.edu/people/nosack/index.html`

An HTML editor that allows you to edit more than one document at a time.

InContext Spider

`http://www.incontext.ca/products/spider1.html`

A commercial Web page tool that supports advanced HTML features.

Symposia

`http://www.grif.fr/prod/sympro.html`

A Web design application for UNIX and Windows.

Webber

`http://www.csdcorp.com/webber.htm`

An HTML editor that includes a validator program to look for invalid HTML markup.

WebMedia Publisher

`http://www.wbmedia.com/publisher/`

A Web page tool that supports the latest Microsoft and Netscape HTML extensions.

Web Wizard

`http://www.halcyon.com/webwizard/index.html`

An HTML editor available in 16-bit and 32-bit versions.

HTML Document Development

HTML 2.0 Specification

`http://www.w3.org/hypertext/WWW/MarkUp/html-spec/index.html`

A full description of the final draft of HTML 2.

HTML 3.2 Draft Specification

`http://www.w3.org/pub/WWW/MarkUp/`

A full description of the current draft of HTML 3.2.

HTML Style Guide

`http://www.w3.org/hypertext/WWW/Provider/Style/Overview.html`

Tim Berners-Lee's excellent guide to designing WWW documents.

NetSpace Guide for HTML Developers

`http://netspace.org/netspace/wwwdoc.html`

Lots of links to documents on creating effective HTML documents.

Subjective Electronic Information Repository

`http://cbl.leeds.ac.uk/nikos/doc/repository.html`

Links to hundreds of WWW development documents.

URL Descriptions

`http://www.w3.org/hypertext/WWW/Addressing/Addressing.html`

Definitions of the various types of URLs, as well as discussion of URNs and URIs.

WWW Development Page (Virtual Library)

`http://www.charm.net/~web/Vlib/`

Links to a wide range of HTML development documents.

Net Tips for Writers and Designers

`http://www.dsiegel.com/tips/`

Design tips for effective Web pages from a leading designer.

Frames Tutorial

`http://www.newbie.net/frames/`

A step-by-step tutorial for creating pages using frames.

Common Gateway Interface (CGI)

CGI Documentation

`http://hoohoo.ncsa.uiuc.edu/cgi/`

Information on the Common Gateway Interface, including CGI scripts in programs.

CGI Programs (Perl)

`http://www.seas.upenn.edu/~mengwong/perlhtml.html`

A library of commonly used CGI routines, written in Perl.

Forms and Imagemaps

NCSA Forms Documentation

`http://hoohoo.ncsa.uiuc.edu/cgi/forms.html`

Information on using forms in conjunction with CGI scripts.

Image Maps: CERN HTTPD

`http://www.w3.org/hypertext/WWW/Daemon/User/CGI/HTImageDoc.html`

A tutorial for creating imagemaps for the CERN HTTPD server program.

Image Maps: NCSA HTTPD

`http://hoohoo.ncsa.uiuc.edu/docs/tutorials/imagemapping.html`

A tutorial for creating imagemaps for the NCSA HTTPD server program.

Scripting and Multimedia

ActiveX

ActiveX Development Information

`http://www.microsoft.com/intdev/`

Microsoft's guide to its ActiveX resources.

ActiveX Examples

`http://www.rollins-assoc.com/fvbs.html`

Examples of ActiveX and Visual Basic applications for the Web.

Java

Sun's Java Information

`http://java.sun.com/`

Java information from Sun, the company that created the language.

Gamelan Java Applets

`http://www.gamelan.com/`

A repository of hundreds of Java applets.

JavaWorld

`http://www.javaworld.com/`

An online magazine for beginning and experienced Java users.

Java Links

`http://www.sover.net/~manx/java.html`

Links to Java resources across the Web.

Steve's Java Resources

`http://infoweb.magi.com/~steve/java.html`

More information about Java on the Web.

Digitalfocus

`http://www.digitalfocus.com/digitalfocus/faq/`

Frequently asked questions about Java and other links.

JavaScript

Netscape JavaScript Information

`http://home.netscape.com/eng/mozilla/Gold/handbook/javascript/`

JavaScript information from the company that brought it to the Web.

Gamelan JavaScript Scripts

`http://www.gamelan.com/`

A repository of many JavaScript scripts.

JavaScript Scripts

`http://www.geocities.com/SiliconValley/9000/`

A set of useful JavaScript scripts by the same set of authors.

JavaScript Tip of the Week

`http://webreference.com/javascript/`

Numerous tips and tricks on using JavaScript.

Babyak's JavaScript Resources

`http://www.epix.com/~mbabyak/`

Links to JavaScript resources across the Web.

Shockwave

Macromedia Shockwave Information

`http://www.macromedia.com/shockwave/`

Shockwave information and tools to create and view Shockwave files.

VRML

VRML FAQ

`http://vag.vrml.org/VRML_FAQ.html`

Frequently asked questions and resources on Virtual Reality Modeling Language.

VRML Respository

`http://www.sdsc.edu/vrml/`

Links to VRML browsers and viewers, development applications, and VRML sites.

NSCA VRML Information

`http://www.ncsa.uiuc.edu/General/VRML/VRMLHome.html`

More information on VRML.

WWW Usenet Newsgroups

Browsers

`comp.infosystems.www.browsers.mac`

Discussion about Macintosh browsers.

`comp.infosystems.www.browsers.ms-windows`

Discussion about Microsoft Windows browsers.

`comp.infosystems.www.browsers.x`

Discussion about X Window browsers.

`comp.infosystems.www.browsers.misc`

Discussion about other classes of browsers.

Document Authoring Groups

`comp.infosystems.www.authoring.cgi`

Discussion of CGI applications.

`comp.infosystems.www.authoring.html`

Discussion of HTML markup.

`comp.infosystems.www.authoring.images`

Discussion of the use of images in WWW documents.

`comp.infosystems.www.authoring.misc`

Discussion of other questions about document creation not covered in the groups already mentioned.

Servers

`comp.infosystems.www.servers.mac`

Discussion about Macintosh servers.

`comp.infosystems.www.servers.ms-windows`

Discussion about Microsoft Windows servers.

`comp.infosystems.www.servers.unix`

Discussion about UNIX servers.

`comp.infosystems.www.servers.misc`

Discussion about other classes of servers.

Other Discussion and Announcement Groups

`comp.infosystems.www.advocacy`

Discussion (and arguments) about various WWW applications and products.

`comp.infosystems.www.announce`

Announcements (no discussion permitted) of new and improved WWW sites.

`comp.infosystems.www.misc`

Discussion about WWW topics not covered by any of the newsgroups already mentioned.

WWW Mailing Lists

`www-talk@info.cern.ch`

Discussion about WWW among experts. To subscribe, e-mail **`listserv@info.cern.ch`** with the line **`subscribe www-talk`** ***Your Name*** in the body of the message. Subscription requests can also be sent to **`www-talk-request@info.cern.ch`** to be processed by a human.

`www-announce@info.cern.ch`

Used for "low-volume" announcements of products and services. Use the **`listserv`** address to subscribe (replace **`www-talk`** in the body with **`www-announce`**), or e-mail **`www-announce-request@info.cern.ch`**.

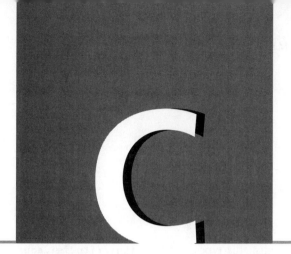

MIME

World Wide Web clients, such as browsers and servers, use MIME protocol to communicate information about the type of data requested and sent via HTTP. The sections of this appendix describe MIME and explain how it is used in the World Wide Web environment.

What Is MIME?

The Multipurpose Internet Mail Extensions (MIME) were developed as an extension to the Internet mail protocol to provide for incorporation of multimedia objects. The original definition for Internet mail dealt primarily with the transmission and reception of plain text messages. This mail protocol, as defined in RFC 822 (for more information, see **http://www.w3.org/pub/WWW/Protocols/rfc822/Overview.html**), specified several message header elements that provided direction for the routing of the mail messages. The development of this protocol provided a standard that all Internet mail programs could use.

The Internet mail protocol, however, left message content largely unmentioned, assuming that most messages would be simple text. In today's world of Internet mail, complex, multipart, and multimedia messages are becoming commonplace. MIME was developed to support these types of complex mail messages. It does so by adding suitable header fields to describe message content and delimit multimedia objects. A standard such as MIME is necessary to provide for interoperability among Internet mail programs that support complex mail messages. For example, the following message represents a multipart message containing text, audio, and PostScript components:

```
MIME-Version: 1.0
Content-type: multipart/mixed; boundary=SomeString

--SomeString
Content-type: text/plain
Text message body
```

continued on next page

continued from previous page

```
--SomeString
Content-type: audio/basic
An audio object

--SomeString
Content-type: application/postscript
A postscript object

--SomeString--
```

(For an official list of registered media types, see URL **ftp://ftp.isi.edu/in-notes/iana/assignments/media-types**.)

The headers define the MIME version and the kind of message being sent. In this case, the message is specified as **multipart/mixed**, with an indication that the string will be used to delimit the subcomponents. Each subcomponent has individual ***type/subtype*** specifications to describe the content of the particular subcomponent. The delimiter string marks the beginning and end of a subcomponent and marks the termination of the message. For more details on MIME, see the specification contained in RFC 1521, which is available at **http://sunsite.auc.dk/RFC/rfc/rfc1521.html**.

MIME Content-type Header and the Web

The portion of MIME protocol that is of central interest to HTML document developers is the **Content-type** header field. The World Wide Web environment uses MIME content-type information in several ways. Table C-1 specifies a set of the more commonly used MIME types that may be encountered in that environment.

Table C-1 MIME types commonly or specifically used with the World Wide Web

MIME TYPE/SUBTYPE	DESCRIPTION	COMMON FILE EXTENSIONS
application/acad	AutoCAD file	dwg
application/arj	ARJ archive file	arj
application/clariscad	ClarisCAD file	CCAD
application/dxf	AutoCAD DXF file	dxf
application/excel	Microsoft Excel	xl
application/mac-binhex40	Binhex archive format	hqx
application/msword	Microsoft Word	doc
application/mswrite	Microsoft Write	wri
application/octet-stream	Binary data	bin
application/oda	Office Document Architecture	oda
application/pdf	Adobe Acrobat PDF format	pdf
application/postscript	PostScript document	ps eps

MIME TYPE/SUBTYPE	DESCRIPTION	COMMON FILE EXTENSIONS
application/rtf	Rich Text Format	rtf
application/set	French CAD standard	set
application/x-csh	C shell script	csh
application/x-cpio	POSIX CPIO format	cpio
application/x-director	Macromedia Director files	dir dcr dxr
application/x-dvi	Device-Independent format	dvi
application/x-gtar	GNU tar format	gtar
application/x-gzip	GNU zip format	gz gzip
application/x-hdf	NCSA HDF data	hdf
application/x-latex	LaTeX document	latex
application/x-mif	FrameMaker MIF files	mif
application/x-netcdf	Net Common Data Format	cdf nc
application/x-pl	Perl script	perl pl
application/x-sh	sh shell script	sh
application/x-shar	Shell archive	shar
application/x-stuffit	Macintosh StuffIt archive	sit sea
application/x-tcl	Tcl script	tcl
application/x-tex	TeX document	tex
application/x-texinfo	TexInfo format	texinfo texi
application/x-troff	troff document	t tr troff
application/x-troff-man	troff with man macros	man
application/x-troff-me	troff with me macros	me
application/x-troff-ms	troff with ms macros	ms
application/x-ustar	POSIX tar format	ustar
application/x-wais-source	WAIS source	src
application/x-winhelp	Windows Help format	hlp
application/zip	Zip compressed document	zip
audio/basic	Basic audio file (8-bit PCM)	au snd
audio/x-aiff	AIFF audio file	aiff aif
audio/x-pn-realaudio	RealAudio	ra ram
audio/x-pn-realaudio-plugin	RealAudio plug-in	rpm
audio/x-wav	Microsoft audio format	wav
image/gif	GIF image	gif
image/ief	Image exchange format	ief
image/jpeg	JPEG image	jpeg jpg jpe

continued on next page

continued from previous page

MIME TYPE/SUBTYPE	DESCRIPTION	COMMON FILE EXTENSIONS
image/pict	PICT image	pict
image/tiff	TIFF image	tiff tif
image/x-portable-anymap	Portable image format	pnm
image/x-portable-bitmap	Portable bitmap format	pbm
image/x-portable-graymap	Portable grayscale image format	pgm
image/x-portable-pixmap	Portable pixmap format	ppm
image/x-rgb	RGB image	rgb
image/x-xwindowdump	X Window dump	xwd
image/x-xbitmap	X bitmap	xbm
image/x-xpixmap	X pixelmap	xpm
message/rfc822	MIME message	mime
multipart/mixed	Multipart messages	
multipart/x-zip	PKZIP archive	zip
multipart/x-gzip	GNU zip archive	gz gzip
text/html	HTML text	html htm
text/plain	Normal text (ASCII)	txt
text/richtext	MIME Rich Text Format	rtx
text/tab-separated-values	Text with tab-separated values	tsv
text/x-setext	Structure enhanced text	etx
video/mpeg	MPEG format video	mpeg mpg mpe
video/msvideo	Microsoft Video format	avi
video/quicktime	QuickTime format video	qt mov
video/x-sgi-movie	SGI format movie	movie
x-world/x-vrml	VRML virtual environment	wrl wrz

In addition, the World Wide Web environment defines several other experimental and nonstandard MIME content types. Table C-2 lists some of them, along with references to the How-To's within this book that describe these particular MIME content types.

Table C-2 World Wide Web–specific MIME types

MIME TYPE/SUBTYPE	DESCRIPTION	HOW-TO REFERENCE
application/x-www-form-urlencode	Encoding for form data	11.1, 14.1
application/x-www-pem-request	PEM authorization request	13.10
application/x-www-pem-reply	PEM authorization reply	13.10
applicaiton/x-www-pgm-request	PGM authorization request	13.10
application/x-www-pgm-reply	PGM authorization reply	13.10

MIME TYPE/SUBTYPE	DESCRIPTION	HOW-TO REFERENCE
`application/x-httpd-cgi`	CGI applications	
	(`cgi` filename extension)	14.4
`magnus-internal/parsed-html`	NS FastTrack-parsed HTML	13.4
`magnus-internal/cgi`	NS FastTrack executable CGI	14.4
`multipart/form-data`	Alternate form data method	11.7, 14.8
`multipart/x-mixed-replace`	Netscape Server Push	15.10
`text/x-server-parsed-html`	NCSA-parsed HTML	13.4

The categories specified in these tables are not a complete list of MIME content types, but they do cover a large percentage of common types. The WWW-specific types described are all nonstandard MIME content types and may not be suitable for all clients, servers, and client/server combinations.

The HTTP protocol specifies the content types of HTTP requests and responses using MIME type/subtype designations. (See Appendix G, "HTML Hypertext Transfer Protocol [HTTP].") When a client issues a **`GET`** request of an HTTP server, the server sends a **`Content-type`** field in the header of its response indicating the type of information enclosed in the response body. When a client issues a **`POST`** request, it includes a **`Content-type`** field in the request header specifying the format of the data being sent to the server:

```
Content-type: application/x-www-form-urlencoded
```

or

```
Content-type: multipart/form-data
```

`Content-type` fields for both MIME and HTTP are composed of the header name, **`Content-type`**, and at least two fields specifying a type and a subtype:

```
Content-type: type/subtype
```

The type specification can be chosen from the following list:

- ✔ **`application`**: The file needs to be processed or manipulated in some manner by the recipient. For example, a PostScript object should be sent to an appropriate PostScript viewer.
- ✔ **`audio`**: The file is an audio object. This object should be rendered using the appropriate software and hardware, if available. If a suitable rendering environment is unavailable, many browsers allow the reader to save the object to a file.
- ✔ **`extension-token`**: This refers to a type beginning with the **`x-`** prefix. Use this prefix for all experimental, nonstandard, or private types. For example, the **`x-world`** type specifies a virtual environment.

- ✔ `image`: The file is an image of some type and should be treated appropriately.
- ✔ `message`: The file conforms to a different message standard, such as RFC 822.
- ✔ `multipart`: The file is composed of multiple objects, each having its own respective type and subtype. The multipart type requires another header element specifying a boundary string to delimit the various component objects.
- ✔ `text`: The message body is composed of text. This text may be in a variety of formats. For example, the text could be an HTML document or a plain text document.
- ✔ `video`: The message body contains a video component. The object should be displayed using appropriate hardware and software.

The second portion of the `Content-type` header field is the subtype. The subtype is used to provide a more detailed specification of the content. For example, the content type `text/plain` represents a plain text file. The content type `text/html` designates an HTML page. The variety of subtypes precludes the delineation of all possible subtypes, but Tables C-1 and C-2 provide a good subset of World Wide Web–related content types, both type and subtype.

MIME and the Web Client

Web clients use MIME content types to determine which external viewer to launch when a server sends it a given document. When a client sends a request to an HTTP server, the server's response includes a response header and possibly a message body, depending on the results of the request. One of the fields in the response header is `Content-type`, which specifies the content type of the response's message body.

Similarly, Gopher servers provide information concerning message content `FILL` (message data type in a Gopher framework). However, when local files are accessed or an FTP transaction occurs, no information concerning the type of information being accessed is available. Therefore, the client must determine the type and present the information in an appropriate manner. The mechanism used by most browsing software is to determine the type based upon the filename extension of the object accessed. Table C-1 provides a list of the most commonly used MIME types with respect to World Wide Web transactions. For the types specified in Table C-2, specific configuration instructions for browsers to support these types are provided in the referenced How-To's. For example, the `multipart/x-mixed-replace` type is currently supported only by the Netscape browser and requires no additional configuration, whereas the `x-www-local-exec` type requires a modification of the browser's configuration files.

Browsers usually maintain a database of file extensions and their associated MIME types. This database is accessed by the client whenever a file needs to be resolved into a type prior to being displayed to the user. This information can usually be modified and extended by the user through configuration control. For example, to modify the MIME database in MacWeb, you modify part of the program resource fork accessible via a pull-down menu in the application. On the other hand, modification of the database for X Window Mosaic involves editing the **mime.types** file.

MIME and the Web Server

Servers also base content-type determination on file-type extensions. When a client makes a request, the server determines the **Content-type** field to use in the response header based on the filename extension of the file. Thus, files on the server with a **.tif** extension generate a **Content-type: image/tiff** field in the response header. Similarly, files with the **.htm** extension are sent with a **Content-type: text/html** in the server's response header.

Additional extensions can be identified to map to the same content type. For example, both the **.htm** and **.html** extensions may signify an HTML document; this is particularly true of PC servers that are limited to three-character file extensions. Whenever additional extensions or new types need to be added to the server, the MIME types database for the server needs to be updated. For the NCSA HTTPD and Netscape FastTrack servers, this database is contained in the **mime.types** file in the **conf** subdirectory.

If the server cannot resolve a filename extension to a type, or if the requested file does not have a filename extension, the server sends a default type in the response header. Many servers use **text/plain** as a default type; however, depending on the server, this default type might be configurable. For example, the **DefaultType** directive in the server resource map file will set this default type for an NCSA HTTPD server.

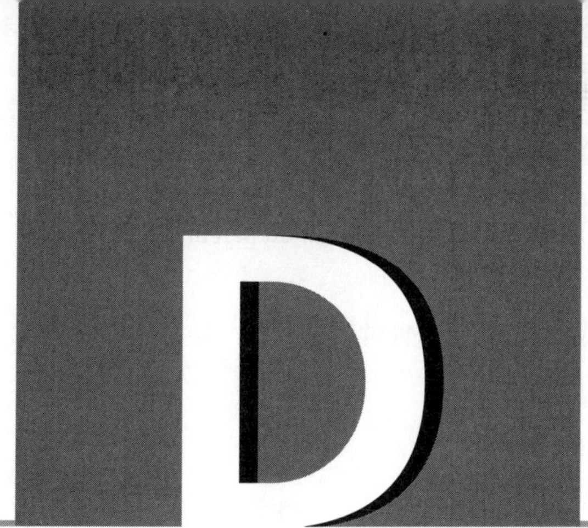

UNIX QUICK REFERENCE

Even though you might be creating your documents on a Windows or Macintosh system, you will find that many aspects of HTML, such as directory paths in URLs, are borrowed directly from UNIX. Despite UNIX's reputation as a user-unfriendly operating system, basic UNIX commands can be easily learned and used. In fact, if you have used DOS on a PC before, you will find UNIX very similar (but with some differences). Here's a brief list of UNIX commands that might be useful to you.

Changing Directories

To change from the current directory to a subdirectory, type

```
cd directoryname
```

To change from the current directory to a subdirectory several levels down, type

```
cd directoryname1/directoryname2/directoryname3
```

NOTE

UNIX uses forward slashes to separate directory names, unlike DOS, which uses back slashes.

To change from the current directory to the parent directory (one level up), type

```
cd ..
```

To change from the current directory to a directory several levels up, type

```
cd ../../..
```

To change to a directory that branches off from a common parent directory, type

```
cd ../directoryname
```

To go to your home directory, regardless of your current location, type

```
cd
```

Listing the Contents of a Directory

To list the contents of a directory, simply type

```
ls
```

To display a long listing, including the filename, size, date created or modified, and owner, type

```
ls -l
```

To list all files, including hidden files (whose filenames begin with a period), type

```
ls -a
```

To place symbols beside specific names (a `/` after directory names or a `*` after executable files), type

```
ls -F
```

Moving and Deleting Files and Changing Filenames

To change the name of a file from `file1` to `file2`, type

```
mv file1 file2
```

To move `file1` to a subdirectory, type

```
mv file1 directoryname/file1
```

To move `file1` to a parent directory, type

```
mv file1 ../file1
```

To move a group of files that begins with the name `file` to a subdirectory, type

```
mv file* directoryname/
```

To delete a file named `file1`, type

```
rm file1
```

To delete the entire contents of a directory, type

```
rm *
```

(Use this command with care. After you delete a file, it's gone for good.)

Creating and Removing Directories

To create a subdirectory in the current directory, type

```
mkdir directoryname
```

To remove an empty subdirectory from the current directory, type

```
rmdir directoryname
```

To remove a subdirectory and all the files and directories contained within it, type

```
rm -r directoryname
```

Setting File and Directory Permissions

To change the permissions on a file to allow or prevent others from accessing it, type

```
chmod nnn filename
```

To change the permissions on all files in a directory to allow or prevent others from accessing them, type

```
chmod nnn directoryname
```

where `nnn` are three digits that define how a file or directory can be accessed by various users. The first digit represents the user, the second digit represents the user's group (a subset of users on the computer system), and the third digit represents all users on a system. The various number values the digits usually take are

0 No access

4 Read-only access

5 Read and executable access

6 Read and write access

7 Read, write, and executable access

For example, to make a file readable, writable, and executable for yourself, but only readable and executable for other users, type

```
chmod 755 file1
```

or to allow all users to read and write to a document, type

```
chmod 666 file2
```

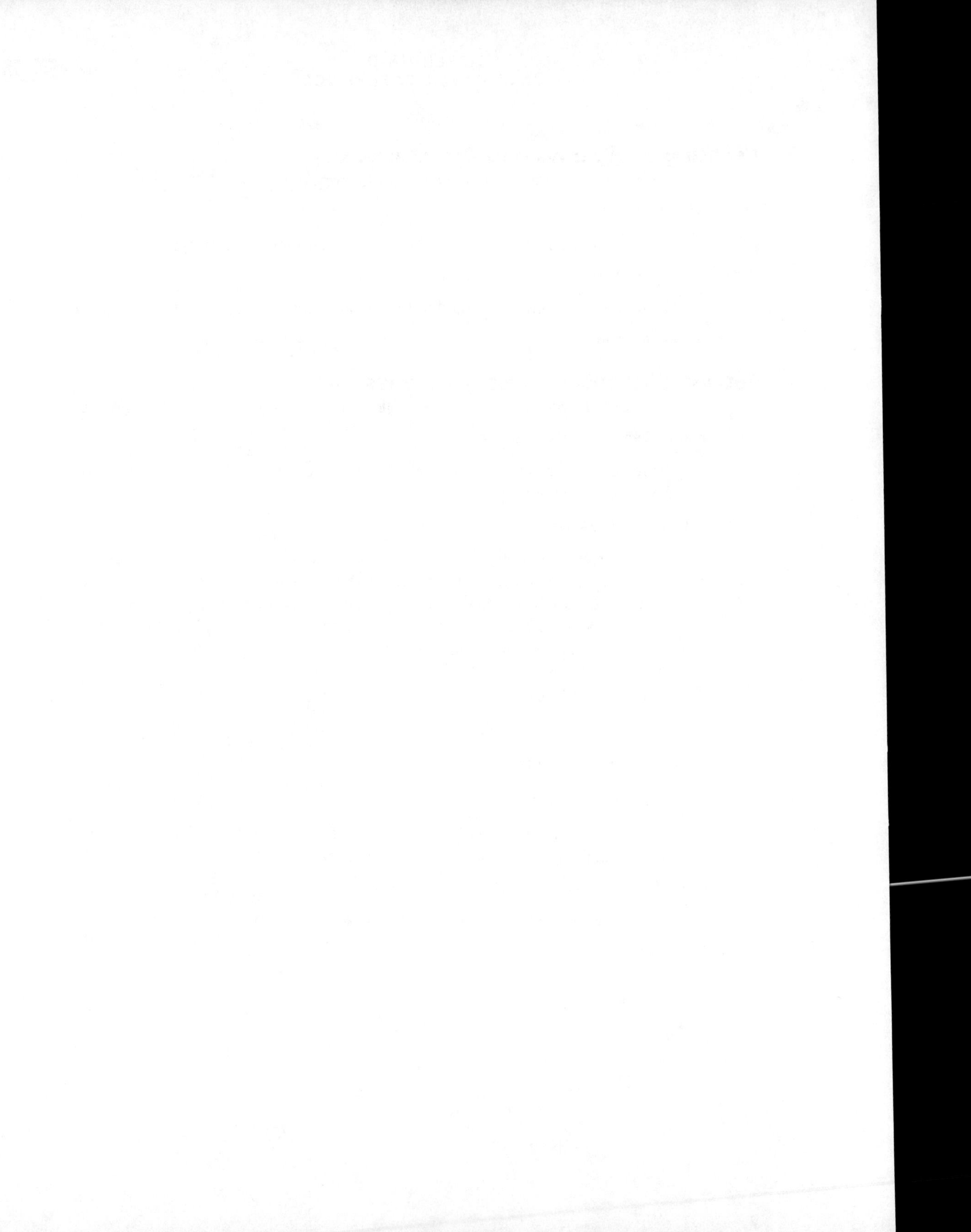

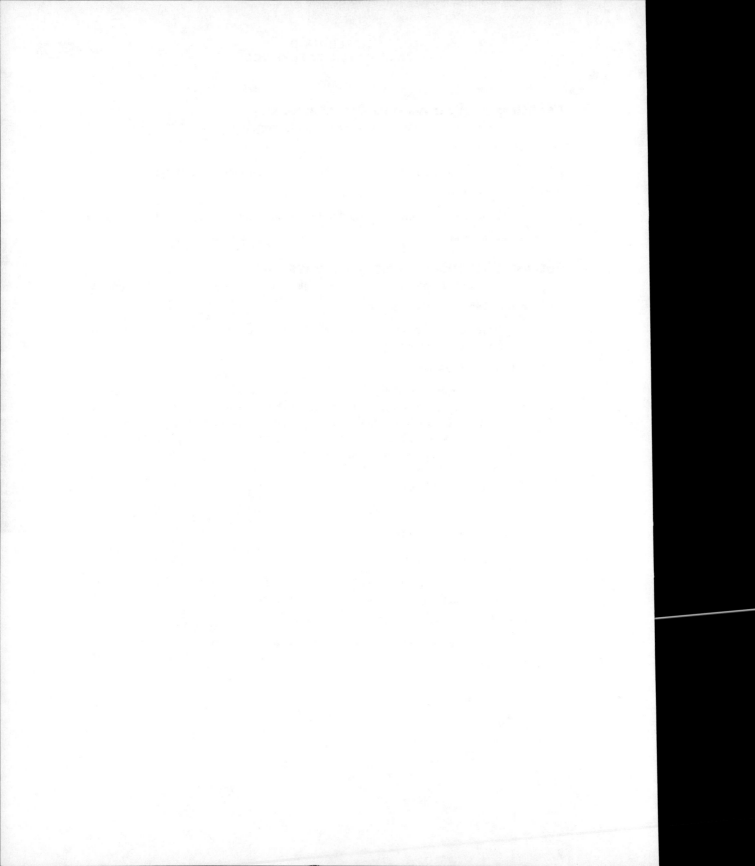

E

HTML STYLE GUIDE

Suggestions for Do's and Don'ts

The Web is a wide-open, freewheeling place. No set rules govern what a person should or shouldn't do with his or her pages. Much of what appears on a page is left to a combination of the creator's individual style and the browser's predetermined set of standards. The following Do's and Don'ts are meant only as guidelines and suggestions for creating readable, nonfrustrating home pages.

Do's

The following Do's, although certainly not carved in stone, will help make your pages more readable. They are general enough to apply to almost any page.

- ✔ Name your pages. With search utilities and Web crawlers, readers can find your pages in any number of ways. Help them locate your pages by using a label to identify each page.
- ✔ List an author somewhere on your pages, preferably on the top or bottom. Take credit for the work you put into your pages.
- ✔ Use informative titles in `<TITLE>` tags. This enables users to jump easily to where they want to go in their "history list." This also makes it easy for users to add your pages to their hot lists.
- ✔ Give readers an idea of how complete your pages are. It sometimes seems as though 90 percent of the Web is always under construction and the other 10 percent isn't working. It's a good idea to let readers know the current state of your pages. However, "under construction" should not be synonymous with "lots of stuff here doesn't work."
- ✔ Give an e-mail address where users can contact you if they have comments or problems.

- ✔ Give warnings with any links that lead to explicit documents or images. Not everybody on the Web is as open-minded as you are.
- ✔ Give warnings with any links that lead to large images or documents. It's a considerate touch to label links with the size of documents or images. This way, users have a general idea of how long it might take for the document to load.
- ✔ A last-modified date is always good to have. It lets readers know how current your information is.
- ✔ A creation date on your page, although not essential, is certainly a nice feature. It lets readers know how long you've been around.
- ✔ If you include browser-specific tags (such as the Netscape enhancements) in your documents, add a statement to the document so that people who don't use the browser in question know why things look so strange.
- ✔ Use the **ALT** attribute with the **<IMG>** tag so that people with nongraphical browsers can get an idea of what they could be seeing.
- ✔ When loading images, use the **WIDTH** and **HEIGHT** attributes in the **<IMG>** tag. This will shorten the time the images need to load.
- ✔ When possible, make smaller images such as icons with backgrounds that are transparent. They look cleaner and more professional that way.
- ✔ Remember, you are writing an electronic document, not a paper document. Things that look fine on paper, such as multiple columns, might not work so well on a scrollable document. The medium is different. It is up to you to figure out how you want to make the most of that difference.
- ✔ If you think your document is something people might be interested in printing and referring to later, make a nonhypertext copy available for people to print.
- ✔ If you are using frames, make sure you also use the **<NOFRAMES>... </NOFRAMES>** tags to either have a nonframe version, or at least tell readers whose browsers don't support frames that your pages use frames. Also, try not to go too frame-crazy. Although frames are a powerful tool, they can also be abused—used in places where, instead of being a navigational aid, they become a real distraction or space waster.
- ✔ Take some time to "optimize" any graphics you might have. With a little work with a program such as Photoshop, you might be able to reduce a graphic's size without hurting its quality.
- ✔ Try to use proper (or at least understandable) grammar and syntax. It will make your pages smoother to read. Try to have several people proofread your pages.

- Before you do any actual encoding of your documents into HTML, outline your page's structure. Remember, learning HTML is easy. The hard part is designing your pages so that people can easily access the information you are providing.

Don'ts (General)

Following is a list of suggestions of what to avoid on your Web pages. These are very general suggestions meant to work with any pages.

- Don't use links to documents that don't exist. There is nothing more frustrating than the message

```
Error Code XXX file not found.
```

- Don't insult your readers unless they have a pretty good idea when they come to your page that they might be insulted.
- Don't copy images from somebody else's page unless you get his or her permission first.
- Avoid anchoring links to words that are device dependent and don't really describe what the link leads to—for example,

```
You may <A HREF="manual.html">Click here</A> for users manual.
```

Instead, try to use

```
A <A HREF="manual.html">User's manual</A> is available.
```

- Don't include trailing blanks or punctuation marks in tags. They don't look nice—for example,

```
Here is <A HREF="mydoc.html">my document!</A>
```

Instead, this could be

```
Here is <A HREF="mydoc.html">my document</A>!
```

It is a simple change, but it looks much cleaner.

- Don't load your page with a lot of big images unless you are certain that most of your readers will have fast (ISDN or better) connections. As a general rule, remember that a page with 60KB of text and graphics will take about a minute to load over a 14.4 connection. Another general rule of thumb is not to use graphics of over 40KB on a page.
- Be careful with animated GIFs. One or two can go a long way; any more than that can really overpower a browser. Also, try to avoid GIFs that loop forever; certain versions of Netscape might have cache problems with this.

Don’ts (Conservative)

Following is a list of conservative Don’ts. Authors don’t usually follow these Don’ts, but other more purist types do. You can decide whether you want to follow them or not.

- ✔ Don’t use browser-specific tags and elements. Too many browser-specific tags make a document unreadable to somebody not using that browser. There are people out there who don’t like the way Netscape incorporates tags into browsers either not supported by HTML 4.0 or supported in a different manner.
- ✔ Don’t use more than one or two horizontal rules per page.
- ✔ Don’t use graphic lines (colored or horizontal lines with pictures in them); they needlessly slow down the server.
- ✔ Don’t use heading levels out of order. In other words, don’t do something like the following:

```
<HTML>
<HEAD><TITLE>Bad example?</TITLE></HEAD>
<BODY>
<H4>Going!</H4>
<H2>Going!!</H4>
<H1>Gone!</H1>
</BODY>
</HTML>
```

- ✔ Don’t use a lot of bold or italic type or exclamation marks. Italics seem to be especially hard to read with some browsers.
- ✔ Don’t put a lot of WORDS IN CAPITALS. Usually there is no need to shout on the Web.
- ✔ Don’t change the default colors of the text and links.

Making Your Page Shine

Follow these suggestions if you want to make your pages more memorable:

- ✔ Use a distinct background, but make sure that it is not too large.
- ✔ Start your page with a nice graphic logo. Take a little time with a good graphics program to optimize the image by using a minimal number of colors and, if possible, anti-aliasing.
- ✔ Center titles.

- ✔ Don't be afraid to use icons or images to make your page more readable and more pleasing to the eye. Even if you are not an artist, there are plenty of sites around that offer icons to be downloaded. Because these sites change often, it's best to search for icons or consult a big index such as Yahoo!, the Whole Internet Catalog, or AltaVista.
- ✔ Take time to plan the navigational aids you use in your pages. It's a good idea to include a navigational marker at the top or bottom of each page. The marker can contain the basic **`Next`**, **`Previous`**, **`Top of Server`**, and **`Home Page`** links.
- ✔ Now that Netscape and Internet Explorer both support tables with backgrounds and background colors, you can create many interesting effects simply by changing the background color of related cells.
- ✔ Use frames wisely. Frames can be a great aid to navigating a Web site or they can make a site seem much more complex than it really is.
- ✔ With layers interacting with JavaScript, it is possible to make some truly interactive sites that until recently could have been created only using Java. Just be careful not to go overboard with the use of layers or JavaScript, or you might end up slowing your page down. Experiment to see what works best.
- ✔ Plan and structure your links. Ideally, you want to set up your documents so that readers have numerous ways of finding information, but you want to avoid cluttering your pages with excess or redundant links. It takes practice, common sense, and experimentation to work out the optimal blend of information and links to that information.

HTML STYLE GUIDE

F

SUMMARY OF SELECTED SERVER SOFTWARE

Described here are some of the HTTP servers available. Each description concludes with a reference to a URL where additional and up-to-date information can be found.

The servers listed are those most commonly used. If none of these is suitable, examine URL `http://www.yahoo.com/Computers_and_Internet/Software/Internet/World_Wide_Web/Servers/` for an up-to-date list of available server software.

UNIX

This platform has the greatest variety of servers available. Since the original HTTP servers were developed on this platform, most new developments and enhancements appear first on UNIX servers. Several popular UNIX servers are discussed here.

Apache Server

The Apache server is a freeware server based upon NCSA HTTPD. This application is one of the more popular Web servers.

The server software is available as source code or precompiled binaries. The software architecture is extremely modular, which allows for very selective control over the features available in a particular compilation of the server.

This product supports the standard CGI/1.1 interface for handling gateway applications. A variety of modules support many standard and experimental authentication mechanisms. A modification of this software is available for supporting SSL connections (see URL **http://www.algroup.co.uk/Apache-SSL**).

Further information on the Apache server is available at the URL

```
http://www.apache.org
```

CERN HTTP Server

One of the best features of this server is its ability to act as a proxy server, allowing you to run a server and access outside servers through an Internet firewall. Further, this software is fully CGI/1.1 compliant and comes packaged with a variety of gateway applications, including active image support. This server supports **HEAD**, **GET**, **POST**, and **PUT** client requests. Several How-To's in Chapter 13, "Handling Server Security," provide information on specific configuration tasks with respect to the CERN server. For information, as well as the software itself, use this URL:

```
http://www.w3.org/hypertext/WWW/Daemon/Status.html
```

GN

This freeware server software provides both HTTP and Gopher service. Use is restricted per the standard GNU license (**http://hopf.math.nwu.edu/docs/Gnu_License**). Security is handled through domain or IP address restrictions on a per-directory basis, or over the entire server. However, user authentication is not supported. Unlike most other servers, the default is to deny access to information unless explicit permission is given. Installation and configuration of this server are similar in many ways to creating a standard Gopher server. Therefore, those familiar with Gopher should have an easier time installing this package. The server supports **GET**, **HEAD**, and **POST** requests. Further information on this server is available at the following URL:

```
http://hopf.math.nwu.edu:70/
```

NCSA HTTPD

This application, freely available from the National Center for Supercomputing Applications, supports **GET**, **HEAD**, and **POST** HTTP requests. Security is provided for host filtering through specification of domains or IP addresses; in addition, password security is supported. These measures provide access protection at the directory level. Server-side includes and directives are supported via a parsed HTML type that is processed by the server prior to transmission to a browser. (See How-To 13.4 for additional information on server-side includes and directives.) Several How-To's in Chapter 12, "Server Basics," and Chapter 13 provide additional information on the use of this server. This software and relevant information can be found at this URL:

```
http://hoohoo.ncsa.uiuc.edu/docs/Overview.html
```

Netscape Servers

The Netscape Communications Corporation markets two server packages: the FastTrack server, an upgrade of its Communications Server; and the Enterprise Server, an enhancement of its Commerce Server. The primary difference between these two applications is the level of security capabilities and the suite of power tools packaged with the server. Both servers support the basic, digest, and Kerberos authentication and directory/file-level domain and address restrictions, as well as encrypted SSL connections, but the Enterprise Server supports more extensive security measures and additional administrative and programmatic support capabilities. These servers are fully CGI/1.1 compliant, and they support a variety of package-specific components. Both applications support **GET**, **HEAD**, **PUT**, and **POST** requests. Several How-To's in Chapter 12 and Chapter 13 provide information on the configuration and use of these servers. Additional information is available at the following URL:

http://home.netscape.com/

WN

This is another freeware HTTP server application distributed under the GNU license (**http://hopf.math.nwu.edu/docs/Gnu_License**). It provides a variety of cutting-edge features that are both useful and experimental. WN provides security features that include IP address and domain restrictions, user authentication support by password, and digest authentication process. Like GN, the default access to documents is to deny access. This package is fully CGI/1.1 compliant, and it also includes a full suite of built-in search capabilities. Server-side includes are supported, as well as conditional server includes. **GET**, **HEAD**, and **POST** requests are currently supported. Further information can be found at this URL:

http://hopf.math.nwu.edu

VMS

Currently, only two servers have been developed for the VMS platform. The first of these is a port of the CERN HTTP server. The second was developed for the VMS platform. Thus, this server is reputedly better adapted to the VMS environment.

CERN HTTP Server

This is a port of the popular UNIX server. The features are identical to those of the original package. This server software can be found at the URL

http://delonline.cern.ch/delphi$www/public/vms/distribution.html

Cheetah Cross-Platform Server

The Cheetah server is a commercial product available for a variety of platforms, including OpenVMS 6.1 or later. This server provides support for many features of the UNIX servers including authentication, basic, and digest, and it also provides CGI/1.1 support. Additional information and an evaluation copy are available through this URL:

http://www.tgv.com/public/cheetah/cheetah_welcome.html

DECthread HTTP Server

As a native VMS server, his software is reputed to exploit the features of the VMS operating system better than the CERN server. The DECthread server was developed using the DECthreads model, which should lead to significantly faster access than the CERN server, particularly when multiple simultaneous requests are made. This server is CGI compliant and comes equipped with a variety of useful gateway applications. Finally, the server supports **GET** and **HEAD** requests. Information and software can be found at the URL

`http://kcgl1.eng.ohio-state.edu/www/doc/serverinfo.html`

Windows NT and Windows 95

Several server software options are available for these platforms. They support a large variety of standard features while being in an environment comfortable for Windows NT and Windows 95 users. Several of these servers are described here.

HTTPS

This server supports **GET**, **HEAD**, and **POST** client requests. It is CGI compliant; however, it does not support either access control or user authentication security. Additional information about this product is available at URL

`http://emwac.ed.ac.uk/html/internet_toolchest/https/CONTENTS.HTM`

Microsoft Servers

Microsoft supports two levels of Web servers: a personal Web server (PWS) and a more powerful commercial Web server, the Internet Information Server (IIS).

IIS provides three servers in one for the Windows NT platform. This server supports the HTTP, FTP, and Gopher protocols. Server security is fully integrated with the NT security model. Further, IIS supports encrypted connections using SSL. Gateway applications written in Perl are supported, as well as integrated support for ActiveX-based embedded object controls. The Internet Service Manager provides administration of IIS through any machine with network access to the server. This server is freely available through Microsoft at this URL:

`http://www.microsoft.com/infoserv/`

Microsoft has recently released a small-scale Web server product, PWS, for its Windows 95 platform. This server supports Internet information dissemination via the HTTP and FTP protocols. This new server product is available with Microsoft's Internet Explorer Starter Kit. Consult the following URL for download and installation information:

`http://www.microsoft.com/ie/isk/pws.htm`

Netscape Servers

Netscape markets servers for the Windows NT and 95 platforms that provide the same capabilities as the servers described in the UNIX section. Both the Enterprise

Server and the FastTrack server are available. See Netscape's home page for more information on these products:

```
http://home.netscape.com
```

WebSite

The WebSite server is a commercial package developed by the O'Reilly and Associates publishing firm. The package runs on both the Windows NT and 95 platforms. The basis for this application is the WinHTTP server developed for the Windows 3.1 platform. WebSite is CGI compliant and supports **GET**, **HEAD**, and **POST** requests. Beyond standard CGI, it has some additional capabilities to run Windows applications such as Excel and Visual Basic within HTML documents. For security, both basic authentication and IP address and domain restrictions are supported. The following specifies the minimum requirements for running this application:

- ✔ 80386 or higher processor
- ✔ VGA or better display
- ✔ 3.5-inch disk drive
- ✔ 12+MB RAM (16MB suggested)
- ✔ At least 5MB of free hard disk space
- ✔ Windows NT 3.5 or 95 with TCP/IP connectivity

An enhanced version that supports increased security, WebSite Professional, is also available. This enhanced version provides for encrypted connections using either SSL or SHTTP.

Additional information and ordering information are available through the URL

```
http://website.ora.com/
```

OS/2

Several server packages have been developed for OS/2. This section describes three of them—Apache, GoServe, and HTTPD. URLs specifying up-to-date information are provided at the end of each description. For more information on OS/2 server options, use URL

```
http://www.yahoo.com/Computers_and_Internet/Software/Internet/
World_Wide_Web/Servers/OS_2/
```

Apache for OS/2

This server is a port of the popular UNIX freeware server of the same name. This port provides most of the features and capabilities of its parent. To download this server or to view additional information, consult URL

```
http://www.slink.com/ApacheOS2/
```

GoServe

The GoServe package supports both HTTP and Gopher protocols. This product is distributed freely under the IBM OS/2 Employee Written Software program and is subject to the IBM license agreement (`http://ww2.hursley.ibm.com/goserve/license.txt`) for OS/2 Tools. The server supports HTTP/1.0, including **GET**, **HEAD**, and **POST** requests. Further, CGI standards for gateway applications are included. Security is provided by the basic authentication package. Directory access security is provided by domain and address restrictions. Some proposed HTTP/1.1 features have been added.

Additional information concerning this package can be found at URL

```
http://www2.hursley.ibm.com/goserve
```

OS2HTTPD

This port of the NCSA HTTPD server to the OS/2 platform supports many of the original's features. Currently, it does not support encrypted connections through SSL or SHTTP. For further information on this product, see URL

```
ftp://ftp.netcom.com/pub/kf/kfan/overview.html
```

Macintosh

Currently, the only HTTP server available for Macintosh users is the MacHTTP server, now also known as WebSTAR.

MacHTTP (WebSTAR)

This server will run on a Macintosh running the System 7 operating system with at least 8 megabytes of RAM. MacTCP is also required. MacHTTP will service **GET**, **HEAD**, and **POST** requests. It also supports a number of built-in search capabilities, but use of these features requires that AppleScript be installed. This server is CGI compliant and loads AppleScript, MacPerl, HyperCard, or custom applications developed with its own set of AppleEvents.

MacHTTP supports several security features. Access control can be limited on a domain or machine basis by restricting access to particular IP addresses or domain specifications. In addition, folder- and document-level security can be established through username and password access control. MacHTTP is the shareware version of this product.

WebSTAR is the commercial version of this server. It supports a variety of enhancements over its shareware predecessor. These improvements include quicker response time, increased capacity, support for additional security, and other advanced features. The price tag for WebSTAR is consequently higher than that of MacHTTP.

How-To 13.8 examines issues in configuring security for a MacHTTP server. You can find registration information and download an evaluation copy of MacHTTP from the following URL:

```
http://www.starnine.com
```

Windows 3.1

Several server packages have been developed for the Windows and Windows for Workgroups environments. These servers are fairly full featured, but they suffer from a lack of true multitasking and task separation. The WinHTTPD server package is briefly described here.

WinHTTPD

This port of the NCSA HTTPD UNIX server to the Windows environment retains many of the features supported by its UNIX parent. The server supports `GET`, `HEAD`, and `POST` method requests; CGI 1.1 compliance; directory-level access control via domain restriction and the basic authentication package; and automatic directory indexing.

WinHTTPD supports gateway applications written as DOS batch files, Visual Basic programs, and Perl scripts. A variety of such programs have been developed and are available for this platform.

For commercial use, this package requires a registration fee. Further information, restrictions, and the software itself are available at URL

`http://www.city.net/win-httpd`

G

HTML HYPERTEXT TRANSFER PROTOCOL (HTTP)

The Hypertext Transfer Protocol (HTTP) was developed as the standard exchange protocol for use with the World Wide Web. This is the language that is spoken between Web clients and Web servers.

Client/server communication can be viewed as a telephone conversation between two individuals. However, the vocabulary and grammar of the conversation are restricted to the HTTP language. The conversation is started by a client (a Web browser) dialing the exchange of the desired server. When the server picks up the connection, the client starts the conversation by making a request, stating its requirements and a description of itself. The server responds with an answer to the request, followed by a description of itself and the results of the request. At this point, the conversation ends, and the phone receiver is placed back on the hook.

These conversations are very structured. Each party speaks only once in a particular conversation involving a single request and a single response. What this means in a Web sense is that, if you attempt to load an HTML document with four inline images, your client will have to hold five discrete conversations to load the entire document: one to request the base document followed by four more to retrieve the images.

Further, clients and servers have exceedingly limited memories of previous conversations. Thus, if you have entered information in an HTML form, this data is passed to the appropriate gateway application (see Chapter 14, "The Common Gateway Interface [CGI]"). However, the server simply acts as a translator passing on the information. It does not keep a copy of this information. Therefore, many gateway applications encode this information back into the documents that they generate as hidden input fields. If they did not, the same information would need to be requested at several levels of nested HTML forms.

Each conversation between a client and a server is composed of four parts:

- ✔ Open connection
- ✔ Request
- ✔ Response
- ✔ Close connection

This HTTP communications process is shown in Figure G-1 and explained in detail.

Open Connection

The first stage of HTTP communications involves the client requesting a connection to a particular server. If a port number is given, the client will attempt to connect to that port; otherwise, the default port number 80 is used for the connection. For example, if you request that a server open the URL list in the following code, the client attempts to establish a connection with the **www.mysite.edu** machine at port 8080.

```
http://www.mysite.edu:8080/new/index.htm
```

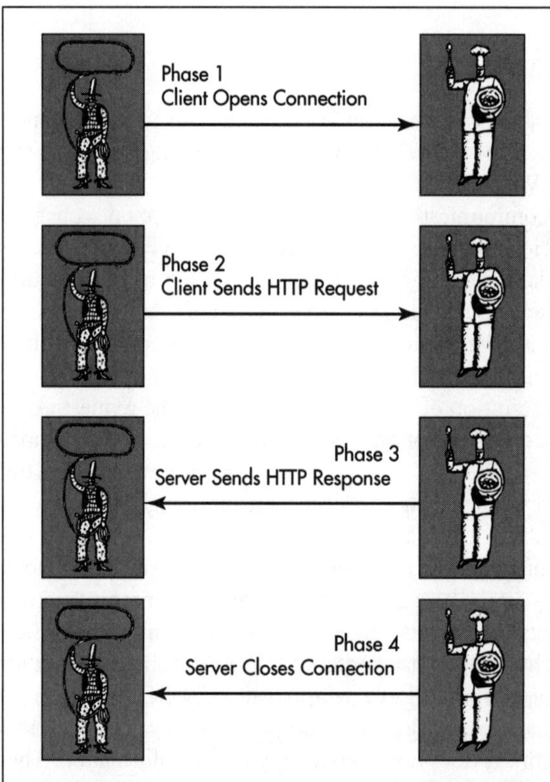

Figure G-1 HTTP communications process

HTTP Request

Once a connection has been established, the client sends an HTTP request. An HTTP request is composed of two parts: the request header and the request body.

The request header also contains two components. The first line of the header contains the method field. In the case of the example in this appendix, a simple **GET** method request would be generated. The method field that might be associated with this request appears as follows:

```
GET /new/index.htm HTTP/1.0
```

The remainder of the header is a series of attributes describing the client and its capabilities to the server. For example, the following might be the remainder of the request header sent for retrieving the document in this appendix:

```
Accept: text/plain
Accept: text/html
...
Accept: */*
User Agent: Mozilla/1.1N (X11; I; SunOS 4.1.3_U1 sun4m)
```

The request header ends with a blank line. The remainder of the request is the request body.

The body of a request is often empty. When it is not, it is most frequently used to send an encrypted actual request, to send input data via a **POST** method request, or to provide the information entity for a **PUT** method request. The header and body are separated by a blank line. This blank line must be included even if a request body is empty. The blank line is a signal to the server that the request header component is ended.

The first line of the request header is the method line. This line follows the format specified here:

```
Method          Identifier          Version
```

The ***Method*** is the HTTP method that the client wishes to use; Table G-1 presents several commonly used methods. (For a comprehensive list of methods, you may want to examine **http://www.w3.org/pub/WWW/Protocols/HTTP/Methods.html**.) The ***Identifier*** is the path to the information to use with the specified method. The ***Version*** field states the protocol and version of the protocol being used, most often HTTP/1.0.

Table G-1 Commonly used HTTP/1.0 requests

METHOD	EXPLANATION
GET	Retrieves the information entity specified by the identifier
HEAD	Retrieves the header information concerning the information entity specified by the identifier
PUT	Places the information contained in the request body at the location specified by the identifier
POST	Passes the information contained in the request body to the entity specified by the identifier and returns the results

The method line is followed by a series of attributes supplied by the client that the server may use as desired. Table G-2 presents a description of several commonly used HTTP/1.0 attributes. (For more information about additional attributes, you may want to reference URL `http://www.w3.org/pub/WWW/Protocols/HTTP/HTRQ_Headers.html`.)

Table G-2 Commonly used HTTP/1.0 request header attributes

ATTRIBUTE	EXPLANATION
`Accept:` *`type/subtype`*	Describes the MIME types of the documents supported by the client making the request. Each such MIME type should be declared in an `Accept` element. The asterisk (*) may be used as a wildcard.
`Content-length:` *`number`*	The number of bytes contained in the request body.
`Content-type:` *`MIME`*	Specifies the MIME type of file contained in the request body.
`UserAgent:` *`string`*	Tells the server the specific type of client making the request.

No request body is necessary for a `GET` method request. The body will depend upon the request type. For example, if the client makes a `PUT` method request, the body will contain the information entity to place on the server. The request body may be used when secure transactions are required. In this case, the request body contains the encrypted request.

NOTE

The request header is terminated with a blank line whether or not a request body follows.

HTTP Response

The server follows up a request with a suitable response. The response also contains two parts: a header and a body.

As in a request, the response header has two components. The first line of the response header is the status line. The status line includes the HTTP version, a status code, and a status message.

The status line has the following format:

```
Version          StatusCode          StatusMessage
```

The *`Version`* represents the version of HTTP used for the communication (usually HTTP/1.0). The *`StatusCode`* and *`StatusMessage`* inform the client of the results of a request. A complete listing of standard status codes and messages is provided at URL `http://www.w3.org/pub/WWW/Protocols/HTTP/HTRESP.html`. Some of the more commonly used status codes and messages are presented in Table G-3. The status codes are three-digit numbers that can be categorized in terms of the first digit of the code.

- ✔ If the first digit is `1`, the result is informational.
- ✔ If the first digit is `2`, the request was understood and successfully completed.
- ✔ If the first digit is `3`, additional actions are required to complete the request.
- ✔ If the first digit is `4`, an error was found in the client's request.
- ✔ If the first digit is `5`, the client sent a valid request, but the server was unable to fulfill the request.

Table G-3 Commonly used HTTP/1.0 status codes and messages

CODE	MESSAGE
200	Completed successfully.
201	Created. Server-side resource created through either `PUT` or `POST` request.
202	Request has been queued, but results are unknown.
203	Completed, but all information was not returned.
204	No content. No new information available. Client should not alter current document.
301	Moved permanently. Requested information moved to another location.
302	Request completed, but desired data is at another location.
304	Not modified. Document that was requested conditionally based upon modification date has not been modified. Client should not alter current document.
400	Syntax error in request.
403	Forbidden. Authorization to access requested information not allowed.
404	Not found. Information requested was not found at the location specified.
500	Internal server error. The server encountered a problem and was unable to service the request.
501	Server does not support requested method.

So for the retrieval started in the example, the following status line might be generated:

```
HTTP/1.0 200 OK
```

The status line is followed by a series of attributes describing both the document being retrieved as well as the server providing the document.

Table G-4 displays many of the commonly used response header attributes. A complete specification of the HTTP response headers for HTTP/1.0 can be found at URL `http://www.w3.org/pub/WWW/Protocols/HTTP/Object_Headers.html`.

Table G-4 Commonly used HTTP/1.0 response header attributes

ATTRIBUTE	EXPLANATION
`Public: methods`	Describes the nonstandard methods that this server supports
`Content-length: number`	The number of bytes contained in the response body
`Content-type: MIME`	Specifies the MIME type of the information entity contained in the response body
`Date: date`	The date and time the request was serviced
`Title: string`	The title of the document that was requested
`Server: string`	Tells the client the specific type of server responding
`WWW-Link: links`	Provides the client with information from the <LINK> element of the HTML 3 document retrieved

The following is a sample set of attributes:

```
Date: Sunday, 17-Dec-1995 11:30:00 GMT
Server: NCSA/1.4.1
MIME-version: 1.0
Content-type: text/html
Last-modified: 16-Jun-1995 10:35:39 GMT
Content-length: 247
```

The response header ends with a blank line.

The remainder of the response is the body. This contains the actual data being transferred. This could be an HTML 3 document, a GIF image, or any other document type supported by the server.

Close Connection

The conversation is complete, and the connection between the server and the client is closed.

The HTTP standard, like the HTML standard, is continuing to develop. The HTTP/1.1 standard is currently under consideration. The proposed new standard would support many additional features and request types. If you are interested in the progress of HTTP/1.1, you should examine the information at URL **http://www.w3.org/pub/WWW/Protocols/**. Links on this page provide access to the latest information on HTTP development.

H

HTML COLOR TABLE

The following table lists some of the more popular colors and their RGB values. You can use these values to change background color, text color, and link colors. The values are given in hexadecimal, where the first two digits represent the red value; the next two, the green; and the last two, the blue. Each red, green, or blue value can go from `00` (none of that color) to `FF` (all of that color).

COLOR	RRGGBB
White	FFFFFF
Red	FF0000
Green	00FF00
Blue	0000FF
Magenta	FF00FF
Cyan	00FFFF
Yellow	FFFF00
Black	000000
Aliceblue	F0F8FF
Aquamarine	70DB93
Baker's chocolate	5C3317
Blue violet	9F5F9F
Brass	B5A642
Bright gold	D9D919
Brown	A62AA2
Bronze	8C7853
Bronze II	A67D3D
Cadet blue	5F9F9F
Cool bopper	D98719
Copper	B87333
Coral	FF7F00
Cornflower blue	42426F
Dark brown	5C4033
Dark green	2F4F2F
Dark green copper	4A766E
Dark olive green	4F4F2F
Dark orchid	9932CD
Dark purple	871F78
Dark slate blue	6B238E
Dark slate gray	2F4F4F

continued on next page

continued from previous page

COLOR	RRGGBB
Dark tan	97694F
Dark turquoise	7093DB
Dark wood	855E42
Dim gray	545454
Dusty rose	856363
Feldspar	D19275
Firebrick	8E2323
Forest green	238E23
Gold	CD7F32
Goldenrod	DBDB70
Gray	C0C0C0
Green copper	527F76
Green yellow	93DB70
Hunter green	215E21
Indian red	4E2F2F
Khaki	9F9F5F
Light blue	C0D9D9
Light gray	A8A8A8
Light steel blue	8F8FBD
Light wood	E9C2A6
Light green	32CD32
Mandarin orange	E47833
Maroon	8E236B
Medium aquamarine	32CD99
Medium blue	3232CD
Medium forest green	6B8E23
Medium goldenrod	EAEAAE
Medium orchid	9370DB
Medium sea green	426F42
Medium slate blue	7F00FF
Medium spring green	7FFF00
Medium turquoise	70DBDB
Medium violet red	DB7093
Medium wood	A68064
Midnight blue	2F2F4F

COLOR	RRGGBB
Navy blue	23238E
Neon blue	4D4DFF
Neon pink	FF6EC7
New midnight blue	00009C
New tan	EBC79E
Old gold	CFB53B
Orange	FF7F00
Orange red	FF2400
Orchid	DB70DB
Pale green	8FBC8F
Pink	BC8F8F
Plum	EAADEA
Quartz	D9D9F3
Rich blue	5959AB
Salmon	6F4242
Scarlet	8C1717
Sea green	238E68
Semi-sweet chocolate	6B42226
Sienna	8E6B23
Silver	E6E8FA
Sky blue	3299CC
Slate blue	007FFF
Spicy pink	FF1CAE
Spring green	00FF7F
Steel blue	236B8E
Summer sky	38B0DE
Tan	DB9370
Thistle	D8BFD8
Turquoise	ADEAEA
Very dark brown	5C4033
Very light gray	CDCDCD
Violet	4F2F4F
Violet red	CC3299
Wheat	D8D8BF
Yellow green	99CC32

INTERNET EXPLORER 3: A FIELD GUIDE

A new day dawned. The sun reached its fingers over the digital outback. The mighty Navigators *(Netscapus navigatorus)*—a species that reproduced like rabbits and ran nearly as fast—covered the landscape. Yonder, on a cliff that seemed to be beyond the horizon, a trembling new creature looked out over the Internet jungle. This strange new creature, calling itself the Explorer *(Microsoftus interneticus explorus)*, sniffed around, considering whether it should enter the fragile ecosystem. Netscape gators gnashed their teeth, but the Explorer was not daunted. Explorer was a formidable beast. It became a part of the jungle and thrived. And even though it began as a mere pup, it evolved, and it evolved, and it evolved.

Now the jungle is rife with two intelligent species.

What follows is a guide to domesticating Internet Explorer. You will learn how to care for your Explorer and even how to teach it tricks. Before long, you shall find truth behind the old axiom that the Explorer is man's (and woman's) best friend.

Introducing the Explorer to Your Ecosystem

Whether you're running a Macintosh, Windows, Windows NT, or Windows 95, installing Internet Explorer is easy. Internet Explorer's own installation program makes setup a breeze, and you need only to select the appropriate file on the CD-ROM to launch this installer. Make sure the CD-ROM included with this book is in the CD-ROM drive; then follow the directions for your operating system.

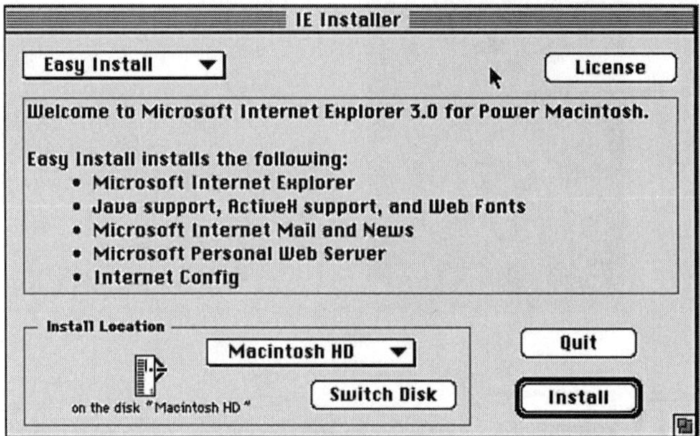

Figure I-1 The Macintosh IE Installer box

Macintosh Installation Instructions

1. Insert the CD-ROM into your CD-ROM drive.
2. You will see a CD-ROM icon when the CD-ROM is mounted by your Macintosh. Double-click on the CD-ROM icon.
3. You will see four folders: `3RDPARTY`, `ARCHIVES`, `SOURCE`, and `EXPLORER`. Double-click on the `EXPLORER` folder.
4. Launch Internet Explorer's installer by double-clicking on IE Installer. A dialog box similar to the one shown in Figure I-1 appears. Follow the onscreen prompts to finish the installation.

Windows 95 Installation

1. Click the Start button in the lower-left corner of your screen.
2. Click on the Run... option in the Start menu. A dialog box similar to the one shown in Figure I-2 appears.
3. Using the Run dialog box, type in a pathname and specify the location of the Internet Explorer installation program. `IE302M95.EXE` is in the CD-ROM's `\EXPLORER` directory, so if your CD-ROM drive is designated as D:, you'd type

```
d:\explorer\ie302m95.exe
```

Figure I-2 The Windows 95 Run dialog box

If your CD-ROM drive has a different designation letter, type in the appropriate drive designation letter in place of D:.

4. After typing the proper pathname, click the OK button to start Internet Explorer's installation program. Depending upon your system, it may take a moment to load.

5. Once the installation program loads, follow the onscreen prompts to set up Internet Explorer on your computer.

Windows NT 4 Installation

1. Click the Start button in the lower-left corner of your screen.

2. Click on the Run... option in the Start menu. A dialog box similar to the one shown in Figure I-3 appears.

3. Using the Run dialog box, type in a pathname and specify the location of the Internet Explorer installation program. `IE302MNT.EXE` is in the CD-ROM's `\EXPLORER` directory, so if your CD-ROM drive is designated as D:, you'd type

```
d:\explorer\ie302mnt.exe
```

If your CD-ROM drive has a different designation letter, type in the appropriate drive designation letter in place of D:.

4. After typing the proper pathname, click the OK button to start Internet Explorer's installation program. Depending upon your system, it may take a moment to load.

5. Once the installation program loads, follow the onscreen prompts to set up Internet Explorer on your computer.

Windows 3.1 and Windows NT 3.51 Installation

1. Click on File in the main menu bar in Program Manager.

2. Click on Run... option in the File menu. A dialog box similar to the one shown in Figure I-4 appears.

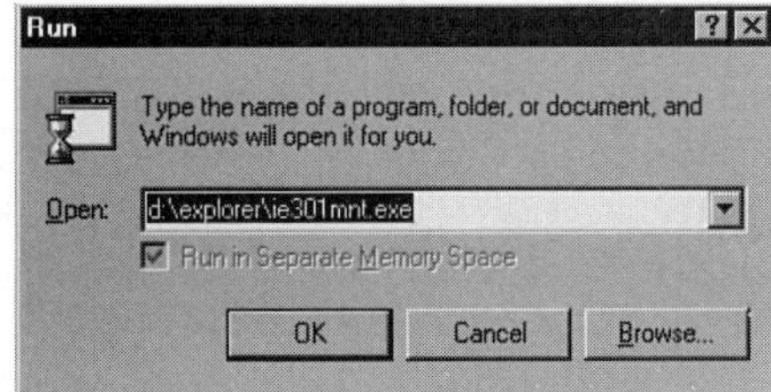

Figure I-3 The Windows NT Run dialog box

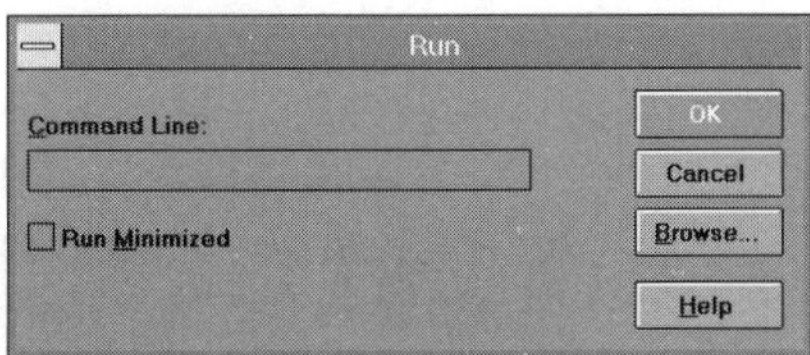

Figure I-4 Windows 3.1 and Windows NT 3.51 Run dialog box

3. Using the Run dialog box, type in a pathname and specify the location of the Internet Explorer installation program. **SETUP.EXE** is in the **\EXPLORER\WIN31NT3.51** directory. If your CD-ROM drive is designated D:, type:

```
d:\explorer\win31nt3.51\setup.exe
```

If your CD-ROM drive has a different designation letter, type in the appropriate drive designation letter in place of D:.

4. After typing the proper pathname, click the OK button to start Internet Explorer's installation program. Depending on your system, it may take a moment to load.

5. Once the installation program loads, follow the onscreen prompts to set up Internet Explorer on your computer.

Once you've run the installation, you'll need to restart your system. You can then click on the Internet icon on your desktop. If you've already selected an Internet provider with Windows dial-up networking, you'll be connected. If not, you'll be walked through the dial-in process. You'll need to enter the phone number of your Internet provider, your modem type, and other related information. Ultimately, you'll be taken to Microsoft's home page, where you can register your Internet Explorer and find out about its latest features.

NOTE

The Explorer is a constantly evolving animal. For the latest updates, plug-ins, and versions, be sure to regularly check out Microsoft's neck of the woods at `http://www.microsoft.com/ie/`.

Internet Explorer Components

Internet Explorer is more than a plain-Jane Web browser. As you work through the installation, you'll be able to choose a variety of components. You can select the following add-ons:

- ✔ *Internet Mail*—This is a comprehensive e-mail package. Using simple icons, you can write and read your mail off-line and then log on quickly to send and receive your latest batch of correspondence. See Figure I-5.
- ✔ *Internet News*—This is a window that lets you browse through thousands of newsgroups, read through the threads, and post your own messages. The News system is very easy to use. You can easily keep track of your favorite topics and automatically update with the latest news.

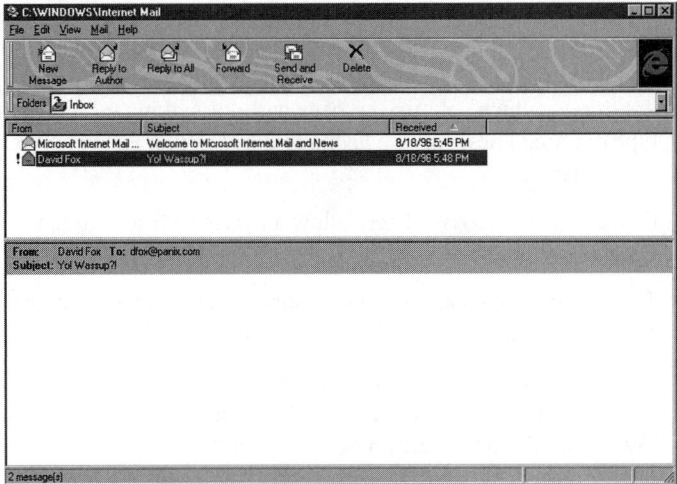

Figure I-5 The Internet Mail main window

- *ActiveMovie*—This feature of Explorer lets you watch all sorts of video clips—MPEG, AVI, and QuickTime formats. It even supports a special streaming version of video that downloads movies as you watch them, letting you view video with little delay. The ActiveMovie system also lets you listen to all popular formats of audio files—AU, WAV, MIDI, MPEG, and AIFF. This makes it easy to add background sound to Web pages.
- *VRML Support*—This feature is a separate module that lets you download and coast through Virtual Reality Modeling Language worlds. This allows you to explore true 3D landscapes and objects.
- *NetMeeting*—This is a full-featured package that lets you hold entire meetings over the Internet. You can chat with one person or with dozens. If you have a microphone, you can use the Internet phone feature to hold voice conversations with other people. You can share applications. For example, you and a client can edit the same word processing document together. A whiteboard feature lets you draw on a "digital blackboard" that can be updated live across the Internet.
- *HTML Layout Control*—This tool lets Web page publishers create spiffy versions of HTML pages, the way professional designers would lay out a magazine page or a newspaper. Designers can choose exactly where to place elements within a Web page. You can make objects transparent and layer objects over each other, which helps make a Web page eye-catching yet uncluttered.

The Nature of the Beast

Internet Explorer features very up-to-date HTML. It supports HTML 3.2, including the following:

- *Frames*—These break up the Web page window into several areas. For example, you can keep an unchanging row of navigation controls along the top of the page while constantly updating the bottom. You can use *borderless frames*, which split up the page without making it seem split. A special type of frame known as the *floating frame* lets you view one Web page within another.
- *Cascading Style Sheets*—These allow all your Web sites to have the same general look and feel.
- *Tables*—You can create or view all sorts of fancy tables, with or without graphics, borders, and columns.
- *Embedded Objects*—Internet Explorer can handle Java applets, ActiveX controls, and even Netscape plug-ins. These objects are discussed later, in the "Symbiotic Partners" section of this appendix.
- *Fonts*—Internet Explorer supports many fonts, allowing Web pages to have a variety of exciting designs.

From the get-go, Internet Explorer has included a few special bells and whistles. For example, it's easy to create and view marquees across Web pages. This lets you scroll a long, attention-drawing message, similar to a tickertape, that puts a great deal of information in a very small space.

Training the Explorer

By its very nature, the Explorer is a friendly beast. You can access the full range of the Explorer's talents by pushing its buttons. These buttons, which appear in the toolbar at the top of the screen as depicted in Figure I-6, are as follows:

- *Back*—Use this to return to the Web page you've just come from. This will help you retrace your steps as you take your Explorer through the Internet maze.
- *Forward*—Use this after you've used the Back button, to jump forward again to the page from which you began.
- *Stop*—If a Web page is taking too long to load, press this button. Any text and graphics will immediately stop downloading.
- *Refresh*—If your Web page is missing some graphics, or if you've previously stopped its loading using the Stop button, you can reload it using Refresh.
- *Home*—This takes you to your preset home page. By default, this is Microsoft's main Web page, but you can set your home to any page you'd like. See the "Taming the Beast" section.
- *Search*—This takes you to a special page that allows you to search for a Web page, using a number of cool search engines. See the "Hunting Skills" section.

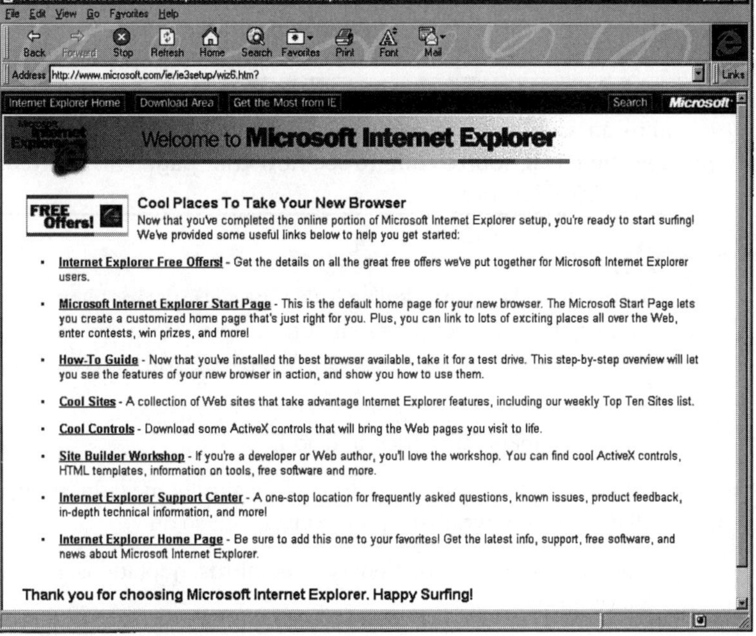

Figure I-6 A cosmetic look at Explorer

- ✔ *Favorites*—This button lets you access a list of your favorite Web sites. See the "Favorite Haunts" section.
- ✔ *Print*—This allows you to print out the current Web page, allowing you to keep a perfect hard copy of it.
- ✔ *Font*—Find yourself squinting at a Web page? Just click here to zoom in. The font size will grow several degrees. Too big now? Click a few more times and the size will shrink once again.
- ✔ *Mail*—This will launch the Internet Mail program, which allows you to send and receive e-mail and to access newsgroups.

Playing Fetch

Your Explorer is a devoted friend. It can scamper anywhere within the Internet, bringing back exactly what you desire.

If you know where you want to go, just type the URL into Internet Explorer's Address box at the top of the screen. If you like, you can omit the `http://` prefix. The Web page will be loaded up. You can also search for a page or load up a previously saved page.

You can now click on any hyperlink—an underlined or colored word or picture—to zoom to that associated Web page or Internet resource. Some hyperlinked graphics may not be obvious. Internet Explorer will tell you when you are positioned over a valid hyperlink, because the cursor will change into a pointing finger.

Continue following these links as long as you like. It's not uncommon to start researching knitting needles and end up reading about porcupines.

NOTE

If you're an aspiring Web page writer, you might want to take a peek at the HTML source code to see how that page was created. Just select View | Source.

Hunting Skills

If you want to find Web pages dealing with a specific category, Internet Explorer makes it easy to find them. Click the Search button. The Search screen will appear, as in Figure I-7. You can search for more than Web pages. With Internet Explorer, it's easy to find

- ✔ Phone numbers, ZIP codes, and addresses
- ✔ Information on a number of topics—health, home, education, consumer affairs, finance, weather, sports, travel, and so on
- ✔ References—maps, a dictionary, a thesaurus, quotations, and an encyclopedia
- ✔ Online books, newspapers, and magazines

TIP

You can also quickly hunt for any idea, word, or category. Simply type GO in the Address box at the top of the screen, followed by the word or phrase you want to search for.

Favorite Haunts

It's easy to keep track of the Web pages you visit most. When you want to save a page for future reference, simply click the Favorites button or choose the Favorites menu item. Select the Add To Favorites option. The current Web page will now be added to the list of favorites, which appears each time you click on the Favorites button or menu.

After a while, your list of favorites will get long and cluttered. It's simple to keep track of huge lists of favorites—just put them into separate folders. Organize your favorites, as shown in Figure I-8, by selecting Favorites|Organize Favorites.

To create a new folder, click on the New Folder icon (the folder with the little glint on it) at the top of the window. Now drag and drop your Web page bookmarks into the appropriate folders. You can also move, rename, or delete a folder by selecting it and using the corresponding buttons at the bottom of the screen.

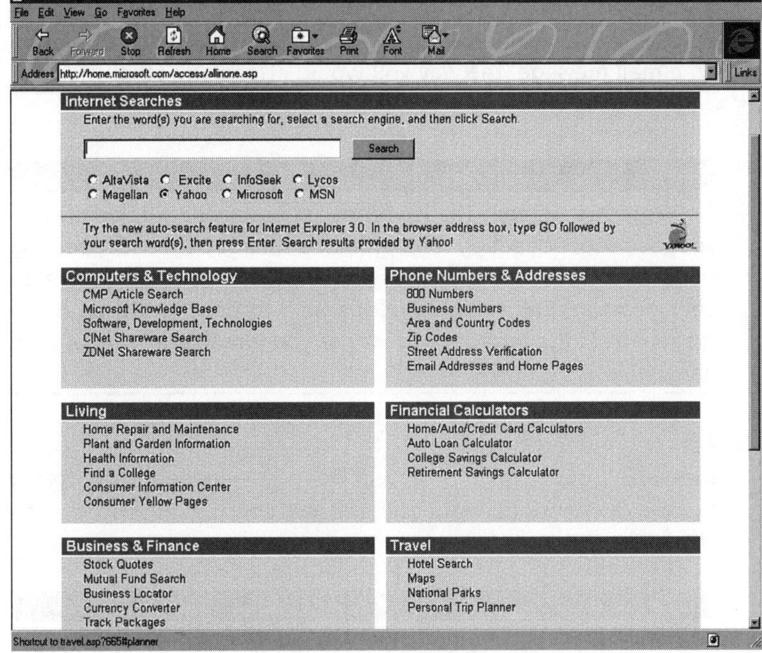

Figure I-7 The Search screen

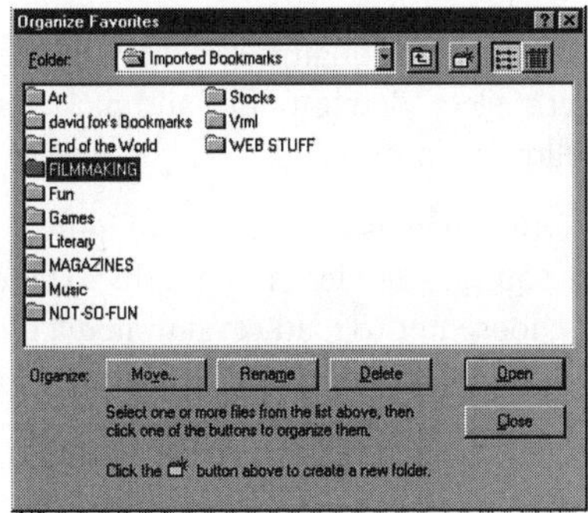

Figure I-8 Organizing the Favorites list

TIP

You can even include or attach a favorite Web document within an e-mail message, the way you would attach any other file.

NOTE

On Windows systems, the Favorites list is actually a folder within your Windows directory. This reflects a Microsoft trend—treating the entire World Wide Web as just another folder to explore on your desktop. Eventually, you'll be able to drag and drop documents across the Internet as easily as you would within your own hard drive.

Memory

Internet Explorer keeps track of every Web page you visit. This is kept in a vast History list. You can view the entire History list, in chronological order, by clicking the View History button. Just click on any page you'd like to revisit.

NOTE

By default, the History list is cleared every 20 days—you can set this value within the Navigation properties sheet.

Taming the Beast

Now that you and your Explorer are getting acquainted, why not tame it so that it acts and looks exactly like you want? Select View|Options and pick a tab at the top of the window to customize the following properties:

✔ *General*—The General properties sheet is illustrated in Figure I-9. Since multimedia content (such as sounds, movies, and graphics) takes longer to load in Web pages, you can choose not to load certain media types. You can also easily customize the color of the text and hyperlinks. Finally, you can decide how little or how much information appears in your toolbar.

NOTE

You can change the size and position of your toolbar simply by clicking on its borders and dragging it to a desired location.

✔ *Connection*—You can adjust your connections settings, as shown in Figure I-10, by clicking on this tab. This lets you choose your Internet provider. If you're connecting to the Internet through a network firewall, you can also set your proxy server information here.

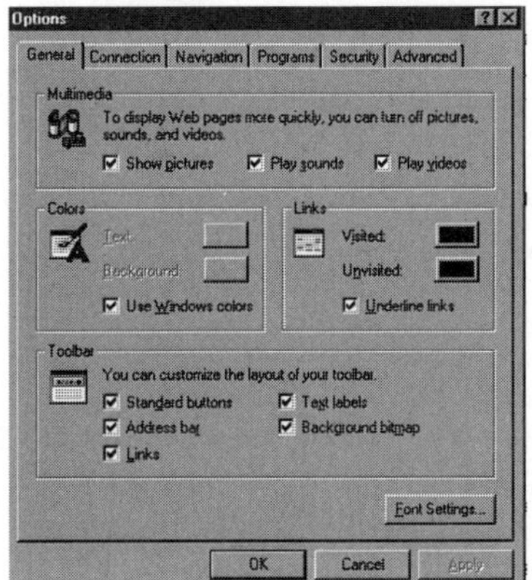

Figure I-9 The General properties sheet

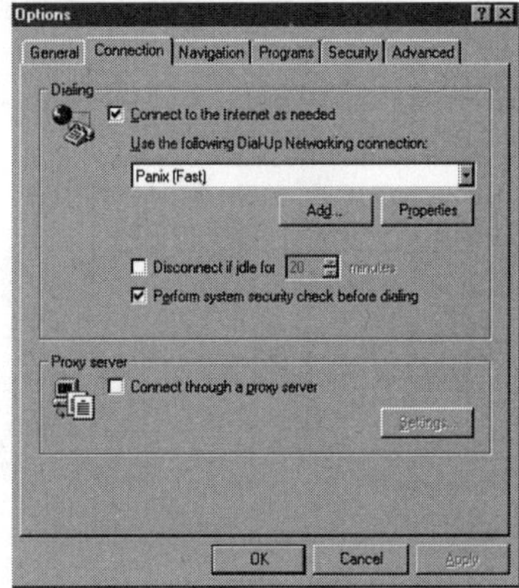

Figure I-10 The Connection property sheet

- ✔ *Navigation*—You can customize which page you'd like to use as your starting home page. Just enter its URL in the Address box here.
- ✔ *Programs*—This allows you to set which programs you'd like to use for e-mail and for Usenet news. By default, you can use Microsoft's Internet Mail and Internet News, which are included with Internet Explorer. You can also tell Internet Explorer how to handle various types of files by selecting the File Types button. It allows you to designate which program or plug-in should be launched whenever Internet Explorer comes across various unfamiliar file formats.
- ✔ *Security*—You are able to customize how securely documents will be handled by Internet Explorer. If you want to keep your computer extremely safe, you may tell Internet Explorer not to download possible security risks such as ActiveX controls, Java applets, or other plug-ins. Another nice feature is a Content Advisor. Click on Settings; the Content Advisor window will appear as in Figure I-11. You may now decide which Web pages to skip based on Adult Language, Nudity, Sex, and Violence. Many questionable Web pages are written with certain tags so that the pages can be weeded out by people who don't want to see them. This is a great option to use if your kids surf the Internet, or if your sensibilities are offended by these kinds of pages. To turn ratings on, click on the Enable Ratings button. You can also lock this window with a password.
- ✔ *Advanced*—This properties sheet lets you customize when Internet Explorer will issue warnings. This is useful if you deal with sensitive information and want to know which Web pages are secure and which are not. You can also set a number of other advanced Java and Security options here.

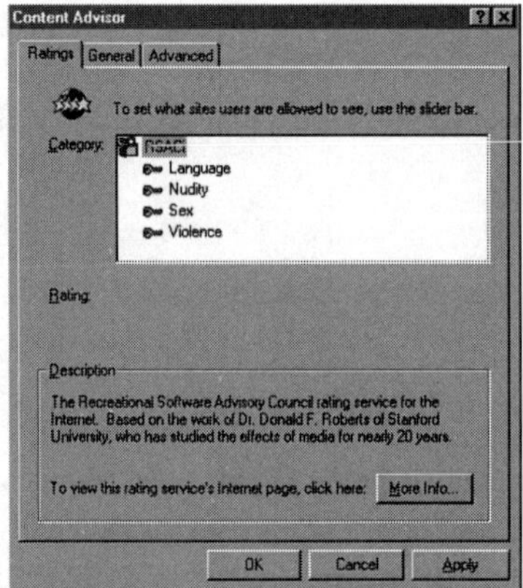

Figure I-11 The Content Advisor window

Symbiotic Partners

Internet Explorer includes many of the latest Web technologies. These make your Web pages sing, dance, and even act as entire applications. The line between what a computer can do in general and what a computer can do over the Internet is thinning.

ActiveX

Microsoft's proprietary ActiveX technology lets you drop controls into your Web pages. Controls are software components such as specialized buttons, input forms, graphics viewers, sound players, and so forth.

When you load a page with an ActiveX control, Internet Explorer will check if you already have that control on your system. If not, you'll be asked whether you'd like to download it. You'll be told whether the control has been authenticated by Microsoft. If the control is secure, it'll automatically be downloaded and installed for you. The resulting Web page may look more like a software program than a Web page. Don't be surprised to find all new types of buttons, such as the up and down arrow controls in Figure I-12.

Scripts

Internet Explorer allows Web page writers to add different types of scripts right into the source code of the Web page itself. This means you can get instantaneous feedback and control of the Web browser, ActiveX controls, Java applets, and other plug-ins. This makes interactivity fast and easy. Internet Explorer supports Visual Basic, Scripting Edition and JavaScript languages.

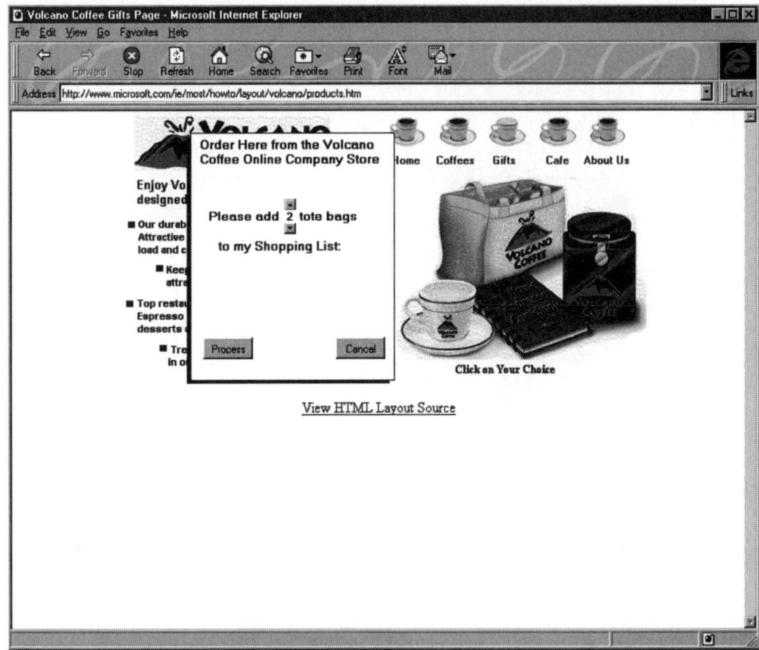

Figure I-12 Loading a page with an ActiveX control

Java

Finally, Internet Explorer fully supports the popular Java language. Java is a programming language that lets you write full applications that run directly within your Web browser. Java is great for writing games, graphics demonstrations, databases, spreadsheets, and much more.

Total Mastery

Now that you are fully in control of your Explorer, you can learn, work, and have fun using it with the greatest of ease. Wandering through the Internet faster than ever, you are ready to investigate new paths of adventure with your trusty, obedient Explorer guiding you every step of the way.

INDEX

SYMBOLS

A

B

C

E

G

J

K - L

M

N

O

P

S

T

U

V

W

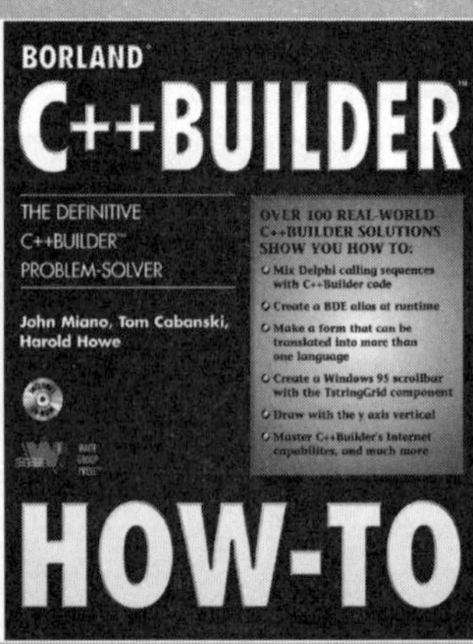

BORLAND C++ BUILDER HOW-TO

John Miano, Tom Cabanski, Harold Howe

Borland C++ Builder How-To presents over 100 clear solutions to real-life C++ Builder programming challenges. The popular "how-to" format covers ways to collect input and provide output, "spy" on other programs and their windows, create animated icons that report information while the program is minimalized, and create Windows user interfaces with simple point-and-click operations.

Available now • 750 pages
ISBN: 1-57169-109-X
U.S. $49.99 • 1 CD-ROM

HTML 4 INTERACTIVE COURSE

Kent Cearly

This personalized, Web-based course gets you started writing HTML-based Web pages from the very first chapter. You'll create a Web page that grows more sophisticated lesson-by-lesson. Includes free enrollment in the eZone (a Web-based education site) and the opportunity to earn continuing education units from Marquette University. Use the eZone for real-time testing, live "mentors" to answer questions, and many other online resources.

Available November 1997
575 pages
ISBN: 1-57169-130-8
U.S. $49.99 • 1 CD-ROM

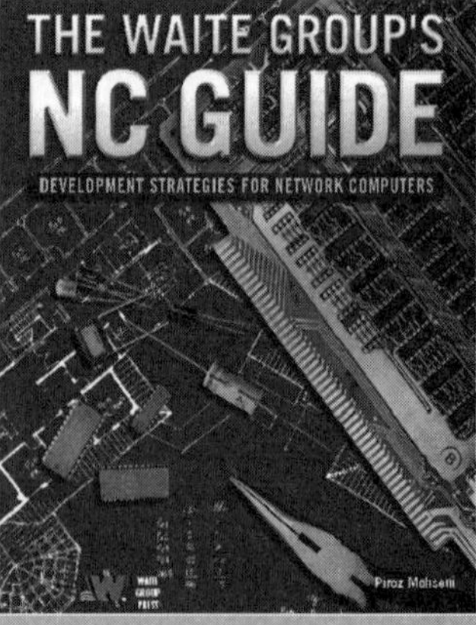

THE WAITE GROUP'S NC GUIDE

Piroz Mohseni

The Waite Group's NC Guide explores the concept of network computers. It examines existing and proposed NC standards and specifications, provides a strong background on hardware and architecture issues of application development on the NC, focuses on Java and its role in application development, and explores design, maintenance, and management perspectives.

Available Now • 350 pages
ISBN: 1-57169-106-5
U.S. $29.99

Send for our unique catalog to get more information about these books as well as our other outstanding and award-winning titles.

Message from the **Publisher**

WELCOME TO OUR NERVOUS SYSTEM

Some people say that the World Wide Web is a graphical extension of the information superhighway, just a network of humans and machines sending each other long lists of the equivalent of digital junk mail.

I think it is much more than that. To me, the Web is nothing less than the nervous system of the entire planet—not just a collection of computer brains connected together, but more like a billion silicon neurons entangled and recirculating electro-chemical signals of information and data, each contributing to the birth of another CPU and another Web site.

Think of each person's hard disk connected at once to every other hard disk on earth, driven by human navigators searching like Columbus for the New World. Seen this way, the Web is more of a superentity, a growing, living thing, controlled by the universal human will to expand, to be more. Yet, unlike a purposeful business plan with rigid rules, the Web expands in a nonlinear, unpredictable, creative way that echoes natural evolution.

We created our Web site not just to extend the reach of our computer book products but to be part of this synaptic neural network, to experience, like a nerve in the body, the flow of ideas and then to pass those ideas up the food chain of the mind. Your mind. Even more, we wanted to pump some of our own creative juices into this rich wine of technology.

TASTE OUR DIGITAL WINE

And so we ask you to taste our wine by visiting the body of our business. Begin by understanding the metaphor we have created for our Web site—a universal learning center, situated in outer space in the form of a space station. A place where you can journey to study any topic from the convenience of your own screen. Right now we are focusing on computer topics, but the stars are the limit on the Web.

If you are interested in discussing this Web site or finding out more about the Waite Group, please send me email with your comments, and I will be happy to respond. Being a programmer myself, I love to talk about technology and find out what our readers are looking for.

Sincerely,

Mitchell Waite

Mitchell Waite, CEO and Publisher

200 Tamal Plaza
Corte Madera, CA 94925
415-924-2575
415-924-2576 fax

Website:
http://www.waite.com/waite

CREATING THE HIGHEST QUALITY COMPUTER BOOKS IN THE INDUSTRY

Waite Group Press

Come Visit

WAITE.COM

Waite Group Press World Wide Web Site

Now find all the latest information on Waite Group books at our new Web site, **http://www.waite.com/waite.** You'll find an online catalog where you can examine and order any title, review upcoming books, and send email to our authors and editors. Our FTP site has all you need to update your book: the latest program listings, errata sheets, most recent versions of Fractint, POV Ray, Polyray, DMorph, and all the programs featured in our books. So download, talk to us, ask questions, on **http://www.waite.com/waite.**

The New Arrivals Room has all our new books listed by month. Just click for a description, Index, Table of Contents, and links to authors.

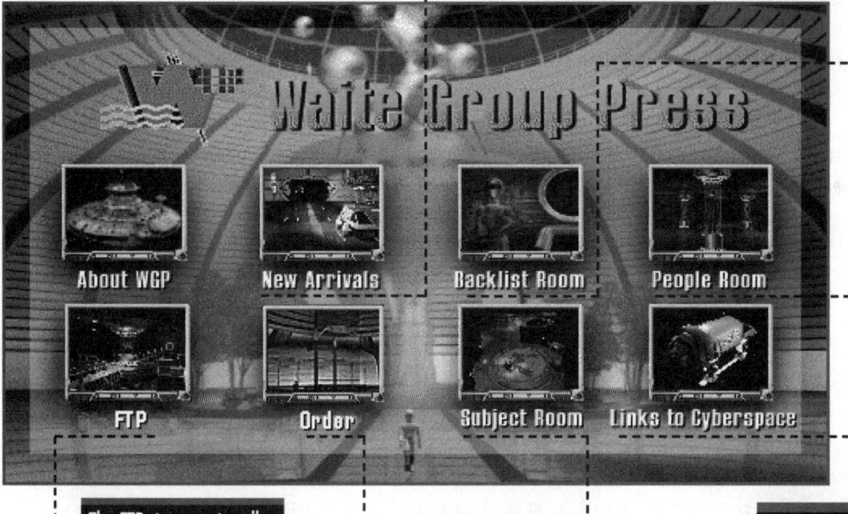

The Backlist Room has all our books listed alphabetically.

The People Room is where you'll interact with Waite Group employees.

Links to Cyberspace get you in touch with other computer book publishers and other interesting Web sites.

The FTP site contains all program listings, errata sheets, etc.

The Order Room is where you can order any of our books online.

The Subject Room contains typical book pages that show description, Index, Table of Contents, and links to authors.

World Wide Web:

COME SURF OUR TURF—THE WAITE GROUP WEB

http://www.waite.com/waite
Gopher: gopher.waite.com
FTP: ftp.waite.com

This is a legal agreement between you, the end user and purchaser, and The Waite Group®, Inc., and the authors of the programs contained in the disc. By opening the sealed disc package, you are agreeing to be bound by the terms of this Agreement. If you do not agree with the terms of this Agreement, promptly return the unopened disc package and the accompanying items (including the related book and other written material) to the place you obtained them for a refund.

SOFTWARE LICENSE

1. The Waite Group, Inc., grants you the right to use one copy of the enclosed software programs (the programs) on a single computer system (whether a single CPU, part of a licensed network, or a terminal connected to a single CPU). Each concurrent user of the program must have exclusive use of the related Waite Group, Inc., written materials.

2. The program, including the copyrights in each program, is owned by the respective author and the copyright in the entire work is owned by The Waite Group, Inc., and they are therefore protected under the copyright laws of the United States and other nations, under international treaties. You may make only one copy of the disc containing the programs exclusively for backup or archival purposes, or you may transfer the programs to one hard disk drive, using the original for backup or archival purposes. You may make no other copies of the programs, and you may make no copies of all or any part of the related Waite Group, Inc., written materials.

3. You may not rent or lease the programs, but you may transfer ownership of the programs and related written materials (including any and all updates and earlier versions) if you keep no copies of either, and if you make sure the transferee agrees to the terms of this license.

4. You may not decompile, reverse engineer, disassemble, copy, create a derivative work, or otherwise use the programs except as stated in this Agreement.

GOVERNING LAW

This Agreement is governed by the laws of the State of California.

LIMITED WARRANTY

The following warranties shall be effective for 90 days from the date of purchase: (i) The Waite Group, Inc., warrants the enclosed disc to be free of defects in materials and workmanship under normal use; and (ii) The Waite Group, Inc., warrants that the programs, unless modified by the purchaser, will substantially perform the functions described in the documentation provided by The Waite Group, Inc., when operated on the designated hardware and operating system. The Waite Group, Inc., does not warrant that the programs will meet purchaser's requirements or that operation of a program will be uninterrupted or error-free. The program warranty does not cover any program that has been altered or changed in any way by anyone other than The Waite Group, Inc. The Waite Group, Inc., is not responsible for problems caused by changes in the operating characteristics of computer hardware or computer operating systems that are made after the release of the programs, nor for problems in the interaction of the programs with each other or other software.

THESE WARRANTIES ARE EXCLUSIVE AND IN LIEU OF ALL OTHER WARRANTIES OF MERCHANTABILITY OR FITNESS FOR A PARTICULAR PURPOSE OR OF ANY OTHER WARRANTY, WHETHER EXPRESSED OR IMPLIED.

EXCLUSIVE REMEDY

The Waite Group, Inc., will replace any defective disk without charge if the defective disc is returned to The Waite Group, Inc., within 90 days from date of purchase.

This is Purchaser's sole and exclusive remedy for any breach of warranty or claim for contract, tort, or damages.

LIMITATION OF LIABILITY

THE WAITE GROUP, INC., AND THE AUTHORS OF THE PROGRAMS SHALL NOT IN ANY CASE BE LIABLE FOR SPECIAL, INCIDENTAL, CONSEQUENTIAL, INDIRECT, OR OTHER SIMILAR DAMAGES ARISING FROM ANY BREACH OF THESE WARRANTIES EVEN IF THE WAITE GROUP, INC., OR ITS AGENT HAS BEEN ADVISED OF THE POSSIBILITY OF SUCH DAMAGES.

THE LIABILITY FOR DAMAGES OF THE WAITE GROUP, INC., AND THE AUTHORS OF THE PROGRAMS UNDER THIS AGREEMENT SHALL IN NO EVENT EXCEED THE PURCHASE PRICE PAID.

COMPLETE AGREEMENT

This Agreement constitutes the complete agreement between The Waite Group, Inc., and the authors of the programs, and you, the purchaser.

Some states do not allow the exclusion or limitation of implied warranties or liability for incidental or consequential damages, so the above exclusions or limitations may not apply to you. This limited warranty gives you specific legal rights; you may have others, which vary from state to state.

Technical Support:

If you cannot get the CD/Disk to install properly, or you need assistance with a particular situation in the book, please feel free to check out the Knowledge Base on our Web site at **http://www.superlibrary.com/general/support**. We have answers to our most Frequently Asked Questions listed there. If you do not find your specific question answered, please contact Macmillan Technical Support at **(317) 581-3833**. We can also be reached by email at **support@mcp.com**.

SATISFACTION REPORT CARD

Please fill out this card if you wish to know of future updates to *HTML 4 How-To*, or to receive our catalog.

First Name: ____________ **Last Name:** ____________

Street Address: ____________

City: ____________ **State:** ____________ **Zip:** ____________

Email Address: ____________

Daytime Telephone: ( ) ____________

Date product was acquired: **Month** **Day** **Year** **Your Occupation:**

Overall, how would you rate *HTML 4 How-To*?

☐ Excellent ☐ Very Good ☐ Good
☐ Fair ☐ Below Average ☐ Poor

What did you like MOST about this book? ____________

What did you like LEAST about this book? ____________

Please describe any problems you may have encountered with installing or using the disc: ____________

How did you use this book (problem-solver, tutorial, reference...)?

What is your level of computer expertise?

☐ New ☐ Dabbler ☐ Hacker
☐ Power User ☐ Programmer ☐ Experienced Professional

What computer languages are you familiar with? ____________

Please describe your computer hardware:

Computer ____________ Hard disk ____________
5.25" disk drives ____________ 3.5" disk drives ____________
Video card ____________ Monitor ____________
Printer ____________ Peripherals ____________
Sound Board ____________ CD-ROM ____________

Where did you buy this book?

☐ Bookstore (name): ____________
☐ Discount store (name): ____________
☐ Computer store (name): ____________
☐ Catalog (name): ____________
☐ Direct from WGP ☐ Other ____________

What price did you pay for this book? ____________

What influenced your purchase of this book?

☐ Recommendation ☐ Advertisement
☐ Magazine review ☐ Store display
☐ Mailing ☐ Book's format
☐ Reputation of Waite Group Press ☐ Other

How many computer books do you buy each year? ____________

How many other Waite Group books do you own? ____________

What is your favorite Waite Group book? ____________

Is there any program or subject you would like to see Waite Group Press cover in a similar approach? ____________

Additional comments? ____________

Please send to: **Waite Group Press**
200 Tamal Plaza
Corte Madera, CA 94925

☐ **Check here for a free Waite Group catalog**

SATISFACTION CARD

INSTALLING THE CD-ROM

The companion CD-ROM contains all source code listed in the book, as well as third-party utilities useful for developing HTML pages.

Windows 3.*x* and Windows NT 3.5*x*

1. Insert the CD-ROM into your CD-ROM drive. If you have more than one CD-ROM drive, insert the disc into the first drive.

2. From the File Manager or Program Manager, choose Run from the File menu.

3. Type `<drive>\WSETUP` and press Enter, where `<drive>` corresponds to the drive letter of your CD-ROM. For example, if your CD-ROM drive is D:, type `D:\WSETUP` and press Enter.

4. Follow the onscreen instructions in the installation program.

Windows 95 and Windows NT 4.0

1. Insert the CD-ROM into your CD-ROM drive. If you have more than one CD-ROM drive, insert the disc into the first drive.

2. From the Start button, choose Run.

3. Type `<drive>\WSETUP` and press Enter, where `<drive>` corresponds to the drive letter of your CD-ROM. For example, if your CD-ROM drive is D:, type `D:\WSETUP` and press Enter.

4. Follow the onscreen instructions in the installation program.

BEFORE YOU OPEN THE DISK OR CD-ROM PACKAGE ON THE FACING PAGE, CAREFULLY READ THE LICENSE AGREEMENT.